µC/OS-III®
The Real-Time Kernel

Jean J. Labrosse

Micriµm®
Press
Weston, FL 33326

Micriµm Press
1290 Weston Road, Suite 306
Weston, FL 33326
USA
www.micrium.com

Designations used by companies to distinguish their products are often claimed as trademarks. In all instances where Micriµm Press is aware of a trademark claim, the product name appears in initial capital letters, in all capital letters, or in accordance with the vendor's capitalization preference. Readers should contact the appropriate companies for more complete information on trademarks and trademark registrations. All trademarks and registered trademarks in this book are the property of their respective holders.

The programs and code examples in this book are presented for instructional value. The programs and examples have been carefully tested, but are not guaranteed to any particular purpose. The publisher does not offer any warranties and does not guarantee the accuracy, adequacy, or completeness of any information herein and is not responsible for any errors or omissions. The publisher assumes no liability for damages resulting from the use of the information in this book or for any infringement of the intellectual property rights of third parties that would result from the use of this information.

Library of Congress Control Number: 2009934275

Library of Congress subject headings:

1. Embedded computer systems
2. Real-time data processing
3. Computer software - Development

For bulk orders, please contact Micrium Press at: +1 954 217 2036

Micriµm®
📖 *Press*

ISBN: 978-1-935772-20-0
100-uCOS-III-Infineon-XMC4500-001

To my loving and caring wife, Manon,
and our two children James and Sabrina.

Table of Contents

Part I: µC/OS-III – The Real-Time Kernel

Part II: μC/OS-III and the Infineon XMC4500

Table of Contents

Foreword to µC/OS-III — by Jack Ganssle

Your system has to read a keyboard and update the display. That's pretty easy to handle in a simple loop.

Oh, wait, then there's the A/D converter which needs service once a millisecond. The data is noisy so ten samples must be averaged and the result fed into a computation which is sent to the display. But you can't do the math till the results of the encoder become available, and that can only be read on 20 msec intervals.

But don't forget to monitor the radiation source; if it goes out of limits a safety protocol has to be invoked to avoid harming users. That has to be monitored every 250 milliseconds.

How would one write this code? Sure, it's possible to write an interrupt handler that takes clock ticks and then, via a number of tortured loops, sequences off the proper activities. It'll be tough to debug and harder to maintain. You can be sure the boss will come in, red-faced, wondering why the heck the system only looks at safety parameters every quarter second when any idiot knows the rate should be 0.230 sec, no matter how he wrote the spec. The loops grow more complex and the program ever more convoluted.

This is a very old problem, one solved by the use of a Real-Time Operating System (RTOS). Write each activity as a separate task. The code is simple, crystal clear, and easy to change.

An old problem, yes. But there's surprisingly little written about the use of an RTOS. Jean Labrosse wrote one of the first and best books on the subject: the first edition of this volume. I'm told the first edition, and the subsequent second edition, are the best selling books ever published about embedded systems, and I'm not surprised. Extremely-well written, they covered the subject in depth and with finesse. He wrote using the µC/OS and µC/OS-II RTOSes as examples.

Now Jean and the crew at Micriµm have a new and hugely improved version of that RTOS: µC/OS-III. Where µC/OS-II is a commercial quality product, one that even meets the highest safety-critical requirements, µC/OS-III takes that quality and reliability level to even the most demanding applications.

Jean has supplemented the new RTOS with this book. It's much weightier than his previous RTOS books as this volume goes in depth into the nuances of using an operating system in real applications. µC/OS-III lays out the rationale behind an RTOS, and then in a very logical fashion presents each of the resources provided by an RTOS and how one goes about using those features in a product. Though µC/OS-III is used as an example, it is not presented as the canonical RTOS, and users of any real-time operating system will find this material immensely usable.

I have long counted Jean a friend, and have great respect for his perfectionism. That is clear when reading the µC/OS source code, which is probably the most beautiful code I have read, and, since it has been used in products certified to DO-178B level A, also works!

That perfectionism also manifests itself in this book, in which it's clear he has taken pains to get every fact right, every drawing clear, all while maintaining a very consistent style.

This is a book by an engineer, for engineers (including engineering students). Devoid of fluff, it's packed with information about using an RTOS in a real system... today. What do I need to do to get started? What are all those files? Where is the information I need located?

Are you using an RTOS? If so, read this book. If you're not using one, read this book; not every embedded system needs an operating system, but there are too many that have been cobbled together through the painful use of ad hoc loops that an RTOS would vastly improve.

Preface

WHAT IS µC/OS-III?

µC/OS-III (pronounced "Micro C O S Three) is a scalable, ROMable, preemptive real-time kernel that manages an unlimited number of tasks. µC/OS-III is a third-generation kernel and offers all of the services expected from a modern real-time kernel, such as resource management, synchronization, inter-task communications, and more. However, µC/OS-III offers many unique features not found in other real-time kernels, such as the ability to complete performance measurements at run-time, to directly signal or send messages to tasks, achieve pending on multiple kernel objects, and more.

WHY A NEW µC/OS VERSION?

The µC/OS series, first introduced in 1992, has undergone a number of changes over the years based on feedback from thousands of people using and deploying its evolving versions.

µC/OS-III is the sum of this feedback and experience. Rarely used µC/OS-II features were eliminated and newer, more efficient features and services, were added. Probably the most common request was to add round robin scheduling, which was not possible for µC/OS-II, but is now a feature of µC/OS-III.

µC/OS-III also provides additional features that better exploit the capabilities of today's newer processors. Specifically, µC/OS-III was designed with 32-bit processors in mind, although it certainly works well with 16- and even several 8-bit processors.

WHAT'S NEW ABOUT THIS BOOK?

The MicroC/OS-II book focused primarily on documenting the µC/OS-II product with a great, yet brief, RTOS introduction. This book changes that focus. This time, the spotlight is on real-time kernels and Real-Time Operating Systems (RTOS), with µC/OS-III used as a reference. In-depth product documentation is now provided in the appendices.

By taking this approach, the intent is to reach a larger target audience, especially those from industry and academia alike that are completely new to the topic of RTOS, This book is also suitable for use as the foundation of a generic RTOS class.

From a didactic perspective, every person has four different learning styles:

- Activist (A)

- Observational (O)

- Theoretical (T)

- Pragmatic (P)

The style that is more dominant differs from person to person. Based on these learning styles, there are strong improvements over the previous book, MicroC/OS-II, The Real-Time Kernel, which primarily focused on theoretical and, thanks to the good illustrations, also the observational learning styles. However, activist and pragmatic styles were somewhat missing. This book answers more questions for the pragmatist concerning: Why would I be interested in this? What could I use this for? What does this mean for my project? How does this help me get the job done?

Typically, books completely lack an activist learning style. This is a tricky one for a book because the question then becomes, how do you get readers to become active and do something with the material? That's where the companion evaluation board and tools come in. This two-part text, combined with tools and evaluation board, enable readers to receive the material, and begin to have a hands-on experience right away.

This book is split into two parts. The first part describes real-time kernels in generic terms, using µC/OS-III as a real-life example. The second part, which actually looks like a completely different book, provides examples using a popular microprocessor or microcontroller. As mentioned, the book is accompanied by a matching evaluation board and such tools as a compiler, assembler, linker, and debugger, which enable the reader to experiment with µC/OS-III and become proficient with its use.

In summary, the general topic of RTOS is now the prevailing topic of this book. Explaining the concept of RTOS in combination with µC/OS-III, an evaluation board and tools simply makes sense.

µC/OS-III GOALS

The main goal of µC/OS-III is to provide a best-in-class real-time kernel that literally shaves months of development time from an embedded-product schedule. Using a commercial real-time kernel such as µC/OS-III provides a solid foundation and framework to the design engineer dealing with the growing complexity of embedded designs.

Another goal for µC/OS-III, and therefore this book, is to explain inner workings of a commercial-grade kernel. This understanding will assist the reader in making logical design decisions and informed tradeoffs between hardware and software that make sense.

INTENDED AUDIENCE

This book is written for embedded systems programmers, consultants, hobbyists and students interested in understanding the inner workings of a real-time kernel. µC/OS-III is not just a great learning platform, but also a commercial-grade software package ready to be part of a range of products.

To get the most from this book, it is assumed that the reader has a good working knowledge of microprocessors, microcontrollers, and/or Digital Signal Processors (DSPs). That knowledge should extend to CPU instructions, interrupts, I/O devices, RAM and ROM or Flash, memory addresses, and stack pointers.

It is also expected that the reader will have a good working knowledge of the C programming language and assembly language.

THE µC/OS STORY

The µC/OS story started when, in 1989, I joined Dynalco Controls in Fort Lauderdale, Florida, and began working on the design of a new microprocessor-based ignition control system for a large industrial reciprocating engine.

Given that I had experience using a kernel, I was convinced that an operating system would substantially benefit this project and other planned projects at Dynalco. Time to market was of paramount importance for this ignition control system, and I knew that a kernel would help meet scheduling requirement. I also knew that new features would be added to this product in the future, and a preemptive operating system would allow for such updates without negatively impacting system responsiveness.

The kernel that I initially considered was one that had served me well in the past. However, it carried a hefty price tag, and my budget was somewhat meager. The alternative was a kernel that I had not used before, but it was five-times cheaper than my original choice. Ultimately, I decided that the financial benefits of using the unfamiliar operating system outweighed the potential advantages that its higher-priced counterpart could offer.

I quickly realized, however, that I would pay for the seemingly cheaper operating system with my time. During the two months after receiving the kernel, I was in constant contact with technical support, trying fruitlessly to determine why even the simplest applications would not run. The operating system, said to be written in C, required me to initialize all of the kernel's internal variables in assembly language, a task laden with problems. I eventually discovered that I was one of the first customers to purchase this operating system and was essentially an unknowing beta tester.

Frustrated with the software's many shortcomings, I turned to the relatively expensive operating system that I originally rejected. It seems that if a project is late, money is no object. Within two days, I was running simple applications that the cheap operating system seemed unable to support. My kernel-related problems seemed to be over.

Before long, however, I would find myself at another impasse. My second set of problems began when one of my engineers reported that the new operating system seemed to contain a bug. I promptly relayed the engineer's findings to the software vendor, assuming that the company would be interested. Instead of receiving assurance that the bug would be fixed, I was notified that the 90-day warranty expired. Unless I purchased a maintenance contract, the bug would not be eliminated, which was absurd to me. The software provider thought otherwise, and I forked over the maintenance fee.

While my popularity as a speaker rose, interest in my book also picked up steam. After its slow start, µC/OS, The Real-Time Kernel, went on to sell more than 15,000 copies.

Thanks to the success of my book, the number of engineers using µC/OS increased substantially throughout the 1990s. Developers easily adapted the operating system to new hardware platforms, and were designing a myriad of µC/OS-based applications. Although several µC/OS users simply tinkered with the operating system in their spare time, many engineers used the software commercially in complex and demanding projects. Comments and suggestions from µC/OS users helped me to continue to refine and evolve the operating system.

For several years, only minor changes were made to µC/OS. However, when R & D asked me to write a second edition, I decided that a substantial update of both the operating system and the book was warranted. The updated operating system became µC/OS-II.

A quick glance at the µC/OS-II files revealed that this operating system was different from µC/OS. Whereas all of the processor-independent code incorporated by µC/OS was contained in a single C file, µC/OS-II spanned multiple files, each corresponding to one of the operating system's services. µC/OS-II also offered many features that its predecessor lacked, including stack-checking capabilities, hook functions, and a safe means to dynamically allocate memory.

To fully describe all of the new operating system's features, I nearly doubled the size of the book. Just as the latest version of the software received a new name, the new edition became MicroC/OS-II, The Real-Time Kernel. ("Micro" was used in place of "µ" because titles incorporating Greek letters posed problems for many book retailers.) Unlike my first text, the new book would be a hardcover.

MicroC/OS-II, The Real-Time Kernel was released in 1998. This new text was accompanied by the source code that it described and I would again have thousands of developers testing the kernel and providing valuable feedback.

Among the thousands of readers of my books using the software, there were many kernel rookies. For them, the book provided thorough and accessible coverage of operating system fundamentals. Many university professors recognized the book's appeal to new kernel users and started designing entire courses around µC/OS-II. Soon college graduates whose kernel training focused on the operating system made their way into the workforce, where they continued to use µC/OS-II.

While students gravitated to µC/OS-II because of my book and readily available source code, a substantial number of engineers using µC/OS-II commercially selected the software for its reliability. Definitive proof of the operating system's reliability was provided in July 2000, when DO-178B Level A certification was conferred on an avionics product incorporating µC/OS-II. This certification, recognized by the Federal Avionics Administration (FAA), is awarded to software deemed safe enough to be used in aircraft. To this day, there are few operating systems that have successfully completed the rigorous testing that certified software must undergo.

DO-178B certification is only one of µC/OS-II's credentials. Additional certifications include Food and Drug Administration (FDA) pre-market notification (510(k)), pre-market approval (PMA) for medical devices, and IEC-61508 for industrial controls. Compliance with such standards is critical within industry segments; however, the certifications also have value for engineers in other industries as they evidence reliability, documentation, and time-to-market advantages beneficial to any design.

As the decade came to a close, I still worked full time at Dynalco, and experienced difficulty keeping up with the demand for the operating system. I felt obligated to respond to each µC/OS-II user that contacted me, and the flow of messages into my inbox was unrelenting. Since I could no longer treat the operating system as a side project, I made the decision to found my own software company. In September 1999, Micriµm, officially came into being. Micriµm comes from the word 'Micro' (for microprocessors or microcontrollers) and 'ium' (which means the Universe of) and thus, Micriµm means the Universe of Microprocessors (as seen through the eyes of software).

In the months before incorporating Micriµm, I began working on a second edition of the µC/OS-II book, which made its debut in November 1999 and was accompanied by a new version of the kernel. Two major features to the operating system were added: event flags and mutual exclusion semaphores. These new features, fully described in the book, were heartily welcomed by µC/OS-II users. The book itself was similarly embraced; the second edition of MicroC/OS-II, The Real-Time Kernel quickly became common sight on the bookshelves of embedded software developers. In fact, the MicroC/OS-II book is the most popular embedded systems book ever sold.

Micriµm expanded. Engineers were hired to adapt µC/OS-II to new hardware platforms and develop a bevy of example projects and application notes. A long-time friend of mine, Christian Legare joined Micriµm as Vice President in 2002, and his substantial corporate and technical expertise further accelerated the company's rapid growth. Since Christian joined Micriµm, the company expanded from a one-product company to one with a portfolio of 15 products.

Meanwhile, new features were added to satisfy the ever-evolving needs of µC/OS-II users, including a variety of new API functions to the operating system and expanding the maximum number of tasks supported by the kernel from 64 to 255.

As Micriµm's president, I remain dedicated to writing world-class kernel code, most recently µC/OS-III. The product of countless hours of meticulous programming and testing, this robust operating system has its roots in µC/OS-II, yet is an entirely new kernel. Addressing input received from customers and all of the lessons learned along the way, several additional important µC/OS-III features were included (see Introduction).

I am highly circumspect of fads and unproven technology as I write new software. Although I like to keep abreast of the latest developments in the high-tech world, the focus is on solving engineers' problems and providing a solid and complete infrastructure, rather than on how to prematurely exploit emerging trends.

This philosophy has yielded considerable success. Micriµm, now in its tenth year, is a highly respected embedded software provider. Industry surveys consistently show the operating systems to be among the most popular in the embedded space. My goal has always been, and continues to be to provide effective solutions for the same types of problems that I confronted at Dynalco, and that millions of embedded systems developers continue to face today.

ACKNOWLEDGEMENTS

First and foremost, I'd like to thank my loving and caring wife Manon for her unconditional support, encouragement, understanding and patience. This new book and μC/OS-III software was again a huge undertaking, and I could not have done it without her.

I would also like to thank many fine people at Micrium who have tested the code and reviewed the book. In alphabetic order:

- Brian Nagel

- Eric Shufro

- Hong Soong

- Freddy Torres

A special thanks to Frank Voorburg from Feaser and to Ian Hall and Robert Mongrain from Renesas for feedback and corrections to the book, to Michael Barr for sharing his real life RTOS experiences, and to Carolyn Mathas for the incredible job of editing this huge project.

A very special thanks to my long-time friend, colleague and partner, Christian Legare, who has provided his advice and support throughout this project and on a day-to-day basis at Micrium. Thank you also to the dozens of people who provided feedback about the μC/OS-III code, as well as reviewers of the book.

Finally, I listen to music when I write software, and artist Gino Vannelli's awesome music has provided a creative environment for me for over three decades. I would be remiss if I did not acknowledge his contribution here as well.

Introduction

Real-time systems are systems whereby the correctness of the computed values and their timeliness are at the forefront. There are two types of real-time systems, hard and soft real time.

What differentiates hard and soft real-time systems is their tolerance to missing deadlines and the consequences associated with those misses. Correctly computed values after a deadline has passed are often useless.

For hard real-time systems, missing deadlines is not an option. In fact, in many cases, missing a deadline often results in catastrophe, which may involve human lives. For soft real-time systems, however, missing deadlines is generally not as critical.

Real-time applications cover a wide range, but many real-time systems are embedded. An embedded system is a computer built into a system and not acknowledged by the user as being a computer. Embedded systems are also typically dedicated systems. In other words, systems that are designed to perform a dedicated function. The following list shows just a few examples of embedded systems:

Aerospace
- Flight management systems
- Jet engine controls
- Weapons systems

Audio
- MP3 players
- Amplifiers and tuners

Automotive
- Antilock braking systems
- Climate control
- Engine controls
- Navigation systems (GPS)

Communications
- Routers
- Switches
- Cell phones

Computger peripherals
- Printers
- Scanners

Domestic
- Air conditioning units
- Thermostats
- White goods

Office automation
- FAX machines / copiers

Process control
- Chemical plants
- Factory automation
- Food processing

Robots

Video
- Broadcasting equipment
- HD Televisions

And many more

Real-time systems are typically more complicated to design, debug, and deploy than non-real-time systems.

1-1 FOREGROUND/BACKGROUND SYSTEMS

Small systems of low complexity are typically designed as foreground/background systems or super-loops. An application consists of an infinite loop (F1-1(1)) that calls modules (i.e., tasks) to perform the desired operations (background). Interrupt Service Routines (ISRs) shown in F1-1(3) handle asynchronous events (foreground). Foreground is also called interrupt level; background is called task level.

Critical operations that should be performed at the task level must unfortunately be handled by the ISRs to ensure that they are dealt with in a timely fashion. This causes ISRs to take longer than they should. Also, information for a background module that an ISR makes available is not processed until the background routine gets its turn to execute, which is called the task-level response. The worst-case task-level response time depends on how long a background loop takes to execute and, since the execution time of typical code is not constant, the time for successive passes through a portion of the loop is nondeterministic. Furthermore, if a code change is made, the timing of the loop is affected.

Most high-volume and low-cost microcontroller-based applications (e.g., microwave ovens, telephones, toys, etc.) are designed as foreground/background systems.

Figure 1-1 **Foreground/Background (SuperLoops) systems**

1-2 REAL-TIME KERNELS

A real-time kernel is software that manages the time and resources of a microprocessor, microcontroller or Digital Signal Processor (DSP).

The design process of a real-time application involves splitting the work into tasks, each responsible for a portion of the job. A task (also called a thread) is a simple program that thinks it has the Central Processing Unit (CPU) completely to itself. On a single CPU, only one task executes at any given time. A task is also typically implemented as an infinite loop.

The kernel is responsible for the management of tasks. This is called multitasking. Multitasking is the process of scheduling and switching the CPU between several tasks. The CPU switches its attention between several sequential tasks. Multitasking provides the illusion of having multiple CPUs and maximizes the use of the CPU. Multitasking also helps in the creation of modular applications. One of the most important aspects of multitasking is that it allows the application programmer to manage the complexity inherent in real-time applications. Application programs are easier to design and maintain when multitasking is used.

µC/OS-III is a preemptive kernel, which means that µC/OS-III always runs the most important task that is ready-to-run as shown in Figure 1-2.

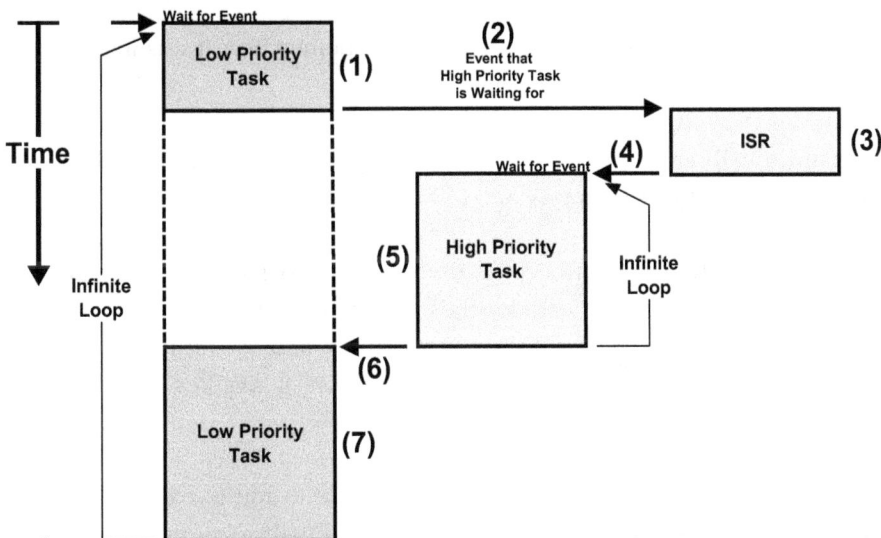

Figure 1-2 µC/OS-III is a preemptive kernel

F1-2(1)   A low-priority task is executing.

F1-2(2)   An interrupt occurs, and the CPU vectors to the ISR responsible for servicing the interrupting device.

F1-2(3)   The ISR services the interrupt device, but actually does very little work. The ISR will typically signal or send a message to a higher-priority task that will be responsible for most of the processing of the interrupting device. For example, if the interrupt comes from an Ethernet controller, the ISR simply signals a task, which will process the received packet.

F1-2(4)   When the ISR finishes, µC/OS-III notices that a more important task has been made ready-to-run by the ISR and will not return to the interrupted task, but instead context switch to the more important task.

F1-2(5)   The higher-priority task executes and performs the necessary processing in response to the interrupt device.

F1-2(6)   When the higher-priority task completes its work, it loops back to the beginning of the task code and makes a µC/OS-III function call to wait for the next interrupt from the device.

F1-2(7)   The low-priority task resumes exactly at the point where it was interrupted, not knowing what happened.

Kernels such as µC/OS-III are also responsible for managing communication between tasks, and managing system resources (memory and I/O devices).

A kernel adds overhead to a system because the services provided by the kernel require time to execute. The amount of overhead depends on how often these services are invoked. In a well-designed application, a kernel uses between 2% and 4% of a CPU's time. And, since µC/OS-III is software that is added to an application, it requires extra ROM (code space) and RAM (data space).

Low-end single-chip microcontrollers are generally not able to run a real-time kernel such as µC/OS-III since they have access to very little RAM. µC/OS-III requires between 1 Kbyte and 4 Kbytes of RAM, plus each task requires its own stack space. It is possible for µC/OS-III to work on processors having as little as 4 Kbytes of RAM.

Finally, μC/OS-III allows for better use of the CPU by providing approximately 70 indispensable services. After designing a system using a real-time kernel such as μC/OS-III, you will not return to designing a foreground/background system.

1-3 RTOS (REAL-TIME OPERATING SYSTEM)

A Real Time Operating System generally contains a real-time kernel and other higher-level services such as file management, protocol stacks, a Graphical User Interface (GUI), and other components. Most additional services revolve around I/O devices.

Micriμm offers a complete suite of RTOS components including: μC/FS (an Embedded File System), μC/TCP-IP (a TCP/IP stack), μC/GUI (a Graphical User Interface), μC/USB (a USB device and host stack), and more. Most of these components are designed to work standalone. Except for μC/TCP-IP, a real-time kernel is not required to use the components in an application. In fact, users can pick and choose only the components required for the application. Contact Micriμm (www.micrium.com) for additional details and pricing.

1-4 μC/OS-III

μC/OS-III is a scalable, ROMable, preemptive real-time kernel that manages an unlimited number of tasks. μC/OS-III is a third-generation kernel, offering all of the services expected from a modern real-time kernel including resource management, synchronization, inter-task communication, and more. However, μC/OS-III also offers many unique features not found in other real-time kernels, such as the ability to perform performance measurements at run time, directly signal or send messages to tasks, and pending (i.e., waiting) on such multiple kernel objects as semaphores and message queues.

Here is a list of features provided by μC/OS-III:

Source Code: μC/OS-III is provided in ANSI-C source form. The source code for μC/OS-III is arguably the cleanest and most consistent kernel code available. Clean source is part of the corporate culture at Micriμm. Although many commercial kernel vendors provide source code for their products, unless the code follows strict coding standards and is accompanied by complete documentation with examples to show how the code works, these products may be cumbersome and difficult to harness. With this book, you will gain a deep understanding of the inner workings of μC/OS-III, which will protect your investment.

Intuitive Application Programming Interface (API): µC/OS-III is highly intuitive. Once familiar with the consistent coding conventions used, it is simple to predict the functions to call for the services required, and even predict which arguments are needed. For example, a pointer to an object is always the first argument, and a pointer to an error code is always the last one.

Preemptive multitasking: µC/OS-III is a preemptive multi-tasking kernel and therefore, µC/OS-III always runs the most important ready-to-run task.

Round robin scheduling of tasks at equal priority: µC/OS-III allows multiple tasks to run at the same priority level. When multiple tasks at the same priority are ready-to-run, and that priority level is the most important level, µC/OS-III runs each task for a user-specified time called a time quanta. Each task can define its own time quanta, and a task can also give up the CPU to another task at the same priority if it does not require the full time quanta.

Low interrupt disable time: µC/OS-III has a number of internal data structures and variables that it needs to access atomically. To ensure this, µC/OS-III is able to protect these critical regions by locking the scheduler instead of disabling interrupts. Interrupts are therefore disabled for very little time. This ensures that µC/OS-III is able to respond to some of the fastest interrupt sources.

Deterministic: Interrupt response with µC/OS-III is deterministic. Also, execution times of most services provided by µC/OS-III are deterministic.

Scalable: The footprint (both code and data) can be adjusted based on the requirements of the application. Adding and removing features (i.e., services) is performed at compile time through approximately 40 #defines (see os_cfg.h). µC/OS-III also performs a number of run-time checks on arguments passed to µC/OS-III services. Specifically, µC/OS-III verifies that the user is not passing NULL pointers, not calling task level services from ISRs, that arguments are within allowable range, and options specified are valid, etc.. These checks can be disabled (at compile time) to further reduce the code footprint and improve performance. The fact that µC/OS-III is scalable allows it to be used in a wide range of applications and projects.

Portable: µC/OS-III can be ported to a large number of CPU architectures. Most µC/OS-II ports are easily converted to work on µC/OS-III with minimal changes in just a matter of minutes and therefore benefit from more than 45 CPU architectures already supported by µC/OS-II.

ROMable: µC/OS-III was designed especially for embedded systems and can be ROMed along with the application code.

Run-time configurable: µC/OS-III allows the user to configure the kernel at run time. Specifically, all kernel objects such as tasks, stacks, semaphores, event-flag groups, message queues, number of messages, mutual exclusion semaphores, memory partitions and timers, are allocated by the user at run time. This prevents over-allocating resources at compile time.

Unlimited number of tasks: µC/OS-III supports an unlimited number of tasks. From a practical standpoint, however, the number of tasks is actually limited by the amount of memory (both code and data space) that the processor has access to. Each task requires its own stack space and, µC/OS-III provides features to allow stack growth of the tasks to be monitored at run-time.

µC/OS-III does not impose any limitations on the size of each task, except that there be a minimum size based on the CPU used.

Unlimited number of priorities: µC/OS-III supports an unlimited number of priority levels. However, configuring µC/OS-III for between 32 and 256 different priority levels is more than adequate for most applications.

Unlimited number of kernel objects: µC/OS-III allows for any number of tasks, semaphores, mutual exclusion semaphores, event flags, message queues, timers, and memory partitions. The user allocates all kernel objects at run-time.

Services: µC/OS-III provides all the services expected from a high-end real-time kernel, such as task management, time management, semaphores, event flags, mutexes, message queues, software timers, fixed-size memory pools, etc.

Mutual Exclusion Semaphores (Mutexes): Mutexes are provided for resource management. Mutexes are special types of semaphores that have built-in priority inheritance, which eliminate unbounded priority inversions. Accesses to a mutex can be nested and therefore, a task can acquire the same mutex up to 250 times. Of course, the mutex owner needs to release the mutex an equal number of times.

Nested task suspension: μC/OS-III allows a task to suspend itself or another task. Suspending a task means that the task will not be allowed to execute until the task is resumed by another task. Suspension can be nested up to 250 levels deep. In other words, a task can suspend another task up to 250 times. Of course, the task must be resumed an equal number of times for it to become eligible to run on the CPU.

Software timers: You can define any number of "one-shot" and/or "periodic" timers. Timers are countdown counters that perform a user-definable action upon counting down to 0. Each timer can have its own action and, if a timer is periodic, the timer is automatically reloaded and the action is executed every time the countdown reaches zero.

Pend on multiple objects: μC/OS-III allows an application to wait (i.e., pend) on multiple events at the same time. Specifically, a task can wait on multiple semaphores and/or message queues to be posted. The waiting task wakes up as soon as one of the events occurs.

Task Signals: μC/OS-III allows an ISR or task to directly signal a task. This avoids having to create an intermediate kernel object such as a semaphore or event flag just to signal a task, and results in better performance.

Task Messages: μC/OS-III allows an ISR or a task to send messages directly to a task. This avoids having to create and use a message queue, and also results in better performance.

Task registers: Each task can have a user-definable number of "task registers." Task registers are different than CPU registers. Task registers can be used to hold "errno" type variable, IDs, interrupt disable time measurement on a per-task basis, and more.

Error checking: μC/OS-III verifies that **NULL** pointers are not passed, that the user is not calling task-level services from ISRs, that arguments are within allowable range, that options specified are valid, that a pointer to the proper object is passed as part of the arguments to services that manipulate the desired object, and more. Each μC/OS-III API function returns an error code concerning the outcome of the function call.

Built-in performance measurements: μC/OS-III has built-in features to measure the execution time of each task, stack usage of each task, number of times a task executes, CPU usage, ISR-to-task and task-to-task response time, peak number of entries in certain lists, interrupt disable and scheduler lock time on a per-task basis, and more.

Can easily be optimized: μC/OS-III was designed so that it could easily be optimized based on the CPU architecture. Most data types used in μC/OS-III can be changed to make better use of the CPU's natural word size. Also, the priority resolution algorithm can easily be written in assembly language to benefit from special instructions such as bit set and clear, as well as count-leading-zeros (CLZ), or find-first-one (FF1) instructions.

Deadlock prevention: All of the μC/OS-III "pend" services include timeouts, which help avoid deadlocks.

Tick handling at task level: The clock tick manager in μC/OS-III is accomplished by a task that receives a trigger from an ISR. Handling delays and timeouts by a task greatly reduces interrupt latency. Also, μC/OS-III uses a hashed delta list mechanism, which further reduces the amount of overhead in processing delays and timeouts of tasks.

User definable hooks: μC/OS-III allows the port and application programmer to define "hook" functions, which are called by μC/OS-III. A hook is simply a defined function that allows the user to extend the functionality of μC/OS-III. One such hook is called during a context switch, another when a task is created, yet another when a task is deleted, etc.

Timestamps: For time measurements, μC/OS-III requires that a 16-bit or 32-bit free running counter be made available. This counter can be read at run time to make time measurements of certain events. For example, when an ISR posts a message to a task, the timestamp counter is automatically read and saved as part of the message posted. When the recipient receives the message, the timestamp is provided to the recipient, and by reading the current timestamp, the time it took for the message to be received can be determined.

Built-in support for Kernel Awareness debuggers: This feature allows kernel awareness debuggers to examine and display μC/OS-III variables and data structures in a user-friendly way. The kernel awareness support in μC/OS-III can be used by μC/Probe to display this information at run-time.

Object names: Each μC/OS-III kernel object can have a name associated with it. This makes it easy to recognize what the object is assigned to. You can thus assign an ASCII name to a task, a semaphore, a mutex, an event flag group, a message queue, a memory partition, and a timer. The object name can have any length, but must be NUL terminated.

1-5 µC/OS, µC/OS-II AND µC/OS-III FEATURES COMPARISON

Table 1-1 shows the evolution of µC/OS over the years, comparing the features available in each version.

Feature	µC/OS	µC/OS-II	µC/OS-III
Year introduced	1992	1998	2009
Book	Yes	Yes	Yes
Source code available	Yes	Yes	Yes
Preemptive Multitasking	Yes	Yes	Yes
Maximum number of tasks	64	255	Unlimited
Number of tasks at each priority level	1	1	Unlimited
Round Robin Scheduling	No	No	Yes
Semaphores	Yes	Yes	Yes
Mutual Exclusion Semaphores	No	Yes	Yes (Nestable)
Event Flags	No	Yes	Yes
Message Mailboxes	Yes	Yes	No (not needed)
Message Queues	Yes	Yes	Yes
Fixed Sized Memory Management	No	Yes	Yes
Signal a task without requiring a semaphore	No	No	Yes
Option to Post without scheduling	No	No	Yes
Send messages to a task without requiring a message queue	No	No	Yes
Software Timers	No	Yes	Yes
Task suspend/resume	No	Yes	Yes (Nestable)
Deadlock prevention	Yes	Yes	Yes
Scalable	Yes	Yes	Yes
Code Footprint	3K to 8K	6K to 26K	6K to 24K
Data Footprint	1K+	1K+	1K+
ROMable	Yes	Yes	Yes

Feature	µC/OS	µC/OS-II	µC/OS-III
Run-time configurable	No	No	Yes
Compile-time configurable	Yes	Yes	Yes
ASCII names for each kernel object	No	Yes	Yes
Pend on multiple objects	No	Yes	Yes
Task registers	No	Yes	Yes
Built-in performance measurements	No	Limited	Extensive
User definable hook functions	No	Yes	Yes
Time stamps on posts	No	No	Yes
Built-in Kernel Awareness support	No	Yes	Yes
Optimizable Scheduler in assembly language	No	No	Yes
Catch a task that returns	No	No	Yes
Tick handling at task level	No	No	Yes
Source code available	Yes	Yes	Yes
Number of services	~20	~90	~70
MISRA-C:1998	No	Yes (except 10 rules)	N/A
MISRA-C:2004	No	No	Yes (except 7 rules)
DO178B Level A and EUROCAE ED-12B	No	Yes	In progress
Medical FDA pre-market notification (510(k)) and pre-market approval (PMA)	No	Yes	In progress
SIL3/SIL4 IEC for transportation and nuclear systems	No	Yes	In progress
IEC-61508	No	Yes	In progress

Table 1-1 **µC/OS, µC/OS-II and µC/OS-III Features Comparison Chart**

1-6 HOW THE BOOK IS ORGANIZED

This book actually consists of two books in one.

Part I describes μC/OS-III and is not tied to any specific CPU architecture. Here, the reader will learn about real-time kernels through μC/OS-III. Specifically, critical sections, task management, the ready list, scheduling, context switching, interrupt management, wait lists, time management, timers, resource management, synchronization, memory management, how to use μC/OS-III's API, how to configure μC/OS-III, and how to port μC/OS-III to different CPU architectures, are all covered.

Part II describes the port of a popular CPU architecture. Here, you will learn about this CPU architecture and how μC/OS-III gets the most out of the CPU. Examples are provided to actually run code on the evaluation board that is available with this book.

As I just mentioned, this book assumes the presence of an evaluation board that allows the user to experiment with the wonderful world of real-time kernels, and specifically μC/OS-III. The book and board are complemented by a full set of tools that are provided free of charge either in a companion CD/DVD, or downloadable through the Internet. The tools and the use of μC/OS-III are free as long as they are used with the evaluation board, and there is no commercial intent to use them on a project. In other words, there is no additional charge except for the initial cost of the book, evaluation board and tools, as long as they are used for educational purposes.

The book also comes with a trial version of an award-winning tool from Micriμm called μC/Probe. The trial version allows the user to monitor and change up to eight (8) variables in a target system.

1-7 μC/PROBE

μC/Probe is a Microsoft Windows™ based application that enables the user to visualize variables in a target at run time. Specifically, you can display or change the value of any variable in a system while the target is running. These variables can be displayed using such graphical elements as gauges, meters, bar graphs, virtual LEDs, numeric indicators, and many more. Sliders, switches, and buttons can be used to change variables. This is accomplished without the user having to write a single line of code!

µC/Probe interfaces to any target (8-, 16-, 32-, 64-bit, or even DSPs) through one of the many interfaces supported (J-Tag, RS-232C, USB, Ethernet, etc.). µC/Probe displays or changes any variable (as long as they are global) in the application, including µC/OS-III's internal variables.

µC/Probe works with any compiler/assembler/linker able to generate an ELF/DWARF or IEEE695 file. This is the exact same file that the user will download to the evaluation board or a final target. From this file, µC/Probe is able to extract symbolic information about variables, and determine where variables are stored in RAM or ROM.

µC/Probe also allows users to log the data displayed into a file for analysis of the collected data at a later time. µC/Probe also provides µC/OS-III kernel awareness as a built-in feature.

The trial version that accompanies the book is limited to the display or change of up to eight (8) variables.

µC/Probe is a tool that serious embedded software engineers should have in their toolbox. The full version of µC/Probe is available from Micrium, see www.micrium.com for more details.

1-8 CONVENTIONS

There are a number of conventions in this book.

First, you will notice that when a specific element in a figure is referenced, the element has a number next to it in parenthesis. A description of this element follows the figure and in this case, the letter "F" followed by the figure number, and then the number in parenthesis. For example, F3-4(2) indicates that this description refers to Figure 3-4 and the element (2) in that figure. This convention also applies to listings (starts with an "L") and tables (starts with a "T").

Second, you will notice that sections and listings are started where it makes sense. Specifically, do not be surprised to see the bottom half of a page empty. New sections begin on a new page, and listings are found on a single page, instead of breaking listings on two pages.

Third, code quality is something I've been avidly promoting throughout my whole career. At Micriμm, we pride ourselves in having the cleanest code in the industry. Examples of this are seen in this book. I created and published a coding standard in 1992 that was published in the original µC/OS book. This standard has evolved over the years, but the spirit of the standard has been maintained throughout. The Micriμm coding standard is available for download from the Micriμm website, www.micrium.com

One of the conventions used is that all functions, variables, macros and **#define** constants are prefixed by "OS" (which stands for Operating System) followed by the acronym of the module (e.g., **Sem**), and then the operation performed by the function. For example **OSSemPost()** indicates that the function belongs to the OS (µC/OS-III), that it is part of the Semaphore services, and specifically that the function performs a **Post** (i.e., signal) operation. This allows all related functions to be grouped together in the reference manual, and makes those services intuitive to use.

You should notice that signaling or sending a message to a task is called posting, and waiting for a signal or a message is called pending. In other words, an ISR or a task signals or sends a message to another task by using **OS???Post()**, where **???** is the type of service: **Sem**, **TaskSem**, **Flag**, **Mutex**, **Q**, and **TaskQ**. Similarly, a task can wait for a signal or a message by calling **OS???Pend()**.

1-9 CHAPTER CONTENTS

Figure 1-3 shows the layout and flow of Part I of the book. This diagram should be useful to understand the relationship between chapters. The first column on the left indicates chapters that should be read in order to understand µC/OS-III's structure. The second column shows chapters that are related to additional services provided by µC/OS-III. The third column relates to chapters that will help port µC/OS-III to different CPU architectures. The top of the fourth column explains how to obtain valuable run-time and compile-time statistics from µC/OS-III. This is especially useful if developing a kernel awareness plug-in for a debugger, or using µC/Probe. The middle of column four contains the µC/OS-III API and configuration manuals. You will be referencing these sections regularly when designing a product using µC/OS-III. Finally, the bottom of the last column contains miscellaneous appendices.

Figure 1-3 **µC/OS-III Book Layout**

Chapter 1, Introduction. This chapter.

Chapter 2, Directories and Files. This chapter explains the directory structure and files needed to build a µC/OS-III-based application. Here, you will learn about the files that are needed, where they should be placed, which module does what, and more.

Chapter 3, Getting Started with µC/OS-III. In this chapter, you will learn how to properly initialize and start a µC/OS-III-based application.

Chapter 4, Critical Sections. This chapter explains what critical sections are, and how they are protected.

Chapter 5, Task Management. This chapter is an introduction to one of the most important aspects of a real-time kernel, the management of tasks in a multitasking environment.

Chapter 6, The Ready List. In this chapter, you will learn how µC/OS-III efficiently keeps track of all of the tasks that are waiting to execute on the CPU.

Chapter 7, Scheduling. This chapter explains the scheduling algorithms used by µC/OS-III, and how it decides which task will run next.

Chapter 8, Context Switching. This chapter explains what a context switch is, and describes the process of suspending execution of a task and resuming execution of a higher-priority task.

Chapter 9, Interrupt Management. Here is how µC/OS-III deals with interrupts and an overview of services that are available from Interrupt Service Routines (ISRs). Here you will learn how µC/OS-III supports nearly any interrupt controller.

Chapter 10, Pend Lists (or Wait Lists). Tasks that are not able to run are most likely blocked waiting for specific events to occur. Pend Lists (or wait lists), are used to keep track of tasks that are waiting for a resource or event. This chapter describes how µC/OS-III maintains these lists.

Chapter 11, Time Management. In this chapter, you will find out about µC/OS-III's services that allow users to suspend a task until some time expires. With µC/OS-III, you can specify to delay execution of a task for an integral number of clock ticks or until the clock-tick counter reaches a certain value. The chapter will also show how a delayed task can be resumed, and describe how to get the current value of the clock tick counter, or set this counter, if needed.

Chapter 12, Timer Management. µC/OS-III allows users to define any number of software timers. When a timer expires, a function can be called to perform some action. Timers can be configured to be either periodic or one-shot. This chapter also explains how the timer-management module works.

Chapter 13, Resource Management. In this chapter, you will learn different techniques so that tasks share resources. Each of these techniques has advantages and disadvantages that will be discussed. This chapter also explains the internals of semaphores, and mutual exclusion semaphore management.

Chapter 14, Synchronization. µC/OS-III provides two types of services for synchronization: semaphores and event flags and these are explained in this chapter, as well as what happens when calling specific services provided in this module.

Chapter 15, Message Passing. μC/OS-III allows a task or an ISR to send messages to a task. This chapter describes some of the services provided by the message queue management module.

Chapter 16, Pending on multiple objects. In this chapter, see how μC/OS-III allows an application to pend (or wait) on multiple kernel objects (semaphores or message queues) at the same time. This feature makes the waiting task ready-to-run as soon as any one of the objects is posted (i.e., OR condition), or a timeout occurs.

Chapter 17, Memory Management. Here is how μC/OS-III's fixed-size memory partition manager can be used to allocate and deallocate dynamic memory.

Chapter 18, Porting μC/OS-III. This chapter explains, in generic terms, how to port μC/OS-III to any CPU architecture.

Chapter 19, Run-Time Statistics. μC/OS-III provides a wealth of information about the run-time environment, such as number of context switches, CPU usage (as a percentage), stack usage on a per-task basis, μC/OS-III RAM usage, maximum interrupt disable time, maximum scheduler lock time, and more.

Chapter 20, Thread Safety of the Compiler's Run-Time Library. μC/OS-III now provides built-in support for run-time library thread safety through the use of Task Local Storage (TLS) for storage of task-specific run-time library static data and mutual exclusion semaphores to protect accesses to shared resources.

Appendix A, μC/OS-III API Reference Manual. This appendix provides a alphabetical reference for all user-available services provided by μC/OS-III.

Appendix B, μC/OS-III Configuration Manual. This appendix describes how to configure a μC/OS-III-based application. os_cfg.h configures the μC/OS-III features (semaphores, queues, event flags, etc.), while os_cfg_app.h configures the run-time characteristics (tick rate, tick wheel size, stack size for the idle task, etc.).

Appendix C, Migrating from μC/OS-II to μC/OS-III. μC/OS-III has its roots in μC/OS-II and, in fact, most of the μC/OS-II ports can be easily converted to μC/OS-III. However, most APIs have changed from μC/OS-II to μC/OS-III, and this appendix describes some of the differences.

Appendix D, MISRA-C:2004 rules and μC/OS-III. μC/OS-III follows most of the MISRA-C:2004, except for a few of these rules.

Appendix E, Bibliography.

Appendix F, Licensing μC/OS-III.

Directories and Files

µC/OS-III is fairly easy to use once it is understood exactly which source files are needed to make up a µC/OS-III-based application. This chapter will discuss the modules available for µC/OS-III and how everything fits together.

Figure 2-1 shows the µC/OS-III architecture and its relationship with hardware. Of course, in addition to the timer and interrupt controller, hardware would most likely contain such other devices as Universal Asynchronous Receiver Transmitters (UARTs), Analog to Digital Converters (ADCs), Ethernet controller(s) and more.

This chapter assumes development on a Windows®-based platform and makes references to typical Windows-type directory structures (also called Folder). However, since µC/OS-III is provided in source form, it can also be used on Unix, Linux or other development platforms.

Figure 2-1 µC/OS-III Architecture

F2-1(1)   The application code consists of project or product files. For convenience, these are simply called **app.c** and app.h, however an application can contain any number of files that do not have to be called **app.***. The application code is typically where one would find the **main( )**.

F2-1(2)   Semiconductor manufacturers often provide library functions in source form for accessing the peripherals on their CPU or MCU. These libraries are quite useful and often save valuable time. Since there is no naming convention for these files, ***.c** and ***.h** are assumed.

F2-1(3)   The Board Support Package (BSP) is code that is typically written to interface to peripherals on a target board. For example such code can turn on and off LEDs, turn on and off relays, or read switches, temperature sensors, and more.

F2-1(4)   This is the µC/OS-III processor-independent code. This code is written in highly portable ANSI C.

F2-1(5)   This is the µC/OS-III code that is adapted to a specific CPU architecture and is called a port. µC/OS-III has its roots in µC/OS-II and benefits from being able to use most of the 45 or so ports available for µC/OS-II. µC/OS-II ports, however, will require small changes to work with µC/OS-III. These changes are described in Appendix C, "Migrating from µC/OS-II to µC/OS-III" on page 711.

F2-1(6)   At Micriµm, we encapsulate CPU functionality. These files define functions to disable and enable interrupts, **CPU_???** data types to be independent of the CPU and compiler used, and many more functions.

F2-1(7)   µC/LIB is of a series of source files that provide common functions such as memory copy, string, and ASCII-related functions. Some are occasionally used to replace **stdlib** functions provided by the compiler. The files are provided to ensure that they are fully portable from application to application and especially, from compiler to compiler. µC/OS-III does not use these files, but µC/CPU does.

F2-1(8)   Some compilers provide extensions to make library functions 'thread safe'. The adaptation of those functions is performed in the **os_tls.c** file which is found under the **uCOS-III\TLS\<tool>** folder. **<tool>** is the name of the tool manufacturer or, the tool name.

F2-1(9)   Configuration files are used to define µC/OS-III features (**os_cfg.h**) to include in the application, specify the size of certain variables and data structures expected by µC/OS-III (**os_cfg_app.h**), such as idle task stack size, tick rate, size of the message pool, configure the µC/CPU features available to the application programmer (**cpu_cfg.h**) and also configure µC/LIB options (**lib_cfg.h**).

2-1 APPLICATION CODE

When Micriµm provides example projects, they are placed in a directory structure shown below. Of course, a directory structure that suits a particular project/product can also be used.

```
\Micrium
    \Software
        \EvalBoards
            \<manufacturer>
                \<board_name>
                    \<compiler>
                        \<project name>
                            \*.*
```

\Micrium
This is where we place all software components and projects provided by Micriµm. This directory generally starts from the root directory of the computer.

\Software
This sub-directory contains all software components and projects.

\EvalBoards
This sub-directory contains all projects related to evaluation boards supported by Micriµm.

\<manufacturer>
This is the name of the manufacturer of the evaluation board. The "<" and ">" are not part of the actual name.

\<board name>

This is the name of the evaluation board. A board from Micrium will typically be called **uC-Eval-xxxx** where "**xxxx**" represents the CPU or MCU used on the board. The "<" and ">" are not part of the actual name.

\<compiler>

This is the name of the compiler or compiler manufacturer used to build the code for the evaluation board. The "<" and ">" are not part of the actual name.

\<project name>

The name of the project that will be demonstrated. For example, a simple μC/OS-III project might have a project name of "**OS-Ex1**". The "**-Ex1**" represents a project containing only μC/OS-III.

.

These are the project source files. Main files can optionally be called **app*.***. This directory also contains configuration files **os_cfg.h**, **os_cfg_app.h** and other required source files.

2-2 CPU

The directory where you will find semiconductor manufacturer peripheral interface source files is shown below. Any directory structure that suits the project/product may be used.

```
\Micrium
    \Software
        \CPU
            \<manufacturer>
                \<architecture>
                    \*.*
```

\Micrium

The location of all software components and projects provided by Micrium.

\Software

This sub-directory contains all software components and projects.

\CPU

This sub-directory is always called CPU.

\<manufacturer>

Is the name of the semiconductor manufacturer providing the peripheral library.

\<architecture>

The name of the specific library, generally associated with a CPU name or an architecture.

.

Indicates library source files. The semiconductor manufacturer names the files.

2-3 BOARD SUPPORT PACKAGE (BSP)

The Board Support Package (BSP) is generally found with the evaluation or target board as it is specific to that board. In fact, when well written, the BSP should be used for multiple projects.

```
\Micrium
    \Software
        \EvalBoards
            \<manufacturer>
                \<board name>
                    \<compiler>
                        \BSP
                            \*.*
```

\Micrium

Contains all software components and projects provided by Micriµm.

\Software

This sub-directory contains all software components and projects.

\EvalBoards

This sub-directory contains all projects related to evaluation boards.

\<manufacturer>

The name of the manufacturer of the evaluation board. The "<" and ">" are not part of the actual name.

\<board name>

The name of the evaluation board. A board from Micriµm will typically be called **uC-Eval-xxxx** where "**xxxx**" is the name of the CPU or MCU used on the evaluation board. The "<" and ">" are not part of the actual name.

\<compiler>

The name of the compiler or compiler manufacturer used to build code for the evaluation board. The "<" and ">" are not part of the actual name.

\BSP

This directory is always called BSP.

.

The source files of the BSP. Typically all of the file names start with BSP. It is therefore normal to find **bsp.c** and **bsp.h** in this directory. BSP code should contain such functions as LED control functions, initialization of timers, interface to Ethernet controllers and more.

2-4 µC/OS-III, CPU INDEPENDENT SOURCE CODE

The files in these directories are µC/OS-III processor independent files provided in source form. See Appendix F, "Licensing Policy" on page 755.

```
\Micrium
    \Software
        \uCOS-III
            \Cfg\Template
                \os_app_hooks.c
                \os_cfg.h
                \os_cfg_app.h
            \Source
                \os_cfg_app.c
                \os_core.c
                \os_dbg.c
                \os_flag.c
                \os_int.c
                \os_mem.c
                \os_msg.c
```

```
            \os_mutex.c
            \os_pend_multi.c
            \os_prio.c
            \os_q.c
            \os_sem.c
            \os_stat.c
            \os_task.c
            \os_tick.c
            \os_time.c
            \os_tmr.c
            \OS_VAR
            \os.h
            \os_type.h
        \TLS
            \<tool>
                \os_tls.c
```

\Micrium

Contains all software components and projects provided by Micriµm.

\Software

This sub-directory contains all software components and projects.

\uCOS-III

This is the main µC/OS-III directory.

\Cfg\Template

This directory contains examples of configuration files to copy to the project directory. You will then modify these files to suit the needs of the application.

os_app_hooks.c shows how to write hook functions that are called by µC/OS-III. Specifically, this file contains eight empty functions.

os_cfg.h specifies which features of µC/OS-III are available for an application. The file is typically copied into an application directory and edited based on which features are required from µC/OS-III. See Appendix B, "µC/OS-III Configuration Manual" on page 691.

os_cfg_app.h is a configuration file that is typically copied into an application directory and edited based on application requirements. This file enables the user to determine the size of the idle task stack, the tick rate, the number of messages available in the message pool and more. See Appendix B, "µC/OS-III Configuration Manual" on page 691.

\Source

The directory containing the CPU-independent source code for µC/OS-III. All files in this directory should be included in the build. Features that are not required will be compiled out based on the value of #define constants in **os_cfg.h** and **os_cfg_app.h**.

os_cfg_app.c declares variables and arrays based on the values in **os_cfg_app.h**.

os_core.c contains core functionality for µC/OS-III such as OSInit() to initialize µC/OS-III, OSSched() for the task level scheduler, OSIntExit() for the interrupt level scheduler, pend list (or wait list) management (see Chapter 10, "Pend Lists (or Wait Lists)" on page 195), ready list management (see Chapter 6, "The Ready List" on page 139), and more.

os_dbg.c contains declarations of constant variables used by a kernel aware debugger or µC/Probe.

os_flag.c contains the code for event flag management. See Chapter 14, "Synchronization" on page 271 for details about event flags.

os_int.c contains code for the interrupt handler task, which is used when **OS_CFG_ISR_POST_DEFERRED_EN** (see os_cfg.h) is set to 1. See Chapter 9, "Interrupt Management" on page 173 for details regarding the interrupt handler task.

os_mem.c contains code for the µC/OS-III fixed-size memory manager, see Chapter 17, "Memory Management" on page 341.

os_msg.c contains code to handle messages. µC/OS-III provides message queues and task specific message queues. **os_msg.c** provides common code for these two services. See Chapter 15, "Message Passing" on page 307.

os_mutex.c contains code to manage mutual exclusion semaphores, see Chapter 13, "Resource Management" on page 229.

os_pend_multi.c contains the code to allow code to pend on multiple semaphores or message queues. This is described in Chapter 16, "Pending On Multiple Objects" on page 331.

os_prio.c contains the code to manage the bitmap table used to keep track of which tasks are ready-to-run, see Chapter 6, "The Ready List" on page 139. This file can be replaced by an assembly language equivalent to improve performance if the CPU used provides bit set, clear and test instructions, and a count leading zeros instruction.

os_q.c contains code to manage message queues. See Chapter 15, "Message Passing" on page 307.

os_sem.c contains code to manage semaphores used for resource management and/or synchronization. See Chapter 13, "Resource Management" on page 229 and Chapter 14, "Synchronization" on page 271.

os_stat.c contains code for the statistic task, which is used to compute the global CPU usage and the CPU usage of each task. See Chapter 5, "Task Management" on page 91.

os_task.c contains code for managing tasks using `OSTaskCreate()`, `OSTaskDel()`, `OSTaskChangePrio()`, and many more. See Chapter 5, "Task Management" on page 91.

os_tick.c contains code to manage tasks that have delayed themselves or that are pending on a kernel object with a timeout. See Chapter 5, on page 91.

os_time.c contains code to allow a task to delay itself until some time expires. See Chapter 11, "Time Management" on page 201.

os_tmr.c contains code to manage software timers. See Chapter 12, "Timer Management" on page 211.

os_var.c contains the µC/OS-III global variables. These variables are for µC/OS-III to manage and should not be accessed by application code.

os.h contains the main µC/OS-III header file, which declares constants, macros, µC/OS-III global variables (for use by µC/OS-III only), function prototypes, and more.

os_type.h contains declarations of µC/OS-III data types that can be changed by the port designer to make better use of the CPU architecture. In this case, the file would typically be copied to the port directory and then modified. See Appendix B, "µC/OS-III Configuration Manual" on page 691.

\TLS\<tool>

The directory containing the compiler interface functions that allow library functions to be thread safe. If this feature is not required then you can omit the files in this directory.

os_tls.c provides the compiler specific thread safe interface functions.

2-5 µC/OS-III, CPU SPECIFIC SOURCE CODE

The µC/OS-III port developer provides these files. See also Chapter 18, "Porting µC/OS-III" on page 353.

```
\Micrium
    \Software
        \uCOS-III
            \Ports
                \<architecture>
                    \<compiler>
                        \os_cpu.h
                        \os_cpu_a.asm
                        \os_cpu_c.c
```

\Micrium
Contains all software components and projects provided by Micriµm.

\Software
This sub-directory contains all software components and projects.

\uCOS-III
The main µC/OS-III directory.

\Ports
The location of port files for the CPU architecture(s) to be used.

\<architecture>

This is the name of the CPU architecture that µC/OS-III was ported to. The "<" and ">" are not part of the actual name.

\<compiler>

The name of the compiler or compiler manufacturer used to build code for the port. The "<" and ">" are not part of the actual name.

The files in this directory contain the µC/OS-III port, see Chapter 18, "Porting µC/OS-III" on page 353 for details on the contents of these files.

os_cpu.h contains a macro declaration for OS_TASK_SW(), as well as the function prototypes for at least the following functions: OSCtxSw(), OSIntCtxSw() and OSStartHighRdy().

os_cpu_a.asm contains the assembly language functions to implement at least the following functions: OSCtxSw(), OSIntCtxSw() and OSStartHighRdy().

os_cpu_c.c contains the C code for the port specific hook functions and code to initialize the stack frame for a task when the task is created.

2-6 µC/CPU, CPU SPECIFIC SOURCE CODE

µC/CPU consists of files that encapsulate common CPU-specific functionality and CPU and compiler-specific data types. See Chapter 18, "Porting µC/OS-III" on page 353.

```
\Micrium
    \Software
        \uC-CPU
            \cpu_core.c
            \cpu_core.h
            \cpu_def.h
            \Cfg\Template
                \cpu_cfg.h
            \<architecture>
                \<compiler>
                    \cpu.h
```

\cpu_a.asm
\cpu_c.c

\Micrium
Contains all software components and projects provided by Micriµm.

\Software
This sub-directory contains all software components and projects.

\uC-CPU
This is the main µC/CPU directory.

cpu_core.c contains C code that is common to all CPU architectures. Specifically, this file contains functions to measure the interrupt disable time of the **CPU_CRITICAL_ENTER()** and **CPU_CRITICAL_EXIT()** macros, a function that emulates a count leading zeros instruction in case the CPU does not provide such an instruction, and a few other functions.

cpu_core.h contains function prototypes for the functions provided in **cpu_core.c** and allocation of the variables used by the module to measure interrupt disable time.

cpu_def.h contains miscellaneous **#define** constants used by the µC/CPU module.

\Cfg\Template
This directory contains a configuration template file (**cpu_cfg.h**) that must be copied to the application directory to configure the µC/CPU module based on application requirements.

cpu_cfg.h determines whether to enable measurement of the interrupt disable time, whether the CPU implements a count leading zeros instruction in assembly language, or whether it will be emulated in C, and more.

\<architecture>
The name of the CPU architecture that µC/CPU was ported to. The "<" and ">" are not part of the actual name.

\<compiler>
The name of the compiler or compiler manufacturer used to build code for the µC/CPU port. The "<" and ">" are not part of the actual name.

The files in this directory contain the μC/CPU port, see Chapter 18, "Porting μC/OS-III" on page 353 for details on the contents of these files.

cpu.h contains type definitions to make μC/OS-III and other modules independent of the CPU and compiler word sizes. Specifically, one will find the declaration of the CPU_INT16U, CPU_INT32U, CPU_FP32 and many other data types. This file also specifies whether the CPU is a big or little endian machine, defines the CPU_STK data type used by μC/OS-III, defines the macros CPU_CRITICAL_ENTER() and CPU_CRITICAL_EXIT(), and contains function prototypes for functions specific to the CPU architecture, and more.

cpu_a.asm contains the assembly language functions to implement code to disable and enable CPU interrupts, count leading zeros (if the CPU supports that instruction), and other CPU specific functions that can only be written in assembly language. This file may also contain code to enable caches, setup MPUs and MMU, and more. The functions provided in this file are accessible from C.

cpu_c.c contains C code of functions that are based on a specific CPU architecture but written in C for portability. As a general rule, if a function can be written in C then it should be, unless there is significant performance benefits available by writing it in assembly language.

2-7 μC/LIB, PORTABLE LIBRARY FUNCTIONS

μC/LIB consists of library functions meant to be highly portable and not tied to any specific compiler. This facilitates third-party certification of Micriμm products. μC/OS-III does not use any μC/LIB functions, however μC/OS-III and μC/CPU assumes the presence of lib_def.h for such definitions as: DEF_YES, DEF_NO, DEF_TRUE, DEF_FALSE, DEF_ON, DEF_OFF and more.

```
\Micrium
    \Software
        \uC-LIB
            \lib_ascii.c
            \lib_ascii.h
            \lib_def.h
            \lib_math.c
            \lib_math.h
```

> **\lib_mem.c**
> **\lib_mem.h**
> **\lib_str.c**
> **\lib_str.h**
> \Cfg\Template
> > **\lib_cfg.h**
> \Ports
> > \<architecture>
> > > \<compiler>
> > > > **\lib_mem_a.asm**

\Micrium

Contains all software components and projects provided by Micrium.

\Software

This sub-directory contains all software components and projects.

\uC-LIB

This is the main µC/LIB directory.

lib_ascii.c and lib_ascii.h contain source code to replace some standard library functions such as tolower(), toupper(), isalpha(), isdigit(), etc. with µC/LIB equivalent functions ASCII_ToLower(), ASCII_ToUpper(), ASCII_IsAlpha(), and ASCII_IsDig(), respectively.

lib_def.h defines constants for many common values such as TRUE/FALSE, YES/NO, ENABLED/DISABLED; as well as for integer, octet, and bit values. However, all #define in this file starts with DEF_ so those constants are actually called DEF_TRUE/DEF_FALSE, DEF_YES/DEF_NO, DEF_ENABLED/DEF_DISABLED, etc. This file also contains macros for common mathematical operations like min(), max(), abs(), bit_set(), bit_clr(), etc. with DEF_MIN(), DEF_MAX(), DEF_ABS(), DEF_BIT_SET(), DEF_BIT_CLR(), respectively.

lib_math.c and lib_math.h contain source code to replace some standard library functions such as rand(), srand(), etc. with µC/LIB equivalent functions Math_Rand(), Math_SetSeed(), respectively.

`lib_mem.c` and `lib_mem.h` contain source code to replace some standard library functions such as `memclr()`, `memset()`, `memcpy()`, `memcmp()`, etc. with μC/LIB equivalent functions `Mem_Clr()`, `Mem_Set()`, `Mem_Copy()`, `Mem_Cmp()`, respectively.

`lib_str.c` and `lib_str.h` contain source code to replace some standard library functions such as `strlen()`, `strcpy()`, `strcmp()`, `memcmp()`, etc. with μC/LIB equivalent functions `Str_Lenr()`, `Str_Copy()`, `Str_Cmp()`, respectively.

\Cfg\Template

This directory contains a configuration template file (`lib_cfg.h`) that should be copied to the application directory to configure the μC/LIB module based on application requirements.

lib_cfg.h determines whether to enable assembly language optimization (assuming there is an assembly language file for the processor, i.e., `lib_mem_a.asm`) and a few other `#defines`.

\Ports\Architecture\Compiler

This directory contains optimized assembly language files specific to the CPU architecture to replace C functions with much faster assembly language implementations. The presence of this folder depends on whether such assembly language functions were implemented by the port developer of the μC/LIB module.

`lib_mem_a.asm` contains optimized versions of the `lib_mem.c` functions.

2-8 SUMMARY

Below is a summary of all directories and files involved in a μC/OS-III-based project. The "<-Cfg" on the far right indicates that these files are typically copied into the application (i.e., project) directory and edited based on the project requirements.

```
\Micrium
    \Software
        \EvalBoards
            \<manufacturer>
                \<board name>
                    \<compiler>
```

```
            \<project name>
                  \app.c
                  \app.h
                  \other
\CPU
    \<manufacturer>
        \<architecture>
            \*.*
\uCOS-III
    \Cfg\Template
        \os_app_hooks.c
        \os_cfg.h                              <-Cfg
        \os_cfg_app.h                          <-Cfg
    \Source
        \os_cfg_app.c
        \os_core.c
        \os_dbg.c
        \os_flag.c
        \os_int.c
        \os_mem.c
        \os_msg.c
        \os_mutex.c
        \os_pend_multi.c
        \os_prio.c
        \os_q.c
        \os_sem.c
        \os_stat.c
        \os_task.c
        \os_tick.c
        \os_time.c
        \os_tmr.c
        \os_var.c
        \os.h
        \os_type.h                             <-Cfg
    \Ports
        \<architecture>
            \<compiler>
                \os_cpu.h
                \os_cpu_a.asm
```

```
                    \os_cpu_c.c
        \TLS
            \<tool>
                \os_tls.c
\uC-CPU
    \cpu_core.c
    \cpu_core.h
    \cpu_def.h
    \Cfg\Template
        \cpu_cfg.h                                  <-Cfg
    \<architecture>
        \<compiler>
            \cpu.h
            \cpu_a.asm
            \cpu_c.c
\uC-LIB
    \lib_ascii.c
    \lib_ascii.h
    \lib_def.h
    \lib_math.c
    \lib_math.h
    \lib_mem.c
    \lib_mem.h
    \lib_str.c
    \lib_str.h
    \Cfg\Template
        \lib_cfg.h                                  <-Cfg
    \Ports
        \<architecture>
            \<compiler>
                \lib_mem_a.asm
```

3

Getting Started with µC/OS-III

µC/OS-III provides services to application code in the form of a set of functions that perform specific operations. µC/OS-III offers services to manage tasks, semaphores, message queues, mutual exclusion semaphores and more. As far as the application is concerned, it calls the µC/OS-III functions as if they were any other functions. In other words, the application now has access to a library of approximately 70 new functions.

In this chapter, the reader will appreciate how easy it is to start using µC/OS-III. Refer to Appendix A, "µC/OS-III API Reference" on page 453, for the full description of several of the µC/OS-III services presented in this chapter.

It is assumed that the project setup (files and directories) is as described in the previous chapter, and that a C compiler exists for the target processor that is in use. However, this chapter makes no assumptions about the tools or the processor that is used.

3

3-1 SINGLE TASK APPLICATION

Listing 3-1 shows the top portion of a simple application file called **app.c**.

```
/*
************************************************************************************
*                              INCLUDE FILES
************************************************************************************
*/
#include <app_cfg.h>                                                      (1)
#include <bsp.h>
#include <os.h>
/*
************************************************************************************
*                          LOCAL GLOBAL VARIABLES
************************************************************************************
*/
static  OS_TCB          AppTaskStartTCB;                                  (2)
static  CPU_STK         AppTaskStartStk[APP_TASK_START_STK_SIZE];         (3)
/*
************************************************************************************
*                           FUNCTION PROTOTYPES
************************************************************************************
*/
static  void  AppTaskStart (void *p_arg);                                 (4)
```

Listing 3-1 **app.c (1st Part)**

L3-1(1)   As with any C programs, you need to include the necessary headers to build the application.

app_cfg.h is a header file that configures the application. For our example, app_cfg.h contains #**define** constants to establish task priorities, stack sizes, and other application specifics.

bsp.h is the header file for the Board Support Package (BSP), which **defines** #**defines** and function prototypes, such as BSP_Init(), BSP_LED_On(), OS_TS_GET() and more.

os.h is the main header file for µC/OS-III, and includes the following header files:

```
os_cfg.h
cpu.h
cpu_core.h
lib_def.h
os_type.h
os_cpu.h
```

L3-1(2)   We will be creating an application task and it is necessary to allocate a task control block (**OS_TCB**) for this task. The **OS_TCB** data type will be described in Chapter 5, "Task Management" on page 91.

L3-1(3)   Each task created requires its own stack. A stack must be declared using the **CPU_STK** data type as shown. The stack can be allocated statically as shown here, or dynamically from the heap using **malloc()**. It should not be necessary to free the stack space, because the task should never be destroyed, and thus, the stack would always be used.

L3-1(4)   This is the function prototype of the task that we will create.

Most C applications start at **main()** as shown in Listing 3-2.

```
void  main (void)
{
    OS_ERR  err;

    BSP_IntDisAll();                                                        (1)
    OSInit(&err);                                                           (2)
    if (err != OS_ERR_NONE) {
        /* Something didn't get initialized correctly ...          */
        /* ... check os.h for the meaning of the error code, see OS_ERR_xxxx */
    }
    OSTaskCreate((OS_TCB      *)&AppTaskStartTCB,                           (3)
                 (CPU_CHAR    *)"App Task Start",                          (4)
                 (OS_TASK_PTR )AppTaskStart,                               (5)
                 (void        *)0,                                         (6)
                 (OS_PRIO     )APP_TASK_START_PRIO,                        (7)
                 (CPU_STK     *)&AppTaskStartStk[0],                       (8)
                 (CPU_STK_SIZE)APP_TASK_START_STK_SIZE / 10,               (9)
                 (CPU_STK_SIZE)APP_TASK_START_STK_SIZE,                    (10)
                 (OS_MSG_QTY  )0,
                 (OS_TICK     )0,
                 (void        *)0,
                 (OS_OPT      )(OS_OPT_TASK_STK_CHK | OS_OPT_TASK_STK_CLR), (11)
                 (OS_ERR      *)&err);                                     (12)
    if (err != OS_ERR_NONE) {
        /* The task didn't get created.  Lookup the value of the error code ... */
        /* ... in os.h for the meaning of the error                  */
    }
    OSStart(&err);                                                         (13)
    if (err != OS_ERR_NONE) {
        /* Your code is NEVER supposed to come back to this point.    */
    }
}
```

Listing 3-2 **app.c (2nd Part)**

L3-2(1)   The startup code for the compiler will bring the CPU to **main()**. **main()** then starts by calling a BSP function that disables all interrupts. On most processors, interrupts are disabled at startup until explicitly enabled by application code. However, it is safer to turn off all peripheral interrupts during startup.

L3-2(2)   **OSInit()** is the called to initialize μC/OS-III. **OSInit()** initializes internal variables and data structures, and also creates between two (2) and five (5) internal tasks. At a minimum, μC/OS-III creates the idle task (**OS_IdleTask()**), which executes when no other task is ready-to-run. μC/OS-III also creates the tick task, which is responsible for keeping track of time.

Depending on the value of **#define** constants, µC/OS-III will create the statistic task (**OS_StatTask()**), the timer task (**OS_TmrTask()**), and the interrupt handler queue management task (**OS_IntQTask()**). Those are all discussed in Chapter 5, "Task Management" on page 91.

Most of µC/OS-III's functions return an error code via a pointer to an **OS_ERR** variable, err in this case. If **OSInit()** was successful, err will be set to **OS_ERR_NONE**. If **OSInit()** encounters a problem during initialization, it will return immediately upon detecting the problem and set err accordingly. If this occurs, look up the error code value in **os.h**. Specifically, all error codes start with **OS_ERR_**.

It is important to note that **OSInit()** must be called before any other µC/OS-III function.

L3-2(3) You create a task by calling **OSTaskCreate()**. **OSTaskCreate()** requires 13 arguments. The first argument is the address of the **OS_TCB** that is declared for this task (see L3-1(2)). Chapter 5, "Task Management" on page 91 provides additional information about tasks.

L3-2(4) **OSTaskCreate()** allows a name to be assigned to each of the tasks. µC/OS-III stores a pointer to the task name inside the **OS_TCB** of the task. There is no limit on the number of ASCII characters used for the name.

L3-2(5) The third argument is the address of the task code. A typical µC/OS-III task is implemented as an infinite loop as shown:

```
void  MyTask (void *p_arg)
{
    /* Do something with "p_arg".
    while (1) {
        /* Task body */
    }
}
```

The task receives an argument when it first starts. As far as the task is concerned, it looks like any other C function that can be called by the code. However, your code *must not* call **MyTask()**. The call is actually performed through µC/OS-III.

L3-2(6)   The fourth argument of **OSTaskCreate()** is the actual argument that the task receives when it first begins. In other words, the "**p_arg**" of **MyTask()**. In the example a **NULL** pointer is passed, and thus "**p_arg**" for **AppTaskStart()** will be a **NULL** pointer.

The argument passed to the task can actually be any pointer. For example, the user may pass a pointer to a data structure containing parameters for the task.

L3-2(7)   The next argument to **OSTaskCreate()** is the priority of the task. The priority establishes the relative importance of this task with respect to the other tasks in the application. A low-priority number indicates a high priority (or more important task). You can set the priority of the task to any value between 1 and **OS_CFG_PRIO_MAX-2**, inclusively. Avoid using priority #0, and priority **OS_CFG_PRIO_MAX-1**, because these are reserved for µC/OS-III. **OS_CFG_PRIO_MAX** is a compile time configuration constant, which is declared in **os_cfg.h**.

L3-2(8)   The sixth argument to **OSTaskCreate()** is the base address of the stack assigned to this task. The base address is always the lowest memory location of the stack.

L3-2(9)   The next argument specifies the location of a "watermark" in the task's stack that can be used to determine the allowable stack growth of the task. See Chapter 5, "Task Management" on page 91 for more details on using this feature. In the code above, the value represents the amount of stack space (in **CPU_STK** elements) before the stack is empty. In other words, in the example, the limit is reached when there is 10% of the stack left.

L3-2(10)   The eighth argument to **OSTaskCreate()** specifies the size of the task's stack in number of **CPU_STK** elements (not bytes). For example, if you want to allocate 1 Kbyte of stack space for a task and the **CPU_STK** is a 32-bit word, then you need to pass 256.

L3-2(11)   The next three arguments are skipped as they are not relevant for the current discussion. The 12th argument to **OSTaskCreate()** specifies options. In this example, we specify that the stack will be checked at run time (assuming the statistic task was enabled in **os_cfg.h**), and that the contents of the stack will be cleared when the task is created.

L3-2(12)   The last argument of **OSTaskCreate()** is a pointer to a variable that will receive an error code. If **OSTaskCreate()** is successful, the error code will be **OS_ERR_NONE** otherwise, you can look up the value of the error code in **os.h** (see **OS_ERR_xxxx**) to determine the cause of the error.

L3-2(13)   The final step in **main()** is to call **OSStart()**, which starts the multitasking process. Specifically, µC/OS-III will select the highest-priority task that was created before calling **OSStart()**.

You should note that the highest-priority task is always **OS_IntQTask()** if that task is enabled in **os_cfg.h** (through the **OS_CFG_ISR_POST_DEFERRED_EN** constant). If this is the case, **OS_IntQTask()** will perform some initialization of its own and then µC/OS-III will switch to the next most important task that was created.

A few important points are worth noting. For one thing, you can create as many tasks as you want before calling **OSStart()**. However, it is recommended to only create one task as shown in the example because, having a single application task allows µC/OS-III to determine the relative speed of the CPU. This allows µC/OS-III to determine the percentage of CPU usage at run-time. Also, if the application needs other kernel objects such as semaphores and message queues then it is recommended that these be created prior to calling **OSStart()**. Finally, notice that interrupts are not enabled. This will be discussed next by examining the contents of **AppTaskStart()**, which is shown in Listing 3-3.

```
static  void  AppTaskStart (void *p_arg)                      (1)
{
    OS_ERR  err;


    p_arg = p_arg;
    BSP_Init();                                               (2)
    CPU_Init();                                               (3)
    BSP_Cfg_Tick();                                           (4)
    BSP_LED_Off(0);                                           (5)
    while (1) {                                               (6)
        BSP_LED_Toggle(0);                                    (7)
        OSTimeDlyHMSM((CPU_INT16U)  0,                        (8)
                      (CPU_INT16U)  0,
                      (CPU_INT16U)  0,
                      (CPU_INT32U)100,
                      (OS_OPT    )OS_OPT_TIME_HMSM_STRICT,
                      (OS_ERR    *)&err);
        /* Check for 'err' */
    }
}
```

Listing 3-3 **app.c (3rd Part)**

L3-3(1)   As previously mentioned, a task looks like any other C function. The argument
            "p_arg" is passed to **AppTaskStart()** by **OSTaskCreate()**, as discussed in the
            previous listing description.

L3-3(2)   **BSP_Init()** is a Board Support Package (BSP) function that is responsible for
            initializing the hardware on an evaluation or target board. The evaluation
            board might have General Purpose Input Output (GPIO) lines that might
            need to be configured, relays, sensors and more. This function is found in a
            file called **bsp.c**.

L3-3(3)   **CPU_Init()** initializes the µC/CPU services. µC/CPU provides services to measure
            interrupt latency, obtain time stamps, and provides emulation of the count leading
            zeros instruction if the processor used does not have that instruction, and more.

L3-3(4)   **BSP_Cfg_Tick()** sets up the µC/OS-III tick interrupt. For this, the function
            needs to initialize one of the hardware timers to interrupt the CPU at a rate of:
            OSCfg_TickRate_Hz,   which   is   defined   in   **os_cfg_app.h**   (See
            OS_CFG_TICK_RATE_HZ).

L3-3(5)   `BSP_LED_Off()` is a function that will turn off all LEDs. `BSP_LED_Off()` is written such that a zero argument means all the LEDs.

L3-3(6)   Most µC/OS-III tasks will need to be written as an infinite loop.

L3-3(7)   This BSP function toggles the state of the specified LED. Again, a zero indicates that all the LEDs should be toggled on the evaluation board. You simply change the zero to 1 and this will cause LED #1 to toggle. Exactly which LED is LED #1? That depends on the BSP developer. Specifically, access to LEDs are encapsulated through the functions: `BSP_LED_On()`, `BSP_LED_Off()` and `BSP_LED_Toggle()`. Also, for sake of portability, we prefer to assign LEDs logical values (1, 2, 3, etc.) instead of specifying which port and which bit on each port.

L3-3(8)   Finally, each task in the application must call one of the µC/OS-III functions that will cause the task to "wait for an event." The task can wait for time to expire (by calling `OSTimeDly()`, or `OSTimeDlyHMSM()`), or wait for a signal or a message from an ISR or another task. In the code shown, we used `OSTimeDlyHMSM()` which allows a task to be suspended until the specified number of hours, minutes, seconds and milliseconds have expired. In this case, 100 ms. Chapter 11, "Time Management" on page 201 provides additional information about time delays.

3-2 MULTIPLE TASKS APPLICATION WITH KERNEL OBJECTS

The code of Listing 3-4 through Listing 3-8 shows a more complete example and contains three tasks: a mutual exclusion, semaphore, and a message queue.

```
/*
*******************************************************************************
*                               INCLUDE FILES
*******************************************************************************
*/
#include <app_cfg.h>
#include <bsp.h>
#include <os.h>
/*
*******************************************************************************
*                           LOCAL GLOBAL VARIABLES
*******************************************************************************
*/
static  OS_TCB          AppTaskStartTCB;                         (1)
static  OS_TCB          AppTask1_TCB;
static  OS_TCB          AppTask2_TCB;
static  OS_MUTEX        AppMutex;                                (2)
static  OS_Q            AppQ;                                    (3)
static  CPU_STK         AppTaskStartStk[APP_TASK_START_STK_SIZE];  (4)
static  CPU_STK         AppTask1_Stk[128];
static  CPU_STK         AppTask2_Stk[128];
/*
*******************************************************************************
*                           FUNCTION PROTOTYPES
*******************************************************************************
*/
static  void  AppTaskStart (void *p_arg);                       (5)
static  void  AppTask1     (void *p_arg);
static  void  AppTask2     (void *p_arg);
```

Listing 3-4 **app.c (1st Part)**

L3-4(1)   Here we allocate storage for the **OS_TCB**s of each task.

L3-4(2)   A mutual exclusion semaphore (a.k.a. a mutex) is a kernel object (a data structure) that is used to protect a shared resource from being accessed by more than one task. A task that wants to access the shared resource must obtain the mutex before it is allowed to proceed. The owner of the resource relinquishes the mutex when it has finished accessing the resource. This process is demonstrated in this example.

L3-4(3)   A message queue is a kernel object through which Interrupt Service Routines (ISRs) and/or tasks send messages to other tasks. The sender "formulates" a message and sends it to the message queue. The task(s) wanting to receive these messages wait on the message queue for messages to arrive. If there are already messages in the message queue, the receiver immediately retrieves those messages. If there are no messages waiting in the message queue, then the receiver will be placed in a wait list associated with the message queue. This process will be demonstrated in this example.

L3-4(4)   A stack is allocated for each task.

L3-4(5)   The prototype of the tasks are declared.

Listing 3-5 shows the C entry point, i.e. **main()**.

```
void  main (void)
{
    OS_ERR  err;

    BSP_IntDisAll();
    OSInit(&err);
    /* Check for 'err' */

    OSMutexCreate((OS_MUTEX  *)&AppMutex,                                          (1)
                  (CPU_CHAR  *)"My App. Mutex",
                  (OS_ERR    *)&err);
    /* Check for 'err' */

    OSQCreate    ((OS_Q      *)&AppQ,                                              (2)
                  (CPU_CHAR  *)"My App Queue",
                  (OS_MSG_QTY )10,
                  (OS_ERR    *)&err);
    /* Check for 'err' */

    OSTaskCreate((OS_TCB     *)&AppTaskStartTCB,                                   (3)
                 (CPU_CHAR    *)"App Task Start",
                 (OS_TASK_PTR )AppTaskStart,
                 (void        *)0,
                 (OS_PRIO     )APP_TASK_START_PRIO,
                 (CPU_STK     *)&AppTaskStartStk[0],
                 (CPU_STK_SIZE)APP_TASK_START_STK_SIZE / 10,
                 (CPU_STK_SIZE)APP_TASK_START_STK_SIZE,
                 (OS_MSG_QTY  )0,
                 (OS_TICK     )0,
                 (void        *)0,
                 (OS_OPT      )(OS_OPT_TASK_STK_CHK | OS_OPT_TASK_STK_CLR),
                 (OS_ERR     *)&err);
    /* Check for 'err' */

    OSStart(&err);
    /* Check for 'err' */
}
```

Listing 3-5 **app.c (2nd Part)**

L3-5(1)   Creating a mutex is simply a matter of calling **OSMutexCreate()**. You need to specify the address of the **OS_MUTEX** object that will be used for the mutex. Chapter 13, "Resource Management" on page 229 provides additional information about mutual exclusion semaphores.

You can assign an ASCII name to the mutex, which is useful when debugging.

L3-5(2)   You create the message queue by calling **OSQCreate()** and specify the address of the **OS_Q** object. Chapter 15, "Message Passing" on page 307 provides additional information about message queues.

You can assign an ASCII name to the message queue which can also be useful during debugging.

You need to specify how many messages the message queue is allowed to receive. This value must be greater than zero. If the sender sends messages faster than they can be consumed by the receiving task, messages will be lost. This can be corrected by either increasing the size of the message queue, or increasing the priority of the receiving task.

L3-5(3)   The first application task is created.

Listing 3-6 shows how to create other tasks once multitasking as started.

```
static  void  AppTaskStart (void *p_arg)
{
    OS_ERR  err;


    p_arg = p_arg;
    BSP_Init();
    CPU_Init();
    BSP_Cfg_Tick();
    OSTaskCreate((OS_TCB     *)&AppTask1_TCB,                                  (1)
                (CPU_CHAR    *)"App Task 1",
                (OS_TASK_PTR )AppTask1,
                (void        *)0,
                (OS_PRIO     )5,
                (CPU_STK     *)&AppTask1_Stk[0],
                (CPU_STK_SIZE)0,
                (CPU_STK_SIZE)128,
                (OS_MSG_QTY  )0,
                (OS_TICK     )0,
                (void        *)0,
                (OS_OPT      )(OS_OPT_TASK_STK_CHK | OS_OPT_TASK_STK_CLR),
                (OS_ERR      *)&err);

    OSTaskCreate((OS_TCB     *)&AppTask2_TCB,                                  (2)
                (CPU_CHAR    *)"App Task 2",
                (OS_TASK_PTR )AppTask2,
                (void        *)0,
                (OS_PRIO     )6,
                (CPU_STK     *)&AppTask2_Stk[0],
                (CPU_STK_SIZE)0,
                (CPU_STK_SIZE)128,
                (OS_MSG_QTY  )0,
                (OS_TICK     )0,
                (void        *)0,
                (OS_OPT      )(OS_OPT_TASK_STK_CHK | OS_OPT_TASK_STK_CLR),
                (OS_ERR      *)&err);
    BSP_LED_Off(0);
    while (1) {
        BSP_LED_Toggle(0);
        OSTimeDlyHMSM((CPU_INT16U)  0,
                     (CPU_INT16U)  0,
                     (CPU_INT16U)  0,
                     (CPU_INT32U)100,
                     (OS_OPT     )OS_OPT_TIME_HMSM_STRICT,
                     (OS_ERR    *)&err);
    }
}
```

Listing 3-6 **app.c (3rd Part)**

L3-6(1)   Task #1 is created by calling **OSTaskCreate()**. If this task happens to have a higher priority than the task that creates it, µC/OS-III will immediately start Task #1. If the created task has a lower priority, **OSTaskCreate()** will return to **AppTaskStart()** and continue execution.

L3-6(2)   Task #2 is created and if it has a higher priority than **AppTaskStart()**, µC/OS-III will immediately switch to that task.

```
static  void  AppTask1 (void *p_arg)
{
    OS_ERR   err;
    CPU_TS   ts;


    p_arg = p_arg;
    while (1) {
        OSTimeDly ((OS_TICK      )1,                             (1)
                   (OS_OPT       )OS_OPT_TIME_DLY,
                   (OS_ERR       *)&err);
        OSQPost    ((OS_Q        *)&AppQ,                        (2)
                   (void         *)1;
                   (OS_MSG_SIZE)sizeof(void *),
                   (OS_OPT       )OS_OPT_POST_FIFO,
                   (OS_ERR       *)&err);
        OSMutexPend((OS_MUTEX    *)&AppMutex,                    (3)
                   (OS_TICK      )0,
                   (OS_OPT       )OS_OPT_PEND_BLOCKING;
                   (CPU_TS       *)&ts,
                   (OS_ERR       *)&err);
        /* Access shared resource */                            (4)
        OSMutexPost((OS_MUTEX    *)&AppMutex,                    (5)
                   (OS_OPT       )OS_OPT_POST_NONE,
                   (OS_ERR       *)&err);
    }
}
```

Listing 3-7 **app.c (4th Part)**

L3-7(1)   The task starts by waiting for one tick to expire before it does anything useful. If the µC/OS-III tick rate is configured for 1000 Hz, the task will be suspended for 1 millisecond.

L3-7(2)   The task then sends a message to another task using the message queue **AppQ**. In this case, the example sends a fixed message of value "1," but the message could have consisted of the address of a buffer, the address of a function, or whatever would need to be sent.

L3-7(3)   The task then waits on the mutual exclusion semaphore since it needs to access a shared resource with another task. If the resource is already owned by another task, **AppTask1()** will wait forever for the mutex to be released by its current owner. The forever wait is specified by passing 0 as the second argument of the call.

L3-7(4)   When **OSMutexPend()** returns, the task owns the resource and can therefore access the shared resource. The shared resource may be a variable, an array, a data structure, an I/O device, etc. You should note that we didn't actually show the access to the shared resource. This is not relevant at this point.

L3-7(5)   When the task is done with the shared resource, it must call **OSMutexPost()** to release the mutex.

```
static  void  AppTask2 (void *p_arg)
{
    OS_ERR        err;
    void          *p_msg;
    OS_MSG_SIZE   msg_size;
    CPU_TS        ts;
    CPU_TS        ts_delta;


    p_arg = p_arg;
    while (1) {
        p_msg = OSQPend((OS_Q         *)&AppQ,                          (1)
                        (OS_MSG_SIZE *)&msg_size,
                        (OS_TICK      )0,
                        (OS_OPT       )OS_OPT_PEND_BLOCKING,
                        (CPU_TS      *)&ts,
                        (OS_ERR      *)&err);
        ts_delta = OS_TS_GET() - ts;                                   (2)
        /* Process message received */                                (3)
    }
}
```

Listing 3-8 app.c (5th Part)

L3-8(1) Task #2 starts by waiting for messages to be sent through the message queue **AppQ**. The task waits forever for a message to be received because the third argument specifies an infinite timeout.

When the message is received **p_msg** will contain the message (i.e., a pointer to "something"). In our case, **AppTask2()** will always receive a message value of '**1**'. Both the sender and receiver must agree as to the meaning of the message. The size of the message received is saved in "**msg_size**". Note that "**p_msg**" could point to a buffer and "**msg_size**" would indicate the size of this buffer.

Also, when the message is received, "**ts**" will contain the timestamp of when the message was sent. A timestamp is the value read from a fairly fast free-running timer. The timestamp is typically an unsigned 32-bit (or more) value.

L3-8(2) Knowing when the message was sent allows the user to determine how long it took this task to get the message. This is done by reading the current timestamp and subtracting the timestamp of when the message was sent allows users to know how long it took for the message to be received. Note that the receiving task may not get the message immediately since ISRs or other higher-priority tasks might execute before the receiver gets to run.

L3-8(3) Here you would add your own code to process the received message.

Critical Sections

A critical section of code, also called a *critical region*, is code that needs to be treated indivisibly. There are many critical sections of code contained in µC/OS-III. If a critical section is accessible by an Interrupt Service Routine (ISR) and a task, then disabling interrupts is necessary to protect the critical region. If the critical section is only accessible by task level code, the critical section may be protected through the use of a *preemption lock*.

Within µC/OS-III, the critical section access method depends on which ISR post method is used by interrupts (see Chapter 9, "Interrupt Management" on page 173). If OS_CFG_ISR_POST_DEFERRED_EN is set to 0 (see os_cfg.h) then µC/OS-III will disable interrupts when accessing internal critical sections. If OS_CFG_ISR_POST_DEFERRED_EN is set to 1 then µC/OS-III will lock the scheduler when accessing most of its internal critical sections.

Chapter 9, "Interrupt Management" on page 173 discusses how to select the method to use.

µC/OS-III defines one macro for entering a critical section and two macros for leaving:

```
OS_CRITICAL_ENTER(),
OS_CRITICAL_EXIT() and
OS_CRITICAL_EXIT_NO_SCHED()
```

These macros are internal to µC/OS-III and must not be invoked by the application code. However, if you need to access critical sections in your application code, consult Chapter 13, "Resource Management" on page 229.

4-1 DISABLING INTERRUPTS

When setting OS_CFG_ISR_POST_DEFERRED_EN to 0, µC/OS-III will disable interrupts before entering a critical section and re-enable them when leaving the critical section.

OS_CRITICAL_ENTER() invokes the µC/CPU macro CPU_CRITICAL_ENTER() that, in turn, calls CPU_SR_Save(). CPU_SR_Save() is a function typically written in assembly language that saves the current interrupt disable status and then disables interrupts. The saved interrupt disable status is returned to the caller and in fact, it is stored onto the caller's stack in a variable called "cpu_sr".

OS_CRITICAL_EXIT() and OS_CRITICAL_EXIT_NO_SCHED() both invoke the µC/CPU macro CPU_CRITICAL_EXIT(), which maps to CPU_SR_Restore(). CPU_SR_Restore() is passed the value of the saved "cpu_sr" variable to re-establish interrupts the way they were prior to calling OS_CRITICAL_ENTER().

The typical code for the macros is shown in Listing 4-1.

```
#define  OS_CRITICAL_ENTER()          { CPU_CRITICAL_ENTER(); }
#define  OS_CRITICAL_EXIT()           { CPU_CRITICAL_EXIT();  }
#define  OS_CRITICAL_EXIT_NO_SCHED()  { CPU_CRITICAL_EXIT();  }
```

Listing 4-1 **Critical section code – Disabling interrupts**

4-1-1 MEASURING INTERRUPT DISABLE TIME

µC/CPU provides facilities to measure the amount of time interrupts are disabled. This is done by setting the configuration constant CPU_CFG_INT_DIS_MEAS_EN to 1 in cpu_cfg.h.

The measurement is started each time interrupts are disabled and ends when interrupts are re-enabled. The measurement keeps track of two values: a global interrupt disable time, and an interrupt disable time for each task. Therefore, it is possible to know how long a task disables interrupts, enabling the user to better optimize their code.

The per-task interrupt disable time is saved in the task's OS_TCB during a context switch (see OSTaskSwHook() in os_cpu_c.c and described in Chapter 8, "Context Switching" on page 163).

The unit of measure for the measured time is in CPU_TS (timestamp) units. It is necessary to find out the resolution of the timer used to measure these timestamps. For example, if the timer used for the timestamp is incremented at 1 MHz then the resolution of **CPU_TS** is 1 microsecond.

Measuring the interrupt disable time obviously adds measurement artifacts and thus increases the amount of time the interrupts are disabled. However, as far as the measurement is concerned, measurement overhead is accounted for and the measured value represents the actual interrupt disable time as if the measurement was not present.

Interrupt disable time is obviously greatly affected by the speed at which the processor accesses instructions and thus, the memory access speed. In this case, the hardware designer might have introduced wait states to memory accesses, which affects overall performance of the system. This may show up as unusually long interrupt disable times.

4-2 LOCKING THE SCHEDULER

When setting **OS_CFG_ISR_POST_DEFERRED_EN** to 1, µC/OS-III locks the scheduler before entering a critical section and unlocks the scheduler when leaving the critical section.

OS_CRITICAL_ENTER( ) simply increments **OSSchedLockNestingCtr** to lock the scheduler. This is the variable the scheduler uses to determine whether or not the scheduler is locked. It is locked when the value is non-zero.

OS_CRITICAL_EXIT( ) decrements **OSSchedLockNestingCtr** and when the value reaches zero, invokes the scheduler.

OS_CRITICAL_EXIT_NO_SCHED( ) also decrements **OSSchedLockNestingCtr**, but does not invoke the scheduler when the value reaches zero.

The code for the macros is shown in Listing 4-2.

```
#define  OS_CRITICAL_ENTER()           {                                                    \
                                           CPU_CRITICAL_ENTER();                             \
                                           OSSchedLockNestingCtr++;                          \
                                           CPU_CRITICAL_EXIT();                              \
                                       }
#define  OS_CRITICAL_EXIT()            {                                                     \
                                           CPU_CRITICAL_ENTER();                             \
                                           OSSchedLockNestingCtr--;                          \
                                           if (OSSchedLockNestingCtr == (OS_NESTING_CTR)0) { \
                                               CPU_CRITICAL_EXIT();                          \
                                               OSSched();                                    \
                                           } else {                                          \
                                               CPU_CRITICAL_EXIT();                          \
                                           }                                                 \
                                       }
#define  OS_CRITICAL_EXIT_NO_SCHED()   {
                                           CPU_CRITICAL_ENTER();                             \
                                           OSSchedLockNestingCtr--;                          \
                                           CPU_CRITICAL_EXIT();                              \
                                       }
```

Listing 4-2 **Critical section code – Locking the Scheduler**

4-2-1 MEASURING SCHEDULER LOCK TIME

μC/OS-III provides facilities to measure the amount of time the scheduler is locked. This is done by setting the configuration constant **OS_CFG_SCHED_LOCK_TIME_MEAS_EN** to 1 in **os_cfg.h**.

The measurement is started each time the scheduler is locked and ends when the scheduler is unlocked. The measurement keeps track of two values: a global scheduler lock time, and a per-task scheduler lock time. It is therefore possible to know how long each task locks the scheduler allowing the user to better optimize code.

The per-task scheduler lock time is saved in the task's **OS_TCB** during a context switch (see **OSTaskSwHook()** in **os_cpu_c.c** and described in Chapter 8, "Context Switching" on page 163).

The unit of measure for the measured time is in **CPU_TS** (timestamp) units so it is necessary to find the resolution of the timer used to measure the timestamps. For example, if the timer used for the timestamp is incremented at 1 MHz then the resolution of **CPU_TS** is 1 microsecond.

Measuring the scheduler lock time adds measurement artifacts and thus increases the amount of time the scheduler is actually locked. However, measurement overhead is accounted for and the measured value represents the actual scheduler lock time as if the measurement was not present.

4-3 µC/OS-III FEATURES WITH LONGER CRITICAL SECTIONS

Table 4-1 shows several µC/OS-III features that have potentially longer critical sections. Knowledge of these will help the user decide whether to direct µC/OS-III to use one critical section over another.

Feature	Reason
Multiple tasks at the same priority	Although this is an important feature of µC/OS-III, multiple tasks at the same priority create longer critical sections. However, if there are only a few tasks at the same priority, interrupt latency would be relatively small. If multiple tasks are not created at the same priority, use the interrupt disable method.
Event Flags Chapter 14, "Synchronization" on page 271	If multiple tasks are waiting on different events, going through all of the tasks waiting for events requires a fair amount of processing time, which means longer critical sections. If only a few tasks (approximately one to five) are waiting on an event flag group, the critical section would be short enough to use the interrupt disable method.
Pend on multiple objects Chapter 16, "Pending On Multiple Objects" on page 331	Pending on multiple objects is probably the most complex feature provided by µC/OS-III, requiring interrupts to be disabled for fairly long periods of time should the interrupt disable method be selected. If pending on multiple objects, it is highly recommended that the user select the scheduler-lock method. If the application does not use this feature, the interrupt disable method is an alternative.
Broadcast on Post calls See `OSSemPost()` and `OSQPost()` descriptions in Appendix A, "µC/OS-III API Reference" on page 453.	µC/OS-III disables interrupts while processing a post to multiple tasks in a broadcast. When not using the broadcast option, you can use the interrupt disable method.

Table 4-1 **Disabling interrupts or locking the Scheduler**

4

4-4 SUMMARY

µC/OS-III needs to access critical sections of code, which it protects by either disabling interrupts (OS_CFG_ISR_POST_DEFERRED_EN set to 0 in **os_cfg.h**), or locking the scheduler (OS_CFG_ISR_POST_DEFERRED_EN set to 1 in **os_cfg.h**).

The application code must not use:

    OS_CRITICAL_ENTER()
    OS_CRITICAL_EXIT()
    OS_CRITICAL_EXIT_NO_SCHED()

When setting CPU_CFG_INT_DIS_MEAS_EN in **cpu_cfg.h**, µC/CPU measures the maximum interrupt disable time. There are two values available, one for the global maximum and one for each task.

When setting OS_CFG_SCHED_LOCK_TIME_MEAS_EN to 1 in **os_cfg.h**, µC/OS-III will measure the maximum scheduler lock time.

Task Management

The design process of a real-time application generally involves splitting the work to be completed into tasks, each responsible for a portion of the problem. µC/OS-III makes it easy for an application programmer to adopt this paradigm. A task (also called a *thread*) is a simple program that thinks it has the Central Processing Unit (CPU) all to itself. On a single CPU, only one task can execute at any given time.

µC/OS-III supports multitasking and allows the application to have any number of tasks. The maximum number of task is actually only limited by the amount of memory (both code and data space) available to the processor. Multitasking is the process of *scheduling* and *switching* the CPU between several tasks (this will be expanded upon later). The CPU switches its attention between several *sequential* tasks. Multitasking provides the illusion of having multiple CPUs and, actually maximizes the use of the CPU. Multitasking also helps in the creation of modular applications. One of the most important aspects of multitasking is that it allows the application programmer to manage the complexity inherent in real-time applications. Application programs are typically easier to design and maintain when multitasking is used.

Tasks are used for such chores as monitoring inputs, updating outputs, performing computations, control loops, update one or more displays, reading buttons and keyboards, communicating with other systems, and more. One application may contain a handful of tasks while another application may require hundreds. The number of tasks does not establish how good or effective a design may be, it really depends on what the application (or product) needs to do. The amount of work a task performs also depends on the application. One task may have a few microseconds worth of work to perform while another task may require tens of milliseconds.

Tasks look like just any other C function except for a few small differences. There are two types of tasks: run-to-completion (Listing 5-1) and infinite loop (Listing 5-2). In most embedded systems, tasks typically take the form of an infinite loop. Also, no task is allowed to return as other C functions can. Given that a task is a regular C function, it can declare local variables.

5

When a μC/OS-III task begins executing, it is passed an argument, **p_arg**. This argument is a pointer to a **void**. The pointer is a universal vehicle used to pass your task the address of a variable, a structure, or even the address of a function, if necessary. With this pointer, it is possible to create many identical tasks, that all use the same code (or task body), but, with different run-time characteristics. For example, you may have four asynchronous serial ports that are each managed by their own task. However, the task code is actually identical. Instead of copying the code four times, you can create the code for a "generic" task that receives a pointer to a data structure, which contains the serial port's parameters (baud rate, I/O port addresses, interrupt vector number, etc.) as an argument. In other words, you can instantiate the same task code four times and pass it different data for each serial port that each instance will manage.

A run-to-completion task must *delete* itself by calling **OSTaskDel()**. The task starts, performs its function, and terminates. There would typically not be too many such tasks in the embedded system because of the overhead associated with "creating" and "deleting" tasks at run-time. In the task body, you can call most of μC/OS-III's functions to help perform the desired operation of the task.

```
void MyTask (void *p_arg)
{
    OS_ERR  err;
    /* Local variables                          */


    /* Do something with 'p_arg'                */
    /* Task initialization                      */
    /* Task body ... do work!                   */
    OSTaskDel((OS_TCB *)0, &err);
}
```

Listing 5-1 **Run-To-Completion task**

With μC/OS-III, you either can call a C or assembly language functions from a task. In fact, it is possible to call the same C function from different tasks as long as the functions are reentrant. A *reentrant* function is a function that does not use static or otherwise global variables unless they are protected (μC/OS-III provides mechanisms for this) from multiple access. If shared C functions only use local variables, they are generally reentrant (assuming that the compiler generates reentrant code). An example of a non-reentrant function is the famous **strtok()** provided by most C compilers as part of the standard library. This function is used to parse an ASCII string for "tokens." The first time you call this function, you specify the ASCII string to parse and a list of token delimiters. As soon as the function finds the first token, it returns. The function "remembers" where it was last so when called again, it can extract additional tokens, which is clearly non-reentrant.

The use of an infinite loop is more common in embedded systems because of the repetitive work needed in such systems (reading inputs, updating displays, performing control operations, etc.). This is one aspect that makes a task different than a regular C function. Note that one could use a "**while (1)**" or "**for (;;)**" to implement the infinite loop, since both behave the same. The one used is simply a matter of personal preference. At Micrium, we like to use "**while (DEF_ON)**". The infinite loop *must* call a µC/OS-III service (i.e., function) that will cause the task to wait for an event to occur. It is important that each task wait for an event to occur, otherwise the task would be a true infinite loop and there would be no easy way for other lower priority tasks to execute. This concept will become clear as more is understood regarding µC/OS-III.

```c
void MyTask (void *p_arg)
{
    /* Local variables                                     */


    /* Do something with "p_arg"                           */
    /* Task initialization                                 */
    while (DEF_ON) {        /* Task body, as an infinite loop.    */
        :
        /* Task body ... do work!                          */
        :
        /* Must call one of the following services:        */
        /*      OSFlagPend()                               */
        /*      OSMutexPend()                              */
        /*      OSPendMulti()                              */
        /*      OSQPend()                                  */
        /*      OSSemPend()                                */
        /*      OSTimeDly()                                */
        /*      OSTimeDlyHMSM()                            */
        /*      OSTaskQPend()                              */
        /*      OSTaskSemPend()                            */
        /*      OSTaskSuspend()     (Suspend self)         */
        /*      OSTaskDel()         (Delete self)          */
        :
        /* Task body ... do work!                          */
        :
    }
}
```

Listing 5-2 **Infinite Loop task**

5

The event the task is waiting for may simply be the passage of time (when OSTimeDly() or OSTimeDlyHMSM() is called). For example, a design may need to scan a keyboard every 100 milliseconds. In this case, you would simply delay the task for 100 milliseconds then see if a key was pressed on the keyboard and, possibly perform some action based on which key was pressed. Typically, however, a keyboard scanning task should just buffer an "identifier" unique to the key pressed and use another task to decide what to do with the key(s) pressed.

Similarly, the event the task is waiting for could be the arrival of a packet from an Ethernet controller. In this case, the task would call one of the OS???Pend() calls (pend is synonymous with wait). The task will have nothing to do until the packet is received. Once the packet is received, the task processes the contents of the packet, and possibly moves the packet along a network stack.

It's important to note that when a task waits for an event, it does not consume CPU time.

Tasks must be created in order for μC/OS-III to know about tasks. You create a task by simply calling OSTaskCreate() as we've seen in Chapter 3. The function prototype for OSTaskCreate() is shown below:

```
void  OSTaskCreate (OS_TCB        *p_tcb,
                    OS_CHAR       *p_name,
                    OS_TASK_PTR   p_task,
                    void          *p_arg,
                    OS_PRIO       prio,
                    CPU_STK       *p_stk_base,
                    CPU_STK_SIZE  stk_limit,
                    CPU_STK_SIZE  stk_size,
                    OS_MSG_QTY    q_size,
                    OS_TICK       time_slice,
                    void          *p_ext,
                    OS_OPT        opt,
                    OS_ERR        *p_err)
```

A complete description of OSTaskCreate() and its arguments is provided in Appendix A, "μC/OS-III API Reference" on page 453. However, it is important to understand that a task needs to be assigned a *Task Control Block* (i.e., TCB), a stack, a priority and a few other parameters which are initialized by OSTaskCreate(), as shown in Figure 5-1.

Figure 5-1 **OSTaskCreate() initializes the task's TCB and stack**

F5-1(1)   When calling **OSTaskCreate()**, you pass the base address of the stack (**p_stk_base**) that will be used by the task, the watermark limit for stack growth (**stk_limit**) which is expressed in number of **CPU_STK** entries before the stack is empty, and the size of that stack (**stk_size**), also in number of **CPU_STK** elements.

F5-1(2)   When specifying **OS_OPT_TASK_STK_CHK + OS_OPT_TASK_STK_CLR** in the opt argument of **OSTaskCreate()**, µC/OS-III initializes the task's stack with all zeros.

5

F5-1(3)   μC/OS-III then initializes the top of the task's stack with a copy of the CPU registers in the same stacking order as if they were all saved at the beginning of an ISR. This makes it easy to perform context switches as we will see when discussing the context switching process. For illustration purposes, the assumption is that the stack grows from high memory to low memory, but the same concept applies for CPUs that use the stack in the reverse order.

F5-1(4)   The new value of the stack pointer (SP) is saved in the TCB. Note that this is also called the **top-of-stack**.

F5-1(5)   The remaining fields of the TCB are initialized: task priority, task name, task state, internal message queue, internal semaphore, and many others.

Next, a call is made to a function that is defined in the CPU port, **OSTaskCreateHook()** (see **os_cpu_c.c**). **OSTaskCreateHook()** is passed the pointer to the new TCB and this function allows you (or the port designer) to extend the functionality of **OSTaskCreate()**. For example, one could printout the contents of the fields of the newly created TCB onto a terminal for debugging purposes.

The task is then placed in the ready-list (see Chapter 6, "The Ready List" on page 139) and finally, if multitasking has started, μC/OS-III will invoke the scheduler to see if the created task is now the highest priority task and, if so, will context switch to this new task.

The body of the task can invoke other services provided by μC/OS-III. Specifically, a task can create another task (i.e., call **OSTaskCreate()**), suspend and resume other tasks (i.e., call **OSTaskSuspend()** and **OSTaskResume()** respectively), post signals or messages to other tasks (i.e., call **OS??Post()**), share resources with other tasks, and more. In other words, tasks are not limited to only make "wait for an event" function calls.

Figure 5-2 shows the resources with which a task typically interacts.

Figure 5-2 **Tasks interact with resources**

F5-2(1)   An important aspect of a task is its code. As previously mentioned, the code looks like any other C function, except that it is typically implemented as an infinite loop and, a task is not allowed to return.

F5-2(2)   Each task is assigned a priority based on its importance in the application. μC/OS-III's job is to decide which task will run on the CPU. The general rule is that μC/OS-III will run the most important *ready-to-run* task (highest priority).

With μC/OS-III, a low priority number indicates a high priority. In other words, a task at priority 1 is more important than a task at priority 10.

μC/OS-III supports a compile-time user configurable number of different priorities (see **OS_PRIO_MAX** in **os_cfg.h**). Thus, μC/OS-III allows the user to determine the number of different priority levels the application is allowed to use. Also, μC/OS-III supports an unlimited number of tasks at the same priority. For example, μC/OS-III can be configured to have 64 different priority levels and one can assign dozens of tasks at each priority level.

See section 5-1 "Assigning Task Priorities" on page 100.

F5-2(3)   A task has its own set of CPU registers. As far as a task is concerned, the task thinks it actually has the CPU all to itself.

F5-2(4)   Because µC/OS-III is a preemptive kernel, each task must have its own stack area. The stack always resides in RAM and is used to keep track of local variables, function calls, and possibly ISR (Interrupt Service Routine) nesting.

Stack space can be allocated either statically (at compile-time) or dynamically (at run-time). A static stack declaration is shown below. This declaration is made outside of a function.

```
static  CPU_STK MyTaskStk[???];
```

or,

```
CPU_STK MyTaskStk[???];
```

Note that "**???**" indicates that the size of the stack (and thus the array) depends on the task stack requirements. Stack space may be allocated dynamically by using the C compiler's heap management function (i.e., **malloc()**) as shown below. However, care must be taken with fragmentation. If creating and deleting tasks, the process of allocating memory might not be able to provide a stack for the task(s) because the heap will eventually become fragmented. For this reason, allocating stack space dynamically in an embedded system is typically allowed but, once allocated, stacks should not be deallocated. Said another way, it's fine to create a task's stack from the heap as long as you don't free the stack space back to the heap.

```
void SomeCode (void)
{
    CPU_STK *p_stk;
    :
    :
    p_stk = (CPU_STK *)malloc(stk_size);
    if (p_stk != (CPU_STK *)0) {
        Create the task and pass it "p_stk" as the base address of the stack;
    }
    :
    :
}
```

See section 5-2 "Determining the Size of a Stack" on page 102.

F5-2(5)   A task can also have access to global variables. However, because µC/OS-III is a preemptive kernel care must be taken with code when accessing such variables as they may be shared between multiple tasks. Fortunately, µC/OS-III provides mechanisms to help with the management of such shared resources (semaphores, mutexes and more).

F5-2(6)   A task may also have access to one or more Input/Output (I/O) devices (also known as *peripherals*). In fact, it is common practice to assign tasks to manage I/O devices.

5-1 ASSIGNING TASK PRIORITIES

Sometimes task priorities are both obvious and intuitive. For example, if the most important aspect of the embedded system is to perform some type of control and it is known that the control algorithm must be responsive then it is best to assign the control task(s) a high priority while display and operator interface tasks are assigned low priority. However, most of the time, assigning task priorities is not so cut and dry because of the complex nature of real-time systems. In most systems, not all tasks are considered critical, and non-critical tasks should obviously be given low priorities.

An interesting technique called rate monotonic scheduling (RMS) assigns task priorities based on how often tasks execute. Simply put, tasks with the highest rate of execution are given the highest priority. However, RMS makes a number of assumptions, including:

■ All tasks are periodic (they occur at regular intervals).

■ Tasks do not synchronize with one another, share resources, or exchange data.

■ The CPU must always execute the highest priority task that is ready-to-run. In other words, preemptive scheduling must be used.

Given a set of n tasks that are assigned RMS priorities, the basic RMS theorem states that all task hard real-time deadlines are always met if the following inequality holds true:

$$\sum_i \frac{E_i}{T_i} \le n \left(2^{\frac{1}{n}} - 1 \right)$$

Where E_i corresponds to the maximum execution time of task i, and T_i corresponds to the execution period of task i. In other words, E_i/T_i corresponds to the fraction of CPU time required to execute task i.

Table 5-1 shows the value for size $n(2^{1/n} - 1)$ based on the number of tasks. The upper bound for an infinite number of tasks is given by $\ln(2)$, or 0.693, which means that you meet all hard real-time deadlines based on RMS, CPU usage of all time-critical tasks should be less than 70 percent!

Note that you can still have non time-critical tasks in a system and thus use close to 100 percent of the CPU's time. However, using 100 percent of your CPU's time is not a desirable goal as it does not allow for code changes and added features. As a rule of thumb, always design a system to use less than 60 to 70 percent of the CPU.

RMS says that the highest rate task has the highest priority. In some cases, the highest rate task might not be the most important task. The application should dictate how to assign priorities. However, RMS is an interesting starting point.

Number of Tasks	$n(2^{1/n}-1)$
1	1.00
2	0.828
3	0.779
4	0.756
5	0.743
:	:
:	:
:	:
Infinite	0.693

Table 5-1 **Allowable CPU usage based on number of tasks**

5

5-2 DETERMINING THE SIZE OF A STACK

The size of the stack required by the task is application specific. When sizing the stack, however, one must account for the nesting of all the functions called by the task, the number of local variables to be allocated by all functions called by the task, and the stack requirements for all nested interrupt service routines. In addition, the stack must be able to store all CPU registers and possibly Floating-Point Unit (FPU) registers if the processor has a FPU. In addition, as a general rule in embedded systems, avoid writing recursive code.

It is possible to manually figure out the stack space needed by adding all the memory required by all function call nesting (1 pointer each function call for the return address), plus all the memory required by all the arguments passed in those function calls, plus storage for a full CPU context (depends on the CPU), plus another full CPU context for each nested ISRs (if the CPU doesn't have a separate stack to handle ISRs), plus whatever stack space is needed by those ISRs. Adding all this up is a tedious chore and the resulting number is a minimum requirement. Most likely you would not make the stack size that precise in order to account for "surprises." The number arrived at should probably be multiplied by some safety factor, possibly 1.5 to 2.0. This calculation assumes that the exact path of the code is known at all times, which is not always possible. Specifically, when calling a function such as `printf()` or some other library function, it might be difficult or nearly impossible to even guess just how much stack space `printf()` will require. In this case, start with a fairly large stack space and monitor the stack usage at run-time to see just how much stack space is actually used after the application runs for a while.

There are really cool and clever compilers/linkers that provide this information in a link map. For each function, the link map indicates the worst-case stack usage. This feature clearly enables you to better evaluate stack usage for each task. It is still necessary to add the stack space for a **full CPU** context plus, another **full CPU** context for each nested ISR (if the CPU does not have a separate stack to handle ISRs), plus whatever stack space is needed by those ISRs. Again, allow for a safety net and multiply this value by some factor.

Always monitor stack usage at run-time while developing and testing the product as stack overflows occur often and can lead to some curious behaviors. In fact, whenever someone mentions that his or her application behaves "strangely," insufficient stack size is the first thing that comes to mind.

5-3 DETECTING TASK STACK OVERFLOWS

1) USING AN MMU OR MPU

Stack overflows are easily detected if the processor has a Memory Management Unit (MMU) or a Memory Protection Unit (MPU). Basically, MMUs and MPUs are special hardware devices integrated alongside the CPU that can be configured to detect when a task attempts to access invalid memory locations, whether code, data, or stack. However, setting up an MMU or MPU is well beyond the scope of this book.

2) USING A CPU WITH STACK OVERFLOW DETECTION

Some processors, however, do have simple stack pointer overflow detection registers. When the CPU's stack pointer goes below (or above depending on stack growth) the value set in this register, an exception is generated and the exception handler ensures that the offending code does not do further damage (possibly issue a warning about the faulty code or even terminate it). The `.StkLimitPtr` field in the `OS_TCB` (see Task Control Blocks) is provided for this purpose as shown in Figure 5-3. Note that the position of the stack limit is typically set at a valid location in the task's stack with sufficient room left on the stack to handle the exception itself (assuming the CPU does not have a separate exception stack). In most cases, the position can be fairly close to `&MyTaskStk[0]`.

Figure 5-3 **Hardware detection of stack overflows**

As a reminder, the location of the **.StkLimitPtr** is determined by the "**stk_limit**" argument passed to **OSTaskCreate()**, when the task is created as shown below:

```
OS_TCB  MtTaskTCB;
CPU_STK MyTaskStk[1000];


OSTaskCreate(&MyTaskTCB,
             "MyTaskName",
             MyTask,
             &MyTaskArg,
             MyPrio,
             &MyTaskStk[0],  /* Stack base address                         */
             100,            /* Used to set .StkLimitPtr to trigger exception ... */
                             /* ... at stack usage > 90%                   */
             1000,           /* Total stack size (in CPU_STK elements)     */
             MyTaskQSize,
             MyTaskTimeQuanta,
             (void *)0,
             MY_TASK_OPT,
             &err);
```

Of course, the value of **.StkLimitPtr** used by the CPU's stack overflow detection hardware needs to be changed whenever µC/OS-III performs a context switch. This can be tricky because the value of this register may need to be changed so that it first points to **NULL**, then the CPU's stack pointer is changed, and finally the value of the stack checking register is set to the value saved in the TCB's **.StkLimitPtr**. Why? Because if the sequence is not followed, the exception could be generated as soon as the stack pointer or the stack overflow detection register is changed. You can avoid this problem by first changing the stack overflow detection register to point to a location that ensures the stack pointer is never invalid (thus the **NULL** as described above). Note that I assumed here that the stack grows from high memory to low memory but the concept works in a similar fashion if the stack grows in the opposite direction.

3) SOFTWARE-BASED STACK OVERFLOW DETECTION

Whenever µC/OS-III switches from one task to another, it calls a "hook" function (**OSTaskSwHook()**), which allows the µC/OS-III port programmer to extend the capabilities of the context switch function. So, if the processor doesn't have hardware stack pointer overflow detection, it's still possible to "simulate" this feature by adding code in the context switch hook function and, perform the overflow detection in software. Specifically, before a task is *switched* in, the code should ensure that the stack pointer to load into the CPU does not exceed the "limit" placed in **.StkLimitPtr**. Because the software implementation cannot detect the stack overflow "as soon" as the stack pointer exceeds the value of .StkLimitPtr, it is important to position the value of **.StkLimitPtr** in the stack fairly far from **&MyTaskStk[0]**, as shown in Figure 5-4. A software implementation such as this is not as reliable as a hardware-based detection mechanism but still prevents a possible stack overflow. Of course, the **.StkLimitPtr** field would be set using **OSTaskCreate()** as shown above but this time, with a location further away from **&MyTaskStk[0]**.

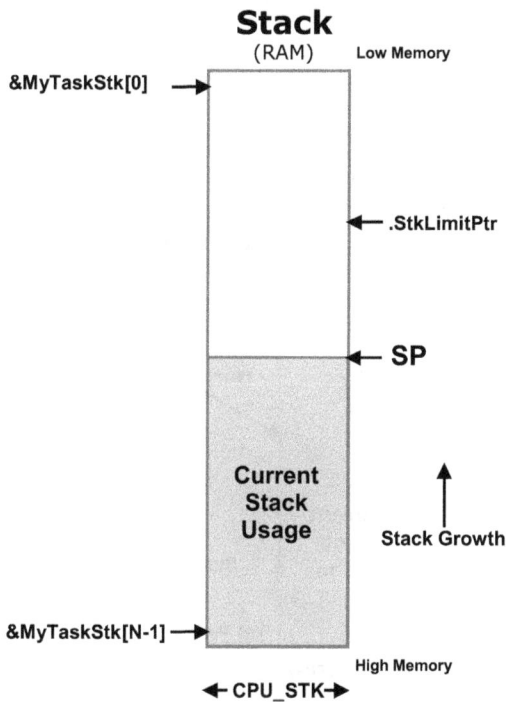

Stack
(RAM)   Low Memory

&MyTaskStk[0] →

←— .StkLimitPtr

←— **SP**

Current Stack Usage   ↑ **Stack Growth**

&MyTaskStk[N-1] →

High Memory

←— **CPU_STK** →

Figure 5-4 **Software detection of stack overflows, monitoring .StkLimitPtr**

4) COUNTING THE AMOUNT OF FREE STACK SPACE

Another way to check for stack overflows is to allocate more stack space than is anticipated to be used for the stack, then, monitor and possibly display actual maximum stack usage at run-time. This is fairly easy to do. First, the task stack needs to be cleared (i.e., filled with zeros) when the task is created. Next, a low priority task *walks the stack* of each task created, from the bottom (**&MyTaskStk[0]**) towards the top, counting the number of zero entries. When the task finds a non-zero value, the process is stopped and the usage of the stack can be computed (in number of bytes used or as a percentage). Then, you can adjust the size of the stacks (by recompiling the code) to allocate a more *reasonable* value (either increase or decrease the amount of stack space for each task). For this to be effective, however, you need to run the application long enough for the stack to grow to its highest value. This is illustrated in Figure 5-5. μC/OS-III provides a function that performs this calculation at run-time, `OSTaskStkChk()` and in fact, this function is called by `OS_StatTask()` to compute stack usage for every task created in the application (to be described later).

Figure 5-5 **Software detection of stack overflows, walking the stack**

5

5-4 TASK MANAGEMENT SERVICES

µC/OS-III provides a number of task-related services to call from the application. These services are found in **os_task.c** and they all start with **OSTask???()**. The type of service they perform groups task-related services:

Group	Functions
General	OSTaskCreate() OSTaskDel() OSTaskChangePrio() OSTaskRegSet() OSTaskRegGet() OSTaskSuspend() OSTaskResume() OSTaskTimeQuantaSet()
Signaling a Task (See Chapter 14, "Synchronization" on page 271)	OSTaskSemPend() OSTaskSemPost() OSTaskSemPendAbort()
Sending Messages to a Task (See Chapter 15, "Message Passing" on page 307)	OSTaskQPend() OSTaskQPost() OSTaskQPendAbort() OSTaskQFlush()

Table 5-2 **Task Management Services**

A complete description of all µC/OS-III task related services is provided in Appendix A, "µC/OS-III API Reference" on page 453.

5

5-5 TASK MANAGEMENT INTERNALS

5-5-1 TASK STATES

From a μC/OS-III user point of view, a task can be in any one of five states as shown in Figure 5-6. Internally, μC/OS-III does not need to keep track of the dormant state and the other states are tracked slightly differently. The actual μC/OS-III states will be discussed after a discussion on task states from the user's point of view. Figure 5-6 also shows which μC/OS-III functions are used to move from one state to another. The diagram is actually simplified as state transitions are a bit more complicated than this.

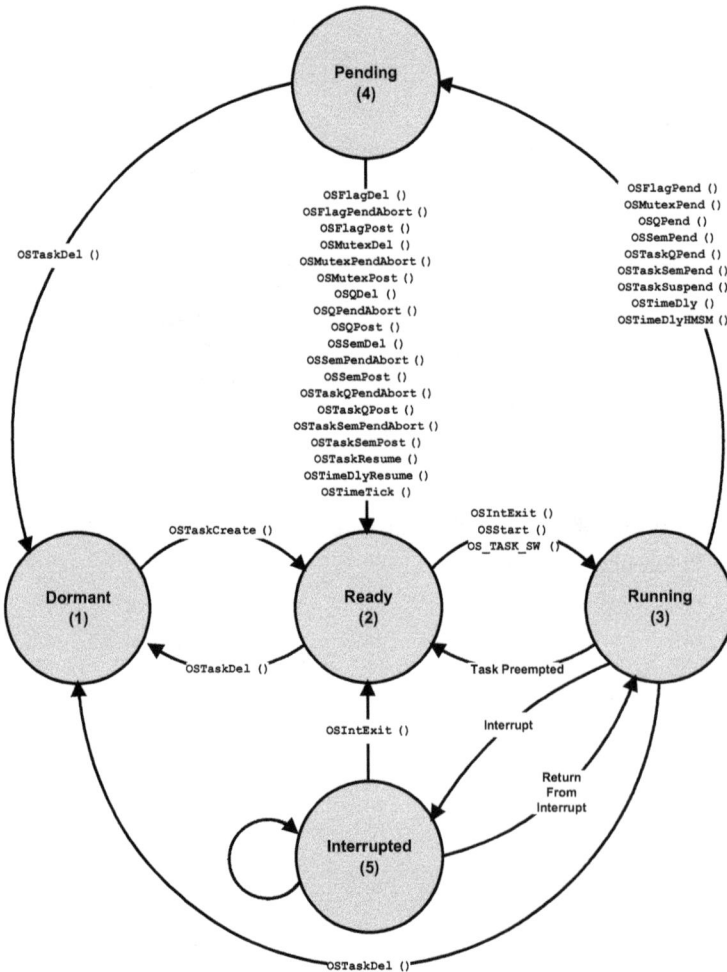

Figure 5-6 **Five basic states of a task**

F5-6(1)   The *Dormant* state corresponds to a task that resides in memory but has not been made available to µC/OS-III.

A task is made available to µC/OS-III by calling a function to create the task, **OSTaskCreate()**. The task code actually resides in code space but µC/OS-III needs to be informed about it.

When it is no longer necessary for µC/OS-III to manage a task, your code can call the task delete function, **OSTaskDel()**. **OSTaskDel()** does not actually delete the code of the task, it is simply not eligible to access the CPU.

F5-6(2)   A task is in the *Ready* state when it is ready-to-run. There can be any number of tasks ready and µC/OS-III keeps track of all ready tasks in a **ready list** (discussed later). This list is sorted by priority.

F5-6(3)   The most important ready-to-run task is placed in the *Running* state. On a single CPU, only one task can be running at any given time.

The task selected to run on the CPU is *switched in* by µC/OS-III when the application code calls **OSStart()**, or when µC/OS-III calls either **OSIntExit()** or **OS_TASK_SW()**.

As previously discussed, tasks must wait for an event to occur. A task waits for an event by calling one of the functions that brings the task to the pending state if the event has not occurred.

F5-6(4)   Tasks in the *Pending* state are placed in a special list called a *pend-list* (or wait list) associated with the event the task is waiting for. When waiting for the event to occur, the task does not consume CPU time. When the event occurs, the task is placed back into the ready list and µC/OS-III decides whether the newly readied task is the most important ready-to-run task. If this is the case, the currently running task will be preempted (placed back in the ready list) and the newly readied task is given control of the CPU. In other words, the newly readied task will run immediately if it is the most important task.

Note that the **OSTaskSuspend()** function unconditionally blocks a task and this task will not actually wait for an event to occur but in fact, waits until another task calls **OSTaskResume()** to make the task ready-to-run.

F5-6(5)   Assuming that CPU interrupts are enabled, an interrupting device will suspend execution of a task and execute an Interrupt Service Routine (ISR). ISRs are typically events that tasks wait for. Generally speaking, an ISR should simply notify a task that an event occurred and let the task process the event. ISRs should be as short as possible and most of the work of handling the interrupting devices should be done at the task level where it can be managed by µC/OS-III. ISRs are only allowed to make "Post" calls (i.e., **OSFlagPost()**, **OSQPost()**, **OSSemPost()**, **OSTaskQPost()** and **OSTaskSemPost()**). The only post call not allowed to be made from an ISR is **OSMutexPost()** since mutexes, as will be addressed later, are assumed to be services that are only accessible at the task level.

As the state diagram indicates, an interrupt can interrupt another interrupt. This is called **interrupt nesting** and most processors allow this. However, interrupt nesting easily leads to stack overflow if not managed properly.

Internally, µC/OS-III keeps track of task states using the state machine shown in Figure 5-7. The task state is actually maintained in a variable that is part of a data structure associated with each task, the task's TCB. The task state diagram was referenced throughout the design of µC/OS-III when implementing most of µC/OS-III's services. The number in parentheses is the state number of the task and thus, a task can be in any one of eight (8) states (see **os.h, OS_TASK_STATE_???**).

Note that the diagram does not keep track of a dormant task, as a dormant task is not known to µC/OS-III. Also, interrupts and interrupt nesting is tracked differently as will be explained further in the text.

This state diagram should be quite useful to understand how to use several functions and their impact on the state of tasks. In fact, I'd highly recommend that the reader bookmark the page of the diagram.

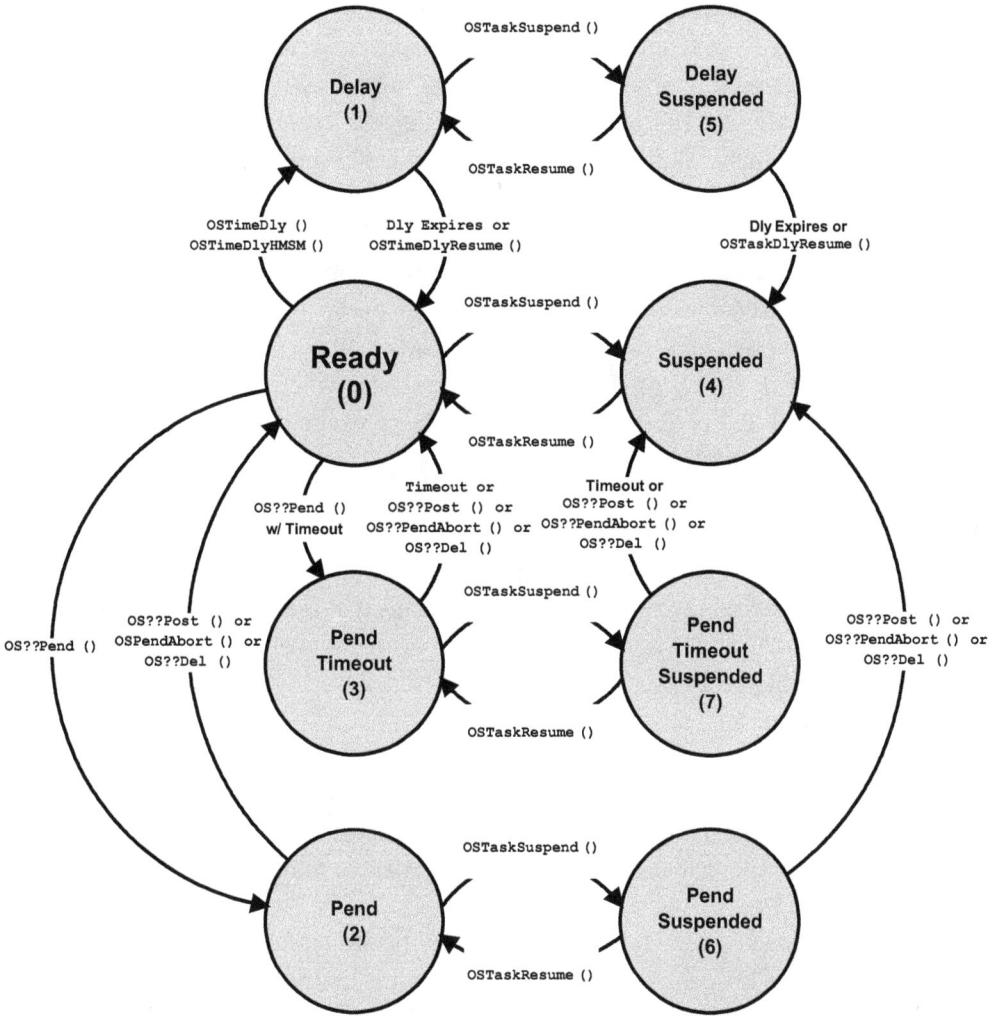

Figure 5-7 **µC/OS-III's internal task state machine**

F5-7(0)   A task is in State 0 when a task is ready-to-run. Every task "wants" to be
           ready-to-run as that is the only way it gets to perform their duties.

F5-7(1)   A task can decide to wait for time to expire by calling either **OSTimeDly()** or
           OSTimeDlyHMSM(). When the time expires or the delay is cancelled (by calling
           OSTimeDlyResume()), the task returns to the ready state.

5

F5-7(2)   A task can wait for an event to occur by calling one of the pend (i.e., wait) functions (OSFlagPend( ), OSMutexPend( ), OSQPend( ), OSSemPend( ), OSTaskQPend( ), or OSTaskSemPend( )), and specify to wait forever for the event to occur. The pend terminates when the event occurs (i.e., a task or an ISR performs a "post"), the awaited object is deleted or, another task decides to abort the pend.

F5-7(3)   A task can wait for an event to occur as indicated, but specify that it is willing to wait a certain amount of time for the event to occur. If the event is not posted within that time, the task is readied, then the task is notified that a timeout occurred. Again, the pend terminates when the event occurs (i.e., a task or an ISR performs a "post"), the object awaited is deleted or, another task decides to abort the pend.

F5-7(4)   A task can suspend itself or another task by calling OSTaskSuspend( ). The only way the task is allowed to resume execution is by calling OSTaskResume( ). Suspending a task means that a task will not be able to run on the CPU until it is resumed. If a task suspends itself then it must be resumed by another task.

F5-7(5)   A delayed task can also be suspended by another task. In this case, the effect is additive. In other words, the delay must complete (or be resumed by OSTimeDlyResume( )) and the suspension must be removed (by another task which would call OSTaskResume( )) in order for the task to be able to run.

F5-7(6)   A task waiting on an event to occur may be suspended by another task. Again, the effect is additive. The event must occur and the suspension removed (by another task) in order for the task to be able to run. Of course, if the object that the task is pending on is deleted or, the pend is aborted by another task, then one of the above two condition is removed. The suspension, however, must be explicitly removed.

F5-7(7)   A task can wait for an event, but only for a certain amount of time, and the task could also be suspended by another task. As one might expect, the suspension must be removed by another task (or the same task that suspended it in the first place), and the event needs to either occur or timeout while waiting for the event.

5

5-5-2 TASK CONTROL BLOCKS (TCBs)

A task control block (TCB) is a data structure used by kernels to maintain information about a task. Each task requires its own TCB and, for µC/OS-III, the user assigns the TCB in user memory space (RAM). The address of the task's TCB is provided to µC/OS-III when calling task-related services (i.e., **OSTask???()** functions). The task control block data structure is declared in **os.h** as shown in Listing 5-3. Note that the fields are actually commented in **os.h**, and some of the fields are conditionally compiled based on whether or not certain features are desired. Both are not shown here for clarity.

Also, it is important to note that even when the user understands what the different fields of the **OS_TCB** do, the application code must never directly access these (especially change them). In other words, **OS_TCB** fields must only be accessed by µC/OS-III and not the code.

```
struct os_tcb {
    CPU_STK          *StkPtr;
    void             *ExtPtr;
    CPU_STK          *StkLimitPtr;
    OS_TCB           *NextPtr;
    OS_TCB           *PrevPtr;
    OS_TCB           *TickNextPtr;
    OS_TCB           *TickPrevPtr;
    OS_TICK_SPOKE    *TickSpokePtr;
    OS_CHAR          *NamePtr;
    CPU_STK          *StkBasePtr;
    OS_TASK_PTR       TaskEntryAddr;
    void             *TaskEntryArg;
    OS_PEND_DATA     *PendDataTblPtr;
    OS_STATE          PendOn;
    OS_STATUS         PendStatus;
    OS_STATE          TaskState;
    OS_PRIO           Prio;
    CPU_STK_SIZE      StkSize;
    OS_OPT            Opt;
    OS_OBJ_QTY        PendDataEntries;
    CPU_TS            TS;
    OS_SEM_CTR        SemCtr;
    OS_TICK           TickCtrPrev;
    OS_TICK           TickCtrMatch;
    OS_TICK           TickRemain;
    OS_TICK           TimeQuanta;
    OS_TICK           TimeQuantaCtr;
    void             *MsgPtr;
```

5

```
    OS_MSG_SIZE          MsgSize;
    OS_MSG_Q             MsgQ;
    CPU_TS               MsgQPendTime;
    CPU_TS               MsgQPendTimeMax;
    OS_REG               RegTbl[OS_TASK_REG_TBL_SIZE];
    OS_FLAGS             FlagsPend;
    OS_FLAGS             FlagsRdy;
    OS_OPT               FlagsOpt;
    OS_NESTING_CTR       SuspendCtr;
    OS_CPU_USAGE         CPUUsage;
    OS_CTX_SW_CTR        CtxSwCtr;
    CPU_TS               CyclesDelta;
    CPU_TS               CyclesStart;
    OS_CYCLES            CyclesTotal;
    OS_CYCLES            CyclesTotalPrev;
    CPU_TS               SemPendTime;
    CPU_TS               SemPendTimeMax;
    CPU_STK_SIZE         StkUsed;
    CPU_STK_SIZE         StkFree;
    CPU_TS               IntDisTimeMax;
    CPU                  SchedLockTimeMax;
    OS_TCB               DbgNextPtr;
    OS_TCB               DbgPrevPtr;
    CPU_CHAR             DbgNamePtr;
};
```

Listing 5-3 **OS_TCB Data Structure**

.StkPtr

This field contains a pointer to the current top-of-stack for the task. µC/OS-III allows each task to have its own stack and each stack can be any size. **.StkPtr** should be the only field in the **OS_TCB** data structure accessed from assembly language code (for the context-switching code). This field is therefore placed as the first entry in the structure making access easier from assembly language code (it will be at offset zero in the data structure).

.ExtPtr

This field contains a pointer to a user-definable data area used to extend the TCB as needed. This pointer is provided as an argument passed in **OSTaskCreate()**. This pointer is easily accessible from assembly language since it always follows the **.StkPtr**. **.ExtPtr** can be used to add storage for saving the context of a FPU (Floating-Point Unit) if the processor you are using has a FPU.

.StkLimitPtr

The field contains a pointer to a location in the task's stack to set a *watermark* limit for stack growth and is determined from the value of the "**stk_limit**" argument passed to **OSTaskCreate()**. Some processors have special registers that automatically check the value of the stack pointer at run-time to ensure that the stack does not overflow. **.StkLimitPtr** may be used to set this register during a context switch. Alternatively, if the processor does not have such a register, this can be "simulated" in software. However, this is not as reliable as a hardware solution. If this feature is not used then you can set the value of "**stk_limit**" can be set to **0** when calling **OSTaskCreate()**. See also section 5-3 "Detecting Task Stack Overflows" on page 103).

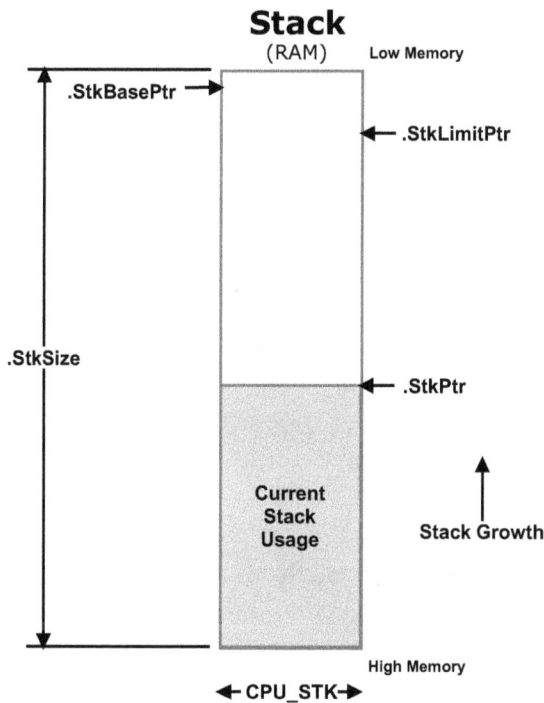

.NextPtr and **.PrevPtr**

These pointers are used to doubly link **OS_TCBs** in the ready list. A doubly linked list allows **OS_TCBs** to be quickly inserted and removed from the list.

.TickNextPtr and **.TickPrevPtr**

These pointers are used to doubly link **OS_TCBs** in the list of tasks waiting for time to expire or to timeout from pend calls. Again, a doubly linked list allows **OS_TCBs** to be quickly inserted and removed from the list.

.TickSpokePtr

This pointer is used to know which spoke in the "tick wheel" the task is linked to. The tick wheel will be described in "Chapter 9, "Interrupt Management" on page 173."

.NamePtr

This pointer allows a name (an ASCII string) to be assigned to each task. Having a name is useful when debugging, since it is user friendly compared to displaying the address of the OS_TCB. Storage for the ASCII string is assumed to be in user space, either in code memory (ASCII string declared as a const) or in RAM.

.StkBasePtr

This field points to the base address of the task's stack. The stack base is typically the lowest address in memory where the stack for the task resides. A task stack is declared as follows:

```
CPU_STK MyTaskStk[???];
```

CPU_STK is the data type you must use to declare task stacks and ??? is the size of the stack associated with the task. The base address is always &MyTaskStk[0].

.TaskEntryAddr

This field contains the entry address of the task. As previously mentioned, a task is declared as shown below and this field contains the address of MyTask.

```
void  MyTask (void *p_arg);
```

.TaskEntryArg

This field contains the value of the argument that is passed to the task when the task starts. As previously mentioned, a task is declared as shown below and this field contains the value of p_arg.

```
void  MyTask (void *p_arg);
```

.PendDataTblPtr

µC/OS-III allows the task to pend on any number of semaphores or message queues simultaneously. This pointer points to a table containing information about the pended objects. This is described in Chapter 10, "Pend Lists".

.PendOn

This field indicates what the task is pending on and contains one of the following values declared in **os.h**:

```
OS_TASK_PEND_ON_NOTHING
OS_TASK_PEND_ON_FLAG
OS_TASK_PEND_ON_TASK_Q
OS_TASK_PEND_ON_MULTI
OS_TASK_PEND_ON_MUTEX
OS_TASK_PEND_ON_Q
OS_TASK_PEND_ON_SEM
OS_TASK_PEND_ON_TASK_SEM
```

.PendStatus

This field indicates the outcome of a pend and contains one of the values declared in **os.h**:

```
OS_STATUS_PEND_OK
OS_STATUS_PEND_ABORT
OS_STATUS_PEND_DEL
OS_STATUS_PEND_TIMEOUT
```

.TaskState

This field indicates the current state of a task and contains one of the eight (8) task states that a task can be in. These states are declared in **os.h**:

```
OS_TASK_STATE_RDY
OS_TASK_STATE_DLY
OS_TASK_STATE_PEND
OS_TASK_STATE_PEND_TIMEOUT
OS_TASK_STATE_SUSPENDED
OS_TASK_STATE_DLY_SUSPENDED
OS_TASK_STATE_PEND_SUSPENDED
OS_TASK_STATE_PEND_TIMEOUT_SUSPENDED
```

.Prio

This field contains the current priority of a task. **.Prio** is a value between 0 and OS_CFG_PRIO_MAX-1. In fact, the idle task is the only task at priority OS_CFG_PRIO_MAX-1.

.StkSize

This field contains the size (in number of `CPU_STK` elements) of the stack associated with the task. Recall that a task stack is declared as follows:

```
CPU_STK MyTaskStk[???];
```

`.StkSize` is the number of elements in the above array.

.Opt

This field saves the "options" passed to `OSTaskCreate()` when the task is created as shown below. Note that task options are additive.

```
OS_OPT_TASK_NONE
OS_OPT_TASK_STK_CHK
OS_OPT_TASK_STK_CLR
OS_OPT_TASK_SAVE_FP
```

.PendDataTblEntries

This field works with the `.PendDataTblPtr` and indicates the number of objects a task is pending on at the same time.

.TS

This field is used to store a "time stamp" of when an event that the task was waiting on occurred. When the task resumes execution, this time stamp is returned to the caller.

.SemCtr

This field contains a semaphore counter associated with the task. Each task has its own semaphore built-in. An ISR or another task can signal a task using this semaphore. `.SemCtr` is therefore used to keep track of how many times the task is signaled. `.SemCtr` is used by `OSTaskSem???()` services.

.TickCtrPrev

This field stores the previous value of `OSTickCtr` when `OSTimeDly()` is called with the `OS_OPT_TIME_PERIODIC` option.

.TickCtrMatch

When a task is waiting for time to expire, or pending on an object with a timeout, the task is placed in a special list of tasks waiting for time to expire. When in this list, the task waits for .TickCtrMatch to match the value of the "tick counter" (OSTickCtr). When a match occurs, the task is removed from that list.

.TickRemain

This field is computed at run time by OS_TickTask() to compute the amount of time (expressed in "ticks") left before a delay or timeout expires. This field is useful for debuggers or run-time monitors for display purposes.

.TimeQuanta and .TimeQuantaCtr

These fields are used for time slicing. When multiple tasks are ready-to-run at the same priority, .TimeQuanta determines how much time (in ticks) the task will execute until it is preempted by µC/OS-III so that the next task at the same priority gets a chance to execute. .TimeQuantaCtr keeps track of the remaining number of ticks for this to happen and is loaded with .TimeQuanta at the beginning of the task's time slice.

.MsgPtr

When a message is sent to a task, this field contains the message received. This field only exists in a TCB if message queue services (OS_CFG_Q_EN is set to 1 in os_cfg.h), or task message queue services, are enabled (OS_CFG_TASK_Q_EN is set to 1 in os_cfg.h) at compile time.

.MsgSize

When a message is sent to a task, this field contains the size (in number of bytes) of the message received. This field only exists in a TCB if message queue services (OS_CFG_Q_EN is set to 1 in os_cfg.h), or task message queue services, (OS_CFG_TASK_Q_EN is set to 1 in os_cfg.h) are enabled at compile time.

.MsgQ

µC/OS-III allows tasks or ISRs to send messages directly to tasks. Because of this, a message queue is actually built into each TCB. This field only exists in a TCB if task message queue services are enabled at compile time (OS_CFG_TASK_Q_EN is set to 1 in os_cfg.h). .MsgQ is used by the OSTaskQ???() services.

.MsgQPendTime

This field contains the amount of time it took for a message to arrive. When OSTaskQPost() is called, the current time stamp is read and stored in the message. When OSTaskQPend() returns, the current time stamp is read again and the difference between the two times is stored in this variable. A debugger or μC/Probe can be used to indicate the time taken for a message to arrive by displaying this field.

This field is only available if setting OS_CFG_TASK_PROFILE_EN to 1 in os_cfg.h.

.MsgQPendTimeMax

This field contains the maximum amount of time it takes for a message to arrive. It is a peak detector of the value of .MsgQPendTime. The peak can be reset by calling OSStatReset().

This field is only available if setting OS_CFG_TASK_PROFILE_EN to 1 in os_cfg.h.

.RegTbl[]

This field contains a table of "registers" that are task-specific. These registers are different than CPU registers. Task registers allow for the storage of such task-specific information as task ID, "errno" common in some software components, and more. Task registers may also store task-related data that needs to be associated with the task at run time. Note that the data type for elements of this array is OS_REG, which can be declared at compile time to be nearly anything. However, all registers must be of this data type. This field only exists in a TCB if task registers are enabled at compile time (OS_CFG_TASK_REG_TBL_SIZE is greater than 0 in os_cfg.h).

.FlagsPend

When a task pends on event flags, this field contains the event flags (i.e., bits) that the task is pending on. This field only exists in a TCB if event flags services are enabled at compile time (OS_CFG_FLAG_EN is set to 1 in os_cfg.h).

.FlagsRdy

This field contains the event flags that were posted and that the task was waiting on. In other words, it allows a task to know which event flags made the task ready-to-run. This field only exists in a TCB if event flags services are enabled at compile time (OS_CFG_FLAG_EN is set to 1 in os_cfg.h).

.FlagsOpt

When a task pends on event flags, this field contains the type of pend (pend on any event flag bit specified in .FlagsPend or all event flag bits specified in .FlagsPend). This field only exists in a TCB if event flags services are enabled at compile time (OS_CFG_FLAG_EN is set to 1 in os_cfg.h). There can be up to eight main values as shown below plus add-on options. Possible values are:

```
OS_OPT_PEND_FLAG_CLR_ALL
OS_OPT_PEND_FLAG_CLR_ANY
OS_OPT_PEND_FLAG_CLR_AND
OS_OPT_PEND_FLAG_CLR_OR
OS_OPT_PEND_FLAG_SET_ALL
OS_OPT_PEND_FLAG_SET_ANY
OS_OPT_PEND_FLAG_SET_AND
OS_OPT_PEND_FLAG_SET_OR
```

You can also 'add' **OS_OPT_PEND_FLAG_CONSUME** and either **OS_OPT_PEND_BLOCKING** or **OS_OPT_PEND_NON_BLOCKING** to the above options.

.SuspendCtr

This field is used by **OSTaskSuspend()** and **OSTaskResume()** to keep track of how many times a task is suspended. Task suspension can be nested. When **.SuspendCtr** is 0, all suspensions are removed. This field only exists in a TCB if task suspension is enabled at compile time (**OS_CFG_TASK_SUSPEND_EN** is set to 1 in **os_cfg.h**).

.CPUUsage

This field is computed by **OS_StatTask()** if **OS_CFG_TASK_PROFILE_EN** is set to 1 in **os_cfg.h**. **.CPUUsage** contains the CPU usage of a task in percent (0 to 100%). As of version V3.03.00, **.CPUUsage** is multiplied by 100. In other words, 10000 represents 100.00%.

.CtxSwCtr

This field keeps track of how often the task has executed (not how long it has executed). This field is generally used by debuggers or run-time monitors to see if a task is executing (the value of this field would be non-zero and would be incrementing). The field is enabled at compile time when **OS_CFG_TASK_PROFILE_EN** is set to 1 in **os_cfg.h**.

.CyclesDelta

.CyclesDelta is computed during a context switch and contains the value of the current time stamp (obtained by calling **OS_TS_GET()**) minus the value of **.CyclesStart**. This field is generally used by debuggers or a run-time monitor to see how long a task had control of the CPU until it got ·switched out. The field is enabled at compile time when **OS_CFG_TASK_PROFILE_EN** is set to 1 in **os_cfg.h**.

.CyclesStart

This field is used to measure how long a task had control of the CPU. .CyclesStart is updated when µC/OS-III performs a context switch. .CyclesStart contains the value of the current time stamp (it calls OS_TS_GET()) when a task is switched-in. The field is enabled at compile time when OS_CFG_TASK_PROFILE_EN is set to 1 in os_cfg.h.

.CyclesTotal

This field accumulates the value of .CyclesDelta, so it contains the total execution time of a task during a set period of time. .CyclesTotal is used by OS_StatTask() to determine CPU usage on a per-task basis. This is typically a 32-bit value because of the accumulation of cycles over time. On the other hand, using a 64-bit value ensures that we can accumulate CPU cycles for almost 600 years even if the CPU is running at 1 GHz! Of course, it's assumed that the compiler supports 64-bit data types. The field is enabled at compile time when OS_CFG_TASK_PROFILE_EN is set to 1 in os_cfg.h.. .CyclesTotal is used by OS_StatTask() to determine CPU usage on a per-task basis.

.SemPendTime

This field contains the amount of time taken for the semaphore to be signaled. When OSTaskSemPost() is called, the current time stamp is read and stored in the OS_TCB (see .TS). When OSTaskSemPend() returns, the current time stamp is read again and the difference between the two times is stored in this variable. This field can be displayed by a debugger or µC/Probe to indicate how much time it took for the task to be signaled.

This field is only available when setting OS_CFG_TASK_PROFILE_EN to 1 in os_cfg.h.

.SemPendTimeMax

This field contains the maximum amount of time it took for the task to be signaled. It is a peak detector of the value of .SemPendTime. The peak can be reset by calling OSStatReset().

This field is only available if setting OS_CFG_TASK_PROFILE_EN to 1 in os_cfg.h.

.StkUsed and .StkFree

µC/OS-III is able to compute (at run time) the amount of stack space a task actually uses and how much stack space remains. This is accomplished by a function called OSTaskStkChk(). Stack usage computation assumes that the task's stack is "cleared" when the task is created. In other words, when calling OSTaskCreate(), it is expected that the following options be specified: OS_TASK_OPT_STK_CLR and OS_TASK_OPT_STK_CHK. OSTaskCreate() will then clear all the RAM used for the task's stack.

µC/OS-III provides an internal task called OS_StatTask() that checks the stack of each of the tasks at run-time. OS_StatTask() typically runs at a low priority so that it does not interfere with the application code. OS_StatTask() saves the value computed for each task in the TCB of each task in these fields, which represents the maximum number of stack bytes used and the amount of stack space still unused by the task. These fields only exist in a TCB if the statistic task is enabled at compile time (OS_CFG_STAT_TASK_STK_CHK_EN is set to 1 in os_cfg.h).

.IntDisTimeMax

This field keeps track of the maximum interrupt disable time of the task. The field is updated only if µC/CPU supports interrupt disable time measurements. This field is available only if setting OS_CFG_TASK_PROFILE_EN to 1 in os_cfg.h and µC/CPU's CPU_CFG_INT_DIS_MEAS_EN is defined in cpu_cfg.h.

.SchedLockTimeMax

The field keeps track of the maximum scheduler lock time of the task. In other words, the maximum amount of time the task locks the scheduler.

This field is available only if you set OS_CFG_TASK_PROFILE_EN to 1 and OS_CFG_SCHED_LOCK_TIME_MEAS_EN is set to 1 in os_cfg.h.

.DbgNextPtr

This field contains a pointer to the next OS_TCB in a doubly linked list of OS_TCBs. OS_TCBs are placed in this list by OSTaskCreate(). This field is only present if OS_CFG_DBG_EN is set to 1 in os_cfg.h.

.DbgPrevPtr

This field contains a pointer to the previous OS_TCB in a doubly linked list of OS_TCBs. OS_TCBs are placed in this list by OSTaskCreate(). This field is only present if OS_CFG_DBG_EN is set to 1 in os_cfg.h.

.DbgNamePtr

This field contains a pointer to the name of the object that the task is pending on when the task is pending on either an event flag group, a semaphore, a mutual exclusion semaphore or a message queue. This information is quite useful during debugging and thus, this field is only present if OS_CFG_DBG_EN is set to 1 in os_cfg.h.

5-6 INTERNAL TASKS

During initialization, µC/OS-III creates a minimum of two (2) internal tasks (OS_IdleTask() and OS_TickTask()) and, three (3) optional tasks (OS_StatTask(), OS_TmrTask() and OS_IntQTask()). The optional tasks are created based on the value of compile-time #defines found in os_cfg.h.

OS_CFG_STAT_TASK_EN	enables OS_StatTask()
OS_CFG_TMR_EN	enables OS_TmrTask()
OS_CFG_ISR_POST_DEFERRED_EN	enables OS_IntQTask()

5-6-1 THE IDLE TASK (OS_IdleTask(), os_core.c)

OS_IdleTask() is the very first task created by µC/OS-III and always exists in a µC/OS-III-based application. The priority of the idle task is always set to OS_CFG_PRIO_MAX-1. In fact, OS_IdleTask() is the only task that is ever allowed to be at this priority and, as a safeguard, when other tasks are created, OSTaskCreate() ensures that there are no other tasks created at the same priority as the idle task. The idle task runs whenever there are no other tasks that are ready-to-run. The important portions of the code for the idle task are shown below (refer to os_core.c for the complete code).

```
void  OS_IdleTask (void *p_arg)
{
    while (DEF_ON) {                    (1)
        OS_CRITICAL_ENTER();
        OSIdleTaskCtr++;                (2)
        OSStatTaskCtr++;
        OS_CRITICAL_EXIT();
        OSIdleTaskHook();               (3)
    }
}
```

Listing 5-4 **Idle Task**

L5-4(1)   The idle task is a "true" infinite loop that never calls functions to "wait for an event". This is because, on most processors, when there is "nothing to do," the processor still executes instructions. When µC/OS-III determines that there is no other higher-priority task to run, μC/OS-III "parks" the CPU in the idle task. However, instead of having an empty "infinite loop" doing nothing, μC/OS-III uses this "idle" time to do something useful.

L5-4(2)   Two counters are incremented whenever the idle task runs.

OSIdleTaskCtr is typically defined as a 32-bit unsigned integer (see **os.h**). **OSIdleTaskCtr** is reset once when μC/OS-III is initialized. **OSIdleTaskCtr** is used to indicate "activity" in the idle task. In other words, if your code monitors and displays **OSIdleTaskCtr**, you should expect to see a value between **0x00000000** and **0xFFFFFFFF**. The rate at which **OSIdleTaskCtr** increments depend on how busy the CPU is at running the application code. The faster the increment, the less work the CPU has to do in application tasks.

OSStatTaskCtr is also typically defined as a 32-bit unsigned integer (see **os.h**) and is used by the statistic task (described later) to get a sense of CPU utilization at run time.

L5-4(3)   Every time through the loop, **OS_IdleTask()** calls **OSIdleTaskHook()**, which is a function that is declared in the μC/OS-III port for the processor used. **OSIdleTaskHook()** allows the implementer of the μC/OS-III port to perform additional processing during idle time. It is very important for this code to not make calls that would cause the idle task to "wait for an event". This is generally not a problem as most programmers developing μC/OS-III ports know to follow this simple rule.

OSIdleTaskHook() may be used to place the CPU in low-power mode for battery-powered applications and thus avoid wasting energy. However, doing this means that **OSStatTaskCtr** cannot be used to measure CPU utilization (described later).

```
void  OSIdleTaskHook (void)
{
    /* Place the CPU in low power mode */
}
```

Typically, most processors exit low-power mode when an interrupt occurs. Depending on the processor, however, the Interrupt Service Routine (ISR) may have to write to "special" registers to return the CPU to its full or desired speed. If the ISR wakes up a high-priority task (every task is higher in priority than the idle task) then the ISR will not immediately return to the interrupted idle task, but instead switch to the higher-priority task. When the higher-priority task completes its work and waits for its event to occur, µC/OS-III causes a context switch to return to **OSIdleTaskHook( )** just "after" the instruction that caused the CPU to enter low-power mode. In turn, **OSIdleTaskHook( )** returns to **OS_IdleTask( )** and causes another iteration through the "infinite loop" which places the CPU back in the low power state.

5-6-2 THE TICK TASK (OS_TickTask(), os_tick.c)

Nearly every RTOS requires a periodic time source called a *Clock Tick* or *System Tick* to keep track of time delays and timeouts. µC/OS-III's clock tick handling is encapsulated in the file **os_tick.c**.

OS_TickTask( ) is a task created by µC/OS-III and its priority is configurable by the user through µC/OS-III's configuration file **os_cfg_app.h** (see **OS_CFG_TICK_TASK_PRIO**). Typically **OS_TickTask( )** is set to a relatively high priority. In fact, the priority of this task is set slightly lower than your most important tasks.

OS_TickTask( ) is used by µC/OS-III to keep track of tasks waiting for time to expire or, for tasks that are pending on kernel objects with a timeout. **OS_TickTask( )** is a periodic task and it waits for signals from the tick ISR (described in Chapter 9, "Interrupt Management" on page 173) as shown in Figure 5-8.

Figure 5-8 **Tick ISR and Tick Task relationship**

F5-8(1)   A hardware timer is generally used and configured to generate an interrupt at a rate between 10 and 1000 Hz (see **OS_CFG_TICK_RATE** in **os_cfg_app.h**). This timer is generally called the *Tick Timer*. The actual rate to use depends on such factors as: processor speed, desired time resolution, and amount of allowable overhead to handle the tick timer, etc.

The tick interrupt does not have to be generated by a timer and, in fact, it can come from other regular time sources such as the power-line frequency (50 or 60 Hz), which are known to be fairly accurate over long periods of time.

F5-8(2)   Assuming CPU interrupts are enabled, the CPU accepts the tick interrupt, preempts the current task, and vectors to the tick ISR. The tick ISR must call **OSTimeTick()** (see **os_time.c**), which accomplishes most of the work needed by μC/OS-III. The tick ISR then clears the timer interrupt (and possibly reloads the timer for the next interrupt). However, some timers may need to be taken care of prior to calling **OSTimeTick()** instead of after as shown below.

```
void  TickISR (void)
{
    OSTimeTick();
    /* Clear tick interrupt source          */
    /* Reload the timer for the next interrupt */
}
```

or,

```
void  TickISR (void)
{
    /* Clear tick interrupt source          */
    /* Reload the timer for the next interrupt */
    OSTimeTick();
}
```

OSTimeTick() calls **OSTimeTickHook()** at the very beginning of **OSTimeTick()** to give the opportunity to the μC/OS-III port developer to react as soon as possible upon servicing the tick interrupt.

F5-8(3)   **OSTimeTick()** calls a service provided by μC/OS-III to signal the tick task and make that task ready-to-run. The tick task executes as soon as it becomes the most important task. The reason the tick task might not run immediately is that

5

the tick interrupt could have interrupted a task higher in priority than the tick task and, upon completion of the tick ISR, µC/OS-III will resume the interrupted task.

F5-8(4)   When the tick task executes, it goes through a list of all tasks that are waiting for time to expire or are waiting on a kernel object with a timeout. From this point forward, this will be called the tick list. The tick task will make ready-to-run all of the tasks in the tick list for which time or timeout has expired. The process is explained below.

µC/OS-III may need to place literally hundreds of tasks (if an application has that many tasks) in the tick list. The tick list is implemented in such a way that it does not take much CPU time to determine if time has expired for those tasks placed in the tick list and, possibly makes those tasks ready-to-run. The tick list is implemented as shown in Figure 5-9.

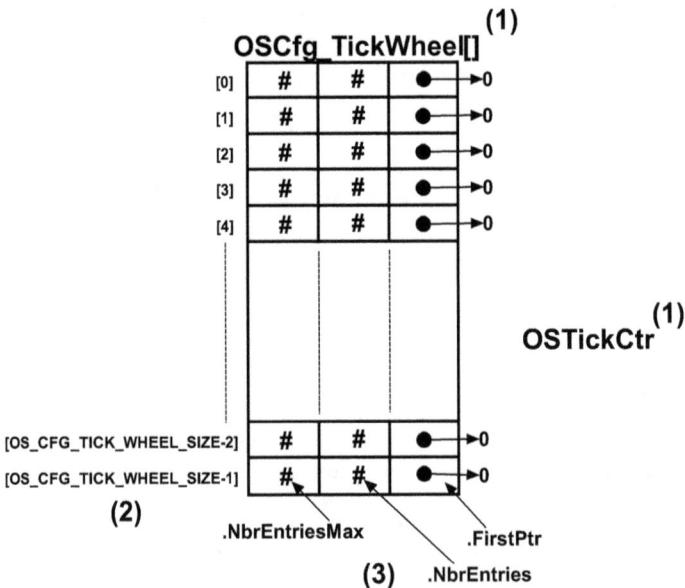

Figure 5-9 **Empty Tick List**

F5-9(1)   The tick list consists of a table (OSCfg_TickWheel[ ], see os_cfg_app.c) and a counter (OSTickCtr).

F5-9(2)   The table contains up to **OS_CFG_TICK_WHEEL_SIZE** entries (see **os_cfg_app.h**), which is a compile time configuration value. The number of entries depends on the amount of memory (RAM) available to the processor and the maximum number of tasks in the application. A good starting point for **OS_CFG_TICK_WHEEL_SIZE** may be: **#Tasks / 4**. It is recommended not to make **OS_CFG_TICK_WHEEL_SIZE** an even multiple of the tick rate. If the tick rate is 1000 Hz and you have 50 tasks in the application, you should avoid setting **OS_CFG_TICK_WHEEL_SIZE** to 10 or 20 (use 11 or 23 instead). Actually, prime numbers are good choices. Although it is not really possible to plan at compile time what will happen at run time, ideally, the number of tasks waiting in each entry of the table will be distributed uniformly.

F5-9(3)   Each entry in the table contains three fields: **.NbrEntriesMax**, **.NbrEntries** and **.FirstPtr**.

.NbrEntries indicates the number of tasks linked to this table entry.

.NbrEntriesMax keeps track of the highest number of entries in the table. This value is reset when the application code calls **OSStatReset()**.

.FirstPtr contains a pointer to a doubly linked list of tasks (through the tasks **OS_TCB**) belonging to the list, at that table position.

OSTickCtr is incremented by **OS_TickTask()** each time the task is signaled by the tick ISR.

Tasks are automatically inserted in the tick list when the application programmer calls a **OSTimeDly???()** function, or when an **OS???Pend()** call is made with a non-zero timeout value.

Example 5-1
Using an example to illustrate the process of inserting a task in the tick list, let's assume that the tick list is completely empty, **OS_CFG_TICK_WHEEL_SIZE** is configured to 12, and the current value of **OSTickCtr** is 10 as shown in Figure 5-10. A task is placed in the tick list when **OSTimeDly()** is called and let's assume **OSTimeDly()** is called as follows:

```
    :
  OSTimeDly(1, OS_OPT_TIME_DLY, &err);
    :
```

Referring to the µC/OS-III reference manual in Appendix A, notice that this action indicates to µC/OS-III to delay the current task for 1 tick. Since `OSTickCtr` has a value of 10, the task will be put to sleep until `OSTickCtr` reaches 11 and thus sleep until the very next clock tick interrupt. Tasks are inserted in the `OSCfg_TickWheel[]` table using the following equation:

```
MatchValue                      = OSTickCtr + dly
Index into OSCfg_TickWheel[] = MatchValue % OS_CFG_TICK_WHEEL_SIZE
```

Where "`dly`" is the value passed in the first argument of `OSTimeDly()` or, 1 in this example. We therefore obtain the following:

```
MatchValue                      =  10 + 1
Index into OSCfg_TickWheel[] = (10 + 1) % 12
```

or,

```
MatchValue                      = 11
Index into OSCfg_TickWheel[] = 11
```

Because of the "circular" nature of the table (a modulo operation using the size of the table), the table is referred to as a *tick wheel* and each entry is a *spoke* in the wheel.

The `OS_TCB` of the task being delayed is entered at index 11 in `OSCfg_TickWheel[]` (i.e., spoke 11 using the wheel analogy). The `OS_TCB` of the task is inserted in the first entry of the list (i.e., pointed to by `OSCfg_TickWheel[11].FirstPtr`), and the number of entries at spoke 11 is incremented (i.e., `OSCfg_TickWheel[11].NbrEntries` will be 1). Notice that the `OS_TCB` also links back to `&OSCfg_TickWheel[11]` and the "MatchValue" is placed in the `OS_TCB` field `.TickCtrMatch`. Since this is the first task inserted in the tick list at spoke 11, the `.TickNextPtr` and `.TickPrevPtr` of the task's `OS_TCB` both point to `NULL`.

OSCfg_TickWheel[]

[0]	0	0	●——►0
[1]	0	0	●——►0
[2]	0	0	●——►0
[3]	0	0	●——►0
[4]	0	0	●——►0
[5]	0	0	●——►0
[6]	0	0	●——►0
[7]	0	0	●——►0
[8]	0	0	●——►0
[9]	0	0	●——►0
[10]	0	0	●——►0
[11]	1	1	●

OSTickCtr == 10

.NbrEntriesMax   .FirstPtr
.NbrEntries

●.TickSpokePtr
.TickNextPtr ●——►0
0◄——● .TickPrevPtr
.TickRemain = 1
.TickCtrMatch = 11

OS_TCB

Figure 5-10 **Inserting a task in the tick list**

OSTimeDly() takes care of a few other details. Specifically, the task is removed from µC/OS-III's ready list (described in Chapter 6, "The Ready List" on page 139) since the task is no longer eligible to run (because it is waiting for time to expire). Also, the scheduler is called because µC/OS-III will need to run the next most important ready-to-run task.

If the next task to run also happens to call OSTimeDly() "before" the next tick arrives and calls OSTimeDly() as follows:

```
    :
    OSTimeDly(13, OS_OPT_TIME_DLY, &err);
    :
```

µC/OS-III will calculate the match value and spoke as follows:

131

```
MatchValue                        =  10 + 13
OSCfg_TickWheel[] spoke number = (10 + 13) % 12
```

or,

```
MatchValue                        =  23
OSCfg_TickWheel[] spoke number =  11
```

The "second task" will be inserted at the same table entry as shown in Figure 5-11. Tasks sharing the same spoke are sorted in ascending order such that the task with the least amount of time remaining is placed at the head of the list.

Figure 5-11 **Inserting a second task in the tick list**

When the tick task executes (see OS_TickTask() and also OS_TickListUpdate() in os_tick.c), it starts by incrementing OSTickCtr and determines which table entry (i.e., which spoke) needs to be processed. Then, if there are tasks in the list at this entry (i.e., .FirstPtr is not NULL), each OS_TCB is examined to determine whether the .TickCtrMatch value "matches" OSTickCtr and, if so, we remove the OS_TCB from the list. If the task is only waiting for time to expire, it will be placed in the ready list (described later). If the task is pending on an object, not only will the task be removed from the tick list, but it will also be removed from the list of tasks waiting on that object. The search through the list terminates as soon as **OSTickCtr** does not match the task's **.TickCtrMatch** value; since there is no point in looking any further in the list.

Note that **OS_TickTask()** does most of its work in a critical section when the tick list is updated. However, because the list is sorted, the critical section has a chance to be fairly short.

5-6-3 THE STATISTIC TASK (OS_StatTask(), os_stat.c)

µC/OS-III contains an internal task that provides such run-time statistics as overall CPU utilization (0.00 to 100.00%), per-task CPU utilization (0.00 to 100.00%), and per-task stack usage. As of V3.03.00, CPU utilization is represented as a integer from 0 to 10,000 (0.00% to 100.00%). Prior to V3.03.00, CPU utilization was represented an integer ranging from 0 to 100.

The statistic task is optional in a µC/OS-III application and its presence is controlled by a compile-time configuration constant **OS_CFG_STAT_TASK_EN** defined in **os_cfg.h**. Specifically, the code is included in the build when **OS_CFG_STAT_TASK_EN** is set to 1.

Also, the priority of this task and the location and size of the statistic task's stack is configurable via **OS_CFG_STAT_TASK_PRIO** declared in **os_cfg_app.h** ().

If the application uses the statistic task, it should call **OSStatTaskCPUUsageInit()** from the first, and only application task created in the **main()** function as shown in Listing 5-5. The startup code should create only one task before calling **OSStart()**. The single task created is, of course, allowed to create other tasks, but only after calling **OSStatTaskCPUUsageInit()**.

133

5

```
void main (void)                       (1)
{
    OS_ERR  err;
    :
    OSInit(&err);                      (2)
    if (err != OS_ERR_NONE) {
        /* Something wasn't configured properly, µC/OS-III not properly initialized */
    }
    /* (3) Create ONE task (we'll call it AppTaskStart() for sake of discussion)    */
    :
    OSStart(&err);                     (4)
}


void AppTaskStart (void *p_arg)
{
    OS_ERR  err;
    :
    /* (5) Initialize the tick interrupt                                            */
#if OS_CFG_STAT_TASK_EN > 0
    OSStatTaskCPUUsageInit(&err);      (6)
#endif
    :
    /* (7) Create other tasks                                                       */
    while (DEF_ON) {
        /* AppTaskStart() body                                                      */
    }
}
```

Listing 5-5 **Proper startup for computing CPU utilization**

L5-5(1)   The C compiler should start up the CPU and bring it to **main()** as is typical in most C applications.

L5-5(2)   **main()** calls **OSInit()** to initialize µC/OS-III. It is assumed that the statistics task was enabled by setting **OS_CFG_STAT_TASK_EN** to 1 in **os_cfg.h**. You should always examine µC/OS-III's returned error code to make sure the call was done properly. Refer to **os.h** for a list of possible errors, **OS_ERR_???**.

L5-5(3)   As the comment indicates, you should create a single task called **AppTaskStart()** in the example (its name is left to the creator's discretion). When creating this task, give it a fairly high priority (do not use priority 0 since it's reserved for µC/OS-III).

Normally, µC/OS-III allows the user to create as many tasks as are necessary prior to calling **OSStart()**. However, when the statistic task is used to compute overall CPU utilization, it is necessary to create only one task.

L5-5(4)   You need to call **OSStart()** to let µC/OS-III start the highest-priority task which, in our case is **AppTaskStart()**. At this point, there should be either four (4) to six (6) tasks created depending on configuration option: **OS_IdleTask()**, **OS_TickTask()**, **OS_StatTask()**, **OS_TmrTask()** (optional), **OS_IntQTask()** (optional) and now **AppTaskStart()**.

L5-5(5)   The start task should then configure and enable tick interrupts. This most likely requires that the user initialize the hardware timer used for the clock tick and have it interrupt at the rate specified by **OS_CFG_TICK_RATE_HZ** (see **os_cfg_app.h**). Additionally, Micriµm provides sample projects that include a basic board-support package (BSP). The BSP initializes many aspects of the CPU as well as the periodic time source required by µC/OS-III. If available, the user may utilize BSP services by calling **BSP_Init()** from the startup task. After this point, no further time source initialization is required by the user.

L5-5(6)   **OSStatTaskCPUUsageInit()** is called to determine the maximum value that **OSStatTaskCtr** (see **OS_IdleTask()**) can count up to for 1/OS_CFG_STAT_TASK_RATE_HZ second when there are no other tasks running in the system (apart for the other µC/OS-III tasks). For example, if the system does not contain an application task and **OSStatTaskCtr** counts from 0 to 10,000,000 for 1/OS_CFG_STAT_TASK_RATE_HZ second, when adding tasks, and the test is redone every 1/OS_CFG_STAT_TASK_RATE_HZ second, the **OSStatTaskCtr** will not reach 10,000,000 and actual CPU utilization is determined as follows:

$$CPU\_Utilization_\% = \left(100 - \frac{100 \times OSStatTaskCtr}{OSStatTaskCtrMax}\right)$$

For example, if when redoing the test, **OSStatTaskCtr** reaches 7,500,000 the CPU is busy 25% of its time running application tasks:

$$25\% = \left(100 - \frac{100 \times 7,500,000}{10,000,000}\right)$$

5

L5-5(7)   **AppTaskStart()** can then create other application tasks as needed.

As previously described, µC/OS-III stores run-time statistics for each task in each task's **OS_TCB**.

OS_StatTask() also computes stack usage of all created tasks by calling **OSTaskStkChk()** (see **os_task.c**) and stores the return values of this function (free and used stack space) in the **.StkFree** and **.StkUsed** field of the task's **OS_TCB**, respectively.

5-6-4 THE TIMER TASK (OS_TmrTask(), os_tmr.c)

µC/OS-III provides timer services to the application programmer and this code is found in **os_tmr.c**.

The timer task is optional in a µC/OS-III application and its presence is controlled by the compile-time configuration constant **OS_CFG_TMR_EN** defined in **os_cfg.h**. Specifically, the code is included in the build when **OS_CFG_TMR_EN** is set to 1.

Timers are countdown counters that perform an action when the counter reaches zero. The action is provided by the user through a callback function. A callback function is a function that the user declares and that will be called when the timer expires. The callback can thus be used to turn on or off a light, a motor, or perform whatever action needed. It is important to note that the callback function is called from the context of the timer task. The application programmer may create an unlimited number of timers (limited only by the amount of available RAM). Timer management is fully described in Chapter 12, "Timer Management" on page 211 and the timer services available to the application programmer are described in Appendix A, "µC/OS-III API Reference" on page 453.

OS_TmrTask() is a task created by µC/OS-III (this assumes setting **OS_CFG_TMR_EN** to 1 in **os_cfg.h**) and its priority is configurable by the user through µC/OS-III's configuration constant **OS_CFG_TMR_TASK_PRIO** found in **os_cfg_app.h**. **OS_TmrTask()** is typically set to a medium priority.

OS_TmrTask() is a periodic task using the same interrupt source that was used to generate clock ticks. However, timers are generally updated at a slower rate (i.e., typically 10 Hz). This is accomplished by dividing down the timer tick rate in software. In other words, if the tick rate is 1000 Hz and the desired timer rate is 10 Hz, the timer task will be signaled every

100th tick interrupt as shown in Figure 5-12.

Figure 5-12 **Tick ISR and Timer Task relationship**

5-6-5 THE ISR HANDLER TASK (OS_IntQTask(), os_int.c)

When setting the compile-time configuration constant OS_CFG_ISR_POST_DEFERRED_EN in os_cfg.h to 1, µC/OS-III creates a task (called OS_IntQTask()) responsible for "deferring" the action of OS post service calls from ISRs.

As described in Chapter 4, "Critical Sections" on page 85, µC/OS-III manages critical sections either by disabling/enabling interrupts, or by locking/unlocking the scheduler. If selecting the latter method (i.e., setting OS_CFG_ISR_POST_DEFERRED_EN to 1), µC/OS-III "post" functions called from interrupts are not allowed to manipulate such internal data structures as the ready list, pend lists, and others.

When an ISR calls one of the "post" functions provided by µC/OS-III, a copy of the data posted and the desired destination is placed in a special "holding" queue. When all nested ISRs complete, µC/OS-III context switches to the ISR handler task (OS_IntQTask()), which "re-posts" the information placed in the holding queue to the appropriate task(s). This extra step is performed to reduce the amount of interrupt disable time that would otherwise be necessary to remove tasks from wait lists, insert them in the ready list, and perform other time-consuming operations.

5

Figure 5-13 **ISR Handler Task**

`OS_IntQTask()` is created by µC/OS-III and always runs at priority 0 (i.e., the highest priority). If `OS_CFG_ISR_POST_DEFERRED_EN` is set to 1, no other task will be allowed to use priority 0.

5-7 SUMMARY

A task is a simple program that thinks it has the CPU all to itself. On a single CPU, only one task executes at any given time. µC/OS-III supports multitasking and allows the application to have any number of tasks. The maximum number of tasks is actually only limited by the amount of memory (both code and data space) available to the processor.

A task can be implemented as a run-to-completion task in which the task deletes itself when it is finished or more typically as an infinite loop, waiting for events to occur and processing those events.

A task needs to be created. When creating a task, it is necessary to specify the address of an `OS_TCB` to be used by the task, the priority of the task, an area in RAM for the task's stack and a few more parameters. A task can perform computations (CPU bound task), or manage one or more I/O (Input/Output) devices.

µC/OS-III creates up to five internal tasks: the idle task, the tick task, the ISR handler task, the statistics task, the ISR handler task and the timer task. The idle and tick tasks are always created while statistics, timer and the ISR handler tasks are optional.

6

The Ready List

Tasks that are ready to execute are placed in the Ready List. The ready list consists of two parts: a bitmap containing the priority levels that are ready and a table containing pointers to all the tasks ready.

6-1 PRIORITY LEVELS

Figure 6-1 to Figure 6-3 show the bitmap of priorities that are ready. The "width" of the table depends on the data type **CPU_DATA** (see **cpu.h**), which can either be 8-, 16- or 32-bits. The width depends on the processor used.

µC/OS-III allows up to **OS_CFG_PRIO_MAX** different priority levels (see **os_cfg.h**). In µC/OS-III, a low-priority number corresponds to a high-priority level. Priority level zero (0) is thus the highest priority level. Priority **OS_CFG_PRIO_MAX-1** is the lowest priority level. µC/OS-III uniquely assigns the lowest priority to the idle task and thus, no other tasks are allowed at this priority level. If there are tasks that are ready-to-run at a given a priority level, then its corresponding bit is set (i.e., 1) in the bitmap table. Notice in Figures 5-1 to 5-3 that "priority levels" are numbered from left to right and, the priority level increases (moves toward lower priority) with an increase in table index. The order was chosen to be able to use a special instruction called Count Leading Zeros (CLZ), which is found on many modern processors. This instruction greatly accelerates the process of determining the highest priority level.

Figure 6-1 **CPU_DATA declared as a CPU_INT08U**

Figure 6-2 **CPU_DATA declared as a CPU_INT16U**

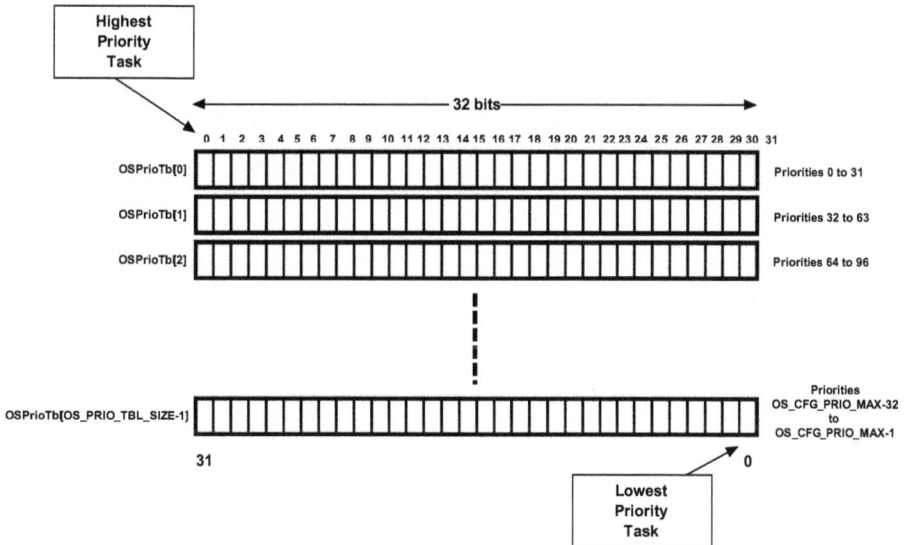

Figure 6-3 **CPU_DATA declared as a CPU_INT32U**

`os_prio.c` contains the code to set, clear, and search the bitmap table. These functions are internal to µC/OS-III and are placed in **os_prio.c** to allow them to be optimized in assembly language by replacing **os_prio.c** with an assembly language equivalent **os_prio.asm**, if necessary.

Function	Description
OS_PrioGetHighest()	Find the highest priority level
OS_PrioInsert()	Set bit corresponding to priority level in the bitmap table
OS_PrioRemove()	Clear bit corresponding to priority level in the bitmap table

Table 6-1 **Priority Level access functions**

To determine the highest priority level that contains ready-to-run tasks, the bitmap table is scanned until the first bit set in the lowest bit position is found using **OS_PrioGetHighest()**. The code for this function is shown in Listing 6-1.

```
OS_PRIO  OS_PrioGetHighest (void)
{
    CPU_DATA  *p_tbl;
    OS_PRIO    prio;


    prio  = (OS_PRIO)0;
    p_tbl = &OSPrioTbl[0];
    while (*p_tbl == (CPU_DATA)0) {        (1)
        prio += DEF_INT_CPU_NBR_BITS;      (2)
        p_tbl++;
    }
    prio += (OS_PRIO)CPU_CntLeadZeros(*p_tbl);  (3)
    return (prio);
}
```

Listing 6-1 **Finding the highest priority level**

L6-1(1)   **OS_PrioGetHighest()** scans the table from **OSPrioTbl[0]** until a non-zero entry is found. The loop will always terminate because there will always be a non-zero entry in the table because of the idle task.

L6-1(2)   Each time a zero entry is found, we move to the next table entry and increment "**prio**" by the width (in number of bits) of each entry. If each entry is 32-bits wide, "**prio**" is incremented by 32.

L6-1(3)   Once the first non-zero entry is found, the number of "**leading zeros**" of that entry is simply added and we return the priority level back to the caller. Counting the number of zeros is a CPU-specific function so that if a particular CPU has a built-in CLZ instruction, it is up to the implementer of the CPU port to take advantage of this feature. If the CPU used does not provide that instruction, the functionality must be implemented in C.

The function **CPU_CntLeadZeros()** simply counts how many zeros there are in a **CPU_DATA** entry starting from the left (i.e., most significant bit). For example, assuming 32 bits, **0xF0001234** results in 0 leading zeros and **0x00F01234** results in 8 leading zeros.

At first view, the linear path through the table might seem inefficient. However, if the number of priority levels is kept low, the search is quite fast. In fact, there are several optimizations to streamline the search. For example, if using a 32-bit processor and you are satisfied with limiting the number of different priority levels to 64, the above code can be optimized as shown in Listing 6-2. In fact, some processors have built-in "Count Leading Zeros" instructions and thus, the code can even be written with just a few lines of assembly language instead of C. Remember that with µC/OS-III, 64 priority levels does not mean that the user is limited to 64 tasks since with µC/OS-III, any number of tasks are possible at a given priority level (except **0** and **OS_CFG_PRIO_MAX-1**).

```
OS_PRIO  OS_PrioGetHighest (void)
{
    OS_PRIO  prio;


    if (OSPrioTbl[0] != (OS_PRIO_BITMAP)0) {
        prio = OS_CntLeadZeros(OSPrioTbl[0]);
    } else {
        prio = OS_CntLeadZeros(OSPrioTbl[1]) + 32;
    }
    return (prio);
}
```

Listing 6-2 **Finding the highest priority level within 64 levels**

6-2 THE READY LIST

Tasks that are ready-to-run are placed in the Ready List. As shown in Figure 6-4, the ready list is an array (OSRdyList[ ]) containing OS_CFG_PRIO_MAX entries, with each entry defined by the data type OS_RDY_LIST (see os.h). An OS_RDY_LIST entry consists of three fields: .Entries, .TailPtr and .HeadPtr.

.Entries contains the number of ready-to-run tasks at the priority level corresponding to the entry in the ready list. .Entries is set to zero (0) if there are no tasks ready-to-run at a given priority level.

.TailPtr and .HeadPtr are used to create a doubly linked list of all the tasks that are ready at a specific priority. .HeadPtr points to the head of the list and .TailPtr points to its tail.

The "index" into the array is the priority level associated with a task. For example, if a task is created at priority level 5 then it will be inserted in the table at OSRdyList[5] if that task is ready-to-run.

Table 6-2 shows the functions that µC/OS-III uses to manipulate entries in the ready list. These functions are found in **os_core.c** and are internal to µC/OS-III so, the application code must never call them.

Function	Description
OS_RdyListInit()	Initialize the ready list to "empty" (see Figure 6-4)
OS_RdyListInsert()	Insert a TCB into the ready list
OS_RdyListInsertHead()	Insert a TCB at the head of the list
OS_RdyListInsertTail()	Insert a TCB at the tail of the list
OS_RdyListMoveHeadToTail()	Move a TCB from the head to the tail of the list
OS_RdyListRemove()	Remove a TCB from the ready list

Table 6-2 **Ready List access functions**

OS_RDY_LIST OSRdyList[OS_CFG_PRIO_MAX]

Figure 6-4 **Empty Ready List**

Assuming all internal µC/OS-III's tasks are enabled, Figure 6-5 shows the state of the ready list after calling **OSInit()** (i.e., µC/OS-III's initialization). It is assumed that each µC/OS-III task had a unique priority. With µC/OS-III, this does not have to be the case.

F6-4(1) There is only one entry in **OSRdyList[OS_CFG_PRIO_MAX-1]**, the idle task.

F6-4(2) The list points to OS_TCBs. Only relevant fields of the TCB are shown. The **.PrevPtr** and **.NextPtr** are used to form a doubly linked list of **OS_TCBs** associated to tasks at the same priority. For the idle task, these fields always point to **NULL**.

F6-4(3) **Priority 0** is reserved to the ISR handler task when **OS_CFG_ISR_DEFERRED_EN** is set to 1 in **os_cfg.h**. In this case, this is the only task that can run at priority 0.

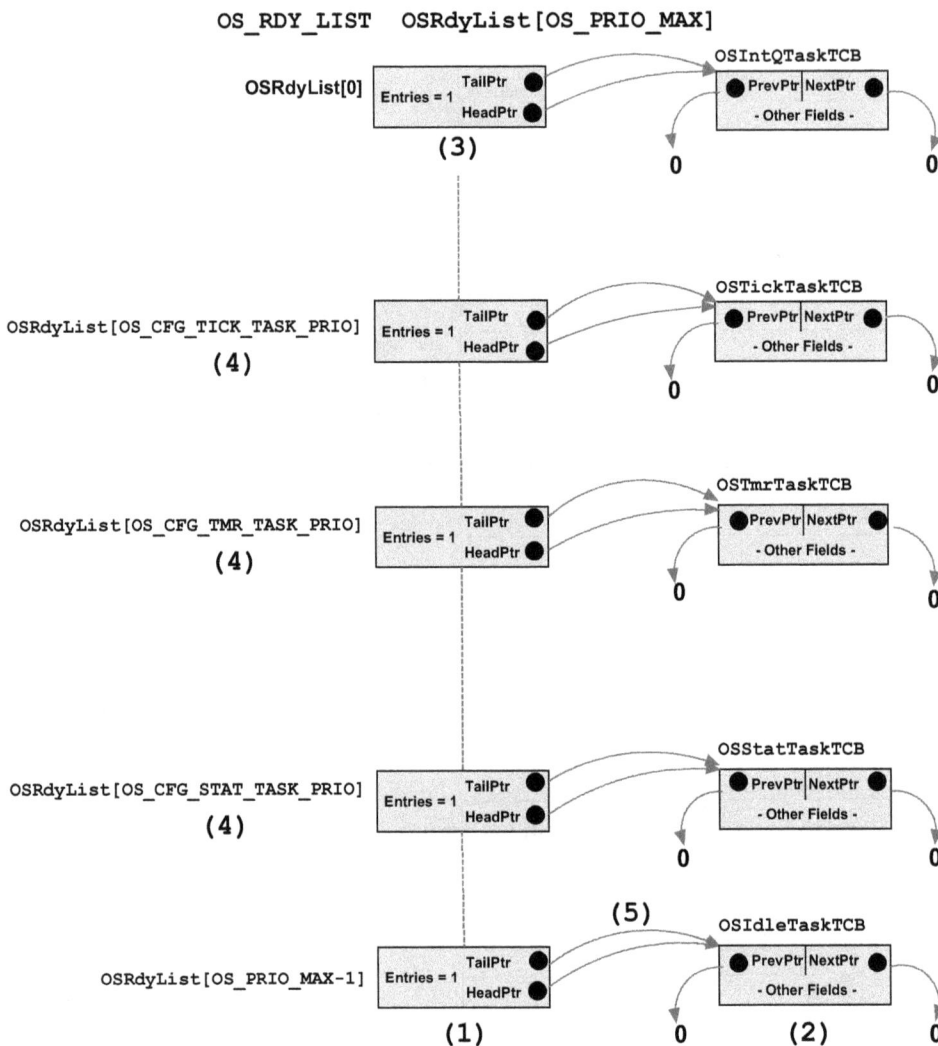

Figure 6-5 **Ready List after calling OSInit()**

F6-5(1)   The tick task and the other three optional tasks have their own priority level, as shown. Typically, you would set the priority of the tick task higher than the timer task and, the timer task higher in priority than the statistic task.

F6-5(2)   Both the tail and head pointers point to the same TCB when there is only one TCB at a given priority level.

6-3 ADDING TASKS TO THE READY LIST

Tasks are added to the ready list by a number of μC/OS-III services. The most obvious service is `OSTaskCreate()`, which always creates a task in the ready-to-run state and adds the task to the ready list. As shown in Figure 6-6, we created a task, and specified a priority level where tasks already existed (two in this example) in the ready list at the desired priority level. `OSTaskCreate()` will then insert the new task at the end of the list of tasks at that priority level.

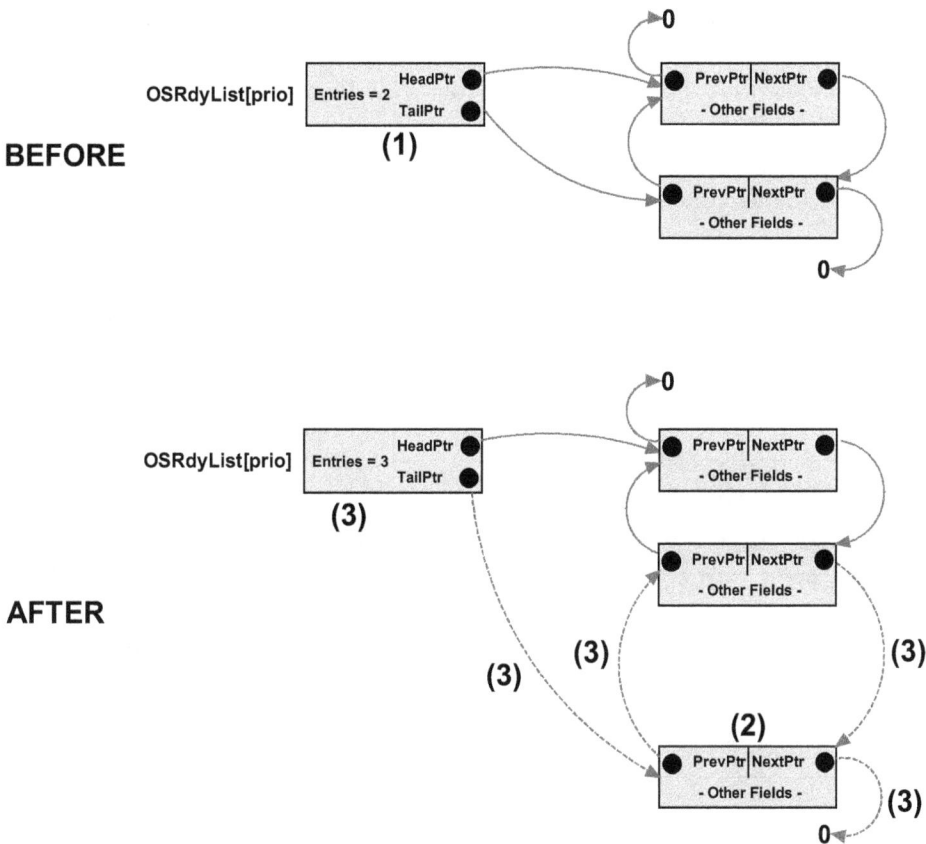

Figure 6-6 **Inserting a newly created task in the ready list**

F6-6(1) Before calling `OSTaskCreate()` (in this example), two tasks were in the ready list at priority "`prio`".

F6-6(2) A new TCB is passed to `OSTaskCreate()` and, μC/OS-III initialized the contents of that TCB.

147

F6-6(3)   `OSTaskCreate()` calls `OS_RdyListInsertTail()`, which links the new TCB to the ready list by setting up four pointers and also incrementing the `.Entries` field of `OSRdyList[prio]`. Not shown in Figure 6-6 is that `OSTaskCreate()` also calls `OS_PrioInsert()` to set the bit in the bitmap table. Of course, this operation is not necessary as there are already entries in the list at this priority. However, `OS_PrioInsert()` is a very fast call and thus it should not affect performance.

The reason the new TCB is added to the end of the list is that the current head of the list could be the task creator and it could be at the same priority. So, there is no reason to make the new task the next task to run. In fact, a task being made ready will be inserted at the tail of the list if the current task is at the same priority. However, if a task is being made ready at a different priority than the current task, it will be inserted at the head of the list.

6-4 SUMMARY

µC/OS-III supports any number of different priority levels. However, 256 different priority levels should be sufficient for the most complex applications and most systems will not require more than 64 levels.

The ready list consist of two data structures: a bitmap table that keeps track of which priority level is ready, and a table containing a list of all the tasks ready at each priority level.

Processors having "count leading zeros" instructions can accelerate the table lookup process used in determining the highest priority task.

7

Scheduling

The scheduler, also called the dispatcher, is a part of µC/OS-III responsible for determining which task runs next. µC/OS-III is a *preemptive, priority-based kernel*. As we have seen, each task is assigned a priority based on its importance. The priority for each task depends on the application, and µC/OS-III supports multiple tasks at the same priority level.

The word preemptive means that when an event occurs, and that event makes a more important task ready-to-run, then µC/OS-III will immediately give control of the CPU to that task. Thus, when a task signals or sends a message to a higher-priority task, the current task is suspended and the higher-priority task is given control of the CPU. Similarly, if an Interrupt Service Routine (ISR) signals or sends a message to a higher priority task, when the message has been sent, the interrupted task remains suspended, and the new higher priority task resumes.

7-1 PREEMPTIVE SCHEDULING

µC/OS-III handles event posting from interrupts using two different methods: Direct and Deferred Post. These will be discussed in greater detail in Chapter 9, "Interrupt Management" on page 173. From a scheduling point of view, the end result of the two methods is the same; the highest priority ready task will receive the CPU as shown in Figures 6-1 and 6-2.

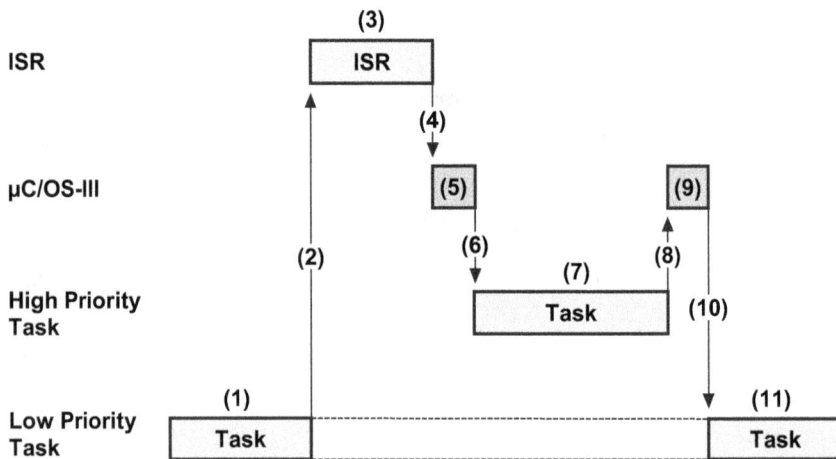

Figure 7-1 **Preemptive scheduling – Direct Method**

F7-1(1)   A low priority task is executing, and an interrupt occurs.

F7-1(2)   If interrupts are enabled, the CPU vectors (i.e., jumps) to the ISR that is responsible for servicing the interrupting device.

F7-1(3)   The ISR services the device and signals or sends a message to a higher-priority task waiting to service this device. This task is thus ready-to-run.

F7-1(4)   When the ISR completes its work it makes a service call to µC/OS-III.

F7-1(5)

F7-1(6)   Since there is a more important ready-to-run task, µC/OS-III decides to not return to the interrupted task but switches to the more important task. See Chapter 8, "Context Switching" on page 163 for details on how this works.

150

F7-1(7)

F7-1(8)   The higher priority task services the interrupting device and, when finished, calls µC/OS-III asking it to wait for another interrupt from the device.

F7-1(9)

F7-1(10)   µC/OS-III blocks the high-priority task until the next time the device needs servicing. Since the device has not interrupted a second time, µC/OS-III switches back to the original task (the one that was interrupted).

F7-1(11)   The interrupted task resumes execution, exactly at the point where it was interrupted.

Figure 7-2 shows that µC/OS-III performs a few extra steps when it is configured for the Deferred Post method. Notice that the end results is the same; the high-priority task preempts the low-priority one.

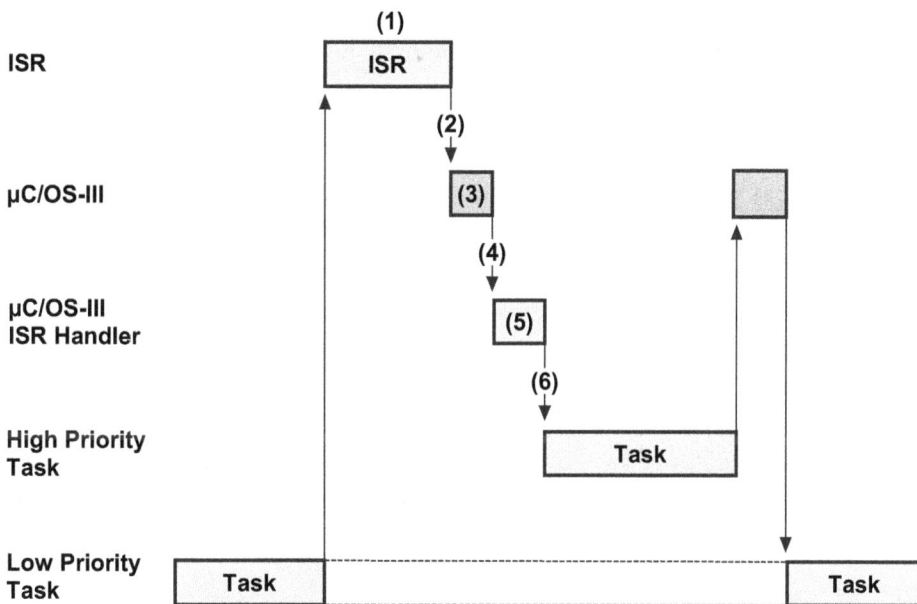

Figure 7-2 **Preemptive scheduling – Deferred Post Method**

7

F7-2(1)   The ISR services the device and, instead of signaling or sending the message to the task, μC/OS-III (through the POST call) places the post call into a special queue and makes a very high-priority task (actually the highest-possible priority) ready-to-run. This task is called the *ISR Handler Task*.

F7-2(2)   When the ISR completes its work, it makes a service call to μC/OS-III.

F7-2(3)
F7-2(4)   Since the ISR made the ISR Handler Task ready-to-run, μC/OS-III switches to that task.

F7-2(5)
F7-2(6)   The ISR Handler Task then removes the post call from the message queue and reissues the post. This time, however, it does it at the task level instead of the ISR level. The reason this extra step is performed is to keep interrupt disable time as small as possible. See Chapter 9, "Interrupt Management" on page 173 to find out more on the subject. When the queue is emptied, μC/OS-III removes the ISR Handler Task from the ready list and switches to the task that was signaled or sent a message.

7-2 SCHEDULING POINTS

Scheduling occurs at scheduling points and nothing special must be done in the application code since scheduling occurs automatically based on the conditions described below.

A task signals or sends a message to another task:
This occurs when the task signaling or sending the message calls one of the post services, OS???Post(). Scheduling occurs towards the end of the OS???Post() call. Note that scheduling does not occur if one specifies (as part of the post call) to not invoke the scheduler (i.e., by setting the option argument to OS_OPT_POST_NO_SCHED).

A task calls OSTimeDly() or OSTimeDlyHMSM():
If the delay is non-zero, scheduling always occurs since the calling task is placed in a list waiting for time to expire. Scheduling occurs as soon as the task is inserted in the wait list and this call will always result in a context switch to the next task that is ready-to-run at the same or lower priority than the task that called OSTimeDly() or OSTimeDlyHMSM().

A task waits for an event to occur and the event has not yet occurred:
This occurs when one of the OS???Pend() functions are called. The task is placed in the wait list for the event and, if a non-zero timeout is specified, the task is also inserted in the list of tasks waiting to timeout. The scheduler is then called to select the next most important task to run.

If a task aborts a pend:
A task is able to abort the wait (i.e., pend) of another task by calling OS???PendAbort(). Scheduling occurs when the task is removed from the wait list for the specified kernel object.

If a task is created:
The newly created task may have a higher priority than the task's creator. In this case, the scheduler is called.

If a task is deleted:
When terminating a task, the scheduler is called if the current task is deleted.

If a kernel object is deleted:
If you delete an event flag group, a semaphore, a message queue, or a mutual exclusion semaphore, if tasks are waiting on the kernel object, those tasks will be made ready-to-run and the scheduler will be called to determine if any of the tasks have a higher priority than the task that deleted the kernel object. Those tasks will be notified that the kernel object was deleted.

A task changes the priority of itself or another task:
The scheduler is called when a task changes the priority of another task (or itself) and the new priority of that task is higher than the task that changed the priority.

A task suspends itself by calling OSTaskSuspend():
The scheduler is called since the task that called OSTaskSuspend() is no longer able to execute. The suspended task must be resumed by another task.

A task resumes another task that was suspended by OSTaskSuspend():
The scheduler is called if the resumed task has a higher priority than the task that calls OSTaskResume().

At the end of all nested ISRs:
The scheduler is called at the end of all nested ISRs to determine whether a more important task is made ready-to-run by one of the ISRs. The scheduling is actually performed by OSIntExit() instead of OSSched().

The scheduler is unlocked by calling OSSchedUnlock():
The scheduler is unlocked after being locked. You can lock the scheduler by calling OSSchedLock(). Note that locking the scheduler can be nested and the scheduler must be unlocked a number of times equal to the number of locks.

A task gives up its time quanta by calling OSSchedRoundRobinYield():
This assumes that the task is running alongside with other tasks at the same priority and the currently running task decides that it can give up its time quanta and let another task run.

The user calls OSSched():
The application code can call OSSched() to run the scheduler. This only makes sense if calling OS???Post() functions and specifying OS_OPT_POST_NO_SCHED so that multiple posts can be accomplished without running the scheduler on every post. However, in the above situation, the last post can be a post without the OS_OPT_POST_NO_SCHED option.

7-3 ROUND-ROBIN SCHEDULING

When two or more tasks have the same priority, µC/OS-III allows one task to run for a predetermined amount of time (called a *Time Quanta*) before selecting another task. This process is called *Round-Robin Scheduling* or *Time Slicing*. If a task does not need to use its full time quanta it can voluntarily give up the CPU so that the next task can execute. This is called *Yielding*. µC/OS-III allows the user to enable or disable round robin scheduling at run time.

Figure 7-3 shows a timing diagram with tasks running at the same priority. There are three tasks that are ready-to-run at priority "X". For sake of illustration, the time quanta occurs every 4th clock tick. This is shown as a darker tick mark.

Figure 7-3 **Round Robin Scheduling**

F7-3(1)   Task #3 is executing. During that time, a tick interrupt occurs but the time quanta have not expired yet for Task #3.

F7-3(2)   On the 4th tick interrupt, the time quanta for Task #3 expire.

F7-3(3)   µC/OS-III resumes Task #1 since it was the next task in the list of tasks at priority "X" that was ready-to-run.

F7-3(4)   Task #1 executes until its time quanta expires (i.e., after four ticks).

F7-3(5)
F7-3(6)
F7-3(7)   Here Task #3 executes but decides to give up its time quanta by calling the µC/OS-III function **OSSchedRoundRobinYield( )**, which causes the next task in the list of tasks ready at priority "X" to execute. An interesting thing occurred when µC/OS-III scheduled Task #1. It reset the time quanta for that task to four ticks so that the next time quanta will expire four ticks from this point.

F7-3(8)   Task #1 executes for its full time quanta.

μC/OS-III allows the user to change the default time quanta at run time through the **OSSchedRoundRobinCfg()** function (see Appendix A, "μC/OS-III API Reference" on page 453). This function also allows round robin scheduling to be enabled/disabled, and the ability to change the default time quanta.

μC/OS-III also enables the user to specify the time quanta on a per-task basis. One task could have a time quanta of 1 tick, another 12, another 3, and yet another 7, etc. The time quanta of a task is specified when the task is created. The time quanta of a task may also be changed at run time through the function **OSTaskTimeQuantaSet()**.

7-4 SCHEDULING INTERNALS

Scheduling is performed by two functions: **OSSched()** and **OSIntExit()**. **OSSched()** is called by task level code while **OSIntExit()** is called by ISRs. Both functions are found in **os_core.c**.

Figure 7-1 illustrates the two sets of data structures that the scheduler uses; the priority ready bitmap and the ready list as described in Chapter 6, "The Ready List" on page 139.

Figure 7-4 **Priority ready bitmap and Ready list**

7-4-1 OSSched()

The pseudo code for the task level scheduler, **OSSched()** (see **os_core.c**) is shown in Listing 7-1.

```
void  OSSched (void)
{
    Disable interrupts;
    if (OSIntNestingCtr > 0) {                              (1)
        return;
    }
    if (OSSchedLockNestingCtr > 0) {                        (2)
        return;
    }
    Get highest priority ready;                             (3)
    Get pointer to OS_TCB of next highest priority task;   (4)
    if (OSTCBNHighRdyPtr != OSTCBCurPtr) {                  (5)
        Perform task level context switch;
    }
    Enable interrupts;
}
```

Listing 7-1 **OSSched() pseudocode**

L7-1(1)   **OSSched()** starts by making sure it is not called from an ISR as **OSSched()** is the task level scheduler. Instead, an ISR must call **OSIntExit()**. If **OSSched()** is called by an ISR, **OSSched()** simply returns.

L7-1(2)   The next step is to make sure the scheduler is not locked. If your code called **OSSchedLock()** then the user does not want to run the scheduler and **OSSchedLock()** just returns.

L7-1(3)   **OSSched()** determines the priority of the highest priority task ready by scanning the bitmap **OSPrioTbl[]** as described in Chapter 6, "The Ready List" on page 139.

L7-1(4)   Once it is known which priority is ready, the priority is used as an index into the **OSRdyList[]** and we extract the **OS_TCB** at the head of the list (i.e., **OSRdyList[highest priority].HeadPtr**). At this point, we know which

7

OS_TCB to switch to and which OS_TCB to save to as this was the task that called OSSched(). Specifically, OSTCBCurPtr points to the current task's OS_TCB and OSTCBHighRdyPtr points to the new OS_TCB to switch to.

L7-1(5)   If the user is not attempting to switch to the same task that is currently running, OSSched() calls the code that will perform the context switch (see Chapter 8, "Context Switching" on page 163). As the code indicates, however, the task level scheduler calls a task-level function to perform the context switch.

Notice that the scheduler and the context switch runs with interrupts disabled. This is necessary because this process needs to be atomic.

7-4-2 OSIntExit()

The pseudo code for the ISR level scheduler, OSIntExit() (see os_core.c) is shown in Listing 7-2. Note that interrupts are assumed to be disabled when OSIntExit() is called.

```
void  OSIntExit (void)
{
    if (OSIntNestingCtr == 0) {                             (1)
        return;
    }
    OSIntNestingCtr--;
    if (OSIntNestingCtr > 0) {                              (2)
        return;
    }
    if (OSSchedLockNestingCtr > 0) {                        (3)
        return;
    }
    Get highest priority ready;                             (4)
    Get pointer to OS_TCB of next highest priority task;   (5)
    if (OSTCBHighRdyPtr != OSTCBCurPtr) {                   (6)
        Perform ISR level context switch;
    }
}
```

Listing 7-2 **OSIntExit() pseudocode**

L7-2(1)   OSIntExit() starts by making sure that the call to OSIntExit() will not cause OSIntNestingCtr to wrap around. This would be an unlikely occurrence, but not worth verifying that it's not.

L7-2(2)   **OSIntExit()** decrements the nesting counter as **OSIntExit()** is called at the end of an ISR. If all ISRs have not nested, the code simply returns. There is no need to run the scheduler since there are still interrupts to return to.

L7-2(3)   **OSIntExit()** checks to see that the scheduler is not locked. If it is, **OSIntExit()** does not run the scheduler and simply returns to the interrupted task that locked the scheduler.

L7-2(4)   Finally, this is the last nested ISR (we are returning to task-level code) and the scheduler is not locked. Therefore, we need to find the highest priority task that needs to run.

L7-2(5)   Again, we extract the highest priority **OS_TCB** from **OSRdyList[]**.

L7-2(6)   If the highest-priority task is not the current task, µC/OS-III performs an ISR level context switch. The ISR level context switch is different as it is assumed that the interrupted task's context was saved at the beginning of the ISR and we only need to restore the context of the new task to run. This is described in Chapter 8, "Context Switching" on page 163.

7-4-3 OS_SchedRoundRobin()

When the time quanta for a task expires and there are multiple tasks at the same priority, µC/OS-III will select and run the next task that is ready-to-run at the current priority. **OS_SchedRoundRobin()** is the code used to perform this operation. **OS_SchedRoundRobin()** is either called by **OSTimeTick()** or **OS_IntQTask()**. **OS_SchedRoundRobin()** is found in **os_core.c**.

OS_SchedRoundRobin() is called by **OSTimeTick()** if you selected the Direct Method of posting (see Chapter 9, "Interrupt Management" on page 173). **OS_SchedRoundRobin()** is called by **OS_IntQTask()** if you selected the Deferred Post Method of posting, described in Chapter 8.

The pseudo code for the round-robin scheduler is shown in Listing 7-3.

```
void  OS_SchedRoundRobin (void)
{
    if (OSSchedRoundRobinEn != TRUE) {                (1)
        return;
    }
    if (Time quanta counter > 0) {                    (2)
        Decrement time quanta counter;
    }
    if (Time quanta counter > 0) {
        return;
    }
    if (Number of OS_TCB at current priority level < 2) {  (3)
        return;
    }
    if (OSSchedLockNestingCtr > 0) {                  (4)
        return;
    }
    Move OS_TCB from head of list to tail of list;    (5)
    Reload time quanta for current task;              (6)
}
```

Listing 7-3 **OS_SchedRoundRobin() pseudocode**

L7-3(1)   **OS_SchedRoundRobin()** starts by making sure that round robin scheduling is enabled. Recall that to enable round robin scheduling, your code must call **OSSchedRoundRobinCfg()**.

L7-3(2)   The time quanta counter, which resides inside the **OS_TCB** of the running task, is decremented. If the value is still non-zero then **OS_SchedRoundRobin()** returns.

L7-3(3)   Once the time quanta counter reaches zero, **OS_SchedRoundRobin()** checks to see that there are other ready-to-run tasks at the current priority. If there are none, the function returns. Round robin scheduling only applies when there are multiple tasks at the same priority and the task doesn't completes its work within its time quanta.

L7-3(4)   **OS_SchedRoundRobin()** also returns if the scheduler is locked.

L7-3(5)   Next, **OS_SchedRoundRobin()** moves the **OS_TCB** of the current task from the head of the ready list to the end.

L7-3(6)   The time quanta for the task at the head of the list is loaded. Each task may specify its own time quanta when the task is created or through **OSTaskTimeQuantaSet()**. If you set the task time quanta to 0 then μC/OS-III assumes the default time quanta, which corresponds to the value in the variable **OSSchedRoundRobinDfltTimeQuanta**.

7-5 SUMMARY

μC/OS-III is a preemptive scheduler so it will always execute the highest priority task that is ready-to-run.

μC/OS-III allows for multiple tasks at the same priority. If there are multiple ready-to-run tasks, μC/OS-III will round robin between these tasks.

Scheduling occurs at specific scheduling points when the application calls μC/OS-III functions.

μC/OS-III has two schedulers: **OSSched()**, which is called by task-level code, and **OSIntExit()** called at the end of each ISR.

7

Context Switching

When µC/OS-III decides to run a different task (see Chapter 7, "Scheduling" on page 149), it saves the current task's context, which typically consists of the CPU registers, onto the current task's stack and restores the context of the new task and resumes execution of that task. This process is called a *Context Switch*.

Context switching adds overhead. The more registers a CPU has, the higher the overhead. The time required to perform a context switch is generally determined by how many registers must be saved and restored by the CPU.

The context switch code is generally part of a processor's *port* of µC/OS-III. A port is the code needed to adapt µC/OS-III to the desired processor. This code is placed in special C and assembly language files: **os_cpu.h**, **os_cpu_c.c** and **os_cpu_a.asm**. Chapter 18, "Porting µC/OS-III" on page 353 provides more details on the steps needed to port µC/OS-III to different CPU architectures.

In this chapter, we will discuss the context switching process in generic terms using a fictitious CPU as shown in Figure 8-1. Our fictitious CPU contains 16 integer registers (R0 to R15), a separate ISR stack pointer, and a separate status register (SR). Every register is 32 bits wide and each of the 16 integer registers can hold either data or an address. The program counter (or instruction pointer) is R15 and there are two separate stack pointers labeled R14 and R14'. R14 represents a task stack pointer (TSP), and R14' represents an ISR stack pointer (ISP). The CPU automatically switches to the ISR stack when servicing an exception or interrupt. The task stack is accessible from an ISR (i.e., we can push and pop elements onto the task stack when in an ISR), and the interrupt stack is also accessible from a task.

Figure 8-1 **Fictitious CPU**

In µC/OS-III, the stack frame for a ready task is always setup to look as if an interrupt has just occurred and all processor registers were saved onto it. Tasks enter the ready state upon creation and thus their stack frames are pre-initialized by software in a similar manner. Using our fictitious CPU, we'll assume that a stack frame for a task that is ready to be restored is shown in Figure 8-2.

The task stack pointer points to the last register saved onto the task's stack. The program counter (**PC** or **R15**) and status register (**SR**) are the first registers saved onto the stack. In fact, these are saved automatically by the CPU when an exception or interrupt occurs (assuming interrupts are enabled) while the other registers are pushed onto the stack by software in the exception handler. The stack pointer (**SP** or **R14**) is not actually saved on the stack but instead is saved in the task's **OS_TCB**.

The interrupt stack pointer points to the current top-of-stack for the interrupt stack, which is a different memory area. When an ISR executes, the processor uses R14' as the stack pointer for function calls and local arguments.

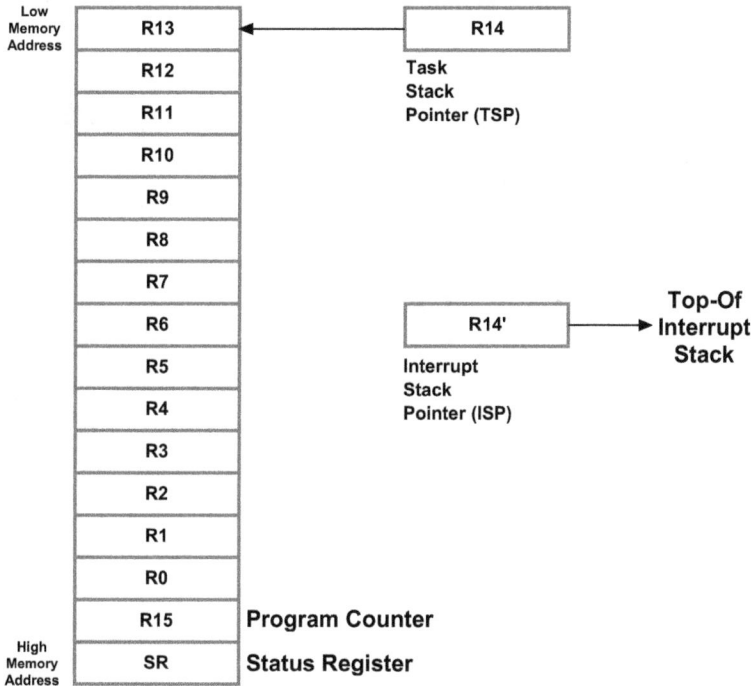

Figure 8-2 **CPU register stacking order of ready task**

There are two types of context switches: one performed from a task and another from an ISR. The task level context switch is implemented by the code in OSCtxSw(), which is actually invoked by the macro OS_TASK_SW(). A macro is used as there are many ways to invoke OSCtxSw() such as software interrupts, trap instructions, or simply calling the function.

The ISR context switch is implemented by OSIntCtxSw(). The code for both functions is typically written in assembly language and is found in a file called os_cpu_a.asm

8-1 OSCtxSw()

OSCtxSw() (see os_cpu_a.asm) is called when the task level scheduler (OSSched()) determines that a new high priority task needs to execute. Figure 8-3 shows the state of several µC/OS-III variables and data structures just prior to calling OSCtxSw().

Figure 8-3 **Variables and data structures prior to calling OSCtxSw()**

F8-3(1)   OSTCBCurPtr points to the OS_TCB of the task that is currently running and that called OSSched().

F8-3(2)   OSSched() finds the new task to run by having OSTCBHighRdyPtr point to its OS_TCB.

F8-3(3)   `OSTCBHighRdyPtr->StkPtr` points to the top of stack of the new task to run.

F8-3(4)   When µC/OS-III creates or suspends a task, it always leaves the stack frame to look as if an interrupt just occurred and all the registers saved onto it. This represents the expected state of the task so it can be resumed.

F8-3(5)   The CPU's stack pointer points within the stack area (i.e., RAM) of the task that called `OSSched()`. Depending on how `OSCtxSw()` is invoked, the stack pointer may be pointing at the return address of `OSCtxSw()`.

Figure 8-4 shows the steps involved in performing the context switch as implemented by `OSCtxSw()`.

Figure 8-4 **Operations performed by OSCtxSw()**

F8-4(1)   OSCtxSw() begins by saving the status register and program counter of the current task onto the current task's stack. The saving order of register depends on how the CPU expects the registers on the stack frame when an interrupt occurs. In this case, it is assumed that the SR is stacked first. The remaining registers are then saved onto the stack.

F8-4(2)   OSCtxSw() saves the contents of the CPU's stack pointer into the OS_TCB of the task being context switched out. In other words, OSTCBCurPtr->StkPtr = R14.

F8-4(3)   OSCtxSw() then loads the CPU stack pointer with the saved top-of-stack from the new task's OS_TCB. In other words, R14 = OSTCBHighRdyPtr->StkPtr.

F8-4(4)   Finally, OSCtxSw() retrieves the CPU register contents from the new stack. The program counter and status registers are generally retrieved at the same time by executing a return from interrupt instruction.

8-2 OSIntCtxSw()

OSIntCtxSw() (see os_cpu_a.asm) is called when the ISR level scheduler (OSIntExit()) determines that a new high priority task is ready to execute. Figure 8-5 shows the state of several µC/OS-III variables and data structures just prior to calling OSIntCtxSw().

Figure 8-5 **Variables and data structures prior to calling OSIntCtxSw()**

µC/OS-III assumes that CPU registers are saved onto the task's stack at the beginning of an ISR (see Chapter 9, "Interrupt Management" on page 173). Because of this, notice that OSTCBCurPtr->StkPtr contains a pointer to the top-of-stack pointer of the task being suspended (the one on the left). OSIntCtxSw() does not have to worry about saving the CPU registers of the suspended task since that has already been done.

Figure 8-6 shows the operations performed by OSIntCtxSw() to complete the second half of the context switch. This is exactly the same process as the second half of OSCtxSw().

8

Figure 8-6 **Operations performed by OSIntCtxSw()**

F8-6(1)   `OSIntCtxSw()` loads the CPU stack pointer with the saved top-of-stack from the new task's `OS_TCB`. `R14 = OSTCBHighRdyPtr->StkPtr`.

F8-6(2)   `OSIntCtxSw()` then retrieves the CPU register contents from the new stack. The program counter and status registers are generally retrieved at the same time by executing a return from interrupt instruction.

8-3 SUMMARY

A context switch consists of saving the context (i.e., CPU registers) associated with one task and restoring the context of a new, higher-priority task.

The new task to be switched to is determined by OSSched() when a context switch is initiated by task level code, and OSIntExit() when initiated by an ISR.

OSCtxSw() performs the context switch for OSSched() and OSIntCtxSw() performs the context switch for OSIntExit(). However, OSIntCtxSw() only needs to perform the second half of the context switch because it is assumed that the ISR saved CPU registers upon entry to the ISR.

8

8

9

Interrupt Management

An *interrupt* is a hardware mechanism used to inform the CPU that an asynchronous event occurred. When an interrupt is recognized, the CPU saves part (or all) of its context (i.e., registers) and jumps to a special subroutine called an *Interrupt Service Routine* (ISR). The ISR processes the event, and – upon completion of the ISR – the program either returns to the interrupted task, or the highest priority task, if the ISR made a higher priority task ready-to-run.

Interrupts allow a microprocessor to process events when they occur (i.e., asynchronously), which prevents the microprocessor from continuously *polling* (looking at) an event to see if it occurred. Task level response to events is typically better using interrupt mode as opposed to polling mode. Microprocessors allow interrupts to be ignored or recognized through the use of two special instructions: disable interrupts and enable interrupts, respectively.

In a real-time environment, interrupts should be disabled as little as possible. Disabling interrupts affects interrupt latency possibly causing interrupts to be missed.

Processors generally allow interrupts to be nested, which means that while servicing an interrupt, the processor recognizes and services other (more important) interrupts.

One of the most important specifications of a real-time kernel is the maximum amount of time that interrupts are disabled. This is called *interrupt disable time*. All real-time systems disable interrupts to manipulate critical sections of code and re-enable interrupts when critical sections are completed. The longer interrupts are disabled, the higher the interrupt latency.

Interrupt response is defined as the time between the reception of the interrupt and the start of the user code that handles the interrupt. Interrupt response time accounts for the entire overhead involved in handling an interrupt. Typically, the processor's context (CPU registers) is saved on the stack before the user code is executed.

Interrupt recovery is defined as the time required for the processor to return to the interrupted code or to a higher priority task if the ISR made such a task ready-to-run.

Task latency is defined as the time it takes from the time the interrupt occurs to the time task level code resumes.

9-1 HANDLING CPU INTERRUPTS

There are many popular CPU architectures on the market today, and most processors typically handle interrupts from a multitude of sources. For example, a UART receives a character, an Ethernet controller receives a packet, a DMA controller completes a data transfer, an Analog-to-Digital Converter (ADC) completes an analog conversion, a timer expires, *etc.*

In most cases, an *interrupt controller* captures all of the different interrupts presented to the processor as shown in Figure 9-1 (note that the "CPU Interrupt Enable/Disable" is typically part of the CPU, but is shown here separately for sake of the illustration).

Interrupting devices signal the interrupt controller, which then prioritizes the interrupts and presents the highest-priority interrupt to the CPU.

Figure 9-1 **Interrupt controllers**

Modern interrupt controllers have built-in intelligence that enable the user to prioritize interrupts, remember which interrupts are still pending and, in many cases, have the interrupt controller provide the address of the ISR (also called the vector address) directly to the CPU.

If "global" interrupts (i.e., the switch in Figure 9-1) are disabled, the CPU will ignore requests from the interrupt controller, but they will be held pending by the interrupt controller until the CPU re-enables interrupts.

CPUs deal with interrupts using one of two models:

1   All interrupts *vector* to a single interrupt handler.

2   Each interrupt *vectors* directly to an interrupt handler.

Before discussing these two methods, it is important to understand how µC/OS-III handles CPU interrupts.

9-2 TYPICAL µC/OS-III INTERRUPT SERVICE ROUTINE (ISR)

µC/OS-III requires that an interrupt service routine be written in assembly language. However, if a C compiler supports in-line assembly language, the ISR code can be placed directly into a C source file. The pseudo-code for a typical ISR when using µC/OS-III is shown in Listing 9-1.

```
MyISR:                                                      (1)
    Disable all interrupts;                                 (2)
    Save the CPU registers;                                 (3)
    OSIntNestingCtr++;                                      (4)
    if (OSIntNestingCtr == 1) {                             (5)
        OSTCBCurPtr->StkPtr = Current task's CPU stack pointer register value;
    }
    Clear interrupting device;                              (6)
    Re-enable interrupts (optional);                        (7)
    Call user ISR;                                          (8)
    OSIntExit();                                            (9)
    Restore the CPU registers;                            (10)
    Return from interrupt;                                 (11)
```

Listing 9-1 **ISRs under µC/OS-III (assembly language)**

9

L9-1(1)   As mentioned above, an ISR is typically written in assembly language. **MyISR** corresponds to the name of the handler that will handle the interrupting device.

L9-1(2)   It is important that all interrupts are disabled before going any further. Some processors have interrupts disabled whenever an interrupt handler starts. Others require the user to explicitly disable interrupts as shown here. This step may be tricky if a processor supports different interrupt priority levels. However, there is always a way to solve the problem.

L9-1(3)   The first thing the interrupt handler must do is save the context of the CPU onto the interrupted task's stack. On some processors, this occurs automatically. However, on most processors it is important to know how to save the CPU registers onto the task's stack. You should save the full "context" of the CPU, which may also include Floating-Point Unit (FPU) registers if the CPU used is equipped with an FPU.

Certain CPUs also automatically switch to a special stack just to process interrupts (i.e., an interrupt stack). This is generally beneficial as it avoids using up valuable task stack space. However, for μC/OS-III, the context of the interrupted task needs to be saved onto that task's stack.

If the processor does not have a dedicated stack pointer to handle ISRs then it is possible to implement one in software. Specifically, upon entering the ISR, simply save the current task stack, switch to a dedicated ISR stack, and when done with the ISR switch back to the task stack. Of course, this means that there is additional code to write, however the benefits are enormous since it is not necessary to allocate extra space on the task stacks to accommodate for worst case interrupt stack usage including interrupt nesting.

L9-1(4)   Next, either call **OSIntEnter()**, or simply increment the variable **OSIntNestingCtr** in assembly language. This is generally quite easy to do and is more efficient than calling **OSIntEnter()**. As its name implies, **OSIntNestingCtr** keeps track of the interrupt nesting level.

L9-1(5)   If this is the first nested interrupt, you need to save the current value of the stack pointer of the interrupted task into its **OS_TCB**. The global pointer **OSTCBCurPtr** conveniently points to the interrupted task's **OS_TCB**. The very first field in **OS_TCB** is where the stack pointer needs to be saved. In other words, **OSTCBCurPtr->StkPtr** happens to be at offset 0 in the **OS_TCB** (this greatly simplifies assembly language).

L9-1(6)   At this point, you need to clear the interrupting device so that it does not generate the same another interrupt. However, most people defer the clearing of the source and prefer to perform the action within the user ISR handler in "C."

L9-1(7)   At this point, it is safe to re-enable interrupts you want to support nested interrupts. This step is optional.

L9-1(8)   At this point, further processing can be deferred to a C function called from assembly language. This is especially useful if there is a large amount of processing to do in the ISR handler. However, as a general rule, keep the ISRs as short as possible. In fact, it is best to simply signal or send a message to a task and let the task handle the details of servicing the interrupting device.

The ISR must call one of the following functions: **OSSemPost()**, **OSTaskSemPost()**, **OSFlagPost()**, **OSQPost()** or **OSTaskQPost()**. This is necessary since the ISR will notify a task, which will service the interrupting device. These are the only functions able to be called from an ISR and they are used to signal or send a message to a task. However, if the ISR does not need to call one of these functions, consider writing the ISR as a "Non Kernel-Aware Interrupt Service Routine," as described in the next section.

L9-1(9)   When the ISR completes, you must call **OSIntExit()** to tell µC/OS-III that the ISR has completed. **OSIntExit()** simply decrements **OSIntNestingCtr** and, if **OSIntNestingCtr** reaches 0, this indicates that the ISR is about to return to task-level code (instead of a previously interrupted ISR). µC/OS-III will need to determine whether there is a higher priority task that needs to run because of one of the nested ISRs. In other words, the ISR might have signaled or sent a message to a higher- priority task waiting for this signal or message. In this case, µC/OS-III will context switch to this higher priority task instead of returning to the interrupted task. In this latter case, **OSIntExit()** does not actually return, but takes a different path.

9

L9-1(10)   If the ISR signaled or sent a message to a lower-priority task than the interrupted task, **OSIntExit()** returns. This means that the interrupted task is still the highest-priority task to run and it is important to restore the previously saved registers.

L9-1(11)   The ISR performs a return from interrupts and so resumes the interrupted task.

NOTE: From this point on, (1) to (6) will be referred to as the *ISR Prologue* and (9) to (11) as the ISR Epilogue.

9-3 NON KERNEL-AWARE INTERRUPT SERVICE ROUTINE (ISR)

The above sequence assumes that the ISR signals or sends a message to a task. However, in many cases, the ISR may not need to notify a task and can simply perform all of its work within the ISR (assuming it can be done quickly). In this case, the ISR will appear as shown in Listing 9-2.

```
MyShortISR:                                       (1)
    Save enough registers as needed by the ISR;   (2)
    Clear interrupting device;                    (3)
    DO NOT re-enable interrupts;                  (4)
    Call user ISR;                                (5)
    Restore the saved CPU registers;              (6)
    Return from interrupt;                        (7)
```

Listing 9-2 **Non-Kernel Aware ISRs with µC/OS-III**

L9-2(1)   As mentioned above, an ISR is typically written in assembly language. **MyShortISR** corresponds to the name of the handler that will handle the interrupting device.

L9-2(2)   Here, you save sufficient registers as required to handle the ISR.

L9-2(3)   The user probably needs to clear the interrupting device to prevent it from generating the same interrupt once the ISR returns.

L9-2(4)   *Do not* re-enable interrupts at this point since another interrupt could make µC/OS-III calls, forcing a context switch to a higher-priority task. This means that the above ISR would complete, but at a much later time.

L9-2(5)   Now you can take care of the interrupting device in assembly language or call a C function, if necessary.

L9-2(6)   Once finished, simply restore the saved CPU registers.

L9-2(7)   Perform a return from interrupt to resume the interrupted task.

9-4 PROCESSORS WITH MULTIPLE INTERRUPT PRIORITIES

There are some processors that actually supports multiple interrupt levels as shown in Figure 9-2.

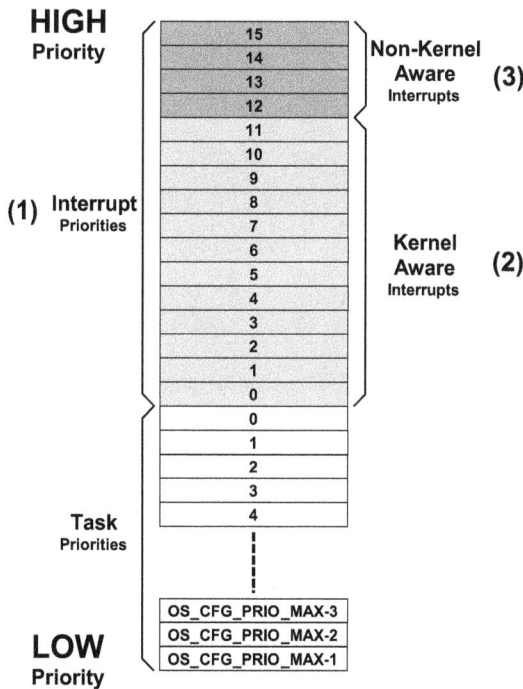

Figure 9-2 **Kernel Aware and Non-Kernel Aware Interrupts**

F9-2(1)   Here, we are assuming that the processor supports 16 different interrupt priority levels. Priority 0 is the lowest priority while 15 is the highest. As shown, interrupts are always higher in priority than tasks (assuming interrupts are enabled).

F9-2(2)   The designed of the product decided that interrupt levels 0 through 12 will be allowed to make µC/OS-III 'post' calls to notify tasks that are assigned to service these interrupts. It's important to note that disabling interrupts (when entering critical sections) for task aware interrupts means raising the interrupt mask to level 12. In other words, interrupt levels 0 through 11 would be disabled but, levels 12 and above would be allowed.

F9-2(3)   Interrupt levels 12 through 15 will **not** be allowed to make any µC/OS-III function calls and are thus implemented as shown in Listing 9-2. It's important to note that since µC/OS-III cannot disable these interrupts, interrupt latency for these interrupts is very short.

Listing 9-3 shows how to implement non-kernel aware ISRs when the processor supports multiple interrupt priorities.

```
MyNonKernelAwareISR:                                          (1)
    Save enough registers as needed by the ISR;               (2)
    Clear interrupting device;                                (3)
    Call user ISR;                                            (4)
    Restore the saved CPU registers;                          (5)
    Return from interrupt;                                    (6)
```

Listing 9-3 **Non-Kernel Aware ISRs for Processors with Multiple Priority Levels**

L9-3(1)   As mentioned above, an ISR is typically written in assembly language. **MyNonKernelAwareISR** corresponds to the name of the handler that will handle the interrupting device.

L9-3(2)   Here, you save sufficient registers as required to handle the ISR.

L9-3(3)   The user probably needs to clear the interrupting device to prevent it from generating the same interrupt once the ISR returns.

L9-3(4)   Now you can take care of the interrupting device in assembly language or call a C function, if necessary.

L9-3(5)   Once finished, simply restore the saved CPU registers.

L9-3(6)   Perform a return from interrupt to resume the interrupted task.

9-5 ALL INTERRUPTS VECTOR TO A COMMON LOCATION

Even though an interrupt controller is present in most designs, some CPUs still vector to a common interrupt handler, and the ISR queries the interrupt controller to determine the source of the interrupt. At first glance, this might seem silly since most interrupt controllers are able to force the CPU to jump directly to the proper interrupt handler. It turns out, however, that for µC/OS-III, it is easier to have the interrupt controller vector to a single ISR handler than to vector to a unique ISR handler for each source. Listing 9-4 describes the sequence of events to be performed when the interrupt controller forces the CPU to vector to a single location.

```
An interrupt occurs;                                (1)
The CPU vectors to a common location;               (2)
The ISR code performs the "ISR prologue"            (3)
The C handler performs the following:               (4)
    while (there are still interrupts to process) { (5)
        Get vector address from interrupt controller;
        Call interrupt handler;
    }
The "ISR epilogue" is executed;                     (6)
```

Listing 9-4 **Single interrupt vector for all interrupts**

L9-4(1)   An interrupt occurs from any device. The interrupt controller activates the interrupt pin on the CPU. If there are other interrupts that occur after the first one, the interrupt controller will latch them and properly prioritize the interrupts.

L9-4(2)   The CPU vectors to a single interrupt handler address. In other words, all interrupts are to be handled by this one interrupt handler.

9

L9-4(3)   The ISR executes the "ISR prologue" code needed by μC/OS-III. as previously described. This ensures that all ISRs will be able to make μC/OS-III "post" calls.

L9-4(4)   You call a μC/OS-III C handler, which will continue processing the ISR. This makes the code easier to write (and read). Notice that interrupts are not re-enabled.

L9-4(5)   The μC/OS-III C handler then interrogates the interrupt controller and asks it: "Who caused the interrupt?" The interrupt controller will either respond with a number (0 to N-1) or with the address of the interrupt handler for the highest priority interrupting device. Of course, the μC/OS-III C handler will know how to handle the specific interrupt controller since the C handler is written specifically for that controller.

If the interrupt controller provides a number between 0 and N-1, the C handler simply uses this number as an index into a table (in ROM or RAM) containing the address of the interrupt service routine associated with the interrupting device. A RAM table is handy to change interrupt handlers at run-time. For many embedded systems, however, the table may also reside in ROM.

If the interrupt controller responds with the address of the interrupt service routine, the C handler only needs to call this function.

In both of the above cases, all interrupt handlers need to be declared as follows:

```
void MyISRHandler (void);
```

There is one such handler for each possible interrupt source (obviously, each having a unique name).

The "**while**" loop terminates when there are no other interrupting devices to service.

L9-4(6)   The μC/OS-III "ISR epilogue" is executed to see if it is necessary to return to the interrupted task, or switch to a more important one.

A couple of interesting points to note:

- If another device caused an interrupt before the C handler had a chance to query the interrupt controller, most likely the interrupt controller will capture that interrupt. In fact, if that second device happens to be a higher-priority interrupting device, it will most likely be serviced first, as the interrupt controller will prioritize the interrupts.

- The loop will not terminate until all pending interrupts are serviced. This is similar to allowing nested interrupts, but better, since it is not necessary to redo the ISR prologue and epilogue.

The disadvantage of this method is that a high priority interrupt that occurs after the servicing of another interrupt that has already started must wait for that interrupt to complete before it will be serviced. So, the latency of any interrupt, regardless of priority, can be as long as it takes to process the longest interrupt.

9-6 EVERY INTERRUPT VECTORS TO A UNIQUE LOCATION

If the interrupt controller vectors directly to the appropriate interrupt handler, each of the ISRs must be written in assembly language as described in section 9-2 "Typical µC/OS-III Interrupt Service Routine (ISR)" on page 175. This, of course, slightly complicates the design. However, you can copy and paste the majority of the code from one handler to the other and just change what is specific to the actual device.

If the interrupt controller allows the user to query it for the source of the interrupt, it may be possible to simulate the mode in which all interrupts vector to the same location by simply setting all vectors to point to the same location. Most interrupt controllers that vector to a unique location, however, do not allow users to query it for the source of the interrupt since, by definition, having a unique vector for all interrupting devices should not be necessary.

9-7 DIRECT AND DEFERRED POST METHODS

µC/OS-III handles event posting from interrupts using two different methods: Direct and Deferred Post. The method used in the application is selected by changing the value of OS_CFG_ISR_POST_DEFERRED_EN in os_cfg.h. When set to 0, µC/OS-III uses the Direct Post Method and when set to 1, µC/OS-III uses the Deferred Post Method.

As far as application code and ISRs are concerned, these two methods are completely transparent. It is not necessary to change anything except the configuration value OS_CFG_ISR_POST_DEFERRED_EN to switch between the two methods. Of course, changing the configuration constant will require recompiling the product and µC/OS-III.

Before explaining why to use one versus the other, let us review their differences.

9-7-1 DIRECT POST METHOD

The Direct Post Method is used by µC/OS-II and is replicated in µC/OS-III. Figure 9-3 shows a task diagram of what takes place in a Direct Post.

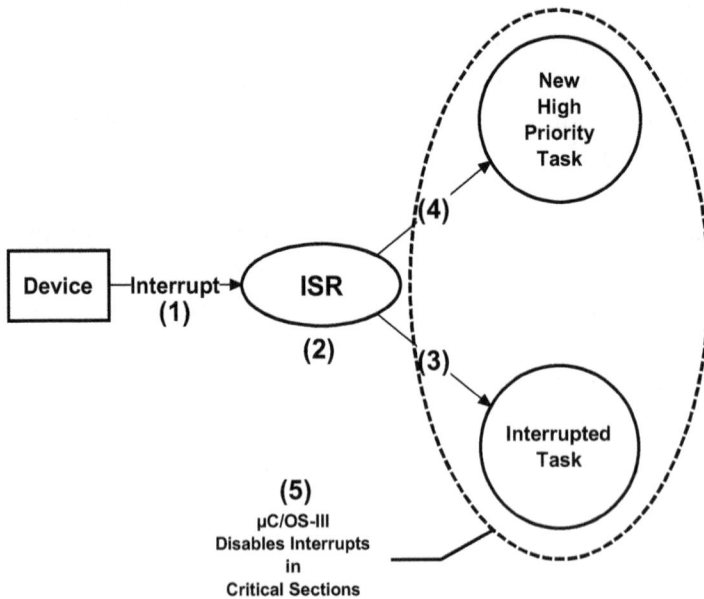

Figure 9-3 **Direct Post Method**

F9-3(1)   A device generates an interrupt.

F9-3(2)   The Interrupt Service Routine (ISR) responsible to handle the device executes (assuming interrupts are enabled). The device interrupt is generally the event a task is waiting for. The task waiting for this interrupt to occur either has a higher priority than the interrupted task, or lower (or equal) in priority.

F9-3(3)   If the ISR made a lower (or equal) priority task ready-to-run then upon completion of the ISR, μC/OS-III returns to the interrupted task exactly at the point the interrupt occurred.

F9-3(4)   If the ISR made a higher priority task ready-to-run, μC/OS-III will context switch to the new higher-priority task since the more important task was waiting for this device interrupt.

F9-3(5)   In the Direct Post Method, μC/OS-III must protect critical sections by disabling interrupts as some of these critical sections can be accessed by ISRs.

The above discussion assumed that interrupts were enabled and that the ISR could respond quickly to the interrupting device. However, if the application code makes μC/OS-III service calls (and it will at some point), it is possible that interrupts would be disabled. When **OS_CFG_ISR_POST_DEFERRED_EN** is set to 0, μC/OS-III disables interrupts while accessing critical sections. Thus, interrupts will not be responded to until μC/OS-III re-enables interrupts. Of course, everything was done to keep interrupt disable times as short as possible, but there are complex features of μC/OS-III that disable interrupts for relatively long periods of time.

The key factor in determining whether to use the Direct Post Method is generally the μC/OS-III interrupt disable time. This is fairly easy to determine since the μC/CPU files provided with the μC/OS-III port for the processor used includes code to measure maximum interrupt disable time. This code can be enabled testing purposes and removed when ready to deploy the product. The user would typically not want to leave measurement code in production code to avoid introducing measurement artifacts.

You can determine the interrupt latency, interrupt response, interrupt recovery, and task latency by adding the execution times of the code involved for each, as shown below.

> Interrupt Latency   = Maximum interrupt disable time;
>
> Interrupt Response = Interrupt latency
>   + Vectoring to the interrupt handler
>   + ISR prologue;
>
> Interrupt Recovery = Handling of the interrupting device
>   + Posting a signal or a message to a task
>   + `OSIntExit()`
>   + `OSIntCtxSw();`
>
> Task Latency   = Interrupt response
>   + Interrupt recovery
>   + Time scheduler is locked;

The execution times of the µC/OS-III ISR prologue, ISR epilogue, `OSIntExit()`, and `OSIntCtxSw()`, can be measured independently and should be fairly constant.

It should also be easy to measure the execution time of a post call by using `OS_TS_GET()`.

In the Direct Post Method, the scheduler is locked only when handling timers and therefore, task latency should be fast if there are few timers with short callbacks expiring at the same time. See Chapter 12, "Timer Management" on page 211. µC/OS-III is also able to measure the amount of time the scheduler is locked, providing task latency.

9-7-2 DEFERRED POST METHOD

In the Deferred Post Method (`OS_CFG_ISR_POST_DEFERRED_EN` is set to 1), instead of disabling interrupts to access critical sections, µC/OS-III locks the scheduler. This avoids having other tasks access critical sections while allowing interrupts to be recognized and serviced. In the Deferred Post Method, interrupts are almost never disabled. The Deferred

Post Method is, however, a bit more complex as shown in Figure 9-4.

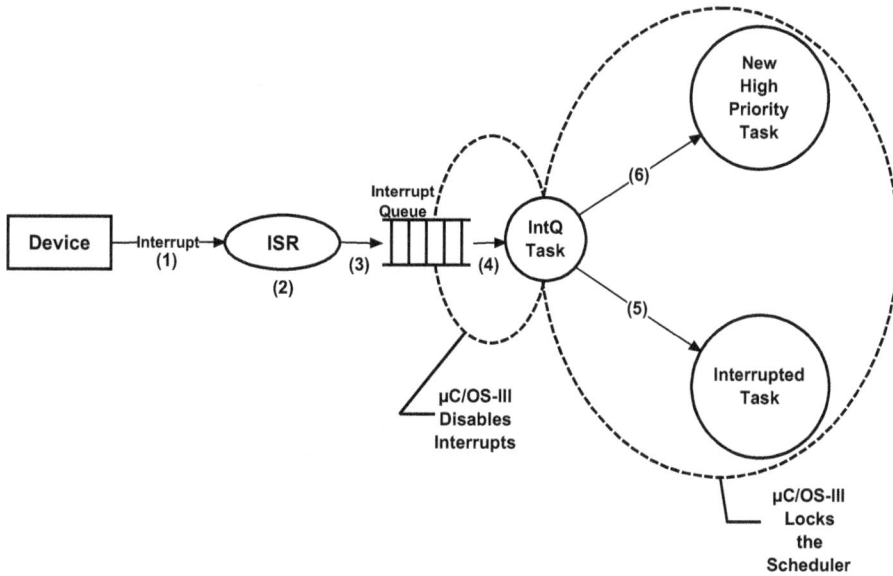

Figure 9-4 **Deferred Post Method block diagram**

F9-4(1)   A device generates an interrupt.

F9-4(2)   The ISR responsible for handling the device executes (assuming interrupts are enabled). The device interrupt is the event that a task was waiting for. The task waiting for this interrupt to occur is either higher in priority than the interrupted task, lower, or equal in priority.

F9-4(3)   The ISR calls one of the post services to signal or send a message to a task. However, instead of performing the post operation, the ISR queues the actual post call along with arguments in a special queue called the *Interrupt Queue*. The ISR then makes the *Interrupt Queue Handler Task* ready-to-run. This task is internal to µC/OS-III and is always the highest priority task (i.e., Priority 0).

F9-4(4)   At the end of the ISR, µC/OS-III always context switches to the interrupt queue handler task, which then extracts the post command from the queue. We disable interrupts to prevent another interrupt from accessing the interrupt queue while the queue is being emptied. The task then re-enables interrupts, locks the scheduler, and performs the post call as if the post was performed at the task level all along. This effectively manipulates critical sections at the task level.

F9-4(5)   When the interrupt queue handler task empties the interrupt queue, it makes itself not ready-to-run and then calls the scheduler to determine which task must run next. If the original interrupted task is still the highest priority task, µC/OS-III will resume that task.

F9-4(6)   If, however, a more important task was made ready-to-run because of the post, µC/OS-III will context switch to that task.

All the extra processing is performed to avoid disabling interrupts during critical sections of code. The extra processing time only consist of copying the post call and arguments into the queue, extracting it back out of the queue, and performing an extra context switch.

Similar to the Direct Post Method, it is easy to determine interrupt latency, interrupt response, interrupt recovery, and task latency, by adding execution times of the pieces of code involved for each as shown below.

Interrupt Latency   =   Maximum interrupt disable time;

Interrupt Response   =   Interrupt latency
                          + Vectoring to the interrupt handler
                          + ISR prologue;

Interrupt Recovery   =   Handling of the interrupting device
                          + Posting a signal or a message to the Interrupt Queue
                          + `OSIntExit()`
                          + `OSIntCtxSw()` to Interrupt Queue Handler Task;

Task Latency   =   Interrupt response
                          + Interrupt recovery
                          + Re-issue the post to the object or task
                          + Context switch to task
                          + Time scheduler is locked;

The execution times of the µC/OS-III ISR prologue, ISR epilogue, `OSIntExit()`, and `OSIntCtxSw()`, can be measured independently and should be constant.

It should also be easy to measure the execution time of a post call by using `OS_TS_GET()`. In fact, the post calls should be short in the Deferred Post Method because it only involves copying the post call and its arguments into the interrupt queue.

The difference is that in the Deferred Post Method, interrupts are disabled for a very short amount of time and thus, the first three metrics should be fast. However, task latency is higher as µC/OS-III locks the scheduler to access critical sections.

9

9-8 DIRECT VS. DEFERRED POST METHOD

In the Direct Post Method, µC/OS-III disables interrupts to access critical sections. In comparison, while in the Deferred Post Method, µC/OS-III locks the scheduler to access the same critical sections.

In the Deferred Post Method, µC/OS-III must still disable interrupts to access the interrupt queue. However, the interrupt disable time is very short and fairly constant.

Direct Post Method   **Deferred Post Method**

Figure 9-5 **Direct vs. Deferred Post Methods**

If interrupt disable time is critical in the application because there are very fast interrupt sources, and the interrupt disable time of µC/OS-III is not acceptable using the Direct Post Method, use the Deferred Post Method.

Nonetheless, if you are planning on using the features listed in Table 9-1, consider using the Deferred Post Method.

Feature	Reason
Multiple tasks at the same priority	Although this is an important feature of µC/OS-III, multiple tasks at the same priority create longer critical sections. However, if there are only a few tasks at the same priority, interrupt latency will be relatively small. If the user does not create multiple tasks at the same priority, the Direct Post Method is recommended.
Event Flags Chapter 14, "Synchronization" on page 271	If multiple tasks are waiting on different events, going through all of the tasks waiting for events requires a fair amount of processing time, which means longer critical sections. If only a few tasks (approximately one to five) are waiting on an event flag group, the critical section will be short enough to use the Direct Post Method.
Pend on multiple objects Chapter 16, "Pending On Multiple Objects" on page 331	Pending on multiple objects is probably the most complex feature provided by µC/OS-III and requires interrupts to be disabled for fairly long periods of time when using the Direct Post Method. If pending on multiple objects, the Deferred Post Method is highly recommended. If the application does not use this feature, the user may select the Direct Post Method.
Broadcast on Post calls See OSSemPost() and OSQPost() descriptions.	µC/OS-III disables interrupts while processing a post to multiple tasks in a broadcast. If not using the broadcast option, use the Direct Post Method. Note that broadcasts only apply to semaphores and message queues.

Table 9-1 **µC/OS-III features to avoid when using the Direct Post Method**

9-9 THE CLOCK TICK (OR SYSTEM TICK)

µC/OS-III-based systems generally require the presence of a periodic time source called the *clock tick* or *system tick*.

A hardware timer configured to generate an interrupt at a rate between 10 and 1000 Hz provides the clock tick. A tick source may also be obtained by generating an interrupt from an AC power line (typically 50 or 60 Hz). In fact, you can easily derive 100 or 120 Hz by detecting zero crossings of the power line. That being said, if your product is subject to be used in regions that use both power line frequencies then you may need to have the user specify which frequency to use or, have the product automatically detect which region it's in.

The clock tick interrupt can be viewed as the system's heartbeat. The rate is application specific and depends on the desired resolution of this time source. However, the faster the tick rate, the higher the overhead imposed on the system.

The clock tick interrupt allows µC/OS-III to delay tasks for an integral number of clock ticks and provide timeouts when tasks are waiting for events to occur.

The clock tick interrupt must call **OSTimeTick()**. The pseudocode for **OSTimeTick()** is shown in Listing 9-5.

```
void  OSTimeTick (void)
{
    OSTimeTickHook();                                       (1)
#if OS_CFG_ISR_POST_DEFERRED_EN > 0u
    Get timestamp;                                          (2)
    Post "time tick" to the Interrupt Queue;
#else
    Signal the Tick Task;                                   (3)
    Run the round-robin scheduling algorithm;              (4)
    Signal the timer task;                                  (5)
#endif
}
```

Listing 9-5 **OSTimeTick() pseudocode**

L9-5(1)   The time tick ISR starts by calling a hook function, **OSTimeTickHook()**. The hook function allows the implementer of the µC/OS-III port to perform additional processing when a tick interrupt occurs. In turn, the tick hook can call a user-defined tick hook if its corresponding pointer, **OS_AppTimeTickHookPtr**, is non-**NULL**. The reason the hook is called first is to give the application immediate access to this periodic time source. This can be useful to read sensors at a regular interval (not as subject to jitter), update Pulse Width Modulation (PWM) registers, and more.

L9-5(2)   If µC/OS-III is configured for the Deferred Post Method, µC/OS-III reads the current timestamp and defers the call to signal the tick task by placing an appropriate entry in the interrupt queue. The tick task will thus be signaled by the Interrupt Queue Handler Task.

L9-5(3)   If µC/OS-III is configured for the Direct Post Method, µC/OS-III signals the tick task so that it can process the time delays and timeouts.

L9-5(4)   µC/OS-III runs the round-robin scheduling algorithm to determine whether the time slot for the current task has expired.

L9-5(5)   The tick task is also used as the time base for the timers (see Chapter 13, "Resource Management" on page 229).

A common misconception is that a system tick is always needed with µC/OS-III. In fact, many low-power applications may not implement the system tick because of the power required to maintain the tick list. In other words, it is not reasonable to continuously power down and power up the product just to maintain the system tick. Since µC/OS-III is a preemptive kernel, an event other than a tick interrupt can wake up a system placed in low power mode by either a keystroke from a keypad or other means. Not having a system tick means that the user is not allowed to use time delays and timeouts on system calls. This is a decision required to be made by the designer of the low-power product.

9-10 SUMMARY

µC/OS-III provides services to manage interrupts. An ISR should be short in length, and signal or send a message to a task, which is responsible for servicing the interrupting device.

ISRs that are short and do not need to signal or send a message to a task, are not required to do so. In other words, µC/OS-III allows you to have non -kernel-aware ISRs.

µC/OS-III supports processors that vector to a single ISR for all interrupting devices, or to a unique ISR for each device.

µC/OS-III supports two methods: Direct and Deferred Post. The Direct Post Method assumes that µC/OS-III critical sections are protected by disabling interrupts. The Deferred Post Method locks the scheduler when µC/OS-III accesses critical sections of code. The method used depends greatly on your interrupt response as well as the task response needs.

µC/OS-III assumes the presence of a periodic time source for applications requiring time delays and timeouts on certain services.

Chapter 9

9

Pend Lists (or Wait Lists)

A task is placed in a *Pend List* (also called a *Wait List*) when it is waiting on a semaphore to be signaled, a mutual exclusion semaphore to be released, an event flag group to be posted, or a message queue to be posted.

See ...	For ...	Kernel Object
Chapter 13, "Resource Management" on page 229	Semaphores Mutual Exclusion Semaphores	OS_SEM OS_MUTEX
Chapter 14, "Synchronization" on page 271	Semaphores Event Flags	OS_SEM OS_FLAG_GRP
Chapter 15, "Message Passing" on page 307	Message Queues	OS_Q

Table 10-1 **Kernel objects that have Pend Lists**

A pend list is similar to the *Ready List*, except that instead of keeping track of tasks that are ready-to-run, the pend list keeps track of tasks waiting for an object to be posted. In addition, the pend list is sorted by priority; the highest priority task waiting on the object is placed at the head of the list, and the lowest priority task waiting on the object is placed at the end of the list.

A pend list is a data structure of type **OS_PEND_LIST**, which consists of three fields as shown in Figure 10-1.

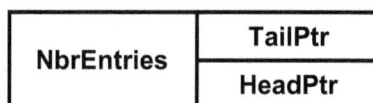

NbrEntries	TailPtr
	HeadPtr

Figure 10-1 **Pend List**

.NbrEntries Contains the current number of entries in the pend list. Each entry in the pend list points to a task that is waiting for the kernel object to be posted.

.TailPtr Is a pointer to the last task in the list (i.e., the lowest priority task).

.HeadPtr Is a pointer to the first task in the list (i.e., the highest priority task).

Figure 10-2 indicates that each kernel object using a pend list contains the same three fields at the beginning of the kernel object that we called an **OS_PEND_OBJ**. Notice that the first field is always a "Type" which allows μC/OS-III to know if the kernel object is a semaphore, a mutual exclusion semaphore, an event flag group, or a message queue object.

Figure 10-2 **OS_PEND_OBJ at the beginning of certain kernel objects**

Table 10-2 shows that the "Type" field of each of the above objects is initialized to contain four ASCII characters when the respective object is created. This allows the user to identify these objects when performing a memory dump using a debugger.

Kernel Object	Type
Semaphore	'S' 'E' 'M' 'A'
Mutual Exclusion Semaphore	'M' 'U' 'T' 'X'
Event Flag Group	'F' 'L' 'A' 'G'
Message Queue	'Q' 'U' 'E' 'U'

Table 10-2 **Kernel objects with initialized "Type" field**

A pend list does not actually point to a task's OS_TCB, but instead points to OS_PEND_DATA objects as shown in Figure 10-3. Also, an OS_PEND_DATA structure is allocated dynamically on the current task's stack when a task is placed on a pend list. This implies that a task stack needs to be able to allocate storage for this data structure.

OS_PEND_DATA

PrevPtr
NextPtr
TCBPtr
PendObjPtr
RdyObjPtr
RdyMsgPtr
RdyMsgSize
RdyTS

Figure 10-3 **Pend Data**

.PrevPtr   Is a pointer to an OS_PEND_DATA entry in the pend list. This pointer points to a higher or equal priority task waiting on the kernel object.

.NextPtr   Is a pointer to an OS_PEND_DATA entry in the pend list. This pointer points to a lower or equal priority task waiting on the kernel object.

.TCBPtr   Is a pointer to the OS_TCB of the task waiting on the pend list.

.PendObjPtr   Is a pointer to the kernel object that the task is pending on. In other words, this pointer can point to an OS_SEM, OS_MUTEX, OS_FLAG_GRP or OS_Q by using an OS_PEND_OBJ as the common data structure.

.RdyObjPtr   Is a pointer to the kernel object that is ready if the task actually waits for multiple kernel objects. See Chapter 16, "Pending On Multiple Objects" on page 331 for more on this.

.RdyMsgPtr   Is a pointer to the message posted through OSQPost() if the task is pending on multiple kernel objects. Again, see Chapter 16, "Pending On Multiple Objects" on page 331.

.RdyTS Is a timestamp of when the kernel object was posted. This is used when a task pends on multiple kernel objects as described in Chapter 16, "Pending On Multiple Objects" on page 331.

Figure 10-4 shows how all data structures connect to each other when tasks are inserted in a pend list. This drawing assumes that there are two tasks waiting on a semaphore.

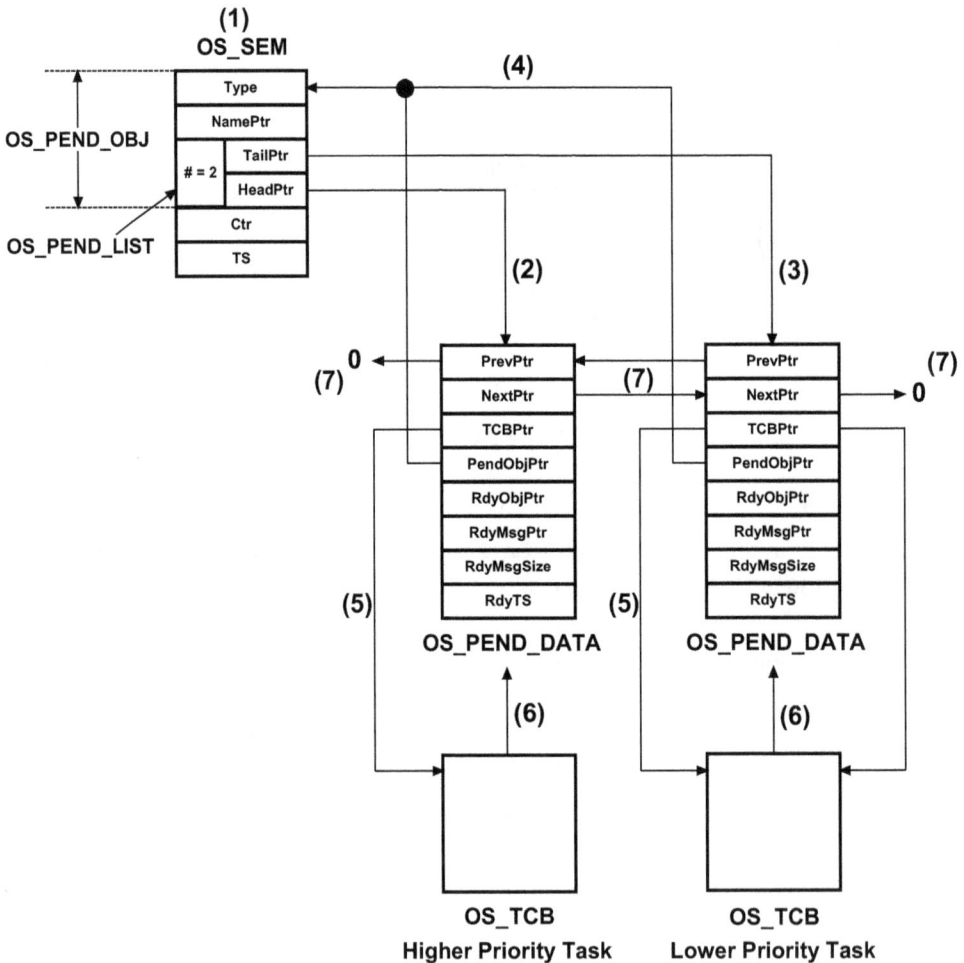

Figure 10-4 **Pend Data**

F10-4(1) The OS_SEM data type contains an OS_PEND_OBJ, which in turn contains an OS_PEND_LIST. The .NbrEntries field in the pend list indicates that there are two tasks waiting on the semaphore.

F10-4(2)   The **.HeadPtr** field of the pend list points to the **OS_PEND_DATA** structure associated with the highest priority task waiting on the semaphore.

F10-4(3)   The **.TailPtr** field of the pend list points to the **OS_PEND_DATA** structure associated with the lowest priority task waiting on the semaphore.

F10-4(4)   Both **OS_PEND_DATA** structures in turn point back to the **OS_SEM** data structure. The pointers think they are pointing to an **OS_PEND_OBJ**. We know that the **OS_PEND_OBJ** is a semaphore by examining the **.Type** field of the **OS_PEND_OBJ**. **.Type** will contain the four (4) ASCII characters 'S', 'E', 'M' and 'A'.

F10-4(5)   Each **OS_PEND_DATA** structure points to its respective **OS_TCB**. In other words, we know which task is pending on the semaphore.

F10-4(6)   Each task points back to the **OS_PEND_DATA** structure.

F10-4(7)   Finally, the **OS_PEND_DATA** structure forms a doubly linked list so that the µC/OS-III can easily add or remove entries in this list.

Although this may seem complex, the reasoning will become apparent in Chapter 16, "Pending On Multiple Objects" on page 331. For now, you should assume that all of the links are necessary.

Table 10-3 shows the functions that µC/OS-III uses to manipulate entries in a pend list. These functions are internal to µC/OS-III and the application code must never call them. The code is found in **os_core.c**.

Function	Description
OS_PendListChangePrio()	Change the priority of a task in a pend list
OS_PendListInit()	Initialize a pend list
OS_PendListInsertHead()	Insert an OS_PEND_DATA at the head of the pend list
OS_PendListInsertPrio()	Insert an OS_PEND_DATA in priority order in the pend list
OS_PendListRemove()	Remove multiple OS_PEND_DATA from the pend list
OS_PendListRemove1()	Remove single OS_PEND_DATA from the pend list

Table 10-3 **Pend List access functions**

10-1 SUMMARY

µC/OS-III keeps track of tasks waiting for semaphores, mutual exclusion semaphores, event flag groups and message queues using pend lists.

A pend list consists of a data structure of type **OS_PEND_LIST**. The pend list is further encapsulated into another data type called an **OS_PEND_OBJ**.

Tasks are not directly linked to the pend list but instead are linked through an intermediate data structure called an **OS_PEND_DATA** which is allocated on the stack of the task waiting on the kernel object.

Application code must not access pend lists, since these are internal to µC/OS-III.

Time Management

µC/OS-III provides time-related services to the application programmer.

In Chapter 9, "Interrupt Management" on page 173, it was established that µC/OS-III generally requires (as do most kernels) that the user provide a periodic interrupt to keep track of time delays and timeouts. This periodic time source is called a clock tick and should occur between 10 and 1000 times per second, or Hertz (see **OS_CFG_TICK_RATE_HZ** in **os_cfg_app.h**). The actual frequency of the clock tick depends on the desired tick resolution of the application. However, the higher the frequency of the ticker, the higher the overhead.

µC/OS-III provides a number of services to manage time as summarized in Table 11-1, and the code is found in **os_time.c**.

Function Name	Operation
OSTimeDly()	Delay execution of a task for "n" ticks
OSTimeDlyHMSM()	Delay a task for a user specified time in HH:MM:SS.mmm
OSTimeDlyResume()	Resume a delayed task
OSTimeGet()	Obtain the current value of the tick counter
OSTimeSet()	Set the tick counter to a new value
OSTimeTick()	Signal the occurrence of a clock tick

Table 11-1 **Time Services API summary**

The application programmer should refer to Appendix A, "µC/OS-III API Reference" on page 453 for a detailed description of these services.

11-1 OSTimeDly()

A task calls this function to suspend execution until some time expires. The calling function will not execute until the specified time expires. This function allows three modes: relative, periodic and absolute.

Listing 11-1 shows how to use OSTimeDly() in relative mode.

```
void  MyTask (void *p_arg)
{
    OS_ERR  err;
    :
    :
    while (DEF_ON) {
        :
        :
        OSTimeDly(2,                        (1)
                  OS_OPT_TIME_DLY,          (2)
                  &err);                    (3)
        /* Check "err" */                   (4)
        :
        :
    }
}
```

Listing 11-1 **OSTimeDly() - Relative**

L11-1(1)   The first argument specifies the amount of time delay (in number of ticks) from when the function is called. For the example in L11-1, if the tick rate (**OS_CFG_TICK_RATE_HZ** in **os_cfg_app.h**) is set to 1000 Hz, the user is asking to suspend the current task for approximately 2 milliseconds. However, the value is not accurate since the count starts from the next tick which could occur almost immediately. This will be explained shortly.

L11-1(2)   Specifying **OS_OPT_TIME_DLY** indicates that the user wants to use "relative" mode.

L11-1(3)   As with most µC/OS-III services an error return value will be returned. The example should return **OS_ERR_NONE** because the arguments are all valid.

L11-1(4)   You should always check the error code returned by μC/OS-III. If "**err**" does not contain **OS_ERR_NONE**, **OSTimeDly()** did not perform the intended work. For example, another task could remove the time delay suspension by calling **OSTimeDlyResume()** and when **MyTask()** returns, it would not have returned because the time had expired.

As mentioned above, the delay is not accurate. Refer to Figure 11-1 and its description below to understand why.

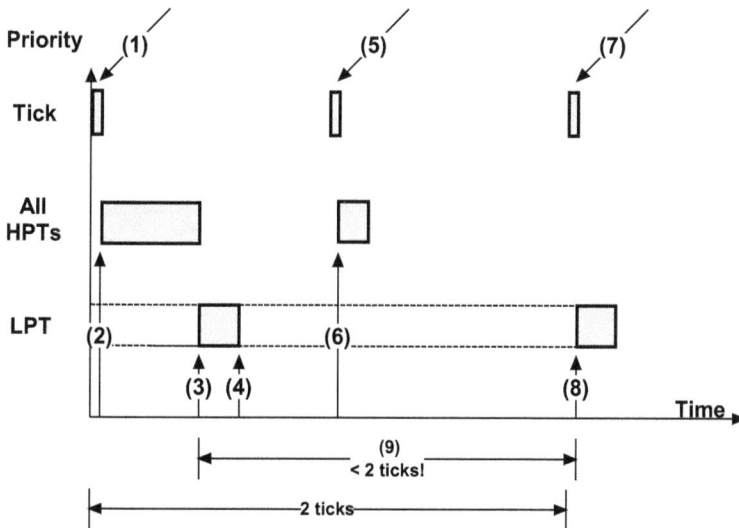

Figure 11-1 **OSTimeDly() - Relative**

F11-1(1)   We get a tick interrupt and μC/OS-III services the ISR.

F11-1(2)   At the end of the ISR, all Higher Priority Tasks (HPTs) execute. The execution time of HPTs is unknown and can vary.

F11-1(3)   Once all HPTs have executed, μC/OS-III runs the task that has called **OSTimeDly()** as shown in L11-1. For the sake of discussion, it is assumed that this task is a lower priority task (LPT).

F11-1(4)   The task calls **OSTimeDly()** and specifies to delay for two ticks in "relative" mode. At this point, µC/OS-III places the current task in the tick list where it will wait for two ticks to expire. The delayed task consumes zero CPU time while waiting for the time to expire.

F11-1(5)   The next tick occurs. If there are HPTs waiting for this particular tick, µC/OS-III will schedule them to run at the end of the ISR.

F11-1(6)   The HPTs execute.

F11-1(7)   The next tick interrupt occurs. This is the tick that the LPT was waiting for and will now be made ready-to-run by µC/OS-III.

F11-1(8)   Since there are no HPTs to execute on this tick, µC/OS-III switches to the LPT.

F11-1(9)   Given the execution time of the HPTs, the time delay is not exactly two ticks, as requested. In fact, it is virtually impossible to obtain a delay of exactly the desired number of ticks. You might ask for a delay of two ticks, but the very next tick could occur almost immediately after calling **OSTimeDly()**! Just imagine what might happen if all HPTs took longer to execute and pushed (3) and (4) further to the right. In this case, the delay would actually appear as one tick instead of two.

OSTimeDly() can also be called with the **OS_OPT_TIME_PERIODIC** option as shown in Listing 11-2. This option allows delaying the task until the tick counter reaches a certain periodic match value and thus ensures that the spacing in time is always the same as it is not subject to CPU load variations.

µC/OS-III determines the "match value" of **OSTickCtr** to determine when the task will need to wake up based on the desired period. This is shown in Figure 11-2. µC/OS-III checks to ensure that if the match is computed such that it represents a value that has already gone by then, the delay will be zero.

Figure 11-2 **OSTimeDly() - Periodic**

```
void  MyTask (void *p_arg)
{
    OS_ERR    err;
    :
    :
    while (DEF_ON) {
        OSTimeDly(4,                            (1)
                    OS_OPT_TIME_PERIODIC,       (2)
                    &err);
        /* Check "err" */                       (3)
        :
        :
    }
}
```

Listing 11-2 **OSTimeDly() - Periodic**

L11-2(1)   The first argument specifies the period for the task to execute, specifically every four ticks. Of course, if the task is a low-priority task, µC/OS-III only schedules and runs the task based on its priority relative to what else needs to be executed.

L11-2(2)   Specifying **OS_OPT_TIME_PERIODIC** indicates that the task is to be ready-to-run when the tick counter reaches the desired period from the previous call.

L11-2(3)   You should always check the error code returned by µC/OS-III.

205

Relative and Periodic modes might not look different, but they are. In Relative mode, it is possible to miss one of the ticks when the system is heavily loaded, missing a tick or more on occasion. In Periodic mode, the task may still execute later, but it will always be synchronized to the desired number of ticks. In fact, Periodic mode is the preferred mode to use to implement a time-of-day clock.

Finally, you can use the absolute mode to perform a specific action at a fixed time after power up. For example, turn off a light 10 seconds after the product powers up. In this case, you would specify **OS_OPT_TIME_MATCH** while "**dly**" actually corresponds to the desired value of **OSTickCtr** you want to reach.

To summarize, the task will wake up when **OSTickCtr** reaches the following value:

Value of "opt"	Task wakes up when
OS_OPT_TIME_DLY	OSTickCtr + dly
OS_OPT_TIME_PERIODIC	OSTCBCurPtr->TickCtrPrev + dly
OS_OPT_TIME_MATCH	dly

11-2 OSTimeDlyHMSM()

A task may call this function to suspend execution until some time expires by specifying the length of time in a more user-friendly way. Specifically, you can specify the delay in hours, minutes, seconds, and milliseconds (thus the HMSM). This function only works in "Relative" mode.

Listing 11-3 indicates how to use OSTimeDlyHMSM().

```
void  MyTask (void *p_arg)
{
    OS_ERR  err;
    :
    :
    while (DEF_ON) {
        :
        :
        OSTimeDlyHMSM(0,                         (1)
                      0,
                      1,
                      0,
                      OS_OPT_TIME_HMSM_STRICT,    (2)
                      &err);                      (3)
        /* Check "err" */
        :
        :
    }
}
```

Listing 11-3 **OSTimeDlyHMSM()**

L11-3(1)   The first four arguments specify the amount of time delay (in hours, minutes, seconds, and milliseconds) from this point in time. In the above example, the task should delay for 1 second. The resolution greatly depends on the tick rate. For example, if the tick rate (OS_CFG_TICK_RATE_HZ in os_cfg_app.h) is set to 1000 Hz there is technically a resolution of 1 millisecond. If the tick rate is 100 Hz then the delay of the current task is in increments of 10 milliseconds. Again, given the relative nature of this call, the actual delay may not be accurate.

L11-3(2)   Specifying `OS_OPT_TIME_HMSM_STRICT` verifies that the user strictly passes valid values for hours, minutes, seconds and milliseconds. Valid hours are 0 to 99, valid minutes are 0 to 59, valid seconds are 0 to 59, and valid milliseconds are 0 to 999.

If specifying `OS_OPT_TIME_HMSM_NON_STRICT`, the function will accept nearly any value for hours (between 0 to 999), minutes (from 0 to 9999), seconds (any value, up to `65,535`), and milliseconds (any value, up to `4,294,967,295`). `OSTimeDlyHMSM(203, 101, 69, 10000)` may be accepted. Whether or not this makes sense is a different story.

The reason hours is limited to 999 is that time delays typically use 32-bit values to keep track of ticks. If the tick rate is set at 1000 Hz then, it is possible to only track 4,294,967 seconds, which corresponds to 1,193 hours, and therefore 999 is a reasonable limit.

L11-3(3)   As with most µC/OS-III services the user will receive an error return value. The example should return `OS_ERR_NONE` since the arguments in L11-3 are all valid. Refer to Appendix A, "µC/OS-III API Reference" on page 453 for a list of possible error codes.

Even though µC/OS-III allows for very long delays for tasks, it is actually not recommended to delay tasks for a long time. The reason is that there is no indication that the task is actually "alive" unless it is possible to monitor the amount of time remaining for the delay. It is better to have the task wake up approximately every minute or so, and have it "tell you" that it is still ok.

`OSTimeDly()` is often used to create periodic tasks (tasks that execute periodically). For example, it is possible to have a task that scans a keyboard every 50 milliseconds and another task that reads analog inputs every 10 milliseconds, etc.

11-3 OSTimeDlyResume()

A task can resume another task that called OSTimeDly() or OSTimeDlyHMSM() by calling OSTimeDlyResume(). Listing 11-4 shows how to use OSTimeDlyResume(). The task that delayed itself will not know that it was resumed, but will think that the delay expired. Because of this, use this function with great care.

```
OS_TCB  MyTaskTCB;


void  MyTask (void *p_arg)
{
    OS_ERR  err;
    :
    :
    while (DEF_ON) {
        :
        :
        OSTimeDly(10,
                  OS_OPT_TIME_DLY,
                  &err);
        /* Check "err" */
        :
        :
    }
}


void  MyOtherTask (void *p_arg)
{
    OS_ERR  err;
    :
    :
    while (DEF_ON) {
        :
        :
        OSTimeDlyResume(&MyTaskTCB,
                        &err);
        /* Check "err" */
        :
        :
    }
}
```

Listing 11-4 **OSTimeDlyResume()**

11-4 OSTimeSet() AND OSTimeGet()

µC/OS-III increments a tick counter every time a tick interrupt occurs. This counter allows the application to make coarse time measurements and have some notion of time (after power up).

OSTimeGet() allows the user to take a snapshot of the tick counter. You can use this value to delay a task for a specific number of ticks and repeat this periodically without losing track of time.

OSTimeSet() allows the user to change the current value of the tick counter. Although µC/OS-III allows for this, it is recommended to use this function with great care.

11-5 OSTimeTick()

The tick Interrupt Service Routine (ISR) must call this function every time a tick interrupt occurs. µC/OS-III uses this function to update time delays and timeouts used by other system calls. OSTimeTick() is considered an internal function to µC/OS-III.

11-6 SUMMARY

µC/OS-III provides services to applications so that tasks can suspend their execution for user-defined time delays. Delays are either specified by a number of clock ticks or hours, minutes, seconds, and milliseconds.

Application code can resume a delayed task by calling OSTimeDlyResume(). However, its use is not recommended because resumed task will not know that they were resumed as opposed to the time delay expired.

µC/OS-III keeps track of the number of ticks that occurred since power up or since the number of ticks counter was last changed by OSTimeSet(). The counter may be read by the application code using OSTimeGet().

Timer Management

µC/OS-III provides timer services to the application programmer and code to handle timers is found in **os_tmr.c**. Timer services are enabled when setting **OS_CFG_TMR_EN** to 1 in **os_cfg.h**.

Timers are down counters that perform an *action* when the counter reaches zero. The user provides the action through a *callback* function (or simply *callback*). A callback is a user-declared function that will be called when the timer expires. The callback can be used to turn a light on or off, start a motor, or perform other actions. However, it is important to never make blocking calls within a callback function (i.e., call **OSTimeDly()**, **OSTimeDlyHMSM()**, **OS???Pend()**, or anything that causes the timer task to block or be deleted).

Timers are useful in protocol stacks (retransmission timers, for example), and can also be used to poll I/O devices at predefined intervals.

An application can have any number of timers (limited only by the amount of RAM available). Timer services (i.e. functions) in µC/OS-III start with the **OSTmr???()** prefix, and the services available to the application programmer are described in Appendix A, "µC/OS-III API Reference" on page 453.

The resolution of all the timers managed by µC/OS-III is determined by the configuration constant: **OS_CFG_TMR_TASK_RATE_HZ**, which is expressed in Hertz (Hz). So, if the timer task (described later) rate is set to 10, all timers have a resolution of 1/10th of a second (ticks in the diagrams to follow). In fact, this is the typical recommended value for the timer task. Timers are to be used with "coarse" granularity.

µC/OS-III provides a number of services to manage timers as summarized in Table 12-1.

Function Name	Operation
OSTmrCreate()	Create and specify the operating mode of the timer.
OSTmrDel()	Delete a timer.
OSTmrRemainGet()	Obtain the remaining time left before the timer expires.
OSTmrStart()	Start (or restart) a timer.
OSTmrStateGet()	Obtain the current state of a timer.
OSTmrStop()	Stop the countdown process of a timer.

Table 12-1 **Timer API summary**

A timer needs to be created before it can be used. You create a timer by calling **OSTmrCreate()** and specify a number of arguments to this function based on how the timer is to operate. Once the timer operation is specified, its operating mode cannot be changed unless the timer is deleted and recreated. The function prototype for **OSTmrCreate()** is shown below as a quick reference:

```
void  OSTmrCreate (OS_TMR              *p_tmr,            /* Pointer to timer       */
                   CPU_CHAR            *p_name,           /* Name of timer, ASCII */
                   OS_TICK             dly,               /* Initial delay          */
                   OS_TICK             period,            /* Repeat period          */
                   OS_OPT              opt,               /* Options                */
                   OS_TMR_CALLBACK_PTR p_callback,        /* Fnct to call at 0      */
                   void                *p_callback_arg,   /* Arg. to callback       */
                   OS_ERR              *p_err)
```

Once created, a timer can be started (or restarted) and stopped as often as is necessary. Timers can be created to operate in one of three modes: One-shot, Periodic (no initial delay), and Periodic (with initial delay).

12-1 ONE-SHOT TIMERS

As its name implies, a one-shot timer will countdown from its initial value, call the callback function when it reaches zero, and stop. Figure 12-1 shows a timing diagram of this operation. The countdown is initiated by calling **OSTmrStart()**. At the completion of the time delay, the callback function is called, assuming a callback function was provided when the timer was created. Once completed, the timer does not do anything unless restarted by calling **OSTmrStart()**, at which point the process starts over.

You terminate the countdown process of a timer (before it reaches zero) by calling **OSTmrStop()**. In this case, you can specify that the callback function be called or not.

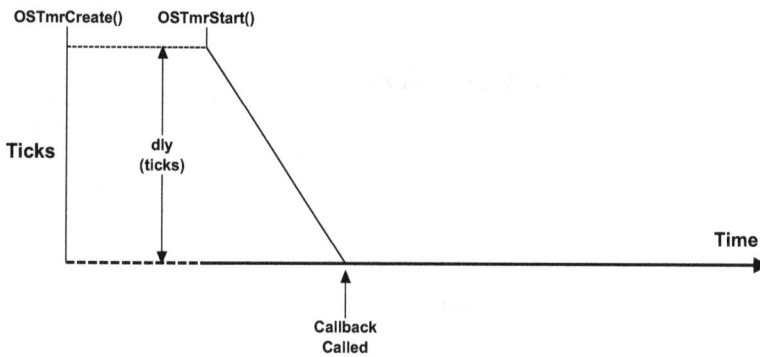

Figure 12-1 One Shot Timers (dly > 0, period == 0)

As shown in Figure 12-2, a one-shot timer can be retriggered by calling **OSTmrStart()** before the timer reaches zero. This feature can be used to implement watchdogs and similar safeguards.

213

Figure 12-2 **Retriggering a One Shot Timer**

12-2 PERIODIC (NO INITIAL DELAY)

As indicated in Figure 12-3, timers can be configured for periodic mode. When the countdown expires, the callback function is called, the timer is automatically reloaded, and the process is repeated. If specifying a delay of zero (i.e., **dly == 0**) when the timer is created and, when started, the timer immediately uses the "**period**" as the reload value. You can call OSTmrStart() at any point in the countdown to restart the process.

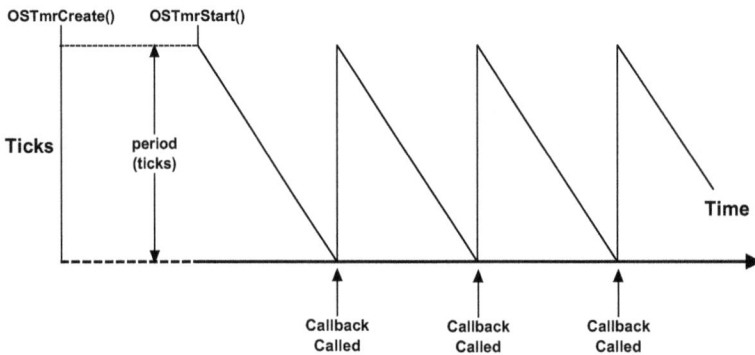

Figure 12-3 **Periodic Timers (dly == 0, period > 0)**

12-3 PERIODIC (WITH INITIAL DELAY)

As shown in Figure 12-4, timers can be configured for periodic mode with an initial delay that is different than its period. The first countdown count comes from the "**dly**" argument passed in the **OSTmrCreate()** call, and the reload value is the "**period**". You can call **OSTmrStart()** to restart the process including the initial delay.

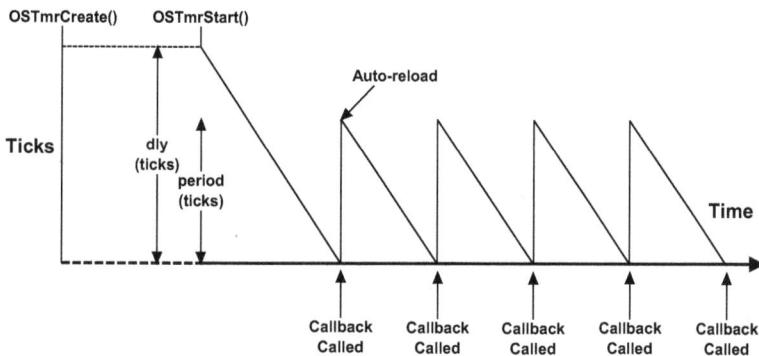

Figure 12-4 **Periodic Timers (dly > 0, period > 0)**

12-4 TIMER MANAGEMENT INTERNALS

12-4-1 TIMER MANAGEMENT INTERNALS - TIMERS STATES

Figure 12-5 shows the state diagram of a timer.

Tasks can call **OSTmrStateGet()** to find out the state of a timer. Also, at any time during the countdown process, the application code can call **OSTmrRemainGet()** to find out how much time remains before the timer reaches zero (0). The value returned is expressed in "timer ticks." If timers are decremented at a rate of 10 Hz then a count of 50 corresponds to 5 seconds. If the timer is in the stop state, the time remaining will correspond to either the initial delay (one shot or periodic with initial delay), or the period if the timer is configured for periodic without initial delay.

215

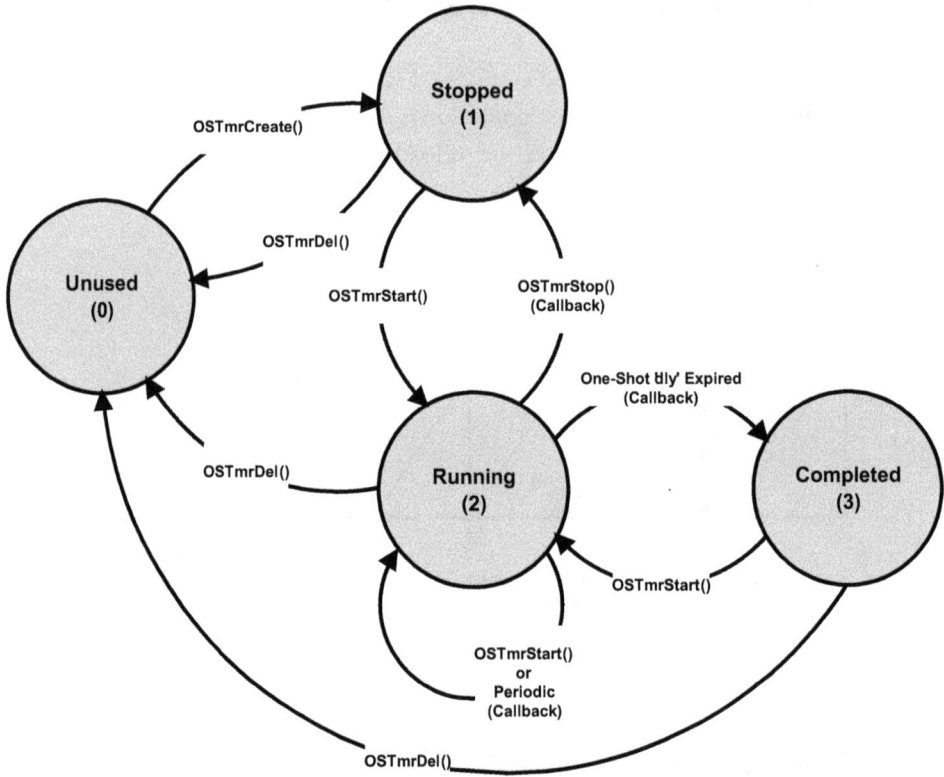

Figure 12-5 **Timer State Diagram**

F12-5(0)   The "Unused" state is a timer that has not been created or has been "deleted." In other words, µC/OS-III does not know about this timer.

F12-5(1)   When creating a timer or calling **OSTmrStop()**, the timer is placed in the "stopped" state.

F12-5(2)   A timer is placed in running state when calling **OSTmrStart()**. The timer stays in that state unless it's stopped, deleted, or completes its one shot.

F12-5(3)   The "Completed" state is the state a one-shot timer is in when its delay expires.

12-4-2 TIMER MANAGEMENT INTERNALS - OS_TMR

A timer is a kernel object as defined by the OS_TMR data type (see **os.h**) as shown in Listing 12-1.

The services provided by µC/OS-III to manage timers are implemented in the file **os_tmr.c**. Timer services are enabled at compile time by setting the configuration constant OS_CFG_TMR_EN to 1 in **os_cfg.h**.

```
typedef  struct  os_tmr  OS_TMR;              (1)


struct  os_tmr {
    OS_OBJ_TYPE          Type;                (2)
    CPU_CHAR             *NamePtr;            (3)
    OS_TMR_CALLBACK_PTR  CallbackPtr;         (4)
    void                 *CallbackPtrArg;     (5)
    OS_TMR               *NextPtr;            (6)
    OS_TMR               *PrevPtr;
    OS_TICK              Match;               (7)
    OS_TICK              Remain;              (8)
    OS_TICK              Dly;                 (9)
    OS_TICK              Period;              (10)
    OS_OPT               Opt;                 (11)
    OS_STATE             State;               (12)
};
```

Listing 12-1 **OS_TMR data type**

L12-1(1)   In µC/OS-III, all structures are given a data type. In fact, all data types start with "OS_" and are all uppercase. When a timer is declared, you simply use OS_TMR as the data type of the variable used to declare the timer.

L12-1(2)   The structure starts with a "**Type**" field, which allows it to be recognized by µC/OS-III as a timer. Other kernel objects will also have a "**Type**" as the first member of the structure. If a function is passed a kernel object, µC/OS-III is able to confirm that it is passed the proper data type (assuming OS_CFG_OBJ_TYPE_CHK_EN is set to 1 in **os_cfg.h**). For example, if passing a message queue (OS_Q) to a timer service (for example OSTmrStart()) then µC/OS-III will be able to recognize that an invalid object was passed, and return an error code accordingly.

L12-1(3)   Each kernel object can be given a name for easier recognition by debuggers or μC/Probe. This member is simply a pointer to an ASCII string which is assumed to be NUL terminated.

L12-1(4)   The **.CallbackPtr** member is a pointer to a function that is called when the timer expires. If a timer is created and passed a **NULL** pointer, a callback would not be called when the timer expires.

L12-1(5)   If there is a non-**NULL** **.CallbackPtr** then the application code could have also specified that the callback be called with an argument when the timer expires. This is the argument that would be passed in this call.

L12-1(6)   **.NextPtr** and **.PrevPtr** are pointers used to link a timer in a doubly linked list. These are described later.

L12-1(7)   A timer expires when the timer manager variable **OSTmrTickCtr** reaches the value stored in a timer's **.Match** field. This is also described later.

L12-1(8)   The **.Remain** field contains the amount of time remaining for the timer to expire. This value is updated once per **OS_CFG_TMR_WHEEL_SIZE** (see **os_cfg_app.h**) that the timer task executes (described later). The value is expressed in multiples of 1/**OS_CFG_TMR_TASK_RATE_HZ** of a second (see **os_cfg_app.h**).

L12-1(9)   The **.Dly** field contains the one-shot time when the timer is configured (i.e., created) as a one-shot timer and the initial delay when the timer is created as a periodic timer. The value is expressed in multiples of 1/**OS_CFG_TMR_TASK_RATE_HZ** of a second (see **os_cfg_app.h**).

L12-1(10)   The **.Period** field is the timer period when the timer is created to operate in periodic mode. The value is expressed in multiples of 1/**OS_CFG_TMR_TASK_RATE_HZ** of a second (see **os_cfg_app.h**).

L12-1(11)   The **.Opt** field contains options that are passed to **OSTmrCreate()**.

L12-1(12)   The **.State** field represents the current state of the timer (see Figure 12-5).

Even if the internals of the OS_TMR data type are understood, the application code should never access any of the fields in this data structure directly. Instead, you should always use the Application Programming Interfaces (APIs) provided with µC/OS-III.

12-4-3 TIMER MANAGEMENT INTERNALS - TIMER TASK

OS_TmrTask() is a task created by µC/OS-III (assumes setting OS_CFG_TMR_EN to 1 in os_cfg.h) and its priority is configurable by the user through µC/OS-III's configuration file os_cfg_app.h (see OS_CFG_TMR_TASK_PRIO). OS_TmrTask() is typically set to a medium priority.

OS_TmrTask() is a periodic task and uses the same interrupt source used to generate clock ticks. However, timers are generally updated at a slower rate (i.e., typically 10 Hz or so) and thus, the timer tick rate is divided down in software. If the tick rate is 1000 Hz and the desired timer rate is 10 Hz then the timer task will be signaled every 100th tick interrupt as shown in Figure 12-6.

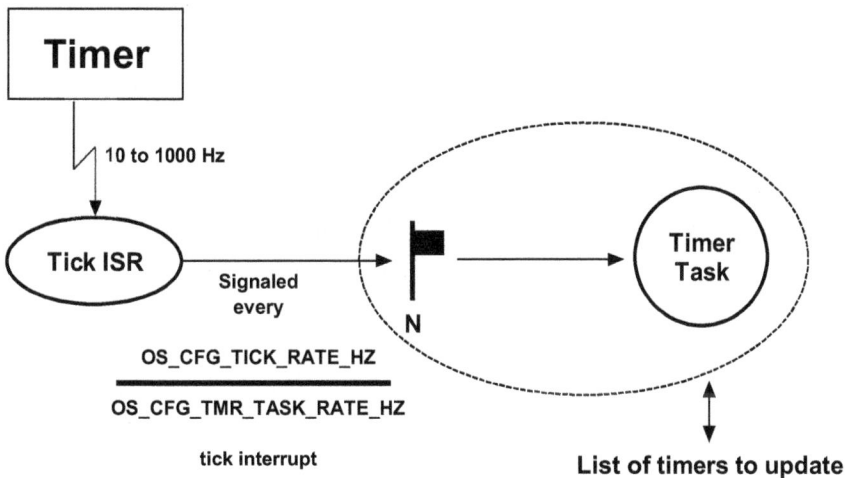

Figure 12-6 **Tick ISR and Timer Task relationship**

Figure 12-7 shows timing diagram associated with the timer management task.

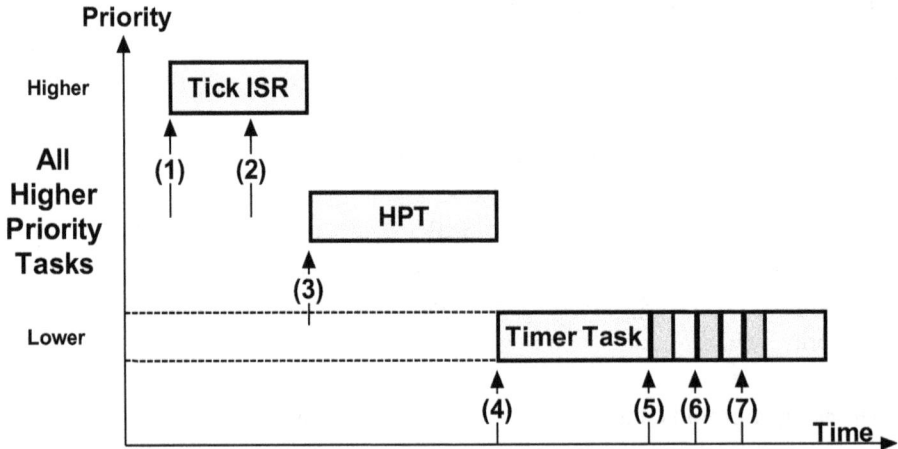

Figure 12-7 **Timing Diagram**

F12-7(1)   The tick ISR occurs and assumes interrupts are enabled and executes.

F12-7(2)   The tick ISR signals the tick task that it is time for it to update timers.

F12-7(3)   The tick ISR terminates, however there might be higher priority tasks that need to execute (assuming the timer task has a lower priority). Therefore, µC/OS-III runs the higher priority task(s).

F12-7(4)   When all higher priority tasks have executed, µC/OS-III switches to the timer task and determines that there are three timers that expired.

F12-7(5)   The callback for the first timer is executed.

F12-7(6)   The callback for the second expired timer is executed.

F12-7(7)   The callback for the third expired timer is executed.

There are a few interesting things to notice:

■   Execution of the callback functions is performed within the context of the timer task. This means that the application code will need to make sure there is sufficient stack space for the timer task to handle these callbacks.

■ The callback functions are executed one after the other based on the order they are found in the timer list.

■ The execution time of the timer task greatly depends on how many timers expire and how long each of the callback functions takes to execute. Since the callbacks are provided by the application code they have a large influence on the execution time of the timer task.

■ The timer callback functions must never wait on events because this would delay the timer task for excessive amounts of time, if not forever.

■ Callbacks are called with the scheduler locked, so you should ensure that callbacks execute as quickly as possible.

12-4-4 TIMER MANAGEMENT INTERNALS - TIMER LIST

μC/OS-III might need to literally maintain hundreds of timers (if an application requires that many). The timer list management needs to be implemented such that it does not take too much CPU time to update the timers. The timer list works similarly to a tick list as shown in Figure 12-8.

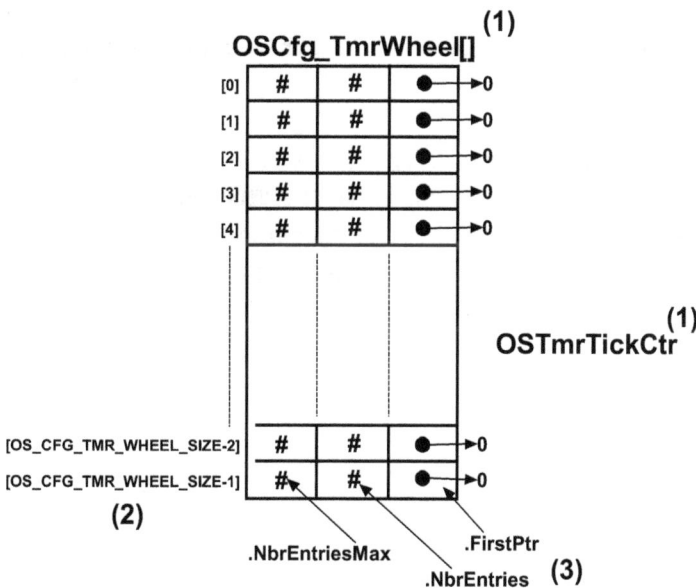

Figure 12-8 **Empty Timer List**

F12-8(1)   The timer list consists of a table (OSCfg_TmrWheel[], declared in os_cfg_app.c) and a counter (OSTmrTickCtr, declared on os.h).

F12-8(2)   The table contains up to OS_CFG_TMR_WHEEL_SIZE entries, which is a compile time configuration value (see os_cfg_app.h). The number of entries depends on the amount of RAM available to the processor and the maximum number of timers in the application. A good starting point for OS_CFG_TMR_WHEEL_SIZE might be: #Timers/4. It is not recommended to make OS_CFG_TMR_WHEEL_SIZE an even multiple of the timer task rate. In other words, if the timer task is 10 Hz, avoid setting OS_CFG_TMR_WHEEL_SIZE to 10 or 100 (use 11 or 101 instead). Also, use prime numbers for the timer wheel size. Although it is not really possible to plan at compile time what will happen at run time, ideally the number of timers waiting in each entry of the table is distributed uniformly.

F12-8(3)   Each entry in the table contains three fields: .NbrEntriesMax, .NbrEntries and .FirstPtr. .NbrEntries indicates how many timers are linked to this table entry. .NbrEntriesMax keeps track of the highest number of entries in the table. Finally, .FirstPtr contains a pointer to a doubly linked list of timers (through the tasks OS_TMR) belonging into the list at that table position.

OSTmrTickCtr is incremented by OS_TmrTask() every time the tick ISR signals the task.

Timers are inserted in the timer list by calling OSTmrStart(). However, a timer must be created before it can be used.

An example to illustrate the process of inserting a timer in the timer list is as follows. Let's assume that the timer list is completely empty, OS_CFG_TMR_WHEEL_SIZE is configured to 9, and the current value of OSTmrTickCtr is 12 as shown in Figure 12-9. A timer is placed in the timer list when calling OSTmrStart(), and assumes that the timer was created with a delay of 1 and that this timer will be a one-shot timer as follows:

```
OS_TMR  MyTmr1;
OS_TMR  MyTmr2;


void MyTmrCallbackFnct1 (void *p_arg)
{
    /* Do something when timer #1 expires */
}


void MyTmrCallbackFnct2 (void *p_arg)
{
    /* Do something when timer #2 expires */
}


void MyTask (void *p_arg)
{
    OS_ERR  err;


    while (DEF_ON) {
        :
        OSTmrCreate((OS_TMR              *)&MyTmr1,
                    (OS_CHAR             *)"My Timer #1",
                    (OS_TICK             )1,
                    (OS_TICK             )0,
                    (OS_OPT              )OS_OPT_TMR_ONE_SHOT,
                    (OS_TMR_CALLBACK_PTR)MyTmrCallbackFnct1,
                    (void                *)0,
                    (OS_ERR              *)&err);
        /* Check 'err" */
        OSTmrStart ((OS_TMR *)&MyTmr1,
                    (OS_ERR *)&err);
        /* Check "err" */
        // Continues in the next code listing!
```

Listing 12-2 **Creating and Starting a timer**

Since `OSTmrTickCtr` has a value of 12, the timer will expire when `OSTmrTickCtr` reaches 13, or during the next time the timer task is signaled. Timers are inserted in the `OSCfg_TmrWheel[]` table using the following equation:

```
MatchValue                      = OSTmrTickCtr + dly
Index into OSCfg_TmrWheel[]      = MatchValue % OS_CFG_TMR_WHEEL_SIZE
```

Where "dly" (in this example) is the value passed in the third argument of OSTmrCreate() (i.e., 1 in this example). Again, using the example, we arrive at the following:

```
MatchValue                      = 12 + 1
Index into OSCfg_TickWheel[]     = 13 % 9
```

or,

```
MatchValue                      = 13
Index into OSCfg_TickWheel[]     = 4
```

Because of the "circular" nature of the table (a modulo operation using the size of the table), the table is referred to as a timer wheel, and each entry is a spoke in the wheel.

The timer is entered at index 4 in the timer wheel, OSCfg_TmrWheel[]. In this case, the OS_TMR is placed at the head of the list (i.e., pointed to by OSCfg_TmrWheel[4].FirstPtr), and the number of entries at index 4 is incremented (i.e., OSCfg_TmrWheel[4].NbrEntries will be 1). "MatchValue" is placed in the OS_TMR field .Match. Since this is the first timer inserted in the timer list at index 4, the .NextPtr and .PrevPtr both point to NULL.

Figure 12-9 **Inserting a timer in the timer list**

The code below shows creating and starting another timer. This is performed "before" the timer task is signaled.

```
// Continuation of code from previous code listing.
:
:
OSTmrCreate((OS_TMR              *)&MyTmr2,
            (OS_CHAR             *)"My Timer #2",
            (OS_TICK             )10,
            (OS_TICK             )0,
            (OS_OPT              .  )OS_OPT_TMR_ONE_SHOT,
            (OS_TMR_CALLBACK_PTR)MyTmrCallbackFnct2,
            (void                *)0,
            (OS_ERR              *)&err);
   /* Check 'err" */
OSTmrStart ((OS_TMR *)&MyTmr,
            (OS_ERR *)&err);
   /* Check 'err" */
}
}
```

Listing 12-3 **Creating and Starting a timer - continued**

µC/OS-III will calculate the match value and index as follows:

```
MatchValue                   = 12 + 10
Index into OSCfg_TmrWheel[]  = 22 % 9
```

or,

```
MatchValue                   = 22
Index into OSCfg_TickWheel[] =  4
```

The "second timer" will be inserted at the same table entry as shown in Figure 12-10, but sorted so that the timer with the least amount of time remaining before expiration is placed at the head of the list, and the timer with the longest to wait at the end.

Figure 12-10 **Inserting a second timer in the tick list**

When the timer task executes (see OS_TmrTask( ) in os_tmr.c), it starts by incrementing OSTmrTickCtr and determines which table entry (i.e., spoke) it needs to update. Then, if there are timers in the list at this entry (i.e., .FirstPtr is not NULL), each OS_TMR is examined to determine whether the .Match value "matches" OSTmrTickCtr and, if so, the OS_TMR is removed from the list and OS_TmrTask( ) calls the timer callback function, assuming one was defined when the timer was created. The search through the list terminates as soon as OSTmrTickCtr does not match the timer's .Match value. In other words, there is no point in looking any further in the list since the list is already sorted.

Note that OS_TmrTask( ) does most of its work with the scheduler locked. However, because the list is sorted, and the search through the list terminates as soon as there no longer is a match, the critical section should be fairly short.

12-5 SUMMARY

Timers are down counters that perform an action when the counter reaches zero. The action is provided by the user through a callback function.

µC/OS-III allows application code to create any number of timers (limited only by the amount of RAM available).

The callback functions are executed in the context of the timer task with the scheduler locked. You must keep callback functions as short and as fast as possible and do not have the callbacks make blocking calls.

12

Chapter

13

Resource Management

This chapter will discuss services provided by µC/OS-III to manage shared resources. A shared resource is typically a variable (static or global), a data structure, table (in RAM), or registers in an I/O device.

When protecting a shared resource it is preferred to use mutual exclusion semaphores, as will be described in this chapter. Other methods are also presented.

Tasks can easily share data when all tasks exist in a single address space and can reference global variables, pointers, buffers, linked lists, ring buffers, etc. Although sharing data simplifies the exchange of information between tasks, it is important to ensure that each task has exclusive access to the data to avoid contention and data corruption.

For example, when implementing a module that performs a simple time-of-day algorithm in software, the module obviously keeps track of hours, minutes and seconds. The **TimeOfDay()** task may appear as shown in Listing 13-1.

Imagine if this task was preempted by another task because an interrupt occurred, and, the other task was more important than the **TimeOfDay()** task) after setting the Minutes to 0. Now imagine what will happen if this higher priority task wants to know the current time from the time-of-day module. Since the Hours were not incremented prior to the interrupt, the higher-priority task will read the time incorrectly and, in this case, it will be incorrect by a whole hour.

The code that updates variables for the **TimeOfDay()** task must treat all of the variables indivisibly (or atomically) whenever there is possible preemption. Time-of-day variables are considered shared resources and any code that accesses those variables must have exclusive access through what is called a critical section. µC/OS-III provides services to protect shared resources and enables the easy creation of critical sections.

```
CPU_INT08U  Hours;
CPU_INT08U  Minutes;
CPU_INT08U  Seconds;


void  TimeOfDay (void *p_arg)
{
    OS_ERR  err;


    (void)&p_arg;
    while (DEF_ON) {
        OSTimeDlyHMSM(0,
                      0,
                      1,
                      0,
                      OS_OPT_TIME_HMSM_STRICT,
                      &err);
        /* Examine "err" to make sure the call was successful */
        Seconds++;
        if (Seconds > 59) {
            Seconds = 0;
            Minutes++;
            if (Minutes > 59) {
                Minutes = 0;
                Hours++;
                if (Hours > 23) {
                    Hours = 0;
                }
            }
        }
    }
}
```

Listing 13-1 **Faulty Time-Of-Day clock task**

The most common methods of obtaining exclusive access to shared resources and to create *critical sections* are:

▨ disabling interrupts

▨ disabling the scheduler

▨ using semaphores

▨ using mutual exclusion semaphores (a.k.a. a mutex)

The mutual exclusion mechanism used depends on how fast the code will access a shared resource, as shown in Table 13-1.

Resource Sharing Method	When should you use?
Disable/Enable Interrupts	When access to shared resource is very quick (reading from or writing to few variables) and access is faster than μC/OS-III's interrupt disable time. It is highly recommended to not use this method as it impacts interrupt latency.
Locking/Unlocking the Scheduler	When access time to the shared resource is longer than μC/OS-III's interrupt disable time, but shorter than μC/OS-III's scheduler lock time. Locking the scheduler has the same effect as making the task that locks the scheduler the highest-priority task. It is recommended not to use this method since it defeats the purpose of using μC/OS-III. However, it is a better method than disabling interrupts, as it does not impact interrupt latency.
Semaphores	When all tasks that need to access a shared resource do not have deadlines. This is because semaphores may cause unbounded priority inversions (described later). However, semaphore services are slightly faster (in execution time) than mutual-exclusion semaphores.
Mutual Exclusion Semaphores	This is the preferred method for accessing shared resources, especially if the tasks that need to access a shared resource have deadlines. μC/OS-III's mutual exclusion semaphores have a built-in priority inheritance mechanism, which avoids unbounded priority inversions. However, mutual exclusion semaphore services are slightly slower (in execution time) than semaphores since the priority of the owner may need to be changed, which requires CPU processing.

Table 13-1 **Resource sharing**

231

13-1 DISABLE/ENABLE INTERRUPTS

The easiest and fastest way to gain exclusive access to a shared resource is by disabling and enabling interrupts, as shown in the pseudo-code in Listing 13-2.

```
Disable Interrupts;
Access the resource;
Enable  Interrupts;
```

Listing 13-2 **Disabling and Enabling Interrupts**

µC/OS-III uses this technique (as do most, if not all, kernels) to access certain internal variables and data structures, ensuring that these variables and data structures are manipulated atomically. However, disabling and enabling interrupts are actually CPU-related functions rather than OS-related functions and functions in CPU-specific files are provided to accomplish this (see the **cpu.h** file of the processor being used). The services provided in the CPU module are called µC/CPU. Each different target CPU architecture has its own set of µC/CPU-related files.

```
void YourFunction (void)
{
    CPU_SR_ALLOC();            (1)


    CPU_CRITICAL_ENTER();      (2)
    Access the resource;       (3)
    CPU_CRITICAL_EXIT();       (4)
}
```

Listing 13-3 **Using CPU macros to disable and enable interrupts**

L13-3(1)   The **CPU_SR_ALLOC()** macro is required when the other two macros that disable/enable interrupts are used. This macro simply allocates storage for a local variable to hold the value of the current interrupt disable status of the CPU. If interrupts are already disabled we do not want to enable them upon exiting the critical section.

L13-3(2)   **CPU_CRITICAL_ENTER()** saves the current state of the CPU interrupt disable flag(s) in the local variable allocated by **CPU_SR_ALLOC()** and disables all maskable interrupts.

L13-3(3)   The critical section of code is then accessed without fear of being changed by either an ISR or another task because interrupts are disabled. In other words, this operation is now atomic.

L13-3(4)   **CPU_CRITICAL_EXIT()** restores the previously saved interrupt disable status of the CPU from the local variable.

CPU_CRITICAL_ENTER() and **CPU_CRITICAL_EXIT()** are always used in pairs. Interrupts should be disabled for as short a time as possible as disabling interrupts impacts the response of the system to interrupts. This is known as interrupt latency. Disabling and enabling is used only when changing or copying a few variables.

Note that this is the only way that a task can share variables or data structures with an ISR.

μC/CPU provides a way to actually measure interrupt latency.

When using μC/OS-III, interrupts may be disabled for as much time as μC/OS-III does, without affecting *interrupt latency*. Obviously, it is important to know how long μC/OS-III disables interrupts, which depends on the CPU used.

Although this method works, you should avoid disabling interrupts as it affects the responsiveness of the system to real-time events.

13-2 LOCK/UNLOCK

If the task does not share variables or data structures with an ISR, you can disable and enable µC/OS-III's scheduler while accessing the resource, as shown in Listing 13-4.

```
void YourFunction (void)
{
    OS_ERR  err();                 (1)


    OSSchedLock(&err);             (2)
    Access the resource;          (3)
    OSSchedUnlock(&err);          (4)
}
```

Listing 13-4 **Accessing a resource with the scheduler locked**

Using this method, two or more tasks share data without the possibility of contention. Note that while the scheduler is locked, interrupts are enabled and if an interrupt occurs while in the critical section, the ISR is executed immediately. At the end of the ISR, the kernel always returns to the interrupted task even if a higher priority task is made ready-to-run by the ISR. Since the ISR returns to the interrupted task, the behavior of the kernel is similar to that of a non-preemptive kernel (while the scheduler is locked).

OSSchedLock() and OSSchedUnlock() can be nested up to 250 levels deep. The scheduler is invoked only when OSSchedUnlock() is called the same number of times the application called OSSchedLock().

After the scheduler is unlocked, µC/OS-III performs a context switch if a higher priority task is ready-to-run.

µC/OS-III will not allow the user to make blocking calls when the scheduler is locked. If the application were able to make blocking calls, the application would most likely fail.

Although this method works well, you can avoid disabling the scheduler as it defeats the purpose of having a preemptive kernel. Locking the scheduler makes the current task the highest priority task.

13-3 SEMAPHORES

A semaphore was originally a mechanical signaling mechanism. The railroad industry used the device to provide a form of mutual exclusion for railroads tracks shared by more than one train. In this form, the semaphore signaled trains by closing a set of mechanical arms to block a train from a section of track that was currently in use. When the track became available, the arm would swing up and the waiting train would then proceed.

The notion of using a semaphore in software as a means of mutual exclusion was invented by the Dutch computer scientist Edgser Dijkstra in 1959. In computer software, a semaphore is a protocol mechanism offered by most multitasking kernels. Semaphores, originally used to control access to shared resources, but now they are used for synchronization as described in Chapter 14, "Synchronization" on page 271. However, it is useful to describe how semaphores can be used to share resources. The pitfalls of semaphores will be discussed in a later section.

A semaphore was originally a "lock mechanism" and code acquired the key to this lock to continue execution. Acquiring the key means that the executing task has permission to enter the section of otherwise locked code. Entering a section of locked code causes the task to wait until the key becomes available.

Typically, two types of semaphores exist: binary semaphores and counting semaphores. As its name implies, a binary semaphore can only take two values: 0 or 1. A counting semaphore allows for values between 0 and 255, 65,535, or 4,294,967,295, depending on whether the semaphore mechanism is implemented using 8, 16, or 32 bits, respectively. For µC/OS-III, the maximum value of a semaphore is determined by the data type **OS_SEM_CTR** (see **os_type.h**), which can be changed as needed. Along with the semaphore's value, µC/OS-III also keeps track of tasks waiting for the semaphore's availability.

Only tasks are allowed to use semaphores when semaphores are used for sharing resources; ISRs are not allowed.

A semaphore is a kernel object defined by the **OS_SEM** data type, which is defined by the structure **os_sem** (see **os.h**). The application can have any number of semaphores (limited only by the amount of RAM available).

There are a number of operations the application is able to perform on semaphores, summarized in Table 13-2. In this chapter, only three functions used most often are discussed: **OSSemCreate()**, **OSSemPend()**, and **OSSemPost()**. Other functions are described in Appendix A, "μC/OS-III API Reference" on page 453. When semaphores are used for sharing resources, every semaphore function must be called from a task and never from an ISR. The same limitation does not apply when using semaphores for signaling, as described later in Chapter 13.

Function Name	Operation
OSSemCreate()	Create a semaphore.
OSSemDel()	Delete a semaphore.
OSSemPend()	Wait on a semaphore.
OSSemPendAbort()	Abort the wait on a semaphore.
OSSemPost()	Release or signal a semaphore.
OSSemSet()	Force the semaphore count to a desired value.

Table 13-2 **Semaphore API summary**

13-3-1 BINARY SEMAPHORES

A task that wants to acquire a resource must perform a Wait (or Pend) operation. If the semaphore is available (the semaphore value is greater than 0), the semaphore value is set to 0, and the task continues execution (owning the resource). If the semaphore's value is 0, the task performing a Wait on the semaphore is placed in a waiting list. μC/OS-III allows a timeout to be specified. If the semaphore is not available within a certain amount of time, the requesting task is made ready-to-run, and an error code (indicating that a timeout has occurred) is returned to the caller.

A task releases a semaphore by performing a Signal (or Post) operation. If no task is waiting for the semaphore, the semaphore value is simply set to 1. If there is at least one task waiting for the semaphore, the highest-priority task waiting on the semaphore is made ready-to-run, and the semaphore value is not incremented. If the readied task has a higher priority than the current task (the task releasing the semaphore), a context switch occurs and the higher-priority task resumes execution. The current task is suspended until it again becomes the highest-priority task that is ready-to-run.

The operations described above are summarized using the pseudo-code shown in Listing 13-5.

```
OS_SEM  MySem;                       (1)


void  main (void)
{
    OS_ERR  err;
    :
    :
    OSInit(&err);
    :
    OSSemCreate(&MySem,              (2)
                "My Semaphore",      (3)
                1,                   (4)
                &err);               (5)
    /* Check "err" */
    :
    /* Create task(s) */
    :
    OSStart(&err);
    (void)err;
}
```

Listing 13-5 **Using a semaphore to access a shared resource**

L13-5(1)   The application must declare a semaphore as a variable of type **OS_SEM**. This variable will be referenced by other semaphore services.

L13-5(2)   You create a semaphore by calling **OSSemCreate()** and pass the address to the semaphore allocated in (1). The semaphore must be created before it can be used by other tasks. Here, the semaphore is initialized in startup code (i.e., **main** ()), however it could also be initialized by a task (but it must be initialized before it is used).

L13-5(3)   You can assign an ASCII name to the semaphore, which can be used by debuggers or µC/Probe to easily identify the semaphore. Storage for the ASCII characters is typically in ROM, which is typically more plentiful than RAM. If it is necessary to change the name of the semaphore at runtime, you can store the characters in an array in RAM and simply pass the address of the array to **OSSemCreate()**. Of course, the array must be NUL terminated.

L13-5(4)   You specify the initial value of the semaphore. You should initialize the semaphore to 1 when the semaphore is used to access a single shared resource (as in this example).

L13-5(5)   **OSSemCreate()** returns an error code based on the outcome of the call. If all the arguments are valid, **err** will contain **OS_ERR_NONE**. Refer to the description of **OSSemCreate()** in Appendix A, "µC/OS-III API Reference" on page 453 for a list of other error codes and their meaning.

```
void  Task1 (void *p_arg)
{
    OS_ERR  err;
    CPU_TS  ts;


    while (DEF_ON) {
        :
        OSSemPend(&MySem,                       (1)
                  0,                            (2)
                  OS_OPT_PEND_BLOCKING,         (3)
                  &ts,                          (4)
                  &err);                        (5)
        switch (err) {
            case OS_ERR_NONE:
                Access Shared Resource;         (6)
                OSSemPost(&MySem,               (7)
                          OS_OPT_POST_1,        (8)
                          &err);                (9)
                /* Check "err" */
                break;

            case OS_ERR_PEND_ABORT:
                /* The pend was aborted by another task    */
                break;

            case OS_ERR_OBJ_DEL:
                /* The semaphore was deleted            */
                break;

            default:
                /* Other errors                        */
        }
        :
    }
}
```

Listing 13-6 **Using a semaphore to access a shared resource**

L13-6(1) The task pends (or waits) on the semaphore by calling **OSSemPend()**. The application must specify the desired semaphore to wait upon, and the semaphore must have been previously created.

L13-6(2) The next argument is a timeout specified in number of clock ticks. The actual timeout depends on the tick rate. If the tick rate (see **os_cfg_app.h**) is set to 1000, a timeout of 10 ticks represents 10 milliseconds. Specifying a timeout of zero (0) means waiting forever for the semaphore.

L13-6(3)   The third argument specifies how to wait. There are two options: OS_OPT_PEND_BLOCKING and OS_OPT_PEND_NON_BLOCKING. The blocking option means that if the semaphore is not available, the task calling OSSemPend() will wait until the semaphore is posted or until the timeout expires. The non-blocking option indicates that if the semaphore is not available, OSSemPend() will return immediately and not wait. This last option is rarely used when using a semaphore to protect a shared resource.

L13-6(4)   When the semaphore is posted, µC/OS-III reads a "timestamp" and returns this timestamp when OSSemPend() returns. This feature allows the application to know "when" the post happened and the semaphore was released. At this point, OS_TS_GET() is read to get the current timestamp and you can compute the difference, indicating the length of the wait.

L13-6(5)   OSSemPend() returns an error code based on the outcome of the call. If the call is successful, **err** will contain OS_ERR_NONE. If not, the error code will indicate the reason for the error. See Appendix A, "µC/OS-III API Reference" on page 453 for a list of possible error code for OSSemPend(). Checking for error return values is important since other tasks might delete or otherwise abort the pend. However, it is not a recommended practice to delete kernel objects at run time as the action may cause serious problems.

L13-6(6)   The resource can be accessed when OSSemPend() returns, if there are no errors.

L13-6(7)   When finished accessing the resource, you simply call OSSemPost() and specify the semaphore to be released.

L13-6(8)   OS_OPT_POST_1 indicates that the semaphore is signaling a single task, if there are many tasks waiting on the semaphore. In fact, you should always specify this option when a semaphore is used to access a shared resource.

L13-6(9)   As with most µC/OS-III functions, you specify the address of a variable that will receive an error message from the call.

```
void  Task2 (void *p_arg)
{
    OS_ERR  err;
    CPU_TS  ts;


    while (DEF_ON) {
        :
        OSSemPend(&MySem,                                (1)
                  0,
                  OS_OPT_PEND_BLOCKING,
                  &ts,
                  &err);
        switch (err) {
            case OS_ERR_NONE:
                Access Shared Resource;
                OSSemPost(&MySem,
                          OS_OPT_POST_1,
                          &err);
                /* Check "err" */
                break;

            case OS_ERR_PEND_ABORT:
                /* The pend was aborted by another task    */
                break;

            case OS_ERR_OBJ_DEL:
                /* The semaphore was deleted               */
                break;

            default:
                /* Other errors                            */
        }
        :
    }
}
```

Listing 13-7 **Using a semaphore to access a shared resource**

L13-7(1)   Another task wanting to access the shared resource needs to use the same procedure to access the shared resource.

241

Semaphores are especially useful when tasks share I/O devices. Imagine what would happen if two tasks were allowed to send characters to a printer at the same time. The printer would contain interleaved data from each task. For instance, the printout from Task 1 printing "I am Task 1," and Task 2 printing "I am Task 2," could result in "I Ia amm T Tasask k1 2". In this case, you can use a semaphore and initialize it to 1 (i.e., a binary semaphore). The rule is simple: to access the printer each task must first obtain the resource's semaphore. Figure 13-1 shows tasks competing for a semaphore to gain exclusive access to the printer. Note that a key, indicating that each task must obtain this key to use the printer, represents the semaphore symbolically.

Figure 13-1 **Using a semaphore to access a printer**

The above example implies that each task knows about the existence of the semaphore to access the resource. It is almost always better to encapsulate the critical section and its protection mechanism. Each task would therefore not know that it is acquiring a semaphore when accessing the resource. For example, an RS-232C port is used by multiple tasks to send commands and receive responses from a device connected at the other end as shown in Figure 13-2.

Figure 13-2 **Hiding a semaphore from a task**

The function **CommSendCmd( )** is called with three arguments: the ASCII string containing the command, a pointer to the response string from the device, and finally, a timeout in case the device does not respond within a certain amount of time. The pseudo-code for this function is shown in Listing 13-8.

```
APP_ERR  CommSendCmd (CPU_CHAR  *cmd,
                      CPU_CHAR  *response,
                      OS_TICK   timeout)
{
    Acquire serial port's semaphore;
    Send "cmd" to device;
    Wait for response with "timeout";
    if (timed out) {
        Release serial port's semaphore;
        return (error code);
    } else {
        Release serial port's semaphore;
        return (no error);
    }
}
```

Listing 13-8 **Encapsulating the use of a semaphore**

Each task that needs to send a command to the device must call this function. The semaphore is assumed to be initialized to 1 (i.e., available) by the communication driver initialization routine. The first task that calls CommSendCmd() acquires the semaphore, proceeds to send the command, and waits for a response. If another task attempts to send a command while the port is busy, this second task is suspended until the semaphore is released. The second task appears simply to have made a call to a normal function that will not return until the function performs its duty. When the semaphore is released by the first task, the second task acquires the semaphore and is allowed to use the RS-232C port.

13-3-2 COUNTING SEMAPHORES

A counting semaphore is used when elements of a resource can be used by more than one task at the same time. For example, a counting semaphore is used in the management of a buffer pool, as shown in Figure 13-3. Let's assume that the buffer pool initially contains 10 buffers. A task obtains a buffer from the buffer manager by calling BufReq(). When the buffer is no longer needed, the task returns the buffer to the buffer manager by calling BufRel(). The pseudo-code for these functions is shown in Listing 13-9.

The buffer manager satisfies the first 10 buffer requests because the semaphore is initialized to 10. When all buffers are used, a task requesting a buffer is suspended until a buffer becomes available. You use µC/OS-III's OSMemGet() and OSMemPut() (see Chapter 17, "Memory Management" on page 341) to obtain a buffer from the buffer pool. When a task is finished with the buffer it acquired, the task calls BufRel() to return the buffer to the buffer manager and the buffer is inserted into the linked list before the semaphore is signaled. By encapsulating the interface to the buffer manager in BufReq() and BufRel(), the caller does not need to be concerned with actual implementation details.

Figure 13-3 **Using a counting semaphore**

```
BUF  *BufReq (void)
{
    BUF  *ptr;


    Wait on semaphore;
    ptr = OSMemGet(...) ;              /* Get a buffer    */
    return (ptr);
}


void  BufRel (BUF *ptr)
{
    OSMemPut(..., (void *)ptr, ...);   /* Return the buffer */
    Signal semaphore;
}
```

Listing 13-9 **Buffer management using a semaphore.**

245

Note that the details of creating the memory partition are removed since this is discussed in Chapter 17, "Memory Management" on page 341. The semaphore is used here to extend the memory management capabilities of µC/OS-III, and to provide it with a blocking mechanism. However, only tasks can make **BufReq( )** and **BufRel( )** calls.

13-3-3 NOTES ON SEMAPHORES

Using a semaphore to access a shared resource does not increase interrupt latency. If an ISR or the current task makes a higher priority task ready-to-run while accessing shared data, the higher priority task executes immediately.

An application may have as many semaphores as required to protect a variety of different resources. For example, one semaphore may be used to access a shared display, another to access a shared printer, another for shared data structures, and another to protect a pool of buffers, etc. However, it is preferable to use semaphores to protect access to I/O devices rather than memory locations.

Semaphores are often overused. The use of a semaphore to access a simple shared variable is overkill in most situations. The overhead involved in acquiring and releasing the semaphore consumes valuable CPU time. You can perform the job more efficiently by disabling and enabling interrupts, however there is an indirect cost to disabling interrupts: even higher priority tasks that do not share the specific resource are blocked from using the CPU. Suppose, for instance, that two tasks share a 32-bit integer variable. The first task increments the variable, while the second task clears it. When considering how long a processor takes to perform either operation, it is easy to see that a semaphore is not required to gain exclusive access to the variable. Each task simply needs to disable interrupts before performing its operation on the variable and enable interrupts when the operation is complete. A semaphore should be used if the variable is a floating-point variable and the microprocessor does not support hardware floating-point operations. In this case, the time involved in processing the floating-point variable may affect interrupt latency if interrupts are disabled.

Semaphores are subject to a serious problem in real-time systems called priority inversion, which is described in section 13-3-5 "Priority Inversions" on page 252.

13-3-4 SEMAPHORE INTERNALS (FOR RESOURCE SHARING)

As previously mentioned, a semaphore is a kernel object as defined by the OS_SEM data type, which is derived from the structure os_sem (see os.h) as shown in Listing 13-10.

The services provided by µC/OS-III to manage semaphores are implemented in the file os_sem.c. Semaphore services are enabled at compile time by setting the configuration constant OS_CFG_SEM_EN to 1 in os_cfg.h.

```
typedef  struct  os_sem  OS_SEM;            (1)


struct  os_sem {
    OS_OBJ_TYPE         Type;              (2)
    CPU_CHAR            *NamePtr;          (3)
    OS_PEND_LIST        PendList;          (4)
    OS_SEM_CTR          Ctr;               (5)
    CPU_TS              TS;                (6)
};
```

Listing 13-10 **OS_SEM data type**

L13-10(1)   In µC/OS-III, all structures are given a data type. All data types start with "OS_" and are uppercase. When a semaphore is declared, you simply use OS_SEM as the data type of the variable used to declare the semaphore.

L13-10(2)   The structure starts with a "Type" field, which allows it to be recognized by µC/OS-III as a semaphore. Other kernel objects will also have a ".Type" as the first member of the structure. If a function is passed a kernel object, µC/OS-III will confirm that it is being passed the proper data type (assuming OS_CFG_OBJ_TYPE_CHK_EN is set to 1 in os_cfg.h). For example, if you pass a message queue (OS_Q) to a semaphore service (for example OSSemPend()), µC/OS-III will recognize that an invalid object was passed, and return an error code accordingly.

L13-10(3)   Each kernel object can be given a name for easier recognition by debuggers or µC/Probe. This member is simply a pointer to an ASCII string, which is assumed to be NUL terminated.

247

L13-10(4)   Since it is possible for multiple tasks to wait (or pend) on a semaphore, the semaphore object contains a pend list as described in Chapter 10, "Pend Lists (or Wait Lists)" on page 195.

L13-10(5)   A semaphore contains a counter. As explained above, the counter can be implemented as either an 8-, 16- or 32-bit value, depending on how the data type **OS_SEM_CTR** is declared in **os_type.h**.

µC/OS-III does not make a distinction between binary and counting semaphores. The distinction is made when the semaphore is created. If creating a semaphore with an initial value of 1, it is a binary semaphore. When creating a semaphore with a value > 1, it is a counting semaphore. In the next chapter, you will discover that a semaphore is more often used as a signaling mechanism and therefore, the semaphore counter is initialized to zero.

L13-10(6)   A semaphore contains a timestamp used to indicate the last time the semaphore was posted. µC/OS-III assumes the presence of a free-running counter that allows the application to make time measurements. When the semaphore is posted, the free-running counter is read and the value is placed in this field, which is returned when **OSSemPend()** is called. The value of this field is more useful when a semaphore is used as a signaling mechanism (see Chapter 14, "Synchronization" on page 271), as opposed to a resource-sharing mechanism.

Even if the user understands the internals of the **OS_SEM** data type, the application code should never access any of the fields in this data structure directly. Instead, you should always use the APIs provided with µC/OS-III.

As previously mentioned, semaphores must be created before they can be used by an application.

A task waits on a semaphore before accessing a shared resource by calling **OSSemPend()** as shown in Listing 13-11 (see Appendix A, "µC/OS-III API Reference" on page 453 for details regarding the arguments).

```
OS_SEM  MySem;


void MyTask (void *p_arg)
{
    OS_ERR  err;
    CPU_TS  ts;


    :
    while (DEF_ON) {
        :
        OSSemPend(&MySem,             /* (1) Pointer to semaphore                       */
                  10,                 /*     Wait up until this time for the semaphore  */
                  OS_OPT_PEND_BLOCKING, /*   Option(s)                                  */
                  &ts,                /*     Returned timestamp of when sem. was released */
                  &err);              /*     Pointer to Error returned                  */
        :
        /* Check "err" */             /* (2)                                            */
        :
        OSSemPost(&MySem,             /* (3) Pointer to semaphore                       */
                  OS_OPT_POST_1,      /*     Option(s) ... always OS_OPT_POST_1         */
                  &err);              /*     Pointer to Error returned                  */
        /* Check "err" */
        :
        :

    }
}
```

Listing 13-11 **Pending on and Posting to a Semaphore**

L13-11(1)   When called, **OSSemPend()** starts by checking the arguments passed to this function to make sure they have valid values (assuming **OS_CFG_ARG_CHK_EN** is set to 1 in **os_cfg.h**).

If the semaphore counter (**.Ctr** of **OS_SEM**) is greater than zero, the counter is decremented and **OSSemPend()** returns. If **OSSemPend()** returns without error, then the task now owns the shared resource.

If the semaphore counter is zero, then another task owns the semaphore, and the calling task will need to wait for the semaphore to be released. If you specify **OS_OPT_PEND_NON_BLOCKING** as the option (the application does not want the task to block), **OSSemPend()** returns immediately to the caller and the returned error code indicates that the semaphore is unavailable. You use this option if the task does not want to wait for the resource to be available, and would prefer to do something else and check back later.

If you specify the **OS_OPT_PEND_BLOCKING** option, the calling task will be inserted in the list of tasks waiting for the semaphore to become available. The task is inserted in the list by priority order and therefore, the highest priority task waiting on the semaphore is at the beginning of the list.

If you specify a non-zero timeout, the task will also be inserted in the tick list. A zero value for a timeout indicates that the user is willing to wait forever for the semaphore to be released. Most of the time, you would specify an infinite timeout when using the semaphore in resource sharing. Adding a timeout may temporarily break a deadlock, however, there are better ways of preventing deadlock at the application level (e.g., never hold more than one semaphore at the same time; resource ordering; etc.).

Assuming blocking, the scheduler is called since the current task is no longer able to run (it is waiting for the semaphore to be released). The scheduler will then run the next highest-priority task that is ready-to-run.

When the semaphore is released and the task that called **OSSemPend()** is again the highest-priority task, µC/OS-III examines the task status to determine the reason why **OSSemPend()** is returning to its caller. The possibilities are:

1) The semaphore was given to the waiting task. This is the preferred outcome.

2) The pend was aborted by another task

3) The semaphore was not posted within the specified timeout

4) The semaphore was deleted

When **OSSemPend()** returns, the caller is notified of the above outcome through an appropriate error code.

L13-11(2)   If OSSemPend() returns with **err** set to **OS_ERR_NONE**, your code can assume that it now has access to the resource.

If **err** contains anything else, OSSemPend() either timed out (if the timeout argument was non-zero), the pend was aborted by another task, or the semaphore was deleted by another task. It is always important to examine the returned error code and not assume that everything went well.

L13-11(3)   When the task is finished accessing the resource, it needs to call OSSemPost() and specify the same semaphore. Again, OSSemPost() starts by checking the arguments passed to this function to make sure there are valid values (assuming **OS_CFG_ARG_CHK_EN** is set to **1** in **os_cfg.h**).

OSSemPost() then calls **OS_TS_GET()** to obtain the current timestamp so it can place that information in the semaphore to be used by OSSemPend(). This feature is not as useful when semaphores are used to share resources as it is when used as a signaling mechanism.

OSSemPost() checks to see if any tasks are waiting for the semaphore. If not, OSSemPost() simply increments **p_sem->Ctr**, saves the timestamp in the semaphore, and returns.

If there are tasks waiting for the semaphore to be released, OSSemPost() extracts the highest-priority task waiting for the semaphore. This is a fast operation as the pend list is sorted by priority order.

When calling OSSemPost(), it is possible to specify as an option to not call the scheduler. This means that the post is performed, but the scheduler is not called even if a higher priority task waits for the semaphore to be released. This allows the calling task to perform other post functions (if needed) and make all posts take effect simultaneously without the possibility of context switching in between each post.

13

13-3-5 PRIORITY INVERSIONS

Priority inversion is a problem in real-time systems, and occurs only when using a priority-based preemptive kernel. Figure 13-4 illustrates a priority-inversion scenario. Task H (high priority) has a higher priority than Task M (medium priority), which in turn has a higher priority than Task L (low priority).

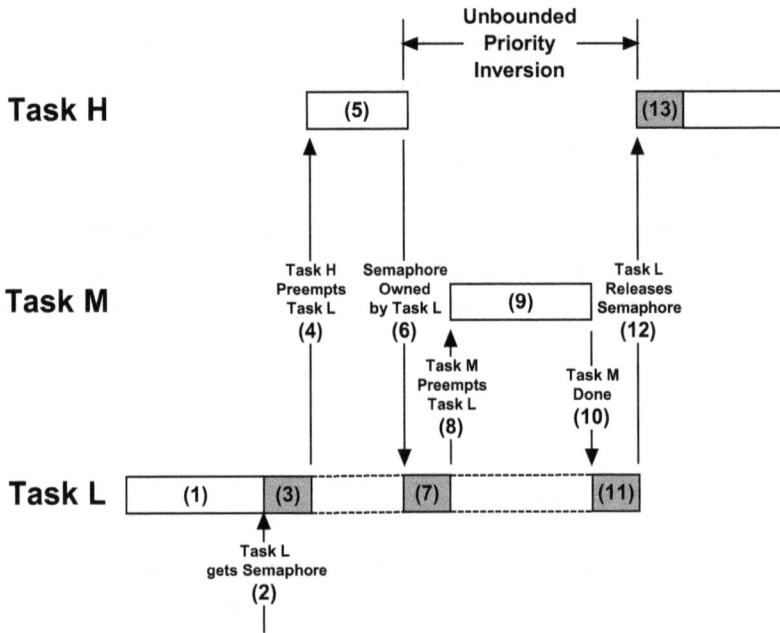

Figure 13-4 **Unbounded priority Inversion**

F13-4(1)   Task H and Task M are both waiting for an event to occur and Task L is executing.

F13-4(2)   At some point, Task L acquires a semaphore, which it needs before it can access a shared resource.

F13-4(3)   Task L performs operations on the acquired resource.

F13-4(4)   The event that Task H was waiting for occurs, and the kernel suspends Task L and start executing Task H since Task H has a higher priority.

F13-4(5)   Task H performs computations based on the event it just received.

F13-4(6)   Task H now wants to access the resource that Task L currently owns (i.e., it attempts to get the semaphore that Task L owns). Because Task L owns the resource, Task H is placed in a list of tasks waiting for the semaphore to be available.

F13-4(7)   Task L is resumed and continues to access the shared resource.

F13-4(8)   Task L is preempted by Task M since the event that Task M was waiting for occurred.

F13-4(9)   Task M handles the event.

F13-4(10)   When Task M completes, the kernel relinquishes the CPU back to Task L.

F13-4(11)   Task L continues accessing the resource.

F13-4(12)   Task L finally finishes working with the resource and releases the semaphore. At this point, the kernel knows that a higher-priority task is waiting for the semaphore, and a context switch takes place to resume Task H.

F13-4(13)   Task H has the semaphore and can access the shared resource.

So, what happened here is that the priority of Task H has been reduced to that of Task L since it waited for the resource that Task L owned. The trouble begins when Task M preempted Task L, further delaying the execution of Task H. This is called an *unbounded priority inversion*. It is unbounded because any medium priority can extend the time Task H has to wait for the resource. Technically, if all medium-priority tasks have known worst-case periodic behavior and bounded execution times, the priority inversion time is computable. This process, however, may be tedious and would need to be revised every time the medium priority tasks change.

This situation can be corrected by raising the priority of Task L, only during the time it takes to access the resource, and restore the original priority level when the task is finished. The priority of Task L should be raised up to the priority of Task H. In fact, μC/OS-III contains a special type of semaphore that does just that and is called a mutual-exclusion semaphore.

13-4 MUTUAL EXCLUSION SEMAPHORES (MUTEX)

µC/OS-III supports a special type of binary semaphore called a mutual exclusion semaphore (also known as a mutex) that eliminates unbounded priority inversions. Figure 13-5 shows how priority inversions are bounded using a Mutex.

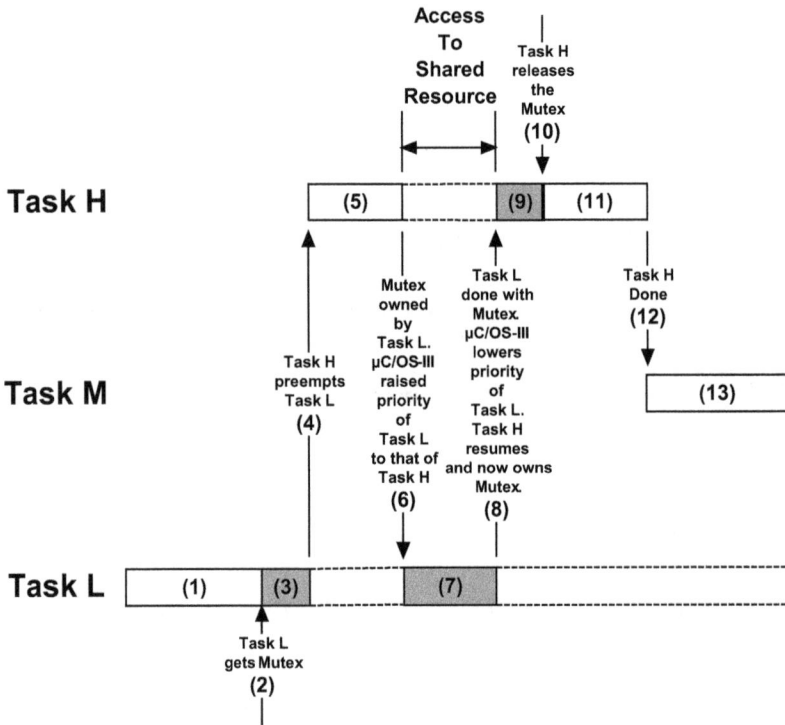

Figure 13-5 **Using a mutex to share a resource**

F13-5(1)   Task H and Task M are both waiting for an event to occur and Task L is executing.

F13-5(2)   At some point, Task L acquires a mutex, which it needs before it is able to access a shared resource.

F13-5(3)   Task L performs operations on the acquired resource.

F13-5(4)   The event that Task H waited for occurs and the kernel suspends Task L and begins executing Task H since Task H has a higher priority.

F13-5(5)   Task H performs computations based on the event it just received.

F13-5(6)   Task H now wants to access the resource that Task L currently owns (i.e., it attempts to get the mutex from Task L). Given that Task L owns the resource, µC/OS-III raises the priority of Task L to the same priority as Task H to allow Task L to finish with the resource and prevent Task L from being preempted by medium-priority tasks.

F13-5(7)   Task L continues accessing the resource, however it now does so while it is running at the same priority as Task H. Note that Task H is not actually running since it is waiting for Task L to release the mutex. In other words, Task H is in the mutex wait list.

F13-5(8)   Task L finishes working with the resource and releases the mutex. µC/OS-III notices that Task L was raised in priority and thus lowers Task L to its original priority. After doing so, µC/OS-III gives the mutex to Task H, which was waiting for the mutex to be released.

F13-5(9)   Task H now has the mutex and can access the shared resource.

F13-5(10)   Task H is finished accessing the shared resource, and frees up the mutex.

F13-5(11)   There are no higher-priority tasks to execute, therefore Task H continues execution.

F13-5(12)   Task H completes and decides to wait for an event to occur. At this point, µC/OS-III resumes Task M, which was made ready-to-run while Task H or Task L were executing. Task M was made ready-to-run because an interrupt (not shown in figure 13-5) occurred which Task M was waiting for.

F13-5(13)   Task M executes.

Note that there is no priority inversion, only resource sharing. Of course, the faster Task L accesses the shared resource and frees up the mutex, the better.

µC/OS-III implements full-priority inheritance and therefore if a higher priority requests the resource, the priority of the owner task will be raised to the priority of the new requestor.

A mutex is a kernel object defined by the **OS_MUTEX** data type, which is derived from the structure **os_mutex** (see **os.h**). An application may have an unlimited number of mutexes (limited only by the RAM available).

Only tasks are allowed to use mutual exclusion semaphores (ISRs are not allowed).

µC/OS-III enables the user to nest ownership of mutexes. If a task owns a mutex, it can own the same mutex up to 250 times. The owner must release the mutex an equivalent number of times. In several cases, an application may not be immediately aware that it called **OSMutexPend()** multiple times, especially if the mutex is acquired again by calling a function as shown in Listing 13-12.

```
OS_MUTEX          MyMutex;
SOME_STRUCT       MySharedResource;


void  MyTask (void *p_arg)
{
    OS_ERR  err;
    CPU_TS  ts;

    :
    while (DEF_ON) {
        OSMutexPend((OS_MUTEX *)&MyMutex,                       (1)
                    (OS_TICK   )0,
                    (OS_OPT    )OS_OPT_PEND_BLOCKING,
                    (CPU_TS   *)&ts,
                    (OS_ERR   *)&err);
        /* Check 'err" */                          */      (2)
        /* Acquire shared resource if no error     */
        MyLibFunction();                                       (3)
        OSMutexPost((OS_MUTEX *)&MyMutex,                      (7)
                    (OS_OPT    )OS_OPT_POST_NONE,
                    (OS_ERR   *)&err);
        /* Check "err" */                          */
    }
}
```

```
void  MyLibFunction (void)
{
    OS_ERR   err;
    CPU_TS   ts;


    OSMutexPend((OS_MUTEX *)&MyMutex,                        (4)
                (OS_TICK   )0,
                (OS_OPT    )OS_OPT_PEND_BLOCKING,
                (CPU_TS   *)&ts,
                (OS_ERR   *)&err);
    /* Check "err"                         */
    /* Access shared resource if no error  */            (5)
    OSMutexPost((OS_MUTEX *)&MyMutex,                        (6)
                (OS_OPT    )OS_OPT_POST_NONE,
                (OS_ERR   *)&err);
    /* Check "err"                         */
}
```

Listing 13-12 **Nesting calls to OSMutexPend()**

L13-12(1)   A task starts by pending on a mutex to access shared resources. **OSMutexPend()** sets a nesting counter to 1.

L13-12(2)   You should check the error return value. If no errors exist, **MyTask()** owns **MySharedResource**.

L13-12(3)   A function is called that will perform additional work.

L13-12(4)   The designer of **MyLibFunction()** knows that, to access **MySharedResource**, it must acquire the mutex. Since the calling task already owns the mutex, this operation should not be necessary. However, **MyLibFunction()** could have been called by yet another function that might not need access to **MySharedResource**. μC/OS-III allows nested mutex pends, so this is not a problem. The mutex nesting counter is thus incremented to 2.

L13-12(5)   **MyLibFunction()** can access the shared resource.

L13-12(6)   The mutex is released and the nesting counter is decremented back to 1. Since this indicates that the mutex is still owned by the same task, nothing further needs to be done, and **OSMutexPost()** simply returns. **MyLibFunction()** returns to its caller.

L13-12(7)   The mutex is released again and, this time, the nesting counter is decremented back to 0 indicating that other tasks can now acquire the mutex.

You should always check the return value of **OSMutexPend()** (and any kernel call) to ensure that the function returned because you properly obtained the mutex, and not because the return from **OSMutexPend()** was caused by the mutex being deleted, or because another task called **OSMutexPendAbort()** on this mutex.

As a general rule, do not make function calls in critical sections. All mutual exclusion semaphore calls should be in the leaf nodes of the source code (e.g., in the low level drivers that actually touches real hardware or in other reentrant function libraries).

There are a number of operations that can be performed on a mutex, as summarized in Table 13-3. However, in this chapter, we will only discuss the three functions that are most often used: **OSMutexCreate()**, **OSMutexPend()**, and **OSMutexPost()**. Other functions are described in Appendix A, "µC/OS-III API Reference" on page 453.

Function Name	Operation
OSMutexCreate()	Create a mutex.
OSMutexDel()	Delete a mutex.
OSMutexPend()	Wait on a mutex.
OSMutexPendAbort()	Abort the wait on a mutex.
OSMutexPost()	Release a mutex.

Table 13-3 **Mutex API summary**

13-4-1 MUTUAL EXCLUSION SEMAPHORE INTERNALS

A mutex is a kernel object defined by the **OS_MUTEX** data type, which is derived from the structure **os_mutex** (see **os.h**) as shown in Listing 13-13:

```
typedef  struct  os_mutex  OS_MUTEX;          (1)


struct  os_mutex {
    OS_OBJ_TYPE          Type;                (2)
    CPU_CHAR             *NamePtr;            (3)
    OS_PEND_LIST         PendList;            (4)
    OS_TCB               *OwnerTCBPtr;        (5)
    OS_PRIO              OwnerOriginalPrio;   (6)
    OS_NESTING_CTR       OwnerNestingCtr;     (7)
    CPU_TS               TS;                  (8)
};
```

Listing 13-13 **OS_MUTEX data type**

L13-13(1)   In µC/OS-III, all structures are given a data type. All data types begin with "**OS_**" and are uppercase. When a mutex is declared, you simply use **OS_MUTEX** as the data type of the variable used to declare the mutex.

L13-13(2)   The structure starts with a "Type" field, which allows it to be recognized by µC/OS-III as a mutex. Other kernel objects will also have a "**.Type**" as the first member of the structure. If a function is passed a kernel object, µC/OS-III will be able to confirm that it is being passed the proper data type (assuming **OS_CFG_OBJ_TYPE_CHK_EN** is set to 1 in **os_cfg.h**). For example, if passing a message queue (**OS_Q**) to a mutex service (for example **OSMutexPend()**), µC/OS-III will recognize that the application passed an invalid object and return an error code accordingly.

L13-13(3)   Each kernel object can be given a name to make them easier to recognize by debuggers or µC/Probe. This member is simply a pointer to an ASCII string, which is assumed to be **NUL** terminated.

L13-13(4)   Because it is possible for multiple tasks to wait (or pend on a mutex), the mutex object contains a pend list as described in Chapter 10, "Pend Lists (or Wait Lists)" on page 195.

259

L13-13(5)   If the mutex is owned by a task, it will point to the **OS_TCB** of that task.

L13-13(6)   If the mutex is owned by a task, this field contains the "original" priority of the task that owns the mutex. This field is required in case the priority of the task must be raised to a higher priority to prevent unbounded priority inversions.

L13-13(7)   μC/OS-III allows a task to "acquire" the same mutex multiple times. In order for the mutex to be released, the owner must release the mutex the same number of times that it was acquired. Nesting can be performed up to 250-levels deep.

L13-13(8)   A mutex contains a timestamp, used to indicate the last time it was released. μC/OS-III assumes the presence of a free-running counter that allows applications to make time measurements. When the mutex is released, the free-running counter is read and the value is placed in this field, which is returned when **OSMutexPend( )** returns.

Application code should never access any of the fields in this data structure directly. Instead, you should always use the APIs provided with μC/OS-III.

A mutual exclusion semaphore (mutex) must be created before it can be used by an application. Listing 13-14 shows how to create a mutex.

```
OS_MUTEX  MyMutex;                       (1)


void  MyTask (void *p_arg)
{
    OS_ERR  err;
    :
    :
    OSMutexCreate(&MyMutex,              (2)
             "My Mutex",                 (3)
             &err);                      (4)
    /* Check "err" */
    :
    :
}
```

Listing 13-14 **Creating a mutex**

L13-14(1)   The application must declare a variable of type **OS_MUTEX**. This variable will be referenced by other mutex services.

L13-14(2)   You create a mutex by calling **OSMutexCreate()** and pass the address to the mutex allocated in L13-14(1).

L13-14(3)   You can assign an ASCII name to the mutex, which can be used by debuggers or µC/Probe to easily identify this mutex. There are no practical limits to the length of the name since µC/OS-III stores a pointer to the ASCII string, and not to the actual characters that makes up the string.

L13-14(4)   **OSMutexCreate()** returns an error code based on the outcome of the call. If all the arguments are valid, **err** will contain **OS_ERR_NONE**.

Note that since a mutex is always a binary semaphore, there is no need to initialize a mutex counter.

A task waits on a mutual exclusion semaphore before accessing a shared resource by calling **OSMutexPend()** as shown in Listing 13-15 (see Appendix A, "µC/OS-III API Reference" on page 453 for details regarding the arguments).

```
OS_MUTEX  MyMutex;


void MyTask (void *p_arg)
{
    OS_ERR  err;
    CPU_TS  ts;
    :
    while (DEF_ON) {
        :
        OSMutexPend(&MyMutex,             /* (1) Pointer to mutex                     */
                    10,                   /*     Wait up until this time for the mutex */
                    OS_OPT_PEND_BLOCKING, /*     Option(s)                            */
                    &ts,                  /*     Timestamp of when mutex was released */
                    &err);                /*     Pointer to Error returned            */
        :
        /* Check "err"                        (2)                                     */
        :
        OSMutexPost(&MyMutex,             /* (3) Pointer to mutex                     */
                    OS_OPT_POST_NONE,
                    &err);                /*     Pointer to Error returned            */
        /* Check "err"                                                                */
        :
        :
    }
}
```

Listing 13-15 **Pending (or waiting) on a Mutual Exclusion Semaphore**

L13-15(1)   When called, **OSMutexPend( )** starts by checking the arguments passed to this function to make sure they have valid values. This assumes that **OS_CFG_ARG_CHK_EN** is set to 1 in **os_cfg.h**).

If the mutex is available, **OSMutexPend( )** assumes the calling task is now the owner of the mutex and stores a pointer to the task's **OS_TCB** in **p_mutex->OwnerTCPPtr**, saves the priority of the task in **p_mutex->OwnerOriginalPrio**, and sets a mutex nesting counter to 1. **OSMutexPend( )** then returns to its caller with an error code of **OS_ERR_NONE**.

If the task that calls **OSMutexPend( )** already owns the mutex, **OSMutexPend( )** simply increments a nesting counter. Applications can nest calls to **OSMutexPend( )** up to 250-levels deep. In this case, the error returned will indicate **OS_ERR_MUTEX_OWNER**.

If the mutex is already owned by another task and OS_OPT_PEND_NON_BLOCKING is specified, OSMutexPend() returns since the task is not willing to wait for the mutex to be released by its owner.

If the mutex is owned by a lower-priority task, µC/OS-III will raise the priority of the owner to match the priority of the current task.

If you specify OS_OPT_PEND_BLOCKING as the option, the calling task will be inserted in the list of tasks waiting for the mutex to be available. The task is inserted in the list by priority order and thus, the highest priority task waiting on the mutex is at the beginning of the list.

If you further specify a non-zero timeout, the task will also be inserted in the tick list. A zero value for a timeout indicates a willingness to wait forever for the mutex to be released.

The scheduler is then called since the current task is no longer able to run (it is waiting for the mutex to be released). The scheduler will then run the next highest-priority task that is ready-to-run.

When the mutex is finally released and the task that called OSMutexPend() is again the highest-priority task, a task status is examined to determine the reason why OSMutexPend() is returning to its caller. The possibilities are:

1) The mutex was given to the waiting task. This is the desired outcome.

2) The pend was aborted by another task.

3) The mutex was not posted within the specified timeout.

4) The mutex was deleted.

When OSMutexPend() returns, the caller is notified of the outcome through an appropriate error code.

L13-15(2)   If OSMutexPend() returns with **err** set to OS_ERR_NONE, assume that the calling task now owns the resource and can proceed with accessing it. If **err** contains anything else, then OSMutexPend() either timed out (if the timeout argument was non-zero), the pend was aborted by another task, or the mutex was deleted by another task. It is always important to examine returned error codes and not assume everything went as planned.

If "**err**" is OS_ERR_MUTEX_NESTING, then the caller attempted to pend on the same mutex.

L13-15(3)   When your task is finished accessing the resource, it must call OSMutexPost() and specify the same mutex. Again, OSMutexPost() starts by checking the arguments passed to this function to make sure they contain valid values (Assuming OS_CFG_ARG_CHK_EN is set to 1 in os_cfg.h).

OSMutexPost() now calls OS_TS_GET() to obtain the current timestamp and place that information in the mutex, which will be used by OSMutexPend().

OSMutexPost() decrements the nesting counter and, if still non-zero, OSMutexPost() returns to the caller. In this case, the current owner has not fully released the mutex. The error code will be OS_ERR_MUTEX_NESTING.

If there are no tasks waiting for the mutex, OSMutexPost() sets p_mutex->OwnerTCBPtr to a NULL pointer and clears the mutex nesting counter.

If μC/OS-III had to raise the priority of the mutex owner, it is returned to its original priority at this time.

The highest-priority task waiting on the mutex is then extracted from the pend list and given the mutex. This is a fast operation since the pend list is sorted by priority.

If the option to OSMutexPost() is not OS_OPT_POST_NO_SCHED then, the scheduler is called to see if the new mutex owner has a higher priority than the current task. If so, μC/OS-III will switch context to the new mutex owner.

You should note that you should only acquire one mutex at a time. In fact, it's highly recommended that when you acquire a mutex, you don't acquire any other kernel objects.

13-5 SHOULD YOU USE A SEMAPHORE INSTEAD OF A MUTEX?

A semaphore can be used instead of a mutex if none of the tasks competing for the shared resource have deadlines to be satisfied.

However, if there are deadlines to meet, you should use a mutex prior to accessing shared resources. Semaphores are subject to unbounded priority inversions, while mutex are not.

13-6 DEADLOCKS (OR DEADLY EMBRACE)

A *deadlock*, also called a **deadly embrace**, is a situation in which two tasks are each unknowingly waiting for resources held by the other.

Assume Task T1 has exclusive access to Resource R1 and Task T2 has exclusive access to Resource R2 as shown in the pseudo-code of Listing 13-16.

```
void T1 (void *p_arg)
{
    while (DEF_ON) {
        Wait for event to occur;      (1)
        Acquire M1;                   (2)
        Access  R1;                   (3)
        :
        :
        \--------  Interrupt!         (4)
        :
        :                             (8)
        Acquire M2;                   (9)
        Access  R2;
    }
}
```

```
void  T2 (void *p_arg)
{
    while (DEF_ON) {
        Wait for event to occur;        (5)
        Acquire M2;                     (6)
        Access  R2;
        :
        :
        Acquire M1;                     (7)
        Access  R1;
    }
}
```

Listing 13-16 **Deadlock problem**

L13-16(1)   Assume that the event that task T1 is waiting for occurs and T1 is now the highest priority task that must execute.

L13-16(2)   Task T1 executes and acquires Mutex M1.

L13-16(3)   Resource R1 is accessed.

L13-16(4)   An interrupt occurs causing the CPU to switch to task T2 since T2 has a higher priority than task T1.

L13-16(5)   The ISR is the event that task T2 was waiting for and therefore T2 resumes execution.

L13-16(6)   Task T2 acquires mutex M2 and is able to access resource R2.

L13-16(7)   Task T2 tries to acquire mutex M1, but µC/OS-III knows that mutex M1 is owned by another task.

L13-16(8)   µC/OS-III switches back to task T1 because Task T2 can no longer continue. It needs mutex M1 to access resource R1.

L13-16(9)   Task T1 now tries to access mutex M2 but, unfortunately, mutex M2 is owned by task T2. At this point, the two tasks are deadlocked, neither one can continue because each owns a resource that the other one wants.

Techniques used to avoid deadlocks are for tasks to:

▪ Acquire all resources before proceeding

▪ Always acquire resources in the same order

▪ Use timeouts on pend calls

μC/OS-III allows the calling task to specify a timeout when acquiring a mutex. This feature allows a deadlock to be broken, but the same deadlock may then recur later, or many times later. If the mutex is not available within a certain period of time, the task requesting the resource resumes execution. μC/OS-III returns an error code indicating that a timeout occurred. A return error code prevents the task from thinking it has properly obtained the resource.

The pseudo-code avoids deadlocks by first acquiring all resources as shown in Listing 13-17.

```
void T1 (void *p_arg)
{
    while (DEF_ON) {
        Wait for event to occur;
        Acquire M1;
        Acquire M2;
        Access  R1;
        Access  R2;
    }
}


void  T2 (void *p_arg)
{
    while (DEF_ON) {
        Wait for event to occur;
        Acquire M1;
        Acquire M2;
        Access  R1;
        Access  R2;
    }
}
```

Listing 13-17 **Deadlock avoidance – acquire all first and in the same order**

The pseudo-code to acquire all of the mutexes in the same order is shown in Listing 13-18. This is similar to the previous example, except that it is not necessary to acquire all the mutexes first, only to make sure that the mutexes are acquired in the same order for both tasks.

```
void T1 (void *p_arg){
    while (DEF_ON) {
        Wait for event to occur;
        Acquire M1;
        Access  R1;
        Acquire M2;
        Access  R2;
    }
}


void  T2 (void *p_arg)
{
    while (DEF_ON) {
        Wait for event to occur;
        Acquire M1;
        Access  R1;
        Acquire M2;
        Access  R2;
    }
}
```

Listing 13-18 **Deadlock avoidance – acquire in the same order**

13-7 SUMMARY

The mutual exclusion mechanism used depends on how fast code will access the shared resource, as shown in Table 13-4.

Resource Sharing Method	When should you use?
Disable/Enable Interrupts	When access to shared resource is very quick (reading from or writing to just a few variables) and the access is actually faster than µC/OS-III's interrupt disable time. It is highly recommended to not use this method as it impacts interrupt latency.
Locking/Unlocking the Scheduler	When access time to the shared resource is longer than µC/OS-III's interrupt disable time, but shorter than µC/OS-III's scheduler lock time. Locking the scheduler has the same effect as making the task that locks the scheduler the highest priority task. It is recommended to not use this method since it defeats the purpose of using µC/OS-III. However, it's a better method than disabling interrupts as it does not impact interrupt latency.
Semaphores	When all tasks that need to access a shared resource do not have deadlines. This is because semaphores can cause unbounded priority inversions. However, semaphore services are slightly faster (in execution time) than mutual exclusion semaphores.
Mutual Exclusion Semaphores	This is the preferred method for accessing shared resources, especially if the tasks that need to access a shared resource have deadlines. Remember that mutual exclusion semaphores have a built-in priority inheritance mechanism, which avoids unbounded priority inversions. However, mutual exclusion semaphore services are slightly slower (in execution time) than semaphores, because the priority of the owner may need to be changed, which requires CPU processing.

Table 13-4 **Resource sharing summary**

13

Synchronization

This chapter focuses on how tasks can synchronize their activities with Interrupt Service Routines (ISRs), or other tasks.

When an ISR executes, it can signal a task telling the task that an event of interest has occurred. After signaling the task, the ISR exits and, depending on the signaled task priority, the scheduler is run. The signaled task may then service the interrupting device, or otherwise react to the event. Servicing interrupting devices from task level is preferred whenever possible, since it reduces the amount of time that interrupts are disabled and the code is easier to debug.

There are two basic mechanisms for synchronizations in µC/OS-III: semaphores and event flags.

14-1 SEMAPHORES

As defined in Chapter 13, "Resource Management" on page 229, a semaphore is a protocol mechanism offered by most multitasking kernels. Semaphores were originally used to control access to shared resources. However, better mechanisms exist to protect access to shared resources, as described in Chapter 12. Semaphores are best used to synchronize an ISR to a task, or synchronize a task with another task as shown in Figure 14-1.

Note that the semaphore is drawn as a flag to indicate that it is used to signal the occurrence of an event. The initial value for the semaphore is typically zero (0), indicating the event has not yet occurred.

The value "N" next to the flag indicates that the semaphore can accumulate *events* or *credits*. An ISR (or a task) can post (or signal) multiple times to a semaphore and the semaphore will remember how many times it was posted. It is possible to initialize the semaphore with a value other than zero, indicating that the semaphore initially contains that number of events.

Also, the small hourglass close to the receiving task indicates that the task has an option to specify a timeout. This timeout indicates that the task is willing to wait for the semaphore to be signaled (or posted to) within a certain amount of time. If the semaphore is not signaled within that time, µC/OS-III resumes the task and returns an error code indicating that the task was made ready-to-run because of a timeout and not the semaphore was signaled.

Figure 14-1 **µC/OS-III Semaphore Services**

There are a number of operations to perform on semaphores as summarized in Table 14-1 and Figure 14-1. However, in this chapter, we will only discuss the three functions used most often: OSSemCreate(), OSSemPend(), and OSSemPost(). The other functions are described in Appendix A, "µC/OS-III API Reference" on page 453. Also note that every semaphore function is callable from a task, but only OSSemPost() can be called by an ISR.

Function Name	Operation
OSSemCreate()	Create a semaphore.
OSSemDel()	Delete a semaphore.
OSSemPend()	Wait on a semaphore.
OSSemPendAbort()	Abort the wait on a semaphore.
OSSemPost()	Signal a semaphore.
OSSemSet()	Force the semaphore count to a desired value.

Table 14-1 **Semaphore API summary**

When used for synchronization, a semaphore keeps track of how many times it was signaled using a counter. The counter can take values between 0 and 255, 65,535, or 4,294,967,295, depending on whether the semaphore mechanism is implemented using 8, 16, or 32 bits, respectively. For µC/OS-III, the maximum value of a semaphore is determined by the data type **OS_SEM_CTR** (see **os_type.h**), which is changeable, as needed (assuming access to µC/OS-III's source code). Along with the semaphore's value, µC/OS-III keeps track of tasks waiting for the semaphore to be signaled.

14-1-1 UNILATERAL RENDEZ-VOUS

Figure 14-2 shows that a task can be synchronized with an ISR (or another task) by using a semaphore. In this case, no data is exchanged, however there is an indication that the ISR or the task (on the left) has occurred. Using a semaphore for this type of synchronization is called a unilateral rendez-vous.

Figure 14-2 **Unilateral Rendezvous**

A unilateral rendez-vous is used when a task initiates an I/O operation and waits (i.e., call OSSemPend()) for the semaphore to be signaled (posted). When the I/O operation is complete, an ISR (or another task) signals the semaphore (i.e., calls OSSemPost()), and the task is resumed. This process is also shown on the timeline of Figure 14-3 and described below. The code for the ISR and task is shown in Listing 14-1.

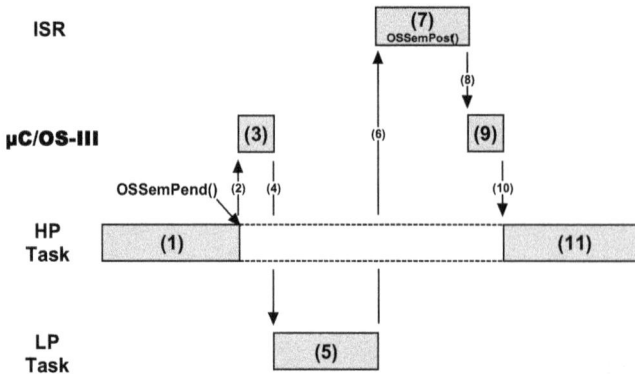

Figure 14-3 **Unilateral Rendezvous, Timing Diagram**

F14-3(1)   A high priority task is executing. The task needs to synchronize with an ISR (i.e., wait for the ISR to occur) and call OSSemPend( ).

F14-3(2)
F14-3(3)
F14-3(4)   Since the ISR has not occurred, the task will be placed in the waiting list for the semaphore until the event occurs The scheduler in µC/OS-III will then select the next most important task and context switch to that task.

F14-3(5)   The low-priority task executes.

F14-3(6)   The event that the original task was waiting for occurs. The lower-priority task is immediately preempted (assuming interrupts are enabled), and the CPU vectors to the interrupt handler for the event.

F14-3(7)
F14-3(8)   The ISR handles the interrupting device and then calls OSSemPost( ) to signal the semaphore. When the ISR completes, µC/OS-III is called (i.e. OSIntExit( )).

F14-3(9)
F14-3(10)   µC/OS-III notices that a higher-priority task is waiting for this event to occur and context switches back to the original task.

F14-3(11)   The original task resumes execution immediately after the call to OSSemPend( ).

14

```
OS_SEM  MySem;


void MyISR (void)
{
    OS_ERR  err;


    /* Clear the interrupting device */
    OSSemPost(&MySem,                   (7)
            OS_OPT_POST_1,
            &err);
    /* Check "err" */
}


void MyTask (void *p_arg)
{
    OS_ERR  err;
    CPU_TS  ts;
    :
    :
    while (DEF_ON) {
        OSSemPend(&MySem,               (1)
                10,
                OS_OPT_PEND_BLOCKING,
                &ts,
                &err);
        /* Check "err" */              (11)
        :
        :
    }
}
```

Listing 14-1 **Pending (or waiting) on a Semaphore**

A few interesting things are worth noting about this process. First, the task does not need to know about the details of what happens behind the scenes. As far as the task is concerned, it called a function (**OSSemPend( )**) that will return when the event it is waiting for occurs. Second, µC/OS-III maximizes the use of the CPU by selecting the next most important task, which executes until the ISR occurs. In fact, the ISR may not occur for many milliseconds and, during that time, the CPU will work on other tasks. As far as the task that is waiting for the semaphore is concerned, it does not consume CPU time while it is waiting. Finally, the task waiting for the semaphore will execute immediately after the event occurs (assuming it is the most important task that needs to run).

14-1-2 CREDIT TRACKING

As previously mentioned, a semaphore "remembers" how many times it was signaled (or posted to). In other words, if the ISR occurs multiple times before the task waiting for the event becomes the highest-priority task, the semaphore will keep count of the number of times it was signaled. When the task becomes the highest priority ready-to-run task, it will execute without blocking as many times as there were ISRs signaled. This is called *Credit Tracking* and is illustrated in Figure 14-4 and described below.

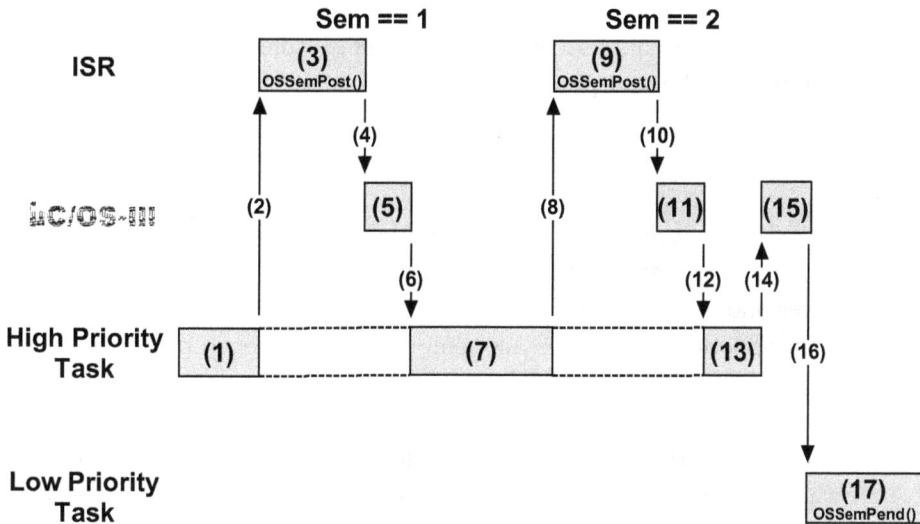

Figure 14-4 **Semaphore Credit Tracking**

F14-4(1)   A high-priority task is executing.

F14-4(2)

F14-4(3)   An event meant for a lower-priority task occurs which preempts the task (assuming interrupts are enabled). The ISR executes and posts the semaphore. At this point the semaphore count is 1.

F14-4(4)

F14-4(5)

F14-4(6)   μC/OS-III is called at the end of the ISR to see if the ISR caused a higher-priority task to be ready-to-run. Since the ISR was an event that a lower-priority task was waiting for, μC/OS-III will resume execution of the higher-priority task at the exact point where it was interrupted.

F14-4(7)   The high-priority task is resumed and continues execution.

F14-4(8)

F14-4(9)   The interrupt occurs a second time. The ISR executes and posts the semaphore. At this point the semaphore count is 2.

F14-4(10)

F14-4(11)

F14-4(12)   μC/OS-III is called at the end of the ISR to see if the ISR caused a higher-priority task to be ready-to-run. Since the ISR was an event that a lower-priority task was waiting for, μC/OS-III resumes execution of the higher-priority task at the exact point where it was interrupted.

F14-4(13)

F14-4(14)   The high-priority task resumes execution and actually terminates the work it was doing. This task will then call one of the μC/OS-III services to wait for "its" event to occur.

F14-4(15)

F14-4(16)   μC/OS-III will then select the next most important task, which happens to be the task waiting for the event and will context switch to that task.

F14-4(17)   The new task executes and will know that the ISR occurred twice since the semaphore count is two. The task will handle this accordingly.

14-1-3 MULTIPLE TASKS WAITING ON A SEMAPHORE

It is possible for more than one task to wait on the same semaphore, each with its own timeout as illustrated in Figure 14-5.

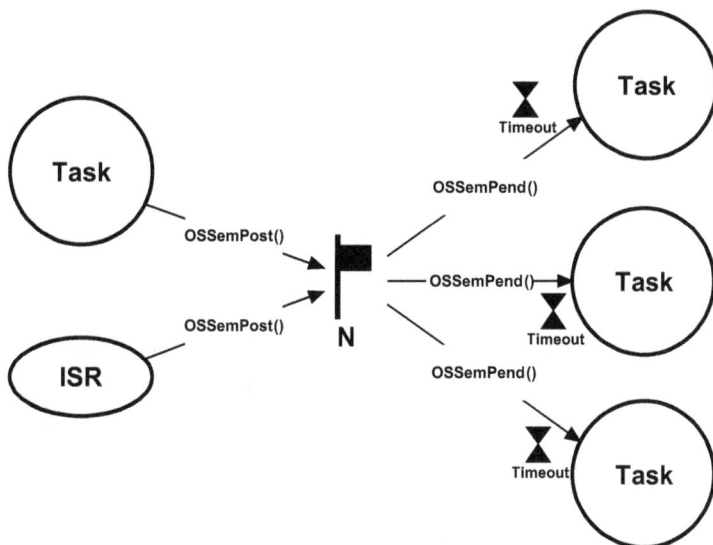

Figure 14-5 **Multiple Tasks waiting on a Semaphore**

When the semaphore is signaled (whether by an ISR or task), µC/OS-III makes the highest-priority task waiting on the semaphore ready-to-run. However, it is also possible to specify that all tasks waiting on the semaphore be made ready-to-run. This is called *broadcasting* and is accomplished by specifying OS_OPT_POST_ALL as an option when calling OSSemPost(). If any of the waiting tasks has a higher priority than the previously running task, µC/OS-III will execute the highest-priority task made ready by OSSemPost().

Broadcasting is a common technique used to synchronize multiple tasks and have them start executing at the same time. However, some of the tasks that we want to synchronize might not be waiting for the semaphore. It is fairly easy to resolve this problem by combining semaphores and event flags. This will be described after examining event flags.

14-1-4 SEMAPHORE INTERNALS (FOR SYNCHRONIZATION)

Note that some of the material presented in this section is also contained in Chapter 13, "Resource Management" on page 229, as semaphores were also discussed in that chapter. However, the material presented here will be applicable to semaphores used for synchronization and thus will differ somewhat.

A counting semaphore allows values between 0 and 255, 65,535, or 4,294,967,295, depending on whether the semaphore mechanism is implemented using 8, 16, or 32 bits, respectively. For µC/OS-III, the maximum value of a semaphore is determined by the data type **OS_SEM_CTR** (see **os_type.h**), which can be changed as needed. Along with the semaphore's value, µC/OS-III keeps track of tasks waiting for the semaphore's availability.

The application programmer can create an unlimited number of semaphores (limited only by available RAM). Semaphore services in µC/OS-III start with the **OSSem???()** prefix, and services available to the application programmer are described in Appendix A, "µC/OS-III API Reference" on page 453. Semaphore services are enabled at compile time by setting the configuration constant **OS_CFG_SEM_EN** to 1 in **os_cfg.h**.

Semaphores must be created before they can be used by the application. Listing 14-3 shows how to create a semaphore.

As previously mentioned, a semaphore is a kernel object as defined by the **OS_SEM** data type, which is derived from the structure **os_sem** (see **os.h**) as shown in Listing 14-2. The services provided by µC/OS-III to manage semaphores are implemented in the file **os_sem.c**.

```
typedef  struct  os_sem  OS_SEM;              (1)


struct  os_sem {
    OS_OBJ_TYPE        Type;                  (2)
    CPU_CHAR          *NamePtr;               (3)
    OS_PEND_LIST       PendList;              (4)
    OS_SEM_CTR         Ctr;                   (5)
    CPU_TS             TS;                    (6)
};
```

Listing 14-2 **OS_SEM data type**

L14-2(1)   In µC/OS-III, all structures are given a data type. In fact, all data types start with "OS_" and are all uppercase. When a semaphore is declared, simply use OS_SEM as the data type of the variable used to declare the semaphore.

L14-2(2)   The structure starts with a "**Type**" field, which allows it to be recognized by µC/OS-III as a semaphore. In other words, other kernel objects will also have a "**Type**" as the first member of the structure. If a function is passed a kernel object, µC/OS-III will confirm that it is being passed the proper data type (assuming OS_CFG_OBJ_TYPE_CHK_EN is set to 1 in os_cfg.h). For example, if passing a message queue (OS_Q) to a semaphore service (for example OSSemPend()), µC/OS-III will recognize that an invalid object was passed, and return an error code accordingly.

L14-2(3)   Each kernel object can be given a name to make them easier to be recognized by debuggers or µC/Probe. This member is simply a pointer to an ASCII string, which is assumed to be **NUL** terminated.

L14-2(4)   Since it is possible for multiple tasks to be waiting (or pending) on a semaphore, the semaphore object contains a pend list as described in Chapter 10, "Pend Lists (or Wait Lists)" on page 195.

L14-2(5)   A semaphore contains a counter. As explained above, the counter can be implemented as either an 8-, 16- or 32-bit value, depending on how the data type OS_SEM_CTR is declared in os_type.h. µC/OS-III keeps track of how many times the semaphore is signaled with this counter and this field is typically initialized to zero by OSSemCreate().

L14-2(6)   A semaphore contains a time stamp, which is used to indicate the last time the semaphore was signaled (or posted to). µC/OS-III assumes the presence of a free-running counter that allows the application to make time measurements. When the semaphore is signaled, the free-running counter is read and the value is placed in this field, which is returned when OSSemPend() is called. This value allows the application to determine either when the signal was performed, or how long it took for the task to get control of the CPU from the signal. In the latter case, you should call OS_TS_GET() to determine the current timestamp and compute the difference.

Even for users who understand the internals of the **OS_SEM** data type, the application code should never access any of the fields in this data structure directly. Instead, you should always use the APIs provided with µC/OS-III.

Semaphores must be created before they can be used by an application. Listing 14-3 shows how to create a semaphore.

```
OS_SEM  MySem;                      (1)


void  MyCode (void)
{
    OS_ERR  err;
    :
    OSSemCreate(&MySem,             (2)
                "My Semaphore",     (3)
                (OS_SEM_CTR)0,      (4)
                &err);              (5)
    /* Check "err" */
    :
}
```

Listing 14-3 **Creating a Semaphore**

L14-3(1)   The application must declare a variable of type **OS_SEM**. This variable will be referenced by other semaphore services.

L14-3(2)   You create a semaphore by calling **OSSemCreate()** and pass the address to the semaphore allocated in L14-3(1).

L14-3(3)   You can assign an ASCII name to the semaphore, which can be used by debuggers or µC/Probe to easily identify this semaphore.

L14-3(4)   You need to initialize the semaphore to zero (0) when using a semaphore as a signaling mechanism.

L14-3(5)   **OSSemCreate()** returns an error code based on the outcome of the call. If all arguments are valid, **err** will contain **OS_ERR_NONE**.

OSSemCreate() performs a check on the arguments passed to this function (assuming OS_CFG_ARG_CHK_EN is set to 1 in os_cfg.h) and only initializes the contents of the variable of type OS_SEM used for signaling.

A task waits for a signal from an ISR or another task by calling OSSemPend() as shown in Listing 14-4 (see Appendix A, "μC/OS-III API Reference" on page 453 for details regarding the arguments).

```
void  MyTask (void *p_arg)
{
    OS_ERR  err;
    CPU_TS  ts;
    :
    while (DEF_ON) {
        OSSemPend(&MySem,                     (1)
                  0,
                  OS_OPT_PEND_BLOCKING,
                  &ts,
                  &err);
        /* Check "err" */                     (2)
        :
    }
}
```

Listing 14-4 **Pending (or waiting) on a Semaphore**

L14-4(1)   When called, OSSemPend() starts by checking the arguments passed to this function to make sure they have valid values (assuming OS_CFG_OBJ_TYPE_CHK_EN is set to 1 in os_cfg.h).

If the semaphore counter (.Ctr of OS_SEM) is greater than zero, the counter is decremented and OSSemPend() returns, which indicates that the signal occurred. This is the outcome that the caller expects.

If the semaphore counter is zero, this indicates that the signal has not occurred and the calling task might need to wait for the semaphore to be released. If you specify OS_OPT_PEND_NON_BLOCKING as the option (the task is not to block), OSSemPend() returns immediately to the caller and the returned error code will indicate that the signal did not occur.

If you specify OS_OPT_PEND_BLOCKING as the option, the calling task will be inserted in the list of tasks waiting for the semaphore to be signaled. The task is inserted in the list by priority order with the highest priority task waiting on the semaphore at the beginning of the list as shown in Figure 14-6.

If you further specify a non-zero timeout, the task will also be inserted in the tick list. A zero value for a timeout indicates that the calling task is willing to wait forever for the semaphore to be signaled.

The scheduler is then called since the current task is not able to run (it is waiting for the semaphore to be signaled). The scheduler will then run the next highest-priority task that is ready-to-run.

When the semaphore is signaled and the task that called OSSemPend() is again the highest-priority task, a task status is examined to determine the reason why OSSemPend() is returning to its caller. The possibilities are:

1) The semaphore was signaled which is the desired outcome

2) The pend was aborted by another task

3) The semaphore was not signaled within the specified timeout

4) The semaphore was deleted

When OSSemPend() returns, the caller is notified of the above outcome through an appropriate error code.

L14-4(2)   If OSSemPend() returns with err set to OS_ERR_NONE, you can assume that the semaphore was signaled and the task can proceed with servicing the ISR or task that caused the signal. If err contains anything else, OSSemPend() either timed out (if the timeout argument was non-zero), the pend was aborted by another task, or the semaphore was deleted by another task. It is always important to examine returned error code and not assume everything went as expected.

To signal a task (either from an ISR or a task), simply call OSSemPost() as shown in Listing 14-5.

```
OS_SEM  MySem;


void MyISR (void)
{
    OS_ERR  err;
    :
    OSSemPost(&MySem,                (1)
             OS_OPT_POST_1,          (2)
             &err);                  (3)
    /* Check "err" */
    :
    :

}
```

Listing 14-5 **Posting (or signaling) a Semaphore**

L14-5(1) Your task signals (or posts to) the semaphore by calling OSSemPost(). You specify the semaphore to post by passing its address. The semaphore must have been previously created.

L14-5(2) The next argument specifies how the task wants to post. There are a number of options to choose from.

When you specify OS_OPT_POST_1, you are indicating that you want to post to only one task (in case there are multiple tasks waiting on the semaphore). The task that will be made ready-to-run will be the highest-priority task waiting on the semaphore. If there are multiple tasks at the same priority, only one of them will be made ready-to-run. As shown in Figure 14-6, tasks waiting are in priority order (HPT means High Priority Task and LPT means Low Priority Task). So, it is a fast operation to extract the HPT from the list.

If specifying OS_OPT_POST_ALL, all tasks waiting on the semaphore will be posted and made ready-to-run.

The calling task can "add" the option OS_OPT_POST_NO_SCHED to either of the two previous options to indicate that the scheduler is not to be called at the end of OSSemPost(), possibly because additional postings will be performed, and rescheduling should only take place when finished. This means that the signal is performed, but the scheduler is not called even if a higher-priority task

285

was waiting for the semaphore to be signaled. This allows the calling task to perform other post functions (if needed) and make all the posts take effect simultaneously. Note that OS_OPT_POST_NO_SCHED is "additive," meaning that it can be used with either of the previous options. You can thus specify:

```
OS_OPT_POST_1
OS_OPT_POST_ALL
OS_OPT_POST_1   + OS_OPT_POST_NO_SCHED
OS_OPT_POST_ALL + OS_OPT_POST_NO_SCHED
```

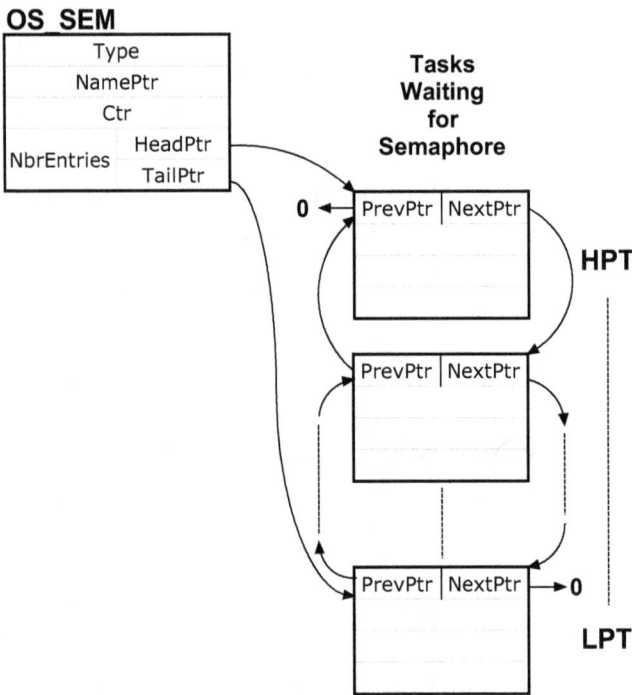

Figure 14-6 **Tasks waiting for semaphore**

L14-5(3)   OSSemPost() returns an error code based on the outcome of the call. If the call was successful, **err** will contain OS_ERR_NONE. If not, the error code will indicate the reason for the error (see Appendix A, "µC/OS-III API Reference" on page 453 for a list of possible error codes for OSSemPost().

14-2 TASK SEMAPHORE

Signaling a task using a semaphore is a very popular method of synchronization and, in µC/OS-III, each task has its own built-in semaphore. This feature not only simplifies code, but is also more efficient than using a separate semaphore object. The semaphore, which is built into each task, is shown in Figure 14-7.

Task semaphore services in µC/OS-III start with the **OSTaskSem???()** prefix, and the services available to the application programmer are described in Appendix A, "µC/OS-III API Reference" on page 453. Task semaphores are built into µC/OS-III and cannot be disabled at compile time as can other services. The code for task semaphores is found in **os_task.c**.

You can use this feature if your code knows which task to signal when the event occurs. For example, if you receive an interrupt from an Ethernet controller, you can signal the task responsible for processing the received packet as it is preferable to perform this processing using a task instead of the ISR.

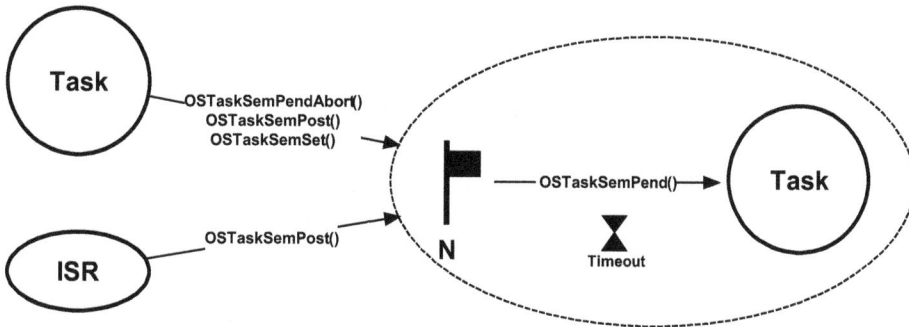

Figure 14-7 **Semaphore built-into a Task**

There is a variety of operations to perform on task semaphores, summarized in Table 14-2.

Function Name	Operation
OSTaskSemPend()	Wait on a task semaphore.
OSTaskSemPendAbort()	Abort the wait on a task semaphore.
OSTaskSemPost()	Signal a task.
OSTaskSemSet()	Force the semaphore count to a desired value.

Table 14-2 **Task Semaphore API summary**

287

14-2-1 PENDING (i.e., WAITING) ON A TASK SEMAPHORE

When a task is created, it automatically creates an internal semaphore with an initial value of zero (0). Waiting on a task semaphore is quite simple, as shown in Listing 14-6.

```
void MyTask (void *p_arg)
{
    OS_ERR  err;
    CPU_TS  ts;
    :
    while (DEF_ON) {
        OSTaskSemPend(10,                     (1)
                      OS_OPT_PEND_BLOCKING,   (2)
                      &ts,                    (3)
                      &err);                  (4)
        /* Check "err" */
        :
        :
    }
}
```

Listing 14-6 **Pending (or waiting) on Task's internal semaphore**

L14-6(1)   A task pends (or waits) on the task semaphore by calling OSTaskSemPend(). There is no need to specify which task, as the current task is assumed. The first argument is a timeout specified in number of clock ticks. The actual timeout obviously depends on the tick rate. If the tick rate (see **os_cfg_app.h**) is set to 1000, a timeout of 10 ticks represents 10 milliseconds. Specifying a timeout of zero (0) means that the task will wait forever for the task semaphore.

L14-6(2)   The second argument specifies how to pend. There are two options: **OS_OPT_PEND_BLOCKING** and **OS_OPT_PEND_NON_BLOCKING**. The blocking option means that, if the task semaphore has not been signaled (or posted to), the task will wait until the semaphore is signaled, the pend is aborted by another task or, until the timeout expires.

L14-6(3)   When the semaphore is signaled, μC/OS-III reads a "timestamp" and places it in the receiving task's **OS_TCB**. When **OSTaskSemPend()** returns, the value of the timestamp is placed in the local variable "**ts**". This feature captures "when" the signal actually happened. You can **call OS_TS_GET()** to read the current timestamp and compute the difference. This establishes how long it took for the task to receive the signal from the posting task or ISR.

L14-6(4)   OSTaskSemPend() returns an error code based on the outcome of the call. If the call was successful, **err** will contain OS_ERR_NONE. If not, the error code will indicate the reason of the error (see Appendix A, "μC/OS-III API Reference" on page 453 for a list of possible error code for OSTaskSemPend().

14-2-2 POSTING (i.e., SIGNALING) A TASK SEMAPHORE

An ISR or a task signals a task by calling OSTaskSemPost(), as shown in Listing 14-7.

```
OS_TCB  MyTaskTCB;


void MyISR (void *p_arg)
{
    OS_ERR  err;
    :
    OSTaskSemPost(&MyTaskTCB,              (1)
                  OS_OPT_POST_NONE,        (2)
                  &err);                   (3)
    /* Check "err" */
    :
    :
}
```

Listing 14-7 **Posting (or signaling) a Semaphore**

L14-7(1)   A task posts (or signals) the task by calling OSTaskSemPost(). It is necessary to pass the address of the desired task's OS_TCB and of course, the task must exist.

L14-7(2)   The next argument specifies how the user wants to post. There are only two choices.

Specify OS_OPT_POST_NONE, which indicates the use of the default option of calling the scheduler after posting the semaphore.

Or, specify OS_OPT_POST_NO_SCHED to indicate that the scheduler is not to be called at the end of OSTaskSemPost(), possibly because there will be additional postings, and rescheduling would take place when finished (the last post would not specify this option).

289

L14-7(3)   OSTaskSemPost() returns an error code based on the outcome of the call. If
the call was successful, **err** will contain OS_ERR_NONE. If not, the error code
will indicate the reason of the error (see Appendix A, "µC/OS-III API
Reference" on page 453 for a list of possible error codes for OSTaskSemPost().

14-2-3 BILATERAL RENDEZ-VOUS

Two tasks can synchronize their activities by using two task semaphores, as shown in
Figure 14-8, and is called a *bilateral rendez-vous*. A bilateral rendez-vous is similar to a
unilateral rendez-vous, except that both tasks must synchronize with one another before
proceeding. A bilateral rendez-vous cannot be performed between a task and an ISR
because an ISR cannot wait on a semaphore.

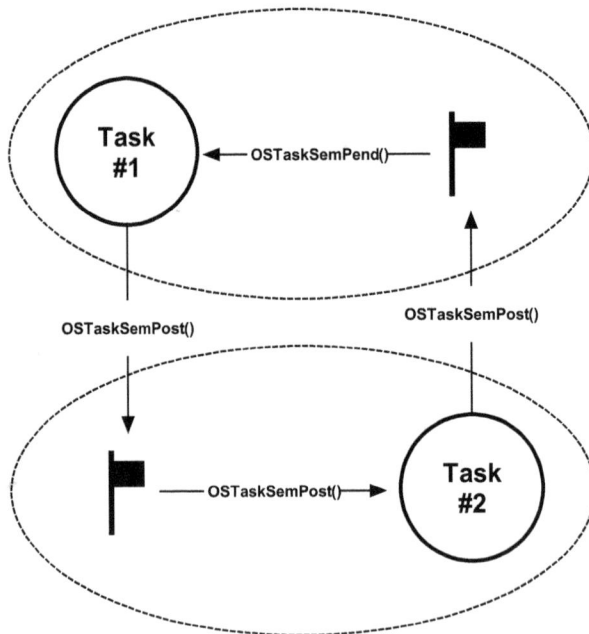

Figure 14-8 **Bilateral Rendezvous**

The code for a bilateral rendez-vous is shown in Listing 14-8. Of course, a bilateral
rendez-vous can use two separate semaphores, but the built-in task semaphore makes
setting up this type of synchronization quite straightforward.

```
OS_TCB  MyTask1_TCB;
OS_TCB  MyTask2_TCB;


void Task1 (void *p_arg)
{
    OS_ERR  err;
    CPU_TS  ts;

    while (DEF_ON) {
        :
        OSTaskSemPost(&MyTask2_TCB,              (1)
                      OS_OPT_POST_NONE,
                      &err);
        /* Check 'err" */
        OSTaskSemPend(0,                         (2)
                      OS_OPT_PEND_BLOCKING,
                      &ts,
                      &err);
        /* Check 'err" */
        :
    }
}


void Task2 (void *p_arg)
{
    OS_ERR  err;
    CPU_TS  ts;

    while (DEF_ON) {
        :
        OSTaskSemPost(&MyTask1_TCB,              (3)
                      OS_OPT_POST_NONE,
                      &err);
        /* Check 'err" */
        OSTaskSemPend(0,                         (4)
                      OS_OPT_PEND_BLOCKING,
                      &ts,
                      &err);
        /* Check 'err" */
        :
    }
}
```

Listing 14-8 **Tasks synchronizing their activities**

L14-8(1)   Task #1 is executing and signals Task #2's semaphore.

L14-8(2)   Task #1 pends on its internal semaphore to synchronize with Task #2. Because Task #2 has not executed yet, Task #1 is blocked waiting on its semaphore to be signaled. μC/OS-III context switches to Task #2.

L14-8(3)   Task #2 executes, and signals Task #1's semaphore.

L14-8(4)   Since it has already been signaled, Task #2 is now synchronized to Task #1. If Task #1 is higher in priority than Task #2, μC/OS-III will switch back to Task #1. If not, Task #2 continues execution.

14-3 EVENT FLAGS

Event flags are used when a task needs to synchronize with the occurrence of multiple events. The task can be synchronized when any of the events have occurred, which is called disjunctive synchronization (logical OR). A task can also be synchronized when all events have occurred, which is called conjunctive synchronization (logical AND). Disjunctive and conjunctive synchronization are shown in Figure 14-9.

The application programmer can create an unlimited number of event flag groups (limited only by available RAM). Event flag services in μC/OS-III start with the **OSFlag???()** prefix. The services available to the application programmer are described in Appendix A, "μC/OS-III API Reference" on page 453.

The code for event flag services is found in the file **os_flag.c**, and is enabled at compile time by setting the configuration constant **OS_CFG_FLAG_EN** to 1 in **os_cfg.h**.

Figure 14-9 **Event Flags**

F14-9(1) A µC/OS-III "event flag group" is a kernel object of type **OS_FLAG_GRP** (see **os.h**), and consists of a series of bits (8-, 16- or 32-bits, based on the data type **OS_FLAGS** defined in **os_type.h**). The event flag group also contains a list of tasks waiting for some (or all) of the bits to be set (1) or clear (0). An event flag group must be created before it can be used by tasks and ISRs. You need to create event flags prior to starting µC/OS-III, or by a startup task in the application code.

F14-9(2) Tasks or ISRs can post to event flags. In addition, only tasks can create, delete, and stop other task from pending on event flag groups.

F14-9(3) A task can wait (i.e., pend) on any number of bits in an event flag group (i.e., a subset of all the bits). As with all µC/OS-III pend calls, the calling task can specify a timeout value such that if the desired bits are not posted within a specified amount of time (in ticks), the pending task is resumed and informed about the timeout.

F14-9(4)   The task can specify whether it wants to wait for "any" subset of bits (OR) to be set (or clear), or wait for "all" bits in a subset of bit (AND) to be set (or clear).

There are a number of operations to perform on event flags, as summarized in Table 14-3.

Function Name	Operation
OSFlagCreate()	Create an event flag group
OSFlagDel()	Delete an event flag group
OSFlagPend()	Pend (i.e., wait) on an event flag group
OSFlagPendAbort()	Abort waiting on an event flag group
OSFlagPendGetFlagsRdy()	Get flags that caused task to become ready
OSFlagPost()	Post flag(s) to an event flag group

Table 14-3 **Event Flags API summary**

14-3-1 USING EVENT FLAGS

When a task or an ISR posts to an event flag group, all tasks that have their wait conditions satisfied will be resumed.

It's up to the application to determine what each bit in an event flag group means and it is possible to use as many event flag groups as needed. In an event flag group you can, for example, define that bit #0 indicates that a temperature sensor is too low, bit #1 may indicate a low battery voltage, bit #2 could indicate that a switch was pressed, etc. The code (tasks or ISRs) that detects these conditions would set the appropriate event flag by calling OSFlagPost() and the task(s) that would respond to those conditions would call OSFlagPend().

Listing 14-9 shows how to use event flags.

```
#define     TEMP_LOW    (OS_FLAGS)0x0001                         (1)
#define     BATT_LOW    (OS_FLAGS)0x0002
#define     SW_PRESSED  (OS_FLAGS)0x0004


OS_FLAG_GRP  MyEventFlagGrp;                                     (2)

void main (void)
{
    OS_ERR  err;

    OSInit(&err);
    :
    OSFlagCreate(&MyEventFlagGrp,                                (3)
                "My Event Flag Group",
                (OS_FLAGS)0,
                &err);
    /* Check 'err" */
    :
    OSStart(&err);
}


void  MyTask (void *p_arg)                                       (4)
{
    OS_ERR  err;
    CPU_TS  ts;

    while (DEF_ON) {
        OSFlagPend(&MyEventFlagGrp,                              (5)
                TEMP_LOW + BATT_LOW,
                (OS_TICK )0,
                (OS_OPT)OS_OPT_PEND_FLAG_SET_ANY,
                &ts,
                &err);
        /* Check 'err" */
        :
    }
}
```

```
void  MyISR (void)                                              (6)
{
    OS_ERR  err;
    :
    OSFlagPost(&MyEventFlagGrp,                                  (7)
               BAT_LOW,
               (OS_OPT)OS_OPT_POST_FLAG_SET,
               &err);
    /* Check 'err" */
    :
}
```

Listing 14-9 **Using Event Flags**

L14-9(1)   You need to define some bits in the event flag group.

L14-9(2)   You have to declare an object of type **OS_FLAG_GRP**. This object will be
            referenced in all subsequent µC/OS-III calls that apply to this event flag group.
            For the sake of discussions, assume that event flags are declared to be 16-bits in
            os_type.h (i.e., of type **CPU_INT16U**).

L14-9(3)   Event flag groups must be "created" before they can be used. The best place to
            do this is in your startup code as it ensures that no tasks, or ISR, will be able to
            use the event flag group until µC/OS-III is started. In other words, the best
            place is to create the event flag group is in **main()**. In the example, the event
            flag was given a name and all bits start in their cleared state (i.e., all zeros).

L14-9(4)   You can assume here that the application created "**MyTask()**" which will be
            pending on the event flag group.

L14-9(5)   To pend on an event flag group, you call **OSFlagPend()** and pass it the address
            of the desired event flag group.

            The second argument specifies which bits the task will be waiting to be set
            (assuming the task is triggered by set bits instead of cleared bits).

            You also need to specify how long to wait for these bits to be set. A timeout
            value of zero (0) indicates that the task will wait forever. A non-zero value
            indicates the number of ticks the task will wait until it is resumed if the desired
            bits are not set.

Specifying **OS_OPT_FLAG_SET_ANY** indicates that the task will wake up if either of the two bits specified is set.

A timestamp is read and saved when the event flag group is posted to. This timestamp can be used to determine the response time to the event.

OSFlagPend( ) performs a number of checks on the arguments passed (i.e., did you pass **NULL** pointers, invalid options, etc.), and returns an error code based on the outcome of the call (assuming **OS_CFG_ARG_CHK_EN** is set to 1 in **os_cfg.h**). If the call was successful "**err**" will be set to **OS_ERR_NONE**.

L14-9(6)   An ISR (it can also be a task) is setup to detect when the battery voltage of the product goes low (assuming the product is battery operated). The ISR signals the task, letting the task perform whatever corrective action is needed.

L14-9(7)   The desired event flag group is specified in the post call as well as which flag the ISR is setting. The third option specifies that the error condition will be "flagged" as a set bit. Again, the function sets "err" based on the outcome of the call.

Event flags are generally used for two purposes: status and transient events. Typically you would use different event flag groups to handle each of these as shown in Listing 14-10.

Tasks or ISRs can report status information such as a temperature that has exceeded a certain value, that RPM is zero on an engine or motor, or there is fuel in the tank, and more. This status information cannot be "consumed" by the tasks waiting for these events, because the status is managed by other tasks or ISRs. Event flags associated with status information are monitored by other task by using non-blocking wait calls.

Tasks will report transient events such as a switch was pressed, an object was detected by a motion sensor, an explosion occurred, etc. The task that responds to these events will typically block waiting for any of those events to occur and "consume" the event.

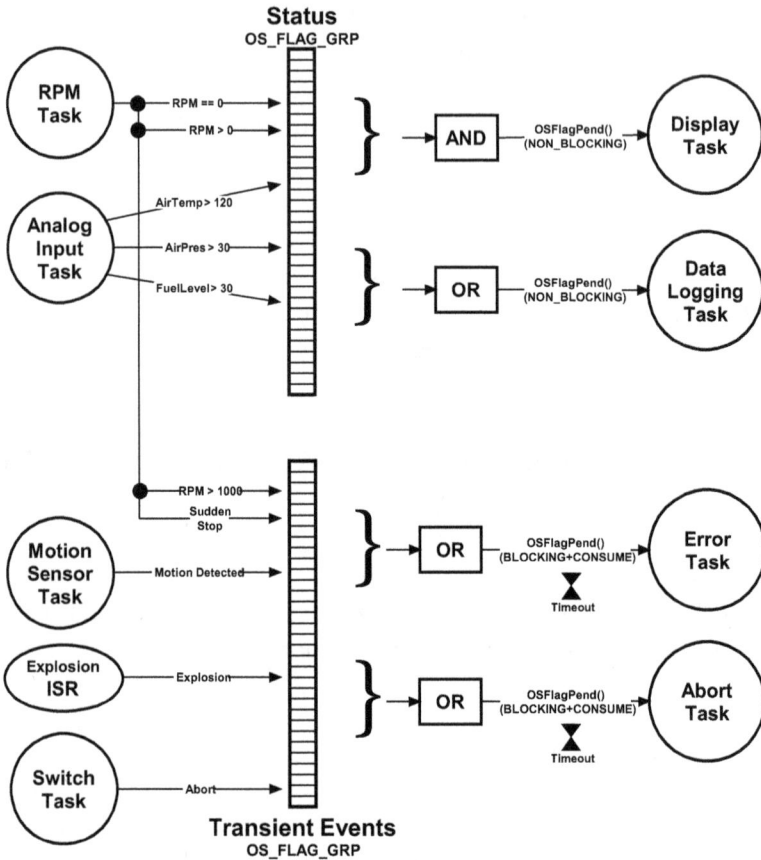

Figure 14-10 **Event Flags used for Status and Transient Events**

14-3-2 EVENT FLAGS INTERNALS

The application programmer can create an unlimited number of event flag groups (limited only by available RAM). Event flag services in µC/OS-III start with **OSFlag** and the services available to the application programmer are described in Appendix A, "µC/OS-III API Reference" on page 453. Event flag services are enabled at compile time by setting the configuration constant **OS_CFG_FLAG_EN** to 1 in **os_cfg.h**.

An event flag group is a kernel object as defined by the **OS_FLAG_GRP** data type, which is derived from the structure **os_flag_grp** (see **os.h**) as shown in Listing 14-10.

The services provided by µC/OS-III to manage event flags are implemented in the file **os_flag.c**.

298

```
typedef  struct  os_flag_grp  OS_FLAG_GRP;    (1)


struct  os_flag_grp {
    OS_OBJ_TYPE           Type;               (2)
    CPU_CHAR              *NamePtr;            (3)
    OS_PEND_LIST          PendList;            (4)
    OS_FLAGS              Flags;               (5)
    CPU_TS                TS;                  (6)
};
```

Listing 14-10 **OS_FLAG_GRP data type**

L14-10(1) In µC/OS-III, all structures are given a data type. In fact, all data types start with "**OS_**" and are uppercase. When an event flag group is declared, you simply use **OS_FLAG_GRP** as the data type of the variable used to declare the event flag group.

L14-10(2) The structure starts with a "**Type**" field, which allows it to be recognized by µC/OS-III as an event flag group. In other words, other kernel objects will also have a "**Type**" as the first member of the structure. If a function is passed a kernel object, µC/OS-III will be able to confirm that it is being passed the proper data type (assuming **OS_CFG_OBJ_TYPE_CHK_EN** is set to 1 in **os_cfg.h**). For example, if passing a message queue (**OS_Q**) to an event flag service (for example **OSFlagPend()**), µC/OS-III will be able to recognize that an invalid object was passed, and return an error code accordingly.

L14-10(3) Each kernel object can be given a name to make them easier to be recognized by debuggers or µC/Probe. This member is simply a pointer to an ASCII string, which is assumed to be **NUL** terminated.

L14-10(4) Because it is possible for multiple tasks to be waiting (or pending) on an event flag group, the event flag group object contains a pend list as described in Chapter 10, "Pend Lists (or Wait Lists)" on page 195.

L14-10(5) An event flag group contains a series of flags (i.e., bits), and this member contains the current state of these flags. The flags can be implemented using either an 8-, 16- or 32-bit value depending on how the data type **OS_FLAGS** is declared in **os_type.h**.

299

L14-10(6)   An event flag group contains a timestamp used to indicate the last time the
              event flag group was posted to. µC/OS-III assumes the presence of a
              free-running counter that allows users to make time measurements. When the
              event flag group is posted to, the free-running counter is read and the value is
              placed in this field, which is returned when **OSFlagPend( )** is called. This value
              allows an application to determine either when the post was performed, or
              how long it took for your code to obtain control of the CPU from the post. In
              the latter case, you can call **OS_TS_GET( )** to determine the current timestamp
              and compute the difference.

Even if the user understands the internals of the **OS_FLAG_GRP** data type, application code
should never access any of the fields in this data structure directly. Instead, you should
always use the APIs provided with µC/OS-III.

Event flag groups must be created before they can be used by an application as shown in
Listing 14-11.

```
OS_FLAG_GRP  MyEventFlagGrp;                    (1)


void  MyCode (void)
{
    OS_ERR  err;
    :
    OSFlagCreate(&MyEventFlagGrp,               (2)
                "My Event Flag Group",          (3)
                (OS_FLAGS)0,                     (4)
                &err);                           (5)
    /* Check 'err" */
    :

}
```

Listing 14-11 **Creating a Event Flag Group**

L14-11(1)   The application must declare a variable of type **OS_FLAG_GRP**. This variable will
              be referenced by other event flag services.

L14-11(2)   You create an event flag group by calling **OSFlagCreate()** and pass the
              address to the event flag group allocated in (1).

L14-11(3)   You can assign an ASCII name to the event flag group, which can be used by debuggers or μC/Probe to easily identify this event flag group. μC/OS-III stores a pointer to the name so there is no practical limit to its size, except that the ASCII string needs to be **NUL** terminated.

L14-11(4)   You initialize the flags inside the event flag group to zero (0) unless the task and ISRs signal events with bits cleared instead of bits set. If using cleared bits, you should initialize all the bits to ones (1).

L14-11(5)   **OSFlagCreate()** returns an error code based on the outcome of the call. If all the arguments are valid, **err** will contain **OS_ERR_NONE**.

A task waits for one or more event flag bits either from an ISR or another task by calling **OSFlagPend()** as shown in Listing 14-12 (see Appendix A, "μC/OS-III API Reference" on page 453 for details regarding the arguments).

14

```
OS_FLAG_GRP   MyEventFlagGrp;


void MyTask (void *p_arg)
{
    OS_ERR   err;
    CPU_TS   ts;
    OS_FLAGS which_flags;
    :
    while (DEF_ON) {
        :
        which_flags = OSFlagPend(&MyEventFlagGrp,     /* (1) Pointer to event flag group       */
                                 (OS_FLAGS)0x0F,      /*      Which bits to wait on            */
                                 10,                  /*      Maximum time to wait             */
                                 OS_OPT_PEND_BLOCKING +
                                 OS_OPT_PEND_FLAG_SET_ANY, /*   Option(s)                      */
                                 &ts,                 /*      Timestamp of when posted to */
                                 &err);               /*      Pointer to Error returned   */
        /* Check "err"                                    (2)                                   */
        :
        :

    }
}
```

Listing 14-12 **Pending (or waiting) on an Event Flag Group**

L14-12(1)   When called, **OSFlagPend( )** starts by checking the arguments passed to this function to ensure they have valid values (assuming **OS_CFG_ARG_CHK_EN** is set to **1** in **os_cfg.h**). If the bits the task is waiting for are set (or cleared depending on the option), **OSFlagPend( )** returns and indicate which flags satisfied the condition. This is the outcome that the caller expects.

If the event flag group does not contain the flags that the caller is looking for, the calling task might need to wait for the desired flags to be set (or cleared). If you specify **OS_OPT_PEND_NON_BLOCKING** as the option (the task is not to block), **OSFlagPend( )** returns immediately to the caller and the returned error code indicates that the bits have not been set (or cleared).

If you specify **OS_OPT_PEND_BLOCKING** as the option, the calling task will be inserted in the list of tasks waiting for the desired event flag bits. The task is not inserted in priority order but simply inserted at the beginning of the list. This is done because whenever bits are set (or cleared), it is necessary to examine all tasks in this list to see if their desired bits have been satisfied.

If you further specify a non-zero **timeout**, the task will also be inserted in the tick list. A zero value for a **timeout** indicates that the calling task is willing to wait forever for the desired bits.

The scheduler is then called since the current task is no longer able to run (it is waiting for the desired bits). The scheduler will run the next highest-priority task that is ready-to-run.

When the event flag group is posted to and the task that called **OSFlagPend( )** has its desired bits set or cleared, a task status is examined to determine the reason why **OSFlagPend( )** is returning to its caller. The possibilities are:

1) The desired bits were set (or cleared)

2) The pend was aborted by another task

3) The bits were not set (or cleared) within the specified timeout

4) The event flag group was deleted

When **OSFlagPend( )** returns, the caller is notified of the above outcome through an appropriate error code.

L14-12(2)   If **OSFlagPend( )** returns with **err** set to **OS_ERR_NONE**, you can assume that the desired bits were set (or cleared) and the task can proceed with servicing the ISR or task that created those events. If **err** contains anything else, **OSFlagPend( )** either timed out (if the timeout argument was non-zero), the pend was aborted by another task or, the event flag group was deleted by another task. It is always important to examine the returned error code and not assume everything went as planned.

To set (or clear) event flags (either from an ISR or a task), you simply call **OSFlagPost( )**, as shown in Listing 14-13.

```
OS_FLAG_GRP  MyEventFlagGrp;

void MyISR (void)
{
    OS_ERR    err;
    OS_FLAGS  flags_cur;
    :
    flags_cur = OSFlagPost(&MyEventFlagGrp,       (1)
                           (OS_FLAGS)0x0C,        (2)
                           OS_OPT_POST_FLAG_SET,  (3)
                           &err);                 (4)
    /* Check 'err" */
    :
    :
}
```

Listing 14-13 **Posting flags to an Event Flag Group**

L14-13(1)   A task posts to the event flag group by calling **OSFlagPost( )**. Specify the desired event flag group to post by passing its address. Of course, the event flag group must have been previously created. **OSFlagPost( )** returns the current value of the event flags in the event flag group after the post has been performed.

L14-13(2)   The next argument specifies which bit(s) the ISR (or task) will be setting or clearing in the event flag group.

L14-13(3)   You can specify **OS_OPT_POST_FLAG_SET** or **OS_OPT_POST_FLAG_CLR**.

If you specify **OS_OPT_POST_FLAG_SET**, the bits specified in the second arguments will set the corresponding bits in the event flag group. For example, if **MyEventFlagGrp.Flags** contains 0x03, the code in Listing 14-13 will change **MyEventFlagGrp.Flags** to 0x0F.

If you specify **OS_OPT_POST_FLAG_CLR**, the bits specified in the second arguments will clear the corresponding bits in the event flag group. For example, if **MyEventFlagGrp.Flags** contains **0x0F**, the code in Listing 14-13 will change **MyEventFlagGrp.Flags** to 0x03.

When calling **OSFlagPost()** you can specify as an option (i.e., **OS_OPT_POST_NO_SCHED**) to not call the scheduler. This means that the post is performed, but the scheduler is not called even if a higher-priority task was waiting for the event flag group. This allows the calling task to perform other post functions (if needed) and make all the posts take effect simultaneously.

L14-13(4)   **OSFlagPost()** returns an error code based on the outcome of the call. If the call was successful, **err** will contain **OS_ERR_NONE**. If not, the error code will indicate the reason of the error (see Appendix A, "µC/OS-III API Reference" on page 453 for a list of possible error codes for **OSFlagPost()**.

14-4 SYNCHRONIZING MULTIPLE TASKS

Synchronizing the execution of multiple tasks by broadcasting to a semaphore is a commonly used technique. It may be important to have multiple tasks start executing at the same time. Obviously, on a single processor, only one task will actually execute at one time. However, the start of their execution will be synchronized to the same time. This is called a multiple task rendez-vous. However, some of the tasks synchronized might not be waiting for the semaphore when the broadcast is performed. It is fairly easy to resolve this problem by combining semaphores and event flags, as shown in Figure 14-11. For this to work properly, the task on the left needs to have a lower priority than the tasks waiting on the semaphore.

Figure 14-11 **Multiple Task Rendezvous**

F14-11(1)   Each task that needs to synchronize at the rendez-vous needs to set an event flag bit (and specify OS_OPT_POST_NO_SCHED).

F14-11(2)   The task needs to wait for the semaphore to be signaled.

F14-11(3)   The task that will be broadcasting must wait for "**all**" of the event flags corresponding to each task to be set.

F14-11(4)   When all waiting tasks are ready, the task that will synchronize the waiting task issues a broadcast to the semaphore.

14-5 SUMMARY

Three methods are presented to allow an ISR or a task to signal one or more tasks: semaphores, task semaphores, and event flags.

Both semaphores and task semaphores contain a counter allowing them to perform credit tracking and accumulate the occurrence of events. If an ISR or task needs to signal a single task (as opposed to multiple tasks when the event occurs), it makes sense to use a task semaphore since it prevents the user from having to declare an external semaphore object. Also, task semaphore services are slightly faster (in execution time) than semaphores.

Event flags are used when a task needs to synchronize with the occurrence of one or more events. However, event flags cannot perform credit tracking since a single bit (as opposed to a counter) represents each event.

14

Message Passing

It is sometimes necessary for a task or an ISR to communicate information to another task. This information transfer is called *inter-task* communication. Information can be communicated between tasks in two ways: through global data, or by sending messages.

As seen in Chapter 13, "Resource Management" on page 229, when using global variables, each task or ISR must ensure that it has exclusive access to variables. If an ISR is involved, the only way to ensure exclusive access to common variables is to disable interrupts. If two tasks share data, each can gain exclusive access to variables either by disabling interrupts, locking the scheduler, using a semaphore, or preferably, using a mutual-exclusion semaphore. Note that a task can only communicate information to an ISR by using global variables. A task is not aware when a global variable is changed by an ISR, unless the ISR signals the task, or the task polls the contents of a variable periodically.

Messages can either be sent to an intermediate object called a *message queue*, or directly to a task since in μC/OS-III, each task has its own built-in message queue. You can use an external message queue if multiple tasks are to wait for messages. You would send a message directly to a task if only one task will process the data received.

When a task waits for a message to arrive, it does not consume CPU time.

15-1 MESSAGES

A message consists of a pointer to data, a variable containing the size of the data being pointed to, and a timestamp indicating when the message was sent. The pointer can point to a data area or even a function. Obviously, the sender and the receiver must agree as to the contents and the meaning of the message. In other words, the receiver of the message will need to know the meaning of the message received to be able to process it. For example, an Ethernet controller receives a packet and sends a pointer to this packet to a task that knows how to handle the packet.

The message contents must always remain in scope since the data is actually sent by reference instead of by value. In other words, data sent is not copied. You might consider using dynamically allocated memory as described in Chapter 17, "Memory Management" on page 341. Alternatively, you can pass a pointer to a global variable, a global data structure, a global array, or a function, etc.

15-2 MESSAGE QUEUES

A message queue is a kernel object allocated by the application. In fact, you can allocate any number of message queues. The only limit is the amount of RAM available.

There are a number of operations that the user can perform on message queues, summarized in Figure 15-1. However, an ISR can only call OSQPost(). A message queue must be created before sending messages through it.

Figure 15-1 **Operations on message queue**

Message queues are drawn as a first-in, first-out pipe (FIFO). However, with µC/OS-III, it is possible to post messages in last-in, first-out order (LIFO). The LIFO mechanism is useful when a task or an ISR must send an "urgent" message to a task. In this case, the message bypasses all other messages already in the message queue. The size of the message queue is configurable at run-time.

The small hourglass close to the receiving task (F15-1) indicates that the task has an option to specify a timeout. This timeout indicates that the task is willing to wait for a message to be sent to the message queue within a certain amount of time. If the message is not sent within that time, µC/OS-III resumes the task and returns an error code indicating that the task was made ready-to-run because of a timeout, and not because the message was received. It is possible to specify an infinite timeout and indicate that the task is willing to wait forever for the message to arrive.

The message queue also contains a list of tasks waiting for messages to be sent to the message queue. Multiple tasks can wait on a message queue as shown in Figure 15-2. When a message is sent to the message queue, the highest priority task waiting on the message queue receives the message. Optionally, the sender can *broadcast* a message to all tasks waiting on the message queue. In this case, if any of the tasks receiving the message from the broadcast has a higher priority than the task sending the message (or interrupted task, if the message is sent by an ISR), µC/OS-III will run the highest-priority task that is waiting. Notice that not all tasks must specify a timeout; some tasks may want to wait forever.

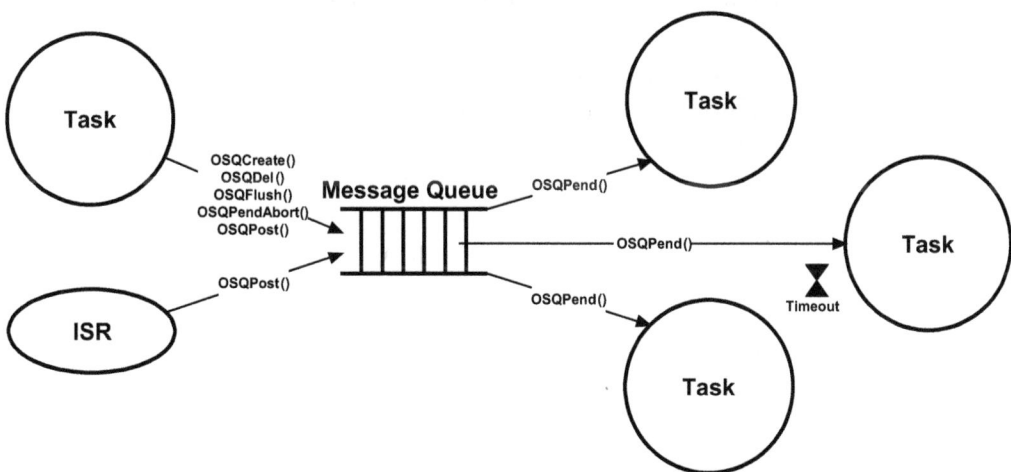

Figure 15-2 **Multiple tasks waiting on a message queue**

15-3 TASK MESSAGE QUEUE

It is fairly rare to find applications where multiple tasks wait on a single message queue. Because of this, a message queue is built into each task and the user can send messages directly to a task without going through an external message queue object. This feature not only simplifies the code but, is also more efficient than using a separate message queue object. The message queue that is built into each task is shown in Figure 15-3.

Figure 15-3 **Task message queue**

Task message queue services in µC/OS-III start with the **OSTaskQ???()** prefix, and services available to the application programmer are described in Appendix A, "µC/OS-III API Reference" on page 453. Setting **OS_CFG_TASK_Q_EN** in **os_cfg.h** enables task message queue services. The code for task message queue management is found in **os_task.c**.

You use this feature if the code knows which task to send the message(s) to. For example, if receiving an interrupt from an Ethernet controller, you can send the address of the received packet to the task that will be responsible for processing the received packet.

15-4 BILATERAL RENDEZ-VOUS

Two tasks can synchronize their activities by using two message queues, as shown in Figure 15-4. This is called a *bilateral rendez-vous* and works the same as with semaphores except that both tasks may send messages to each other. A bilateral rendez-vous cannot be performed between a task and an ISR since an ISR cannot wait on a message queue.

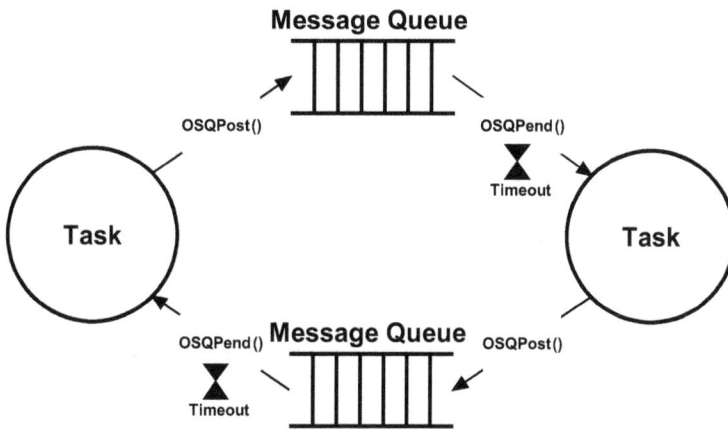

Figure 15-4 **Bilateral Rendez-vous**

In a bilateral rendez-vous, each message queue holds a maximum of one message. Both message queues are initially created empty. When the task on the left reaches the rendez-vous point, it sends a message to the top message queue and waits for a message to arrive on the bottom message queue. Similarly, when the task on the right reaches its rendez-vous point, it sends a message to the message queue on the bottom and waits for a message to arrive on the top message queue.

Figure 15-5 shows how to use task-message queues to perform a bilateral rendez-vous.

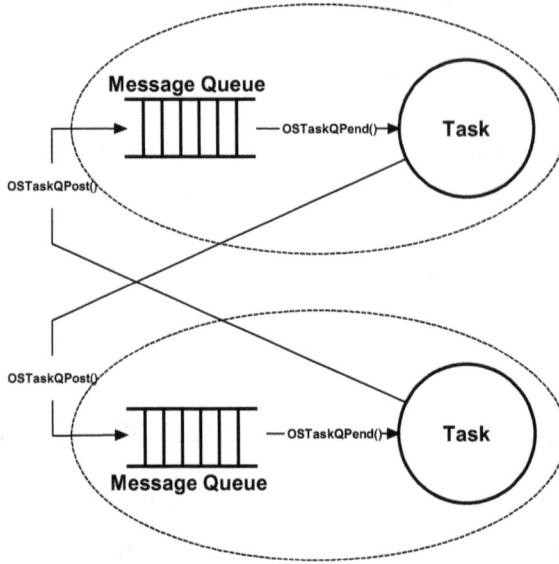

Figure 15-5 **Figure Bilateral Rendez-vous with task message queues**

15-5 FLOW CONTROL

Task-to-task communication often involves data transfer from one task to another. One task produces data while the other *consumes* it. However, data processing takes time and consumers might not consume data as fast as it is produced. In other words, it is possible for the producer to overflow the message queue if a higher-priority task preempts the consumer. One way to solve this problem is to add flow control in the process as shown in Figure 15-6.

Figure 15-6 **Producer and consumer tasks with flow control**

Here, a counting semaphore is used, initialized with the number of allowable messages that can be sent by the consumer. If the consumer cannot queue more than 10 messages, the counting semaphore contains a count of 10.

As shown in the pseudo code of Listing 15-1, the producer must wait on the semaphore before it is allowed to send a message. The consumer waits for messages and, when processed, signals the semaphore.

```
Producer Task:
    Pend on Semaphore;
    Send message to message queue;

Consumer Task:
    Wait for message from message queue;
    Signal the semaphore;
```

Listing 15-1 **Producer and consumer flow control**

Combining the task message queue and task semaphores (see Chapter 14, "Synchronization" on page 271), it is easy to implement flow control as shown in Figure 15-7. In this case, however, OSTaskSemSet() must be called immediately after creating the task to set the value of the task semaphore to the same value as the maximum number of allowable messages in the task message queue.

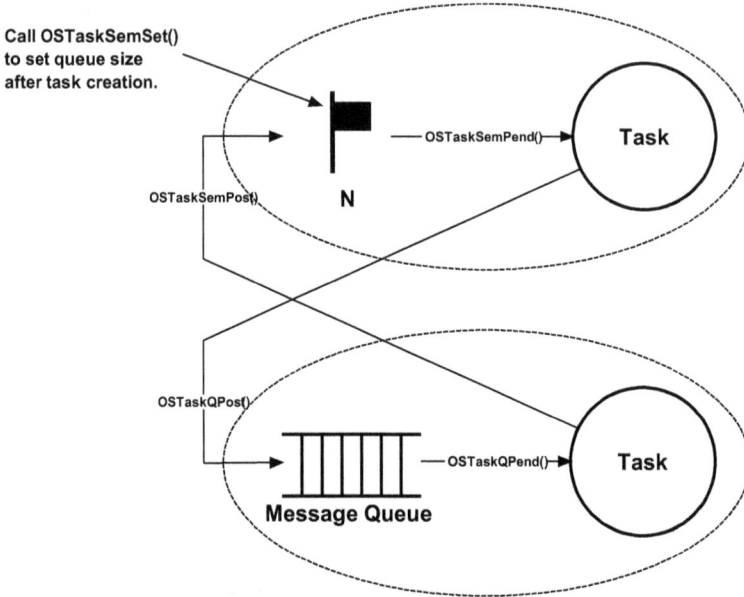

Figure 15-7 **Flow control with task semaphore and task message queue**

15-6 KEEPING THE DATA IN SCOPE

The messages sent typically point to data structures, variables, arrays, tables, etc. However, it is important to realize that the data must remain static until the receiver of the data completes its processing of the data. Once sent, the sender must not touch the sent data. This seems obvious, however it is easy to forget.

One possibility is to use the fixed-size memory partition manager provided with µC/OS-III (see Chapter 17, "Memory Management" on page 341) to dynamically allocate and free memory blocks used to pass the data. Figure 15-8 shows an example. For sake of illustration, assume that a device is sending data bytes to the UART in packets using some protocol. In this case, the first byte of a packet is unique and the end-of-packet byte is also unique.

Figure 15-8 **Using memory partitions for message contents**

F15-8(1)   Here, a UART generates an interrupt when characters are received.

F15-8(2)   The pseudo-code in Listing 15-2 shows what the UART ISR code might look like. There are a lot of details omitted for sake of simplicity. The ISR reads the byte received from the UART and sees if it corresponds to a start of packet. If it is, a buffer is obtained from the memory partition.

F15-8(3)   The received byte is then placed in the buffer.

F15-8(4)   If the data received is an end-of-packet byte, you would simply post the address of the buffer to the message queue so that the task can process the received packet.

F15-8(5)   If the message sent makes the UART task the highest priority task, µC/OS-III will switch to that task at the end of the ISR instead of returning to the interrupted task. The task retrieves the packet from the message queue. Note that the **OSQPend( )** call also returns the number of bytes in the packet and a time stamp indicating when the message was sent.

F15-8(6)   When the task is finished processing the packet, the buffer is returned to the memory partition it came from by calling **OSMemPut( )**.

```
void  UART_ISR (void)
{
    OS_ERR  err;


    RxData = Read byte from UART;
    if (RxData == Start of Packet) {          /* See if we need a new buffer    */
        RxDataPtr = OSMemGet(&UART_MemPool,   /* Yes                            */
                            &err);
      *RxDataPtr++ = RxData;
        RxDataCtr  = 1;
    } if (RxData == End of Packet byte) {      /* See if we got a full packet    */
        *RxDataPtr++ = RxData;
        RxDataCtr++;
        OSQPost((OS_Q      *)&UART_Q,          /* Yes, post to task for processing */
                (void      *)RxDataPtr,
                (OS_MSG_SIZE)RxDataCtr,
                (OS_OPT    )OS_OPT_POST_FIFO,
                (OS_ERR    *)&err);
        RxDataPtr = NULL;                      /* Don't point to sent buffer     */
        RxDataCtr = 0;
    } else; {
        *RxDataPtr++ = RxData;                 /* Save the byte received         */
        RxDataCtr++;
    }
}
```

Listing 15-2 **UART ISR Pseudo-code**

15-7 USING MESSAGE QUEUES

Table 15-1 shows a summary of message-queue services available from μC/OS-III. Refer to Appendix A, "μC/OS-III API Reference" on page 453 for a full description on their use.

Function Name	Operation
OSQCreate()	Create a message queue.
OSQDel()	Delete a message queue.
OSQFlush()	Empty the message queue.
OSQPend()	Wait for a message.
OSQPendAbort()	Abort waiting for a message.
OSQPost()	Send a message through a message queue.

Table 15-1 **Message queue API summary**

Table 15-2 is a summary of task message queue services available from μC/OS-III. Refer to Appendix A, "μC/OS-III API Reference" on page 453, for a full description of their use.

Function Name	Operation
OSTaskQPend()	Wait for a message.
OSTaskQPendAbort()	Abort the wait for a message.
OSTaskQPost()	Send a message to a task.
OSTaskQFlush()	Empty the message queue.

Table 15-2 **Task message queue API summary**

Figure 15-9 shows an example of using a message queue when determining the speed of a rotating wheel.

Figure 15-9 **Measuring RPM**

F15-9(1)   The goal is to measure the RPM of a rotating wheel.

F15-9(2)   A sensor is used to detect the passage of a hole in the wheel. In fact, to receive additional resolution, the wheel could contain multiple holes that are equally spaced.

F15-9(3)   A 32-bit input capture register is used to capture the value of a free-running counter when the hole is detected.

F15-9(4)   An interrupt is generated when the hole is detected. The ISR reads the current count of the input capture register and subtracts the value of the previous capture to determine the time it took for one rotation (assuming only a single hole).

```
Delta Counts    = Current Counts - Previous Counts;
Previous Counts = Current Counts;
```

F15-9(5)

F15-9(6)   The delta counts are sent to a message queue. Since a message is actually a pointer, if the pointer is 32-bits wide on the processor in use, you can simply cast the 32-bit delta counts to a pointer and send this through the message queue. A safer and more portable approach is to dynamically allocate storage to hold the delta counts using a memory block from µC/OS-III's memory management services (see Chapter 17, "Memory Management" on page 341) and send the address of the allocated memory block. The counts read are then saved in 'Previous Counts' to be used on the next interrupt.

F15-9(7)   When the message is sent, the RPM measurement task wakes up and computes the RPM as follows:

```
RPM = 60 * Reference Frequency / Delta Counts;
```

The user may specify a timeout on the pend call and the task will wake up if a message is not sent within the timeout period. This allows the user to easily detect that the wheel is not rotating and therefore, the RPM is 0.

F15-9(8)   Along with computing RPM, the task can also compute average RPM, maximum RPM, and whether the speed is above or below thresholds, etc.

A few interesting things are worth noting about the above example. First, the ISR is very short; it reads the input capture and post the delta counts to the task so it can computer the time-consuming math. Second, with the timeout on the pend, it is easy to detect that the wheel is stopped. Finally, the task can perform additional calculations and can further detect such errors as the wheel spinning too fast or too slow. In fact, the task can notify other tasks about these errors, if needed.

Listing 15-3 shows how to implement the RPM measurement example using µC/OS-III's message queue services. Some of the code is pseudo-code, while the calls to µC/OS-III services are actual calls with their appropriate arguments.

```
OS_Q        RPM_Q;                                              (1)
CPU_INT32U  DeltaCounts;
CPU_INT32U  CurrentCounts;
CPU_INT32U  PreviousCounts;


void main (void)
{
    OS_ERR  err ;
    :
    OSInit(&err) ;                                              (2)
    :
    OSQCreate((OS_Q     *)&RPM_Q,
              (CPU_CHAR *)"My Queue",
              (OS_MSG_QTY)10,
              (OS_ERR   *)&err);
    :
    OSStart(&err);
}


void RPM_ISR (void)                                             (3)
{
    OS_ERR  err;


    Clear the interrupt from the sensor;
    CurrentCounts  = Read the input capture;
    DeltaCounts    = CurrentCounts - PreviousCounts;
    PreviousCounts = CurrentCounts;
    OSQPost((OS_Q     *)&RPM_Q,                                 (4)
            (void      *)DeltaCounts,
            (OS_MSG_SIZE)sizeof(void *),
            (OS_OPT    )OS_OPT_POST_FIFO,
            (OS_ERR    *)&err);
}
```

```
void RPM_Task (void *p_arg)
{
    CPU_INT32U  delta;
    OS_ERR      err;
    OS_MSG_SIZE size;
    CPU_TS      ts;


    DeltaCounts    = 0;
    PreviousCounts = 0;
    CurrentCounts  = 0;
    while (DEF_ON) {
        delta = (CPU_INT32U)OSQPend((OS_Q        *)&RPM_Q,              (5)
                                    (OS_TICK      )OS_CFG_TICK_RATE_HZ * 10,
                                    (OS_OPT       )OS_OPT_PEND_BLOCKING,
                                    (OS_MSG_SIZE *)&size,
                                    (CPU_TS      *)&ts,
                                    (OS_ERR      *)&err);
        if (err == OS_ERR_TIMEOUT) {                                   (6)
            RPM = 0;
        } else {
            if (delta > 0u) {
                RPM = 60 * Reference Frequency / delta;                (7)
            }
        }
        Compute average RPM;                                           (8)
        Detect maximum RPM;
        Check for overspeed;
        Check for underspeed;
        :
        :
    }
}
```

Listing 15-3 **Pseudo-code of RPM measurement**

L15-3(1)   Variables are declared. Notice that it is necessary to allocate storage for the message queue itself.

L15-3(2)   You need to call **OSInit()** and create the message queue before it is used. The best place to do this is in startup code.

L15-3(3)   The RPM ISR clears the sensor interrupt and reads the value of the 32-bit input capture. Note that it is possible to read RPM if there is only a 16-bit input capture. The problem with a 16-bit input capture is that it is easy for it to overflow, especially at low RPMs.

The RPM ISR also computes delta counts directly in the ISR. It is just as easy to post the current counts and let the task compute the delta. However, the subtraction is a fast operation and does not significantly increase ISR processing time.

L15-3(4)   The code then sends the delta counts to the RPM task, which is responsible for computing the RPM and perform additional computations. Note that the message gets lost if the queue is full when the user attempts to post. This happens if data is generated faster than it is processed. Unfortunately, it is not possible to implement flow control in the example because we are dealing with an ISR.

L15-3(5)   The RPM task starts by waiting for a message from the RPM ISR by pending on the message queue. The third argument specifies the timeout. In this case, ten seconds worth of timeout is specified. However, the value chosen depends on the requirements of an application.

Also notice that the **ts** variable contains the timestamp of when the post was completed. You can determine the time it took for the task to respond to the message received by calling **OS_TS_GET( )**, and subtract the value of **ts**:

```
response_time = OS_TS_GET() - ts;
```

L15-3(6)   If a timeout occurs, you can assume the wheel is no longer spinning.

L15-3(7)   The RPM is computed from the delta counts received, and from the reference frequency of the free-running counter.

L15-3(8)   Additional computations are performed as needed. In fact, messages can be sent to different tasks in case error conditions are detected. The messages would be processed by the other tasks. For example, if the wheel spins too fast, another task can initiate a shutdown on the device that is controlling the wheel speed.

In Listing 15-4, **OSQPost()** and **OSQPend()** are replaced with **OSTaskQPost()** and **OSTaskQPend()** for the RPM measurement example. Notice that the code is slightly simpler to use and does not require creating a separate message queue object. However, when creating the RPM task, it is important to specify the size of the message queue used by the task and compile the application code with **OS_CFG_TASK_Q_EN** set to 1. The differences between using message queues and the task's message queue will be explained.

```
OS_TCB      RPM_TCB;                                           (1)
OS_STK      RPM_Stk[1000];
CPU_INT32U  DeltaCounts ;
CPU_INT32U  CurrentCounts ;
CPU_INT32U  PreviousCounts ;


void main (void)
{
    OS_ERR  err ;
    :
    OSInit(&err) ;
    :
    void  OSTaskCreate ((OS_TCB      *)&RPM_TCB,                (2)
                        (CPU_CHAR    *)"RPM Task",
                        (OS_TASK_PTR )RPM_Task,
                        (void        *)0,
                        (OS_PRIO     )10,
                        (CPU_STK     *)&RPM_Stk[0],
                        (CPU_STK_SIZE )100,
                        (CPU_STK_SIZE )1000,
                        (OS_MSG_QTY  )10,
                        (OS_TICK     )0,
                        (void        *)0,
                        (OS_OPT      )(OS_OPT_TASK_STK_CHK + OS_OPT_TASK_STK_CLR),
                        (OS_ERR      *)&err);
    :
    OSStart(&err);
}
```

```
void RPM_ISR (void)
{
    OS_ERR  err;

    Clear the interrupting from the sensor;
    CurrentCounts  = Read the input capture;
    DeltaCounts    = CurrentCounts - PreviousCounts;
    PreviousCounts = CurrentCounts;
    OSTaskQPost((OS_TCB      *)&RPM_TCB,                                    (3)
                (void        *)DeltaCounts,
                (OS_MSG_SIZE )sizeof(DeltaCounts),
                (OS_OPT      )OS_OPT_POST_FIFO,
                (OS_ERR      *)&err);
}

void RPM_Task (void *p_arg)
{
    CPU_INT32U   delta;
    OS_ERR       err;
    OS_MSG_SIZE  size;
    CPU_TS       ts;


    DeltaCounts    = 0;
    PreviousCounts = 0;
    CurrentCounts  = 0;
    while (DEF_ON) {
        delta = (CPU_INT32U)OSTaskQPend((OS_TICK      )OS_CFG_TICK_RATE * 10,  (4)
                                        (OS_OPT       )OS_OPT_PEND_BLOCKING,
                                        (OS_MSG_SIZE *)&size,
                                        (CPU_TS      *)&ts,
                                        (OS_ERR      *)&err);
        if (err == OS_ERR_TIMEOUT) {
            RPM = 0;
        } else {
            if (delta > 0u) {
                RPM = 60 * ReferenceFrequency / delta;
            }
        }
        Compute average RPM;
        Detect maximum RPM;
        Check for overspeed;
        Check for underspeed;
        :
        :
    }
}
```

Listing 15-4 **Pseudo-code of RPM measurement**

L15-4(1)   Instead of declaring a message queue, it is important to know the **OS_TCB** of the task that will be receiving messages.

L15-4(2)   The RPM task is created and a queue size of 10 entries is specified. Of course, hard-coded values should not be specified in a real application, but instead, you should use **#defines**. Fixed numbers are used here for sake of illustration.

L15-4(3)   Instead of posting to a message queue, the ISR posts the message directly to the task, specifying the address of the **OS_TCB** of the task. This is known since the **OS_TCB** is allocated when creating the task.

L15-4(4)   The RPM task starts by waiting for a message from the RPM ISR by calling **OSTaskQPend()**. This is an inherent call so it is not necessary to specify the address of the **OS_TCB** to pend on as the current task is assumed. The second argument specifies the timeout. Here, ten seconds worth of timeout is specified, which corresponds to 6 RPM.

15-8 CLIENTS AND SERVERS

Another interesting use of message queues is shown in Figure 15-10. Here, a task (the server) is used to monitor error conditions that are sent to it by other tasks or ISRs (clients). For example, a client detects whether the RPM of the rotating wheel has been exceeded, another client detects whether an over-temperature exists, and yet another client detects that a user pressed a shutdown button. When the clients detect error conditions, they send a message through the message queue. The message sent indicates the error detected, which threshold was exceeded, the error code that is associated with error conditions, or even suggests the address of a function that will handle the error, and more.

Figure 15-10 **Clients and Servers**

15-9 MESSAGE QUEUES INTERNALS

As previously described, a message consists of a pointer to actual data, a variable indicating the size of the data being pointed to and a timestamp indicating when the message was actually sent. When sent, a message is placed in a data structure of type OS_MSG, shown in Figure 15-11.

The sender and receiver are unaware of this data structure since everything is hidden through the APIs provided by µC/OS-III.

OS_MSG

NextPtr	→ Pointer to next OS_MSG
MsgSize
MsgTS
MsgPtr

Pointer to message contents

Figure 15-11 **OS_MSG structure**

µC/OS-III maintains a pool of free OS_MSGs. The total number of available messages in the pool is determined by the value of OS_CFG_MSG_POOL_SIZE found in os_cfg_app.h. When µC/OS-III is initialized, OS_MSGs are linked in a single linked list as shown in Figure 15-12. Notice that the free list is maintained by a data structure of type OS_MSG_POOL, which contains four (4) fields: .NextPtr, which points to the free list; .NbrFree, which contains the number of free OS_MSGs in the pool, .NbrUsed, which contains the number of OS_MSGs allocated to the application and, .NbrUsedMax which detects the maximum number of messages allocated to the application.

OS_MSG_POOL

NextPtr	NextPtr	NextPtr	NextPtr	→ NULL
NbrFree	MsgSize	MsgSize	MsgSize
NbrUsed	MsgTS	MsgTS	MsgTS
NbrUsedMax	MsgPtr	MsgPtr	MsgPtr

← OS_CFG_MSG_POOL_SIZE →

Figure 15-12 **Pool of free OS_MSGs**

Messages are queued using a data structure of type OS_MSG_Q, as shown in Figure 15-13.

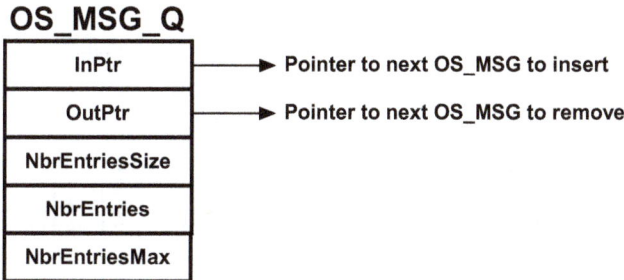

OS_MSG_Q

InPtr	→ **Pointer to next OS_MSG to insert**
OutPtr	→ **Pointer to next OS_MSG to remove**
NbrEntriesSize	
NbrEntries	
NbrEntriesMax	

Figure 15-13 **OS_MSG_Q structure**

.InPtr — This field contains a pointer to where the next OS_MSG will be inserted in the queue. In fact, the OS_MSG will be inserted "after" the OS_MSG pointed to.

.OutPtr — This field contains a pointer to where the next OS_MSG will be extracted.

.NbrEntriesSize — This field contains the maximum number of OS_MSGs that the queue will hold. If an application attempts to send a message and the .NbrEntries matches this value, the queue is considered to be full and the OS_MSG will not be inserted.

.NbrEntries — This field contains the current number of OS_MSGs in the queue.

.NbrEntriesMax — This field contains the highest number of OS_MSGs existing in the queue at any given time.

A number of internal functions are used by μC/OS-III to manipulate the free list and messages. Specifically, OS_MsgQPut() inserts an OS_MSG in an OS_MSG_Q, OS_MsgQGet() extracts an OS_MSG from an OS_MSG_Q, and OS_MsgQFreeAll() returns all OS_MSGs in an OS_MSG_Q to the pool of free OS_MSGs. There are other OS_MsgQ??() functions in os_msg.c that are used during initialization.

Figure 15-14 shows an example of an OS_MSG_Q when four OS_MSGs are inserted.

Figure 15-14 **OS_MSG_Q with four OS_MSGs**

OS_MSG_Qs are used inside two additional data structures: OS_Q and OS_TCB. Recall that an OS_Q is declared when creating a message queue object. An OS_TCB is a task control block and, as previously mentioned, each OS_TCB can have its own message queue when the configuration constant OS_CFG_TASK_Q_EN is set to 1 in os_cfg.h. Figure 15-15 shows the contents of an OS_Q and partial contents of an OS_TCB containing an OS_MSG_Q. The OS_MSG_Q data structure is shown as an "exploded view" to emphasize the structure within the structure.

Figure 15-15 **OS_Q and OS_TCB each contain an OS_MSG_Q**

15-10 SUMMARY

Message queues are useful when a task or an ISR needs to send data to another task. The data sent must remain in scope as it is actually sent by reference instead of by value. In other words, the data sent is not copied.

The task waiting for the data will not consume CPU time while waiting for a message to be sent to it.

If it is known which task is responsible for servicing messages sent by producers, then you should use task message queue (i.e., **OSTaskQ???()**) services since they are simple and fast. Task message queue services are enabled when **OS_CFG_TASK_Q_EN** is set to 1 in **os_cfg.h**.

If multiple tasks must wait for messages from the same message queue, you need to allocate an **OS_Q** and have the tasks wait for messages to be sent to the queue. Alternatively, you can broadcast special messages to all tasks waiting on a message queue. Regular message queue services are enabled when **OS_CFG_Q_EN** is set to 1 in **os_cfg.h**.

Messages are sent using an **OS_MSG** data structure obtained by µC/OS-III from a pool. You need to set the maximum number of messages that can be sent to a message queue, or as many messages as are available in the pool.

15

16

Pending On Multiple Objects

In Chapter 10, "Pend Lists (or Wait Lists)" on page 195 we saw how multiple tasks can pend (or wait) on a single kernel object such as a semaphore, mutual exclusion semaphore, event flag group, or message queue. In this chapter, we will see how tasks can pend on multiple objects. However, µC/OS-III only allows for pend on multiple semaphores and/or message queues. In other words, it is not possible to pend on multiple event flag groups or mutual exclusion semaphores.

As shown in Figure 16-1, a task can pend on any number of semaphores or message queues at the same time. The first semaphore or message queue posted will make the task ready-to-run and compete for CPU time with other tasks in the ready list. As shown, a task pends on multiple objects by calling **OSPendMulti()** and specifies an optional timeout value. The timeout applies to all of the objects. If none of the objects are posted within the specified timeout, the task resumes with an error code indicating that the pend timed out.

Figure 16-1 **Task pending on multiple objects**

Table 16-1 shows the function prototype of **OSPendMulti()** and Figure 16-2 shows an array of **OS_PEND_DATA** elements.

```
OS_OBJ_QTY  OSPendMulti (OS_PEND_DATA  *p_pend_data_tbl,          (1)
                         OS_OBJ_QTY     tbl_size,                 (2)
                         OS_TICK        timeout,                  (3)
                         OS_OPT         opt,                      (4)
                         OS_ERR        *p_err);                   (5)
```

Table 16-1 **OSPendMulti() prototype**

	PrevPtr	NextPtr	TCBPtr	PendObjPtr	RdyObjPtr	RdyMsgPtr	RdyMsgSize	RdyTS
[0]	PrevPtr	NextPtr	TCBPtr	PendObjPtr	RdyObjPtr	RdyMsgPtr	RdyMsgSize	RdyTS
[1]	PrevPtr	NextPtr	TCBPtr	PendObjPtr	RdyObjPtr	RdyMsgPtr	RdyMsgSize	RdyTS
[2]	PrevPtr	NextPtr	TCBPtr	PendObjPtr	RdyObjPtr	RdyMsgPtr	RdyMsgSize	RdyTS
[N-1]	PrevPtr	NextPtr	TCBPtr	PendObjPtr	RdyObjPtr	RdyMsgPtr	RdyMsgSize	RdyTS

OS_PEND_DATA

Figure 16-2 **Array of OS_PEND_DATA**

L16-0(1)   **OSPendMulti()** is passed an array of **OS_PEND_DATA** elements. The caller must instantiate an array of **OS_PEND_DATA**. The size of the array depends on the total number of kernel objects that the task wants to pend on. For example, if the task wants to pend on three semaphores and two message queues then the array contains five **OS_PEND_DATA** elements as shown below:

```
OS_PEND_DATA   my_pend_multi_tbl[5];
```

The calling task needs to initialize the **.PendObjPtr** of each element of the array to point to each of the objects to be pended on. For example:

333

```
OS_SEM  MySem1;
OS_SEM  MySem2;
OS_SEM  MySem3;
OS_Q    MyQ1;
OS_Q    MyQ2;


void  MyTask (void)
{
    OS_ERR          err;
    OS_PEND_DATA  my_pend_multi_tbl[5];
    :
    while (DEF_ON) {
        :
        my_pend_multi_tbl[0].PendObjPtr = (OS_PEND_OBJ)&MySem1;       (6)
        my_pend_multi_tbl[1].PendObjPtr = (OS_PEND_OBJ)&MySem2;
        my_pend_multi_tbl[2].PendObjPtr = (OS_PEND_OBJ)&MySem3;
        my_pend_multi_tbl[3].PendObjPtr = (OS_PEND_OBJ)&MyQ1;
        my_pend_multi_tbl[4].PendObjPtr = (OS_PEND_OBJ)&MyQ2;
        OSPendMulti((OS_PEND_DATA *)&my_pend_multi_tbl[0],
                    (OS_OBJ_QTY    )5,
                    (OS_TICK       )0,
                    (OS_OPT        )OS_OPT_PEND_BLOCKING,
                    (OS_ERR       *)&err);
        /* Check 'err" */
        :
    }
}
```

L16-0(2)   This argument specifies the size of the **OS_PEND_DATA** table. In the above example, this is 5.

L16-0(3)   You specify whether or not to timeout in case none of the objects are posted within a certain amount of time. A non-zero value indicates the number of ticks to timeout. Specifying zero indicates the task will wait forever for any of the objects to be posted.

L16-0(4)   The "**opt**" argument specifies whether to wait for objects to be posted (you would set **opt** to **OS_OPT_PEND_BLOCKING**) or, not block if none of the objects have already been posted (you would set **opt** to **OS_OPT_PEND_NON_BLOCKING**).

F16-2(1)   As with most µC/OS-III function calls, you specify the address of a variable that will receive an error code based on the outcome of the function call. See Appendix A, "µC/OS-III API Reference" on page 453 for a list of possible error codes. As always, it is highly recommended to examine the error return code.

F16-2(2)   Note that all objects are cast to OS_PEND_OBJ data types.

When called, OSPendMulti() first starts by validating that all of the objects specified in the OS_PEND_DATA table are either an OS_SEM or an OS_Q. If not, an error code is returned.

Next, OSPendMulti() goes through the OS_PEND_DATA table to see if any of the objects have already posted. If so, OSPendMulti() fills the following fields in the table: .RdyObjPtr, .RdyMsgPtr, .RdyMsgSize and .RdyTS.

.RdyObjPtr   is a pointer to the object if the object has been posted. For example, if the first object in the table is a semaphore and the semaphore has been posted to, my_pend_multi_tbl[0].RdyObjPtr is set to my_pend_multi_tbl[0].PendObjPtr.

.RdyMsgPtr   is a pointer to a message if the object in the table at this entry is a message queue and a message was received from the message queue.

.RdyMsgSize   is the size of the message received if the object in the table at this entry is a message queue and a message was received from the message queue.

.RdyTS   is the timestamp of when the object posted. This allows the user to know when a semaphore or message queue was posted.

If there are no objects posted, then OSPendMulti() places the current task in the wait list of all the objects that it is pending on. This is a complex and tedious process for OSPendMulti() since there can be other tasks in the pend list of some of these objects we are pending on.

To indicate how tricky things get, Figure 16-3 is an example of a task pending on two semaphores.

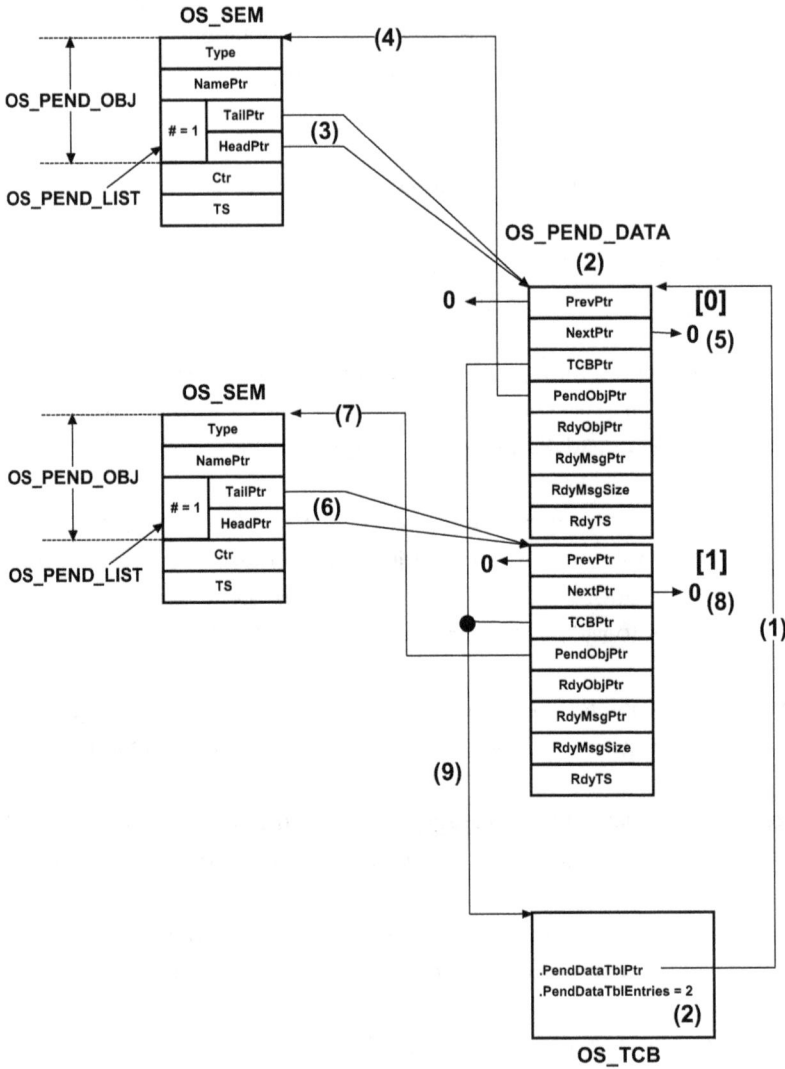

Figure 16-3 **Task pending on two semaphores**

F16-3(1)   A pointer to the base address of the OS_PEND_DATA table is placed in the OS_TCB of the task placed in the pend list of the two semaphores.

F16-3(2)   The number of entries in the OS_PEND_DATA table is also placed in the OS_TCB. Again, this task is waiting on two semaphores and therefore there are two entries in the table.

F16-3(3)   The first semaphore is linked to the first entry in the **OS_PEND_DATA** array.

F16-3(4)   Entry [0] of the **OS_PEND_DATA** table is linked to the semaphore object specified by that entry's **.PendObjPtr**. This pointer was specified by the caller of **OSPendMulti()**.

F16-3(5)   Since there is only one task in the pend list of the semaphore, the **.PrevPtr** and **.NextPtr** are pointing to **NULL**.

F16-3(6)   The second semaphore points to the second entry in the **OS_PEND_DATA** table.

F16-3(7)   The second entry in the **OS_PEND_DATA** array points to the second semaphore. This pointer was specified by the caller of **OSPendMulti()**.

F16-3(8)   The second semaphore only has one entry in its pend list. Therefore the **.PrevPtr** and **.NextPtr** both point to **NULL**.

F16-3(9)   **OSPendMulti()** links back each **OS_PEND_DATA** entry to the task that is waiting on the two semaphores.

Figure 16-4 is a more complex example where one task is pending on two semaphores while another task also pends on one of the two semaphores. The examples presented so far only show semaphores, but they could be combinations of semaphores and message queues.

16

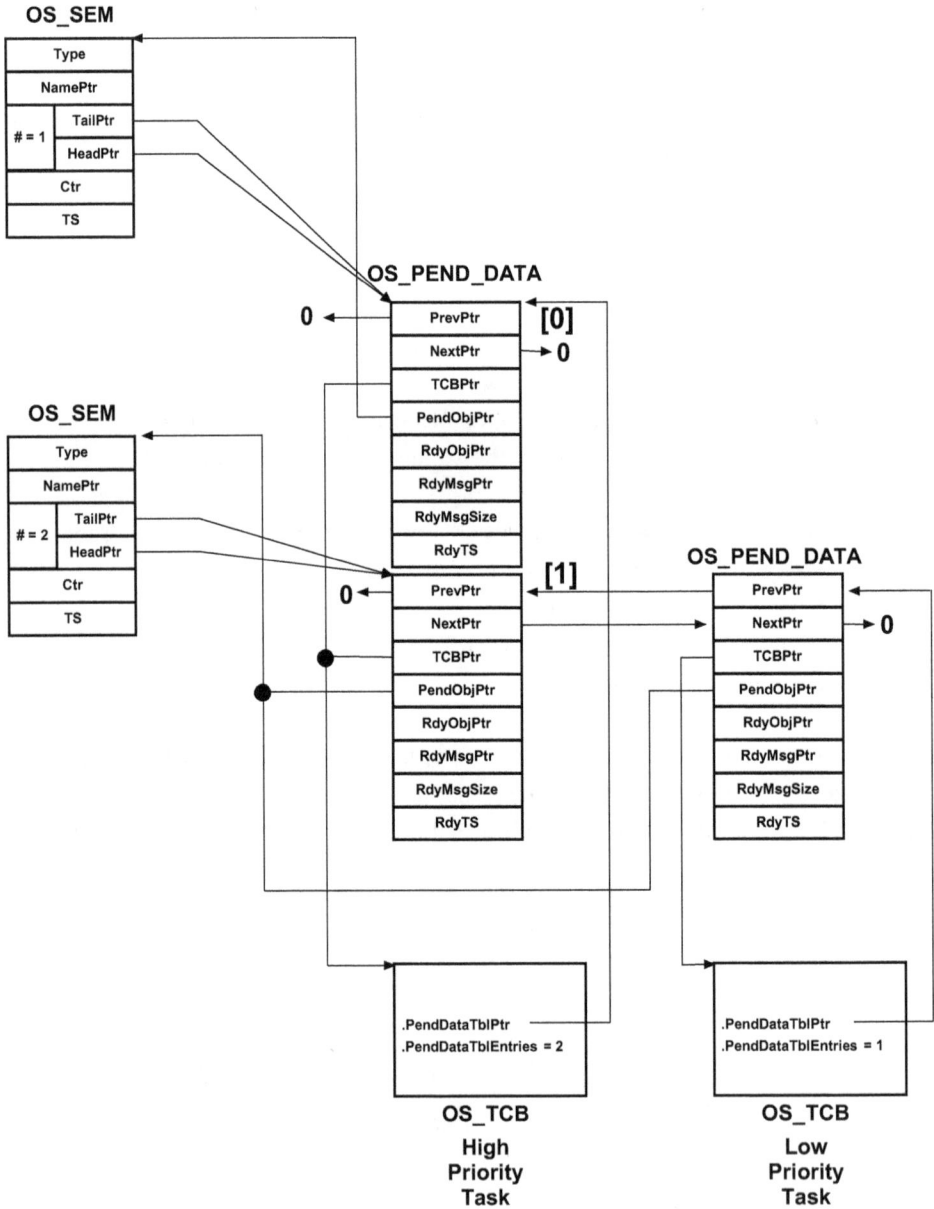

Figure 16-4 **Tasks pending on semaphores**

When either an ISR or a task signals or sends a message to one of the objects that the task is pending on, OSPendMulti() returns, indicating in the OS_PEND_DATA table which object was posted. This is done by only filling in "one" of the .RdyObjPtr entries, the one that corresponds to the object posted.

Only one of the entries in the OS_PEND_DATA table will have a .RdyObjPtr with a non-NULL value while all the other entries have the .RdyObjPtr set to NULL. Going back to the case where a task waits on five semaphores and two message queues, if the first message queue is posted while the task is pending on all those objects, the OS_PEND_DATA table will be as shown in Figure 16-5.

	.PrevPtr	.NextPtr	.TCBPtr	.PendObjPtr	.RdyObjPtr	.RdyMsgPtr	.RdyMsgSize	.RdyTS
[0]	0	0	TCBPtr	PendObjPtr	0	0	0	0
[1]	0	0	TCBPtr	PendObjPtr	0	0	0	0
[2]	0	0	TCBPtr	PendObjPtr	0	0	0	0
[3]	0	0	TCBPtr	&MyQ1	&MyQ1	Msg Ptr	Msg Size	Timestamp
[4]	0	0	TCBPtr	PendObjPtr	0	0	0	0

Figure 16-5 **Message queue #1 posted before timeout expired**

16-1 SUMMARY

µC/OS-III allows tasks to pend on multiple kernel objects.

OSPendMulti() can only pend on multiple semaphores and message queues, not event flags and mutual-exclusion semaphores.

If the objects are already posted when OSPendMulti() is called, µC/OS-III will specify which of the objects (can be more than one) in the list of objects have already been posted.

If none of the objects are posted, OSPendMulti() will place the calling task in the pend list of all the desired objects. OSPendMulti() will return as soon as one of the objects is posted. In this case, OSPendMulti() will indicate which object was posted.

OSPendMulti() is a complex function that has potentially long critical sections.

16

17

Memory Management

An application can allocate and free dynamic memory using any ANSI C compiler's `malloc()` and `free()` functions, respectively. However, using `malloc()` and `free()` in an embedded real-time system may be dangerous. Eventually, it might not be possible to obtain a single contiguous memory area due to fragmentation. Fragmentation is the development of a large number of separate free areas (i.e., the total free memory is fragmented into small, non-contiguous pieces). Execution time of `malloc()` and `free()` is generally nondeterministic given the algorithms used to locate a contiguous block of free memory large enough to satisfy a `malloc()` request.

μC/OS-III provides an alternative to `malloc()` and `free()` by allowing an application to obtain fixed-sized memory blocks from a partition made from a contiguous memory area, as illustrated in Figure 17-1. All memory blocks are the same size, and the partition contains an integral number of blocks. Allocation and deallocation of these memory blocks is performed in constant time and is deterministic. The partition itself is typically allocated statically (as an array), but can also be allocated by using `malloc()` as long as it is never freed.

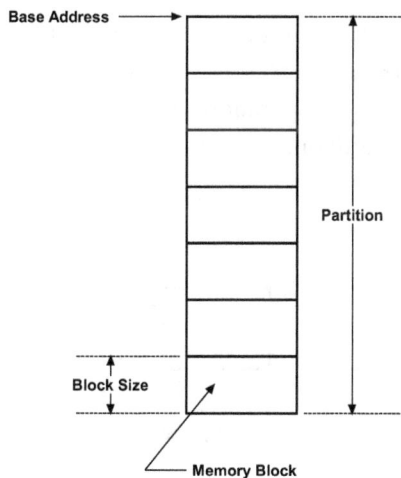

Figure 17-1 **Memory Partition**

As indicated in Figure 17-2, more than one memory partition may exist in an application and each one may have a different number of memory blocks and be a different size. An application can obtain memory blocks of different sizes based upon requirements. However, a specific memory block must always be returned to the partition that it came from. This type of memory management is not subject to fragmentation except that it is possible to run out of memory blocks. It is up to the application to decide how many partitions to have and how large each memory block should be within each partition.

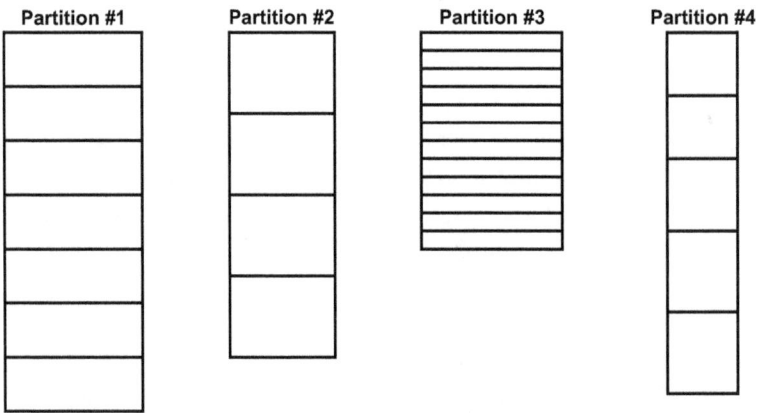

Figure 17-2 **Multiple Memory Partitions**

17-1 CREATING A MEMORY PARTITION

Before using a memory partition, it must be created. This allows µC/OS-III to know something about the memory partition so that it can manage their allocation and deallocation. Once created, a memory partition is as shown in Figure 17-3. Calling OSMemCreate() creates a memory partition.

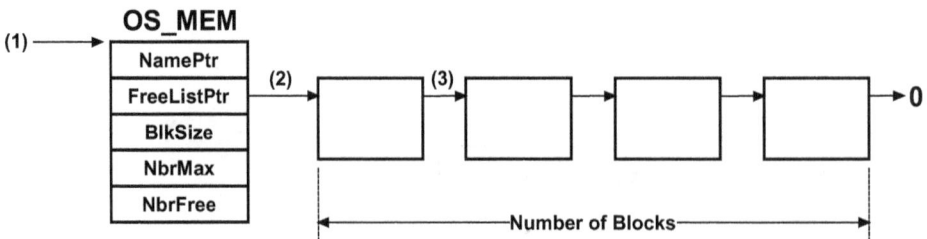

Figure 17-3 **Created Memory Partition**

F17-3(1)   When creating a partition, the application code supplies the address of a memory partition control block (OS_MEM). Typically, this memory control block is allocated from static memory, however it can also be obtained from the heap by calling **malloc()**. The application code should however never deallocate it.

F17-3(2)   **OSMemCreate()** organizes the continuous memory provided into a singly linked list and stores the pointer to the beginning of the list in the OS_MEM structure.

F17-3(3)   Each memory block must be large enough to hold a pointer. Given the nature of the linked list, a block needs to be able to point to the next block.

Listing 17-1 indicates how to create a memory partition with µC/OS-III.

```
OS_MEM       MyPartition;                          (1)
CPU_INT08U   MyPartitionStorage[12][100];          (2)


void  main (void)                                  (3)
{
    OS_ERR  err;
    :
    :
    OSInit(&err);
    :
    OSMemCreate((OS_MEM    *)&MyPartition,          (4)
                (CPU_CHAR  *)"My Partition",        (5)
                (void      *)&MyPartitionStorage[0][0],  (6)
                (OS_MEM_QTY ) 12,                   (7)
                (OS_MEM_SIZE)100,                   (8)
                (OS_ERR    *)&err);                 (9)
    /* Check 'err' */
    :
    :
    OSStart(&err);
}
```

Listing 17-1 **Creating a memory partition**

L17-1(1)   An application needs to allocate storage for a memory partition control block (i.e. OS_MEM structure). This can be a static allocation as shown here or malloc() can be used in the code. However, the application code must not deallocate the memory control block.

L17-1(2)   The application also needs to allocate storage for the memory that will be split into memory blocks. This can also be a static allocation or malloc() can be used. The same reasoning applies. Do not deallocate this storage since other tasks may rely on the existence of this storage.

L17-1(3)   Memory partition must be created before allocating and deallocating blocks from the partition. One of the best places to create memory partitions is in main() prior to starting the multitasking process. Of course, an application can call a function from main() to do this instead of actually placing the code directly in main().

L17-1(4)   You pass the address of the memory partition control block to OSMemCreate(). You should never reference any of the internal members of the OS_MEM data structure. Instead, you should always use μC/OS-III's API.

L17-1(5)   You can assign a name to the memory partition. There is no limit to the length of the ASCII string as μC/OS-III saves a pointer to the ASCII string in the partition control block and not the actual characters.

L17-1(6)   You then need to pass the base address of the storage area reserved for the memory blocks.

L17-1(7)   Here, you specify how many memory blocks are available from this memory partition. Hard coded numbers are used for the sake of the illustration but you should instead use #define constants.

L17-1(8)   You need to specify the size of each memory block in the partition. Again, a hard coded value is used for illustration, which is not recommended in real code.

L17-1(9)   As with most μC/OS-III services, OSMemCreate() returns an error code indicating the outcome of the service. The call is successful if "err" contains OS_ERR_NONE.

Listing 17-2 shows how to create a memory partition with µC/OS-III, but this time, using `malloc()` to allocate storage. Do not deallocate the memory control block or the storage for the partition.

```
OS_MEM      *MyPartitionPtr;                                    (1)


void  main (void)
{
    OS_ERR    err;
    void      *p_storage;
    :
    OSInit(&err);
    :
    MyPartitionPtr = (OS_MEM *)malloc(sizeof(OS_MEM));          (2)
    if (MyPartitionPtr != (OS_MEM *)0) {
        p_storage = malloc(12 * 100);                          (3)
        if (p_storage != (void *)0) {
            OSMemCreate((OS_MEM    *)MyPartitionPtr,           (4)
                        (CPU_CHAR  *)"My Partition",
                        (void      *)p_storage,                (5)
                        (OS_MEM_QTY ) 12,                      (6)
                        (OS_MEM_SIZE)100,                      (6)
                        (OS_ERR    *)&err);
            /* Check 'err" */
        }
    }
    :
    OSStart(&err);
}
```

Listing 17-2 **Creating a memory partition**

L17-2(1)   Instead of allocating static storage for the memory partition control block, you can assign a pointer that receives the **OS_MEM** allocated using `malloc()`.

L17-2(2)   The application allocates storage for the memory control block.

L17-2(3)   We then allocate storage for the memory partition.

L17-2(4)   A pointer is passed to the allocated memory control block to **OSMemCreate()**.

L17-2(5)   The base address of the storage used for the partition is passed to OSMemCreate().

L17-2(6)   Finally, the number of blocks and the size of each block is passed so that μC/OS-III can create the linked list of 12 blocks of 100 bytes each. Again, hard coded numbers are used, but these would typically be replaced by #defines.

17-2 GETTING A MEMORY BLOCK FROM A PARTITION

Application code can request a memory block from a partition by calling OSMemGet() as shown in Listing 17-3. The code assumes that the partition was already created.

```
OS_MEM      MyPartition;                                          (1)
CPU_INT08U *MyDataBlkPtr;


void  MyTask (void *p_arg)
{
    OS_ERR  err;


    :
    while (DEF_ON) {
        :
        MyDataBlkPtr = (CPU_INT08U *)OSMemGet((OS_MEM    *)&MyPartition,  (2)
                                              (OS_ERR    *)&err);
        if (err == OS_ERR_NONE) {                                 (3)
            /* You have a memory block from the partition */
        }
        :
        :
    }
}
```

Listing 17-3 **Obtaining a memory block from a partition**

L17-3(1)   The memory partition control block must be accessible by all tasks or ISRs that will be using the partition.

L17-3(2)   Simply call **OSMemGet()** to obtain a memory block from the desired partition. A pointer to the allocated memory block is returned. This is similar to **malloc()**, except that the memory block comes from a pool that is guaranteed to not fragment. Also, it's assumed that your application knows the size of each block so it doesn't overflow the block with data.

L17-3(3)   It is important to examine the returned error code to ensure that there are free memory blocks and that the application can start putting content in the memory blocks.

17-3 RETURNING A MEMORY BLOCK TO A PARTITION

The application code must return an allocated memory block back to the proper partition when finished. You do this by calling **OSMemPut()** as shown in Listing 17-4. The code assumes that the partition was already created.

```
OS_MEM      MyPartition;                                        (1)
CPU_INT08U *MyDataBlkPtr;


void  MyTask (void *p_arg)
{
   OS_ERR  err;


   :
   while (DEF_ON) {
      :
      OSMemPut((OS_MEM  *)&MyPartition,                         (2)
               (void    *)MyDataBlkPtr,                         (3)
               (OS_ERR  *)&err);
      if (err == OS_ERR_NONE) {                                 (4)
         /* You properly returned the memory block to the partition */
      }
      :
      :
   }
}
```

Listing 17-4 **Returning a memory block to a partition**

L17-4(1)   The memory partition control block must be accessible by all tasks or ISRs that will be using the partition.

347

L17-4(2)   You simply call OSMemPut() to return the memory block back to the memory partition. Note that there is no check to see whether the proper memory block is being returned to the proper partition (assuming you have multiple different partitions). It is therefore important to be careful (as is necessary when designing embedded systems).

L17-4(3)   You pass the pointer to the data area that is allocated so that it can be returned to the pool. Note that a "**void ***" is assumed.

L17-4(4)   You would examine the returned error code to ensure that the call was successful.

17-4 USING MEMORY PARTITIONS

Memory management services are enabled at compile time by setting the configuration constant OS_CFG_MEM_EN to 1 in **os_cfg.h**.

There are a number of operations to perform on memory partitions as summarized in Table 13-1.

Function Name	Operation
OSMemCreate()	Create a memory partition.
OSMemGet()	Obtain a memory block from a memory partition.
OSMemPut()	Return a memory block to a memory partition.

Table 17-1 **Memory Partition API summary**

OSMemCreate() can only be called from task-level code, but OSMemGet() and OSMemPut() can be called by Interrupt Service Routines (ISRs).

Listing 17-4 shows an example of how to use the dynamic memory allocation feature of μC/OS-III, as well as message-passing capabilities (see Chapter 15, "Message Passing" on page 307). In this example, the task on the left reads and checks the value of analog inputs (pressures, temperatures, and voltage) and sends a message to the second task if any of the analog inputs exceed a threshold. The message sent contains information about which channel had the error, an error code, an indication of the severity of the error, and other information.

Error handling in this example is centralized. Other tasks, or even ISRs, can post error messages to the error-handling task. The error-handling task could be responsible for displaying error messages on a monitor (a display), logging errors to a disk, or dispatching other tasks to take corrective action based on the error.

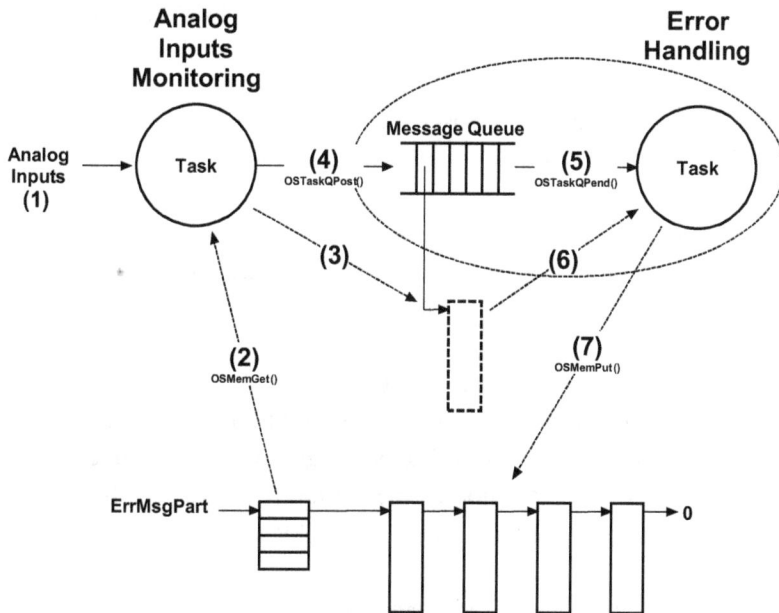

Figure 17-4 **Using a Memory Partition – non blocking**

F17-4(1)   The analog inputs are read by the task. The task determines that one of the inputs is outside a valid range and an error message needs to be sent to the error handler.

F17-4(2)   The task then obtains a memory block from a memory partition so that it can place information regarding the detected error.

F17-4(3)   The task writes this information to the memory block. As mentioned above, the task places the analog channel that is at fault, an error code, an indication of the severity, possible solutions, and more. There is no need to store a timestamp in the message, as time stamping is a built-in feature of μC/OS-III so the receiving task will know when the message was posted.

F17-4(4)   Once the message is complete, it is posted to the task that will handle such error messages. Of course the receiving task needs to know how the information is placed in the message. Once the message is sent, the analog input task is no longer allowed (by convention) to access the memory block since it sent it out to be processed.

F17-4(5)   The error handler task (on the right) normally pends on the message queue. This task will not execute until a message is sent to it.

F17-4(6)   When a message is received, the error handler task reads the contents of the message and performs necessary action(s). As indicated, once sent, the sender will not do anything else with the message.

F17-4(7)   Once the error handler task is finished processing the message, it simply returns the memory block to the memory partition. The sender and receiver therefore need to know about the memory partition or, the sender can pass the address of the memory partition as part of the message and the error handler task will know where to return the memory block to.

Sometimes it is useful to have a task wait for a memory block in case a partition runs out of blocks. μC/OS-III does not support pending on partitions, but it is possible to support this requirement by adding a counting semaphore (see Chapter 13, "Resource Management" on page 229) to guard the memory partition. The initial value of the counting semaphore would be set to the number of blocks in the partition. This is illustrated in Figure 17-5.

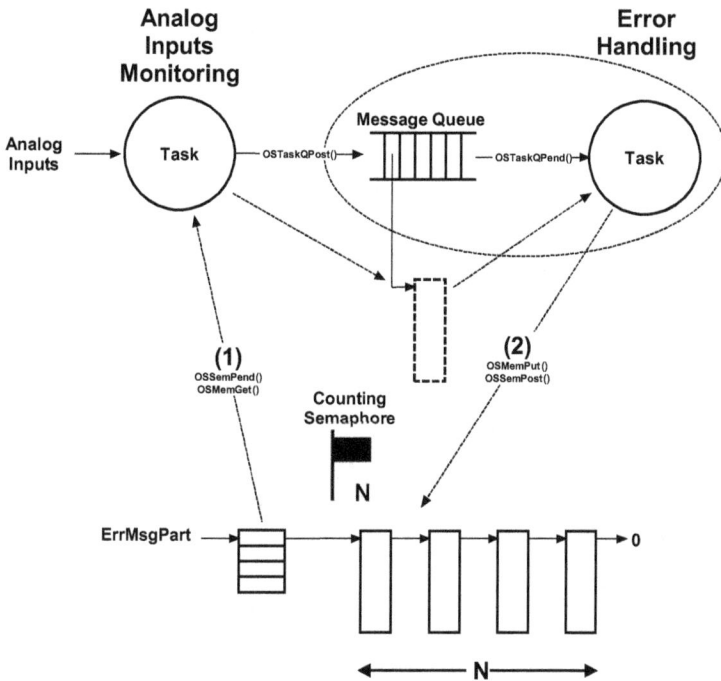

Figure 17-5 **Using a Memory Partition - blocking**

F17-5(1)   To obtain a memory block, your code simply obtain the semaphore by calling
            OSSemPend() and then calls OSMemGet() to receive the memory block.

F17-5(2)   To release a block, you simply return the memory block by calling OSMemPut()
            and then signal the semaphore by calling OSSemPost().

The above operations must be performed in order.

Note that the user may call OSMemGet() and OSMemPut() from an ISR since these functions
do not block and in fact, execute very quickly. However, you cannot use blocking calls from
ISRs.

17-5 SUMMARY

Do not use `malloc()` and `free()` in embedded systems since they lead to fragmentation. However, it is possible to use `malloc()` to allocate memory from the heap, but do not deallocate the memory.

The application programmer can create an unlimited number of memory partitions (limited only by the amount of available RAM).

Memory partition services in µC/OS-III start with the `OSMem???()` prefix, and the services available to the application programmer are described in Appendix A, "µC/OS-III API Reference" on page 453.

Memory management services are enabled at compile time by setting the configuration constant `OS_CFG_MEM_EN` to 1 in `os_cfg.h`.

`OSMemGet()` and `OSMemPut()` can be called from ISRs.

Porting µC/OS-III

This chapter describes how to adapt µC/OS-III to different processors. Adapting µC/OS-III to a microprocessor or a microcontroller is called porting. Most of µC/OS-III is written in C for portability. However, it is still necessary to write processor-specific code in C and assembly language. µC/OS-III manipulates processor registers, which can only be done using assembly language unless the C compiler supports inline assembly language extensions. Porting µC/OS-III to different processors is relatively easy as µC/OS-III was designed to be portable and, since µC/OS-III is similar to µC/OS-II, the user can start from a µC/OS-II port. In fact, this is the easiest way to do a µC/OS-III port.

If there is already a port for the processor to be used, it is not necessary to read this chapter unless, of course, there is an interest in knowing how µC/OS-III processor-specific code works.

µC/OS-III can run on a processor if it satisfies the following general requirements:

- The processor has an ANSI C compiler that generates reentrant code. In fact, the toolchain used must contain an assembler, C compiler and linker/locator. Finding such a toolchain is generally not an issue since there are a number of good toolchains available on the market.

- The processor supports interrupts and can provide an interrupt that occurs at regular intervals (typically between 10 and 1000 Hz). Most processors (especially MCUs) provide timer that can be used for this purpose. Some processors even have dedicated timers for use by an RTOS.

- Interrupts can be disabled and enabled. All current processors that we've worked with offer this. Ideally, the processor allows you to save the current state of the interrupt mask so that it can be restored.

▣ The processor supports a hardware stack that accommodates a fair amount of data (possibly many kilobytes).

▣ The processor has instructions to save and restore the stack pointer and other CPU registers, either on the stack or in memory.

▣ The processor has access to sufficient RAM for µC/OS-III's variables and data structures as well as internal task stacks.

▣ The compiler should support 32-bit data types. For some fast 32-bit processors, the compiler should also support 64-bit data types (typically "`long long`").

Figure 18-1 shows the µC/OS-III architecture and its relationship with other software components and hardware. When using µC/OS-III in an application, the user is responsible for providing application software and the µC/OS-III configuration sections.

Figure 18-1 **µC/OS-III architecture**

F18-1(1)   The port developer is responsible for providing the **µC/OS-III CPU Specific** portion. A µC/OS-III port consists of writing or changing the contents of four kernel-specific files: os_cpu.h, os_cpu_a.asm, os_cpu_a.inc and os_cpu_c.c.

F18-1(2)   A port also involves writing or changing the contents of two CPU specific files: **cpu.h** and **cpu_a.asm**. **cpu_core.c** is generally generic and should not require modifications.

F18-1(3)   A Board Support Package (BSP) is generally necessary to interface μC/OS-III to a timer (which is used for the clock tick) and an interrupt controller.

F18-1(4)   Some semiconductor manufacturers provide source and header files to access on-chip peripherals. These are contained in CPU/MCU specific files. You generally don't need to modify any of these and thus, you can use them as-is.

Porting μC/OS-III is quite straightforward once the subtleties of the target processor and the C compiler/assembler are understood. Depending on the processor, a port consists of writing or changing between 100 and 400 lines of code, which takes a few hours to a few days to accomplish. The easiest thing to do, however, is to modify an existing port from a processor that is similar to the one intended for use.

A μC/OS-III port looks very much like a μC/OS-II port. Since μC/OS-II was ported to well over 45 different CPU architectures it is easy to start from a μC/OS-II port. Converting a μC/OS-II port to μC/OS-III takes approximately an hour. The process is described in Appendix C, "Migrating from μC/OS-II to μC/OS-III" on page 711.

A port involves three aspects: CPU, OS and board-specific code. The board-specific code is often called a *Board Support Package* (BSP) and from μC/OS-III's point of view, requires very little.

In this chapter, we'll present the steps needed to do a port from scratch. Actually, you'll be starting from *templates* files that already contain placeholders for the code you'll need to insert.

The following is the layout for this chapter:

■ Conventions

■ μC/CPU Port Files

■ μC/OS-III Port Files

■ BSP Files

■ Testing a Port

18-1 CONVENTIONS

µC/CPU and µC/OS-III are provided in source form and include template files (C and assembly language) which contain instructions about what code needs to be inserted and where. Specifically, you will need to search the source files for four dollar signs (i.e., $$$$) which are used as placeholders and replace those with the necessary code.

It is assumed that assembly language code use a file extension of **.asm**. Other assembler might require that the extension be **.s** or **.src**. If that's the case with your tools, simply name the assembly language files using the proper extension.

It is assumed that comments in an assembly language file starts with a semicolon, '**;**'.

In assembly language, there are a number of 'directives' that tell the assembler how to process certain pieces of information. Below is a list of such directives and their meaning. The assembler you use may use different syntax for these directives but overall, they should work and mean the same.

- The **PUBLIC** directive indicates that you are declaring a symbol to be globally available. In other words, it's public for all files to see.

- The **EXTERN** directive indicates that the definition of a symbol is found in another file (external to this file).

- The **CODE** directive indicates that what follows needs to be linked with the rest of your executable code. In other words, we are not declaring any variables.

- The **MACRO** directive is used to define an assembly language macro. A macro is basically a series of assembly language instructions that will be replacing the macro name. In other words, when the assembler sees the macro name being invoked in your code, it will replace the macro name with the instructions that are associated with the macro. Macros are useful to avoid repeating sequences of assembly language instructions.

- The **END** directive is generally the last assembly language statement in an assembly language file. The END directive should not appear at the end of a file that defines macros because macro files are generally included in other assembly language files.

18-2 µC/CPU

µC/CPU is a module that provides CPU-specific functionality that is independent of µC/OS-III. Specifically, µC/CPU defines compiler and CPU dependent data types, the word width of the stack, whether the stack grows from high-to-low memory or from low-to-high memory, functions for disabling and enabling interrupts and more. Additional information about this module is provided in the µC/CPU User's Manual (**uC-CPU-Manual.pdf**) which is found in the **\Micrium\Software\uC-CPU\Doc** folder.

Table 18-1 shows the name of µC/CPU files and where they should be placed on the computer used to develop a µC/OS-III-based application. The file names in **bold** are files you will need to create or modify for your own port.

File	Directory
cpu_bsp.c	\Micrium\Software\uC-CPU\BSP\Template\cpu_bsp.c
cpu_def.h	\Micrium\Software\uC-CPU\
cpu_cfg.h	\Micrium\Software\uC-CPU\CFG\Template
cpu_core.c	\Micrium\Software\uC-CPU\
cpu_core.h	\Micrium\Software\uC-CPU\
cpu.h	\Micrium\Software\uC-CPU\<processor>\<compiler>
cpu_c.c	\Micrium\Software\uC-CPU\<processor>\<compiler>
cpu_a.asm	\Micrium\Software\uC-CPU\<processor>\<compiler>

Table 18-1 **µC/CPU files and directories**

<processor> is the name of the processor that the **cpu*.*** files apply to.

<compiler> is the name of the toolchain (compiler, assembler, linker/locator) used. Each has its own directory because they may have different features that makes them different from one another.

18-2-1 CPU_BSP.H

This file contains skeleton functions for **CPU_TS_TmrInit()**, **CPU_TS_TmrRd()** and other time stamp related functions. You can copy this file to your Board Support Package (BSP) directory, modify its content and add it to your build.

18-2-2 CPU_DEF.H

This file should not require any changes. **cpu_def.h** declares **#define** constants that are used by Micriµm software components.

18-2-3 CPU_CFG.H

This is a configuration file to be copied into the product directory and changed based on the options to exercise in µC/CPU. **cpu_cfg.h** is not considered a 'port file' but more an application specific file. However, it's discussed here for completeness. The file contains **#define** constants that may need to be changed based on the desired use of µC/CPU.

CPU_CFG_NAME_EN

This **#define** determines whether you will be assigning a 'name' to the CPU port. This name can then be read by application code.

CPU_CFG_NAME_SIZE

This **#define** specifies the length of the ASCII string used to assign a name to the CPU.

CPU_CFG_TS_32_EN

This **#define** specifies whether 32-bit time stamps are available for this CPU. A 32-bit timestamp is typically the value of a free-running 32-bit counter that is used to make accurate time measurements. The application code can obtain the current value of this free-running timer at any point in time and use such value to determine when an event occurred or, measure the time difference between two events. The free-running counter is generally incremented at a fairly high rate, for example 1 MHz or more.

CPU_CFG_TS_64_EN

This **#define** specifies whether 64-bit time stamps are available for this CPU. A 64-bit timestamp is typically the value of a free-running 64-bit counter (possibly made up by counting overflows of a 32-bit counter) that is used to make accurate time measurements. The application code can obtain the current value of this free-running timer at any point in time and use such value to determine when an event occurred or, measure the time difference between two events. The free-running counter is generally incremented at a fairly high rate, for example 100 MHz or more.

CPU_CFG_TS_TMR_SIZE

This **#define** specifies the size, in number of bytes, of a timestamp. A 32-bit timestamp is 4 bytes long while a 64-bit timestamp is 8 bytes long.

CPU_CFG_INT_DIS_MEAS_EN

This **#define** specifies whether extra code will be inserted to measure interrupt disable time when the code uses **CPU_CRITICAL_ENTER()** and **CPU_CRITICAL_EXIT()**. This extra code obviously adds additional interrupt latency because of the measurement artifacts.

CPU_CFG_INT_DIS_MEAS_OVRHD_NBR

This **#define** is used to account for the interrupt disable time measurement artifacts. The value should typically be 1.

CPU_CFG_LEAD_ZEROS_ASM_PRESENT

This **#define** specifies whether or not your processor offers assembly language instructions to count the number of consecutive zeros from the left most bit position of an integer.

CPU_CFG_TRAIL_ZEROS_ASM_PRESENT

This **#define** specifies whether or not your processor offers assembly language instructions to count the number of consecutive zeros from the right most bit position of an integer.

18-2-4 CPU_CORE.C

This file is generic and does not need to be changed. However it must be included in all builds. **cpu_core.c** defines such functions as **CPU_Init()**, **CPU_CntLeadZeros()**, and code to measure maximum CPU interrupt disable time. A few functions are explained here since they are used in µC/OS-III-based applications.

CPU_Init()

CPU_Init() must be called before calling **OSInit()**.

CPU_CntLeadZeros()

CPU_CntLeadZeros() is used by the µC/OS-III scheduler to find the highest priority ready task (see Chapter 7, "Scheduling" on page 149). **cpu_core.c** implements a count leading zeros in C. However, if the processor used provides a built-in instruction to count leading zeros, define **CPU_CFG_LEAD_ZEROS_ASM_PRESENT**, and replace this function by an assembly language equivalent (in **cpu_a.asm**). It is important to properly declare **CPU_CFG_DATA_SIZE** in **cpu.h** for this function to work.

CPU_TS_TmrFreqSet()

CPU_TS_TmrFreqSet() is a function that needs to be called by the application code to notify µC/CPU about the increment frequency of the timer used for timestamps. In other words, if the timestamp timer is incremented at a rate of 1 MHz then your application code would need to call **CPU_TS_TmrFreqSet()** and pass **1000000**.

CPU_TS_Get32()

CPU_TS_Get32() is a function that returns a 32-bit timestamp. The macro **OS_TS_GET()** (**see os_cpu.h**) generally maps to this function.

18

18-2-5 CPU_CORE.H

This header file is required by **cpu_core.c** to define function prototypes.

Table 18-2 shows the name of µC/CPU 'template' files you should use as a starting point should you decide to start a µC/CPU port from scratch. It's highly recommended that you copy these files to folders that matches the layout shown in Table 18-1. You would then edit these files to build up your own µC/CPU port files. Again, refer to the µC/CPU User's Manual (**uC-CPU-Manual.pdf**) found in **\Micrium\Software\uC-CPU\Doc**.

File	Directory
cpu.h	\Micrium\Software\uC-CPU\Template
cpu_c.c	\Micrium\Software\uC-CPU\Template
cpu_a.asm	\Micrium\Software\uC-CPU\Template

Table 18-2 µC/CPU template files

18-2-6 CPU.H

Many CPUs have different word lengths and **cpu.h** declares a series of type definitions that ensure portability. Specifically, we don't use the C data types **int**, **short**, **long**, **char**, etc. at Micrium. Instead, clearer data types are defined. Consult your compiler documentation to determine whether the standard declarations described below need to be changed for the CPU/compiler you are using. You should note that the **typedef**s below are not all grouped together in **cpu.h** and also, **cpu.h** contains additional comments about these data types.

```
typedef            void        CPU_VOID;
typedef  unsigned  char        CPU_CHAR;
typedef  unsigned  char        CPU_BOOLEAN;
typedef  unsigned  char        CPU_INT08U;
typedef    signed  char        CPU_INT08S;
typedef  unsigned  short       CPU_INT16U;
typedef    signed  short       CPU_INT16S;
typedef  unsigned  int         CPU_INT32U;
typedef    signed  int         CPU_INT32S;
typedef  unsigned  long  long  CPU_INT64U;
typedef    signed  long  long  CPU_INT64S;
typedef            float       CPU_FP32;
typedef            double      CPU_FP64;
typedef  volatile  CPU_INT08U  CPU_REG08;
typedef  volatile  CPU_INT16U  CPU_REG16;
typedef  volatile  CPU_INT32U  CPU_REG32;
typedef  volatile  CPU_INT64U  CPU_REG64;
typedef            void        (*CPU_FNCT_VOID)(void);
typedef            void        (*CPU_FNCT_PTR )(void *);
typedef  CPU_INT32U            CPU_ADDR;
typedef  CPU_INT32U            CPU_DATA;
typedef  CPU_DATA              CPU_ALIGN;
typedef  CPU_ADDR              CPU_SIZE_T;
typedef  CPU_INT32U            CPU_STK;          (1)
typedef  CPU_ADDR              CPU_STK_SIZE;
typedef  CPU_INT16U            CPU_ERR;
typedef  CPU_INT32U            CPU_SR;           (2)
typedef  CPU_INT32U            CPU_TS;           (3)
```

Listing 18-1 **µC/CPU Data Types**

18

L18-1(1)   Especially important for µC/OS-III is the definition of the **CPU_STK** data type, which sets the width of a stack entry. Specifically, is the width of data pushed to and popped from the stack 8 bits, 16 bits, 32 bits or 64 bits?

L18-1(2)   **CPU_SR** defines the data type for the processor's status register (SR) that generally holds the interrupt disable status.

L18-1(3)   The **CPU_TS** is a time stamp used to determine when an operation occurred, or to measure the execution time of code.

cpu.h also declares macros to disable and enable interrupts: CPU_CRITICAL_ENTER() and CPU_CRITICAL_EXIT(), respectively. The documentation in the template file explains how to declare these macros.

cpu.h is also where you need to define configuration constants:

CPU_CFG_ENDIAN_TYPE

This #define specifies whether your CPU is a little-endian machine or a big-endian machine. cpu_def.h offers the following choices:

```
CPU_ENDIAN_TYPE_BIG
CPU_ENDIAN_TYPE_LITTLE
```

CPU_CFG_ADDR_SIZE

This #define specifies the size of an address for the processor, in number of bytes. cpu_def.h offers the following choices:

```
CPU_WORD_SIZE_08
CPU_WORD_SIZE_16
CPU_WORD_SIZE_32
CPU_WORD_SIZE_64
```

CPU_CFG_DATA_SIZE

This #define specifies the 'natural' data width of the processor, in number of bytes. cpu_def.h offers the following choices:

```
CPU_WORD_SIZE_08
CPU_WORD_SIZE_16
CPU_WORD_SIZE_32
CPU_WORD_SIZE_64
```

CPU_DATA_SIZE_MAX

This **#define** specifies the maximum word size of the processor, in number of bytes. **cpu_def.h** offers the following choices:

```
CPU_WORD_SIZE_08
CPU_WORD_SIZE_16
CPU_WORD_SIZE_32
CPU_WORD_SIZE_64
```

CPU_CFG_STK_GROWTH

This **#define** specifies whether the stack grows from high to low memory or from low to high memory addresses. **cpu_def.h** offers the following choices:

```
CPU_STK_GROWTH_LO_TO_HI
CPU_STK_GROWTH_HI_TO_LO
```

CPU_CFG_CRITICAL_METHOD

This **#define** establishes how interrupts will be disabled when processing critical sections. Specifically, will we simply disable interrupts when entering a critical section, irrespective of whether or not interrupts were already disabled? Will we save the status of the interrupt disable state before we disable interrupts? **cpu_def.h** offers the following choices:

```
CPU_CRITICAL_METHOD_INT_DIS_EN
CPU_CRITICAL_METHOD_STATUS_STK
CPU_CRITICAL_METHOD_STATUS_LOCAL
```

cpu.h also declares function prototypes for a number of functions found in either **cpu_c.c** or **cpu_a.asm**

18

18-2-7 CPU_C.C

This is an optional file containing CPU-specific functions to set the interrupt controller, timer prescalers, and more. Most implementations will not contain this file.

18-2-8 CPU_A.ASM

This file contains assembly language code to implement such functions as disabling and enabling interrupts, a more efficient count leading zeros function, and more. At a minimum, this file should implement CPU_SR_Save( ) and CPU_SR_Restore( ).

CPU_SR_Save()

CPU_SR_Save( ) reads the current value of the CPU status register where the current interrupt disable flag resides and returns this value to the caller. However, before returning, CPU_SR_Save( ) must disable all interrupts. CPU_SR_Save( ) is actually called by the macro CPU_CRITICAL_ENTER( ).

CPU_SR_Restore()

CPU_SR_Restore( ) restores the CPU's status register to a previously saved value. CPU_SR_Restore( ) is called from the macro CPU_CRITICAL_EXIT( ).

18-3 µC/OS-III PORT

Table 18-3 shows the name of µC/OS-III files and where they are typically found.

For the purpose of demonstrating how to do a port, we will assume the generic 32-bit processor as described in Chapter 8, "Context Switching" on page 163 and shown in Figure 18-2.

Figure 18-2 **Generic 32-bit CPU**

Our generic CPU contains 16 integer registers (R0 to R15), a separate ISR stack pointer, and a separate status register (SR). Every register is 32 bits wide and each of the 16 integer registers can hold either data or an address. The return address of a function call is placed in the Link Register (**LR**). The program counter (or instruction pointer) is R15 and there are two separate stack pointers labeled R14 and R14'. R14 represents a task stack pointer (TSP), and R14' represents an ISR stack pointer (ISP). The CPU automatically switches to the ISR stack when servicing an exception or interrupt. The task stack is accessible from an ISR (i.e., we can push

367

and pop elements onto the task stack when in an ISR), and the interrupt stack is also accessible from a task. The Status Register (SR) contains the interrupt mask as well as various status such as the Carry, Zero, Sign, Overflow, Parity, etc.

File	Directory
os_cpu.h	\Micrium\Software\uCOS-III\Ports\<processor>\<compiler>\
os_cpu_a.asm	\Micrium\Software\uCOS-III\Ports\<processor>\<compiler>\
os_cpu_a.inc	\Micrium\Software\uCOS-III\Ports\<processor>\<compiler>
os_cpu_c.c	\Micrium\Software\uCOS-III\Ports\<processor>\<compiler>\

Table 18-3 **µC/OS-III files and directories**

Here, **<processor>** is the name of the processor that the **os_cpu*.*** files apply to, and **<compiler>** is the name of the compiler that these files assume because of the different assembly language directives that different toolchain uses.

Table 18-4 shows where you can find template files that will help you create a µC/OS-III port from scratch. You would simply copy these files in a folder specific to your processor/compiler as shown in Table 18-3 and then change the contents of these files per your processor/compiler.

File	Directory
os_cpu.h	\Micrium\Software\uCOS-III\Ports\Template\
os_cpu_a.asm	\Micrium\Software\uCOS-III\Ports\Template\
os_cpu_a.inc	\Micrium\Software\uCOS-III\Ports\Template\
os_cpu_c.c	\Micrium\Software\uCOS-III\Ports\Template\

Table 18-4 **µC/OS-III template files**

18-3-1 OS_CPU.H

OS_TASK_SW()

OS_TASK_SW() is a macro that is called by OSSched() to perform a task-level context switch. The macro can translate directly to a call to OSCtxSw(), trigger a software interrupt, or a TRAP. If a software interrupt or TRAP is used then you would most likely need to add the address of OSCtxSw() in the interrupt vector table. The choice depends on the CPU architecture.

OS_TS_GET()

OS_TS_GET() is a macro that obtains the current time stamp. It is expected that the time stamp is type CPU_TS, which is typically declared as at least a 32-bit value.

OSCtxSw(), OSIntCtxSw() and OSStartHighRdy()

os_cpu.h declares function prototypes for OSCtxSw(), OSIntCtxSw(), OSStartHighRdy() and possibly other functions required by the port.

18-3-2 OS_CPU_C.C

The functions are described in Appendix A on page 453. **os_cpu_c.c** can declare any functions needed by the port, however the functions described below are mandatory. These functions are already implemented in the template file, but those can certainly be extended as needed. You should not have to change this file unless you have specific requirements.

OSIdleTaskHook()

This function is called repeatedly when µC/OS-III doesn't have any task ready-to-run. The port implemented might choose to put the processor in low power mode if the product being designed is battery operated. However, it would be preferable to defer this choice to the application level. You can do this by putting the processor in low power mode in a function called **App_OS_IdleTaskHook()** and let the application decide whether or not it is appropriate to place the processor in low power mode. The template file contains the following code:

```
void  OSIdleTaskHook (void)
{
#if OS_CFG_APP_HOOKS_EN > 0u
    if (OS_AppIdleTaskHookPtr != (OS_APP_HOOK_VOID)0) {
        (*OS_AppIdleTaskHookPtr)();
    }
#endif
}
```

Listing 18-2 **Typical OSIdleTaskHook()**

OSInitHook()

This function is called by **OSInit()** at the very beginning of **OSInit()**. This is done to allow the port implemented to add functionality to the port while hiding the details from the µC/OS-III user. For one thing, the port implementer could setup an ISR stack in **OSInitHook()**. The template file contains the following code:

```
void  OSInitHook (void)
{
}
```

Listing 18-3 **Typical OSInitHook()**

OSStatTaskHook()

This function is called when the statistic task executes. This hook allows the port developer the opportunity to add his or her own statistics. The template file contains the following code:

```
void  OSStatTaskHook (void)
{
#if OS_CFG_APP_HOOKS_EN > 0u
    if (OS_AppStatTaskHookPtr != (OS_APP_HOOK_VOID)0) {
        (*OS_AppStatTaskHookPtr)();
    }
#endif
}
```

Listing 18-4 **Typical OSStatTaskHook()**

OSTaskCreateHook()

This function is called by **OSTaskCreate()** and is passed the address of the **OS_TCB** of the newly created task. **OSTaskCreateHook()** is called by **OSTaskCreate()** after initializing the **OS_TCB** fields and setting up the stack frame for the task. The template file contains the following code:

```
void  OSTaskCreateHook (OS_TCB  *p_tcb)
{
#if OS_CFG_APP_HOOKS_EN > 0u
    if (OS_AppTaskCreateHookPtr != (OS_APP_HOOK_TCB)0) {
        (*OS_AppTaskCreateHookPtr)(p_tcb);
    }
#else
    (void)p_tcb;
}
```

Listing 18-5 **Typical OSTaskCreateHook()**

18

371

OSTaskDelHook()

This function is called by **OSTaskDel()** after the task to delete has been removed either from the ready list or a wait list. The template file contains the following code:

```
void  OSTaskDelHook (OS_TCB  *p_tcb)
{
#if OS_CFG_APP_HOOKS_EN > 0u
    if (OS_AppTaskDelHookPtr != (OS_APP_HOOK_TCB)0) {
        (*OS_AppTaskDelHookPtr)(p_tcb);
    }
#else
    (void)p_tcb;
#endif
}
```

Listing 18-6 **Typical OSTaskDelHook()**

OSTaskReturnHook()

This function is called by **OS_TaskReturn()** if the user accidentally returns from the task code. The template file contains the following code:

```
void  OSTaskReturnHook (OS_TCB  *p_tcb)
{
#if OS_CFG_APP_HOOKS_EN > 0u
    if (OS_AppTaskReturnHookPtr != (OS_APP_HOOK_TCB)0) {
        (*OS_AppTaskReturnHookPtr)(p_tcb);
    }
#else
    (void)p_tcb;
}
```

Listing 18-7 **Typical OSTaskReturnHook()**

OSTaskStkInit()

OSTaskStkInit() is called by OSTaskCreate() and is one of the most difficult port functions to create because it establishes the stack frame of every task created. The template file contains the following code:

```
CPU_STK  *OSTaskStkInit (OS_TASK_PTR    p_task,
                         void           *p_arg,
                         CPU_STK        *p_stk_base,
                         CPU_STK        *p_stk_limit,
                         CPU_STK_SIZE   stk_size,
                         OS_OPT         opt)
{
    CPU_STK  *p_stk;


    (void)opt;

    p_stk    = &p_stk_base[stk_size];             (1)

    *--p_stk = (CPU_STK)0x00000000u;              (2)
    *--p_stk = (CPU_STK)p_task;                   (3)
    *--p_stk = (CPU_STK)p_arg;                    (4)
    *--p_stk = (CPU_STK)0x01010101u;              (5)
    *--p_stk = (CPU_STK)0x02020202u;
    *--p_stk = (CPU_STK)0x03030303u;
    *--p_stk = (CPU_STK)0x04040404u;
    *--p_stk = (CPU_STK)0x05050505u;
    *--p_stk = (CPU_STK)0x06060606u;
    *--p_stk = (CPU_STK)0x07070707u;
    *--p_stk = (CPU_STK)0x08080808u;
    *--p_stk = (CPU_STK)0x09090909u;
    *--p_stk = (CPU_STK)0x10101010u;
    *--p_stk = (CPU_STK)0x11111111u;
    *--p_stk = (CPU_STK)0x12121212u;
    *--p_stk = (CPU_STK)OS_TaskReturn;            (6)

    return (p_stk);                               (7)
}
```

Listing 18-8 **Generic OSTaskStkInit()**

L18-8(1)   You need to initialize the top-of-stack. For our 'generic 32-bit CPU, the top-of-stack (TOS) points at one location beyond the area reserved for the stack. This is because we will decrement the TOS pointer before storing a value into the stack.

373

If the stack for the processor grew from low memory to high memory, most likely you would have setup the TOS to point at the base of the memory or, &p_stk_base[0].

L18-8(2)   Since we are simulating an interrupt and the stacking of registers in the same order as an ISR would place them on the stack, we start by putting the **SR** (Status Register, also called the Program Status Word) of the CPU onto the stack first.

Also, the value stored at this location must be such that, once restored into the CPU, the **SR** must enable ALL interrupts. Here we assumed that a value of **0x00000000** would do this. However, you need to check with the processor you are using to find out how this works on that processor.

L18-8(3)   The address of the task code is then placed onto the next stack location. This way, when you perform a return from interrupt (or exception) instruction the PC will automatically be loaded with the address of the task to run.

L18-8(4)   You should recall that a task is passed an argument, **p_arg**. **p_arg** is a pointer to some user define storage or function and its use is application specific. In the assumptions above, we indicated that a function called with a single argument gets this argument passed in **R0**. You will need to check the compiler documentation to determine where '**p_arg**' is placed for your processor.

L18-8(5)   The remaining registers are placed onto the stack. You will notice that we initialized the value of those registers with a hexadecimal number that corresponds to the register number. In other words, **R12** should have the value **0x12121212** when the task starts, **R11** should have the value **0x11111111** when the task starts and so on. This makes it easy to determine whether the stack frame was setup properly when you test the port. You would simply look at the register contents with a debugger and confirm that all registers have the proper values.

L18-8(6)   Here we place the return address of the task into the location where the Link Register (**LR**) will be retrieved from. In this case, we force the return address to actually be **OS_TaskReturn()** allowing µC/OS-III to catch a task that is attempting to return. You should recall that this is not allowed with µC/OS-III.

L18-8(7) **OSTaskStkInit()** needs to return the new top-of-stack location. In this case, the top-of-stack points at the last element placed onto the stack.

Figure 18-3 shows how the stack frame looks like just before the function returns. **OSTaskCreate()** will actually save the new top-of-stack (**p_stk**) into the **OS_TCB** of the task being created.

Figure 18-3 **Stack frame created by OSTaskStkInit()**

OSTaskSwHook()

The typical code for μC/OS-III's context switch hook is shown below. What `OSTaskSwHook()` does is highly dependent on a number of configuration options.

```
void  OSTaskSwHook (void)
{
#if OS_CFG_TASK_PROFILE_EN > 0u
    CPU_TS  ts;
#endif
#ifdef  CPU_CFG_INT_DIS_MEAS_EN
    CPU_TS  int_dis_time;
#endif


#if OS_CFG_APP_HOOKS_EN > 0u
    if (OS_AppTaskSwHookPtr != (OS_APP_HOOK_VOID)0) {                    (1)
        (*OS_AppTaskSwHookPtr)();
    }
#endif

#if OS_CFG_TASK_PROFILE_EN > 0u
    ts = OS_TS_GET();                                                    (2)
    if (OSTCBCurPtr != OSTCBHighRdyPtr) {
        OSTCBCurPtr->CyclesDelta  = ts - OSTCBCurPtr->CyclesStart;
        OSTCBCurPtr->CyclesTotal += (OS_CYCLES)OSTCBCurPtr->CyclesDelta;
    }

    OSTCBHighRdyPtr->CyclesStart = ts;
#endif

#ifdef  CPU_CFG_INT_DIS_MEAS_EN
    int_dis_time = CPU_IntDisMeasMaxCurReset();                         (3)
    if (OSTCBCurPtr->IntDisTimeMax < int_dis_time) {
        OSTCBCurPtr->IntDisTimeMax = int_dis_time;
    }
#endif

#if OS_CFG_SCHED_LOCK_TIME_MEAS_EN > 0u
    if (OSTCBCurPtr->SchedLockTimeMax < OSSchedLockTimeMaxCur) {        (4)
        OSTCBCurPtr->SchedLockTimeMax = OSSchedLockTimeMaxCur;
    }
    OSSchedLockTimeMaxCur = (CPU_TS)0;
#endif
}
```

Listing 18-9 **Typical OSTaskSwHook()**

L18-9(1)   If the application code defined a hook function to be called during a context switch then this function is called first. You application hook function can assume that **OSTCBCurPtr** points to the **OS_TCB** of the task being switched out while **OSTCBHighRdyPtr** points to the **OS_TCB** of the task being switched in.

L18-9(2)   **OSTaskSwHook()** then computes the amount of time the current task ran. However, this includes the execution time of all the ISRs that happened while the task was running.

We then take a timestamp to mark the beginning of the task being switched in.

L18-9(3)   **OSTaskSwHook()** then stores the highest interrupt disable time into the **OS_TCB** of the task being switched out. This allows a debugger or µC/Probe to display maximum interrupt disable time on a per-task basis.

L18-9(4)   **OSTaskSwHook()** then captures the highest scheduler lock time and stores that in the **OS_TCB** of the task being switched out.

OSTimeTickHook()

This function is called by **OSTimeTick()** and is called before any other code is executed in **OSTimeTick()**. The template file contains the following code. If the application code defines an application hook function then it is called as shown.

```
void  OSTimeTickHook (void)
{
#if OS_CFG_APP_HOOKS_EN > 0u
    if (OS_AppTimeTickHookPtr != (OS_APP_HOOK_VOID)0) {
        (*OS_AppTimeTickHookPtr)();
    }
#endif
}
```

Listing 18-10 **Typical OSTimeTickHook()**

18-3-3 OS_CPU_A.ASM

This file contains the implementation of the following assembly language functions:

OSStartHighRdy()

This function is called by OSStart() to start multitasking. OSStart() will have determined the highest priority task (OSTCBHighRdyPtr will point to the OS_TCB of that task) that was created prior to calling OSStart() and will start executing that task. The pseudo code for this function is shown below (the C-like code needs to be implemented in assembly language):

```
OSStartHighRdy:
    OSTaskSwHook();
    SP = OSTCBHighRdyPtr->StkPtr;                (1)
    OS_CTX_RESTORE                              (2)
    Return from Interrupt/Exception;            (3)
```

Listing 18-11 **OSStartHighRdy() Pseudo Code**

L18-11(1)   The Stack Pointer (SP) for the first task to execute is retrieved from the OS_TCB of the highest priority task that was created prior to calling OSStart(). Figure 18-4 shows the stack frame as pointed to by OSTCBHighRdy->StkPtr.

L18-11(2)   OS_CTX_RESTORE is a macro (see os_cpu_a.inc) that restores the context of the CPU (R0 through R13) from the new task's stack.

L18-11(3)   The Return from Interrupt/Exception restores the Program Counter (PC) and the Status Register (SR) in a single instruction. At this point, the task will start executing. In fact, the task will think it was called by another function and thus, will receive 'p_arg' as its argument. Of course, the task *must not* return.

R13 (LR) = OS_TaskReturn	◄──────── OSTCBHighRdy-StkPtr
R12 = 0x12121212	
R11 = 0x11111111	
R10 = 0x10101010	
R9 = 0x09090909	
R8 = 0x08080808	
R7 = 0x07070707	
R6 = 0x06060606	
R5 = 0x05050505	
R4 = 0x04040404	
R3 = 0x03030303	
R2 = 0x02020202	
R1 = 0x01010101	
R0 = p_arg	
R15 (PC) = p_task	
SR = 0x00000000	

High Memory

Figure 18-4 **Stack Frame pointed to by OSTCBHighRdy->StkPtr**

OSCtxSw()

This function implements the task level context switch which is invoked by the OS_TASK_SW() macro declared in **os_cpu.h**. The pseudo code for this function is shown below (the C-like code needs to be implemented in assembly language). You should also refer to Chapter 8, on page 166.

```
OSCtxSw:                                           (1)
    OS_CTX_SAVE                                    (2)
    OSTCBCurPtr->StkPtr = SP;                      (3)
    OSTaskSwHook();
    OSPrioCur   = OSPrioHighRdy;
    OSTCBCurPtr = OSTCBHighRdyPtr;
    SP          = OSTCBCurPtr->StkPtr;             (4)
    OS_CTX_RESTORE                                 (5)
    Return from Interrupt/Exception;               (6)
```

Listing 18-12 **OSCtxSw() Pseudo Code**

379

L18-12(1)   OSCtxSw() is invoked by OS_TASK_SW() which is typically implemented as a *software interrupt* instruction or, a *trap* instruction. These types of instructions generally simulate the behavior of an interrupt, but is synchronous with the code. OSCtxSw() is thus the *entry point* for this instruction. In other words, if a software interrupt or TRAP is used then you would most likely need to add the address of OSCtxSw() in the interrupt vector table.

L18-12(2)   OS_CTX_SAVE is a macro (see os_cpu_a.inc) that saves the CPU context onto the current task's stack. For our generic 32-bit CPU, OS_CTX_SAVE would push R0 through R13 onto the stack, in that order.

L18-12(3)   OSCtxSw() then needs to save the current top-of-stack pointer (i.e. R14 or SP) into the OS_TCB of the current task.

L18-12(4)   The stack pointer for the new task is retrieved from the OS_TCB of the new current task.

L18-12(5)   OS_CTX_RESTORE is a macro (see os_cpu_a.inc) that restores the context of the CPU from the new task's stack. For our generic 32-bit CPU, OS_CTX_RESTORE would pop CPU registers R13 through R0 from the stack, in that order.

L18-12(6)   The Return from Interrupt/Exception restores the Program Counter (PC) and the Status Register (SR) in a single instruction. At this point, the new task will resume execution, exactly where it was preempted.

OSIntCtxSw()

This function implements the interrupt level context switch which is called by `OSIntExit()` (see **os_core.c**). The pseudo code for this function is shown below (the C-like code needs to be implemented in assembly language). Refer also to Chapter 8, on page 168.

```
OSIntCtxSw:                              (1)
    OSTaskSwHook();
    OSPrioCur   = OSPrioHighRdy;
    OSTCBCurPtr = OSTCBHighRdyPtr;
    SP          = OSTCBCurPtr->StkPtr;   (2)
    OS_CTX_RESTORE                       (3)
    Return from Interrupt/Exception;     (4)
```

Listing 18-13 **OSIntCtxSw() Pseudo Code**

L18-13(1)   `OSIntCtxSw()` is called by `OSIntExit()` at the end of all nested ISRs. The ISR is assumed to have saved the context of the interrupted task onto that task's stack. Also, the ISR is assumed to have saved the new top-of-stack of the interrupted task into the **OS_TCB** of that task.

L18-13(2)   The stack pointer for the new task is then retrieved from the **OS_TCB** of the new current task.

L18-13(3)   **OS_CTX_RESTORE** is a macro (see **os_cpu_a.inc**) that restores the context of the CPU from the new task's stack. For our generic 32-bit CPU, **OS_CTX_RESTORE** would pop CPU registers **R13** through **R0** from the stack, in that order.

L18-13(4)   The Return from Interrupt/Exception restores the Program Counter (**PC**) and the Status Register (**SR**) in a single instruction. At this point, the new task will resume execution, exactly where it was preempted.

OSTickISR()

This function may or may not reside in **os_cpu_a.asm**. It's presence in **os_cpu_a.asm** depends on whether the tick ISR is generic for the CPU and, whether it needs to be implemented in assembly language. In other words, if the CPU or MCU has a dedicated timer that can be assigned for the tick ISR so that it's the same, irrespective of the target application then **OSTickISR()** can be placed in **os_cpu_a.asm**. The pseudo code for this function is shown below (the C-like code needs to be implemented in assembly language). You should note that all ISRs should be modeled after **OSTickISR()**.

```
OSTickISR:                                          (1)
    OS_CTX_SAVE                                      (2)
    Disable Interrupts;                              (3)
    OSIntNestingCtr++;                               (4)
    if (OSIntNestingCtr == 1) {                      (5)
        OSTCBCurPtr->StkPtr = SP;
    }
    Clear tick interrupt;                            (6)
    OSTimeTick();                                    (7)
    OSIntExit();                                     (8)
    OS_CTX_RESTORE                                   (9)
    Return from Interrupt/Exception;                 (10)
```

Listing 18-14 **OSTickISR() Pseudo Code**

L18-14(1)   **OSTickISR()** is generally invoked automatically by the interrupt controller when the tick interrupt occurs. Assuming again our generic 32-bit CPU, it's assumed here that the **SR** and **PC** of the interrupted task are pushed automatically onto the stack of the interrupted task.

L18-14(2)   Again, **OS_CTX_SAVE** saves the CPU context onto the current task's stack. For our generic 32-bit CPU, **OS_CTX_SAVE** would push **R0** through **R13** onto the stack, in that order.

L18-14(3)   Interrupts should be disabled here. On some processors, interrupts are automatically disabled when the processor accepts the interrupt. Some processors support multiple interrupt levels. In fact, some interrupts are allowed to make kernel calls while others are not. Typically, interrupts that do not make kernel calls (called *Non-Kernel Aware Interrupts*) would generally be high priority interrupts and kernel aware interrupts would all be grouped (in priority) below these. For example, if a processor has **16** different interrupt levels and level **0** is the lowest priority interrupt then, all kernel aware interrupts would be assigned from 0 to some number **N** (let's say **12**) and **N+1** to **15** would be assigned to be non-kernel aware interrupts.

L18-14(4)   **OSTickISR()** then needs to increment the interrupt nesting counter. This tells µC/OS-III that the code is servicing an interrupt. The nesting counter indicates how many levels of interrupts we are currently servicing (in case the application supports nested interrupts).

L18-14(5)   If this interrupt interrupts a task then we need to save the stack pointer of that task into the **OS_TCB** of that task.

L18-14(6)   You need to clear the interrupting device so that it doesn't re-issue the same interrupt upon returning from interrupts. This can be done here or, in the device handler (see below).

L18-14(7)   At this point, **OSTickISR()** calls **OSTimeTick()** which is reponsible for notifying the tick task that a tick occurred.

             If you model your ISR like **OSTickISR()** then you would call your own C function to service the interrupting device.

L18-14(8)   **OSIntExit()** is then called at the end of the ISR to notify µC/OS-III that you are done processing the ISR. µC/OS-III decrements the nesting counter and if **OSIntNestingCtr** reaches **0**, µC/OS-III knows it's returning to task level code. So, if the ISR made a more important task ready-to-run (more important than the interrupted task), µC/OS-III will context switch to that task instead of returning to the interrupted task.

L18-14(9)   If the interrupted task is still the most important task then **OSIntExit()** returns and the ISR will needs to restore the saved registers. **OS_CTX_RESTORE** does just that. For our generic 32-bit CPU, **OS_CTX_RESTORE** would pop CPU registers **R13** through **R0** from the stack, in that order.

L18-14(10) Finally, the Return from Interrupt/Exception restores the Program Counter (**PC**) and the Status Register (**SR**) in a single instruction. At this point, the interrupted task will resume execution, exactly where it was interrupted.

It is actually possible to simplify the code for **OSTickISR()** or any of your ISRs. Notice that the code at the beginning and end of the ISR is common for all ISRs. Because of that, it's possible to create two assembly language macros, **OS_ISR_ENTER** and **OS_ISR_EXIT** in **os_cpu_a.inc**. The new **OSTickISR()** code would now look as shown below:

```
OSTickISR:
    OS_ISR_ENTER
    Clear tick interrupt;
    OSTimeTick();
    OS_ISR_EXIT
```

Listing 18-15 **OSTickISR() Pseudo Code using the OS_ISR_ENTER and OS_ISR_EXIT macros**

18-3-4 OS_CPU_A.INC

This file contains the implementation of assembly language macros that are used to simplify the implementation of **os_cpu_a.asm**. A macro replaces many assembly language instructions with a single macro invocation.

OS_CTX_SAVE

This macro is used to save the CPU context onto the current stack. **OS_CTX_SAVE** needs to save the CPU registers in the same order as they are pushed in **OSTaskStkInit()** which is described later. **OS_CTX_SAVE** only saves the CPU registers that are not automatically saved by the CPU when the CPU accepts an interrupt. In other words, if the CPU automatically saves the **PSW** and **PC** onto the stack upon initiating an ISR then **OS_CTX_SAVE** only needs to save the remaining CPU registers.

```
OS_CTX_SAVE
    Save all the CPU registers onto the current task stack
    (in the same order as in OSTaskStkInit())
```

Listing 18-16 **OS_CTX_SAVE macro Pseudo Code**

Assuming our generic 32-bit CPU, **OS_CTX_SAVE** would be implemented as follows.

```
OS_CTX_SAVE  MACRO
    PUSH R0
    PUSH R1
    PUSH R2
    PUSH R3
    PUSH R4
    PUSH R5
    PUSH R6
    PUSH R7
    PUSH R8
    PUSH R9
    PUSH R10
    PUSH R11
    PUSH R12
    PUSH R13
ENDM
```

Listing 18-17 **OS_CTX_SAVE assuming generic 32-bit CPU**

OS_CTX_RESTORE

This macro is used to reverse the process done by **OS_CTX_SAVE**. In other words, **OS_CTX_RESTORE** loads the CPU registers from the stack in the reverse order..

```
OS_CTX_RESTORE
    Restore all the CPU registers from the new task's stack
      (in the reverse order that they were in OSTaskStkInit())
```

Listing 18-18 **OS_CTX_SAVE macro Pseudo Code**

Assuming our generic 32-bit CPU, **OS_CTX_RESTORE** would be implemented as follows.

```
OS_CTX_RESTORE  MACRO
    POP R13
    POP R12
    POP R11
    POP R10
    POP R9
    POP R8
    POP R7
    POP R6
    POP R5
    POP R4
    POP R3
    POP R2
    POP R1
    POP R0
ENDM
```

Listing 18-19 **OS_CTX_RESTORE assuming generic 32-bit CPU**

OS_ISR_ENTER

This macro allows you to simplify your assembly language ISRs. OS_ISR_ENTER is basically the first line of code you would add to the ISR. The pseudo code for OS_ISR_ENTER is shown below.

```
OS_ISR_ENTER
    OS_CTX_SAVE
    OSIntNestingCtr++;
    if (OSIntNestingCtr == 1) {
        OSTCBCurPtr->StkPtr = SP;
    }
```

Listing 18-20 **OS_ISR_ENTER macro Pseudo Code**

Assuming our generic 32-bit CPU, OS_ISR_ENTER would be implemented as follows. You should note that the C-like code would actually be implemented in assembly language.

```
OS_ISR_ENTER  MACRO
    PUSH  R0
    PUSH  R1
    PUSH  R2
    PUSH  R3
    PUSH  R4
    PUSH  R5
    PUSH  R6
    PUSH  R7
    PUSH  R8
    PUSH  R9
    PUSH  R10
    PUSH  R11
    PUSH  R12
    PUSH  R13
    OSIntNestingCtr++;
    if (OSIntNestingCtr == 1) {
        OSTCBCurPtr->StkPtr = SP;
    }
ENDM
```

Listing 18-21 **OS_ISR_ENTER assuming generic 32-bit CPU**

18

387

OS_ISR_EXIT

This macro allows you to simplify your assembly language ISRs. OS_ISR_EXIT is basically the last line of code you would add to the ISR. The pseudo code for OS_ISR_EXIT is shown below.

```
OS_ISR_EXIT
    OSIntExit();
    OS_CTX_RESTORE
    Return from Interrupt/Exception
```

Listing 18-22 **OS_ISR_EXIT macro Pseudo Code**

Assuming our generic 32-bit CPU, OS_ISR_EXIT would be implemented as follows. You should note that the C-like code would actually be implemented in assembly language.

```
OS_ISR_EXIT  MACRO
    OSIntExit();
    POP R13
    POP R12
    POP R11
    POP R10
    POP R9
    POP R8
    POP R7
    POP R6
    POP R5
    POP R4
    POP R3
    POP R2
    POP R1
    POP R0
    Return from Interrupt/Exception;
ENDM
```

Listing 18-23 **OS_ISR_EXIT assuming generic 32-bit CPU**

18-4 BOARD SUPPORT PACKAGE (BSP)

A board support package refers to code associated with the actual evaluation board or the target board used. For example, the BSP defines functions to turn LEDs on or off, reads push-button switches, initializes peripheral clocks, etc., providing nearly any functionality to multiple products/projects.

Names of typical BSP files include:

```
bsp.c
bsp.h
bsp_int.c
bsp_int.h
```

All files are generally placed in a directory as follows:

\Micrium\Software\EvalBoards\<manufacturer>\<board_name>\<compiler>\BSP\

Here, <manufacturer> is the name of the evaluation board or target board manufacturer, <board_name> is the name of the evaluation or target board and <compiler> is the name of the compiler that these files assume, although most should be portable to different compilers since the BSP is typically written in C.

18-4-1 BSP.C AND BSP.H

These files normally contain functions and their definitions such as:

BSP_Init()

This function is called by application code to initialize the BSP functionality. BSP_Init() could initialize I/O ports, setup timers, serial ports, SPI ports and so on.

BSP_LED_On(), BSP_LED_Off() and BSP_LED_Toggle()

This code allows the user to control LEDs by referring to them as 'logical' devices as opposed to controlling ports directly from application code. BSP_LED_On() allows your application to turn a specific LED, BSP_LED_Off() turn off a specific LED and BSP_LED_Toggle() to change the state of a specific LED. The argument to these functions is an ID number 0..N. Each ID refers to a specific LED on the board. It's up to the BSP implementer to define which ID corresponds to what LED. By convention, however, ID 0 refers to all LEDs. In other words, you can turn on all LEDs on the board by calling BSP_LED_On(0).

BSP_PB_Rd()

BSP_PB_Rd() is a function that reads the state of push button switches on the board. Each push button is identified by an ID. It's up to the BSP developer to assign the IDs to the push button switches.

Note: It is up to you to decide if the functions in this file start with the prefix BSP_. In other words, you can use LED_On() and PB_Rd() if this is clearer to you. However, it is a good practice to encapsulate this type of functionality in a BSP type file.

CPU_TS_TmrInit()

CPU_TS_TmrInit() is a function that μC/CPU expects to have in order to initialize the timer that will be used for timestamps. Note that a skeleton of CPU_TS_TmrInit() is can be found in the template file \Micrium\Software\uC-CPU\BSP\Template\cpu_bsp.c.

CPU_TS_TmrRd()

CPU_TS_TmrRd() is responsible for reading the value of a 16-, 32- or 64-bit free-running timer. CPU_TS_TmrRd() returns a CPU_TS_TMR data type which can be configured to be either a CPU_TS32 or a CPU_TS64. If a 16-bit timer is used, the implementer of this function must accumulate 16-bit values into a 32-bit accumulator in order to always have 32-bit timestamps. The timer used for timestamps must count up (0, 1, 2, 3, ...) and must rollover automatically when the maximum count for the resolution of the timer is reached. In other words, a 16-bit counter should go from 0x0000 to 0xFFFF and then roll back to 0x0000. Note that a skeleton of CPU_TS_TmrRd() is can be found in the template file \Micrium\Software\uC-CPU\BSP\Template\cpu_bsp.c.

18-4-2 BSP_INT.C AND BSP_INT.H

These files are typically used to declare interrupt controller related functions. For example, code that enables or disables specific interrupts from the interrupt controller, acknowledges the interrupt controller, and code to handle all interrupts if the CPU vectors to a single location when an interrupt occurs (see Chapter 9, "Interrupt Management" on page 173).

The pseudo code below shows an example of the latter.

```
void  BSP_IntHandler (void)                                  (1)
{
   CPU_FNCT_VOID   p_isr;

   while (interrupts being asserted) {                       (2)
      p_isr = Read the highest priority interrupt from the controller; (3)
      if (p_isr != (CPU_FNCT_VOID)0) {                       (4)
         (*p_isr)();                                         (5)
      }
      Acknowledge interrupt controller;                      (6)
   }
}
```

Listing 18-24 **Generic Interrupt Handler**

L18-24(1)   Here we assume that the handler for the interrupt controller is called from the assembly language code that saves the CPU registers upon entering an ISR (see Chapter 9, "Interrupt Management" on page 173).

L18-24(2)   The handler queries the interrupt controller to ask it for the address of the ISR that needs to be executed in response to the interrupt. Some interrupt controllers return an integer value that corresponds to the source. In this case, you would simply use this integer value as an index into a table (RAM or ROM) where those vectors are placed.

L18-24(3)   The interrupt controller is then asked to provide the highest priority interrupt pending. It is assumed here that the CPU may receive multiple simultaneous interrupts (or closely spaced interrupts), and that the interrupt controller will prioritize the interrupts received. The CPU will then service each interrupt in priority order instead of on a first-come basis. However, the scheme used greatly depends on the interrupt controller itself.

L18-24(4)   Here we check to ensure that the interrupt controller did not return a **NULL** pointer.

L18-24(5)   We then simply call the ISR associated with the interrupt device.

L18-24(6) The interrupt controller generally needs to be acknowledged so that it knows that the interrupt presented is taken care of.

18-5 TESTING A PORT

Testing a port is fairly easy to do if you have the proper tools. Here we will assume that you have access to a good debugging tool, preferably built around an Integrated Development Environment (IDE). The debugger should allow you to load your code into your target, single step through your code, set breakpoint, examine CPU registers, look at memory contents and more.

18-5-1 CREATING A SIMPLE TEST PROJECT

At this point, you should have the μC/CPU and μC/OS-III port file created. To test the port files, you need to create a simple project. When you download and unzip the μC/OS-III source code you will have a directory structure similar to what is shown on the next page. When you see 'My' in front of a directory name it means a directory you will need to create for your tests of the port.

The filenames that are in **bold** are the files you will need to provide for the tests. As you will see, you can start with the template files provided with μC/CPU and μC/OS-III with little or no modifications.

```
\Micrium
  \Software
    \EvalBoards
      \MyBoardManufacturer
        \MyBoardName
          \MyToolsName
            \MyBSP
              bsp.c                <- Created in Section 18-4
              bsp.h                <- Created in Section 18-4
              bsp_int.c            <- Created in Section 18-4
            \MyTest          (1)
              app.c          (2)
              includes.h     (3)
              app_cfg.h      (4)
              app_vect.c     (5)
              cpu_cfg.h      (6) <- Copied from \Micrium\Software\uC-CPU\Cfg\Template
              lib_cfg.h          <- Copied from \Micrium\Software\uC-LIB\Cfg\Template
              os_app_hooks.c     <- Copied from \Micrium\Software\uCOS-III\Cfg\Template
              os_app_hooks.h     <- Copied from \Micrium\Software\uCOS-III\Cfg\Template
              os_cfg.h       (7) <- Copied from \Micrium\Software\uCOS-III\Cfg\Template
              os_cfg_app.h       <- Copied from \Micrium\Software\uCOS-III\Cfg\Template
              os_type.h          <- Copied from \Micrium\Software\uCOS-III\Source
\Micrium
  \Software
    \uC-CPU
      cpu_core.c
      cpu_core.h
      cpu_def.h
      \MyCPUName
        \MyToolsName
          cpu.h                  <- Created in Section 18-2
          cpu_a.asm              <- Created in Section 18-2
\Micrium
  \Software
    \uC-LIB
      lib_ascii.c
      lib_ascii.h
      lib_def.h
      lib_math.c
      lib_math.h
      lib_mem.c
      lib_mem.h
      lib_str.c
      lib_str.h
```

18

```
\Micrium
  \Software
    \uC/OS-III
      \Cfg
        os_app_hooks.c
        os_app_hooks.h
        os_cfg.h
        os_cfg_app.h
      \Ports
        \MyCPUName
          \MyToolsName
            os_cpu.h              <- Created in Section 18-3
            os_cpu_a.asm          <- Created in Section 18-3
            os_cpu_a.inc          <- Created in Section 18-3
            os_cpu_c.c       (8) <- Created in Section 18-3
      \Source
        os.h
        os_cfg_app.c
        os_core.c
        os_dbg.c
        os_flag.c
        os_int.c
        os_mem.c
        os_msg.c
        os_mutex.c
        os_pend_multi.c
        os_prio.c
        os_q.c
        os_sem.c
        os_stat.c
        os_task.c
        os_tick.c
        os_time.c
        os_tmr.c
        os_type.h
        os_var.c
```

Listing 18-25 **Test Code Directory Structure**

L18-25(1)   **MyTest** is the name of the directory that will contain the project source files.

L18-25(2)   **app.c** is the test file that contains **main()** and should look as shown below.

```
/* app.c */

#include  "includes.h"

void  main (void)
{
    OS_ERR  err;

    OSInit(&err);
    OSStart(&err);
}
```

L18-25(3)   **includes.h** is a master include file that **app.c** and other files assume. The contents of this file should be as shown below.

```
/* includes.h */

#include  <stdarg.h>
#include  <stdio.h>
#include  <stdlib.h>
#include  <math.h>

#include  <cpu.h>
#include  <lib_def.h>
#include  <lib_ascii.h>
#include  <lib_math.h>
#include  <lib_mem.h>
#include  <lib_str.h>

#include  <app_cfg.h>
#include  <os_cfg_app.h>
#include  <bsp.h>

#include  <os.h>
```

L18-25(4)   **app_cfg.**h must exist but should be an 'empty' file for now.

L18-25(5)   **app_vect.c** is a file that contains the processor's interrupt vector table. The file must exist but it is should be 'empty' for now.

395

L18-25(6)   The remaining files are copied from the directories shown in Listing 18-25 and should not be changed at this point.

L18-25(7)   You need to edit **os_cfg.h** and set the following **#define**s to the values shown below:

    OS_CFG_ISR_POST_DEFERRED_EN   0u
    OS_CFG_PRIO_MAX   16u
    OS_CFG_STAT_TASK_EN   0u
    OS_CFG_TMR_EN   0u
    OS_CFG_SCHED_ROUNDROBIN_EN   0u

This is done to ensure that we only have two tasks in the test application, **OS_IdleTask()** and **OS_TickTask()**.

For this test, you need to add *one* line of code in **OSIdleTaskHook()** as shown in **bold** below. Once we verify **OSInit()**, **OSTaskStkInit()**, **OSCtxSw()**, **OS_CTX_SAVE** and **OS_CTX_RESTORE**, we'll remove this code:

```
void  OSIdleTaskHook (void)
{
    OSTimeTick();
#if OS_CFG_APP_HOOKS_EN > 0u
    if (OS_AppIdleTaskHookPtr != (OS_APP_HOOK_VOID)0) {
        (*OS_AppIdleTaskHookPtr)();
    }
#endif
}
```

18-5-2 VERIFYING TASK CONTEXT SWITCHES

In this section, we will verify the proper operation of the following functions/macros:

```
OSInit()              (os_core.c)
OSStartHighRdy()      (os_cpu_a.asm)
OSTaskStkInit()       (os_cpu_c.c)
OSCtxSw()             (os_cpu_a.asm)
OS_CTX_SAVE           (os_cpu_a.inc)
OS_CTX_RESTORE        (os_cpu_a.inc)
CPU_SR_Save()         (cpu_a.asm)
CPU_SR_Restore()      (cpu_a.asm)
```

Our first test is to verify that µC/OS-III gets properly initialized and that the code in **OSTaskStkInit()** properly initializes a task's stack.

Recall that our application consist of **app.c** which contains the code shown below:

```
void main (void)
{
    OS_ERR  err;

    OSInit(&err);
    OSStart(&err);                    <- Set a BREAKPOINT here!
}
```

STEP 1

You now need to build and download this project to your target. Building is obviously highly toolchain specific. Of course, if you encounter errors during the build, you will need to resolve those before being able to move to the next step.

Once all build errors have been resolved, you need to download the target code onto the evaluation board you selected for the tests.

STEP 2

You then need to set a breakpoint at the **OSStart()** line. In other words, have your target stop AFTER executing **OSInit()**. You should then examine the contents of '**err**' and confirm that it has the value **OS_ERR_NONE** (or, **0**). If you get anything other than **OS_ERR_NONE**, the error code will tell you where the problem is (see section A-20 on page 485).

STEP 3

If **err** is **OS_ERR_NONE** then you can 'Step Into' **OSStart()** (file **os_core.c**). You should see the following code:

```
void  OSStart (OS_ERR  *p_err)
{
#ifdef OS_SAFETY_CRITICAL
    if (p_err == (OS_ERR *)0) {
        OS_SAFETY_CRITICAL_EXCEPTION();
        return;
    }
#endif

    if (OSRunning == OS_STATE_OS_STOPPED) {
        OSPrioHighRdy    = OS_PrioGetHighest();                     (1)
        OSPrioCur        = OSPrioHighRdy;
        OSTCBHighRdyPtr  = OSRdyList[OSPrioHighRdy].HeadPtr;        (2)
        OSTCBCurPtr      = OSTCBHighRdyPtr;
        OSRunning        = OS_STATE_OS_RUNNING;
        OSStartHighRdy();                                           (3)
        *p_err           = OS_ERR_FATAL_RETURN;
    } else {
        *p_err           = OS_ERR_OS_RUNNING;
    }
}
```

STEP 4

Step into the code and stop just before executing **OSStartHighRdy()**. You should confirm that **OSPrioCur** is the same value as **OS_CFG_TICK_TASK_PRIO** (see **os_cfg_app.h**) and that **OSTCBHighRdyPtr** point at **OSTickTaskTCB**. In other words, the highest priority task should be the tick task because we should only have two task created after **OSInit()** and the tick task always has a higher priority than the idle task.

STEP 5

Now, 'Step Into' **OSStartHighRdy()** (file **os_cpu_a.asm**). You should see the assembly language shown below.

```
OSStartHighRdy:
    OSTaskSwHook();
    SP = OSTCBHighRdyPtr->StkPtr;
    OS_CTX_RESTORE
    Return from Interrupt/Exception;
```

You can 'Step Over' **OSTaskSwHook()** and the code to load the stack pointer. However, you should set a breakpoint at the 'Return from Interrupt/Exception' instruction. Once you executed the **OS_CTX_RESTORE** macro, you should look at the CPU registers and confirm that they all have their expected value (0x12121212 for R12, 0x05050505 for R5, etc.). If not then something is not quite right with either **OSTaskStkInit()** or the **OS_CTX_RESTORE** macro. Basically, **OSTaskStkInit()** sets up the stack and **OS_CTX_RESTORE** sets up the registers based on what's on the stack.

1ε

STEP 6

If the CPU registers appear to have their proper value then you can 'Single Step' and execute the 'Return from Interrupt/Exception' instruction. If all is well, you should be looking at the **OS_TickTask()** code which should look something like this:

```
void  OS_TickTask (void  *p_arg)
{
    OS_ERR  err;
    CPU_TS  ts;


    p_arg = p_arg;
    while (DEF_ON) {
        (void)OSTaskSemPend((OS_TICK  )0,
                            (OS_OPT   )OS_OPT_PEND_BLOCKING,
                            (CPU_TS  *)&ts,
                            (OS_ERR  *)&err);
        if (err == OS_ERR_NONE) {                    <- Set a BREAKPOINT here!
            if (OSRunning == OS_STATE_OS_RUNNING) {
                OS_TickListUpdate();
            }
        }
    }
}
```

If the debugger doesn't show you this code then it's possible that the **PC** and **PSW** are not properly setup on the task stack by **OSTaskStkInit()**.

If you end up in **OS_TickTask()** your code for **OSTaskStkInit()** and the macro **OS_CTX_RESTORE** is correct.

You should now set a breakpoint on the line following **OSTaskSemPend()**.

STEP 7

You need to set another breakpoint in **OSCtxSw( )** as shown below.

```
OSCtxSw:                                          <- Set a BREAKPOINT here!
    OS_CTX_SAVE
    OSTCBCurPtr->StkPtr = SP;
    OSTaskSwHook();
    OSPrioCur   = OSPrioHighRdy;
    OSTCBCurPtr = OSTCBHighRdyPtr;
    SP          = OSTCBCurPtr->StkPtr;
    OS_CTX_RESTORE
    Return from Interrupt/Exception;
```

You can now run the code at full speed. Because of the breakpoint in **OSCtxSw( )**, the debugger should stop and show you the code for **OSCtxSw( )**.

Basically, what's happening here is that **OS_TickTask( )** will be waiting for the tick ISR to signal the task that a tick has expired. Since we haven't setup the tick interrupt (not yet anyway), **OS_TickTask( )** would never get to execute. However, I had you modify the idle task hook to simulate signaling the tick task so µC/OS-III will eventually switch back to this code. In the meantime, µC/OS-III will switch to the next task that's ready-to-run. This happens to be the idle task. We'll be following the code until we get to **OS_IdleTask( )**.

STEP 8

You can 'Step Over' **OS_CTX_SAVE** and verify that the stack (pointed to by **SP**) contains the value of the CPU registers saved in the same order as they are in **OSTaskStkInit( )**. In fact, you can verify this when context switches back out of the idle task in just a few more steps.

STEP 9

'Step Into' the code one more time and verify that the **SP** was saved in **OSTickTaskTCB.StkPtr**.

STEP 10

'Step Into' the code and stop just before executing the 'Return from Interrupt/Exception' instruction. At this point, the CPU registers should contain the proper register values (similar to what we had when we restored the CPU registers for **OSTickTask( )** (but this time it's for **OS_IdleTask( )**).

18

STEP 11

'Step Into' the return from interrupt/exception instruction and the CPU should now jump into the idle task (**os_core.c**) as shown below. You should then set a breakpoint as shown.

```
void  OS_IdleTask (void  *p_arg)
{
    CPU_SR_ALLOC();


    p_arg = p_arg;
    while (DEF_ON) {
        CPU_CRITICAL_ENTER();                          <- Set a BREAKPOINT here!
        OSIdleTaskCtr++;
#if OS_CFG_STAT_TASK_EN > 0u
        OSStatTaskCtr++;
#endif
        CPU_CRITICAL_EXIT();

        OSIdleTaskHook();
    }
}
```

STEP 12

'Step Into' the idle task and then, 'Step Into' **OSIdleTaskHook()**. Recall that I had you modify the idle task hook as shown below. What we're doing here is simulate the occurrence of the tick interrupt.

```
void  OSIdleTaskHook (void)
{
    OSTimeTick();
#if OS_CFG_APP_HOOKS_EN > 0u
    if (OS_AppIdleTaskHookPtr != (OS_APP_HOOK_VOID)0) {
        (*OS_AppIdleTaskHookPtr)();
    }
#endif
}
```

STEP 13

Have your debugger run the code at full speed. You should actually hit the breakpoint in OSCtxSw() as shown below. What happened here is that µC/OS-III signaled the tick task and since the tick task is more important than the idle task, µC/OS-III is switching back to the tick task.

```
OSCtxSw:                                        <- BREAKPOINT here.
    OS_CTX_SAVE
    OSTCBCurPtr->StkPtr = SP;
    OSTaskSwHook();
    OSPrioCur   = OSPrioHighRdy;
    OSTCBCurPtr = OSTCBHighRdyPtr;
    SP          = OSTCBCurPtr->StkPtr;
    OS_CTX_RESTORE
    Return from Interrupt/Exception;
```

STEP 14

You can run the target at full speed and the debugger should bring you back at the breakpoint in OS_TickTask().

If you were to repeatedly run the target at full speed, your debugger should now stop at the following places:

```
OSCtxSw()
OS_IdleTask()
OSCtxSw()
OS_TickTask()
OSCtxSw()
OS_IdleTask()
OSCtxSw()
etc.
```

18-5-3 VERIFYING INTERRUPT CONTEXT SWITCHES

In this section, we will verify the proper operation of the following functions/macros:

OSTickISR( )	(os_cpu_a.asm)
OSIntCtxSw( )	(os_cpu_a.asm)
OS_ISR_ENTER	(os_cpu_a.inc)
OS_ISR_EXIT	(os_cpu_a.inc)
CPU_INT_EN( )	(cpu.h)
CPU_IntEn( )	(cpu_a.asm)

You can now remove the code we added in **OSIdleTaskHook( )**. The code should now be as shown below.

```
void  OSIdleTaskHook (void)
{
#if OS_CFG_APP_HOOKS_EN > 0u
    if (OS_AppIdleTaskHookPtr != (OS_APP_HOOK_VOID)0) {
        (*OS_AppIdleTaskHookPtr)();
    }
#endif
}
```

You should now setup the tick interrupt in **main( )** (**app.c**) as shown below.

```
/* app.c */

#include  "includes.h"

void  main (void)
{
    OS_ERR  err;

    OSInit(&err);
    /* (1) Install interrupt vector for OSTickISR()             */
    /* (2) Initialize the tick timer to generate interrupts every millisecond */
    CPU_INT_EN();        /* (3) Enable interrupts                 */
    OSStart(&err);
}
```

L18-25(8)   You need to setup the interrupt vector for the tick ISR. Where this is done greatly depends on the CPU architecture. On some processors, you would simply insert a pointer to **OSTickISR()** in the interrupt vector table while on others, you would need to call a function to install the vector in a RAM table.

L18-25(9)   You can setup the timer you will use to generate interrupts here. You need to make sure that the interrupt will not occur immediately but instead 1 millisecond after the timer is initialized. You may recall that I told you to always initialize the tick interrupt from the first task that executes when we start multitasking. However, since we are testing the port, it's safe to initialize the timer here since we have control over when the first interrupt will actually occur.

L18-25(10)   This macro is used to enable global CPU interrupts. It's assumed that the startup code runs with interrupts disabled and thus, those need to be explicitly enabled.

At this point, you need to remove all breakpoints you inserted to test the task level context switch code and insert the following breakpoints. You should note that the C-like code should actually be replaced with assembly language instructions for your processor.

```
OSIntCtxSw:                                         <- Set BREAKPOINT here!
    OSTaskSwHook();
    OSPrioCur   = OSPrioHighRdy;
    OSTCBCurPtr = OSTCBHighRdyPtr;
    SP          = OSTCBCurPtr->StkPtr;
    OS_CTX_RESTORE
    Return from Interrupt/Exception;


OSTickISR:                                          <- Set BREAKPOINT here!
    OS_ISR_ENTER
    Clear tick interrupt;
    OSTimeTick();
    OS_ISR_EXIT
```

18

STEP 1

Reset the CPU and run the code until you hit the first breakpoint. If you properly initialized the tick timer then you should be looking at the **OSTickISR()** code. If not, you need to determine why you are not getting the tick interrupt.

If the tick interrupt is properly setup then you should verify that is pointing at **OSIdleTaskTCB** since your application should have been looping around the idle task until the tick interrupt occurred.

STEP 2

You should step into the **OSTickISR()** code and verify that **OS_ISR_ENTER** increments **OSIntNestingCtr** (you should be able to look at that variable with the debugger and notice that it should have a value of **1**). Also, you should verify that the current **SP** is saved in **OSTCBCurPtr->StkPtr** (it should be the same as **OSIdleTaskTCB.StkPtr**).

STEP 3

You should now step through the code that clears the tick interrupt and verify that it's doing the proper thing.

STEP 4

You can now 'Step Over' the call to **OSTimeTick()**. **OSTimeTick()** basically signals the tick task and thus makes it ready-to-run. Instead of returning from interrupt from **OSTickISR()**, μC/OS-III will instead exit through **OSIntCtxSw()** because the tick ISR has a higher priority than the idle task.

STEP 5

You should now 'Step Into' the code for **OS_ISR_EXIT** and 'Step Over' **OSIntExit()** (os_core.c). **OSIntExit()** should not return to its caller but instead, call **OSIntCtxSw()** (os_cpu_a.asm) as shown below. At this point, **OSTCBHighRdyPtr** should point at **OSTickTaskTCB**.

```
OSIntCtxSw:
    OSTaskSwHook();
    OSPrioCur    = OSPrioHighRdy;
    OSTCBCurPtr  = OSTCBHighRdyPtr;
    SP           = OSTCBCurPtr->StkPtr;
    OS_CTX_RESTORE
    Return from Interrupt/Exception;
```

STEP 6

Before going any further in the code, you should set a breakpoint in `OS_TickTask()` (`os_tick.c`) as shown below.

```
void  OS_TickTask (void  *p_arg)
{
    OS_ERR   err;
    CPU_TS   ts;


    p_arg = p_arg;
    while (DEF_ON) {
        (void)OSTaskSemPend((OS_TICK  )0,                    <- Set BREAKPOINT here!
                            (OS_OPT   )OS_OPT_PEND_BLOCKING,
                            (CPU_TS  *)&ts,
                            (OS_ERR  *)&err);
        if (err == OS_ERR_NONE) {
            if (OSRunning == OS_STATE_OS_RUNNING) {
                OS_TickListUpdate();
            }
        }
    }
}
```

STEP 7

You should then go back to `os_cpu_a.asm` and 'Step Into' the code for `OS_CTX_RESTORE` and then execute the Return from Interrupt/Exception instruction.

This should cause the code to context switch into `OS_TickTask()`. In fact, you will be in the context of `OS_TickTask()` but you will not be in the `OS_TickTask()` code itself. This is because μC/OS-III is actually returning to the point where it invoked the scheduler to switch to the idle task. µC/OS-III is simply returning to that point. You can step through code to see the path µC/OS-III is taking. However, this corresponds to quite a few lines of code. It's probably simpler to simply run the CPU at full speed and have the debugger stop when you hit the breakpoint in **OS_TickTask( )**.

If you were to repeatedly run the target at full speed, your debugger should now stop at the following breakpoints:

```
OSTickISR( )
OSIntCtxSw( )
OS_TickTask( )
OSTickISR( )
OSIntCtxSw( )
etc.
```

At this point, the port tests are complete. You should be able to use the µC/OS-III port in your target application.

18-6 SUMMARY

A port involves three aspects: CPU, OS and board specific (BSP) code.

µC/OS-III port consists of writing or changing the contents of four kernel specific files: **os_cpu.h**, **os_cpu_a.asm**, **os_cpu_a.inc** and **os_cpu_c.c**.

It is also necessary to write or change the content of three CPU specific files: **cpu.h**, **cpu_a.asm** and **cpu_c.c**.

Finally, you can create or change a Board Support Package (BSP) for the evaluation board or target board being used.

A µC/OS-III port is similar to a µC/OS-II port, therefore you can start from one of the many µC/OS-II ports already available (see Appendix C, "Migrating from µC/OS-II to µC/OS-III" on page 711).

19

Run-Time Statistics

µC/OS-III performs substantial run-time statistics that can be displayed by kernel-aware debuggers and/or µC/Probe. Specifically, it is possible to ascertain the total number of context switches, maximum interrupt disable time, maximum scheduler lock time, CPU usage, stack space used on a per-task basis, the RAM used by µC/OS-III, and much more.

No other real-time kernel provides as much run-time information as µC/OS-III. This information is quite useful during debugging as it provides a sense of how well an application is running and the resources being used.

µC/OS-III also provides information about the configuration of the system. Specifically, the amount of RAM used by µC/OS-III, including all internal variables and task stacks.

The µC/OS-III variables described in this chapter should be displayed and never changed.

19-1 GENERAL STATISTICS – RUN-TIME

The following is a list of µC/OS-III variables that are not associated to any specific task:

19-1-1 TICK WHEEL

OSCfg_TickWheel[i].NbrEntries
The tick wheel contains up to **OS_CFG_TICK_WHEEL_SIZE** "spokes" (see **os_cfg_app.h**), and each spoke contains the **.NbrEntries** field, which holds the current number of entries in that spoke.

OSCfg_TickWheel[i].NbrEntriesMax
The **.NbrEntriesMax** field holds the maximum (i.e., peak) number of entries in a spoke.

19-1-2 TIMER WHEEL

OSCfg_TmrWheel[i].NbrEntries
The timer wheel contains up to **OS_CFG_TMR_WHEEL_SIZE** "spokes" (see **os_cfg_app.h**), and each spoke contains the **.NbrEntries** field, which holds the current number of entries in that spoke.

OSCfg_TmrWheel[i].NbrEntriesMax
The **.NbrEntriesMax** field holds the maximum (i.e., peak) number of entries in a spoke.\

19-1-3 INTERRUPTS

OSIntNestingCtr
This variable contains the interrupt nesting level. 1 means servicing the first level of interrupt nesting, 2 means the interrupt was interrupted by another interrupt, etc.

OSIntDisTimeMax
This variable contains the maximum interrupt disable time (in **CPU_TS** units).

19-1-4 INTERRUPT QUEUE

OSIntQNbrEntries
This variable indicates the current number of entries in the interrupt handler queue.

OSIntQNbrEntriesMax
This variable contains the maximum (i.e. peak) number of entries in the interrupt handler queue. This variable is reset by **OSStatReset()**.

OSIntQOvfCtr
This variable shows the number of attempts to post a message from an interrupt to the interrupt handler queue, and there was not enough room to place the post call. In other words, how many times an interrupt was not being able to be serviced by its corresponding task. This value should always be 0 if the interrupt handler queue is sized large enough. If the value is non-zero, you should increase the size of the interrupt handler queue. A non-zero value may also indicate that the processor is not fast enough.

OSIntQTaskTimeMax
This variable contains the maximum execution time of the Interrupt Queue Handler Task (in **CPU_TS** units). The total time also includes the time of any ISR that occurred while the Interrupt Handler task was running.

19-1-5 NUMBER OF KERNEL OBJECTS

OSFlagQty
This variable indicates the number of event flag groups created. This variable is declared only if OS_CFG_FLAG_EN is set to 1 in **os_cfg.h**.

OSMemQty
This variable indicates the number of fixed-sized memory partitions created by the application. This variable is declared only if OS_CFG_MEM_EN is set to 1 in **os_cfg.h**.

OSMutexQty
This variable indicates the number of mutual exclusion semaphores created by the application. This variable is declared only if OS_CFG_MUTEX_EN is set to 1 in **os_cfg.h**.

OSSemQty

This variable indicates the number of semaphores created by your application. This variable is declared only if OS_CFG_SEM_EN is set to 1 in **os_cfg.h**.

OSTaskQty

The variable contains the total number of tasks created in the application.

OSTmrQty

This variable indicates the number of timers created by the application. It is declared only if OS_CFG_TMR_EN is set to 1 in **os_cfg.h**.

19-1-6 MESSAGE POOL

OSMsgPool.NbrFree

The variable indicates the number of free OS_MSGs in the message pool. This number should never be zero since that indicate that the application is no longer able to send messages. This variable is declared only if OS_CFG_Q_EN is set to 1, or OS_CFG_TASK_Q_EN is set to 1 in **os_cfg.h**.

OSMsgPool.NbrUsed

This variable indicates the number of OS_MSGs currently used by the application. This variable is declared only if OS_CFG_Q_EN is set to 1, or OS_CFG_TASK_Q_EN is set to 1 in os_cfg.h.

OSMsgPool.NbrUsedMax

This variable indicates the maximum (i.e. peak) number of OS_MSGs that was ever used by the application and is reset by **OSStatReset()**. This variable is declared only if OS_CFG_Q_EN is set to 1, or OS_CFG_TASK_Q_EN is set to 1 in **os_cfg.h**.

19-1-7 READY LIST

OSRdyList[i].NbrEntries

These variable are used to examine how many entries there are in the ready list at each priority.

19-1-8 SCHEDULER

OSSchedLockTimeMax

This variable indicates the maximum amount of time the scheduler was locked irrespective of which task did the locking. It represents the global scheduler lock time. This value is expressed in CPU_TS units. The variable is declared only if OS_CFG_SCHED_LOCK_TIME_MEAS_EN is set to 1 in os_cfg.h.

OSSchedLockTimeMaxCur

This variable indicates the maximum amount of time the scheduler was locked. This value is expressed in CPU_TS units and is reset by the context switch code so that it can track the scheduler lock time on a per-task basis. This variable is declared only if OS_CFG_SCHED_LOCK_TIME_MEAS_EN is set to 1 in os_cfg.h.

OSSchedLockNestingCtr

This variable keeps track of the nesting level of the scheduler lock.

OSSchedRoundRobinEn

When set to 1, this variable indicates that round robin scheduling is enabled.

19-1-9 STATISTICS TASK

OSStatTaskCPUUsage

This variable indicates the CPU usage of the application expressed as a percentage multiplied by 100. A value of 1000 indicates that 10.00% of the CPU is used, while 90.00% of the time the CPU is idling. This variable is declared only if OS_CFG_STAT_TASK_EN is set to 1 in os_cfg.h.

OSStatTaskCtr

This variable contains a counter that is incremented every time the idle task infinite loop runs. This variable is declared only if OS_CFG_STAT_TASK_EN is set to 1 in os_cfg.h.

OSStatTaskCtrMax

This variable contains the maximum number of times the idle task loop runs in 0.1 second. This value is used to measure the CPU usage of the application. This variable is declared only if OS_CFG_STAT_TASK_EN is set to 1 in os_cfg.h.

OSStatTaskTimeMax

This variable contains the maximum execution time of the statistic task (in **CPU_TS** units). It is declared only if **OS_CFG_STAT_TASK_EN** is set to 1 in **os_cfg.h**. The total time also includes the time of any ISR that occurred while the statistic task was running.

19-1-10 TICK TASK

OSTickCtr

This variable is incremented every time the tick task executes.

OSTickTaskTimeMax

This variable contains the maximum execution time of the tick task (in **CPU_TS** units). The total time also includes the time of any ISR that occurred while the tick task was running.

19-1-11 TIMER TASK

OSTmrCtr

This variable is incremented every time the timer task executes.

OSTmrTaskTimeMax

This variable contains the maximum execution time of the timer task (in **CPU_TS** units). It is declared only if **OS_CFG_TMR_EN** is set to 1 in **os_cfg.h**. The total time also includes the time of any ISR that occurred while the timer task was running.

19-1-12 MISCELLANEOUS

OSIdleTaskCtr

This variable contains a counter that is incremented every time the idle task infinite loop runs.

OSRunning

When non-zero, this variable indicates that multitasking has started.

OSTaskCtxSwCtr

This variable accumulates the number of context switches performed by µC/OS-III.

19-2 PER-TASK STATISTICS – RUN-TIME

µC/OS-III maintains statistics for each task at run-time. This information is saved in the task's **OS_TCB**.

.CPUUsage

This variable keeps track of CPU usage of the task (multiplied by 100). For example if the task's **.CPUUsage** is 200 then the task consumes 2.00% of total CPU usage.

The variable is declared only when **OS_CFG_TASK_PROFILE_EN** is set to 1 in **os_cfg.h**.

.CPUUsageMax

This variable keeps track of the maximum (i.e. peak) CPU usage of the task (multiplied by 100). For example if the task's **.CPUUsageMax** is 571 then the task maximum CPU usage that the task consumed at any given time is 5.71% of total CPU usage. This variable is reset by **OSStatReset()**.

The variable is declared only when **OS_CFG_TASK_PROFILE_EN** is set to 1 in **os_cfg.h**.

.CtxSwCtr

This variable keeps track of the number of times a task is context switched-in. This variable should increment. If it does not increment, the task is not running. At a minimum, the counter should at least have a value of one since a task is always created ready-to-run. However, if higher priority tasks prevent the task from ever running, the value would be 0.

This variable is declared only when **OS_CFG_TASK_PROFILE_EN** is set to 1 in **os_cfg.h**.

.IntDisTimeMax

This variable keeps track of the maximum interrupt disable time of a task (in **CPU_TS** units). This variable shows how each task affects interrupt latency.

The variable is declared only when **CPU_CFG_INT_DIS_MEAS_EN** in **cpu_cfg.h** is set to 1.

.MsgQ.NbrEntries

This variable indicates the number of entries currently waiting in the message queue of a task. This variable is declared only when **OS_CFG_TASK_Q_EN** is set to 1 in **os_cfg.h**.

.MsgQ.NbrEntriesMax

This variable indicates the maximum number of entries placed in the message queue of a task. This variable is declared only when **OS_CFG_TASK_Q_EN** is set to 1 in **os_cfg.h**.

.MsgQ.NbrEntriesSize

This variable indicates the maximum number of entries that a task message queue is able to accept before it is full.

This variable is declared only when **OS_CFG_TASK_Q_EN** is set to 1 in **os_cfg.h**.

.MsgQPendTime

This variable indicates the amount of time it took for a task or an ISR to send a message to the task (in **CPU_TS** units).

The variable is declared only when **OS_CFG_TASK_PROFILE_EN** is set to 1 in **os_cfg.h**.

.MsgQPendTimeMax

This variable indicates the maximum amount of time it took for a task or an ISR to send a message to the task (in **CPU_TS** units).

This variable is declared only when **OS_CFG_TASK_PROFILE_EN** is set to 1 in **os_cfg.h**.

.PendOn

This variable indicates what a task is pending on if the task is in a pend state. Possible values are:

0	Nothing
1	Pending on an event flag group
2	Pending on the task's message queue
3	Pending on multiple objects
4	Pending on a mutual exclusion semaphore
5	Pending on a message queue
6	Pending on a semaphore
7	Pending on a task's semaphore

.Prio

This corresponds to the priority of the task. This might change at run time depending on whether or not the task owns a mutual exclusion semaphore, or the user changes the priority of the task by calling OSTaskChangePrio().

.SchedLockTimeMax

This variable keeps track of the maximum time a task locks the scheduler (in CPU_TS units). This variable allows the application to see how each task affects task latency. The variable is declared only when OS_CFG_SCHED_LOCK_TIME_MEAS_EN is set to 1 in os_cfg.h.

.SemPendTime

This variable indicates the amount of time it took for a task or ISR to signal the task (in CPU_TS units).

This variable is declared only when OS_CFG_TASK_PROFILE_EN is set to 1 in os_cfg.h.

.SemPendTimeMax

This variable indicates the maximum amount of time it took for a task or an ISR to signal the task (in CPU_TS units).

This variable is declared only when OS_CFG_TASK_PROFILE_EN is set to 1 in os_cfg.h.

.State

This variable indicates the current state of a task. The possible values are:

0	Ready
1	Delayed
2	Pending
3	Pending with Timeout
4	Suspended
5	Delayed and Suspended
6	Pending and Suspended
7	Pending, Delayed and Suspended

.StkFree

This variable indicates the amount of stack space (in number of stack entries) unused by a task. This value is determined by the statistic task if OS_CFG_TASK_STAT_STK_CHK_EN is set to 1 in os_cfg.h.

.StkUsed

This variable indicates the maximum stack usage (in number of stack entries) of a task. This value is determined by the statistic task if OS_CFG_TASK_STAT_STK_CHK_EN is set to 1 in os_cfg.h.

.TickRemain

This variable indicates the amount of time left (in clock ticks) until a task time delay expires, or the task times out waiting on a kernel object such as a semaphore, message queue, or other.

19-3 KERNEL OBJECT – RUN-TIME

It is possible to examine the run-time values of certain kernel objects as described below.

19-3-1 SEMAPHORES

.NamePtr

This is a pointer to an ASCII string used to provide a name to the semaphore. The ASCII string can have any length as long as it is NUL terminated.

.PendList.NbrEntries

Each semaphore contains a wait list of tasks waiting for the semaphore to be signaled. The variable represents the number of entries in the wait list.

.Ctr

This variable represents the current count of the semaphore.

.TS

This variable contains the timestamp of when the semaphore was last signaled.

19-3-2 MUTUAL EXCLUSION SEMAPHORES

.NamePtr

This is a pointer to an ASCII string used to provide a name to the mutual exclusion semaphore. The ASCII string can have any length as long as it is **NUL** terminated.

.PendList.NbrEntries

Each mutual exclusion semaphore contains a list of tasks waiting for the semaphore to be released. The variable represents the number of entries in the wait list.

.OwnerOriginalPrio

This variable holds the original priority of the task that owns the mutual exclusion semaphore.

.OwnerTCBPtr->Prio

Dereferencing the pointer to the **OS_TCB** of the mutual exclusion semaphore owner allows the application to determine whether a task priority was changed.

.OwnerNestingCtr

This variable indicates how many times the owner of the mutual exclusion semaphore requested the semaphore.

.TS

This variable contains the timestamp of when the mutual exclusion semaphore was last released.

19-3-3 MESSAGE QUEUES

.NamePtr

This is a pointer to an ASCII string used to provide a name to the message queue. The ASCII string can have any length, as long as it is **NUL** terminated.

.PendList.NbrEntries

Each message queue contains a wait list of tasks waiting for messages to be sent to the queue. The variable represents the number of entries in the wait list.

.MsgQ.NbrEntries

This variable represents the number of messages currently in the message queue.

`.MsgQ.NbrEntriesMax`

This variable represents the maximum number of messages ever placed in the message queue.

`.MsgQ.NbrEntriesSize`

This variable represents the maximum number of messages that can be placed in the message queue.

19-3-4 EVENT FLAGS

`.NamePtr`

This is a pointer to an ASCII string used to provide a name to the event flag group. The ASCII string can have any length, as long as it is **NUL** terminated.

`.PendList.NbrEntries`

Each event flag group contains a wait list of tasks waiting for event flags to be set or cleared. This variable represents the number of entries in the wait list.

`.Flags`

This variable contains the current value of the event flags in an event flag group.

`.TS`

This variable contains the timestamp of when the event flag group was last posted.

19-3-5 MEMORY PARTITIONS

`.NamePtr`

This is a pointer to an ASCII string that is used to provide a name to the memory partition. The ASCII string can have any length as long as it is **NUL** terminated.

`.BlkSize`

This variable contains the block size (in bytes) for the memory partition.

`.NbrMax`

This variable contains the maximum number of memory blocks belonging to the memory partition.

.NbrFree

This variable contains the number of memory blocks that are available from memory partition. The number of memory blocks in use is given by:

.NbrMax - .NbrFree

19-4 OS_DBG.C – STATIC

os_dbg.c is provided in µC/OS-III as some debuggers are not able to read the values of **#define** constants. Specifically, **os_dbg.c** contains ROM variables initialized to **#define** constants so that users can read them with any debugger.

Below is a list of ROM variables provided in **os_dbg.c**, along with their descriptions. These variables use approximately 100 bytes of code space.

The application code can examine these variables and you do not need to access them in a critical region as they reside in code space and are therefore not changeable.

ROM Variable	Data Type	Value
OSDbg_DbgEn	CPU_INT08U	OS_CFG_DBG_EN

When 1, this variable indicates that ROM variables in **os_dbg.c** will be compiled. This value is set in **os_cfg.h**.

ROM Variable	Data Type	Value
OSDbg_ArgChkEn	CPU_INT08U	OS_CFG_ARG_CHK_EN

When 1, this variable indicates that run-time argument checking is enabled. This means that µC/OS-III will check the validity of the values of arguments passed to functions. The feature is enabled in **os_cfg.h**.

ROM Variable	Data Type	Value
OSDbg_AppHooksEn	CPU_INT08U	OS_CFG_APP_HOOKS_EN

When 1, the variable indicates whether application hooks will be available to the application programmer, and the pointers listed below are declared. This value is set in **os_cfg.h**.

```
OS_AppTaskCreateHookPtr;
OS_AppTaskDelHookPtr;
OS_AppTaskReturnHookPtr;
OS_AppIdleTaskHookPtr;
OS_AppStatTaskHookPtr;
OS_AppTaskSwHookPtr;
OS_AppTimeTickHookPtr;
```

ROM Variable	Data Type	Value
OSDbg_EndiannessTest	CPU_INT32U	0x12345678

This variable allows a kernel awareness debugger or µC/Probe to determine the endianness of the CPU. This is easily done by looking at the lowest address in memory where this variable is saved. If the value is 0x78 then the CPU is a little endian machine. If it's 0x12, it is a big endian machine.

ROM Variable	Data Type	Value
OSDbg_CalledFromISRChkEn	CPU_INT08U	OS_CFG_CALLED_FROM_ISR_CHK_EN

When 1, this variable indicates that µC/OS-III will perform run-time checking to see if a function that is not supposed to be called from an ISR, is called from an ISR. This value is set in **os_cfg.h**.

ROM Variable	Data Type	Value
OSDbg_FlagEn	CPU_INT08U	OS_CFG_FLAG_EN

When 1, this variable indicates that µC/OS-III's event flag services are available to the application programmer. This value is set in **os_cfg.h**.

ROM Variable	Data Type	Value
OSDbg_FlagDelEn	CPU_INT08U	OS_CFG_FLAG_DEL_EN

When 1, this variable indicates that the **OSFlagDel()** function is available to the application programmer. This value is set in **os_cfg.h**.

ROM Variable	Data Type	Value
OSDbg_FlagModeClrEn	CPU_INT08U	OS_CFG_FLAG_MODE_CLR_EN

When 1, this variable indicates that you can either clear or set flags when posting and pending on event flags. This value is set in **os_cfg.h**.

ROM Variable	Data Type	Value
OSDbg_FlagPendAbortEn	CPU_INT08U	OS_CFG_FLAG_PEND_ABORT_EN

When 1, this variable indicates that the **OSFlagPendAbort()** function is available to the application programmer. This value is set in **os_cfg.h**.

19

ROM Variable	Data Type	Value
OSDbg_FlagGrpSize	CPU_INT16U	sizeof(OS_FLAG_GRP)

This variable indicates the memory footprint (in RAM) of an event flag group (in bytes). This data type is declared in **os.h**.

ROM Variable	Data Type	Value
OSDbg_FlagWidth	CPU_INT16U	sizeof(OS_FLAGS)

This variable indicates the word width (in bytes) of event flags. If event flags are declared as **CPU_INT08U**, this variable will be 1, if declared as a **CPU_INT16U**, this variable will be 2, etc. This **OS_FLAGS** data type is declared in **os_type.h**.

ROM Variable	Data Type	Value
OSDbg_IntQ	CPU_INT16U	sizeof(OS_INT_Q)

This variable indicates the size (in bytes) of the **OS_INT_Q** data type, which is used to queue up deferred posts. The value of this variable is zero if **OS_CFG_ISR_POST_DEFERRED_EN** is 0 in **os_cfg.h**.

ROM Variable	Data Type	Value
OSDbg_ISRPostDeferredEn	CPU_INT08U	OS_CFG_ISR_POST_DEFERRED_EN

When 1, this variable indicates that an ISR will defer posts to task-level code. This value is set in **os_cfg.h**.

ROM Variable	Data Type	Value
OSDbg_MemEn	CPU_INT08U	OS_CFG_MEM_EN

When 1, this variable indicates that µC/OS-III's memory management services are available to the application. This value is set in **os_cfg.h**.

ROM Variable	Data Type	Value
OSDbg_MemSize	CPU_INT16U	sizeof(OS_MEM)

This variable indicates the RAM footprint (in bytes) of a memory partition control block, **OS_MEM**.

ROM Variable	Data Type	Value
OSDbg_MsgEn	CPU_INT08U	OS_MSG_EN

When 1, this variable indicates that the application either enabled message queues, or task message queues, or both. This value is set in **os_cfg.h** by ORing the value of OS_CFG_Q_EN and OS_CFG_TASK_Q_EN.

ROM Variable	Data Type	Value
OSDbg_MsgSize	CPU_INT16U	sizeof(OS_MSG)

This variable indicates the RAM footprint (in bytes) of an **OS_MSG** data structure.

ROM Variable	Data Type	Value
OSDbg_MsgPoolSize	CPU_INT16U	sizeof(OS_MSG_POOL)

This variable indicates the RAM footprint (in bytes) of an **OS_MSG_POOL** data structure.

ROM Variable	Data Type	Value
OSDbg_MsgQSize	CPU_INT16U	sizeof(OS_MSG_Q)

This variable indicates the RAM footprint (in number of bytes) of an **OS_MSG_Q** data type.

ROM Variable	Data Type	Value
OSDbg_MutexEn	CPU_INT08U	OS_CFG_MUTEX_EN

When 1, this variable indicates that μC/OS-III's mutual exclusion semaphore management services are available to the application. This value is set in **os_cfg.h**.

ROM Variable	Data Type	Value
OSDbg_MutexDelEn	CPU_INT08U	OS_CFG_MUTEX_DEL_EN

When 1, this variable indicates that the function **OSMutexDel()** is available to the application. This value is set in **os_cfg.h**.

ROM Variable	Data Type	Value
OSDbg_MutexPendAbortEn	CPU_INT08U	OS_CFG_MUTEX_PEND_ABORT_EN

When 1, the variable indicates that the function **OSMutexPendAbort()** is available to the application. This value is set in **os_cfg.h**.

ROM Variable	Data Type	Value
OSDbg_MutexSize	CPU_INT16U	sizeof(OS_MUTEX)

This variable indicates the RAM footprint (in number of bytes) of an **OS_MUTEX** data type.

ROM Variable	Data Type	Value
OSDbg_ObjTypeChkEn	CPU_INT08U	OS_CFG_OBJ_TYPE_CHK_EN

When 1, this variable indicates that µC/OS-III will check for valid object types at run time. µC/OS-III will make sure the application is accessing a semaphore if calling **OSSem???()** functions, accessing a message queue when calling **OSQ???()** functions, etc. This value is set in **os_cfg.h**.

ROM Variable	Data Type	Value
OSDbg_PendMultiEn	CPU_INT08U	OS_CFG_PEND_MULTI_EN

When 1, this variable indicates that µC/OS-III's service to pend on multiple objects (semaphores or message queues) is available to the application. This value is set in **os_cfg.h**.

ROM Variable	Data Type	Value
OSDbg_PendDataSize	CPU_INT16U	sizeof(OS_PEND_DATA)

This variable indicates the RAM footprint (in bytes) of an **OS_PEND_DATA** data type.

ROM Variable	Data Type	Value
OSDbg_PendListSize	CPU_INT16U	sizeof(OS_PEND_LIST)

This variable indicates the RAM footprint (in bytes) of an **OS_PEND_LIST** data type.

ROM Variable	Data Type	Value
OSDbg_PendObjSize	CPU_INT16U	sizeof(OS_PEND_OBJ)

This variable indicates the RAM footprint (in bytes) of an **OS_PEND_OBJ** data type.

ROM Variable	Data Type	Value
OSDbg_PrioMax	CPU_INT16U	OS_CFG_PRIO_MAX

This variable indicates the maximum number of priorities that the application will support.

ROM Variable	Data Type	Value
OSDbg_PtrSize	CPU_INT16U	sizeof(void *)

This variable indicates the size (in bytes) of a pointer.

ROM Variable	Data Type	Value
OSDbg_QEn	CPU_INT08U	OS_CFG_Q_EN

When 1, this variable indicates that µC/OS-III's message queue services are available to the application. This value is set in **os_cfg.h**.

ROM Variable	Data Type	Value
OSDbg_QDelEn	CPU_INT08U	OS_CFG_Q_DEL_EN

When 1, this variable indicates that the function **OSQDel()** is available to the application. This value is set in **os_cfg.h**.

ROM Variable	Data Type	Value
OSDbg_QFlushEn	CPU_INT08U	OS_CFG_Q_FLUSH_EN

When 1, this variable indicates that the function **OSQFlush()** is available to the application. This value is set in **os_cfg.h**.

ROM Variable	Data Type	Value
OSDbg_QPendAbortEn	CPU_INT08U	OS_CFG_Q_PEND_ABORT_EN

When 1, this variable indicates that the function **OSQPendAbort()** is available to the application. This value is set in **os_cfg.h**.

ROM Variable	Data Type	Value
OSDbg_QSize	CPU_INT16U	

This variable indicates the RAM footprint (in number of bytes) of an **OS_Q** data type.

ROM Variable	Data Type	Value
OSDbg_SchedRoundRobinEn	CPU_INT08U	OS_CFG_SCHED_ROUND_ROBIN_EN

When 1, this variable indicates that the µC/OS-III round-robin scheduling feature is available to the application. This value is set in **os_cfg.h**.

ROM Variable	Data Type	Value
OSDbg_SemEn	CPU_INT08U	OS_CFG_SEM_EN

When 1, this variable indicates that µC/OS-III's semaphore management services are available to the application. This value is set in **os_cfg.h**.

ROM Variable	Data Type	Value
OSDbg_SemDelEn	CPU_INT08U	OS_CFG_SEM_DEL_EN

When 1, this variable indicates that the function **OSSemDel()** is available to the application. This value is set in **os_cfg.h**.

ROM Variable	Data Type	Value
OSDbg_SemPendAbortEn	CPU_INT08U	OS_CFG_SEM_PEND_ABORT_EN

When 1, this variable indicates that the function **OSSemPendAbort()** is available to the application. This value is set in **os_cfg.h**.

ROM Variable	Data Type	Value
OSDbg_SemSetEn	CPU_INT08U	OS_CFG_SEM_SET_EN

When 1, this variable indicates that the function **OSSemSet()** is available to the application. This value is set in **os_cfg.h**.

ROM Variable	Data Type	Value
OSDbg_SemSize	CPU_INT16U	sizeof(OS_SEM)

This variable indicates the RAM footprint (in bytes) of an **OS_SEM** data type.

ROM Variable	Data Type	Value
OSDbg_RdyList	CPU_INT16U	sizeof(OS_RDY_LIST)

This variable indicates the RAM footprint (in bytes) of the **OS_RDY_LIST** data type.

ROM Variable	Data Type	Value
OSDbg_RdyListSize	CPU_INT32U	sizeof(OSRdyList)

This variable indicates the RAM footprint (in bytes) of the ready list.

ROM Variable	Data Type	Value
OSDbg_StkWidth	CPU_INT08U	sizeof(CPU_STK)

This variable indicates the word size of a stack entry (in bytes). If a stack entry is declared as **CPU_INT08U**, this value will be 1, if a stack entry is declared as **CPU_INT16U**, the value will be 2, etc.

ROM Variable	Data Type	Value
OSDbg_StatTaskEn	CPU_INT08U	OS_CFG_STAT_TASK_EN

When 1, this variable indicates that µC/OS-III's statistic task is enabled. This value is set in **os_cfg.h**.

ROM Variable	Data Type	Value
OSDbg_StatTaskStkChkEn	CPU_INT08U	OS_CFG_STAT_TASK_STK_CHK_EN

When 1, this variable indicates that µC/OS-III will perform run-time stack checking by walking the stack of each task to determine the usage of each. This value is set in **os_cfg.h**.

ROM Variable	Data Type	Value
OSDbg_TaskChangePrioEn	CPU_INT08U	OS_CFG_TASK_CHANGE_PRIO_EN

When 1, this variable indicates that the function **OSTaskChangePrio()** is available to the application. This value is set in **os_cfg.h**.

ROM Variable	Data Type	Value
OSDbg_TaskDelEn	CPU_INT08U	OS_CFG_TASK_DEL_EN

When 1, this variable indicates that the function **OSTaskDel()** is available to the application. This value is set in **os_cfg.h**.

ROM Variable	Data Type	Value
OSDbg_TaskQEn	CPU_INT08U	OS_CFG_TASK_Q_EN

When 1, this variable indicates that **OSTaskQ???()** services are available to the application. This value is set in **os_cfg.h**.

ROM Variable	Data Type	Value
OSDbg_TaskQPendAbortEn	CPU_INT08U	OS_CFG_TASK_Q_PEND_ABORT_EN

When 1, this variable indicates that the function OSTaskQPendAbort() is available to the application. This value is set in **os_cfg.h**.

ROM Variable	Data Type	Value
OSDbg_TaskProfileEn	CPU_INT08U	OS_CFG_TASK_PROFILE_EN

When 1, this variable indicates that task profiling is enabled, and that μC/OS-III will perform run-time performance measurements on a per-task basis. Specifically, when 1, μC/OS-III will keep track of how many context switches each task makes, how long a task disables interrupts, how long a task locks the scheduler, and more. This value is set in **os_cfg.h**.

ROM Variable	Data Type	Value
OSDbg_TaskRegTblSize	CPU_INT16U	OS_CFG_TASK_REG_TBL_SIZE

This variable indicates how many entries each task register table can accept.

ROM Variable	Data Type	Value
OSDbg_TaskSemPendAbortEn	CPU_INT08U	OS_CFG_TASK_SEM_PEND_ABORT_EN

When 1, this variable indicates that the function OSTaskSemPendAbort() is available to the application. This value is set in **os_cfg.h**.

ROM Variable	Data Type	Value
OSDbg_TaskSuspendEn	CPU_INT08U	OS_CFG_TASK_SUSPEND_EN

When 1, this variable indicates that the function **OSTaskSuspend()** is available to the application. This value is set in **os_cfg.h**.

ROM Variable	Data Type	Value
OSDbg_TCBSize	CPU_INT16U	sizeof(OS_TCB)

This variable indicates the RAM footprint (in bytes) of an **OS_TCB** data structure.

ROM Variable	Data Type	Value
OSDbg_TickSpokeSize	CPU_INT16U	sizeof(OS_TICK_SPOKE)

This variable indicates the RAM footprint (in bytes) of an **OS_TICK_SPOKE** data structure.

ROM Variable	Data Type	Value
OSDbg_TimeDlyHMSMEn	CPU_INT08U	OS_CFG_TIME_DLY_HMSM_EN

When 1, this variable indicates that the function **OSTimeDlyHMSM()** is available to the application. This value is set in **os_cfg.h**.

ROM Variable	Data Type	Value
OSDbg_TimeDlyResumeEn	CPU_INT08U	OS_CFG_TIME_DLY_RESUME_EN

When 1, this variable indicates that the function **OSTimeDlyResume()** is available to the application. This value is set in **os_cfg.h**.

ROM Variable	Data Type	Value
OSDbg_TLS_TblSize	CPU_INT16U	OS_CFG_TLS_TBL_SIZE

Indicates the size of the .TLS_Tbl[] in an OS_TCB in number of bytes. This value is set in os_cfg.h.

ROM Variable	Data Type	Value
OSDbg_TmrEn	CPU_INT08U	OS_CFG_TMR_EN

When 1, this variable indicates that OSTmr???() services are available to the application. This value is set in os_cfg.h.

ROM Variable	Data Type	Value
OSDbg_TmrDelEn	CPU_INT08U	OS_CFG_TMR_DEL_EN

When 1, this variable indicates that the function OSTmrDel() is available to the application. This value is set in os_cfg.h.

ROM Variable	Data Type	Value
OSDbg_TmrSize	CPU_INT16U	sizeof(OS_TMR)

This variable indicates the RAM footprint (in bytes) of an OS_TMR data structure.

ROM Variable	Data Type	Value
OSDbg_TmrSpokeSize	CPU_INT16U	sizeof(OS_TMR_SPOKE)

This variable indicates the RAM footprint (in bytes) of an OS_TMR_SPOKE data structure.

ROM Variable	Data Type	Value
OSDbg_VersionNbr	CPU_INT16U	OS_VERSION

This variable indicates the current version of µC/OS-III multiplied by 10000. For example version 3.02.00 will show as 30200.

ROM Variable	Data Type	Value
OSDbg_DataSize	CPU_INT32U	Size of all RAM variables

This variable indicates the RAM footprint (in bytes) of the internal µC/OS-III variables for the current configuration.

19-5 OS_CFG_APP.C – STATIC

As with **os_dbg.c**, **os_cfg_app.c** defines a number of ROM variables. These variables, however, reflect the run-time configuration of an application. Specifically, the user will be able to know the RAM footprint (in bytes) of µC/OS-III task stacks, the message pool, and more.

Below is a list of ROM variables provided in **os_app_cfg.c**, along with their descriptions. These variables represent approximately 100 bytes of code space.

Application code can examine these variables and the application does not need to access them in a critical region since they reside in code space and are therefore not changeable.

ROM Variable	Data Type	Value
OSCfg_IdleTaskStkSizeRAM	CPU_INT32U	sizeof(OSCfg_IdleTaskStk)

This variable indicates the RAM footprint (in bytes) of the µC/OS-III idle task stack.

ROM Variable	Data Type	Value
OSCfg_IntQSizeRAM	CPU_INT32U	sizeof(OSCfg_IntQ)

This variable indicates the RAM footprint (in bytes) of the µC/OS-III interrupt handler task queue.

ROM Variable	Data Type	Value
OSCfg_IntQTaskStkSizeRAM	CPU_INT32U	sizeof(OSCfg_IntQTaskStk)

This variable indicates the RAM footprint (in bytes) of the µC/OS-III interrupt queue handler task stack.

ROM Variable	Data Type	Value
OSCfg_ISRStkSizeRAM	CPU_INT32U	sizeof(OSCfg_ISRStk)

This variable indicates the RAM footprint (in bytes) of the dedicated Interrupt Service Routine (ISR) stack.

ROM Variable	Data Type	Value
OSCfg_MsgPoolSizeRAM	CPU_INT32U	sizeof(OSCfg_MsgPool)

This variable indicates the RAM footprint (in bytes) of the message pool.

ROM Variable	Data Type	Value
OSCfg_StatTaskStkSizeRAM	CPU_INT32U	sizeof(OSCfg_StatTaskStk)

This variable indicates the RAM footprint (in bytes) of the µC/OS-III statistic task stack.

ROM Variable	Data Type	Value
OSCfg_TickTaskStkSizeRAM	CPU_INT32U	sizeof(OSCfg_TickTaskStk)

This variable indicates the RAM footprint (in bytes) of the µC/OS-III tick task stack.

ROM Variable	Data Type	Value
OSCfg_TickWheelSizeRAM	CPU_INT32U	sizeof(OSCfg_TickWheel)

This variable indicates the RAM footprint (in bytes) of the tick wheel.

ROM Variable	Data Type	Value
OSCfg_TmrWheelSizeRAM	CPU_INT32U	sizeof(OSCfg_TmrWheel)

This variable indicates the RAM footprint (in bytes) of the timer wheel.

ROM Variable	Data Type	Value
OSCfg_DataSizeRAM	CPU_INT32U	Total of all configuration RAM

This variable indicates the RAM footprint (in bytes) of all of the configuration variables declared in **os_cfg_app.c**.

19-6 SUMMARY

This chapter presented a number of variables that can be read by a debugger and/or μC/Probe.

These variables provide run-time and compile-time (static) information regarding μC/OS-III-based applications. The μC/OS-III variables allow users to monitor RAM footprint, task stack usage, context switches, CPU usage, the execution time of many operations, and more.

The application must never change (i.e., write to) any of these variables.

19

20

Thread Safety of the Compiler's Run-Time Library

As of V3.03.00, µC/OS-III provides built-in support for run-time library thread safety through the use of Task Local Storage (TLS) for storage of task-specific run-time library static data and mutual exclusion semaphores to protect accesses to shared resources.

The run-time environment consists of the run-time library, which contains the functions defined by the C and the C++ standards, and includes files that define the library interface (the system header files).

Compilers provide complete libraries that are compliant with Standard C and C++. These libraries also supports floating-point numbers in IEEE 7+54 format and can be configured to include different levels of support for locale, file descriptors, multi-byte characters, etc. Most parts of the libraries are reentrant, but some functionality and parts are not reentrant because they require the use of static data. Different compilers provide different methods to add reentrancy to their libraries through an API defined by the tool chain supplier.

In a multi-threaded environment the C/C++ library has to handle all library objects with a global state differently. Either an object is a true global object, then any updates of its state has to be guarded by some locking mechanism to make sure that only one task can update it at any one time, or an object is local to each task, then the static variables containing the objects state must reside in a variable area local for the task. This area is commonly named thread local storage or, TLS.

The run-time library may also need to use multiple types of locks. For example, a lock could be necessary to ensure exclusive access to the file stream, another one to the heap, etc. It is thus common to protect the following functions through one or more mutual exclusion semaphores (mutex):

- The heap through the usage of **malloc()**, **free()**, **realloc()**, and **calloc()**.

- The file system through the usage of **fopen()**, **fclose()**, **fdopen()**, **fflush()**, and **freopen()**.

- The signal system through the usage of **signal()**.

- The tempfile system through the usage of **tmpnam()**.

- Initialization of static function objects.

Thread-local storage is typically needed for the following library objects:

- Error functions through **errno** and **strerror**

- Locale functions through the usage of **localeconv()** and **setlocale()**

- Time functions through the usage of **asctime()**, **localtime()**, **gmtime()**, and **mktime()**

- Multibyte functions through the usage of **mbrlen()**, **mbrtowc()**, **mbsrtowc()**, **mbtowc()**, **wcrtomb()**, **wcsrtomb()**, and **wctomb()**

- Random functions through the usage of **rand()** and **srand()**

- Other functions through the usage of **atexit()** and **strtok()**

- C++ exception engine

Different compilers require different implementations and those implementation details are encapsulated into a single file called **os_tls.c**. There is thus one **os_tls.c** file associated with each compiler supported by Micrium and each implementation is placed in its own directory as follows:

`\Micrium\Software\uCOS-III\TLS\<compiler manufacturer>\os_tls.c`

Where 'compiler manufacturer' is the name of the compiler manufacturer or the code name for the compiler for which thread safety has been implemented. Refer to the code distribution to see if your compiler is supported.

20-1 ENABLING THREAD SAFETY

In order to enable thread safety, you need to do the following:

▓ Set OS_CFG_TLS_TBL_SIZE in os_cfg.h to a value greater than 1. The actual value depends on the number of entries needed by the compiler used. In most cases you would only need to set this to 1 but you should consult the os_tls.c that you plan to use for additional information.

▓ Add to your build, the os_tls.c file that corresponds to the compiler you are using.

▓ Depending on the compiler and how TLS is allocated, you may also need to make sure that you have a heap. Consult your compiler documentation on how you can enable the heap and determine its size.

▓ Most likely, os_tls.c will make use of mutexes to guard access to shared resources (such as the heap or files) then you need to make sure OS_CFG_MUTEX_EN is set to 1 in os_cfg.h. Also, the run-time library may already define APIs to lock and unlock sections of code. The implementation of these functions should also be part of os_tls.c.

20-2 TASK SPECIFIC STORAGE

When OS_CFG_TLS_TBL_SIZE is set to 1 or greater, each task's OS_TCB will contain a new array called .TLS_Tbl[] as shown in Figure 20-1. Each array element is of type OS_TLS which is actually a pointer to **void**. This allows an OS_TCB to be extended so that it can have as many TLS areas as needed.

2C

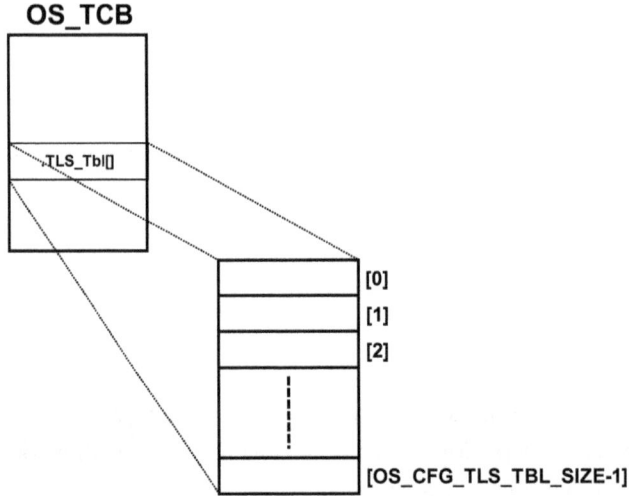

Figure 20-1 **Each OS_TCB contains an array of OS_TLS when OS_CFG_TLS_TBL_Size > 0 in os_cfg.h**

The number of entries (i.e., the value to set **OS_CFG_TLS_TBL_SIZE** to) depends on the compiler being supported as well as whether TLS storage is needed for other purposes.

OS_TLS_GETID()

The index into **.TLS_Tbl[]** is called the TLS ID and TLS IDs are assigned through an API function. In other words, TLS IDs are assigned dynamically as needed. Once a TLS ID is assigned for a specific purpose, it cannot be 'unassigned'. The function used to assign a TLS ID is called **OS_TLS_GetID()** (see Appendix A, "µC/OS-III API Reference" on page 453).

OS_TLS_SETVALUE()

The application can set the value of a **.TLS_Tbl[]** entry by calling **OS_TLS_SetValue()**. Because TLS is specific to a given task then you will need to specify the address of the **OS_TCB** of the task, the TLS ID that you want to set and the value to store into the table entry. Figure 20-2 shows two **.TLS_Tbl[]** entries (i.e., pointers) assigned by **OS_TLS_SetValue()** (see Appendix A, "µC/OS-III API Reference" on page 453).

Figure 20-2 **OS_TLS_SetValue() assigns a pointer to a .TLS_Tbl[] entry**

OS_TLS_GETVALUE()

You can retrieve the value stored into a **.TLS_Tbl[]** entry by calling **OS_TLS_GetValue()**. Again, you will have to specify the address of the **OS_TCB** of the task you are interested in as well as the desired TLS ID. **OS_TLS_GetValue()** returns the value stored in that task's .TLS_Tbl[] entry indexed by the TLS ID (see Appendix A on page 453).

OS_TLS_SETDESTRUCT()

Finally, each **.TLS_Tbl[]** entry can have a 'destructor' associated with it. A destructor is a function that is called when the task is deleted. Destructors are common to all tasks. This means that if a destructor is assigned for a TLS ID, the same destructor will be called for all the tasks for that entry. Also, when a task is deleted, the destructor for all of the TLS IDs will be called – assuming, of course, that a destructor was assigned to the corresponding TLS ID. You set a destructor function by calling **OS_TLS_SetDestruct()** and specify the TLS ID associated with the destructor as well as a pointer to the function that will be called (see Appendix A on page 453). Note that a destructor function must be declared as follows:

```
void  MyDestructFunction (OS_TCB     *p_tcb,
                          OS_TLS_ID  id,
                          OS_TLS     value);
```

445

Figure 20-3 shows the global destructor table. Note that not all implementations of `os_tls.c` will have destructors for the TLS.

Figure 20-3 **Array of pointers to destructor functions (global to all tasks)**

20-3 OS_TLS.C INTERNAL FUNCTIONS

There are four mandatory internal functions that needs to be implemented in `os_tls.c` if `OS_CFG_TLS_TBL_SIZE` is set to a non-zero value.

VOID OS_TLS_INIT (VOID)

This function is called by `OSInit()` and in fact, is called after creating the kernel objects but before creating any of the internal μC/OS-III tasks. This means that `OS_TLS_Init()` is allowed to create event flags, semaphores, mutexes and message queues.

`OS_TLS_Init()` would typically create mutexes to protect access to shared resources such as the heap or streams.

VOID OS_TLS_TASKCREATE (OS_TCB *P_TCB)

This function is called by `OSTaskCreate()` allowing each task to allocate TLS storage as needed at task creation time. If a task needs to use a specific TLS ID, the TLS ID must have been previously assigned, most likely by the startup code in `main()` or in one of the first task that runs.

OS_TLS_TaskCreate() is called immediately after calling OSTaskCreateHook().

You should note that you cannot call OS_TLS_GetValue() or OS_TLS_SetValue() for the specified task, unless the task has been created.

OS_TLS_TaskCreate() should check that TLS is a feature enabled for the task being created. This is done by examining the OS_TCB's option field (i.e., p_tcb->Opt) as follows:

```
void  OS_TLS_TaskCreate (OS_TCB  *p_tcb)
{
    OS_TLS  p_tls;


    if ((p_tcb->Opt & OS_OPT_TASK_NO_TLS) == OS_OPT_NONE) {
        p_tls                   = /* Allocate storage for TLS */
        p_tcb->TLS_Tbl[MyTLS_ID] = p_tls;
    }
}
```

Listing 20-1 **OS_TLS_TaskCreate()**

VOID OS_TLS_TASKDEL (OS_TCB *P_TCB)

This function is called by OSTaskDel() allowing each task to deallocate TLS storage that was allocated by OS_TLS_TaskCreate(). If the os_tls.c file implements destructor functions then OS_TLS_Del() should call all the destructors for the TLS IDs that have been assigned.

OS_TLS_TaskDel() is called by OSTaskDel(), immediately after calling OSTaskDelHook().

The code below shows how OS_TLS_TaskDel() can be implemented.

2C

```
void  OS_TLS_TaskDel (OS_TCB  *p_tcb)
{
    OS_TLS_ID            id;
    OS_TLS_DESTRUCT_PTR  *p_tbl;


    for (id = 0; id < OS_TLS_NextAvailID; id++) {
        p_tbl = &OS_TLS_DestructPtrTbl[id];
        if (*p_tbl != (OS_TLS_DESTRUCT_PTR)0) {
            (*p_tbl)(p_tcb, id, p_tcb->TLS_Tbl[id]);
        }
    }
}
```

Listing 20-2 **OS_TLS_TaskDel()**

OS_TLS_TaskDel() should actually check that TLS was used by the task being deleted. This is done by examining the OS_TCB's option field (i.e., p_tcb->Opt) as follows:

```
void  OS_TLS_TaskDel (OS_TCB  *p_tcb)
{
    OS_TLS_ID            id;
    OS_TLS_DESTRUCT_PTR  *p_tbl;


    if ((p_tcb->Opt & OS_OPT_TASK_NO_TLS) == OS_OPT_NONE) {
        for (id = 0; id < OS_TLS_NextAvailID; id++) {
            p_tbl = &OS_TLS_DestructPtrTbl[id];
            if (*p_tbl != (OS_TLS_DESTRUCT_PTR)0) {
                (*p_tbl)(p_tcb, id, p_tcb->TLS_Tbl[id]);
            }
        }
    }
}
```

Listing 20-3 **Check that TLS was used by the task being deleted**

An alternate implementation is shown below where OS_TLS_TaskDel() needs to deallocate storage for the task is shown below.

```
void  OS_TLS_TaskDel (OS_TCB  *p_tcb)
{
    OS_TLS  p_tls;


    p_tls = p_tcb->TLS_Tbl[MyTLS_ID];
    if ((p_tcb->Opt & OS_OPT_TASK_NO_TLS) == OS_OPT_NONE) {
        /* FREE storage used by TLS */
        p_tcb->TLS_Tbl[MyTLS_ID] = (OS_TLS)0;
    }


}
```

Listing 20-4 **OS_TLS_TaskDel() alternate implementation**

VOID OS_TLS_TASKSW (VOID)

This function is called by OSSched() before invoking OS_TASK_SW() and also, by OSIntExit() before calling OSIntCtxSw(). When OS_TLS_TaskSw() is called, OSTCBCurPtr will point to the task being switched out and OSTCBHighRdyPtr will point to the task being switched in.

OS_TLS_TaskSw() allows you to change the "current TLS" during a context switch. For example, if a compiler uses a global pointer that points to the current TLS then, OS_TLS_TaskSw() could set this pointer to point to the new task's TLS.

OS_TLS_TaskSw() should check that TLS is desired for the task being switched in. This is done by examining the OS_TCB's option field (i.e. p_tcb->Opt) as follows:

```
if ((p_tcb->Opt & OS_OPT_TASK_NO_TLS) == OS_OPT_NONE) {
    /* TLS option enabled for this task */
}
```

Listing 20-5 **Check that TLS is desired for the task being switched in**

20-4 COMPILER-SPECIFIC LOCK APIs

As previously mentioned, some compilers may already have declared API functions that are called to ensure exclusive access to shared resources. For example, APIs such as **_mutex_lock_file_system()** and **_mutex_unlock_file_system()** could be required by the compiler to ensure exclusive access to the file system. **os_tls.c** might then implement these using µC/OS-III as shown below. Note that we also included the code to initialize the mutex in **OS_TLS_Init()**.

```
OS_MUTEX  OS_TLS_FS_Mutex;              /* Mutex needed to ensure exclusive access to the FS */


void  OS_TLS_Init (OS_ERR *p_err)
{
    OS_TLS_NextAvailID = 0u;

    OS_TLS_NewLibID    = OS_TLS_GetID(p_err);
    if (*p_err != OS_ERR_NONE) {
        return;
    }

    OSMutexCreate((OS_MUTEX *)&OS_TLS_FS_Mutex,
                  (CPU_CHAR *)"File System",
                  (OS_ERR   *)p_err);
}


void  _mutex_lock_file_system (void)
{
    OS_ERR   os_err;

    if (OSRunning != OS_STATE_OS_RUNNING) {
        return;
    }
    OSMutexPend((OS_MUTEX *)&OS_TLS_FS_Mutex,
                (OS_TICK  ) 0u,
                (OS_OPT   ) OS_OPT_PEND_BLOCKING,
                (CPU_TS  *) 0,
                (OS_ERR  *)&os_err);
}
```

20

```
void  _mutex_lock_file_system (void)
{
    OS_ERR  err;

    if (OSRunning != OS_STATE_OS_RUNNING) {
        return;
    }
    OSMutexPost((OS_MUTEX *)&OS_TLS_FS_Mutex,
                (OS_OPT    )OS_OPT_POST_NONE,
                (OS_ERR   *)&err);
}
```

Listing 20-6 **Implement mutex_lock_file_system()**

The compiler may require the implementation of many such API functions to ensure exclusive access to the heap, environment variables, etc. These would all be found in os_tls.c.

20-5 SUMMARY

This chapter explained how µC/OS-III provides compiler support for thread safety.

2C

20

µC/OS-III API Reference

This chapter provides a reference to µC/OS-III services. Each of the user-accessible kernel services is presented in alphabetical order. The following information is provided for each entry:

■ A brief description of the service

■ The function prototype

■ The filename of the source code

■ The **#define** constant required to enable code for the service

■ A description of the arguments passed to the function

■ A description of returned value(s)

■ Specific notes and warnings regarding use of the service

■ One or two examples of how to use the function

Most µC/OS-III API functions return an error code. In fact, when present, the error return value is done through the last argument of the API function, as a pointer to an error code. These error codes should be checked by the application to ensure that the µC/OS-III function performed its operation as expected. Also, some of the error codes are conditional based on configuration constants. For example, argument checking error codes are returned only if **OS_CFG_ARG_CHK_EN** is set to 1 in **os_cfg.h**.

The next few pages summarizes most of the services provided by µC/OS-III. The function calls in bold are commonly used.

A-1 Task Management

```
void
OSTaskChangePrio   (OS_TCB      *p_tcb,
                    OS_PRIO      prio_new,
                    OS_ERR      *p_err);
```

```
void
OSTaskCreate       (OS_TCB      *p_tcb,          Values for "opt":
                    CPU_CHAR    *p_name,            OS_OPT_TASK_NONE
                    OS_TASK_PTR  p_task,            OS_OPT_TASK_STK_CHK
                    void        *p_arg,             OS_OPT_TASK_STK_CLR
                    OS_PRIO      prio,              OS_OPT_TASK_SAVE_FP
                    CPU_STK     *p_stk_base,        OS_OPT_TASK_NO_TLS
                    CPU_STK_SIZE stk_limit,
                    CPU_STK_SIZE stk_size,
                    OS_MSG_QTY   q_size,
                    OS_TICK      time_quanta,
                    void        *p_ext,
                    OS_OPT       opt,
                    OS_ERR      *p_err);
```

```
void
OSTaskDel          (OS_TCB      *p_tcb,
                    OS_ERR      *p_err);
```

```
OS_REG
OSTaskRegGet       (OS_TCB      *p_tcb,
                    OS_REG_ID    id,
                    OS_ERR      *p_err);
```

```
void
OSTaskRegSet       (OS_TCB      *p_tcb,
                    OS_REG_ID    id,
                    OS_REG       value,
                    OS_ERR      *p_err);
```

```
void
OSTaskResume       (OS_TCB      *p_tcb,
                    OS_ERR      *p_err);
```

```
void
OSTaskSuspend      (OS_TCB      *p_tcb,
                    OS_ERR      *p_err);
```

```
void
OSTaskStkChk       (OS_TCB      *p_tcb,
                    CPU_STK_SIZE *p_free,
                    CPU_STK_SIZE *p_used,
                    OS_ERR      *p_err);
```

```
void
OSTaskTimeQuantaSet (OS_TCB     *p_tcb,
                    OS_TICK      time_quanta,
                    OS_ERR      *p_err);
```

A-2 Time Management

```
void
OSTimeDly        (OS_TICK     dly,
                 OS_OPT      opt,
                 OS_ERR      *p_err);
```

```
void                                              Values for "opt":
OSTimeDlyHMSM    (CPU_INT16U  hours,                  OS_OPT_TIME_HMSM_STRICT
                 CPU_INT16U  minutes,                 OS_OPT_TIME_HMSM_NON_STRICT
                 CPU_INT16U  seconds
                 CPU_INT32U  milli,
                 OS_OPT      opt,
                 OS_ERR      *p_err);
```

```
void
OSTimeDlyResume (OS_TCB      *p_tcb,
                 OS_ERR      *p_err);
```

```
OS_TICK
OSTimeGet        (OS_ERR      *p_err);
```

```
void
OSTimeSet        (OS_TICK     ticks,
                 OS_ERR      *p_err);
```

A-3 Mutual Exclusion Semaphores – Resource Management

OS_MUTEX

void		
OSMutexCreate	(OS_MUTEX	*p_mutex,
	CPU_CHAR	*p_name,
	OS_ERR	*p_err);

			Values for "opt":
void			
OSMutexDel	(OS_MUTEX	*p_mutex,	OS_OPT_DEL_NO_PEND
	OS_OPT	opt,	OS_OPT_DEL_ALWAYS
	OS_ERR	*p_err);	

			Values for "opt":
void			
OSMutexPend	(OS_MUTEX	*p_mutex,	OS_OPT_PEND_BLOCKING
	OS_TICK	timeout,	OS_OPT_PEND_NON_BLOCKING
	OS_OPT	opt,	
	CPU_TS	*p_ts,	
	OS_ERR	*p_err);	

			Values for "opt":
OS_OBJ_QTY			
OSMutexPendAbort	(OS_MUTEX	*p_mutex,	OS_OPT_PEND_ABORT_1
	OS_OPT	opt,	OS_OPT_PEND_ABORT_ALL
	OS_ERR	*p_err);	OS_OPT_POST_NO_SCHED (additive)

			Values for "opt":
void			
OSMutexPost	(OS_MUTEX	*p_mutex,	OS_OPT_POST_NONE
	OS_OPT	opt,	OS_OPT_POST_NO_SCHED
	OS_ERR	*p_err);	

A-4 Event Flags – Synchronization

OS_FLAG_GRP

```
void
OSFlagCreate           (OS_FLAG_GRP    *p_grp,
                        CPU_CHAR       *p_name,
                        OS_FLAGS       flags,
                        OS_ERR         *p_err);
```

`OS_OBJ_QTY`
`OSFlagDel           (OS_FLAG_GRP    *p_grp,`
`                     OS_OPT         opt,`
`                     OS_ERR         *p_err);`
	Values for "opt":
	  `OS_OPT_DEL_NO_PEND`
	  `OS_OPT_DEL_ALWAYS`

`OS_FLAGS`
`OSFlagPend``          (OS_FLAG_GRP    *p_grp,`
`                     OS_FLAGS       flags,`
`                     OS_TICK        timeout,`
`                     OS_OPT         opt,`
`                     CPU_TS         *p_ts,`
`                     OS_ERR         *p_err);`
	Values for "opt":
	  `OS_OPT_PEND_FLAG_CLR_ALL`
	  `OS_OPT_PEND_FLAG_CLR_ANY`
	  `OS_OPT_PEND_FLAG_SET_ALL`
	  `OS_OPT_PEND_FLAH_SET_ANY`

`OS_OBJ_QTY`
`OSFlagPendAbort      (OS_FLAG_GRP    *p_grp,`
`                     OS_OPT         opt,`
`                     OS_ERR         *p_err);`
	Values for "opt":
	  `OS_OPT_PEND_ABORT_1`
	  `OS_OPT_PEND_ABORT_ALL`
	  `OS_OPT_POST_NO_SCHED (additive)`

`OS_FLAGS` **`OSFlagPendGetFlagsRdy`** `(OS_ERR         *p_err);`	

`OS_FLAGS`
`OSFlagPost``          (OS_FLAG_GRP    *p_grp,`
`                     OS_FLAGS       flags,`
`                     OS_OPT         opt,`
`                     OS_ERR         *p_err);`
	Values for "opt":
	  `OS_OPT_POST_FLAG_SET`
	  `OS_OPT_POST_FLAG_CLR`

457

A-5 Semaphores – Synchronization

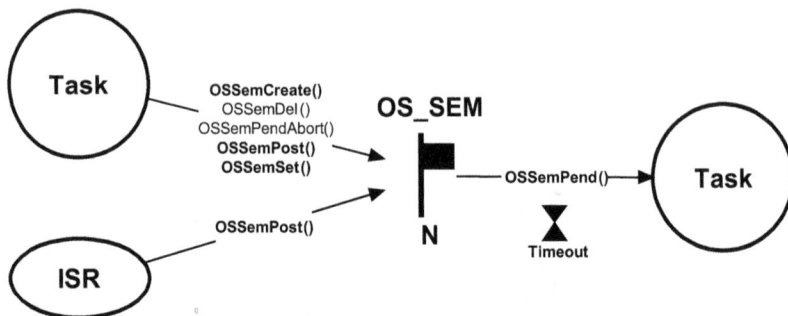

void			
OSSemCreate	(OS_SEM	*p_sem,	
	CPU_CHAR	*p_name,	
	OS_SEM_CTR	cnt,	
	OS_ERR	*p_err);	

			Values for "opt":
OS_OBJ_QTY			
OSSemDel	(OS_SEM	*p_sem,	OS_OPT_DEL_NO_PEND
	OS_OPT	opt,	OS_OPT_DEL_ALWAYS
	OS_ERR	*p_err);	

			Values for "opt":
OS_SEM_CTR			
OSSemPend	(OS_SEM	*p_sem,	OS_OPT_PEND_BLOCKING
	OS_TICK	timeout,	OS_OPT_PEND_NON_BLOCKING
	OS_OPT	opt,	
	CPU_TS	*p_ts,	
	OS_ERR	*p_err);	

			Values for "opt":
OS_OBJ_QTY			
OSSemPendAbort	(OS_SEM	*p_sem,	OS_OPT_PEND_ABORT_1
	OS_OPT	opt,	OS_OPT_PEND_ABORT_ALL
	OS_ERR	*p_err);	OS_OPT_POST_NO_SCHED (additive)

			Values for "opt":
void			
OSSemPost	(OS_SEM	*p_sem,	OS_OPT_POST_1
	OS_OPT	opt,	OS_OPT_POST_ALL
	OS_ERR	*p_err);	OS_OPT_POST_NO_SCHED (additive)

void			
OSSemSet	(OS_SEM	*p_sem,	
	OS_SEM_CTR	cnt,	
	OS_ERR	*p_err);	

A-6 Task Semaphores – Synchronization

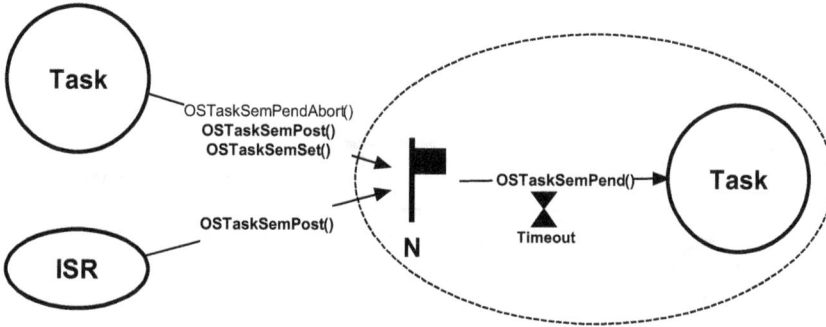

OS_SEM_CTR			Values for "opt":
OSTaskSemPend	(OS_TICK	timeout,	OS_OPT_PEND_BLOCKING
	OS_OPT	opt,	OS_OPT_PEND_NON_BLOCKING
	CPU_TS	*p_ts,	
	OS_ERR	*p_err);	

CPU_BOOLEAN			Values for "opt":
OSTaskSemPendAbort	(OS_TCB	*p_tcb,	OS_OPT_POST_NONE
	OS_OPT	opt,	OS_OPT_POST_NO_SCHED
	OS_ERR	*p_err);	

OS_SEM_CTR			Values for "opt":
OSTaskSemPost	(OS_TCB	*p_tcb,	OS_OPT_POST_NONE
	OS_OPT	opt,	OS_OPT_POST_NO_SCHED
	OS_ERR	*p_err);	

OS_SEM_CTR			
OSTaskSemSet	(OS_TCB	*p_tcb,	
	OS_SEM_CTR	cnt,	
	OS_ERR	*p_err);	

A-7 Message Queues – Message Passing

```
void
OSQCreate    (OS_Q       *p_q,
              CPU_CHAR    *p_name,
              OS_MSG_QTY  max_qty,
              OS_ERR      *p_err);
```

```OS_OBJ_QTY,```
```OSQDel   (OS_Q   *p_q,```
```   OS_OPT   opt,```
```   OS_ERR   *p_err);```
	Values for "opt":
	    OS_OPT_DEL_NO_PEND
	    OS_OPT_DEL_ALWAYS

```
OS_MSG_QTY
OSQFlush  (OS_Q    *p_q,
           OS_ERR  *p_err);
```

```void *```
```OSQPend   (OS_Q   *p_q,```
```   OS_TICK   timeout,```
```   OS_OPT   opt,```
```   OS_MSG_SIZE *p_msg_size,```
```   CPU_TS   *p_ts,```
```   OS_ERR   *p_err);```
	Values for "opt":
	    OS_OPT_PEND_BLOCKING
	    OS_OPT_PEND_NON_BLOCKING

```OS_OBJ_QTY```
```OSQPendAbort (OS_Q   *p_q,```
```   OS_OPT   opt,```
```   OS_ERR   *p_err);```
	Values for "opt":
	    OS_OPT_PEND_ABORT_1
	    OS_OPT_PEND_ABORT_ALL
	    OS_OPT_POST_NO_SCHED (additive)

```void```
```OSQPost   (OS_Q   *p_q,```
```   void   *p_void,```
```   OS_MSG_SIZE msg_size,```
```   OS_OPT   opt,```
```   OS_ERR   *p_err);```
	Values for "opt":
	    OS_OPT_POST_ALL
	    OS_OPT_POST_FIFO
	    OS_OPT_POST_LIFO
	    OS_OPT_POST_NO_SCHED (additive)

A-8 Task Message Queues – Message Passing

```
OS_MSG_QTY
OSTaskQFlush    (OS_TCB    *p_tcb,
                 OS_ERR    *p_err);
```

```
void *
OSTaskQPend    (OS_TICK     timeout,
                OS_OPT      opt,
                OS_MSG_SIZE *p_msg_size,
                CPU_TS      *p_ts,
                OS_ERR      *p_err);
```
Values for "opt":
    OS_OPT_PEND_BLOCKING
    OS_OPT_PEND_NON_BLOCKING

```
CPU_BOOLEAN
OSTaskQPendAbort (OS_TCB    *p_tcb,
                  OS_OPT    opt,
                  OS_ERR    *p_err);
```
Values for "opt":
    OS_OPT_POST_NONE
    OS_OPT_POST_NO_SCHED

```
void
OSTaskQPost    (OS_TCB      *p_tcb,
                void        *p_void,
                OS_MSG_SIZE msg_size,
                OS_OPT      opt,
                OS_ERR      *p_err);
```
Values for "opt":
    OS_OPT_POST_FIFO
    OS_OPT_POST_LIFO
    OS_OPT_POST_NO_SCHED (additive)

A-9 Pending on Multiple Objects

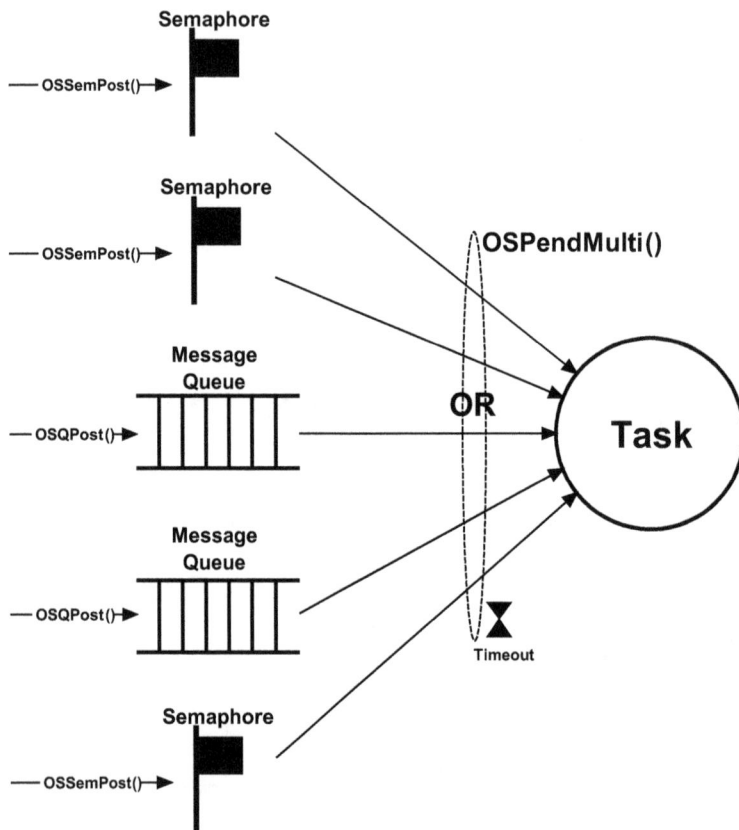

```
OS_OBJ_QTY
OSPendMulti (OS_PEND_DATA  *p_pend_data_tbl,
             OS_OBJ_QTY     tbl_size,
             OS_TICK        timeout,
             OS_OPT         opt,
             OS_ERR         *p_err);
```

```
Values for "opt":
   OS_OPT_PEND_BLOCKING
   OS_OPT_PEND_NON_BLOCKING
```

A-10 Timers

OS_TMR

```
void
OSTmrCreate     (OS_TMR              *p_tmr,
                 CPU_CHAR            *p_name,
                 OS_TICK             dly,
                 OS_TICK             period,
                 OS_OPT              opt,
                 OS_TMR_CALLBACK_PTR p_callback,
                 void                *p_callback_arg,
                 OS_ERR              *p_err);
```

Values for "opt":
    OS_OPT_TMR_ONE_SHOT
    OS_OPT_TMR_PERIODIC

```
CPU_BOOLEAN
OSTmrDel        (OS_TMR              *p_tmr,
                 OS_ERR              *p_err);
```

```
OS_TICK
OSTmrRemainGet  (OS_TMR              *p_tmr,
                 OS_ERR              *p_err);
```

```
OS_STATE
OSTmrStateGet   (OS_TMR              *p_tmr,
                 OS_ERR              *p_err);
```

```
CPU_BOOLEAN
OSTmrStart      (OS_TMR              *p_tmr,
                 OS_ERR              *p_err);
```

```
CPU_BOOLEAN
OSTmrStop       (OS_TMR              *p_tmr,
                 OS_OPT              opt,
                 void                *p_callback_arg,
                 OS_ERR              *p_err);
```

A-11 Fixed-Size Memory Partitions – Memory Management

```
void
OSMemCreate (OS_MEM       *p_mem,
             CPU_CHAR     *p_name,
             void         *p_addr,
             OS_MEM_QTY   n_blks,
             OS_MEM_SIZE  blk_size,
             OS_ERR       *p_err);
```

```
void *
OSMemGet    (OS_MEM       *p_mem,
             OS_ERR       *p_err);
```

```
void
OSMemPut    (OS_MEM       *p_mem,
             void         *p_blk,
             OS_ERR       *p_err);
```

A-12 OSCtxSw()

```
void   OSCtxSw (void)
```

File	Called from	Code enabled by
os_cpu_a.asm	OSSched()	N/A

OSCtxSw() is called from the macro OS_TASK_SW(), which in turn is called from OSSched() to perform a task-level context switch. Interrupts are disabled when OSCtxSw() is called.

Prior to calling OSCtxSw(), OSTCBCurPtr to point at the OS_TCB of the task that is being switched out, and OSSched() sets OSTCBHighRdyPtr to point at the OS_TCB of the task being switched in.

ARGUMENTS

None

RETURNED VALUES

None

NOTES/WARNINGS

None

EXAMPLE

The pseudocode for OSCtxSw() follows:

```
void  OSCtxSw (void)
{
    Save all CPU registers;                      (1)
    OSTCBCurPtr->StkPtr = SP;                     (2)
    OSTaskSwHook();                               (3)
    OSPrioCur          = OSPrioHighRdy;           (4)
    OSTCBCurPtr        = OSTCBHighRdyPtr;          (5)
    SP                 = OSTCBHighRdyPtr->StkPtr;  (6)
    Restore all CPU registers;                    (7)
    Return from interrupt;                        (8)
}
```

(1)   OSCtxSw() must save all of the CPU registers onto the current task's stack. OSCtxSw() is called from the context of the task being switched out. Therefore, the CPU stack pointer is pointing to the proper stack. The user must save all of the registers in the same order as if an ISR started and all the CPU registers were saved on the stack. The stacking order should therefore match that of OSTaskStkInit().

(2)   The current task's stack pointer is then saved into the current task's OS_TCB.

(3)   Next, OSCtxSw() must call OSTaskSwHook().

(4)   OSPrioHighRdy is copied to OSPrioCur.

(5)   OSTCBHighRdyPtr is copied to OSTCBCurPtr since the current task is now the task being switched in.

(6)   The stack pointer of the new task is restored from the OS_TCB of the new task.

(7)   All the CPU registers from the new task's stack are restored.

(8)   Finally, OSCtxSw() must execute a return from interrupt instruction.

A-13 OSFlagCreate()

```
void  OSFlagCreate (OS_FLAG_GRP  *p_grp,
                    CPU_CHAR      *p_name,
                    OS_FLAGS       flags,
                    OS_ERR        *p_err)
```

File	Called from	Code enabled by
os_flag.c	Task or startup code	OS_CFG_FLAG_EN

OSFlagCreate() is used to create and initialize an event flag group. µC/OS-III allows the user to create an unlimited number of event flag groups (limited only by the amount of RAM in the system).

ARGUMENTS

p_grp   This is a pointer to an event flag group that must be allocated in the application. The user will need to declare a "global" variable as shown, and pass a pointer to this variable to OSFlagCreate():

OS_FLAG_GRP MyEventFlag;

p_name   This is a pointer to an ASCII string used for the name of the event flag group. The name can be displayed by debuggers or by µC/Probe.

flags   This contains the initial value of the flags to store in the event flag group. Typically, you would set all flags to 0 events correspond to set bits and all 1s if events correspond to cleared bits.

p_err   This is a pointer to a variable that is used to hold an error code. The error code can be one of the following:

OS_ERR_NONE   If the call is successful and the event flag group has been created.

OS_ERR_CREATE_ISR   if OS_CFG_CALLED_FROM_ISR_CHK_EN set to 1 in os_cfg.h: If attempting to create an event flag group from an ISR, w is not allowed.

OS_ERR_OBJ_CREATED   If the object passed has already been created.

OS_ERR_OBJ_PTR_NULL	if OS_CFG_ARG_CHK_EN is set to 1 in os_cfg.h: If p_grp is a NULL pointer.
OS_ERR_ILLEGAL_CREATE_RUN_TIME	if OS_SAFETY_CRITICAL_IEC61508 is defined: you called this after calling OSSafetyCriticalStart() and thus you are no longer allowed to create additional kernel objects.

RETURNED VALUES

None

NOTES/WARNINGS

Event flag groups must be created by this function before they can be used by the other event flag group services.

EXAMPLE

```
OS_FLAG_GRP  EngineStatus;


void main (void)
{
    OS_ERR  err;

    OSInit(&err);                   /* Initialize µC/OS-III                       */
    :
    :
    OSFlagCreate(&EngineStatus,
             "Engine Status",
             (OS_FLAGS)0,
             &err);                 /* Create a flag grp containing the engine's status */
    /* Check "err" */
    :
    :
    OSStart();                      /* Start Multitasking                         */
}
```

A-14 OSFlagDel()

```
void OSFlagDel (OS_FLAG_GRP *p_grp,
                OS_OPT       opt,
                OS_ERR      *p_err);
```

File	Called from	Code enabled by
os_flag.c	Task only	OS_CFG_FLAG_EN and OS_CFG_FLAG_DEL_EN

OSFlagDel() is used to delete an event flag group. This function should be used with care since multiple tasks may be relying on the presence of the event flag group. Generally, before deleting an event flag group, first delete all of the tasks that access the event flag group. Also, it is recommended that the user not delete kernel objects at run time.

ARGUMENTS

p_grp   is a pointer to the event flag group to delete.

opt   specifies whether the user wants to delete the event flag group only if there are no pending tasks (OS_OPT_DEL_NO_PEND), or whether the event flag group should always be deleted regardless of whether or not tasks are pending (OS_OPT_DEL_ALWAYS). In this case, all pending task are readied.

p_err   is a pointer to a variable used to hold an error code. The error code can be one of the following:

OS_ERR_NONE	if the call is successful and the event flag group has been deleted.
OS_ERR_DEL_ISR	if OS_CFG_CALLED_FROM_ISR_CHK_EN set to 1 in os_cfg.h: if the user attempts to delete an event flag group from an ISR.
OS_ERR_OBJ_PTR_NULL	if OS_CFG_ARG_CHK_EN is set to 1 in os_cfg.h: if p_grp is a NULL pointer.
OS_ERR_OBJ_TYPE	if OS_CFG_OBJ_TYPE_CHK_EN is set to 1 in os_cfg.h: if p_grp is not pointing to an event flag group.

OS_ERR_OPT_INVALID	if OS_CFG_ARG_CHK_EN is set to 1 in os_cfg.h: if the user does not specify one of the options mentioned in the **opt** argument.
OS_ERR_TASK_WAITING	if one or more tasks are waiting on the event flag group and OS_OPT_DEL_NO_PEND is specified.

RETURNED VALUES

0 if no task was waiting on the event flag group, or an error occurs.

> 0 if one or more tasks waiting on the event flag group are now readied and informed

NOTES/WARNINGS

You should use this call with care as other tasks might expect the presence of the event flag group.

EXAMPLE

```
OS_FLAG_GRP  EngineStatusFlags;


void Task (void *p_arg)
{
    OS_ERR      err;
    OS_OBJ_QTY  qty;

    (void)&p_arg;
    while (DEF_ON) {
        :
        :
        qty = OSFlagDel(&EngineStatusFlags,
                        OS_OPT_DEL_ALWAYS,
                        &err);
        /* Check "err" */
        :
        :
    }
}
```

A-15 OSFlagPend()

```
OS_FLAGS   OSFlagPend (OS_FLAG_GRP *p_grp,
                       OS_FLAGS     flags,
                       OS_TICK      timeout,
                       OS_OPT       opt,
                       CPU_TS      *p_ts,
                       OS_ERR      *p_err)
```

File	Called from	Code enabled by
os_flag.c	Task only	OS_CFG_FLAG_EN

OSFlagPend() allows the task to wait for a combination of conditions or events (i.e. bits) to be set (or cleared) in an event flag group. The application can wait for any condition to be set or cleared, or for all conditions to be set or cleared. If the events that the calling task desires are not available, the calling task is blocked (optional) until the desired conditions or events are satisfied, the specified timeout expires, the event flag is deleted, or the pend is aborted by another task.

ARGUMENTS

p_grp   is a pointer to the event flag group.

flags   is a bit pattern indicating which bit(s) (i.e., flags) to check. The bits wanted are specified by setting the corresponding bits in flags. If the application wants to wait for bits 0 and 1 to be set, specify 0x03. The same applies if you'd want to wait for the same 2 bits to be cleared (you'd still specify which bits by passing 0x03).

timeout   allows the task to resume execution if the desired flag(s) is (are) not received from the event flag group within the specified number of clock ticks. A timeout value of 0 indicates that the task wants to wait forever for the flag(s). The timeout value is not synchronized with the clock tick. The timeout count begins decrementing on the next clock tick, which could potentially occur immediately.

opt   specifies whether all bits are to be set/cleared or any of the bits are to be set/cleared. Here are the options:

OS_OPT_PEND_FLAG_CLR_ALL	Check all bits in flags to be clear (0)
OS_OPT_PEND_FLAG_CLR_ANY	Check any bit in flags to be clear (0)
OS_OPT_PEND_FLAG_SET_ALL	Check all bits in flags to be set (1)
OS_OPT_PEND_FLAG_SET_ANY	Check any bit in flags to be set (1)

The caller may also specify whether the flags are consumed by "adding" OS_OPT_PEND_FLAG_CONSUME to the **opt** argument. For example, to wait for any flag in a group and then clear the flags that satisfy the condition, you would set **opt** to:

OS_OPT_PEND_FLAG_SET_ANY + OS_OPT_PEND_FLAG_CONSUME

Finally, you can specify whether you want the caller to block if the flag(s) are available or not. You would then "add" the following options:

OS_OPT_PEND_BLOCKING
OS_OPT_PEND_NON_BLOCKING

Note that the **timeout** argument should be set to **0** when specifying OS_OPT_PEND_NON_BLOCKING, since the timeout value is irrelevant using this option. Having a non-zero value could simply confuse the reader of your code.

p_ts   is a pointer to a timestamp indicating when the flags were posted, the pend was aborted, or the event flag group was deleted. Passing a **NULL** pointer (i.e., (CPU_TS *)0) indicates that the caller does not desire the timestamp. In other words, passing a **NULL** pointer is valid, and indicates that the caller does not need the timestamp.

A timestamp is useful when the task desires to know when the event flag group was posted or how long it took for the task to resume after the event flag group was posted. In the latter case, the user must call OS_TS_GET() and compute the difference between the current value of the timestamp and *p_ts, as shown:

delta = OS_TS_GET() - *p_ts;

p_err	is a pointer to an error code and can be:

OS_ERR_NONE	No error.
OS_ERR_OBJ_PTR_NULL	if OS_CFG_ARG_CHK_EN is set to 1 in os_cfg.h: if p_grp is a NULL pointer.
OS_ERR_OBJ_TYPE	if OS_CFG_OBJ_TYPE_CHK_EN is set to 1 in os_cfg.h: p_grp is not pointing to an event flag group.
OS_ERR_OPT_INVALID	if OS_CFG_ARG_CHK_EN is set to 1 in os_cfg.h: the caller specified an invalid option.
OS_ERR_PEND_ABORT	the wait on the flags was aborted by another task that called OSFlagPendAbort().
OS_ERR_PEND_ISR	if OS_CFG_CALLED_FROM_ISR_CHK_EN set to 1 in os_cfg.h: An attempt was made to call OSFlagPend() from an ISR, which is not allowed.
OS_ERR_SCHED_LOCKED	When calling this function while the scheduler was locked.
OS_ERR_PEND_WOULD_BLOCK	if specifying non-blocking but the flags were not available and the call would block if the caller had specified OS_OPT_PEND_BLOCKING.
OS_ERR_TIMEOUT	the flags are not available within the specified amount of time.

RETURNED VALUES

The flag(s) that cause the task to be ready, 0 if either none of the flags are ready, or indicate an error occurred.

NOTES/WARNINGS

The event flag group must be created before it is used.

EXAMPLE

```
#define   ENGINE_OIL_PRES_OK    0x01
#define   ENGINE_OIL_TEMP_OK    0x02
#define   ENGINE_START          0x04

OS_FLAG_GRP  EngineStatus;

void Task (void *p_arg)
{
    OS_ERR    err;
    OS_FLAGS  value;
    CPU_TS    ts;


    (void)&p_arg;
    while (DEF_ON) {
        value = OSFlagPend(&EngineStatus,
                           ENGINE_OIL_PRES_OK   + ENGINE_OIL_TEMP_OK,
                           OS_FLAG_WAIT_SET_ALL + OS_FLAG_CONSUME,
                           10,
                           OS_OPT_PEND_BLOCKING,
                           &ts,
                           &err);
        /* Check "err" */
        :
        :
    }
}
```

A-16 OSFlagPendAbort()

```
OS_OBJ_QTY  OSFlagPendAbort (OS_SEM   *p_grp,
                             OS_OPT    opt,
                             OS_ERR   *p_err)
```

File	Called from	Code enabled by
os_flag.c	Task only	OS_CFG_FLAG_EN and OS_CFG_FLAG_PEND_ABORT_EN

OSFlagPendAbort() aborts and readies any tasks currently waiting on an event flag group. This function would be used by another task to fault abort the wait on the event flag group, rather than to normally signal the event flag group via **OSFlagPost()**.

ARGUMENTS

p_grp   is a pointer to the event flag group for which pend(s) must be aborted.

opt   determines the type of abort performed.

OS_OPT_PEND_ABORT_1	Aborts the pend of only the highest priority task waiting on the event flag group.
OS_OPT_PEND_ABORT_ALL	Aborts the pend of all the tasks waiting on the event flag group.
OS_OPT_POST_NO_SCHED	Specifies that the scheduler should not be called even if the pend of a higher priority task is aborted. Scheduling will need to occur from another function.
	You would use this option if the task calling **OSFlagPendAbort()** will perform additional pend aborts, rescheduling will take place at completion, and when multiple pend aborts are to take effect simultaneously.

p_err   is a pointer to a variable that holds an error code. `OSFlagPendAbort()` sets
            `*p_err` to one of the following:

OS_ERR_NONE	at least one task waiting on the event flag group was readied and informed of the aborted wait. The return value indicates the number of tasks where a wait on the event flag group was aborted.
OS_ERR_OBJ_PTR_NULL	if OS_CFG_ARG_CHK_EN is set to 1 in os_cfg.h: if p_grp is a NULL pointer.
OS_ERR_OBJ_TYPE	if OS_CFG_OBJ_TYPE_CHK_EN is set to 1 in os_cfg.h: if p_grp is not pointing to an event flag group.
OS_ERR_OPT_INVALID	if OS_CFG_ARG_CHK_EN is set to 1 in os_cfg.h: if specifying an invalid option.
OS_ERR_PEND_ABORT_ISR	if OS_CFG_CALLED_FROM_ISR_CHK_EN set to 1 in os_cfg.h: This function cannot be called from an ISR.
OS_ERR_PEND_ABORT_NONE	No task was aborted since no task was waiting.

RETURNED VALUE

`OSFlagPendAbort()` returns the number of tasks made ready-to-run by this function. Zero indicates that no tasks were pending on the event flag group and thus this function had no effect.

NOTES/WARNINGS

Event flag groups must be created before they are used.

EXAMPLE

```
OS_FLAG_GRP  EngineStatus;


void Task (void *p_arg)
{
    OS_ERR      err;
    OS_OBJ_QTY nbr_tasks;


    (void)&p_arg;
    while (DEF_ON) {
        :
        :
        nbr_tasks = OSFlagPendAbort(&EngineStatus,
                                    OS_OPT_PEND_ABORT_ALL,
                                    &err);
        /* Check "err" */
        :
        :
    }
}
```

A-17 OSFlagPendGetFlagsRdy()

OS_FLAGS OSFlagPendGetFlagsRdy (OS_ERR *p_err)

File	Called from	Code enabled by
os_flag.c	Task only	OS_CFG_FLAG_EN

OSFlagPendGetFlagsRdy() is used to obtain the flags that caused the current task to be ready-to-run. This function allows the user to know "Who did it!"

ARGUMENTS

p_err   is a pointer to an error code and can be:

> OS_ERR_NONE   No error.
>
> OS_ERR_PEND_ISR   if OS_CFG_CALLED_FROM_ISR_CHK_EN set to 1 in os_cfg.h: When attempting to call this function from an ISR.

RETURNED VALUE

The value of the flags that caused the current task to become ready-to-run.

NOTES/WARNINGS

The event flag group must be created before it is used.

EXAMPLE

```
#define  ENGINE_OIL_PRES_OK    0x01
#define  ENGINE_OIL_TEMP_OK    0x02
#define  ENGINE_START          0x04

OS_FLAG_GRP  EngineStatus;


void Task (void *p_arg)
{
    OS_ERR    err;
    OS_FLAGS  value;
    OS_FLAGS  flags_rdy;


    (void)&p_arg;
    while (DEF_ON) {
        value    = OSFlagPend(&EngineStatus,
                              ENGINE_OIL_PRES_OK   + ENGINE_OIL_TEMP_OK,
                              OS_FLAG_WAIT_SET_ALL + OS_FLAG_CONSUME,
                              10,
                              &err);
        /* Check "err" */
        flags_rdy = OSFlagPendGetFlagsRdy(&err);
        /* Check "err" */
        :
        :
    }
}
```

479

A-18 OSFlagPost()

```
OS_FLAGS  OSFlagPost (OS_FLAG_GRP  *p_grp,
                      OS_FLAGS       flags,
                      OS_OPT         opt,
                      OS_ERR        *p_err)
```

File	Called from	Code enabled by
os_flag.c	Task or ISR	OS_CFG_FLAG_EN

You can set or clear event flag bits by calling **OSFlagPost()**. The bits set or cleared are specified in a bit mask (i.e., the flags argument). **OSFlagPost()** readies each task that has its desired bits satisfied by this call. The caller can set or clear bits that are already set or cleared.

ARGUMENTS

p_grp   is a pointer to the event flag group.

flags   specifies which bits to be set or cleared. If **opt** is **OS_OPT_POST_FLAG_SET**, each bit that is set in **flags** will set the corresponding bit in the event flag group. For example to set bits 0, 4, and 5, you would set **flags** to **0x31** (note that bit 0 is the least significant bit). If opt is **OS_OPT_POST_FLAG_CLR**, each bit that is set in **flags** will clear the corresponding bit in the event flag group. For example to clear bits 0, 4, and 5, you would specify **flags** as **0x31** (again, bit 0 is the least significant bit).

opt   indicates whether the flags are set (**OS_OPT_POST_FLAG_SET**) or cleared (**OS_OPT_POST_FLAG_CLR**).

The caller may also "add" **OS_OPT_POST_NO_SCHED** so that μC/OS-III will not call the scheduler after the post.

p_err   is a pointer to an error code and can be:

OS_ERR_NONE	the call is successful.
OS_ERR_FLAG_INVALID_OPT	if OS_CFG_ARG_CHK_EN is set to 1 in os_cfg.h: if you specified an invalid option.
OS_ERR_OBJ_PTR_NULL	if OS_CFG_ARG_CHK_EN is set to 1 in os_cfg.h: if the caller passed a NULL pointer.
OS_ERR_OBJ_TYPE	if OS_CFG_OBJ_TYPE_CHK_EN is set to 1 in os_cfg.h: p_grp is not pointing to an event flag group.

RETURNED VALUE

The new value of the event flags.

NOTES/WARNINGS

1   Event flag groups must be created before they are used.

2   The execution time of this function depends on the number of tasks waiting on the event flag group. However, the execution time is still deterministic.

3   Although the example below shows that we are posting from a task, OSFlagPost() can also be called from an ISR.

EXAMPLE

```
#define  ENGINE_OIL_PRES_OK   0x01
#define  ENGINE_OIL_TEMP_OK   0x02
#define  ENGINE_START         0x04

OS_FLAG_GRP  EngineStatusFlags;


void  TaskX (void *p_arg)
{
    OS_ERR    err;
    OS_FLAGS  flags;


    (void)&p_arg;
    while (DEF_ON) {
        :
        :
        flags = OSFlagPost(&EngineStatusFlags,
                           ENGINE_START,
                           OS_OPT_POST_FLAG_SET,
                           &err);
        /* Check 'err" */
        :
        :
    }
}
```

A-19 OSIdleTaskHook()

```
void  OSIdleTaskHook (void);
```

File	Called from	Code enabled by
os_cpu_c.c	OS_IdleTask() ONLY	N/A

This function is called by OS_IdleTask().

OSIdleTaskHook() is part of the CPU port code and this function *must not* be called by the application code. OSIdleTaskHook() is used by the µC/OS-III port developer.

OSIdleTaskHook() runs in the context of the idle task and thus it is important to make sure there is sufficient stack space in the idle task. OSIdleTaskHook() *must not* make any OS???Pend() calls, call OSTaskSuspend() or OSTimeDly???(). In other words, this function must never be allowed to make a blocking call.

ARGUMENTS

None

RETURNED VALUE

None

NOTES/WARNINGS

■ Never make blocking calls from OSIdleTaskHook().

■ *Do not* call this function from you application.

EXAMPLE

The code below calls an application-specific hook that the application programmer can define. The user can simply set the value of OS_AppIdleTaskHookPtr to point to the desired hook function which in this case is assumed to be defined in os_app_hooks.c. The idle task calls OSIdleTaskHook() which in turns calls App_OS_IdleTaskHook() through OS_AppIdleTaskHookPtr.

This feature is very useful when there is a processor that can enter low-power mode. When µC/OS-III has no other task to run, the processor can be put to sleep waiting for an interrupt to wake it up.

```c
void  App_OS_IdleTaskHook (void)                        /* See os_app_hooks.c    */
{
    /* Your code goes here! */
    /* Put the CPU in low power mode (optional) */
}


void App_OS_SetAllHooks (void)                          /* os_app_hooks.c        */
{
    CPU_SR_ALLOC();

    CPU_CRITICAL_ENTER();
    :
    OS_AppIdleTaskHookPtr = App_OS_IdleTaskHook;
    :
    CPU_CRITICAL_EXIT();
}


void  OSIdleTaskHook (void)                             /* See os_cpu_c.c        */
{
#if OS_CFG_APP_HOOKS_EN > 0u
    if (OS_AppIdleTaskHookPtr != (OS_APP_HOOK_VOID)0) {  /* Call application hook */
        (*OS_AppIdleTaskHookPtr)();
    }
#endif
}
```

A-20 OSInit()

```
void OSInit (OS_ERR *p_err);
```

File	Called from	Code enabled by
os_core.c	Startup code only	N/A

OSInit() initializes µC/OS-III and it must be called prior to calling any other µC/OS-III function. Including OSStart() which will start multitasking. OSInit() returns as soon as an error is detected.

ARGUMENTS

p_err   is a pointer to an error code. Some of the error codes below are issued only if the associated feature is enabled.

> OS_ERR_NONE   initialization was successful.
>
> OS_ERR_INT_Q   if OS_CFG_ISR_POST_DEFERRED_EN is set to 1 in os_cfg.h: OSCfg_IntQBasePtr is NULL. The error is detected by OS_IntQTaskInit() in os_int.c.
>
> OS_ERR_INT_Q_SIZE   if OS_CFG_ISR_POST_DEFERRED_EN is set to 1 in os_cfg.h: OSCfg_IntQSize must have at least 2 elements. The error is detected by OS_IntQTaskInit() in os_int.c.
>
> OS_ERR_INT_Q_STK_INVALID   if OS_CFG_ISR_POST_DEFERRED_EN is set to 1 in os_cfg.h: OSCfg_IntQTaskStkBasePtr is NULL. The error is detected by OS_IntQTaskInit() in os_int.c
>
> OS_ERR_INT_Q_STK_SIZE_INVALID   if OS_CFG_ISR_POST_DEFERRED_EN is set to 1 in os_cfg.h: OSCfg_IntQTaskStkSize is less than OSCfg_StkSizeMin. The error is detected by OS_IntQTaskInit() in os_int.c.

`OS_ERR_MSG_POOL_EMPTY`	if `OS_CFG_ARG_CHK_EN` and `OS_CFG_Q_EN` or `OS_CFG_TASK_Q_EN` are set to 1 in `os_cfg.h`: `OSCfg_MsgPoolSize` is zero. The error is detected by `OS_MsgPoolInit()` in `os_msg.c`.
`OS_ERR_MSG_POOL_NULL_PTR`	if `OS_CFG_ARG_CHK_EN` and `OS_CFG_Q_EN` or `OS_CFG_TASK_Q_EN` are set to 1 in `os_cfg.h`: `OSCfg_MsgPoolBasePtr` is `NULL` in `os_msg.c`. The error is detected by `OS_MsgPoolInit()` in `os_msg.c`.
`OS_ERR_STAT_PRIO_INVALID`	if `OS_CFG_STAT_TASK_EN` is set to 1 in `os_cfg.h`: `OSCfg_StatTaskPrio` is invalid. The error is detected by `OS_StatTaskInit()` in `os_stat.c`.
`OS_ERR_STAT_STK_INVALID`	if `OS_CFG_STAT_TASK_EN` is set to 1 in `os_cfg.h`: `OSCfg_StatTaskStkBasePtr` is `NULL`. The error is detected by `OS_StatTaskInit()` in `os_stat.c`.
`OS_ERR_STAT_STK_SIZE_INVALID`	if`OS_CFG_STAT_TASK_EN` is set to 1 in `os_cfg.h`: `OSCfg_StatTaskStkSize` is less than `OSCfg_StkSizeMin`. The error is detected by `OS_StatTaskInit()` in `os_stat.c`.
`OS_ERR_TICK_PRIO_INVALID`	if `OSCfg_TickTaskPrio` is invalid, The error is detected by `OS_TickTaskInit()` in `os_tick.c`.
`OS_ERR_TICK_STK_INVALID`	`OSCfg_TickTaskStkBasePtr` is `NULL`. The error is detected by `OS_TickTaskInit()` in `os_tick.c`.
`OS_ERR_TICK_STK_SIZE_INVALID`	`OSCfg_TickTaskStkSize` is less than `OSCfg_StkSizeMin`. This error was detected by `OS_TickTaskInit()` in `os_tick.c`.
`OS_ERR_TMR_PRIO_INVALID`	if `OS_CFG_TMR_EN` is set to 1 in `os_cfg.h`: `OSCfg_TmrTaskPrio` is invalid. The error is detected by see `OS_TmrInit()` in `os_tmr.c`.

OS_ERR_TMR_STK_INVALID	if OS_CFG_TMR_EN is set to 1 in **os_cfg.h**: OSCfg_TmrTaskBasePtr is pointing at NULL. The error is detected by OS_TmrInit() in **os_tmr.c**.
OS_ERR_TMR_STK_SIZE_INVALID	if OS_CFG_TMR_EN is set to 1 in **os_cfg.h**: OSCfg_TmrTaskStkSize is less than OSCfg_StkSizeMin. The error is detected by OS_TmrInit() in **os_tmr.c**.

RETURNED VALUES

None

NOTES/WARNINGS

- OSInit() must be called before OSStart().

- OSInit() returns as soon as it detects an error in any of the sub-functions it calls. For example, if OSInit() encounters a problem initializing the task manager, an appropriate error code will be returned and OSInit() will not go any further. It is therefore important that the user checks the error code before starting multitasking.

EXAMPLE

```
void main (void)
{
    OS_ERR  err;

       :
    OSInit(&err);              /* Initialize µC/OS-III          */
    /* Check "err" */
       :
       :
    OSStart(&err);             /* Start Multitasking            */
    /* Check "err" */          /* Code not supposed to end up here! */
}
```

A-21 OSInitHook()

void OSInitHook (void);

File	Called from	Code enabled by
os_cpu_c.c	OSInit()	Always enabled

OSInitHook() is a function that is called by µC/OS-III's initialization code, OSInit(). OSInitHook() is typically implemented by the port implementer for the processor used. This hook allows the port to be extended to do such tasks as setup exception stacks, floating-point registers, and more. OSInitHook() is called at the beginning of OSInit(), before any µC/OS-III task and data structure have been initialized.

ARGUMENTS

None

RETURNED VALUES

None

NOTES/WARNINGS

None

EXAMPLE

```
void OSInitHook (void)                              /* See os_cpu_c.c      */
{
    /* Perform any initialization code necessary by the port */
}
```

A-22 OSIntCtxSw()

void OSIntCtxSw (void)

File	Called from	Code enabled by
os_cpu_a.asm	OSIntExit()	N/A

OSIntCtxSw() is called from OSIntExit() to perform a context switch when all nested interrupts have returned.

Interrupts are disabled when OSIntCtxSw() is called.

OSTCBCurPtr points at the OS_TCB of the task that is switched out when OSIntCtxSw() is called and OSIntExit() sets OSTCBHighRdyPtr to point at the OS_TCB of the task that is switched in.

ARGUMENTS

None

RETURNED VALUES

None

NOTES/WARNINGS

None

EXAMPLE

The pseudocode for OSIntCtxSw() is shown below. Notice that the code does only half of what OSCtxSw() did. The reason is that OSIntCtxSw() is called from an ISR and it is assumed that all of the CPU registers of the interrupted task were saved at the beginning of the ISR. OSIntCtxSw() therefore must only restore the context of the new, high-priority task.

```
void OSIntCtxSw (void)
{
    OSTaskSwHook();                              (1)
    OSPrioCur          = OSPrioHighRdy;          (2)
    OSTCBCurPtr        = OSTCBHighRdyPtr;         (3)
    SP                 = OSTCBHighRdyPtr->StkPtr; (4)
    Restore all CPU registers;                   (5)
    Return from interrupt;                       (6)
}
```

(1)   OSIntCtxSw() must call OSTaskSwHook().

(2)   OSPrioHighRdy needs to be copied to OSPrioCur.

(3)   OSTCBHighRdyPtr needs to be copied to OSTCBCurPtr because the current task will now be the new task.

(4)   The stack pointer of the new task is restored from the OS_TCB of the new task.

(5)   All the CPU registers need to be restored from the new task's stack.

(6)   A return from interrupt instruction must be executed.

A-23 OSIntEnter()

```
void OSIntEnter (void);
```

File	Called from	Code enabled by
os_core.c	ISR only	N/A

OSIntEnter() notifies μC/OS-III that an ISR is being processed. This allows μC/OS-III to keep track of interrupt nesting. OSIntEnter() is used in conjunction with OSIntExit(). This function is generally called at the beginning of ISRs. Note that on some CPU architectures, it must be written in assembly language (shown below in pseudo code):

```
MyISR:
    Save CPU registers;
    OSIntEnter();               /* Or, OSIntNestingCtr++ */
        :
    Process ISR;
        :
    OSIntExit();
    Restore CPU registers;
    Return from interrupt;
```

ARGUMENTS

None

RETURNED VALUES

None

NOTES/WARNINGS

■ This function must not be called by task-level code.

■ You can also increment the interrupt-nesting counter (**OSIntNestingCtr**) directly in the ISR to avoid the overhead of the function call/return. It is safe to increment **OSIntNestingCtr** in the ISR since interrupts are assumed to be disabled when **OSIntNestingCtr** is incremented. However, that is not true for all CPU architectures. You need to make sure that interrupts are disabled in the ISR before directly incrementing **OSIntNestingCtr**.

■ It is possible to nest interrupts up to 250 levels deep.

A-24 OSIntExit()

void OSIntExit (void);

File	Called from	Code enabled by
os_core.c	ISR only	N/A

OSIntExit() notifies µC/OS-III that an ISR is complete. This allows µC/OS-III to keep track of interrupt nesting. OSIntExit() is used in conjunction with OSIntEnter(). When the last nested interrupt completes, OSIntExit() determines if a higher priority task is ready-to-run. If so, the interrupt returns to the higher priority task instead of the interrupted task.

This function is typically called at the end of ISRs as follows, and on some CPU architectures, it must be written in assembly language (shown below in pseudo code):

```
MyISR:
    Save CPU registers;
    OSIntEnter();
        :
    Process ISR;
        :
    OSIntExit();
    Restore CPU registers;
    Return from interrupt;
```

ARGUMENTS

None

RETURNED VALUE

None

NOTES/WARNINGS

This function must not be called by task-level code. Also, if you decide to directly increment OSIntNestingCtr, instead of calling OSIntEnter(), you must still call OSIntExit().

493

A-25 OSMemCreate()

```
void  OSMemCreate (OS_MEM      *p_mem,
                   CPU_CHAR    *p_name,
                   void        *p_addr,
                   OS_MEM_QTY   n_blks,
                   OS_MEM_SIZE  blk_size,
                   OS_ERR      *p_err)
```

File	Called from	Code enabled by
os_mem.c	Task or startup code	OS_CFG_MEM_EN

OSMemCreate() creates and initializes a memory partition. A memory partition contains a user-specified number of fixed-size memory blocks. An application may obtain one of these memory blocks and, when completed, release the block back to the same partition where the block originated.

ARGUMENTS

p_mem   is a pointer to a memory partition control block that must be allocated in the application. It is assumed that storage will be allocated for the memory control blocks in the application. In other words, the user will declare a "global" variable as follows, and pass a pointer to this variable to OSMemCreate():

```
OS_MEM  MyMemPartition;
```

p_name   is a pointer to an ASCII string to provide a name to the memory partition. The name can be displayed by debuggers or µC/Probe.

p_addr   is the address of the start of a memory area used to create fixed-size memory blocks. Memory partitions may be created using either static arrays or malloc() during startup. Note that the partition *must* align on a pointer boundary. Thus, if a pointer is 16-bits wide. the partition must start on a memory location with an address that ends with 0, 2, 4, 6, 8, etc. If a pointer is 32-bits wide, the partition must start on a memory location with an address that ends in 0, 4, 8 or C. The easiest way to ensure this is to create a static array as follows:

```
void *MyMemArray[N][M]
```

You should never deallocate memory blocks that were allocated from the heap to prevent fragmentation of your heap. It is quite acceptable to allocate memory blocks from the heap as long as the user does not deallocate them.

n_blks   contains the number of memory blocks available from the specified partition. You need to specify at least two memory blocks per partition.

blk_size specifies the size (in bytes) of each memory block within a partition. A memory block must be large enough to hold at least a pointer. Also, the size of a memory block must be a multiple of the size of a pointer. If a pointer is 32-bits wide then the block size must be 4, 8, 12, 16, 20, etc. bytes (i.e., a multiple of 4 bytes).

p_err   is a pointer to a variable that holds an error code:

OS_ERR_NONE	if the memory partition is created successfully
OS_ERR_MEM_CREATE_ISR	if OS_CFG_CALLED_FROM_ISR_CHK_EN is set to 1 in os_cfg.h: if you called OSMemCreate() from an ISR.
OS_ERR_MEM_INVALID_BLKS	if OS_CFG_ARG_CHK_EN is set to 1 in os_cfg.h: if the user does not specify at least two memory blocks per partition
OS_ERR_MEM_INVALID_P_ADDR	if OS_CFG_ARG_CHK_EN is set to 1 in os_cfg.h: if specifying an invalid address (i.e., p_addr is a NULL pointer) or the partition is not properly aligned.
OS_ERR_MEM_INVALID_SIZE	if OS_CFG_ARG_CHK_EN is set to 1 in os_cfg.h: if the user does not specify a block size that can contain at least a pointer variable, and if it is not a multiple of a pointer-size variable.
OS_ERR_ILLEGAL_CREATE_RUN_TIME	if OS_SAFETY_CRITICAL_IEC61508 is defined: you called this after calling OSSafetyCriticalStart() and thus you are no longer allowed to create additional kernel objects.

RETURNED VALUE

None

NOTES/WARNINGS

Memory partitions must be created before they are used.

EXAMPLE

```
OS_MEM      CommMem;
CPU_INT32U  *CommBuf[16][32];           /* 16 buffers of 32 words of 32 bits */


void  main (void)
{
    OS_ERR  err;


    OSInit(&err);                       /* Initialize µC/OS-III            */
    :
    :
    OSMemCreate(&CommMem,
                "Comm Buffers",
                &CommBuf[0][0],
                16,
                32 * sizeof(CPU_INT32U),
                &err);
    /* Check "err" */
    :
    :
    OSStart(&err);                      /* Start Multitasking              */
}
```

A-26 OSMemGet()

```
void  *OSMemGet (OS_MEM  *p_mem,
                 OS_ERR  *p_err)
```

File	Called from	Code enabled by
os_mem.c	Task or ISR	OS_CFG_MEM_EN

OSMemGet() obtains a memory block from a memory partition. It is assumed that the application knows the size of each memory block obtained. Also, the application must return the memory block [using OSMemPut()] to the same memory partition when it no longer requires it. OSMemGet() may be called more than once until all memory blocks are allocated.

ARGUMENTS

p_mem   is a pointer to the desired memory partition control block.

p_err   is a pointer to a variable that holds an error code:

OS_ERR_NONE	if a memory block is available and returned to the application.
OS_ERR_MEM_INVALID_P_MEM	if OS_CFG_ARG_CHK_EN is set to 1 in os_cfg.h: if p_mem is a NULL pointer.
OS_ERR_MEM_NO_FREE_BLKS	if the memory partition does not contain additional memory blocks to allocate.

RETURNED VALUE

OSMemGet() returns a pointer to the allocated memory block if one is available. If a memory block is not available from the memory partition, OSMemGet() returns a NULL pointer. It is up to the application to "cast" the pointer to the proper data type since OSMemGet() returns a void *.

NOTES/WARNINGS

■ Memory partitions must be created before they are used.

■ This is a non-blocking call and this function can be called from an ISR.

EXAMPLE

```
OS_MEM  CommMem;


void Task (void *p_arg)
{
    OS_ERR      err;
    CPU_INT32U  *p_msg;


    (void)&p_arg;
    while (DEF_ON) {
        p_msg = (CPU_INT32U *)OSMemGet(&CommMem,
                                       &err);
        /* Check "err" */
        :
        :
    }
}
```

A-27 OSMemPut()

```
void   OSMemPut (OS_MEM  *p_mem,
                 void     *p_blk,
                 OS_ERR   *p_err)
```

File	Called from	Code enabled by
os_mem.c	Task or ISR	OS_CFG_MEM_EN

OSMemPut() returns a memory block back to a memory partition. It is assumed that the user will return the memory block to the same memory partition from which it was allocated.

ARGUMENTS

p_mem   is a pointer to the memory partition control block.

p_blk   is a pointer to the memory block to be returned to the memory partition.

p_err   is a pointer to a variable that holds an error code:

OS_ERR_NONE	if a memory block is available and returned to the application.
OS_ERR_MEM_INVALID_P_BLK	if OS_CFG_ARG_CHK_EN is set to 1 in os_cfg.h: if the user passed a NULL pointer for the memory block being returned to the memory partition.
OS_ERR_MEM_INVALID_P_MEM	if OS_CFG_ARG_CHK_EN is set to 1 in os_cfg.h: if p_mem is a NULL pointer.
OS_ERR_MEM_MEM_FULL	if returning a memory block to an already full memory partition. This would indicate that the user freed more blocks that were allocated and potentially did not return some of the memory blocks to the proper memory partition.

RETURNED VALUE

None

NOTES/WARNINGS

■ Memory partitions must be created before they are used.

■ You must return a memory block to the proper memory partition.

■ You can call this function from an ISR or a task.

EXAMPLE

```
OS_MEM      CommMem;
CPU_INT32U  *CommMsg;


void Task (void *p_arg)
{
    OS_ERR err;


    (void)&p_arg;
    while (DEF_ON) {
        OSMemPut(&CommMem,
                 (void *)CommMsg,
                 &err);
        /* Check "err" */
        :
        :
    }
}
```

A-28 OSMutexCreate()

```
void  OSMutexCreate (OS_MUTEX    *p_mutex,
                     CPU_CHAR    *p_name,
                     OS_ERR      *p_err)
```

File	Called from	Code enabled by
os_mutex.c	Task or startup code	OS_CFG_MUTEX_EN

OSMutexCreate() is used to create and initialize a mutex. A mutex is used to gain exclusive access to a resource.

ARGUMENTS

p_mutex   is a pointer to a mutex control block that must be allocated in the application. The user will need to declare a "global" variable as follows, and pass a pointer to this variable to OSMutexCreate():

   OS_MUTEX MyMutex;

p_name   is a pointer to an ASCII string used to assign a name to the mutual exclusion semaphore. The name may be displayed by debuggers or µC/Probe.

p_err   is a pointer to a variable that is used to hold an error code:

OS_ERR_NONE	if the call is successful and the mutex has been created.
OS_ERR_CREATE_ISR	if OS_CFG_CALLED_FROM_ISR_CHK_EN set to 1 in os_cfg.h: if attempting to create a mutex from an ISR.
OS_ERR_OBJ_PTR_NULL	if OS_CFG_ARG_CHK_EN is set to 1 in os_cfg.h: if p_mutex is a NULL pointer.
OS_ERR_ILLEGAL_CREATE_RUN_TIME	if OS_SAFETY_CRITICAL_IEC61508 is defined: you called this after calling OSSafetyCriticalStart() and thus you are no longer allowed to create additional kernel objects.

RETURNED VALUE

None

NOTES/WARNINGS

Mutexes must be created before they are used.

EXAMPLE

```
OS_MUTEX  DispMutex;


void main (void)
{
    OS_ERR  err;


    :
    OSInit(&err);                       /* Initialize µC/OS-III      */
    :
    :
    OSMutexCreate(&DispMutex,           /* Create Display Mutex      */
               "Display Mutex",
                  &err);
    /* Check "err" */


    :
    :
    OSStart(&err);                      /* Start Multitasking        */
}
```

A-29 OSMutexDel()

```
void  OSMutexDel (OS_MUTEX  *p_mutex,
                  OS_OPT     opt,
                  OS_ERR    *p_err)
```

File	Called from	Code enabled by
os_mutex.c	Task only	OS_CFG_MUTEX_EN and OS_CFG_MUTEX_DEL_EN

OSMutexDel() is used to delete a mutex. This function should be used with care because multiple tasks may rely on the presence of the mutex. Generally speaking, before deleting a mutex, first delete all the tasks that access the mutex. However, as a general rule, do not delete kernel objects at run-time.

ARGUMENTS

p_mutex   is a pointer to the mutex to delete.

opt   specifies whether to delete the mutex only if there are no pending tasks (OS_OPT_DEL_NO_PEND), or whether to always delete the mutex regardless of whether tasks are pending or not (OS_OPT_DEL_ALWAYS). In this case, all pending tasks are readied.

p_err   is a pointer to a variable that is used to hold an error code:

OS_ERR_NONE	if the call is successful and the mutex has been deleted.
OS_ERR_DEL_ISR	if OS_CFG_CALLED_FROM_ISR_CHK_EN set to 1 in os_cfg.h: if attempting to delete a mutex from an ISR.
OS_ERR_OBJ_PTR_NULL	if OS_CFG_ARG_CHK_EN is set to 1 in os_cfg.h: if p_mutex is a NULL pointer.
OS_ERR_OBJ_TYPE	if OS_CFG_OBJ_TYPE_CHK_EN is set to 1 in os_cfg.h: if p_mutex is not pointing to a mutex.
OS_ERR_OPT_INVALID	if the user does not specify one of the two options mentioned in the opt argument.

OS_ERR_TASK_WAITING if one or more task are waiting on the mutex and OS_OPT_DEL_NO_PEND is specified.

RETURNED VALUE

The number of tasks that were waiting for the mutex and 0 if an error occurred.

NOTES/WARNINGS

Use this call with care as other tasks may expect the presence of the mutex.

EXAMPLE

```
OS_MUTEX  DispMutex;


void Task (void *p_arg)
{
    OS_ERR  err;


    (void)&p_arg;
    while (DEF_ON) {
        :
        :
        OSMutexDel(&DispMutex,
                   OS_OPT_DEL_ALWAYS,
                   &err);
        /* Check "err" */
        :
        :
    }
}
```

A-30 OSMutexPend()

```
void  OSMutexPend (OS_MUTEX   *p_mutex,
                   OS_TICK      timeout,
                   OS_OPT       opt,
                   CPU_TS      *p_ts,
                   OS_ERR      *p_err)
```

File	Called from	Code enabled by
os_mutex.c	Task only	OS_CFG_MUTEX_EN

OSMutexPend() is used when a task requires exclusive access to a resource. If a task calls OSMutexPend() and the mutex is available, OSMutexPend() gives the mutex to the caller and returns to its caller. Note that nothing is actually given to the caller except that if **p_err** is set to **OS_ERR_NONE**, the caller can assume that it owns the mutex.

However, if the mutex is already owned by another task, OSMutexPend() places the calling task in the wait list for the mutex. The task waits until the task that owns the mutex releases the mutex and therefore the resource, or until the specified timeout expires. If the mutex is signaled before the timeout expires, µC/OS-III resumes the highest-priority task that is waiting for the mutex.

Note that if the mutex is owned by a lower-priority task, OSMutexPend() raises the priority of the task that owns the mutex to the same priority as the task requesting the mutex. The priority of the owner will be returned to its original priority when the owner releases the mutex (see OSMutexPost()).

OSMutexPend() allows nesting. The same task can call OSMutexPend() multiple times. However, the same task must then call OSMutexPost() an equivalent number of times to release the mutex.

ARGUMENTS

p_mutex   is a pointer to the mutex.

timeout   specifies a timeout value (in clock ticks) and is used to allow the task to resume
           execution if the mutex is not signaled (i.e., posted to) within the specified timeout.
           A timeout value of 0 indicates that the task wants to wait forever for the mutex. The
           timeout value is not synchronized with the clock tick. The timeout count is
           decremented on the next clock tick, which could potentially occur immediately.

opt   determines whether the user wants to block if the mutex is not available or not.
           This argument must be set to either:

           OS_OPT_PEND_BLOCKING, or

           OS_OPT_PEND_NON_BLOCKING

           Note that the timeout argument should be set to 0 when specifying
           OS_OPT_PEND_NON_BLOCKING since the timeout value is irrelevant using this
           option.

p_ts   is a pointer to a timestamp indicating when the mutex was posted, the pend
           was aborted, or the mutex was deleted. If passing a NULL pointer (i.e., (CPU_TS
           *)0), the caller will not receive the timestamp. In other words, passing a NULL
           pointer is valid and indicates that the timestamp is not required.

           A timestamp is useful when it is important for a task to know when the mutex
           was posted, or how long it took for the task to resume after the mutex was
           posted. In the latter case, the user must call OS_TS_GET() and compute the
           difference between the current value of the timestamp and *p_ts. In other
           words:

           delta = OS_TS_GET() - *p_ts;

p_err   is a pointer to a variable that is used to hold an error code:

OS_ERR_NONE	if the call is successful and the mutex is available.
OS_ERR_MUTEX_NESTING	if the calling task already owns the mutex and it has not posted all nested values.
OS_ERR_MUTEX_OWNER	if the calling task already owns the mutex.
OS_ERR_OBJ_PTR_NULL	if OS_CFG_ARG_CHK_EN is set to 1 in os_cfg.h: if p_mutex is a NULL pointer.
OS_ERR_OBJ_TYPE	if OS_CFG_OBJ_TYPE_CHK_EN is set to 1 in os_cfg.h: if the user did not pass a pointer to a mutex.
OS_ERR_OPT_INVALID	if OS_CFG_ARG_CHK_EN is set to 1 in os_cfg.h: if a valid option is not specified.
OS_ERR_PEND_ISR	if OS_CFG_CALLED_FROM_ISR_CHK_EN set to 1 in os_cfg.h: if attempting to acquire the mutex from an ISR.
OS_ERR_SCHED_LOCKED	if calling this function when the scheduler is locked
OS_ERR_TIMEOUT	if the mutex is not available within the specified timeout.

RETURNED VALUE

None

NOTES/WARNINGS

■   Mutexes must be created before they are used.

■   Do not suspend the task that owns the mutex. Also, do not have the mutex owner wait on any other µC/OS-III objects (i.e., semaphore, event flag, or queue), and delay the task that owns the mutex. The code should release the resource as quickly as possible.

EXAMPLE

```
OS_MUTEX  DispMutex;


void  DispTask (void *p_arg)
{
    OS_ERR  err;
    CPU_TS  ts;


    (void)&p_arg;
    while (DEF_ON) {
        :
        OSMutexPend(&DispMutex,
                    0,
                    OS_OPT_PEND_BLOCKING,
                    &ts,
                    &err);
        /* Check "err" */
    }
}
```

A-31 OSMutexPendAbort()

```
void OSMutexPendAbort (OS_MUTEX  *p_mutex,
                       OS_OPT     opt,
                       OS_ERR    *p_err)
```

File	Called from	Code enabled by
os_mutex.c	Task only	OS_CFG_MUTEX_EN and OS_CFG_MUTEX_PEND_ABORT_EN

OSMutexPendAbort() aborts and readies any tasks currently waiting on a mutex. This function should be used to fault-abort the wait on the mutex rather than to normally signal the mutex via OSMutexPost().

ARGUMENTS

p_mutex   is a pointer to the mutex.

opt   specifies whether to abort only the highest-priority task waiting on the mutex or all tasks waiting on the mutex:

OS_OPT_PEND_ABORT_1	to abort only the highest-priority task waiting on the mutex.
OS_OPT_PEND_ABORT_ALL	to abort all tasks waiting on the mutex.
OS_OPT_POST_NO_SCHED	specifies that the scheduler should not be called even if the pend of a higher-priority task has been aborted. Scheduling will need to occur from another function. The user would select this option if the task calling OSMutexPendAbort() will be doing additional pend aborts, rescheduling should not take place until all tasks are completed, and multiple pend aborts should take place simultaneously.

`p_err`   is a pointer to a variable that is used to hold an error code:

OS_ERR_NONE	if at least one task was aborted. Check the return value for the number of tasks aborted.
OS_ERR_OBJ_PTR_NULL	if OS_CFG_ARG_CHK_EN is set to 1 in os_cfg.h: if p_mutex is a NULL pointer.
OS_ERR_OBJ_TYPE	if OS_CFG_OBJ_TYPE_CHK_EN is set to 1 in os_cfg.h: if the caller does not pass a pointer to a mutex.
OS_ERR_OPT_INVALID	if OS_CFG_ARG_CHK_EN is set to 1 in os_cfg.h: if the caller specified an invalid option.
OS_ERR_PEND_ABORT_ISR	if OS_CFG_CALLED_FROM_ISR_CHK_EN set to 1 in os_cfg.h: if attempting to call this function from an ISR
OS_ERR_PEND_ABORT_NONE	if no tasks were aborted.

RETURNED VALUE

OSMutexPendAbort() returns the number of tasks made ready-to-run by this function. Zero indicates that no tasks were pending on the mutex and therefore this function had no effect.

NOTES/WARNINGS

Mutexes must be created before they are used.

EXAMPLE

```
OS_MUTEX  DispMutex;


void  DispTask (void *p_arg)
{
    OS_ERR     err;
    OS_OBJ_QTY qty;


    (void)&p_arg;
    while (DEF_ON) {
        :
        :
        qty = OSMutexPendAbort(&DispMutex,
                               OS_OPT_PEND_ABORT_ALL,
                               &err);
        /* Check "err" */
    }
}
```

A-32 OSMutexPost()

```
void OSMutexPost (OS_MUTEX  *p_mutex,
                  OS_OPT     opt,
                  OS_ERR    *p_err);
```

File	Called from	Code enabled by
os_mutex.c	Task only	OS_CFG_MUTEX_EN

A mutex is signaled (i.e., released) by calling **OSMutexPost()**. You should call this function only if you acquired the mutex by first calling **OSMutexPend()**. If the priority of the task that owns the mutex has been raised when a higher priority task attempted to acquire the mutex, at that point, the original task priority of the task is restored. If one or more tasks are waiting for the mutex, the mutex is given to the highest-priority task waiting on the mutex. The scheduler is then called to determine if the awakened task is now the highest-priority task ready-to-run, and if so, a context switch is performed to run the readied task. If no task is waiting for the mutex, the mutex value is simply set to available.

ARGUMENTS

p_mutex   is a pointer to the mutex.

opt   determines the type of POST performed.

OS_OPT_POST_NONE	No special option selected.
OS_OPT_POST_NO_SCHED	Do not call the scheduler after the post, therefore the caller is resumed even if the mutex was posted and tasks of higher priority are waiting for the mutex. Use this option if the task calling **OSMutexPost()** will be doing additional posts, if the user does not want to reschedule until all is complete, and multiple posts should take effect simultaneously.

p_err   is a pointer to a variable that is used to hold an error code:

OS_ERR_NONE	if the call is successful and the mutex is available.
OS_ERR_MUTEX_NESTING	if the owner of the mutex has the mutex nested and it has not fully un-nested.
OS_ERR_MUTEX_NOT_OWNER	if the caller is not the owner of the mutex and therefore is not allowed to release it.
OS_ERR_OBJ_PTR_NULL	if OS_CFG_ARG_CHK_EN is set to 1 in os_cfg.h: if p_mutex is a NULL pointer.
OS_ERR_OBJ_TYPE	if OS_CFG_OBJ_TYPE_CHK_EN is set to 1 in os_cfg.h: if not passing a pointer to a mutex.
OS_ERR_POST_ISR	if OS_CFG_CALLED_FROM_ISR_CHK_EN set to 1 in os_cfg.h: if attempting to post the mutex from an ISR.

RETURNED VALUE

None

NOTES/WARNINGS

- Mutexes must be created before they are used.

- Do not call this function from an ISR.

EXAMPLE

```
OS_MUTEX  DispMutex;


void  TaskX (void *p_arg)
{
    OS_ERR  err;


    (void)&p_arg;
    while (DEF_ON) {
        :
        OSMutexPost(&DispMutex,
                    OS_OPT_POST_NONE,
                    &err);
        /* Check "err" */
        :
    }
}
```

A-33 OSPendMulti()

```
OS_OBJ_QTY  OSPendMulti(OS_PEND_DATA  *p_pend_data_tbl,
                        OS_OBJ_QTY     tbl_size,
                        OS_TICK        timeout,
                        OS_OPT         opt,
                        OS_ERR         *p_err);
```

File	Called from	Code enabled by
os_pend_multi.c	Task only	OS_CFG_PEND_MULTI_EN && (OS_CFG_Q_EN || OS_CFG_SEM_EN)

OSPendMulti() is used when a task expects to wait on multiple kernel objects, specifically semaphores or message queues. If more than one such object is ready when OSPendMulti() is called, then all available objects and messages, if any, are returned as ready to the caller. If no objects are ready, OSPendMulti() suspends the current task until either:

■ an object becomes ready,

■ a timeout occurs,

■ one or more of the tasks are deleted or pend aborted or,

■ one or more of the objects are deleted.

If an object becomes ready, and multiple tasks are waiting for the object, μC/OS-III resumes the highest-priority task waiting on that object.

A pended task suspended with OSTaskSuspend() can still receive a message from a multi-pended message queue, or obtain a signal from a multi-pended semaphore. However, the task remains suspended until it is resumed by calling OSTaskResume().

ARGUMENTS

p_pend_data_tbl   is a pointer to an OS_PEND_DATA table. This table will be used by the caller to understand the outcome of this call. Also, the caller *must* initialize the .PendObjPtr field of the OS_PEND_DATA field for each object that the caller wants to pend on (see example below).

tbl_size   is the number of entries in the **OS_PEND_DATA** table pointed to by **p_pend_data_tbl**. This value indicates how many objects the task will be pending on.

timeout   specifies the amount of time (in clock ticks) that the calling task is willing to wait for objects to be posted. A timeout value of 0 indicates that the task wants to wait forever for any of the multi-pended objects. The timeout value is not synchronized with the clock tick. The timeout count begins decrementing on the next clock tick, which could potentially occur immediately.

opt   specifies options:

     OS_OPT_PEND_BLOCKING   if the caller desired to wait until any of the objects is posted to, a timeout, the pend is aborted or an object is deleted.

     OS_OPT_PEND_NON_BLOCKING   if the caller is not willing to wait if none of the objects have not already been posted.

p_err   is a pointer to a variable that holds an error code:

     OS_ERR_NONE   if any of the multi-pended objects are ready.

     OS_ERR_OBJ_TYPE   if **OS_CFG_OBJ_TYPE_CHK_EN** is set to 1 in **os_cfg.h**: if any of the **.PendObjPtr** in the **p_pend_data_tbl** is a **NULL** pointer (i.e. is not a semaphore or not a message queue).

     OS_ERR_OPT_INVALID   if **OS_CFG_ARG_CHK_EN** is set to 1 in **os_cfg.h**: if specifying an invalid option.

     OS_ERR_PEND_ABORT   indicates that a multi-pended object was aborted; check the **.RdyObjPtr** of the **p_pend_data_tbl** to know which object was aborted. The first non-**NULL** **.RdyObjPtr** is the object that was aborted.

     OS_ERR_PEND_DEL   indicates that a multi-pended object was deleted; check the **.RdyObjPtr** of the **p_pend_data_tbl** to know which object was deleted. The first non-**NULL** **.RdyObjPtr** is the object that was deleted.

OS_ERR_PEND_ISR	if OS_CFG_CALLED_FROM_ISR_CHK_EN set to 1 in os_cfg.h: if calling this function from an ISR.
OS_ERR_PEND_LOCKED	if calling this function when the scheduler is locked.
OS_ERR_PEND_WOULD_BLOCK	if the caller does not want to block and no object is ready and **opt** was OS_OPT_PEND_NON_BLOCKING.
OS_ERR_PTR_INVALID	if OS_CFG_ARG_CHK_EN is set to 1 in os_cfg.h: if p_pend_data_tbl is a NULL pointer.
OS_ERR_TIMEOUT	if no multi-pended object is ready within the specified timeout.

RETURNED VALUE

OSPendMulti() returns the number of multi-pended objects that are ready. If an object is pend aborted or deleted, the return value will be 1. You should examine the value of *p_err to know the exact outcome of this call. If no multi-pended object is ready within the specified timeout period, or because of any error, the .RdyObjPtr in the p_pend_data_tbl array will all be NULL.

When objects are posted, the OS_PEND_DATA fields of p_pend_data_tbl contains additional information about the posted objects:

.RdyObjPtr	Contains a pointer to the object ready or posted to, or NULL pointer if the object was not ready or posted to.
.RdyMsgPtr	If the object pended on was a message queue and the queue was posted to, this field contains the message.
.RdyMsgSize	If the object pended on was a message queue and the queue was posted to, this field contains the size of the message (in number of bytes).

.RdyTS   If the object pended on was posted to, this field contains the timestamp as to when the object was posted. Note that if the object is deleted or pend-aborted, this field contains the timestamp of when this occurred.

NOTES/WARNINGS

■ Message queue or semaphore objects must be created before they are used.

■ You cannot call **OSPendMulti()** from an ISR.

■ The user cannot multi-pend on event flags and mutexes.

```
OS_SEM  Sem1;
OS_SEM  Sem2;
OS_Q    Q1;
OS_Q    Q2;


void Task(void *p_arg)
{
    OS_PEND_DATA  pend_data_tbl[4];
    OS_ERR        err;
    OS_OBJ_QTY    nbr_rdy;


    (void)&p_arg;
    while (DEF_ON) {
        :
        pend_data_tbl[0].PendObjPtr = (OS_PEND_OBJ *)Sem1;
        pend_data_tbl[1].PendObjPtr = (OS_PEND_OBJ *)Sem2;
        pend_data_tbl[2].PendObjPtr = (OS_PEND_OBJ *)Q1;
        pend_data_tbl[3].PendObjPtr = (OS_PEND_OBJ *)Q2;
        nbr_rdy = OSPendMulti(&pend_data_tbl[0],
                              4,
                              0,
                              OS_OPT_PEND_BLOCKING,
                              &err);
        /* Check "err" */
        :
        :
    }
}
```

A-34 OSQCreate()

```
void  OSQCreate (OS_Q        *p_q,
                 CPU_CHAR    *p_name,
                 OS_MSG_QTY   max_qty,
                 OS_ERR      *p_err)
```

File	Called from	Code enabled by
os_q.c	Task or startup code	OS_CFG_Q_EN and OS_CFG_MSG_EN

OSQCreate() creates a message queue. A message queue allows tasks or ISRs to send pointer-sized variables (messages) to one or more tasks. The meaning of the messages sent are application specific.

ARGUMENTS

p_q   is a pointer to the message queue control block. It is assumed that storage for the message queue will be allocated in the application. The user will need to declare a "global" variable as follows, and pass a pointer to this variable to OSQCreate():

             OS_Q MyMsgQ;

p_name   is a pointer to an ASCII string used to name the message queue. The name can be displayed by debuggers or µC/Probe.

msg_qty   indicates the maximum size of the message queue (must be non-zero). If the user intends to not limit the size of the queue, simply pass a very large number. Of course, if there are not enough OS_MSGs in the pool of OS_MSGs, the post call (i.e., OSQPost()) will simply fail and an error code will indicate that there are no more OS_MSGs to use.

p_err   is a pointer to a variable that is used to hold an error code:

OS_ERR_NONE	if the call is successful and the mutex has been created.
OS_ERR_CREATE_ISR	if OS_CFG_CALLED_FROM_ISR_CHK_EN set to 1 in os_cfg.h: if attempting to create the message queue from an ISR.
OS_ERR_OBJ_PTR_NULL	if OS_CFG_ARG_CHK_EN is set to 1 in os_cfg.h: if p_q is a NULL pointer.
OS_ERR_Q_SIZE	if OS_CFG_ARG_CHK_EN is set to 1 in os_cfg.h: if the size specified is 0.
OS_ERR_ILLEGAL_CREATE_RUN_TIME	if OS_SAFETY_CRITICAL_IEC61508 is defined: you called this after calling OSSafetyCriticalStart() and thus you are no longer allowed to create additional kernel objects.

RETURNED VALUE

None

NOTES/WARNINGS

Queues must be created before they are used.

EXAMPLE

```
OS_Q    CommQ;


void main (void)
{
    OS_ERR   err;


    OSInit(&err);                    /* Initialize µC/OS-III */
    :
    :
    OSQCreate(&CommQ,
             "Comm Queue",
             10,
             &err);                  /* Create COMM Q         */
    /* Check "err" */
    :
    :
    OSStart();                       /* Start Multitasking    */
}
```

A-35 OSQDel()

```
OS_OBJ_QTY  OSQDel (OS_Q    *p_q,
                    OS_OPT   opt,
                    OS_ERR  *p_err)
```

File	Called from	Code enabled by
os_q.c	Task only	OS_CFG_Q_EN and OS_CFG_Q_DEL_EN

OSQDel() is used to delete a message queue. This function should be used with care since multiple tasks may rely on the presence of the message queue. Generally speaking, before deleting a message queue, first delete all the tasks that can access the message queue. However, it is highly recommended that you do not delete kernel objects at run time.

ARGUMENTS

p_q   is a pointer to the message queue to delete.

opt   specifies whether to delete the queue only if there are no pending tasks (OS_OPT_DEL_NO_PEND), or always delete the queue regardless of whether tasks are pending or not (OS_OPT_DEL_ALWAYS). In this case, all pending task are readied.

p_err   is a pointer to a variable that is used to hold an error code. The error code can be one of the following:

OS_ERR_NONE	if the call is successful and the message queue has been deleted.
OS_ERR_DEL_ISR	if OS_CFG_CALLED_FROM_ISR_CHK_EN set to 1 in os_cfg.h: if the user attempts to delete the message queue from an ISR.
OS_ERR_OBJ_PTR_NULL	if OS_CFG_ARG_CHK_EN is set to 1 in os_cfg.h: if passing a NULL pointer for p_q.
OS_ERR_OBJ_TYPE	if OS_CFG_OBJ_TYPE_CHK_EN is set to 1 in os_cfg.h: if p_q is not pointing to a queue.
OS_ERR_OPT_INVALID	if not specifying one of the two options mentioned in the opt argument.

OS_ERR_TASK_WAITING   if one or more tasks are waiting for messages at the message queue and it is specified to only delete if no task is pending.

RETURNED VALUE

The number of tasks that were waiting on the message queue and **0** if an error is detected.

NOTES/WARNINGS

- Message queues must be created before they can be used.

- This function must be used with care. Tasks that would normally expect the presence of the queue *must* check the return code of **OSQPend()**.

EXAMPLE

```
OS_Q  DispQ;


void Task (void *p_arg)
{
    OS_ERR  err;


    (void)&p_arg;
    while (DEF_ON) {
        :
        :
        OSQDel(&DispQ,
               OS_OPT_DEL_ALWAYS,
               &err);
        /* Check "err" */
        :
        :
    }
}
```

A-36 OSQFlush()

```
OS_MSG_QTY OSQFlush (OS_Q     *p_q,
                     OS_ERR  *p_err)
```

File	Called from	Code enabled by
os_q.c	Task only	OS_CFG_Q_EN and OS_CFG_Q_FLUSH_EN

OSQFlush() empties the contents of the message queue and eliminates all messages sent to the queue. This function takes the same amount of time to execute regardless of whether tasks are waiting on the queue (and thus no messages are present), or the queue contains one or more messages. OS_MSGs from the queue are simply returned to the free pool of OS_MSGs.

ARGUMENTS

p_q   is a pointer to the message queue.

p_err   is a pointer to a variable that will contain an error code returned by this function.

OS_ERR_NONE	if the message queue is flushed.
OS_ERR_FLUSH_ISR	if OS_CFG_CALLED_FROM_ISR_CHK_EN set to 1 in os_cfg.h: if calling this function from an ISR
OS_ERR_OBJ_PTR_NULL	if OS_CFG_ARG_CHK_EN is set to 1 in os_cfg.h: if p_q is a NULL pointer.
OS_ERR_OBJ_TYPE	if OS_CFG_OBJ_TYPE_CHK_EN is set to 1 in os_cfg.h: if you attempt to flush an object other than a message queue.

RETURNED VALUE

The number of OS_MSG entries freed from the message queue. Note that the OS_MSG entries are returned to the free pool of OS_MSGs.

NOTES/WARNINGS

■ Queues must be created before they are used.

■ Use this function with great care. When flushing a queue, you lose the references to what the queue entries are pointing to, potentially causing 'memory leaks'. The data that the user is pointing to that is referenced by the queue entries should, most likely, be de-allocated (i.e., freed).

EXAMPLE

```
OS_Q  CommQ;


void Task (void *p_arg)
{
    OS_ERR  err;


    (void)&p_arg;
    while (DEF_ON) {
        :
        :
        entries = OSQFlush(&CommQ,
                           &err);
        /* Check "err" */
        :
        :
    }
}
```

or, to flush a queue that contains entries, instead you can use **OSQPend( )** and specify the **OS_OPT_PEND_NON_BLOCKING** option.

```
OS_Q  CommQ;


void Task (void *p_arg)
{
    OS_ERR      err;
    CPU_TS      ts;
    OS_MSG_SIZE msg_size;


    (void)&p_arg;
    :
    do {
        OSQPend(&CommQ,
                0,
                OS_OPT_PEND_NON_BLOCKING,
                &msg_size,
                &ts,
                &err);
    } while (err != OS_ERR_PEND_WOULD_BLOCK);
    :
    :
}
```

A-37 OSQPend()

```
void  *OSQPend (OS_Q        *p_q,
                OS_TICK      timeout,
                OS_OPT       opt,
                OS_MSG_SIZE  *p_msg_size,
                CPU_TS       *p_ts,
                OS_ERR       *p_err)
```

File	Called from	Code enabled by
os_q.c	Task only	OS_CFG_Q_EN and OS_CFG_MSG_EN

OSQPend() is used when a task wants to receive messages from a message queue. The messages are sent to the task via the message queue either by an ISR, or by another task using the OSQPost() call. The messages received are pointer-sized variables, and their use is application specific. If at least one message is already present in the message queue when OSQPend() is called, the message is retrieved and returned to the caller.

If no message is present in the message queue and **OS_OPT_PEND_BLOCKING** is specified for the **opt** argument, OSQPend() suspends the current task until either a message is received, or a user-specified timeout expires. If a message is sent to the message queue and multiple tasks are waiting for such a message, µC/OS-III resumes the highest priority task that is waiting.

A pended task suspended with **OSTaskSuspend()** can receive a message. However, the task remains suspended until it is resumed by calling **OSTaskResume()**.

If no message is present in the queue and **OS_OPT_PEND_NON_BLOCKING** is specifed for the opt argument, OSQPend() returns to the caller with an appropriate error code, and returns a **NULL** pointer.

ARGUMENTS

p_q   is a pointer to the queue from which the messages are received.

timeout   allows the task to resume execution if a message is not received from the
           message queue within the specified number of clock ticks. A timeout value of
           0 indicates that the task is willing to wait forever for a message. The timeout
           value is not synchronized with the clock tick. The timeout count starts
           decrementing on the next clock tick, which could potentially occur
           immediately.

opt   determines whether or not to block if a message is not available in the queue.
           This argument must be set to either:

           OS_OPT_PEND_BLOCKING, or

           OS_OPT_PEND_NON_BLOCKING

           Note that the timeout argument should be set to 0 when specifying
           OS_OPT_PEND_NON_BLOCKING, since the timeout value is irrelevant using this
           option.

p_msg_size is a pointer to a variable that will receive the size of the message (in number of
           bytes).

p_ts   is a pointer to a variable that will receive the timestamp of when the message
           was received. Passing a NULL pointer is valid, and indicates that the user does
           not need the timestamp.

           A timestamp is useful when the user wants the task to know when the message
           queue was posted, or how long it took for the task to resume after the message
           queue was posted. In the latter case, you would call OS_TS_GET() and
           compute the difference between the current value of the timestamp and *p_ts.
           In other words:

           delta = OS_TS_GET() - *p_ts;

p_err   is a pointer to a variable used to hold an error code.

OS_ERR_NONE	if a message is received.
OS_ERR_OBJ_PTR_NULL	if OS_CFG_ARG_CHK_EN is set to 1 in os_cfg.h: if p_q is a NULL pointer.
OS_ERR_OBJ_TYPE	if OS_CFG_OBJ_TYPE_CHK_EN is set to 1 in os_cfg.h: if p_q is not pointing to a message queue.
OS_ERR_OPT_INVALID	if OS_CFG_ARG_CHK_EN is set to 1 in os_cfg.h: if you specified invalid options.
OS_ERR_PEND_ABORT	if the pend was aborted because another task called OSQPendAbort().
OS_ERR_PEND_ISR	if OS_CFG_CALLED_FROM_ISR_CHK_EN set to 1 in os_cfg.h: if the function is called from an ISR.
OS_ERR_PEND_WOULD_BLOCK	if this function is called with the opt argument set to OS_OPT_PEND_NON_BLOCKING, and no message is in the queue.
OS_ERR_PTR_INVALID	if OS_CFG_ARG_CHK_EN is set to 1 in os_cfg.h: if p_msg_size is a NULL pointer.
OS_ERR_SCHED_LOCKED	if calling this function when the scheduler is locked.
OS_ERR_TIMEOUT	if a message is not received within the specified timeout.

RETURNED VALUE

The message (i.e., a pointer) or a NULL pointer if no messages has been received. Note that it is possible for the actual message to be a NULL pointer, so you should check the returned error code instead of relying on the returned value.

NOTES/WARNINGS

■ Queues must be created before they are used.

■ The user cannot call OSQPend() from an ISR.

EXAMPLE

```
OS_Q   CommQ;


void CommTask (void *p_arg)
{
    OS_ERR       err;
    void         *p_msg;
    OS_MSG_SIZE  msg_size;
    CPU_TS       ts;


    (void)&p_arg;
    while (DEF_ON) {
        :
        :
        p_msg = OSQPend(CommQ,
                        100,
                        OS_OPT_PEND_BLOCKING,
                        &msg_size,
                        &ts,
                        &err);
        /* Check "err" */
        :
        :
    }
}
```

A-38 OSQPendAbort()

```
OS_OBJ_QTY  OSQPendAbort (OS_Q     *p_q,
                          OS_OPT    opt,
                          OS_ERR   *p_err)
```

File	Called from	Code enabled by
os_q.c	Task only	OS_CFG_Q_EN and OS_CFG_Q_PEND_ABORT_EN

OSQPendAbort() aborts and readies any tasks currently waiting on a message queue. This function should be used to fault-abort the wait on the message queue, rather than to signal the message queue via OSQPost().

ARGUMENTS

p_q   is a pointer to the queue for which pend(s) need to be aborted.

opt   determines the type of abort to be performed.

OS_OPT_PEND_ABORT_1	Aborts the pend of only the highest-priority task waiting on the message queue.
OS_OPT_PEND_ABORT_ALL	Aborts the pend of all tasks waiting on the message queue.
OS_OPT_POST_NO_SCHED	specifies that the scheduler should not be called, even if the pend of a higher-priority task has been aborted. Scheduling will need to occur from another function.
	You would use this option if the task calling OSQPendAbort() is doing additional pend aborts, rescheduling is not performed until completion, and multiple pend aborts are to take effect simultaneously.

p_err   is a pointer to a variable that holds an error code:

OS_ERR_NONE	at least one task waiting on the message queue was readied and informed of the aborted wait. Check the return value for the number of tasks whose wait on the message queue was aborted.
OS_ERR_PEND_ABORT_ISR	if OS_CFG_CALLED_FROM_ISR_CHK_EN set to 1 in os_cfg.h: if called from an ISR
OS_ERR_PEND_ABORT_NONE	if no task was pending on the message queue
OS_ERR_OBJ_PTR_NULL	if OS_CFG_ARG_CHK_EN is set to 1 in os_cfg.h: if p_q is a NULL pointer.
OS_ERR_OBJ_TYPE	if OS_CFG_OBJ_TYPE_CHK_EN is set to 1 in os_cfg.h: if p_q is not pointing to a message queue.
OS_ERR_OPT_INVALID	if OS_CFG_ARG_CHK_EN is set to 1 in os_cfg.h: if an invalid option is specified.

RETURNED VALUE

OSQPendAbort() returns the number of tasks made ready-to-run by this function. Zero indicates that no tasks were pending on the message queue, therefore this function had no effect.

NOTES/WARNINGS

Queues must be created before they are used.

EXAMPLE

```
OS_Q   CommQ;


void CommTask(void *p_arg)
{
    OS_ERR      err;
    OS_OBJ_QTY  nbr_tasks;


    (void)&p_arg;
    while (DEF_ON) {
        :
        :
        nbr_tasks = OSQPendAbort(&CommQ,
                                 OS_OPT_PEND_ABORT_ALL,
                                 &err);
        /* Check "err" */
        :
        :
    }
}
```

A-39 OSQPost()

```
void   OSQPost (OS_Q         *p_q,
               void          *p_void,
               OS_MSG_SIZE   msg_size,
               OS_OPT        opt,
               OS_ERR        *p_err)
```

File	Called from	Code enabled by
os_q.c	Task or ISR	OS_CFG_Q_EN

OSQPost() sends a message to a task through a message queue. A message is a pointer-sized variable, and its use is application specific. If the message queue is full, an error code is returned to the caller. In this case, OSQPost() immediately returns to its caller, and the message is not placed in the message queue.

If any task is waiting for a message to be posted to the message queue, the highest-priority task receives the message. If the task waiting for the message has a higher priority than the task sending the message, the higher-priority task resumes, and the task sending the message is suspended; that is, a context switch occurs. Message queues can be first-in first-out (OS_OPT_POST_FIFO), or last-in-first-out (OS_OPT_POST_LIFO) depending of the value specified in the **opt** argument.

If any task is waiting for a message at the message queue, OSQPost() allows the user to either post the message to the highest-priority task waiting at the queue (**opt** set to OS_OPT_POST_FIFO or OS_OPT_POST_LIFO), or to all tasks waiting at the message queue (**opt** is set to OS_OPT_POST_ALL). In either case, scheduling occurs unless **opt** is also set to OS_OPT_POST_NO_SCHED.

ARGUMENTS

p_q   is a pointer to the message queue being posted to.

p_void   is the actual message posted. **p_void** is a pointer-sized variable. Its meaning is application specific.

msg_size specifies the size of the message (in number of bytes).

535

opt   determines the type of POST performed. The last two options may be added to either **OS_OPT_POST_FIFO** or **OS_OPT_POST_LIFO** to create different combinations:

OS_OPT_POST_FIFO	POST message to the end of the queue (FIFO), or send message to a single waiting task.
OS_OPT_POST_LIFO	POST message to the front of the queue (LIFO), or send message to a single waiting task
OS_OPT_POST_ALL	POST message to ALL tasks that are waiting on the queue. This option can be added to either **OS_OPT_POST_FIFO** or **OS_OPT_POST_LIFO**.
OS_OPT_POST_NO_SCHED	This option specifies to not call the scheduler after the post and therefore the caller is resumed, even if the message was posted to a message queue with tasks having a higher priority than the caller.
	You would use this option if the task (or ISR) calling **OSQPost()** will do additional posts, in this case, the caller does not want to reschedule until finished, and, multiple posts are to take effect simultaneously.

p_err   is a pointer to a variable that will contain an error code returned by this function.

OS_ERR_NONE	if no tasks were waiting on the queue. In this case, the return value is also 0.
OS_ERR_MSG_POOL_EMPTY	if there are no more **OS_MSG** structures to use to store the message.
OS_ERR_OBJ_PTR_NULL	if **OS_CFG_ARG_CHK_EN** is set to 1 in **os_cfg.h**: if **p_q** is a NULL pointer.
OS_ERR_OBJ_TYPE	if **OS_CFG_OBJ_TYPE_CHK_EN** is set to 1 in **os_cfg.h**: if **p_q** is not pointing to a message queue.
OS_ERR_Q_MAX	if the queue is full and therefore cannot accept more messages.

RETURNED VALUE

None

NOTES/WARNINGS

- Queues must be created before they are used.

- Possible combinations of options are:

```
OS_OPT_POST_FIFO
OS_OPT_POST_LIFO
OS_OPT_POST_FIFO + OS_OPT_POST_ALL
OS_OPT_POST_LIFO + OS_OPT_POST_ALL
OS_OPT_POST_FIFO + OS_OPT_POST_NO_SCHED
OS_OPT_POST_LIFO + OS_OPT_POST_NO_SCHED
OS_OPT_POST_FIFO + OS_OPT_POST_ALL + OS_OPT_POST_NO_SCHED
OS_OPT_POST_LIFO + OS_OPT_POST_ALL + OS_OPT_POST_NO_SCHED
```

- Although the example below shows calling **OSQPost()** from a task, it can also be called from an ISR.

EXAMPLE

```
OS_Q         CommQ;
CPU_INT08U   CommRxBuf[100];


void CommTaskRx (void *p_arg)
{
    OS_ERR  err;


    (void)&p_arg;
    while (DEF_ON) {
        :
        :
        OSQPost(&CommQ,
                &CommRxBuf[0],
                sizeof(CommRxBuf),
                OS_OPT_POST_OPT_FIFO + OS_OPT_POST_ALL + OS_OPT_POST_NO_SCHED,
                &err);
        /* Check "err" */
        :
        :
    }
}
```

A-40 OSSafetyCriticalStart()

void OSSafetyCriticalStart (void)

File	Called from	Code enabled by
os_core.c	Task only	OS_SAFETY_CRITICAL_IEC61508

OSSafetyCriticalStart() allows your code to notify µC/OS-III that you are done initializing and creating kernel objects. After calling OSSafetyCriticalStart(), your application code will no longer be allowed to create kernel objects. In other words, once your code has called OSSafetyCriticalStart(), you will not be allowed to create tasks, semaphores, mutexes, message queues, event flags and timers.

ARGUMENTS

None

RETURNED VALUE

None

NOTES/WARNINGS

None

EXAMPLE

```
void AppStartTask (void *p_arg)
{
    (void)&p_arg;
    /* Create tasks and other kernel objects                          */
    OSSafetyCriticalStart();
    /* Your code is no longer allowed to create any additional kernel objects */
    while (DEF_ON) {
        :
        :
    }
}
```

A-41 OSSched()

void OSSched (void)

File	Called from	Code enabled by
os_core.c	Task only	N/A

OSSched() allows a task to call the scheduler. You would use this function after doing a series of "posts" where you specified OS_OPT_POST_NO_SCHED as a post option.

OSSched() can only be called by task-level code. Also, if the scheduler is locked (i.e., OSSchedLock() was previously called), then OSSched() will have no effect.

If a higher-priority task than the calling task is ready-to-run, OSSched() will context switch to that task.

ARGUMENTS

None

RETURNED VALUE

None

NOTES/WARNINGS

None

EXAMPLE

```
void TaskX (void *p_arg)
{
    (void)&p_arg;
    while (DEF_ON) {
        :
        OS??Post(…);           /* Posts with OS_OPT_POST_NO_SCHED option        */
        /* Check "err" */
        OS??Post(…);
        /* Check "err" */
        OS??Post(…);
        /* Check "err" */
        :
        OSSched();             /* Run the scheduler                             */
        :
    }
}
```

A-42 OSSchedLock()

void OSSchedLock (OS_ERR *p_err)

File	Called from	Code enabled by
os_core.c	Task only	N/A

OSSchedLock() prevents task rescheduling until its counterpart, OSSchedUnlock(), is called. The task that calls OSSchedLock() retains control of the CPU, even though other higher-priority tasks are ready-to-run. However, interrupts are still recognized and serviced (assuming interrupts are enabled). OSSchedLock() and OSSchedUnlock() must be used in pairs.

µC/OS-III allows OSSchedLock() to be nested up to 250 levels deep. Scheduling is enabled when an equal number of OSSchedUnlock() calls have been made.

ARGUMENTS

p_err   is a pointer to a variable that will contain an error code returned by this function.

OS_ERR_NONE	the scheduler is locked.
OS_ERR_LOCK_NESTING_OVF	if the user called this function too many times.
OS_ERR_OS_NOT_RUNNING	if the function is called before calling OSStart().
OS_ERR_SCHED_LOCK_ISR	if OS_CFG_CALLED_FROM_ISR_CHK_EN set to 1 in os_cfg.h: if you attempted to call OSSchedLock() from an ISR.

RETURNED VALUE

None

NOTES/WARNINGS

After calling OSSchedLock(), the application must not make system calls that suspend execution of the current task; that is, the application cannot call OSTimeDly(), OSTimeDlyHMSM(), OSFlagPend(), OSSemPend(), OSMutexPend(), or OSQPend(). Since the scheduler is locked out, no other task is allowed to run, and the system will lock up.

EXAMPLE

```
void TaskX (void *p_arg)
{
    OS_ERR  err;


    (void)&p_arg;
    while (DEF_ON) {
        :
        OSSchedLock(&err);      /* Prevent other tasks to run        */
        /* Check "err" */
        :                       /* Code protected from context switch */
        OSSchedUnlock(&err);    /* Enable other tasks to run         */
        /* Check "err" */
        :
    }
}
```

A-43 OSSchedRoundRobinCfg()

```
void  OSSchedRoundRobinCfg (CPU_BOOLEAN  en,
                            OS_TICK      dflt_time_quanta,
                            OS_ERR       *p_err)
```

File	Called from	Code enabled by
os_core.c	Task or startup code	OS_CFG_SCHED_ROUND_ROBIN_EN

OSSchedRoundRobinCfg() is used to enable or disable round-robin scheduling.

ARGUMENTS

en   when set to **DEF_ENABLED** enables round-robin scheduling, and when set to **DEF_DISABLED** disables it.

dflt_time_quanta   is the default time quanta given to a task. This value is used when a task is created and you specify a value of 0 for the time quanta. In other words, if the user did not specify a non-zero for the task's time quanta, this is the value that will be used. If passing 0 for this argument, µC/OS-III will assume a time quanta of 1/10 the tick rate. For example, if the tick rate is 1000 Hz and 0 is passed for **dflt_time_quanta** then, µC/OS-III will set the time quanta to 10 milliseconds.

p_err   is a pointer to a variable that is used to hold an error code:

OS_ERR_NONE   if the call is successful.

RETURNED VALUE

None

NOTES/WARNINGS

None

EXAMPLE

```
void main (void)
{
    OS_ERR  err;


    :
    OSInit(&err);                /* Initialize µC/OS-III          */
    :

    :
    OSSchedRoundRobinCfg(DEF_ENABLED,
                    10,
                    &err);
    /* Check "err" */
    :
    :
    OSStart(&err);               /* Start Multitasking            */
}
```

A-44 OSSchedRoundRobinYield()

```
void  OSSchedRoundRobinYield (OS_ERR  *p_err);
```

File	Called from	Code enabled by
os_core.c	Task only	OS_CFG_SCHED_ROUND_ROBIN_EN

OSSchedRoundRobinYield() is used to voluntarily give up a task's time slot, assuming that there are other tasks running at the same priority.

ARGUMENTS

p_err   is a pointer to a variable used to hold an error code:

OS_ERR_NONE	if the call was successful.
OS_ERR_ROUND_ROBIN_1	if there is only one task at the current priority level that is ready-to-run.
OS_ERR_ROUND_ROBIN_DISABLED	if round-robin scheduling has not been enabled. See OSSchedRoundRobinCfg() to enable or disable.
OS_ERR_SCHED_LOCKED	if the scheduler is locked and µC/OS-III cannot switch tasks.
OS_ERR_YIELD_ISR	if OS_CFG_CALLED_FROM_ISR_CHK_EN set to 1 in os_cfg.h: if calling this function from an ISR.

RETURNED VALUE

None

NOTES/WARNINGS

None

EXAMPLE

```
void Task (void *p_arg)
{
    OS_ERR  err;


    (void)&p_arg;
    while (DEF_ON) {
        :
        :
        OSSchedRoundRobinYield(&err); /* Give up the CPU to the next task at same priority */
        /* Check "err" */
        :
        :
    }
}
```

A-45 OSSchedUnlock()

```
void OSSchedUnlock(OS_ERR  *p_err);
```

File	Called from	Code enabled by
os_core.c	Task only	N/A

OSSchedUnlock() re-enables task scheduling whenever it is paired with OSSchedLock().

ARGUMENTS

p_err   is a pointer to a variable that will contain an error code returned by this function.

OS_ERR_NONE	the call is successful and the scheduler is no longer locked.
OS_ERR_OS_NOT_RUNNING	if calling this function before calling OSStart().
OS_ERR_SCHED_LOCKED	if the scheduler is still locked. This would indicate that scheduler lock has not fully unnested
OS_ERR_SCHED_NOT_LOCKED	if the user did not call OSSchedLock().
OS_ERR_SCHED_UNLOCK_ISR	if OS_CFG_CALLED_FROM_ISR_CHK_EN set to 1 in **os_cfg.h**: if you attempted to unlock scheduler from an ISR.

RETURNED VALUE

None

NOTES/WARNINGS

None

EXAMPLE

```c
void TaskX (void *p_arg)
{
    OS_ERR  err;


    (void)&p_arg;
    while (DEF_ON) {
        :
        OSSchedLock(&err);      /* Prevent other tasks to run          */
        /* Check "err" */
        :                       /* Code protected from context switch */
        OSSchedUnlock(&err);    /* Enable other tasks to run           */
        /* Check "err" */
        :
    }
}
```

A-46 OSSemCreate()

```
void  OSSemCreate (OS_SEM      *p_sem,
                   CPU_CHAR    *p_name,
                   OS_SEM_CTR  cnt,
                   OS_ERR      *p_err)
```

File	Called from	Code enabled by
os_sem.c	Task or startup code	OS_CFG_SEM_EN

OSSemCreate() initializes a semaphore. Semaphores are used when a task wants exclusive access to a resource, needs to synchronize its activities with an ISR or a task, or is waiting until an event occurs. You would use a semaphore to signal the occurrence of an event to one or multiple tasks, and use mutexes to guard share resources. However, technically, semaphores allow for both.

ARGUMENTS

p_sem   is a pointer to the semaphore control block. It is assumed that storage for the semaphore will be allocated in the application. In other words, you need to declare a "global" variable as follows, and pass a pointer to this variable to OSSemCreate():

        OS_SEM MySem;

p_name   is a pointer to an ASCII string used to assign a name to the semaphore. The name can be displayed by debuggers or µC/Probe.

cnt   specifies the initial value of the semaphore.

        If the semaphore is used for resource sharing, you would set the initial value of the semaphore to the number of identical resources guarded by the semaphore. If there is only one resource, the value should be set to 1 (this is called a binary semaphore). For multiple resources, set the value to the number of resources (this is called a counting semaphore).

        If using a semaphore as a signaling mechanism, you should set the initial value to 0.

p_err   is a pointer to a variable used to hold an error code:

    OS_ERR_NONE   if the call is successful and the semaphore has
                                                   been created.

    OS_ERR_CREATE_ISR   if OS_CFG_CALLED_FROM_ISR_CHK_EN set to 1
                                                   in os_cfg.h: if you attempted to create a
                                                   semaphore from an ISR.

    OS_ERR_OBJ_PTR_NULL   if OS_CFG_ARG_CHK_EN is set to 1 in
                                                   os_cfg.h: if p_sem is a NULL pointer.

    OS_ERR_OBJ_TYPE   if OS_CFG_OBJ_TYPE_CHK_EN is set to 1 in
                                                   os_cfg.h: if p_sem has been initialized to a
                                                   different object type.

    OS_ERR_ILLEGAL_CREATE_RUN_TIME   if OS_SAFETY_CRITICAL_IEC61508 is
                                                   defined: you called this after calling
                                                   OSSafetyCriticalStart() and thus you are
                                                   no longer allowed to create additional kernel
                                                   objects.

RETURNED VALUE

None

NOTES/WARNINGS

Semaphores must be created before they are used.

EXAMPLE

```
OS_SEM   SwSem;


void main (void)
{
    OS_ERR   err;


    :
    OSInit(&err);                   /* Initialize µC/OS-III        */
    :
    :
    OSSemCreate(&SwSem,             /* Create Switch Semaphore     */
                "Switch Semaphore",
                0,
                &err);
    /* Check "err" */
    :
    :
    OSStart(&err);                  /* Start Multitasking          */
}
```

A-47 OSSemDel()

```
void  OSSemDel (OS_SEM  *p_sem,
               OS_OPT   opt,
               OS_ERR   *p_err)
```

File	Called from	Code enabled by
os_sem.c	Task only	OS_CFG_SEM_EN and OS_CFG_SEM_DEL_EN

OSSemDel() is used to delete a semaphore. This function should be used with care as multiple tasks may rely on the presence of the semaphore. Generally speaking, before deleting a semaphore, first delete all the tasks that access the semaphore. As a rule, it is highly recommended to not delete kernel objects at run time.

Deleting the semaphore will not de-allocate the object. In other words, storage for the variable will still remain at the same location unless the semaphore is allocated dynamically from the heap. The dynamic allocation of objects has its own set of problems. Specifically, it is not recommended for embedded systems to allocate (and de-allocate) objects from the heap given the high likelihood of fragmentation.

ARGUMENTS

p_sem   is a pointer to the semaphore.

opt   specifies one of two options: OS_OPT_DEL_NO_PEND or OS_OPT_DEL_ALWAYS.

OS_OPT_DEL_NO_PEND specifies to delete the semaphore only if no task is waiting on the semaphore. Because no task is "currently" waiting on the semaphore does not mean that a task will not attempt to wait for the semaphore later. How would such a task handle the situation waiting for a semaphore that was deleted? The application code will have to deal with this eventuality.

OS_OPT_DEL_ALWAYS specifies deleting the semaphore, regardless of whether tasks are waiting on the semaphore or not. If there are tasks waiting on the semaphore, these tasks will be made ready-to-run and informed (through an appropriate error code) that the reason the task is readied is that the semaphore it was waiting on was deleted. The same reasoning applies with the other option, how will the tasks handle the fact that the semaphore they want to wait for is no longer available?

p_err   is a pointer to a variable used to hold an error code. The error code may be one of the following:

OS_ERR_NONE	if the call is successful and the semaphore has been deleted.
OS_ERR_DEL_ISR	if OS_CFG_CALLED_FROM_ISR_CHK_EN set to 1 in os_cfg.h: if attempting to delete the semaphore from an ISR.
OS_ERR_OBJ_PTR_NULL	if OS_CFG_ARG_CHK_EN is set to 1 in os_cfg.h: if p_sem is a NULL pointer.
OS_ERR_OBJ_TYPE	if OS_CFG_OBJ_TYPE_CHK_EN is set to 1 in os_cfg.h: if p_sem is not pointing to a semaphore.
OS_ERR_OPT_INVALID	if OS_CFG_ARG_CHK_EN is set to 1 in os_cfg.h: if one of the two options mentioned in the opt argument is not specified.
OS_ERR_TASK_WAITING	if one or more tasks are waiting on the semaphore.

RETURNED VALUE

None

NOTES/WARNINGS

Use this call with care because other tasks might expect the presence of the semaphore.

EXAMPLE

```
OS_SEM  SwSem;


void Task (void *p_arg)
{
    OS_ERR  err;


    (void)&p_arg;
    while (DEF_ON) {
        :
        :
        OSSemDel(&SwSem,
                 OS_OPT_DEL_ALWAYS,
                 &err);
        /* Check "err" */
        :
        :
    }
}
```

A-48 OSSemPend()

```
OS_SEM_CTR  OSSemPend (OS_SEM    *p_sem,
                       OS_TICK    timeout,
                       OS_OPT     opt,
                       CPU_TS     *p_ts,
                       OS_ERR     *p_err)
```

File	Called from	Code enabled by
os_sem.c	Task only	OS_CFG_SEM_EN

OSSemPend() is used when a task wants exclusive access to a resource, needs to synchronize its activities with an ISR or task, or is waiting until an event occurs.

When the semaphore is used for resource sharing, if a task calls OSSemPend() and the value of the semaphore is greater than 0, OSSemPend() decrements the semaphore and returns to its caller. However, if the value of the semaphore is 0, OSSemPend() places the calling task in the waiting list for the semaphore. The task waits until the owner of the semaphore (which is always a task in this case) releases the semaphore by calling OSSemPost(), or the specified timeout expires. If the semaphore is signaled before the timeout expires, μC/OS-III resumes the highest-priority task waiting for the semaphore.

When the semaphore is used as a signaling mechanism, the calling task waits until a task or an ISR signals the semaphore by calling OSSemPost(), or the specified timeout expires. If the semaphore is signaled before the timeout expires, μC/OS-III resumes the highest-priority task waiting for the semaphore.

A pended task that has been suspended with OSTaskSuspend() can obtain the semaphore. However, the task remains suspended until it is resumed by calling OSTaskResume().

OSSemPend() also returns if the pend is aborted or, the semaphore is deleted.

ARGUMENTS

p_sem   is a pointer to the semaphore.

timeout   allows the task to resume execution if a semaphore is not posted within the specified number of clock ticks. A timeout value of 0 indicates that the task waits forever for the semaphore. The timeout value is not synchronized with the clock tick. The timeout count begins decrementing on the next clock tick, which could potentially occur immediately.

opt   specifies whether the call is to block if the semaphore is not available, or not block.

OS_OPT_PEND_BLOCKING	to block the caller until the semaphore is available or a timeout occurs.
OS_OPT_PEND_NON_BLOCKING	if the semaphore is not available, OSSemPend() will not block but return to the caller with an appropriate error code.

p_ts   is a pointer to a variable that will receive a timestamp of when the semaphore was posted, pend aborted, or deleted. Passing a NULL pointer is valid and indicates that a timestamp is not required.

A timestamp is useful when the task must know when the semaphore was posted or, how long it took for the task to resume after the semaphore was posted. In the latter case, call OS_TS_GET() and compute the difference between the current value of the timestamp and *p_ts. In other words:

delta = OS_TS_GET() - *p_ts;

p_err   is a pointer to a variable used to hold an error code:

OS_ERR_NONE	if the semaphore is available.
OS_ERR_OBJ_DEL	if the semaphore was deleted.
OS_ERR_OBJ_PTR_NULL	if OS_CFG_ARG_CHK_EN is set to 1 in os_cfg.h: if p_sem is a NULL pointer.
OS_ERR_OBJ_TYPE	if OS_CFG_OBJ_TYPE_CHK_EN is set to 1 in os_cfg.h: if p_sem is not pointing to a semaphore.

OS_ERR_OPT_INVALID	if OS_CFG_ARG_CHK_EN is set to 1 in os_cfg.h: if opt is not OS_OPT_PEND_NON_BLOCKING or OS_OPT_PEND_BLOCKING.
OS_ERR_PEND_ABORT	if the pend was aborted
OS_ERR_PEND_ISR	if OS_CFG_CALLED_FROM_ISR_CHK_EN set to 1 in os_cfg.h: if this function is called from an ISR.
OS_ERR_PEND_WOULD_BLOCK	if this function is called as specified OS_OPT_PEND_NON_BLOCKING, and the semaphore was not available.
OS_ERR_SCHED_LOCKED	if calling this function when the scheduler is locked.
OS_ERR_TIMEOUT	if the semaphore is not signaled within the specified timeout.

RETURNED VALUE

The new value of the semaphore count.

NOTES/WARNINGS

Semaphores must be created before they are used.

EXAMPLE

```
OS_SEM  SwSem;


void DispTask (void *p_arg)
{
    OS_ERR   err;
    CPU_TS   ts;


    (void)&p_arg;
    while (DEF_ON) {
        :
        :
        (void)OSSemPend(&SwSem,
                        0,
                        OS_OPT_PEND_BLOCKING,
                        &ts,
                        &err);
        /* Check "err" */
    }
}
```

A-49 OSSemPendAbort()

```
OS_OBJ_QTY  OSSemPendAbort (OS_SEM  *p_sem,
                            OS_OPT   opt,
                            OS_ERR  *p_err)
```

File	Called from	Code enabled by
os_sem.c	Task only	OS_CFG_SEM_EN and OS_CFG_SEM_PEND_ABORT_EN

OSSemPendAbort() aborts and readies any task currently waiting on a semaphore. This function should be used to fault-abort the wait on the semaphore, rather than to normally signal the semaphore via OSSemPost().

ARGUMENTS

p_sem   is a pointer to the semaphore for which pend(s) need to be aborted.

opt   determines the type of abort performed.

> OS_OPT_PEND_ABORT_1   Aborts the pend of only the highest-priority task waiting on the semaphore.
>
> OS_OPT_PEND_ABORT_ALL   Aborts the pend of all the tasks waiting on the semaphore.
>
> OS_OPT_POST_NO_SCHED   Specifies that the scheduler should not be called, even if the pend of a higher-priority task has been aborted. Scheduling will need to occur from another function.
>
> You would use this option if the task calling OSSemPendAbort() will be doing additional pend aborts, reschedule takes place when finished, and multiple pend aborts are to take effect simultaneously.

p_err   Is a pointer to a variable that holds an error code:

OS_ERR_NONE	At least one task waiting on the semaphore was readied and informed of the aborted wait. Check the return value for the number of tasks whose wait on the semaphore was aborted.
OS_ERR_OBJ_PTR_NULL	if OS_CFG_ARG_CHK_EN is set to 1 in os_cfg.h: if p_sem is a NULL pointer.
OS_ERR_OBJ_TYPE	if OS_CFG_OBJ_TYPE_CHK_EN is set to 1 in os_cfg.h: if p_sem is not pointing to a semaphore.
OS_ERR_OPT_INVALID	if OS_CFG_ARG_CHK_EN is set to 1 in os_cfg.h: if an invalid option is specified.
OS_ERR_PEND_ABORT_ISR	if OS_CFG_CALLED_FROM_ISR_CHK_EN set to 1 in os_cfg.h: if you called this function from an ISR.
OS_ERR_PEND_ABORT_NONE	No task was aborted because no task was waiting.

RETURNED VALUE

OSSemPendAbort() returns the number of tasks made ready-to-run by this function. Zero indicates that no tasks were pending on the semaphore and therefore, the function had no effect.

NOTES/WARNINGS

Semaphores must be created before they are used.

EXAMPLE

```c
OS_SEM  SwSem;


void CommTask(void *p_arg)
{
    OS_ERR      err;
    OS_OBJ_QTY  nbr_tasks;


    (void)&p_arg;
    while (DEF_ON) {
        :
        :
        nbr_tasks = OSSemPendAbort(&SwSem,
                                   OS_OPT_PEND_ABORT_ALL,
                                   &err);
        /* Check "err" */
        :
        :
    }
}
```

A-50 OSSemPost()

```
OS_SEM_CTR  OSSemPost (OS_SEM  *p_sem,
                       OS_OPT   opt,
                       OS_ERR  *p_err)
```

File	Called from	Code enabled by
os_sem.c	Task or ISR	OS_CFG_SEM_EN

A semaphore is signaled by calling OSSemPost(). If the semaphore value is 0 or more, it is incremented, and OSSemPost() returns to its caller. If tasks are waiting for the semaphore to be signaled, OSSemPost() removes the highest-priority task pending for the semaphore from the waiting list and makes this task ready-to-run. The scheduler is then called to determine if the awakened task is now the highest-priority task that is ready-to-run.

ARGUMENTS

p_sem   is a pointer to the semaphore.

opt   determines the type of post performed.

OS_OPT_POST_1	Post and ready only the highest-priority task waiting on the semaphore.
OS_OPT_POST_ALL	Post to all tasks waiting on the semaphore. You should only use this option if the semaphore is used as a signaling mechanism and never when the semaphore is used to guard a shared resource. It does not make sense to tell all tasks that are sharing a resource that they can all access the resource.
OS_OPT_POST_NO_SCHED	This option indicates that the caller does not want the scheduler to be called after the post. This option can be used in combination with one of the two previous options.

You should use this option if the task (or ISR) calling `OSSemPost()` will be doing additional posting and, the user does not want to reschedule until all done, and multiple posts are to take effect simultaneously.

`p_err`   is a pointer to a variable that holds an error code:

OS_ERR_NONE	if no tasks are waiting on the semaphore. In this case, the return value is also 0.
OS_ERR_OBJ_PTR_NULL	if OS_CFG_ARG_CHK_EN is set to 1 in os_cfg.h: if p_sem is a NULL pointer.
OS_ERR_OBJ_TYPE	if OS_CFG_OBJ_TYPE_CHK_EN is set to 1 in os_cfg.h: if p_sem is not pointing to a semaphore.
OS_ERR_SEM_OVF	if the post would have caused the semaphore counter to overflow.

RETURNED VALUE

The current value of the semaphore count

NOTES/WARNINGS

▪ Semaphores must be created before they are used.

▪ You can also post to a semaphore from an ISR but the semaphore must be used as a signaling mechanism and not to protect a shared resource.

EXAMPLE

```
OS_SEM  SwSem;


void TaskX (void *p_arg)
{
    OS_ERR       err;
    OS_SEM_CTR   ctr;


    (void)&p_arg;
    while (DEF_ON) {
        :
        :
        ctr = OSSemPost(&SwSem,
                        OS_OPT_POST_1 + OS_OPT_POST_NO_SCHED,
                        &err);
        /* Check "err" */
        :
        :
    }
}
```

A-51 OSSemSet()

```
void  OSSemSet (OS_SEM      *p_sem,
               OS_SEM_CTR   cnt,
               OS_ERR       *p_err)
```

File	Called from	Code enabled by
os_sem.c	Task only	OS_CFG_SEM_EN and OS_CFG_SEM_SET_EN

OSSemSet() is used to change the current value of the semaphore count. This function is normally selected when a semaphore is used as a signaling mechanism. OSSemSet() can then be used to reset the count to any value. If the semaphore count is already 0, the count is only changed if there are no tasks waiting on the semaphore.

ARGUMENTS

p_sem   is a pointer to the semaphore that is used as a signaling mechanism.

cnt   is the desired count that the semaphore should be set to.

p_err   is a pointer to a variable used to hold an error code:

OS_ERR_NONE	if the count was changed or, not changed, because one or more tasks was waiting on the semaphore.
OS_ERR_OBJ_PTR_NULL	if OS_CFG_ARG_CHK_EN is set to 1 in os_cfg.h: if p_sem is a NULL pointer.
OS_ERR_OBJ_TYPE	if OS_CFG_OBJ_TYPE_CHK_EN is set to 1 in os_cfg.h: if p_sem is not pointing to a semaphore.
OS_ERR_SET_ISR	if OS_CFG_CALLED_FROM_ISR_CHK_EN set to 1 in os_cfg.h: if this function was called from an ISR.
OS_ERR_TASK_WAITING	if tasks are waiting on the semaphore.

None

NOTES/WARNINGS

Do not use this function if the semaphore is used to protect a shared resource.

EXAMPLE

```
OS_SEM  SwSem;


void Task (void *p_arg)
{
    OS_ERR  err;


    (void)&p_arg;
    while (DEF_ON) {
        OSSemSet(&SwSem,       /* Reset the semaphore count */
                 0,
                 &err);
        /* Check "err" */
        :
        :
    }
}
```

A-52 OSStart()

```
void  OSStart (OS_ERR  *p_err)
```

File	Called from	Code enabled by
os_core.c	Startup code only	N/A

OSStart() starts multitasking under μC/OS-III. This function is typically called from startup code after calling OSInit() and creating at least one application task. OSStart() will not return to the caller. Once μC/OS-III is running, calling OSStart() again will have no effect.

ARGUMENTS

p_err   is a pointer to a variable used to hold an error code:

> OS_ERR_FATAL_RETURN   if we ever return to this function.
>
> OS_ERR_OS_RUNNING   if the kernel is already running. In other words, if this function has already been called.

RETURNED VALUE

None

NOTES/WARNINGS

OSInit() must be called prior to calling OSStart(). OSStart() should only be called once by the application code. However, if you called OSStart() more than once, nothing happens on the second and subsequent calls.

EXAMPLE

```
void main (void)
{
    OS_ERR  err;

                                    /* User Code          */
    :
    OSInit(&err);                   /* Initialize µC/OS-III */
    /* Check "err" */
    :                               /* User Code          */
    :
    OSStart(&err);                  /* Start Multitasking  */
    /* Any code here should NEVER be executed! */
}
```

A-53 OSStartHighRdy()

void OSStartHighRdy (void)

File	Called from	Code enabled by
os_cpu_a.asm	OSStart()	N/A

OSStartHighRdy() is responsible for starting the highest-priority task that was created prior to calling OSStart(). OSStartHighRdy() is a µC/OS-III port function that is generally written in assembly language.

ARGUMENTS

None

RETURNED VALUES

None

NOTES/WARNINGS

None

EXAMPLE

The pseudocode for OSStartHighRdy() is shown below.

```
OSStartHighRdy:
    OSTaskSwHook();                              (1)
    SP = OSTCBHighRdyPtr->StkPtr;                (2)
    Pop CPU registers off the task's stack;      (3)
    Return from interrupt;                       (4)
```

(1)   OSStartHighRdy() must call OSTaskSwHook().

When called, OSTCBCurPtr and OSTCBHighRdyPtr both point to the OS_TCB of the highest-priority task created.

OSTaskSwHook() should check that OSTCBCurPtr is not equal to OSTCBHighRdyPtr as this is the first time OSTaskSwHook() is called and there is not a task being switched out.

(2)   The CPU stack pointer register is loaded with the top-of-stack (TOS) of the task being started. The TOS is found in the .StkPtr field of the OS_TCB. For convenience, the .StkPtr field is the very first field of the OS_TCB data structure. This makes it easily accessible from assembly language.

(3)   The registers are popped from the task's stack frame. Recall that the registers should have been placed on the stack frame in the same order as if they were pushed at the beginning of an interrupt service routine.

(4)   You must execute a return from interrupt. This starts the task as if it was resumed when returning from a real interrupt.

A-54 OSStatReset()

```
void OSStatReset (OS_ERR *p_err)
```

File	Called from	Code enabled by
os_stat.c	Task only	OS_CFG_STAT_TASK_EN

OSStatReset() is used to reset statistical variables maintained by µC/OS-III. Specifically, the per-task maximum interrupt disable time, maximum scheduler lock time, maximum amount of time a message takes to reach a task queue, the maximum amount of time it takes a signal to reach a task and more.

ARGUMENTS

p_err   is a pointer to a variable used to hold an error code:

OS_ERR_NONE	the call was successful.
OS_ERR_STAT_RESET_ISR	if OS_CFG_CALLED_FROM_ISR_CHK_EN set to 1 in **os_cfg.h**: if the call was attempted from an ISR.

RETURNED VALUE

None

NOTES/WARNINGS

None

EXAMPLE

```
void TaskX (void *p_arg)
{
    OS_ERR   err;

    (void)&p_arg;
    while (DEF_ON) {
        :
        :
        if (statistics reset switch is pressed) {
            OSStatReset(&err);
            /* Check "err" */
        }
        :
        :
    }
}
```

A-55 OSStatTaskCPUUsageInit()

void OSStatTaskCPUUsageInit (OS_ERR *p_err)

File	Called from	Code enabled by
os_stat.c	Startup code only	OS_CFG_TASK_STAT_EN

OSStatTaskCPUUsageInit() determines the maximum value that a 32-bit counter can reach when no other task is executing. This function must be called when only one task is created in the application and when multitasking has started. This function must be called from the first and only task created by the application.

ARGUMENTS

p_err   is a pointer to a variable used to hold an error code:

      OS_ERR_NONE   Always returns this value.

RETURNED VALUE

None

NOTES/WARNINGS

None

```
void FirstAndOnlyTask (void *p_arg)
{
    OS_ERR  err;
    :
    :
#if OS_CFG_TASK_STAT_EN > 0
    OSStatTaskCPUUsageInit(&err); /* Compute CPU capacity with no task running */
#endif
    :
    OSTaskCreate(_);               /* Create the other tasks              */
    OSTaskCreate(_);
    :
    while (DEF_ON) {
        :
        :
    }
}
```

A-56 OSStatTaskHook()

void OSStatTaskHook (void);

File	Called from	Code enabled by
os_cpu_c.c	OSStatTask()	Always enabled

OSStatTaskHook() is a function called by μC/OS-III's statistic task, OSStatTask(). OSStatTaskHook() is generally implemented by the port implementer for the processor used. This hook allows the port to perform additional statistics.

ARGUMENTS

None

RETURNED VALUES

None

NOTES/WARNINGS

None

EXAMPLE

The code below calls an application-specific hook that an application programmer can define. For this, the user can simply set the value of OS_AppStatTaskHookPtr to point to the desired hook function (see App_OS_SetAllHooks() in os_app_hooks.c).

In the example below, OSStatTaskHook() calls App_OS_StatTaskHook() if the pointer OS_AppStatTaskHookPtr is set to that function.

```
void  App_OS_StatTaskHook (void)                    /* os_app_hooks.c      */
{
    /* Your code goes here! */
}


void App_OS_SetAllHooks (void)                      /* os_app_hooks.c      */
{
    CPU_SR_ALLOC();

    CPU_CRITICAL_ENTER();
    :
    OS_AppStatTaskHookPtr = App_OS_StatTaskHook;
    :
    CPU_CRITICAL_EXIT();
}


void  OSStatTaskHook (void)                         /* os_cpu_c.c          */
{
#if OS_CFG_APP_HOOKS_EN > 0u
    if (OS_AppStatTaskHookPtr != (OS_APP_HOOK_VOID)0) {   /* Call application hook */
        (*OS_AppStatTaskHookPtr)();
    }
#endif
}
```

A-57 OSTaskChangePrio()

```
void OSTaskChangePrio (OS_TCB    *p_tcb,
                       OS_PRIO    prio_new,
                       OS_ERR    *p_err)
```

File	Called from	Code enabled by
os_task.c	Task only	OS_CFG_TASK_CHANGE_PRIO_EN

When you creating a task (see **OSTaskCreate()**), you specify the priority of the task being created. In most cases, it is not necessary to change the priority of the task at run time. However, it is sometimes useful to do so, and **OSTaskChangePrio()** allows this to take place.

If the task is ready-to-run, **OSTaskChangePrio()** simply changes the position of the task in µC/OS-III's ready list. If the task is waiting on an event, **OSTaskChangePrio()** will change the position of the task in the pend list of the corresponding object, so that the pend list remains sorted by priority.

Because µC/OS-III supports multiple tasks at the same priority, there are no restrictions on the priority that a task can have, except that task priority zero (0) is reserved by µC/OS-III, and priority **OS_PRIO_MAX-1** is used by the idle task.

Note that a task priority cannot be changed from an ISR.

ARGUMENTS

p_tcb   is a pointer to the **OS_TCB** of the task for which the priority is being changed. If you pass a **NULL** pointer, the priority of the current task is changed.

prio_new   is the new task's priority. This value must never be set to **OS_CFG_PRIO_MAX-1**, or higher and you must not use priority 0 since they are reserved for µC/OS-III.

p_err	is a pointer to a variable that will receive an error code:

OS_ERR_NONE	if the task's priority is changed.
OS_ERR_TASK_CHANGE_PRIO_ISR	if OS_CFG_CALLED_FROM_ISR_CHK_EN set to 1 in os_cfg.h: if attempting to change the task's priority from an ISR.
OS_ERR_PRIO_INVALID	if the priority of the task specified is invalid. By specifying a priority greater than or equal to OS_PRIO_MAX-1, or 0.

RETURNED VALUE

None

NOTES/WARNINGS

None

EXAMPLE

```
OS_TCB  MyTaskTCB;


void TaskX (void *p_arg)
{
    OS_ERR  err;


    while (DEF_ON) {
        :
        :
        OSTaskChangePrio(&MyTaskTCB,      /* Change the priority of "MyTask" to 10 */
                         10,
                         &err);
        /* Check "err" */
        :
    }
}
```

A-58 OSTaskCreate()

```
void   OSTaskCreate (OS_TCB          *p_tcb,
                     CPU_CHAR        *p_name,
                     OS_TASK_PTR      p_task,
                     void            *p_arg,
                     OS_PRIO          prio,
                     CPU_STK         *p_stk_base,
                     CPU_STK_SIZE     stk_limit,
                     CPU_STK_SIZE     stk_size,
                     OS_MSG_QTY       q_size,
                     OS_TICK          time_quanta,
                     void            *p_ext,
                     OS_OPT           opt,
                     OS_ERR          *p_err)
```

File	Called from	Code enabled by
os_task.c	Task or startup code	N/A

Tasks must be created in order for µC/OS-III to recognize them as tasks. You create a task by calling **OSTaskCreate()** and by providing arguments specifying to µC/OS-III how the task will be managed. Tasks are always created in the ready-to-run state.

Tasks can be created either prior to the start of multitasking (i.e., before calling **OSStart()**), or by a running task. A task cannot be created by an ISR. A task must either be written as an infinite loop, or delete itself once completed. If the task code returns by mistake, µC/OS-III will terminate the task by calling **OSTaskDel((OS_TCB *)0, &err))**. At Micrium, we like the "**while (DEF_ON)**" to implement infinite loops because, by convention, we use a **while** loop when we don't know how many iterations a loop will do. This is the case of an infinite loop. We prefer to use **for** loops when we know how many iterations a loop will do.

Task as an infinite loop:

```
void MyTask (void *p_arg)
{
    /* Local variables                                           */


    /* Do something with 'p_arg'                                 */
    /* Task initialization                                       */
    while (DEF_ON) {        /* Task body, as an infinite loop.   */
        :
        :
        /* Must call one of the following services:              */
        /*     OSFlagPend()                                      */
        /*     OSMutexPend()                                     */
        /*     OSQPend()                                         */
        /*     OSSemPend()                                       */
        /*     OSTimeDly()                                       */
        /*     OSTimeDlyHMSM()                                   */
        /*     OSTaskQPend()                                     */
        /*     OSTaskSemPend()                                   */
        /*     OSTaskSuspend()     (Suspend self)                */
        /*     OSTaskDel()         (Delete  self)                */
        :
        :
    }
}
```

Run to completion task:

```
void MyTask (void *p_arg)
{
    OS_ERR  err;
    /* Local variables                                           */


    /* Do something with 'p_arg'                                 */
    /* Task initialization                                       */
    /* Task body (do some work)                                  */
    OSTaskDel((OS_TCB *)0, &err);
    /* Check 'err" ... you code should never end up here!        */
}
```

ARGUMENTS

p_tcb   is a pointer to the task's **OS_TCB** to use. It is assumed that storage for the TCB of the task will be allocated by the user code. You can declare a "global" variable as follows, and pass a pointer to this variable to **OSTaskCreate()**:

OS_TCB MyTaskTCB;

p_name   is a pointer to an ASCII string (NUL terminated) to assign a name to the task. The name can be displayed by debuggers or by µC/Probe.

p_task   is a pointer to the task (i.e., the name of the function that defines the task).

p_arg   is a pointer to an optional data area which is used to pass parameters to the task when it is created. When µC/OS-III runs the task for the first time, the task will think that it was invoked, and passed the argument **p_arg**. For example, you could create a generic task that handles an asynchronous serial port. **p_arg** can be used to pass task information about the serial port it will manage: the port address, baud rate, number of bits, parity, and more. **p_arg** is the argument received by the task shown below.

```
void MyTask (void *p_arg)
{
    while (DEF_ON) {
        Task code;
    }
}
```

prio   is the task priority. The lower the number, the higher the priority (i.e., the importance) of the task. If **OS_CFG_ISR_POST_DEFERRED_EN** is set to 1, the user cannot use priority **0.**

Task priority must also have a lower number than **OS_CFG_PRIO_MAX**-Priorities 0, 1, **OS_CFG_PRIO_MAX-2** and **OS_CFG_PRIO_MAX-1** are reserved. In other words, a task should have a priority between 2 and **OOS_CFG_PRIO_MAX-3**, inclusively.

p_stk_base is a pointer to the task's stack base address. The task's stack is used to store local variables, function parameters, return addresses, and possibly CPU registers during an interrupt.

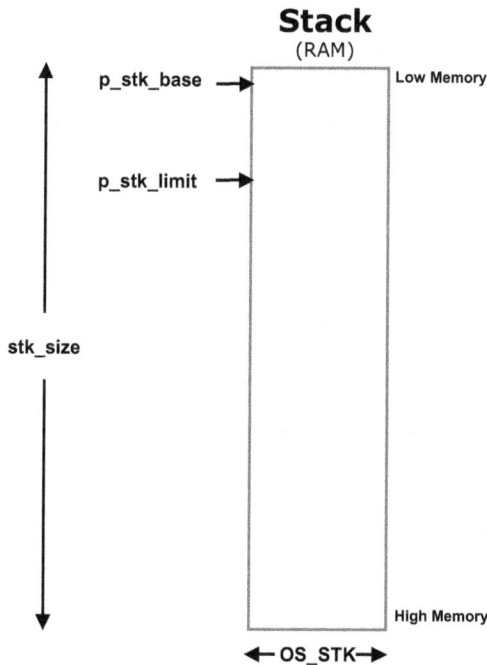

The task stack must be declared as follows:

```
CPU_STK MyTaskStk[???];
```

The user would then pass **p_stk_base** the address of the first element of this array or, **&MyTaskStk[0]**. "???" represents the size of the stack.

The size of this stack is determined by the task's requirements and the anticipated interrupt nesting (unless the processor has a separate stack just for interrupts). Determining the size of the stack involves knowing how many bytes are required for storage of local variables for the task itself, all nested functions, as well as requirements for interrupts (accounting for nesting).

Note that you can allocate stack space for a task from the heap but, in this case, we don't recommend to ever delete the task and free the stack space as this can cause the heap to fragment, which is not desirable in embedded systems.

stk_limit   is used to locate, within the task's stack, a watermark limit that can be used to monitor and ensure that the stack does not overflow.

If the processor does not have hardware stack overflow detection, or this feature is not implemented in software by the port developer, this value may be used for other purposes. For example, some processors have two stacks, a hardware and a software stack. The hardware stack typically keeps track of function call nesting and the software stack is used to pass function arguments. **stk_limit** may be used to set the size of the hardware stack as shown below.

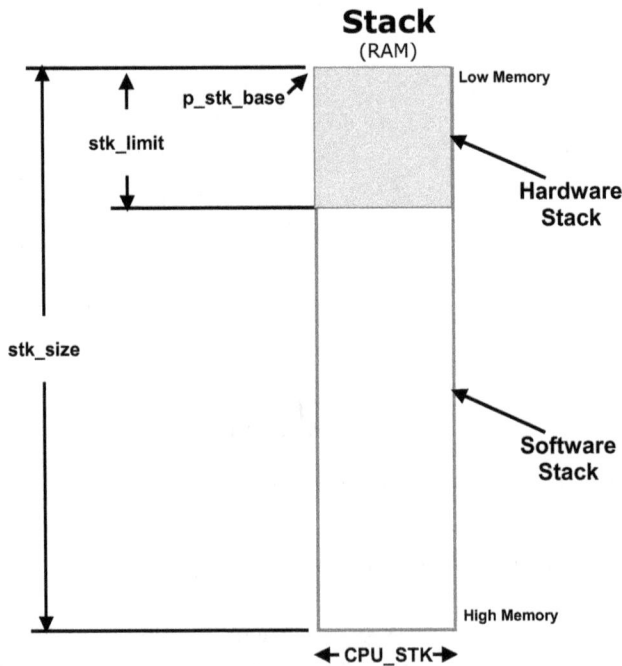

stk_size   specifies the size of the task's stack in number of elements. If **CPU_STK** is set to **CPU_INT08U** (see **os_type.h**), **stk_size** corresponds to the number of bytes available on the stack. If **CPU_STK** is set to **CPU_INT16U**, then **stk_size** contains the number of 16-bit entries available on the stack. Finally, if **CPU_STK** is set to **CPU_INT32U**, **stk_size** contains the number of 32-bit entries available on the stack.

q_size   A µC/OS-III task contains an optional internal message queue (if OS_CFG_TASK_Q_EN > 0). This argument specifies the maximum number of messages that the task can receive through this message queue. The user may specify that the task is unable to receive messages by setting this argument to 0.

time_quanta   the amount of time (in clock ticks) for the time quanta when round robin is enabled. If you specify 0, then the default time quanta will be used which is the tick rate divided by 10.

p_ext   is a pointer to a user-supplied memory location (typically a data structure) used as a TCB extension. For example, the user memory can hold the contents of floating-point registers during a context switch.

opt   contains task-specific options. Each option consists of one bit. The option is selected when the bit is set. The current version of µC/OS-III supports the following options:

OS_OPT_TASK_NONE	specifies that there are no options.
OS_OPT_TASK_STK_CHK	specifies whether stack checking is allowed for the task.
OS_OPT_TASK_STK_CLR	specifies whether the stack needs to be cleared.
OS_OPT_TASK_SAVE_FP	specifies whether floating-point registers are saved. This option is only valid if the processor has floating-point hardware and the processor-specific code saves the floating-point registers.
OS_OPT_TASK_NO_TLS	if the caller doesn't want or need TLS (Thread Local Storage) support for the task being created. If you do not include this option, TLS will be supported by default, assuming Micriµm supports TLS for the toolchain you are using. TLS support was added in V3.03.00.

p_err   is a pointer to a variable that will receive an error code:

OS_ERR_NONE	if the function is successful.

OS_ERR_PRIO_INVALID	if OS_CFG_ARG_CHK_EN is set to 1 in os_cfg.h: if prio is higher than the maximum value allowed (i.e., > OS_PRIO_MAX-1). Also, you will get this error if the user set OS_CFG_ISR_POST_DEFERRED_EN to 1 and tried to use priority 0.
OS_ERR_STK_INVALID	if OS_CFG_ARG_CHK_EN is set to 1 in os_cfg.h: if specifying a NULL pointer for p_stk_base.
OS_ERR_STK_SIZE_INVALID	if OS_CFG_ARG_CHK_EN is set to 1 in os_cfg.h: if specifying a stack size smaller than what is currently specified by OS_CFG_STK_SIZE_MIN (see the os_cfg.h).
OS_ERR_TASK_CREATE_ISR	if OS_CFG_CALLED_FROM_ISR_CHK_EN set to 1 in os_cfg.h: if attempting to create the task from an ISR.
OS_ERR_TASK_INVALID	if OS_CFG_ARG_CHK_EN is set to 1 in os_cfg.h: if specifying a NULL pointer for p_task
OS_ERR_TCB_INVALID	if OS_CFG_ARG_CHK_EN is set to 1 in os_cfg.h: if specifying a NULL pointer for p_tcb.
OS_ERR_ILLEGAL_CREATE_RUN_TIME	if OS_SAFETY_CRITICAL_IEC61508 is defined: you called this after calling OSSafetyCriticalStart() and thus you are no longer allowed to create additional kernel objects.

RETURNED VALUE

None

NOTES/WARNINGS

■ The stack must be declared with the CPU_STK type.

- A task must always invoke one of the services provided by μC/OS-III to wait for time to expire, suspend the task, or wait on an object (wait on a message queue, event flag, mutex, semaphore, a signal or a message to be sent directly to the task). This allows other tasks to gain control of the CPU.

- You should not use task priorities 0, 1, OS_CFG_PRIO_MAX-2 and OS_CFG_PRIO_MAX-1 because they are reserved for use by μC/OS-III.

EXAMPLE

OSTaskCreate() can be called from **main()** (in C), or a previously created task.

```
OS_TCB  MyTaskTCB;                      /*  (1) Storage for task's TCB                  */
CPU_STK MyTaskStk[200];


void  MyTask (void *p_arg)              /*  (3) The address of the task is its name     */
{
    while (DEF_ON) {
        /* Wait for an event */
        /* My task body      */
    }
}


void SomeCode (void)
{
    OS_ERR  err;
    :
    :
    OSTaskCreate (&MyTaskTCB,            /*  (1) Address of TCB assigned to the task     */
                  "My Task",             /*  (2) Name you want to give the task          */
                  MyTask,                /*  (3) Address of the task itself              */
                  (void *)0,             /*  (4) "p_arg" is not used                     */
                  12,                    /*  (5) Priority you want to assign to the task */
                  &MyTaskStk[0],         /*  (6) Base address of task's stack            */
                  10,                    /*  (7) Watermark limit for stack growth        */
                  200,                   /*  (8) Stack size in number of CPU_STK elements */
                  5,                     /*  (9) Size of task message queue              */
                  10,                    /* (10) Time quanta (in number of ticks)        */
                  (void *)0,             /* (11) Extension pointer is not used           */
                  OS_OPT_TASK_STK_CHK + OS_OPT_TASK_STK_CLR, /* (12) Options             */
                  &err);                                     /* (13) Error code          */
    /* Check "err"                                               (14)                    */
    :
    :
}
```

(1)   In order to create a task, you need to allocate storage for a TCB and pass a pointer to this TCB to **OSTaskCreate()**.

(2)   You can assign an ASCII name to the task by passing a pointer to an ASCII string. The ASCII string may be allocated in code space (i.e., ROM), or data space (i.e., RAM). In either case, it is assumed that the code can access that memory. The ASCII string must be **NUL** terminated.

(3)   You pass the address of the task to **OSTaskCreate()**. In C, the address of a function is simply the name of that function.

(4)   To provide additional data to **MyTask()**, you can pass a pointer to such data. In this case, **MyTask()** did not need such data and therefore, a **NULL** pointer is passed.

(5)   The user must assign a priority to the task. The priority specifies the importance of this task with respect to other tasks. A low-priority value indicates a high priority. Priority **0** is the highest priority (reserved for an internal task) and a priority up to **OS_CFG_PRIO_MAX-3** can be specified (see **os_cfg.h**). Note that **OS_CFG_PRIO_MAX-1** is also reserved for an internal task, the idle task.

(6)   The next argument specifies the "base address" of the task's stack. In this case, it is simply the base address of the array **MyTaskStk[ ]**. Note that it is possible to simply specify the name of the array. I prefer to make it clear by writing **&MyTaskStk[0]**.

(7)   This argument sets the watermark limit for stack growth. If the processor port does not use this field then you can set this value to **0**.

(8)   μC/OS-III also needs to know the size of the stack for the task. This allows μC/OS-III to perform stack checking at run time. This argument represents the number of **CPU_STK** elements, not the number of bytes.

(9)   μC/OS-III allows tasks or ISRs to send messages directly to a task. This argument specifies how many such messages can be received by this task.

(10)   This argument specifies how much time (in number of ticks) this task will run on the CPU before μC/OS-III will force the CPU away from this task and run the next task at the same priority (if there are more than one task at the same priority that is ready-to-run).

(11)   μC/OS-III allows the user to "extend" the capabilities of the TCB by allowing passing a pointer to some memory location that could contain additional information about the task. For example, there may be a CPU that supports

floating-point math and the user would likely need to save the floating-point registers during a context switch. This pointer could point to the storage area for these registers.

(12)   When creating a task, options must be specified. Specifically, such options as, whether the stack of the task will be cleared (i.e., filled with 0x00) when the task is created (**OS_OPT_TASK_STK_CLR**), whether µC/OS-III will be allowed to check for stack usage (**OS_OPT_TASK_STK_CHK**), whether the CPU supports floating-point math, and whether the task will make use of the floating-point registers and therefore need to save and restore them during a context switch (**OS_OPT_TASK_SAVE_FP**). The options are additive.

(13)   Most of µC/OS-III's services return an error code indicating the outcome of the call. The error code is always returned as a pointer to a variable of type **OS_ERR**. The user must allocate storage for this variable prior to calling **OSTaskCreate()**.

(14)   It is highly recommended that the user examine the error code whenever calling a µC/OS-III function. If the call is successful, the error code will always be **OS_ERR_NONE**. If the call is not successful, the returned code will indicate the reason for the failure (see **OS_ERR_???** in **os.h**).

A-59 OSTaskCreateHook()

void OSTaskCreateHook (OS_TCB *p_tcb)

File	Called from	Code enabled by
os_cpu_c.c	OSTaskCreate() ONLY	N/A

This function is called by OSTaskCreate() after initializing the OS_TCB fields and setting up the stack frame for the task, just before adding the task to the ready list. When OSTaskCreateHook() is called, all of the OS_TCB fields are assumed to be initialized.

OSTaskCreateHook() is part of the CPU port code and this function *must not* be called by the application code. OSTaskCreateHook() is actually used by the µC/OS-III port developer.

You can use this hook to initialize and store the contents of floating-point registers, MMU registers, or anything else that can be associated with a task. Typically, you would store this additional information in memory allocated by the application.

ARGUMENTS

p_tcb   is a pointer to the TCB of the task being created. Note that the OS_TCB has been validated by OSTaskCreate() and is guaranteed to not be a NULL pointer when OSTaskCreateHook() is called.

RETURNED VALUE

None

NOTES/WARNINGS

Do not call this function from the application.

EXAMPLE

The code below calls an application-specific hook that the application programmer can define. The user can simply set the value of OS_AppTaskCreateHookPtr to point to the desired hook function as shown in the example. OSTaskCreate() calls

591

`OSTaskCreateHook()` which in turns calls **App_OS_TaskCreateHook()** through `OS_AppTaskCreateHookPtr`. As can be seen, when called, the application hook is passed the address of the **OS_TCB** of the newly created task.

```
void  App_OS_TaskCreateHook (OS_TCB *p_tcb)                /* os_app_hooks.c        */
{
    /* Your code goes here! */
}


void App_OS_SetAllHooks (void)                             /* os_app_hooks.c        */
{
    CPU_SR_ALLOC();

    CPU_CRITICAL_ENTER();
    :
    OS_AppTaskCreateHookPtr = App_OS_TaskCreateHook;
    :
    CPU_CRITICAL_EXIT();
}


void  OSTaskCreateHook (OS_TCB *p_tcb)                      /* os_cpu_c.c            */
{
#if OS_CFG_APP_HOOKS_EN > 0u
    if (OS_AppTaskCreateHookPtr != (OS_APP_HOOK_TCB)0) {    /* Call application hook */
        (*OS_AppTaskCreateHookPtr)(p_tcb);
    }
#endif
}
```

A-60 OSTaskDel()

```
void   OSTaskDel (OS_TCB   *p_tcb,
                  OS_ERR   *p_err)
```

File	Called from	Code enabled by
os_task.c	Task only	OS_CFG_TASK_DEL_EN

When a task is no longer needed, it can be deleted. Deleting a task does not mean that the code is removed, but that the task code is no longer managed by µC/OS-III. OSTaskDel() can be used when creating a task that will only run once. In this case, the task must not return but instead call OSTaskDel((OS_TCB *)0, &err) which specifies to µC/OS-III to delete the currently running task.

A task may also delete another task by specifying to OSTaskDel() the address of the OS_TCB of the task to delete.

Once a task is deleted, its OS_TCB and stack may be reused to create another task. This assumes that the task's stack requirement of the new task is satisfied by the stack size of the deleted task.

Even though µC/OS-III allows the user to delete tasks at run time, it is recommend that such actions be avoided. Why? Because a task can "own" resources that are shared with other tasks. Deleting the task that owns resource(s) without first relinquishing the resources could lead to strange behaviors and possible deadlocks.

ARGUMENTS

p_tcb   is a pointer to the TCB of the task to delete or, you can pass a NULL pointer to specify that the calling task delete itself. If deleting the calling task, the scheduler will be invoked so that the next highest-priority task is executed.

p_err   is a pointer to a variable that will receive an error code:

OS_ERR_NONE   'p_err' gets set to OS_ERR_NONE before
                                     OSSched() to allow the returned error code to
                                     be monitored (by another task) even for a task
                                     that is deleting itself. In this case, p_err *must*

point to a global variable that can be accessed by that other task and, you should initialize that variable to OS_ERR_TASK_RUNNING prior to deleting the task.

OS_ERR_TASK_DEL_IDLE   if attempting to delete the idle task.

OS_ERR_TASK_DEL_ISR   if OS_CFG_CALLED_FROM_ISR_CHK_EN set to 1 in os_cfg.h: if you called OSTaskDel() from an ISR.

OS_ERR_TASK_DEL_INVALID   if attempting to delete the ISR Handler task while OS_CFG_ISR_POST_DEFERRED_EN is set to 1.

RETURNED VALUE

None

NOTES/WARNINGS

■ OSTaskDel() verifies that the user is not attempting to delete the µC/OS-III idle task and the ISR handler task.

■ Be careful when deleting a task that owns resources.

EXAMPLE

```
OS_TCB  MyTaskTCB;


void TaskX (void *p_arg)
{
    OS_ERR  err;


    while (DEF_ON) {
        :
        :
        OSTaskDel(&MyTaskTCB,
                  &err);
        /* Check "err" */
        :
        :
    }
}
```

A-61 OSTaskDelHook()

```
void  OSTaskDelHook (OS_TCB  *p_tcb);
```

File	Called from	Code enabled by
os_cpu_c.c	OSTaskDel() only	N/A

This function is called by **OSTaskDel()** after the task is removed from the ready list or any pend list.

You can use this hook to deallocate storage assigned to the task.

OSTaskDelHook() is part of the CPU port code and this function *must not* be called by the application code. **OSTaskDelHook()** is actually used by the µC/OS-III port developer.

ARGUMENTS

p_tcb   is a pointer to the TCB of the task being created. Note that the **OS_TCB** has been validated by **OSTaskDel()** and is guaranteed to not be a **NULL** pointer when **OSTaskDelHook()** is called.

RETURNED VALUE

None

NOTES/WARNINGS

Do not call this function from the application.

EXAMPLE

The code below calls an application-specific hook that the application programmer can define. The user can simply set the value of **OS_AppTaskDelHookPtr** to point to the desired hook function. **OSTaskDel()** calls **OSTaskDelHook()** which in turns calls **App_OS_TaskDelHook()** through **OS_AppTaskDelHookPtr**. As can be seen, when called, the application hook is passed the address of the **OS_TCB** of the task being deleted.

```
void  App_OS_TaskDelHook (OS_TCB *p_tcb)                    /* os_app_hooks.c      */
{
    /* Your code goes here! */
}


void App_OS_SetAllHooks (void)                             /* os_app_hooks.c      */
{
    CPU_SR_ALLOC();

    CPU_CRITICAL_ENTER();
    :
    OS_AppTaskDelHookPtr = App_OS_TaskDelHook;
    :
    CPU_CRITICAL_EXIT();
}



void  OSTaskDelHook (OS_TCB *p_tcb)                         /* os_cpu_c.c          */
{
#if OS_CFG_APP_HOOKS_EN > 0u
    if (OS_AppTaskDelHookPtr != (OS_APP_HOOK_TCB)0) {      /* Call application hook */
        (*OS_AppTaskDelHookPtr)(p_tcb);
    }
#endif
}
```

A-62 OSTaskQFlush()

```
OS_MSG_QTY  OSTaskQFlush (OS_TCB    *p_tcb,
                          OS_ERR  *p_err)
```

File	Called from	Code enabled by
os_task.c	Task only	OS_CFG_TASK_Q_EN

OSTaskQFlush() empties the contents of the task message queue and eliminates all messages sent to the queue. OS_MSGs from the queue are simply returned to the free pool of OS_MSGs.

ARGUMENTS

p_tcb   is a pointer to the TCB of the task that contains the queue to flush. Specifying a NULL pointer tells OSTaskQFlush() to flush the queue of the calling task's built-in message queue.

p_err   is a pointer to a variable that will contain an error code returned by this function.

OS_ERR_NONE	if the message queue is flushed.
OS_ERR_FLUSH_ISR	if OS_CFG_CALLED_FROM_ISR_CHK_EN set to 1 in os_cfg.h: if calling this function from an ISR

RETURNED VALUE

The number of OS_MSG entries freed from the message queue. Note that the OS_MSG entries are returned to the free pool of OS_MSGs.

NOTES/WARNINGS

- Use this function with great care. When flushing a queue, you lose the references to what the queue entries are pointing to, potentially causing 'memory leaks'. The data that the user is pointing to that is referenced by the queue entries should, most likely, be de-allocated (i.e., freed).

```
void Task (void *p_arg)
{
    OS_ERR  err;


    (void)&p_arg;
    while (DEF_ON) {
        :
        :
        entries = OSTaskQFlush((OS_TCB *)0,
                               &err);
        /* Check "err" */
        :
        :
    }
}
```

or, to flush a queue that contains entries, instead you can use **OSTaskQPend()** and specify the **OS_OPT_PEND_NON_BLOCKING** option.

```
void Task (void *p_arg)
{
    OS_ERR       err;
    CPU_TS       ts;
    OS_MSG_SIZE  msg_size;


    (void)&p_arg;
    :
    do {
        OSTaskQPend(0,
                    OS_OPT_PEND_NON_BLOCKING,
                    &msg_size,
                    &ts,
                    &err);
    } while (err != OS_ERR_PEND_WOULD_BLOCK);
    :
    :
}
```

A-63 OSTaskQPend()

```
void  *OSTaskQPend (OS_TICK       timeout,
                    OS_OPT        opt,
                    OS_MSG_SIZE   *p_msg_size,
                    CPU_TS        *p_ts,
                    OS_ERR        *p_err)
```

File	Called from	Code enabled by
os_task.c	Task only	OS_CFG_TASK_Q_EN and OS_CFG_MSG_EN

OSTaskQPend( ) allows a task to receive messages directly from an ISR or another task, without going through an intermediate message queue. In fact, each task has a built-in message queue if the configuration constant OS_CFG_TASK_Q_EN is set to The messages received are pointer-sized variables, and their use is application specific. If at least one message is already present in the message queue when OSTaskQPend( ) is called, the message is retrieved and returned to the caller.

If no message is present in the task's message queue and OS_OPT_PEND_BLOCKING is specified for the opt argument, OSTaskQPend( ) suspends the current task (assuming the scheduler is not locked) until either a message is received, or a user-specified timeout expires. A pended task that is suspended with OSTaskSuspend( ) can receive messages. However, the task remains suspended until it is resumed by calling OSTaskResume( ).

If no message is present in the task's message queue and OS_OPT_PEND_NON_BLOCKING is specified for the opt argument, OSTaskQPend( ) returns to the caller with an appropriate error code and returns a NULL pointer.

ARGUMENTS

timeout   allows the task to resume execution if a message is not received from a task or an ISR within the specified number of clock ticks. A timeout value of 0 indicates that the task wants to wait forever for a message. The timeout value is not synchronized with the clock tick. The timeout count starts decrementing on the next clock tick, which could potentially occur immediately.

opt   determines whether or not the user wants to block if a message is not available in the task's queue. This argument must be set to either:

OS_OPT_PEND_BLOCKING, or
OS_OPT_PEND_NON_BLOCKING

Note that the timeout argument should be set to 0 when OS_OPT_PEND_NON_BLOCKING is specified, since the timeout value is irrelevant using this option.

p_msg_size is a pointer to a variable that will receive the size of the message.

p_ts   is a pointer to a timestamp indicating when the task's queue was posted, or the pend aborted. Passing a **NULL** pointer is valid and indicates that the timestamp is not necessary.

A timestamp is useful when the task must know when the task message queue was posted, or how long it took for the task to resume after the task message queue was posted. In the latter case, call **OS_TS_GET()** and compute the difference between the current value of the timestamp and ***p_ts**. In other words:

delta = OS_TS_GET() - *p_ts;

p_err   is a pointer to a variable used to hold an error code.

OS_ERR_NONE	if a message is received.
OS_ERR_OPT_INVALID	if OS_CFG_ARG_CHK_EN set to 1 in os_cfg.h: if you specified an invalid option.
OS_ERR_PEND_ABORT	if the pend was aborted because another task called OSTaskQPendAbort().
OS_ERR_PEND_ISR	if OS_CFG_CALLED_FROM_ISR_CHK_EN set to 1 in os_cfg.h: if calling this function from an ISR.
OS_ERR_PEND_WOULD_BLOCK	if calling this function with the opt argument set to OS_OPT_PEND_NON_BLOCKING and no message is in the task's message queue.

OS_ERR_PTR_INVALID	if OS_CFG_ARG_CHK_EN set to 1 in os_cfg.h: if p_msg_size is a NULL pointer.
OS_ERR_SCHED_LOCKED	if calling this function when the scheduler is locked and the user wanted to block.
OS_ERR_TIMEOUT	if a message is not received within the specified timeout.

RETURNED VALUE

The message if no error or a NULL pointer upon error. You should examine the error code since it is possible to send NULL pointer messages. In other words, a NULL pointer does not mean an error occurred. *p_err must be examined to determine the reason for the error.

NOTES/WARNINGS

Do not call OSTaskQPend( ) from an ISR.

EXAMPLE

```
void CommTask (void *p_arg)
{
    OS_ERR       err;
    void        *p_msg;
    OS_MSG_SIZE  msg_size;
    CPU_TS       ts;


    (void)&p_arg;
    while (DEF_ON) {
        :
        :
        p_msg = OSTaskQPend(100,
                            OS_OPT_PEND_BLOCKING,
                            &msg_size,
                            &ts,
                            &err);
        /* Check "err" */
        :
        :

    }
}
```

A-64 OSTaskQPendAbort()

```
CPU_BOOLEAN  OSTaskQPendAbort (OS_TCB    *p_tcb,
                               OS_OPT    opt,
                               OS_ERR    *p_err)
```

File	Called from	Code enabled by
os_q.c	Task only	OS_CFG_TASK_Q_EN and OS_CFG_TASK_Q_PEND_ABORT_EN

OSTaskQPendAbort() aborts and readies a task currently waiting on its built-in message queue. This function should be used to fault-abort the wait on the task's message queue, rather than to normally signal the message queue via OSTaskQPost().

ARGUMENTS

p_tcb   is a pointer to the task for which the pend needs to be aborted. Note that it doesn't make sense to pass a NULL pointer or the address of the calling task's TCB since, by definition, the calling task cannot be pending.

opt   provides options for this function.

> OS_OPT_POST_NONE   No option specified.
>
> OS_OPT_POST_NO_SCHED   specifies that the scheduler should not be called even if the pend of a higher priority task has been aborted. Scheduling will need to occur from another function.
>
> Use this option if the task calling OSTaskQPendAbort() will do additional pend aborts, rescheduling will take place when completed, and multiple pend aborts should take effect simultaneously.

p_err   is a pointer to a variable that holds an error code:

> OS_ERR_NONE   the task was readied by another task and it was informed of the aborted wait.

OS_ERR_PEND_ABORT_ISR	if OS_CFG_CALLED_FROM_ISR_CHK_EN set to 1 in **os_cfg.h**: if called from an ISR
OS_ERR_PEND_ABORT_NONE	if the task was not pending on the task's message queue.
OS_ERR_PEND_ABORT_SELF	if OS_CFG_ARG_CHK_EN is set to 1 in **os_cfg.h**: if **p_tcb** is a **NULL** pointer. The user is attempting to pend abort the calling task which makes no sense as the caller, by definition, is not pending.

RETURNED VALUE

OSTaskQPendAbort() returns DEF_TRUE if the task was made ready-to-run by this function. DEF_FALSE indicates that the task was not pending, or an error occurred.

NOTES/WARNINGS

None

EXAMPLE

```
OS_TCB   CommRxTaskTCB;


void CommTask (void *p_arg)
{
    OS_ERR      err;
    CPU_BOOLEAN aborted;


    (void)&p_arg;
    while (DEF_ON) {
        :
        :
        aborted = OSTaskQPendAbort(&CommRxTaskTCB,
                              OS_OPT_POST_NONE,
                              &err);
        /* Check "err" */
        :
        :
    }
}
```

A-65 OSTaskQPost()

```
void  OSTaskQPost (OS_TCB        *p_tcb,
                   void          *p_void,
                   OS_MSG_SIZE   msg_size,
                   OS_OPT        opt,
                   OS_ERR        *p_err)
```

File	Called from	Code enabled by
os_q.c	Task or ISR	OS_CFG_TASK_Q_EN and OS_CFG_MSG_EN

OSTaskQPost() sends a message to a task through its local message queue. A message is a pointer-sized variable, and its use is application specific. If the task's message queue is full, an error code is returned to the caller. In this case, OSTaskQPost() immediately returns to its caller, and the message is not placed in the message queue.

If the task receiving the message is waiting for a message to arrive, it will be made ready-to-run. If the receiving task has a higher priority than the task sending the message, the higher-priority task resumes, and the task sending the message is suspended; that is, a context switch occurs. A message can be posted as first-in first-out (FIFO), or last-in-first-out (LIFO), depending on the value specified in the opt argument. In either case, scheduling occurs unless opt is set to OS_OPT_POST_NO_SCHED.

ARGUMENTS

p_tcb   is a pointer to the TCB of the task. Note that it is possible to post a message to the calling task (i.e., self) by specifying a NULL pointer, or the address of its TCB.

p_void   is the actual message sent to the task. p_void is a pointer-sized variable and its meaning is application specific.

msg_size specifies the size of the message posted (in number of bytes).

opt   determines the type of POST performed. Of course, it does not make sense to post LIFO and FIFO simultaneously, so these options are exclusive:

        OS_OPT_POST_FIFO   POST message to task and place at the end of the queue if the task is not waiting for messages.

        OS_OPT_POST_LIFO   POST message to task and place at the front of the queue if the task is not waiting for messages.

        OS_OPT_POST_NO_SCHED   This option prevents calling the scheduler after the post and therefore the caller is resumed.

                                   You should use this option if the task (or ISR) calling **OSTaskQPost()** will be doing additional posts, the user does not want to reschedule until all done, and multiple posts are to take effect simultaneously.

p_err   is a pointer to a variable that will contain an error code returned by this function.

        OS_ERR_NONE   if the call was successful and the message was posted to the task's message queue.

        OS_ERR_MSG_POOL_EMPTY   if running out of **OS_MSG** to hold the message being posted.

        OS_ERR_Q_MAX   if the task's message queue is full and cannot accept more messages.

RETURNED VALUE

None

NOTES/WARNINGS

None

EXAMPLE

```
OS_TCB       CommRxTaskTCB;
CPU_INT08U   CommRxBuf[100];


void CommTaskRx (void *p_arg)
{
    OS_ERR  err;


    (void)&p_arg;
    while (DEF_ON) {
        :
        OSTaskQPost(&CommRxTaskTCB,
                    (void *)&CommRxBuf[0],
                    sizeof(CommRxBuf),
                    OS_OPT_POST_FIFO,
                    &err);
        /* Check "err" */
        :
    }
}
```

A-66 OSTaskRegGet()

```
OS_REG   OSTaskRegGet (OS_TCB      *p_tcb,
                       OS_REG_ID   id,
                       OS_ERR      *p_err)
```

File	Called from	Code enabled by
os_task.c	Task only	OS_CFG_TASK_REG_TBL_SIZE > 0

µC/OS-III allows the user to store task-specific values in task registers. Task registers are different than CPU registers and are used to save such information as "**errno**," which are common in software components. Task registers can also store task-related data to be associated with the task at run time such as I/O register settings, configuration values, etc. A task may have as many as **OS_CFG_TASK_REG_TBL_SIZE** registers, and all registers have a data type of **OS_REG**. However, **OS_REG** can be declared at compile time (see **os_type.h**) to be nearly anything (8-, 16-, 32-, 64-bit signed or unsigned integer, or floating-point).

As shown below, a task register is changed by calling **OSTaskRegSet()** and read by calling **OSTaskRegGet()**. The desired task register is specified as an argument to these functions and can take a value between 0 and **OS_CFG_TASK_REG_TBL_SIZE-1**.

ARGUMENTS

p_tcb   is a pointer to the TCB of the task the user is receiving a task-register value from. A **NULL** pointer indicates that the user wants the value of a task register of the calling task.

id   is the identifier of the task register and valid values are from **0** to **OS_CFG_TASK_REG_TBL_SIZE-1**.

p_err   is a pointer to a variable that will contain an error code returned by this function.

OS_ERR_NONE	if the call was successful and the function returned the value of the desired task register.
OS_ERR_REG_ID_INVALID	if **OS_CFG_ARG_CHK_EN** is set to **1** in **os_cfg.h**: if a valid task register identifier is not specified.

RETURNED VALUE

The current value of the task register.

NOTES/WARNINGS

None

Appendix A

EXAMPLE

```
OS_TCB  MyTaskTCB;


void TaskX (void *p_arg)
{
    OS_ERR  err;
    OS_REG  reg;


    while (DEF_ON) {
        :
        reg = OSTaskRegGet(&MyTaskTCB,
                           5,
                           &err);
        /* Check "err" */
        :
    }
}
```

A-67 OSTaskRegGetID()

```
OS_REG_ID  OSTaskRegGet (OS_ERR  *p_err)
```

File	Called from	Code enabled by
os_task.c	Task only	OS_CFG_TASK_REG_TBL_SIZE > 0

OSTaskRegGetID() allows your application to assign task register IDs dynamically. In other words, instead of using #define constants to establish a task register number (or index) into the .TaskReg[] shown below, you should always use OSTaskRegGetID(), assign the ID to a variable and use this ID when calling OSTaskRegGet() or OSTaskRegSet().

If successful, OSTaskRegGetID() will return an ID between 0 and OS_CFG_TASK_REG_TBL_SIZE-1.

ARGUMENTS

p_err   is a pointer to a variable that will contain an error code returned by this function.

      OS_ERR_NONE   if the call was successful and the function returned the next available task register ID (or index).

611

OS_ERR_NO_MORE_ID_AVAIL   if you already called **OSTaskRegGetID()** OS_CFG_TASK_REG_TBL_SIZE (see **os_cfg.h**) times and thus there are no more IDs available to be assigned.

RETURNED VALUE

The next available task register ID or **OS_CFG_TASK_REG_TBL_SIZE** if all the IDs have already been assigned.

NOTES/WARNINGS

None

EXAMPLE

```
OS_REG_ID  MyTaskRegID;


void main (void)
{
    OS_ERR  err;

    :
    OSInit(&err);
    :
    MyTaskRegID = OSTaskRegGetID(&err);
    :
    OSStart(&err);
}
```

A-68 OSTaskRegSet()

```
void  OSTaskRegSet (OS_TCB     *p_tcb,
                    OS_REG_ID   id,
                    OS_REG      value,
                    OS_ERR     *p_err)
```

File	Called from	Code enabled by
os_task.c	Task only	OS_CFG_TASK_REG_TBL_SIZE > 0

µC/OS-III allows the user to store task-specific values in task registers. Task registers are different than CPU registers and are used to save such information as "**errno**," which are common in software components. Task registers can also store task-related data to be associated with the task at run time such as I/O register settings, configuration values, etc. A task may have as many as **OS_CFG_TASK_REG_TBL_SIZE** registers, and all registers have a data type of **OS_REG**. However, **OS_REG** can be declared at compile time to be nearly anything (8-, 16-, 32-, 64-bit signed or unsigned integer, or floating-point).

As shown below, a task register is changed by calling **OSTaskRegSet()**, and read by calling **OSTaskRegGet()**. The desired task register is specified as an argument to these functions and can take a value between 0 and OS_CFG_TASK_REG_TBL_SIZE-1.

.TaskReg[ ]

OSTaskRegSet () ⟶ [0] ⟶ OSTaskRegGet ()

[OS_CFG_TASK_REG_TBL_SIZE-1]

◄—OS_REG—►

ARGUMENTS

p_tcb   is a pointer to the TCB of the task you are setting. A **NULL** pointer indicates that the user wants to set the value of a task register of the calling task.

id   is the identifier of the task register and valid values are from **0** to **OS_CFG_TASK_REG_TBL_SIZE-1**.

value   is the new value of the task register specified by **id**.

p_err   is a pointer to a variable that will contain an error code returned by this function.

OS_ERR_NONE	if the call was successful, and the function set the value of the desired task register.
OS_ERR_REG_ID_INVALID	if **OS_CFG_ARG_CHK_EN** is set to **1** in **os_cfg.h**: if a valid task register identifier is not specified.

RETURNED VALUE

None

NOTES/WARNINGS

None

```
OS_TCB  MyTaskTCB;


void TaskX (void *p_arg)
{
    OS_ERR  err;


    while (DEF_ON) {
        :
        reg = OSTaskRegSet(&MyTaskTCB,
                           5,
                           23,
                           &err);
        /* Check "err" */
        :
    }
}
```

A-69 OSTaskReturnHook()

```
void  OSTaskReturnHook (void);
```

File	Called from	Code enabled by
os_cpu_c.c	OS_TaskReturn() ONLY	N/A

This function is called by **OS_TaskReturn()**. **OS_TaskReturn()** is called if the user accidentally returns from the task code. In other words, the task should either be implemented as an infinite loop and never return, or the task must call **OSTaskDel((OS_TCB *)0, &err)** to delete itself to prevent it from exiting.

OSTaskReturnHook() is part of the CPU port code and this function *must not* be called by the application code. **OSTaskReturnHook()** is actually used by the µC/OS-III port developer.

Note that after calling **OSTaskReturnHook()**, **OS_TaskReturn()** will actually delete the task by calling:

```
OSTaskDel((OS_TCB *)0,
          &err)
```

ARGUMENTS

p_tcb   is a pointer to the TCB of the task that is not behaving as expected. Note that the **OS_TCB** is validated by **OS_TaskReturn()**, and is guaranteed to not be a **NULL** pointer when **OSTaskReturnHook()** is called.

RETURNED VALUE

None

NOTES/WARNINGS

Do not call this function from the application.

EXAMPLE

The code below calls an application-specific hook that the application programmer can define. For this, the user can simply set the value of **OS_AppTaskReturnHookPtr** to point to the desired hook function as shown in the example. If a task returns and forgets to call **OSTaskDel((OS_TCB *)0, &err)** then µC/OS-III will call **OSTaskReturnHook()** which in turns calls **App_OS_TaskReturnHook()** through **OS_AppTaskReturnHookPtr**. When called, the application hook is passed the address of the **OS_TCB** of the task returning.

```c
void  App_OS_TaskReturnHook (OS_TCB  *p_tcb)              /* os_app_hooks.c        */
{
    /* Your code goes here! */
}


void App_OS_SetAllHooks (void)                           /* os_app_hooks.c        */
{
    CPU_SR_ALLOC();

    CPU_CRITICAL_ENTER();
    :
    OS_AppTaskReturnHookPtr = App_OS_TaskReturnHook;
    :
    CPU_CRITICAL_EXIT();
}


void  OSTaskReturnHook (OS_TCB *p_tcb)                    /* os_cpu_c.c            */
{
#if OS_CFG_APP_HOOKS_EN > 0u
    if (OS_AppTaskReturnHookPtr != (OS_APP_HOOK_TCB)0) {   /* Call application hook */
        (*OS_AppTaskReturnHookPtr)(p_tcb);
    }
#endif
}
```

A-70 OSTaskResume()

```
void  OSTaskResume (OS_TCB  *p_tcb,
                    OS_ERR  *p_err)
```

File	Called from	Code enabled by
os_task.c	Task only	OS_CFG_TASK_SUSPEND_EN

OSTaskResume() resumes a task suspended through the OSTaskSuspend() function. In fact, OSTaskResume() is the only function that can unsuspend a suspended task. Obviously, the suspended task can only be resumed by another task. If the suspended task is also waiting on another kernel object such as an event flag, semaphore, mutex, message queue etc., the suspension will simply be lifted (i.e., removed), but the task will continue waiting for the object.

The user can "nest" suspension of a task by calling OSTaskSuspend() and therefore must call OSTaskResume() an equivalent number of times to resume such a task. In other words, if suspending a task five times, it is necessary to unsuspend the same task five times to remove the suspension of the task.

ARGUMENTS

p_tcb   is a pointer to the TCB of the task that is resuming. A NULL pointer is not a valid value as one cannot resume the calling task because, by definition, the calling task is running and is not suspended.

p_err   is a pointer to a variable that will contain an error code returned by this function.

OS_ERR_NONE	if the call was successful and the desired task is resumed.
OS_ERR_TASK_RESUME_ISR	if OS_CFG_CALLED_FROM_ISR_CHK_EN set to 1 in os_cfg.h: if calling this function from an ISR.

OS_ERR_TASK_RESUME_SELF	if OS_CFG_ARG_CHK_EN is set to 1 in os_cfg.h: if passing a NULL pointer for p_tcb or, a pointer to the current TCB. It is not possible to resume the calling task since, if suspended, it cannot be executing.
OS_ERR_TASK_NOT_SUSPENDED	if the task attempting to be resumed is not suspended.

RETURNED VALUE

None

NOTES/WARNINGS

None

EXAMPLE

```
OS_TCB   TaskY;


void TaskX (void *p_arg)
{
    OS_ERR err;


    while (DEF_ON) {
        :
        :
        OSTaskResume(&TaskY,
                     &err);        /* Resume suspended task      */
        /* Check "err" */
        :
        :
    }
}
```

A-71 OSTaskSemPend()

```
OS_SEM_CTR  OSTaskSemPend (OS_TICK    timeout,
                           OS_OPT     opt,
                           CPU_TS     *p_ts,
                           OS_ERR     *p_err)
```

File	Called from	Code enabled by
os_task.c	Task only	Always enabled

OSTaskSemPend() allows a task to wait for a signal to be sent by another task or ISR without going through an intermediate object such as a semaphore. If the task was previously signaled when OSTaskSemPend() is called then, the caller resumes.

If no signal was received by the task and OS_OPT_PEND_BLOCKING is specified for the opt argument, OSTaskSemPend() suspends the current task until either a signal is received, or a user-specified timeout expires. A pended task suspended with OSTaskSuspend() can receive signals. However, the task remains suspended until it is resumed by calling OSTaskResume().

If no signals were sent to the task and OS_OPT_PEND_NON_BLOCKING was specified for the opt argument, OSTaskSemPend() returns to the caller with an appropriate error code and returns a signal count of 0.

ARGUMENTS

timeout   allows the task to resume execution if a signal is not received from a task or an ISR within the specified number of clock ticks. A timeout value of 0 indicates that the task wants to wait forever for a signal. The timeout value is not synchronized with the clock tick. The timeout count starts decrementing on the next clock tick, which could potentially occur immediately.

opt   determines whether the user wants to block or not, if a signal was not sent to the task. Set this argument to either:

OS_OPT_PEND_BLOCKING, or
OS_OPT_PEND_NON_BLOCKING

Note that the **timeout** argument should be set to 0 when specifying OS_OPT_PEND_NON_BLOCKING, since the timeout value is irrelevant using this option.

p_ts   is a pointer to a timestamp indicating when the task's semaphore was posted, or the pend was aborted. Passing a **NULL** pointer is valid and indicates that the timestamp is not necessary.

A timestamp is useful when the task is to know when the semaphore was posted, or how long it took for the task to resume after the semaphore was posted. In the latter case, call **OS_TS_GET()** and compute the difference between the current value of the timestamp and ***p_ts**. In other words:

```
delta = OS_TS_GET() - *p_ts;
```

p_err   is a pointer to a variable used to hold an error code.

OS_ERR_NONE	if a signal is received.
OS_ERR_PEND_ABORT	if the pend was aborted because another task called **OSTaskSemPendAbort()**.
OS_ERR_PEND_ISR	if OS_CFG_CALLED_FROM_ISR_CHK_EN set to 1 in **os_cfg.h**: if calling this function from an ISR.
OS_ERR_PEND_WOULD_BLOCK	if calling this function with the **opt** argument set to OS_OPT_PEND_NON_BLOCKING, and no signal was received.
OS_ERR_SCHED_LOCKED	if calling this function when the scheduler is locked and the user wanted the task to block.
OS_ERR_TIMEOUT	if a signal is not received within the specified timeout.

RETURNED VALUE

The current value of the signal counter after it has been decremented. In other words, the number of signals still remaining in the signal counter.

NOTES/WARNINGS

Do not call **OSTaskSemPend( )** from an ISR.

EXAMPLE

```c
void CommTask(void *p_arg)
{
    OS_ERR      err;
    OS_SEM_CTR  ctr;
    CPU_TS      ts;


    (void)&p_arg;
    while (DEF_ON) {
        :
        ctr = OSTaskSemPend(100,
                            OS_OPT_PEND_BLOCKING,
                            &ts,
                            &err);
        /* Check "err" */
        :
    }
}
```

A-72 OSTaskSemPendAbort()

```
CPU_BOOLEAN  OSTaskSemPendAbort (OS_TCB  *p_tcb,
                                 OS_OPT   opt,
                                 OS_ERR  *p_err)
```

File	Called from	Code enabled by
os_task.c	Task only	OS_CFG_TASK_SEM_PEND_ABORT_EN

OSTaskSemPendAbort() aborts and readies a task currently waiting on its built-in semaphore. This function should be used to fault-abort the wait on the task's semaphore, rather than to normally signal the task via OSTaskSemPost().

ARGUMENTS

p_tcb   is a pointer to the task for which the pend must be aborted. Note that it does not make sense to pass a NULL pointer or the address of the calling task's TCB since, by definition, the calling task cannot be pending.

opt   provides options for this function.

OS_OPT_POST_NONE	no option specified, call the scheduler by default.
OS_OPT_POST_NO_SCHED	specifies that the scheduler should not be called even if the pend of a higher-priority task has been aborted. Scheduling will need to occur from another function.
	Use this option if the task calling OSTaskSemPendAbort() will be doing additional pend aborts, rescheduling will not take place until finished, and multiple pend aborts are to take effect simultaneously.
p_err	is a pointer to a variable that holds an error code:
OS_ERR_NONE	the pend was aborted for the specified task.
OS_ERR_PEND_ABORT_ISR	if OS_CFG_CALLED_FROM_ISR_CHK_EN set to 1 in os_cfg.h: if called from an ISR
OS_ERR_PEND_ABORT_NONE	if the task was not waiting for a signal.

623

OS_ERR_PEND_ABORT_SELF   if **p_tcb** is a **NULL** pointer or the TCB of the calling task is specified. The user is attempting to pend abort the calling task, which makes no sense since, by definition, the calling task is not pending.

RETURNED VALUE

OSTaskSemPendAbort() returns **DEF_TRUE** if the task was made ready-to-run by this function. **DEF_FALSE** indicates that the task was not pending, or an error occurred.

NOTES/WARNINGS

None

EXAMPLE

```
OS_TCB  CommRxTaskTCB;


void CommTask (void *p_arg)
{
    OS_ERR      err;
    CPU_BOOLEAN aborted;


    (void)&p_arg;
    while (DEF_ON) {
        :
        :
        aborted = OSTaskSemPendAbort(&CommRxTaskTCB,
                                     OS_OPT_POST_NONE,
                                     &err);
        /* Check "err" */
        :
        :
    }
}
```

A-73 OSTaskSemPost()

```
OS_SEM_CTR  OSTaskSemPost (OS_TCB   *p_tcb,
                           OS_OPT    opt,
                           OS_ERR   *p_err)
```

File	Called from	Code enabled by
os_task.c	Task or ISR	Always enabled

OSTaskSemPost() sends a signal to a task through it's local semaphore.

If the task receiving the signal is actually waiting for a signal to be received, it will be made ready-to-run and, if the receiving task has a higher priority than the task sending the signal, the higher-priority task resumes, and the task sending the signal is suspended; that is, a context switch occurs. Note that scheduling only occurs if **opt** is set to OS_OPT_POST_NONE, because the OS_OPT_POST_NO_SCHED option does not cause the scheduler to be called.

ARGUMENTS

p_tcb　　is a pointer to the TCB of the task being signaled. A **NULL** pointer indicates that the user is sending a signal to itself.

opt　　provides options to the call.

OS_OPT_POST_NONE	No option, by default the scheduler will be called.
OS_OPT_POST_NO_SCHED	Do not call the scheduler after the post, therefore the caller is resumed. You would use this option if the task (or ISR) calling **OSTaskSemPost()** will be doing additional posts, reschedule waits until all is done, and multiple posts are to take effect simultaneously.

p_err   is a pointer to a variable that will contain an error code returned by this function.

> OS_ERR_NONE   if the call was successful and the signal was sent.
>
> OS_ERR_SEM_OVF   the post would have caused the semaphore counter to overflow.

RETURNED VALUE

The current value of the task's signal counter, or **0** if called from an ISR and OS_CFG_ISR_POST_DEFERRED_EN is set to 1.

NOTES/WARNINGS

None

EXAMPLE

```
OS_TCB        CommRxTaskTCB;


void CommTaskRx (void *p_arg)
{
    OS_ERR      err;
    OS_SEM_CTR  ctr;


    (void)&p_arg;
    while (DEF_ON) {
        :
        ctr = OSTaskSemPost(&CommRxTaskTCB,
                            OS_OPT_POST_NONE,
                            &err);
        /* Check "err" */
        :
    }
}
```

A-74 OSTaskSemSet()

```
OS_SEM_CTR  OSTaskSemSet (OS_TCB     *p_tcb,
                          OS_SEM_CTR  cnt;
                          OS_ERR      *p_err)
```

File	Called from	Code enabled by
os_task.c	Task or ISR	Always Enabled

OSTaskSemSet() allows the user to set the value of the task's signal counter. You would set the signal counter of the calling task by passing a NULL pointer for p_tcb.

ARGUMENTS

p_tcb   is a pointer to the task's OS_TCB to clear the signal counter. A NULL pointer indicates that the user wants to clear the caller's signal counter.

cnt   the desired value for the task semaphore counter.

p_err   is a pointer to a variable that will contain an error code returned by this function.

OS_ERR_NONE	if the call was successful and the signal counter was cleared.
OS_ERR_SET_ISR	if OS_CFG_CALLED_FROM_ISR_CHK_EN set to 1 in os_cfg.h: if calling this function from an ISR

RETURNED VALUE

The value of the signal counter prior to setting it.

NOTES/WARNINGS

None

EXAMPLE

```
OS_TCB    TaskY;


void TaskX (void *p_arg)
{
    OS_ERR err;


    while (DEF_ON) {
        :
        :
        OSTaskSemSet(&TaskY,
                     0,
                     &err);
        /* Check "err" */
        :
        :
    }
}
```

A-75 OSStatTaskHook()

```
void  OSStatTaskHook (void);
```

File	Called from	Code enabled by
os_cpu_c.c	OS_StatTask() ONLY	OS_CFG_TASK_STAT_EN

This function is called by OS_StatTask().

OSStatTaskHook() is part of the CPU port code and *must not* be called by the application code. OSStatTaskHook() is actually used by the µC/OS-III port developer.

ARGUMENTS

None

RETURNED VALUE

None

NOTES/WARNINGS

Do not call this function from the application.

EXAMPLE

The code below calls an application-specific hook that the application programmer can define. The user can simply set the value of OS_AppStatTaskHookPtr to point to the desired hook function as shown in the example. The statistic task calls OSStatTaskHook() which in turns calls App_OS_StatTaskHook() through OS_AppStatTaskHookPtr.

```
void  App_OS_StatTaskHook (void)                        /* os_app_hooks.c        */
{
    /* Your code goes here! */
}


void App_OS_SetAllHooks (void)                          /* os_app_hooks.c        */
{
   CPU_SR_ALLOC();

   CPU_CRITICAL_ENTER();
   :
   OS_AppStatTaskHookPtr = App_OS_StatTaskHook;
   :
   CPU_CRITICAL_EXIT();
}


void  OSStatTaskHook (void)                             /* os_cpu_c.c            */
{
#if OS_CFG_APP_HOOKS_EN > 0u
    if (OS_AppStatTaskHookPtr != (OS_APP_HOOK_VOID)0) {   /* Call application hook */
        (*OS_AppStatTaskHookPtr)();
    }
#endif
}
```

A-76 OSTaskStkChk()

```
void  OSTaskStkChk (OS_TCB        *p_tcb,
                    CPU_STK_SIZE  *p_free,
                    CPU_STK_SIZE  *p_used,
                    OS_ERR        *p_err)
```

File	Called from	Code enabled by
os_task.c	Task only	OS_CFG_TASK_STAT_CHK_EN

OSTaskStkChk() determines a task's stack statistics. Specifically, it computes the amount of free stack space, as well as the amount of stack space used by the specified task. This function requires that the task be created with the OS_TASK_OPT_STK_CHK and OS_TASK_OPT_STK_CLR options.

Stack sizing is accomplished by walking from the bottom of the stack and counting the number of 0 entries on the stack until a non-zero value is found.

It is possible to not set the OS_TASK_OPT_STK_CLR when creating the task if the startup code clears all RAM, and tasks are not deleted (this reduces the execution time of OSTaskCreate()).

µC/OS-III's statistic task calls OSTaskStkChk() for each task created and stores the results in each task's OS_TCB so your application doesn't need to call this function if the statistic task is enabled.

ARGUMENTS

p_tcb   is a pointer to the TCB of the task where the stack is being checked. A NULL pointer indicates that the user is checking the calling task's stack.

p_free   is a pointer to a variable of type CPU_STK_SIZE and will contain the number of free CPU_STK elements on the stack of the task being inquired about.

p_used   is a pointer to a variable of type CPU_STK_SIZE and will contain the number of used CPU_STK elements on the stack of the task being inquired about.

p_err   is a pointer to a variable that will contain an error code returned by this function.

OS_ERR_NONE	if the call was successful.
OS_ERR_PTR_INVALID	if OS_CFG_ARG_CHK_EN is set to 1 in os_cfg.h: if either p_free or p_used are NULL pointers.
OS_ERR_TASK_NOT_EXIST	if the stack pointer of the task is a NULL pointer.
OS_ERR_TASK_OPT	if OS_OPT_TASK_STK_CHK is not specifed whencreating the task being checked.
OS_ERR_TASK_STK_CHK_ISR	if OS_CFG_CALLED_FROM_ISR_CHK_EN set to 1 in os_cfg.h: if calling this function from an ISR.

RETURNED VALUE

None

NOTES/WARNINGS

■ Execution time of this task depends on the size of the task's stack.

■ The application can determine the total task stack space (in number of CPU_STK elements) by adding the value of *p_free and *p_used. This number should add up to the task's stack size which is stored in the .StkSize field of the OS_TCB of the task.

■ The #define CPU_CFG_STK_GROWTH must be declared (typically from os_cpu.h). When this #define is set to CPU_STK_GROWTH_LO_TO_HI, the stack grows from low memory to high memory. When this #define is set to CPU_STK_GROWTH_HI_TO_LO, the stack grows from high memory to low memory.

EXAMPLE

```
OS_TCB  MyTaskTCB;


void Task (void *p_arg)
{
    OS_ERR       err;
    CPU_STK_SIZE n_free;
    CPU_STK_SIZE n_used;


    (void)&p_arg;
    while (DEF_ON) {
        :
        :
        OSTaskStkChk(&MyTaskTCB,
                     &n_free,
                     &n_used,
                     &err);
        /* Check "err" */
        :
        :
    }
}
```

A-77 OSTaskStkInit()

```
void OSTaskStkInit (OS_TASK_PTR    p_task,
                    void          *p_arg,
                    CPU_STK       *p_stk_base,
                    CPU_STK       *p_stk_limit,
                    CPU_STK_SIZE   stk_size,
                    OS_OPT         opt);
```

File	Called from	Code enabled by
os_cpu_c.c	OSTaskCreate() ONLY	N/A

This function is called by **OSTaskCreate()** to setup the stack frame of the task being created. Typically, the stack frame will look as if an interrupt just occurred, and all CPU registers were pushed onto the task's stack. The stacking order of CPU registers is very CPU specific.

OSTaskStkInit() is part of the CPU port code and this function *must not* be called by the application code. **OSTaskStkInit()** is actually defined by the µC/OS-III port developer.

ARGUMENTS

p_task   is the address of the task being created (see **MyTask()** below). Tasks must be declared as follows:

```
void   MyTask (void  *p_arg)
{
    /* Do something with "p_arg" (optional) */
    while (DEF_ON) {
        /* Wait for an event to occur */
        /* Do some work              */
    }
}
```

Or,

```
void   MyTask (void  *p_arg)
{
    OS_ERR  err;


    /* Do something with "p_arg" (optional) */
    /* Do some work                          */
    OSTaskDel((OS_TCB *)0,
              &err);
}
```

p_arg   is the argument that the task will receive when the task first start (see code above).

p_stk_base is the base address of the task's stack. This is typically the lowest address of the area of storage reserved for the task stack. In other words, if declaring the task's stack as follows:

```
CPU_STK  MyTaskStk[100];
```

OSTaskCreate() would pass &OSMyTaskStk[0] to p_stk_base.

p_stk_limit is the address of the task's stack limit watermark. This pointer is computed by OSTaskCreate() prior to calling OSTaskStkInit().

stk_size   is the size of the task's stack in number of CPU_STK elements. In the example above, the stack size is 100.

opt   is the options passed to OSTaskCreate() for the task being created.

RETURNED VALUE

The new top of stack after the task's stack is initialized. **OSTaskStkInit()** will place values on the task's stack and will return the new pointer for the stack pointer for the task. The value returned is very processor specific. For some processors, the returned value will point to the last value placed on the stack while, with other processors, the returned value will point at the next free stack entry.

NOTES/WARNINGS

Do not call this function from the application.

EXAMPLE

The pseudo code below shows the typical steps performed by this function. Consult an existing µC/OS-III port for examples. Here it is assumed that the stack grows from high memory to low memory.

```
CPU_STK  *OSTaskStkInit (OS_TASK_PTR   p_task,
                         void          *p_arg,
                         CPU_STK       *p_stk_base,
                         CPU_STK       *p_stk_limit,
                         CPU_STK_SIZE  stk_size,
                         OS_OPT        opt)
{
    CPU_STK  *p_stk;


    p_stk   = &p_stk_base[stk_size - 1u];                      (1)
    *p_stk-- = Initialize the stack as if an interrupt just occurred; (2)
    return (p_stk);                                            (3)
}
```

(1)   **p_stk** is set to the top-of-stack. It is assumed that the stack grows from high memory locations to lower ones. If the stack of the CPU grew from low memory locations to higher ones, the user would simply set **p_stk** to point at the base. However, this also means that it would be necessary to initialize the stack frame in the opposite direction.

636

(2)   The CPU registers are stored onto the stack using the same stacking order as used when an interrupt service routine (ISR) saves the registers at the beginning of the ISR. The value of the register contents on the stack is typically not important. However, there are some values that are critical. Specifically, you need to place the address of the task in the proper location on the stack frame and it may be important to load the value of the CPU register and possibly pass the value of **p_arg** in one of the CPU registers. Finally, if the task is to return by mistake, it is a good idea to place the address of **OS_TaskReturn()** in the proper location on the stack frame. This ensures that a faulty returning task is intercepted by µC/OS-III.

(3)   Finally, your code will need to return the value of the stack pointer at the new top-of-stack frame. Some processors point to the last stored location, while others point to the next empty location. You should consult the processor documentation so that the return value points at the proper location.

Below is an example showing which arguments **OSTaskCreate()** passes to **OSTaskStkInit()**.

```
CPU_STK  MyTaskStk[100];
OS_TCB   MyTaskTCB;


void  MyTask (void *p_arg)
{
    /* Do something with "parg" (optional) */
}


void  main (void)
{
    OS_ERR  err;
    :
    :
    OSInit(&err);
    /* Check "err" */
    :
    OSTaskCreate ((OS_TCB        *)&MyTaskTCB,
                  (CPU_CHAR      *)"My Task",
                  (OS_TASK_PTR   )MyTask,            /* "p_task"     of OSTaskStkInit() */
                  (void          *)0,                /* "p_arg"      of OSTaskStkInit() */
                  (OS_PRIO       )prio,
                  (CPU_STK       *)&MyTaskStk[0],    /* "p_stk_base" of OSTaskStkInit() */
                  (CPU_STK_SIZE  )10,                /* "p_stk_limit" of OSTaskStkInit() */
                  (CPU_STK_SIZE  )100,               /* "stk_size"   of OSTaskStkInit() */
                  (OS_MSG_QTY    )0,
                  (OS_TICK       )0,
                  (void          *)0,
                  (OS_OPT        )(OS_OPT_TASK_STK_CLR + OS_OPT_TASK_STK_CHK),   /* "opt" */
                  (OS_ERR        *)&err);
    /* Check "err" */
    :
    :
    OSStart(&err);
    /* Check "err" */
}
```

A-78 OSTaskSuspend()

```
void    OSTaskSuspend (OS_TCB  *p_tcb,
                       OS_ERR  *p_err)
```

File	Called from	Code enabled by
os_task.c	Task only	OS_CFG_TASK_SUSPEND_EN

OSTaskSuspend() suspends (or blocks) execution of a task unconditionally. The calling task may be suspended by specifying a NULL pointer for p_tcb, or simply by passing the address of its OS_TCB. In this case, another task needs to resume the suspended task. If the current task is suspended, rescheduling occurs, and µC/OS-III runs the next highest priority task ready-to-run. The only way to resume a suspended task is to call OSTaskResume().

Task suspension is additive, which means that if the task being suspended is delayed until N ticks expire, the task is resumed only when both the time expires and the suspension is removed. Also, if the suspended task is waiting for a semaphore and the semaphore is signaled, the task is removed from the semaphore wait list (if it is the highest-priority task waiting for the semaphore), but execution is not resumed until the suspension is removed.

The user can "nest" suspension of a task by calling OSTaskSuspend() and therefore it is important to call OSTaskResume() an equivalent number of times to resume the task. If suspending a task five times, it is necessary to unsuspend the same task five times to remove the suspension of the task.

ARGUMENTS

p_tcb   is a pointer to the TCB of the task the user is suspending. A NULL pointer indicates suspension of the calling task.

p_err   is a pointer to a variable that will contain an error code returned by this function.

OS_ERR_NONE	if the call was successful and the desired task was suspended.
OS_ERR_TASK_SUSPEND_ISR	if OS_CFG_CALLED_FROM_ISR_CHK_EN set to 1 in os_cfg.h: if the function is called from an ISR.

OS_ERR_TASK_SUSPEND_IDLE   if attempting to suspend the idle task. This is not allowed since the idle task must always exist.

OS_ERR_TASK_SUSPEND_INT_HANDLER if attempting to suspend the ISR handler task. This is not allowed since the ISR handler task is a μC/OS-III internal task.

RETURNED VALUE

None

NOTES/WARNINGS

■   OSTaskSuspend() and OSTaskResume() must be used in pairs.

■   A suspended task can only be resumed by OSTaskResume().

EXAMPLE

```
void TaskX (void *p_arg)
{
    OS_ERR  err;

    (void)&p_arg;
    while (DEF_ON) {
        :
        :
        OSTaskSuspend((OS_TCB *)0,
                      &err);       /* Suspend current task                    */
        /* Check "err" */
        :
    }
}
```

A-79 OSTaskSwHook()

```
void   OSTaskSwHook (void)
```

File	Called from	Code enabled by
os_cpu_c.c	OSCtxSw() or OSIntCtxSw()	N/A

OSTaskSwHook() is always called by either OSCtxSw() or OSIntCtxSw() (see os_cpu_a.asm), just after saving the CPU registers onto the task being switched out. This hook function allows the port developer to perform additional operations (if needed) when µC/OS-III performs a context switch.

Before calling OSTaskSwHook(), OSTCBCurPtr points at the OS_TCB of the task being switched out, and OSTCBHighRdyPtr points at the OS_TCB of the new task being switched in.

The code shown in the example below should be included in all implementations of OSTaskSwHook(), and is used for performance measurements. This code is written in C for portability.

ARGUMENTS

None

RETURNED VALUES

None

NOTES/WARNINGS

None

EXAMPLE

The code below calls an application specific hook that the application programmer can define. The user can simply set the value of OS_AppTaskSwHookPtr to point to the desired hook function. When µC/OS-III performs a context switch, it calls OSTaskSwHook() which in turn calls App_OS_TaskSwHook() through OS_AppTaskSwHookPtr.

```
void  App_OS_TaskSwHook (void)                        /* os_app_hooks.c        */
{
    /* Your code goes here! */
}


void App_OS_SetAllHooks (void)                        /* os_app_hooks.c        */
{
    CPU_SR_ALLOC();

    CPU_CRITICAL_ENTER();
    :
    OS_AppTaskSwHookPtr = App_OS_TaskSwHook;
    :
    CPU_CRITICAL_EXIT();
}
```

```c
void  OSTaskSwHook (void)                              /* os_cpu_c.c          */
{
#if OS_CFG_TASK_PROFILE_EN > 0u
    CPU_TS     ts;
#endif
#ifdef  CPU_CFG_TIME_MEAS_INT_DIS_EN
    CPU_TS     int_dis_time;
#endif



#if OS_CFG_APP_HOOKS_EN > 0u
    if (OS_AppTaskSwHookPtr != (OS_APP_HOOK_VOID)0) {
        (*OS_AppTaskSwHookPtr)();
    }
#endif
#if OS_CFG_TASK_PROFILE_EN > 0u
    ts = OS_TS_GET();
    if (OSTCBCurPtr != OSTCBHighRdyPtr) {
        OSTCBCurPtr->CyclesDelta  = ts - OSTCBCurPtr->CyclesStart;
        OSTCBCurPtr->CyclesTotal += OSTCBCurPtr->CyclesDelta;
    }
    OSTCBHighRdyPtr->CyclesStart = ts;
#endif
#ifdef  CPU_CFG_INT_DIS_MEAS_EN
    int_dis_time = CPU_IntDisMeasMaxCurReset();
    if (int_dis_time > OSTCBCurPtr->IntDisTimeMax) {
        OSTCBCurPtr->IntDisTimeMax = int_dis_time;
    }
#endif
#if OS_CFG_SCHED_LOCK_TIME_MEAS_EN > 0u
    if (OSTCBCurPtr->SchedLockTimeMax < OSSchedLockTimeMaxCur) {
        OSTCBCurPtr->SchedLockTimeMax = OSSchedLockTimeMaxCur;
    }
    OSSchedLockTimeMaxCur         = (CPU_TS)0;
#endif
}
```

A-80 OSTaskTimeQuantaSet()

```
void    OSTaskTimeQuantaSet (OS_TCB   *p_tcb,
                             OS_TICK   time_quanta,
                             OS_ERR   *p_err)
```

File	Called from	Code enabled by
os_task.c	Task only	OS_CFG_SCHED_ROUND_ROBIN_EN

OSTaskTimeQuantaSet() is used to change the amount of time a task is given when time slicing multiple tasks running at the same priority.

ARGUMENTS

p_tcb   is a pointer to the TCB of the task for which the time quanta is being set. A NULL pointer indicates that the user is changing the time quanta for the calling task.

time_quanta specifies the amount of time (in ticks) that the task will run when μC/OS-III is time slicing between tasks at the same priority. Specifying 0 indicates that the default time as specified will be used when calling the function OSSchedRoundRobinCfg(), or OS_CFG_TICK_RATE_HZ / 10 if you never called OSSchedRoundRobinCfg().

You should not specify a "large" value for this argument as this means that the task will execute for that amount of time when multiple tasks are ready-to-run at the same priority. The concept of time slicing is to allow other equal-priority tasks a chance to run. Typical time quanta periods should be approximately 10 mS. A too small value results in more overhead because of the additional context switches.

p_err   is a pointer to a variable that will contain an error code returned by this function.

OS_ERR_NONE	if the call was successful and the time quanta for the task was changed.
OS_ERR_SET_ISR	if **OS_CFG_CALLED_FROM_ISR_CHK_EN** set to 1 in **os_cfg.h**: if calling this function from an ISR.

RETURNED VALUE

None

NOTES/WARNINGS

Do not specify a large value for **time_quanta**.

EXAMPLE

```
void TaskX (void *p_arg)
{
    OS_ERR  err;


    while (DEF_ON) {
        :
        :
        OSTaskTimeQuantaSet((OS_TCB *)0,
                            OS_CFG_TICK_RATE_HZ / 4;
                            &err);
        /* Check "err" */
        :
    }
}
```

A-81 OSTickISR()

void OSTickISR (void)

File	Called from	Code enabled by
os_cpu_a.asm	Tick interrupt	N/A

OSTickISR() is invoked by the tick interrupt, and the function is generally written in assembly language. However, this depends on how interrupts are handled by the processor. (see Chapter 9, "Interrupt Management" on page 173).

ARGUMENTS

None

RETURNED VALUES

None

NOTES/WARNINGS

None

EXAMPLE

The code below indicates how to write OSTickISR() if all interrupts vector to a common location, and the interrupt handler simply calls OSTickISR(). As indicated, this code can be written completely in C and can be placed either in **os_cpu_c.c** of the µC/OS-III port, or in the board support package (**bsp.c**) and be reused by applications using the same BSP.

```
void OSTickISR (void)
{
    Clear the tick interrupt;
    OSTimeTick();
}
```

The pseudo code below shows how to write **OSTickISR()** if each interrupt directly vectors to its own interrupt handler. The code, in this case, would be written in assembly language and placed either in **os_cpu_a.asm** of the µC/OS-III port, or in the board support package (**bsp.c**).

```
void  OSTickISR (void)
{
    Save all the CPU registers onto the current task's stack;
    if (OSIntNestingCtr == 0) {
        OSTCBCurPtr->StkPtr = SP;
    }
    OSIntNestingCtr++;
    Clear the tick interrupt;
    OSTimeTick();
    OSIntExit();
    Restore the CPU registers from the stack;
    Return from interrupt;
}
```

A-82 OSTimeDly()

```
void OSTimeDly (OS_TICK   dly,
                OS_OPT    opt,
                OS_ERR    *p_err)
```

File	Called from	Code enabled by
os_time.c	Task only	N/A

OSTimeDly() allows a task to delay itself for an integral number of clock ticks. The delay can either be relative (delay from current time), periodic (delay occurs at fixed intervals) or absolute (delay until we reach some time).

In relative mode, rescheduling always occurs when the number of clock ticks is greater than zero. A delay of **0** means that the task is not delayed, and OSTimeDly() returns immediately to the caller.

In periodic mode, you must specify a non-zero period otherwise the function returns immediately with an appropriate error code. The period is specified in "ticks".

In absolute mode, rescheduling always occurs since all delay values are valid.

The actual delay time depends on the tick rate (see **OS_CFG_TICK_RATE_HZ** if **os_cfg_app.h**).

ARGUMENTS

dly   is the desired delay expressed in number of clock ticks. Depending on the value of the **opt** field, delays can be relative or absolute.

A relative delay means that the delay is started from the "**current time + dly**".

A periodic delay means the period (in number of ticks). µC/OS-III saves the current time + **dly** in **.TcikCtrPrev** so the next time OSTimeDly() is called, we use **.TickDlyPrev + dly**.

An absolute delay means that the task will wake up when OSTickCtr reaches the value specified by **dly**.

opt	is used to indicate whether the delay is absolute or relative:

OS_OPT_TIME_DLY	Specifies a relative delay.
OS_OPT_TIME_PERIODIC	Specifies periodic mode.
OS_OPT_TIME_MATCH	Specifies that the task will wake up when OSTickCtr reaches the value specified by dly

p_err	is a pointer to a variable that will contain an error code returned by this function.

OS_ERR_NONE	if the call was successful, and the task has returned from the desired delay.
OS_ERR_OPT_INVALID	if OS_CFG_ARG_CHK_EN is set to 1 in os_cfg.h: if a valid option is not specified.
OS_ERR_TIME_DLY_ISR	if OS_CFG_CALLED_FROM_ISR_CHK_EN set to 1 in os_cfg.h: if calling this function from an ISR.
OS_ERR_TIME_ZERO_DLY	if specifying a delay of 0 when the option was set to OS_OPT_TIME_DLY. Note that a value of 0 is valid when setting the option to OS_OPT_TIME_MATCH.

RETURNED VALUE

None

NOTES/WARNINGS

None

EXAMPLE

```
void TaskX (void *p_arg)
{
  OS_ERR  err;


  while (DEF_ON) {
    :
    :
    OSTimeDly(10,
              OS_OPT_TIME_PERIODIC,
              &err);
    /* Check "err" */
    :
    :
  }
}
```

A-83 OSTimeDlyHMSM()

```
void  OSTimeDlyHMSM (CPU_INT16U  hours,
                     CPU_INT16U  minutes,
                     CPU_INT16U  seconds,
                     CPU_INT32U  milli,
                     OS_OPT      opt,
                     OS_ERR      *p_err)
```

File	Called from	Code enabled by
os_time.c	Task only	OS_CFG_TIME_DLY_HMSM_EN

OSTimeDlyHMSM() allows a task to delay itself for a user-specified period that is specified in hours, minutes, seconds, and milliseconds. This format is more convenient and natural than simply specifying ticks as in OSTimeDly(). Rescheduling always occurs when at least one of the parameters is non-zero. The delay is relative from the time this function is called.

μC/OS-III allows the user to specify nearly any value when indicating that this function is not to be strict about the values being passed (opt == OS_OPT_TIME_HMSM_NON_STRICT). This is a useful feature, for example, to delay a task for thousands of milliseconds.

ARGUMENTS

hours   is the number of hours the task is delayed. Depending on the opt value, the valid range is 0..99 (OS_OPT_TIME_HMSM_STRICT), or 0..999 (OS_OPT_TIME_HMSM_NON_STRICT). Please note that it *not* recommended to delay a task for many hours because feedback from the task will not be available for such a long period of time.

minutes   is the number of minutes the task is delayed. The valid range of values is 0 to 59 (OS_OPT_TIME_HMSM_STRICT), or 0..9,999 (OS_OPT_TIME_HMSM_NON_STRICT). Please note that it *not* recommended to delay a task for tens to hundreds of minutes because feedback from the task will not be available for such a long period of time.

seconds   is the number of seconds the task is delayed. The valid range of values is 0 to 59 (OS_OPT_TIME_HMSM_STRICT), or 0..65,535 (OS_OPT_TIME_HMSM_NON_STRICT).

---

milli is the number of milliseconds the task is delayed. The valid range of values is 0 to 999 (OS_OPT_TIME_HMSM_STRICT), or 0..4,294,967,295 (OS_OPT_TIME_HMSM_NON_STRICT). Note that the resolution of this argument is in multiples of the tick rate. For instance, if the tick rate is set to 100Hz, a delay of 4 ms results in no delay because the delay is rounded to the nearest tick. Thus, a delay of 15 ms actually results in a delay of 20 ms.

opt is the desired mode and can be either:

OS_OPT_TIME_HMSM_STRICT   (see above)
OS_OPT_TIME_HMSM_NON_STRICT (see above)

p_err is a pointer to a variable that contains an error code returned by this function.

OS_ERR_NONE	if the call was successful and the task has returned from the desired delay.
OS_ERR_TIME_DLY_ISR	if OS_CFG_CALLED_FROM_ISR_CHK_EN set to 1 in **os_cfg.h**: if calling this function from an ISR.
OS_ERR_TIME_INVALID_HOURS	if OS_CFG_ARG_CHK_EN is set to 1 in **os_cfg.h**: if not specifying a valid value for hours.
OS_ERR_TIME_INVALID_MINUTES	if OS_CFG_ARG_CHK_EN is set to 1 in **os_cfg.h**: if not specifying a valid value for minutes.
OS_ERR_TIME_INVALID_SECONDS	if OS_CFG_ARG_CHK_EN is set to 1 in **os_cfg.h**: if not specifying a valid value for seconds.
OS_ERR_TIME_INVALID_MILLISECONDS	if OS_CFG_ARG_CHK_EN is set to 1 in **os_cfg.h**: if not specifying a valid value for milliseconds.
OS_ERR_TIME_ZERO_DLY	if specifying a delay of 0 because all the time arguments are 0.

RETURNED VALUE

None

NOTES/WARNINGS

■ Note that `OSTimeDlyHMSM(0,0,0,0,OS_OPT_TIME_HMSM_???,&err)` (i.e., hours, minutes, seconds, milliseconds are 0) results in no delay, and the function returns to the caller.

■ The total delay (in ticks) must not exceed the maximum acceptable value that an `OS_TICK` variable can hold. Typically `OS_TICK` is a 32-bit value.

EXAMPLE

```
void TaskX (void *p_arg)
{
    OS_ERR  err;


    while (DEF_ON) {
        :
        :
        OSTimeDlyHMSM(0,
                      0,
                      1,
                      0,
                      OS_OPT_TIME_HMSM_STRICT,
                      &err);            /* Delay task for 1 second */
        /* Check "err" */
        :
        :
    }
}
```

A-84 OSTimeDlyResume()

```
void  OSTimeDlyResume (OS_TCB  *p_tcb,
                       OS_ERR  *p_err)
```

File	Called from	Code enabled by
os_time.c	Task only	OS_CFG_TIME_DLY_RESUME_EN

OSTimeDlyResume() resumes a task that has been delayed through a call to either OSTimeDly(), or OSTimeDlyHMSM().

ARGUMENTS

p_tcb   is a pointer to the TCB of the task that is resuming. A **NULL** pointer is not valid since it would indicate that the user is attempting to resume the current task and that is not possible as the caller cannot possibly be delayed.

p_err   is a pointer to a variable that contains an error code returned by this function.

OS_ERR_NONE	if the call was successful and the task was resumed.
OS_ERR_STATE_INVALID	if the task is in an invalid state.
OS_ERR_TIME_DLY_RESUME_ISR	if OS_CFG_CALLED_FROM_ISR_CHK_EN set to 1 in os_cfg.h: if calling this function from an ISR.
OS_ERR_TIME_NOT_DLY	if OS_CFG_ARG_CHK_EN is set to 1 in os_cfg.h: if the task was not delayed or, you passed a NULL pointer for the TCB.
OS_ERR_TASK_SUSPENDED	if the task to resume is suspended and will remain suspended.

RETURNED VALUE

None

NOTES/WARNINGS

Do not call this function to resume a task that is waiting for an event with timeout.

EXAMPLE

```
OS_TCB  AnotherTaskTCB;


void TaskX (void *p_arg)
{
    OS_ERR  err;


    while (DEF_ON) {
        :
        OSTimeDlyResume(&AnotherTaskTCB,
                        &err);
        /* Check "err" */
        :
    }
}
```

A-85 OSTimeGet()

```
OS_TICK   OSTimeGet (OS_ERR   *p_err)
```

File	Called from	Code enabled by
os_time.c	Task or ISR	N/A

OSTimeGet() obtains the current value of the system clock. Specifically, it returns a snapshot of the variable OSTickCtr. The system clock is a counter of type OS_TICK that counts the number of clock ticks since power was applied, or since OSTickCtr was last set by OSTimeSet().

ARGUMENTS

p_err   is a pointer to a variable that contains an error code returned by this function.

OS_ERR_NONE   if the call was successful.

RETURNED VALUE

The current value of OSTickCtr (in number of ticks).

NOTES/WARNINGS

None

EXAMPLE

```
void TaskX (void *p_arg)
{
    OS_TICK  clk;
    OS_ERR   err;


    while (DEF_ON) {
        :
        :
        clk = OSTimeGet(&err);  /* Get current value of system clock */
        /* Check "err" */
        :
        :
    }
}
```

A-86 OSTimeSet()

```
void  OSTimeSet (OS_TICK  ticks,
                 OS_ERR  *p_err)
```

File	Called from	Code enabled by
os_time.c	Task or ISR	N/A

OSTimeSet() sets the system clock. The system clock (OSTickCtr) is a counter, which has a data type of OS_TICK, and it counts the number of clock ticks since power was applied, or since the system clock was last set.

ARGUMENTS

ticks   is the desired value for the system clock, in ticks.

p_err   is a pointer to a variable that will contain an error code returned by this function.

      OS_ERR_NONE   if the call was successful.

RETURNED VALUE

None

NOTES/WARNINGS

You should be careful when using this function because other tasks may depend on the current value of the tick counter (OSTickCtr). Specifically, a task may delay itself (see OSTimeDly()) and specify to wake up when OSTickCtr reaches a specific value.

EXAMPLE

```
void TaskX (void *p_arg)
{
    OS_ERR  err;


    while (DEF_ON) {
        :
        :
        OSTimeSet(0,
                  &err);        /* Reset the system clock  */
        /* Check "err" */
        :
        :
    }
}
```

A-87 OSTimeTick()

```
void  OSTimeTick (void)
```

File	Called from	Code enabled by
os_time.c	ISR only	N/A

OSTimeTick( ) "announces" that a tick has just occurred, and that time delays and timeouts need to be updated. This function must be called from the tick ISR.

ARGUMENTS

None

RETURNED VALUE

None

NOTES/WARNINGS

None

EXAMPLE

```
void MyTickISR (void)
{
    /* Clear interrupt source */
    OSTimeTick();
    :
    :
}
```

A-88 OSTimeTickHook()

```
void OSTimeTickHook (void);
```

File	Called from	Code enabled by
os_cpu_c.c	OSTimeTick() ONLY	N/A

This function is called by **OSTimeTick()**, which is assumed to be called from an ISR. **OSTimeTickHook()** is called at the very beginning of **OSTimeTick()** to give priority to user or port-specific code when the tick interrupt occurs.

If the **#define OS_CFG_APP_HOOKS_EN** is set to 1 in **os_cfg.h**, **OSTimeTickHook()** will call **App_OS_TimeTickHook()**.

OSTimeTickHook() is part of the CPU port code and the function *must not* be called by the application code. **OSTimeTickHook()** is actually used by the µC/OS-III port developer.

ARGUMENTS

None

RETURNED VALUE

None

NOTES/WARNINGS

Do not call this function from the application.

EXAMPLE

The code below calls an application-specific hook that the application programmer can define. The user can simply set the value of **OS_AppTimeTickHookPtr** to point to the desired hook function **OSTimeTickHook()** is called by **OSTimeTick()** which in turn calls **App_OS_TimeTickHook()** through the pointer **OS_AppTimeTickHookPtr**.

```c
void  App_OS_TimeTickHook (void)                      /* os_app_hooks.c      */
{
    /* Your code goes here! */
}


void App_OS_SetAllHooks (void)                        /* os_app_hooks.c      */
{
    CPU_SR_ALLOC();

    CPU_CRITICAL_ENTER();
    :
    OS_AppTimeTickHookPtr = App_OS_TimeTickHook;
    :
    CPU_CRITICAL_EXIT();
}


void  OSTimeTickHook (void)                           /* os_cpu_c.c          */
{
#if OS_CFG_APP_HOOKS_EN > 0u
    if (OS_AppTimeTickHookPtr != (OS_APP_HOOK_VOID)0) {   /* Call application hook */
        (*OS_AppTimeTickHookPtr)();
    }
#endif
}
```

A-89 OS_TLS_GetID()

```
OS_TLS_ID  OS_TLS_GetID (OS_ERR  *p_err);
```

File	Called from	Code enabled by
os_tls.c	Task	OS_CFG_TLS_TBL_SIZE

OS_TLS_GetID() is called by the application to assign a TLS (thread-local storage) ID for a specific purpose. See Chapter 20, "Thread Safety of the Compiler's Run-Time Library" on page 441 for details on TLS. TLS IDs are assigned dynamically as needed by the application. Once assigned, TLS IDs cannot be un-assigned.

ARGUMENTS

p_err   is a pointer to a variable that contains an error code returned by this function. Possible values are:

OS_ERR_NONE   if the call was successful and the caller was returned a TLS ID.

OS_ERR_TLS_NO_MORE_AVAIL   if you called OS_TLS_GetID() more than OS_CFG_TLS_TBL_SIZE times.

RETURNED VALUE

The next available TLS ID or OS_CFG_TLS_TBL_SIZE if there are no more TLS IDs available.

NOTES/WARNINGS

None

EXAMPLE

```
OS_TLS_ID   MyTLS_ID;


void  main (void)
{
    OS_ERR   err;


    :
    OSInit(&err);
    :
    :
    MyTLS_ID = OS_TLS_GetID(&err);   /* Obtain the next available TLS ID      */
    /* Check "err" */
    :
    :
}
```

A-90 OS_TLS_GetValue()

```
OS_TLS  OS_TLS_GetValue (OS_TCB    *p_tcb,
                         OS_TLS_ID  id,
                         OS_ERR    *p_err);
```

File	Called from	Code enabled by
os_tls.c	Task	OS_CFG_TLS_TBL_SIZE

OS_TLS_GetValue() is called by the application to retrieve the current value of a task's TLS (thread-local storage) stored in the task's **p_tcb->TLS_Tbl[id]**. See Chapter 20, "Thread Safety of the Compiler's Run-Time Library" on page 441 for details on TLS.

ARGUMENTS

p_tcb   is a pointer to the **OS_TCB** of the task you wish to retrieve the TLS from. You will get a copy of the **p_tcb->TLS_Tbl[id]** entry and of course, the entry will not be changed.

id   is the TLS ID of the entry you desire.

p_err   is a pointer to a variable that contains an error code returned by this function. Possible values are:

OS_ERR_NONE	if the call was successful and the caller was returned the value.
OS_ERR_OS_NOT_RUNNING	if you called **OS_TLS_GetValue()** and the kernel has not started yet. However, it's acceptable to call this function prior to starting multitasking but in this case, you must specify a non-**NULL** pointer for **p_tcb**.
OS_ERR_TLS_ID_INVALID	if you called **OS_TLS_GetValue()** and specified a TLS ID that has not been assigned. See **OS_TLS_GetID()** about assigning TLS IDs.
OS_ERR_TLS_NOT_EN	if you called **OS_TLS_GetValue()** but the task was created with the option **OS_OPT_TASK_NO_TLS** indicating that the task does not need TLS support.

RETURNED VALUE

The value store in **p_tcb->TLS_Tbl[id]** or **NULL** if an error occurred.

NOTES/WARNINGS

You cannot call **OS_TLS_GetValue()** for a task until that task gets created.

EXAMPLE

```
OS_TLS_ID   MyTLS_ID;


void MyTask (void *p_arg)
{
    OS_ERR      err;
    OS_TLS      p_tls;


    :
    :
    while (DEF_TRUE) {
        p_tls = OSTLS_GetValue((OS_TCB   *)0,
                               (OS_TLS_ID)MyTLS_ID,
                               (OS_ERR  *)&err);
        /* Check "err" */
        :
        :
    }
}
```

A-91 OS_TLS_SetDestruct()

```
void   OS_TLS_SetDestruct (OS_TLS_ID             id,
                           OS_TLS_DESTRUCT_PTR   p_destruct,
                           OS_ERR                *p_err);
```

File	Called from	Code enabled by
os_tls.c	Task	OS_CFG_TLS_TBL_SIZE

OS_TLS_SetDestruct() is called by the application to assign a "destructor function" to a TLS (thread-local storage) ID. All destructor functions that have been set for the TLS IDs will be called when the task is deleted. Destructor functions are thus common to all tasks. Note that a destructor function must be declared as follows:

```
void   MyDestructFunction (OS_TCB    *p_tcb,
                           OS_TLS_ID  id,
                           OS_TLS     value);
```

When the destructor function is called, it will be passed the address of the OS_TCB for the task being deleted, the TLS ID that is being destructed and the value of p_tcb->TLS_Tbl[id] which was set by OS_TLS_SetValue().

ARGUMENTS

id   is the TLS ID for which you want to set the destructor function for.

p_destruct is a pointer to the destructor function you want to assign to the TLS ID.

p_err   is a pointer to a variable that contains an error code returned by this function. Possible values are:

OS_ERR_NONE	if the call was successful and the destructor function was assigned to the TLS ID value.
OS_ERR_TLS_DESTRUCT_ASSIGNED	if a destructor function has already been assigned. You can only assign a destructor function once for each TLS ID.

OS_ERR_TLS_ID_INVALID	if you specified a TLS ID that has not been assigned. See **OS_TLS_GetID( )** about assigning TLS IDs.

RETURNED VALUE

None

NOTES/WARNINGS

You can only call **OS_TLS_SetDestruct( )** once for each TLS ID.

Note that not all implementations of **os_tls.c** will have destructors for TLS IDs.

EXAMPLE

```
void  MyDestructFunction (OS_TCB    *p_tcb,
                          OS_TLS_ID  id,
                          OS_TLS     value);


OS_TLS_ID   MyTLS_ID;


void  main (void)
{
    OS_ERR   err;


    :
    OSInit(&err);
    :
    :
    MyTLS_ID = OS_TLS_GetID(&err);  /* Obtain the next available TLS ID     */
    OS_TSL_SetDestruct((OS_TLS_ID)MyTLS_ID,
                       (OS_TLS_DESTRUCT_PTR)MyTLS_Destructor,
                       (OS_ERR *)&err);
    /* Check "err" */
    :
    :
}


void  MyDestructFunction (OS_TCB    *p_tcb,
                          OS_TLS_ID  id,
                          OS_TLS     value)
{
    /* Note that 'value' is typically a 'void *' that points to storage area for the TLS */
}
```

669

A-92 OS_TLS_SetValue()

```
void  OS_TLS_SetValue (OS_TCB     *p_tcb,
                       OS_TLS_ID  id,
                       OS_TLS     value,
                       OS_ERR     *p_err);
```

File	Called from	Code enabled by
os_tls.c	Task	OS_CFG_TLS_TBL_SIZE

OS_TLS_SetValue() allows your application to set the value of a TLS (thread-local storage) entry in the specified task's OS_TCB. Specifically, this function assigns value to p_tcb->TLS_Tbl[id]. See Chapter 20, "Thread Safety of the Compiler's Run-Time Library" on page 441 for details on TLS.

ARGUMENTS

p_tcb   is a pointer to the OS_TCB of the task you wish to assign the TLS value to. value will thus be assigned to p_tcb->TLS_Tbl[id].

id   is the TLS ID of the entry you are setting.

value   is the value to store at p_tcb->TLS_Tbl[id].

p_err   is a pointer to a variable that contains an error code returned by this function. Possible values are:

OS_ERR_NONE	if the call was successful and the caller was returned the value.
OS_ERR_OS_NOT_RUNNING	if you called OS_TLS_SetValue() and the kernel has not started yet. However, it's acceptable to call this function prior to starting multitasking but in this case, you must specify a non-NULL pointer for p_tcb.
OS_ERR_TLS_ID_INVALID	if you called OS_TLS_GetValue() and specified a TLS ID that has not been assigned. See OS_TLS_GetID() about assigning TLS IDs.

OS_ERR_TLS_NOT_EN	if you called OS_TLS_SetValue() but the task was created with the option OS_OPT_TASK_NO_TLS indicating that the task does not need TLS support.

RETURNED VALUE

None

NOTES/WARNINGS

You cannot call OS_TLS_SetValue() for a task until that task gets created.

EXAMPLE

```
OS_TLS_ID    MyTLS_ID;


void MyTask (void *p_arg)
{
    OS_ERR      err;
    OS_TLS      p_tls;


    :
    :
    while (DEF_TRUE) {
        p_tls = OSTLS_GetValue((OS_TCB   *)0,
                               (OS_TLS_ID)MyTLS_ID,
                               (OS_ERR  *)&err);
        /* Check "err" */
        :
        :
    }
}
```

A-93 OSTmrCreate()

```
void  OSTmrCreate (OS_TMR              *p_tmr,
                   CPU_CHAR            *p_name,
                   OS_TICK             dly,
                   OS_TICK             period,
                   OS_OPT              opt,
                   OS_TMR_CALLBACK_PTR p_callback,
                   void                *p_callback_arg,
                   OS_ERR              *p_err)
```

File	Called from	Code enabled by
os_tmr.c	Task only	OS_CFG_TMR_EN

OSTmrCreate() allows the user to create a software timer. The timer can be configured to run continuously (opt set to OS_TMR_OPT_PERIODIC), or only once (opt set to OS_TMR_OPT_ONE_SHOT). When the timer counts down to 0 (from the value specified in period), an optional "callback" function can be executed. The callback can be used to signal a task that the timer expired, or perform any other function. However, it is recommended to keep the callback function as short as possible.

The timer is created in the "stop" mode and therefore the user *must* call OSTmrStart() to actually start the timer. If configuring the timer for ONE-SHOT mode, and the timer expires, you need to call OSTmrStart() to retrigger the timer, call OSTmrDel() to delete the timer if it is not necessary to retrigger it, or not use the timer anymore. Note: you can use the callback function to delete the timer if using the ONE-SHOT mode.

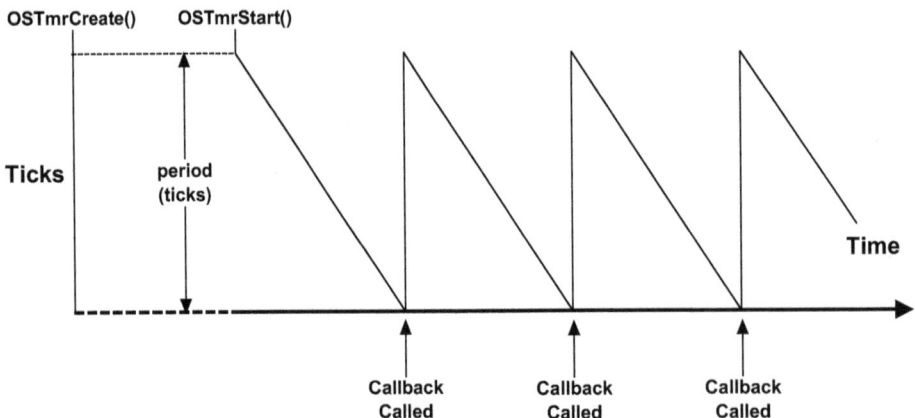

PERIODIC MODE (see "opt") – dly > 0, **period** > 0

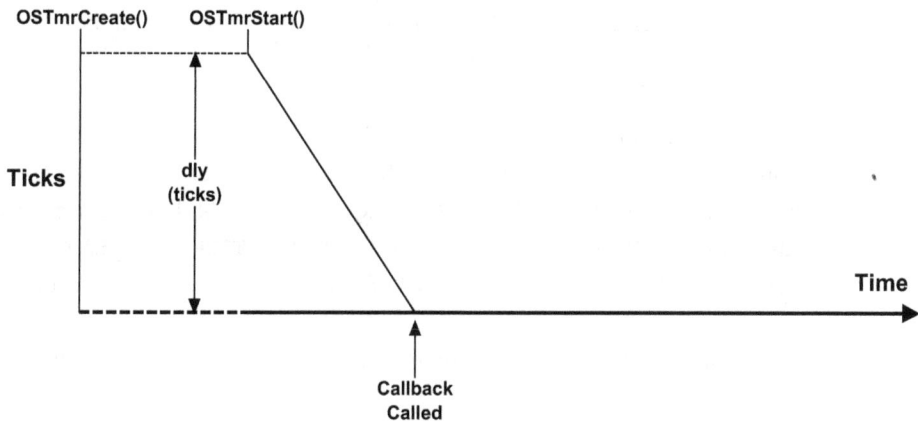

OSTmrCreate()   **OSTmrStart()**

Ticks

period (ticks)

Time

Callback Called   **Callback Called**   **Callback Called**

PERIODIC MODE (see "opt") – "dly == 0, period > 0

OSTmrCreate()   **OSTmrStart()**

Ticks

dly (ticks)

Time

Callback Called

ONE-SHOT MODE (see "opt") – dly > 0, **period** == 0

ARGUMENTS

p_tmr   is a pointer to the timer-control block of the desired timer. It is assumed that storage for the timer will be allocated in the application. In other words, you should declare a "global" variable as follows, and pass a pointer to this variable to OSTmrCreate():

```
OS_TMR MyTmr;
```

p_name   is a pointer to an ASCII string (NUL terminated) used to assign a name to the timer. The name can be displayed by debuggers or µC/Probe.

dly   specifies the initial delay (specified in timer tick units) used by the timer (see drawing above). If the timer is configured for ONE-SHOT mode, this is the timeout used. If the timer is configured for PERIODIC mode, this is the timeout to wait before the timer enters periodic mode. The units of this time depends on how often the user will call OSTmrSignal() (see OSTimeTick()). If OSTmrSignal() is called every 1/10 of a second (i.e., OS_CFG_TMR_TASK_RATE_HZ set to 10), dly specifies the number of 1/10 of a second before the delay expires.

period   specifies the period repeated by the timer if configured for PERIODIC mode. You would set the "period" to 0 when using ONE-SHOT mode. The units of time depend on how often OSTmrSignal() is called. If OSTmrSignal() is called every 1/10 of a second (i.e., OS_CFG_TMR_TASK_RATE_HZ set to 10), the period specifies the number of 1/10 of a second before the timer repeats.

opt   is used to specify whether the timer is to be ONE-SHOT or PERIODIC:

```
OS_OPT_TMR_ONE_SHOT specifies   ONE-SHOT mode
OS_OPT_TMR_PERIODIC specifies   PERIODIC mode
```

p_callback is a pointer to a function that will execute when the timer expires (ONE-SHOT mode), or every time the period expires (PERIODIC mode). A NULL pointer indicates that no action is to be performed upon timer expiration. The callback function must be declared as follows:

```
void MyCallback (OS_TMR *p_tmr, void *p_arg);
```

When called, the callback will be passed the pointer to the timer as well as an argument (**p_callback_arg**), which can be used to indicate to the callback what to do. Note that the user is allowed to call all of the timer related functions (i.e., **OSTmrCreate()**, **OSTmrDel()**, **OSTmrStateGet()**, **OSTmrRemainGet()**, **OSTmrStart()**, and **OSTmrStop()**) from the callback function.

Do not make blocking calls within callback functions.

p_callback_arg   is an argument passed to the callback function when the timer expires (ONE-SHOT mode), or every time the period expires (PERIODIC mode). The pointer is declared as a "**void ***" so it can point to any data.

p_err   is a pointer to a variable that contains an error code returned by this function.

OS_ERR_NONE	if the call was successful.
OS_ERR_OBJ_PTR_NULL	if **OS_CFG_ARG_CHK_EN** is set to 1 in **os_cfg.h**: if **p_tmr** is a **NULL** pointer
OS_ERR_TMR_INVALID_DLY	if **OS_CFG_ARG_CHK_EN** is set to 1 in **os_cfg.h**: if specifying an invalid delay in ONE-SHOT mode. In other words, it is not allowed to delay for **0** in ONE-SHOT mode.
OS_ERR_TMR_INVALID_PERIOD	if **OS_CFG_ARG_CHK_EN** is set to 1 in **os_cfg.h**: if specifying an invalid period in PERIODIC mode. It is not allowed to have a **0** period in PERIODIC.
OS_ERR_OPT_INVALID	if **OS_CFG_ARG_CHK_EN** is set to 1 in **os_cfg.h**: if not specifying a valid options.
OS_ERR_TMR_ISR	if **OS_CFG_CALLED_FROM_ISR_CHK_EN** set to 1 in **os_cfg.h**: if calling this function from an ISR.
OS_ERR_ILLEGAL_CREATE_RUN_TIME	if **OS_SAFETY_CRITICAL_IEC61508** is defined: you called this after calling **OSSafetyCriticalStart()** and thus you are no longer allowed to create additional kernel objects.

RETURNED VALUES

None.

NOTES/WARNINGS

■ *Do not* call this function from an ISR.

■ The timer is *not* started when it is created. To start the timer, simply call **OSTmrStart()**.

■ *Do not* make blocking calls within callback functions.

■ Keep callback functions as short as possible.

EXAMPLE

```
OS_TMR  CloseDoorTmr;


void Task (void *p_arg)
{
    OS_ERR   err;


    (void)&p_arg;
    while (DEF_ON) {
        OSTmrCreate(&CloseDoorTmr,          /* p_tmr           */
                    "Door close",           /* p_name          */
                     10,                     /* dly             */
                     100,                    /* period          */
                     OS_OPT_TMR_PERIODIC,    /* opt             */
                     DoorCloseFnct,          /* p_callback      */
                     0,                      /* p_callback_arg  */
                     &err);                  /* p_err           */
            /* Check "err" */
    }
}


void  DoorCloseFnct (OS_TMR  *p_tmr,
                     void    *p_arg)
{
    /* Close the door! */
}
```

A-94 OSTmrDel()

```
CPU_BOOLEAN  OSTmrDel(OS_TMR    *p_tmr,
                      OS_ERR     *p_err)
```

File	Called from	Code enabled by
os_tmr.c	Task only	OS_CFG_TMR_EN and OS_CFG_TMR_DEL_EN

OSTmrDel() allows the user to delete a timer. If a timer was running it will be stopped and then deleted. If the timer has already timed out and is therefore stopped, it will simply be deleted.

It is up to the user to delete unused timers. If deleting a timer, you must not reference it again.

ARGUMENTS

p_tmr   is a pointer to the timer to be deleted.

p_err   a pointer to an error code and can be any of the following:

OS_ERR_NONE	if the timer was deleted.
OS_ERR_OBJ_TYPE	if OS_CFG_OBJ_TYPE_CHK_EN is set to 1 in os_cfg.h: if the user did not pass a pointer to a timer.
OS_ERR_TMR_INVALID	if OS_CFG_ARG_CHK_EN is set to 1 in os_cfg.h: if p_tmr is a NULL pointer.
OS_ERR_TMR_ISR	if OS_CFG_CALLED_FROM_ISR_CHK_EN set to 1 in os_cfg.h: This function is called from an ISR, which is *not* allowed.
OS_ERR_TMR_INACTIVE	p_tmr is pointing to an inactive timer. In other words, this error appears when pointing to a timer that has been deleted.
OS_ERR_TMR_INVALID_STATE	the timer is in an invalid state.

RETURNED VALUES

DEF_TRUE if the timer was deleted, **DEF_FALSE** if not.

NOTES/WARNINGS

■ *Do not* call this function from an ISR.

■ When deleting a timer, *do not* reference it again unless you re-create the timer by calling OSTmrCreate().

EXAMPLE

```
OS_TMR  CloseDoorTmr;


void Task (void *p_arg)
{
    OS_ERR       err;
    CPU_BOOLEAN  deleted;


    (void)&p_arg;
    while (DEF_ON) {
        deleted = OSTmrDel(&CloseDoorTmr,
                           &err);
        /* Check "err" */
    }
}
```

A-95 OSTmrRemainGet()

```
OS_TICK  OSTmrRemainGet(OS_TMR *p_tmr,
                        OS_ERR *p_err);
```

File	Called from	Code enabled by
os_tmr.c	Task only	OS_CFG_TMR_EN

OSTmrRemainGet() allows the user to obtain the time remaining (before timeout) of the specified timer. The value returned depends on the rate (in Hz) at which the timer task is signaled (see OS_CFG_TMR_TASK_RATE_HZ). If OS_CFG_TMR_TASK_RATE_HZ is set to 10, the value returned is the number of 1/10 of a second before the timer times out. If the timer has timed out, the value returned is 0.

ARGUMENTS

p_tmr   is a pointer to the timer the user is inquiring about.

p_err   a pointer to an error code and can be any of the following:

OS_ERR_NONE	if the function returned the time remaining for the timer.
OS_ERR_OBJ_TYPE	if OS_CFG_OBJ_TYPE_CHK_EN is set to 1 in os_cfg.h: 'p_tmr" is not pointing to a timer.
OS_ERR_TMR_INVALID	if OS_CFG_ARG_CHK_EN is set to 1 in os_cfg.h: if p_tmr is a NULL pointer.
OS_ERR_TMR_ISR	if OS_CFG_CALLED_FROM_ISR_CHK_EN set to 1 in os_cfg.h: This function is called from an ISR, which is *not* allowed.
OS_ERR_TMR_INACTIVE	p_tmr is pointing to an inactive timer. In other words, this error will appear when pointing to a timer that has been deleted.
OS_ERR_TMR_INVALID_STATE	the timer is in an invalid state.

RETURNED VALUES

The time remaining for the timer. The value returned depends on the rate (in Hz) at which the timer task is signaled (see OS_CFG_TMR_TASK_RATE_HZ). If OS_CFG_TMR_TASK_RATE_HZ is set to 10 the value returned is the number of 1/10 of a second before the timer times out. If specifying an invalid timer, the returned value will be 0. If the timer expired, the returned value will be 0.

NOTES/WARNINGS

■ *Do not* call this function from an ISR.

EXAMPLE

```
OS_TICK    TimeRemainToCloseDoor;
OS_TMR     CloseDoorTmr;


void Task (void *p_arg)
{
    OS_ERR    err;


    (void)&p_arg;
    while (DEF_ON) {
        TimeRemainToCloseDoor = OSTmrRemainGet(&CloseDoorTmr,
                                               &err);
        /* Check "err" */
    }
}
```

A-96 OSTmrStart()

```
CPU_BOOLEAN  OSTmrStart (OS_TMR   *p_tmr,
                         OS_ERR   *p_err);
```

File	Called from	Code enabled by
os_tmr.c	Task only	OS_CFG_TMR_EN

OSTmrStart() allows the user to start (or restart) the countdown process of a timer. The timer *must* have previously been created.

ARGUMENTS

p_tmr   is a pointer to the timer to start (or restart).

p_err   a pointer to an error code and can be any of the following:

OS_ERR_NONE	if the timer was started.
OS_ERR_OBJ_TYPE	if OS_CFG_OBJ_TYPE_CHK_EN is set to 1 in os_cfg.h: 'p_tmr" is not pointing to a timer.
OS_ERR_TMR_INVALID	if OS_CFG_ARG_CHK_EN is set to 1 in os_cfg.h: if p_tmr is a NULL pointer.
OS_ERR_TMR_INACTIVE	p_tmr is pointing to an inactive timer. In other words, this error occurs if pointing to a timer that has been deleted or was not created.
OS_ERR_TMR_INVALID_STATE	the timer is in an invalid state.
OS_ERR_TMR_ISR	if OS_CFG_CALLED_FROM_ISR_CHK_EN set to 1 in os_cfg.h: This function was called from an ISR, which is *not* allowed.

RETURNED VALUES

DEF_TRUE   if the timer was started

DEF_FALSE   if an error occurred.

NOTES/WARNINGS

■ *Do not* call this function from an ISR.

■ The timer *must* have previously been created.

EXAMPLE

```
OS_TMR      CloseDoorTmr;


void Task (void *p_arg)
{
    OS_ERR      err;
    CPU_BOOLEAN status;


    (void)&p_arg;
    while (DEF_ON) {
        status = OSTmrStart(&CloseDoorTmr,
                            &err);
        /* Check "err" */
    }
}
```

A-97 OSTmrStateGet()

```
OS_STATE  OSTmrStateGet(OS_TMR  *p_tmr,
                        OS_ERR  *p_err);
```

File	Called from	Code enabled by
os_tmr.c	Task only	OS_CFG_TMR_EN

OSTmrStateGet() allows the user to obtain the current state of a timer. A timer can be in one of four states:

OS_TMR_STATE_UNUSED	the timer has not been created
OS_TMR_STATE_STOPPED	the timer is created but has not yet started, or has been stopped.
OS_TMR_STATE_COMPLETED	the timer is in *one-shot* mode, and has completed its delay.
OS_TMR_STATE_RUNNING	the timer is currently running

ARGUMENTS

p_tmr   is a pointer to the timer that the user is inquiring about.

p_err   a pointer to an error code and can be any of the following:

OS_ERR_NONE	if the function returned the state of the timer.
OS_ERR_OBJ_TYPE	if OS_CFG_OBJ_TYPE_CHK_EN is set to 1 in os_cfg.h: p_tmr is not pointing to a timer.
OS_ERR_TMR_INVALID	if OS_CFG_ARG_CHK_EN is set to 1 in os_cfg.h: if p_tmr is a NULL pointer.
OS_ERR_TMR_INVALID_STATE	the timer is in an invalid state.
OS_ERR_TMR_ISR	if OS_CFG_CALLED_FROM_ISR_CHK_EN set to 1 in os_cfg.h: This function was called from an ISR, which is *not* allowed.

RETURNED VALUES

The state of the timer (see description).

NOTES/WARNINGS

■ *Do not* call this function from an ISR.

EXAMPLE

```
OS_STATE    CloseDoorTmrState;
OS_TMR      CloseDoorTmr;


void Task (void *p_arg)
{
    OS_ERR   err;


    (void)&p_arg;
    while (DEF_ON) {
        CloseDoorTmrState = OSTmrStateGet(&CloseDoorTmr,
                                          &err);

        /* Check "err" */
    }
}
```

A-98 OSTmrStop()

```
CPU_BOOLEAN    OSTmrStop (OS_TMR    *p_tmr,
                          OS_OPT    opt,
                          void      *p_callback_arg,
                          OS_ERR    *p_err)
```

File	Called from	Code enabled by
os_tmr.c	Task only	OS_CFG_TMR_EN

OSTmrStop() allows the user to stop a timer. The user may execute the callback function of the timer when it is stopped, and pass this callback function a different argument than was specified when the timer was started. This allows the callback function to know that the timer was stopped since the callback argument can be set to indicate this (this is application specific). If the timer is already stopped, the callback function is not called.

ARGUMENTS

p_tmr   is a pointer to the timer control block of the desired timer.

opt   is used to specify options:

OS_OPT_TMR_NONE	No option
OS_OPT_TMR_CALLBACK	Run the callback function with the argument specified when the timer was created.
OS_OPT_TMR_CALLBACK_ARG	Run the callback function, but use the argument passed in OSTmrStop() instead of the one specified when the task was created.

p_callback_arg   is a new argument to pass the callback functions (see options above).

p_err   is a pointer to a variable that contains an error code returned by this function.

OS_ERR_NONE	if the call was successful.
OS_ERR_OBJ_TYPE	if OS_CFG_OBJ_TYPE_CHK_EN is set to 1 in os_cfg.h: if p_tmr is not pointing to a timer object.

OS_ERR_TMR_INACTIVE	the timer cannot be stopped since it is inactive.
OS_ERR_TMR_INVALID	if OS_CFG_ARG_CHK_EN is set to 1 in os_cfg.h: if you passed a NULL pointer for the p_tmr argument.
OS_ERR_TMR_INVALID_OPT	if the user did not specify a valid option.
OS_ERR_TMR_INVALID_STATE	the timer is in an invalid state.
OS_ERR_TMR_ISR	if OS_CFG_CALLED_FROM_ISR_CHK_EN set to 1 in os_cfg.h: if calling this function from an ISR.
OS_ERR_TMR_NO_CALLBACK	if the timer lacks a callback function. This should have been specified when the timer was created.
OS_ERR_TMR_STOPPED	if the timer is currently stopped.

RETURNED VALUES

DEF_TRUE   if the timer was stopped (even if it was already stopped).

DEF_FALSE if an error occurred.

NOTES/WARNINGS

- *Do not* call this function from an ISR.

- The callback function is *not* called if the timer is already stopped.

EXAMPLE

```
OS_TMR  CloseDoorTmr;


void Task (void *p_arg)
{
    OS_ERR    err;


    (void)&p_arg;
    while (DEF_ON) {
        OSTmrStop(&CloseDoorTmr,
                  OS_TMR_OPT_CALLBACK,
                  (void *)0,
                  &err);
        /* Check "err" */
    }
}
```

A-99 OSVersion()

```
CPU_INT16U OSVersion (OS_ERR  *p_err);
```

File	Called from	Code enabled by
os_core.c	Task or ISR	N/A

OSVersion() obtains the current version of µC/OS-III.

ARGUMENTS

p_err   is a pointer to a variable that contains an error code returned by this function. Currently, OSVersion() always return:

OS_ERR_NONE

RETURNED VALUE

The version is returned as **x.yy.zz** multiplied by **10,000**. For example, V3.00.00 is returned as **30000**.

NOTES/WARNINGS

None

EXAMPLE

```
void TaskX (void *p_arg)
{
    CPU_INT16U  os_version;
    OS_ERR      err;


    while (DEF_ON) {
        :
        :
        os_version = OSVersion(&err);  /* Obtain µC/OS-III's version      */
        /* Check "err" */
        :
        :
    }
}
```

Appendix A

B

µC/OS-III Configuration Manual

Three (3) files are used to configure µC/OS-III as highlighted in Figure B-1: os_cfg.h, os_cfg_app.h and os_type.h.

Table B-1 shows where these files are typically located on your on a computer.

File	Directory
os_cfg.h	\Micrium\Software\uCOS-III\Cfg\Template
os_cfg_app.h	\Micrium\Software\uCOS-III\Cfg\Template
os_type.h	\Micrium\Software\uCOS-III\Source

Table B-1 **Configuration files and directories**

µC/OS-III Configuration	Application Code
(1) os_cfg.h **(3)** os_cfg_app.h	app.c app.h

µC/OS-III
CPU Independent

os_cfg_app.c
(2) os_type.h
os_core.c
os_dbg.c
os_flag.c
os_int.c
os_mem.c
os_msg.c
os_mutex.c
os_pend_multi.c
os_prio.c
os_q.c
os_sem.c
os_stat.c
os_task.c
os_tick.c
os_time.c
os_tmr.c
os_var.c
os.h

µC/LIB
Libraries

lib_ascii.c
lib_ascii.h
lib_def.h
lib_mat.c
lib_math.h
lib_mem_a.asm
lib_mem.c
lib_mem.h
lib_str.c
lib_str.h

µC/OS-III CPU Specific	µC/CPU CPU Specific	BSP Board Support Package	CPU
os_cpu.h os_cpu_a.asm os_cpu_c.c	cpu.h cpu_a.asm cpu_core.c	bsp.c bsp.h	*.c *.h

Software/Firmware
- -
Hardware

CPU	Timer	Interrupt Controller

Figure B-1 µC/OS-III File Structure

FB-1(1)   **µC/OS-III Features (os_cfg.h):**

os_cfg.h is used to determine which features are needed from µC/OS-III for an application (i.e., product). Specifically, this file allows a user to determine whether to include semaphores, mutexes, event flags, run-time argument checking, etc.

FB-1(2)   **µC/OS-III Data Types (os_type.h):**

os_type.h establishes µC/OS-III-specific data types used when building an application. It specifies the size of variables used to represent task priorities, the size of a semaphore count, and more. This file contains recommended data types for µC/OS-III, however these can be altered to make better use of the CPU's natural word size. For example, on some 32-bit CPUs, it is better to declare boolean variables as 32-bit values for performance considerations, even though an 8-bit quantity is more space efficient (assuming performance is more important than footprint).

The port developer typically makes those decisions, since altering the contents of the file requires a deep understanding of the CPU and, most important, how data sizes affect µC/OS-III.

FB-1(3)   **µC/OS-III Stacks, Pools and other data sizes (os_cfg_app.h):**

µC/OS-III can be configured at the application level through **#define** constants in **os_cfg_app.h**. The **#defines** allows a user to specify stack sizes for all µC/OS-III internal tasks: the idle task, statistic task, tick task, timer task, and the ISR handler task. **os_cfg_app.h** also allows users to specify task priorities (except for the idle task since it is always the lowest priority), the tick rate, tick wheel size, the timer wheel size, and more.

The contents of the three configuration files will be described in the following sections.

B-1 μC/OS-III FEATURES (OS_CFG.H)

Compile-time configuration allows users to determine which features to enable and those features that are not needed. With compile-time configuration, the code and data sizes of μC/OS-III (i.e., its footprint) can be reduced by enabling only the desired functionality.

Compile-time configuration is accomplished by setting a number of **#define** constants in a file called **os_cfg.h** that the application is expected to provide. You simply copy **os_cfg.h** into the application directory and change the copied file to satisfy the application's requirements. This way, **os_cfg.h** is not recreated from scratch.

The compile-time configuration **#defines** are listed below in alphabetic order and are not necessarily found in this order in **os_cfg.h**.

OS_CFG_APP_HOOKS_EN
When set to 1, this **#define** specifies that application-defined hooks can be called from μC/OS-III's hooks. This allows the application code to extend the functionality of μC/OS-III. Specifically:

The μC/OS-III hook ...	Calls the Application-define hook through...
OSIdleTaskHook()	OS_AppIdleTaskHookPtr
OSInitHook()	None
OSStatTaskHook()	OS_AppStatTaskHookPtr
OSTaskCreateHook()	OS_AppTaskCreateHookPtr
OSTaskDelHook()	OS_AppTaskDelHookPtr
OSTaskReturnHook()	OS_AppTaskReturnHookPtr
OSTaskSwHook()	OS_AppTaskSwHookPtr
OSTimeTickHook()	OS_AppTimeTickHookPtr

Application hook functions could be declared as shown in the code below.

```
void  App_OS_TaskCreateHook (OS_TCB *p_tcb)
{
    /* Your code here */
}


void  App_OS_TaskDelHook (OS_TCB *p_tcb)
{
    /* Your code here */
}


void  App_OS_TaskReturnHook (OS_TCB *p_tcb)
{
    /* Your code here */
}


void  App_OS_IdleTaskHook (void)
{
    /* Your code here */
}


void  App_OS_StatTaskHook (void)
{
    /* Your code here */
}


void  App_OS_TaskSwHook (void)
{
    /* Your code here */
}


void  App_OS_TimeTickHook (void)
{
    /* Your code here */
}
```

It's also up to a user to set the value of the pointers so that they point to the appropriate functions as shown below. The pointers do not have to be set in **main()** but, you can set them after calling OSInit().

```
void  main (void)
{
    OS_ERR  err;


    OSInit(&err);
    :
    :
    OS_AppTaskCreateHookPtr = (OS_APP_HOOK_TCB )App_OS_TaskCreateHook;
    OS_AppTaskDelHookPtr    = (OS_APP_HOOK_TCB )App_OS_TaskDelHook;
    OS_AppTaskReturnHookPtr = (OS_APP_HOOK_TCB )App_OS_TaskReturnHook;
    OS_AppIdleTaskHookPtr   = (OS_APP_HOOK_VOID)App_OS_IdleTaskHook;
    OS_AppStatTaskHookPtr   = (OS_APP_HOOK_VOID)App_OS_StatTaskHook;
    OS_AppTaskSwHookPtr     = (OS_APP_HOOK_VOID)App_OS_TaskSwHook;
    OS_AppTimeTickHookPtr   = (OS_APP_HOOK_VOID)App_OS_TimeTickHook;
    :
    :
    OSStart(&err);
}
```

Note that not every hook function need to be defined, only the ones the user wants to place in the application code.

Also, if you don't intend to extend μC/OS-III's hook through these application hooks, you can set **OS_CFG_APP_HOOKS_EN** to 0 to save RAM (i.e., the pointers).

OS_CFG_ARG_CHK_EN

OS_CFG_ARG_CHK_EN determines whether the user wants most of μC/OS-III functions to perform argument checking. When set to 1, μC/OS-III ensures that pointers passed to functions are non-NULL, that arguments passed are within allowable range, that options are valid, and more. When set to 0, **OS_CFG_ARG_CHK_EN** those arguments are not checked and the amount of code space and processing time required by μC/OS-III is reduced. You would set **OS_CFG_ARG_CHK_EN** to 0 if you are certain that the arguments are correct.

μC/OS-III performs argument checking in over 40 functions. Therefore, you can save a few hundred bytes of code space by disabling this check. However, you should always enable argument checking until you are certain the code can be trusted.

OS_CFG_CALLED_FROM_ISR_CHK_EN

OS_CFG_CALLED_FROM_ISR_CHK_EN determines whether most of μC/OS-III functions are to confirm that the function is not called from an ISR. In other words, most of the functions from μC/OS-III should be called by task-level code except "post" type functions (which can also be called from ISRs). By setting this #define to 1 µC/OS-III is told to make sure that functions that are only supposed to be called by tasks are not called by ISRs. It's highly recommended to set this #define to 1 until you are absolutely certain that the code is behaving correctly and that task-level functions are always called from tasks. You can set this #define to 0 to save code space and, of course, processing time.

µC/OS-III performs this check in approximately 50 functions. Therefore, you can save a few hundred bytes of code space by disabling this check.

OS_CFG_DBG_EN

When set to **1**, this #define adds ROM constants located in **os_dbg.c** to help support kernel aware debuggers. Specifically, a number of named ROM variables can be queried by a debugger to find out about compiled-in options. For example, a debugger can find out the size of an **OS_TCB**, µC/OS-III's version number, the size of an event flag group (OS_FLAG_GRP), and much more.

OS_CFG_FLAG_EN

OS_CFG_FLAG_EN enables (when set to **1**) or disables (when set to 0) code generation of event flag services and data structures. This reduces the amount of code and data space needed when an application does not require event flags. When OS_CFG_FLAG_EN is set to 0, it is not necessary to enable or disable any of the other OS_CFG_FLAG_xxx #define constants in this section.

OS_CFG_FLAG_DEL_EN

OS_CFG_FLAG_DEL_EN enables (when set to 1) or disables (when set to **0**) code generation of the function OSFlagDel().

OS_CFG_FLAG_MODE_CLR_EN

OS_CFG_FLAG_MODE_CLR_EN enables (when set to 1) or disables (when set to **0**) code generation used to wait for event flags to be 0 instead of 1. Generally, you would wait for event flags to be set. However, the user may also want to wait for event flags to be clear and in this case, enable this option.

OS_CFG_FLAG_PEND_ABORT_EN

OS_CFG_FLAG_PEND_ABORT_EN enables (when set to 1) or disables (when set to **0**) code generation of the function OSFlagPendAbort().

OS_CFG_ISR_POST_DEFERRED_EN

When set to 1, OS_CFG_ISR_POST_DEFERRED_EN reduces interrupt latency since interrupts are not disabled during most critical sections of code within μC/OS-III. Instead, the scheduler is locked during the processing of these critical sections. The advantage of setting OS_CFG_ISR_POST_DEFERRED_EN to 1 is that interrupt latency is lower, however, ISR to task response is slightly higher. It is recommended to set OS_CFG_ISR_POST_DEFERRED_EN to 1 when enabling the following services, since setting this #define to 0 would potentially make interrupt latency unacceptably high:

μC/OS-III Services	Enabled by ...
Event Flags	OS_CFG_FLAG_EN
Multiple Pend	OS_CFG_PEND_MULTI_EN
OS???Post() with broadcast	
OS???Del() with OS_OPT_DEL_ALWAYS	
OS???PendAbort()	

The compromise to make is:

OS_CFG_ISR_POST_DEFERRED_EN set to 1
Short interrupt latency, longer ISR-to-task response.

OS_CFG_ISR_POST_DEFERRED_EN set to 0
Long interrupt latency (see table above), shorter ISR-to-task response.

OS_CFG_MEM_EN

OS_CFG_MEM_EN enables (when set to 1) or disables (when set to 0) code generation of the μC/OS-III partition memory manager and its associated data structures. This feature allows users to reduce the amount of code and data space needed when an application does not require the use of memory partitions.

OS_CFG_MUTEX_EN

OS_CFG_MUTEX_EN enables (when set to **1**) or disables (when set to 0) the code generation of all mutual exclusion semaphore services and data structures. This feature allows users to reduce the amount of code and data space needed when an application does not require the use of mutexes. When OS_CFG_MUTEX_EN is set to 0, there is no need to enable or disable any of the other OS_CFG_MUTEX_XXX #define constants in this section.

OS_CFG_MUTEX_DEL_EN

OS_CFG_MUTEX_DEL_EN enables (when set to 1) or disables (when set to **0**) code generation of the function OSMutexDel().

OS_CFG_MUTEX_PEND_ABORT_EN

OS_CFG_MUTEX_PEND_ABORT_EN enables (when set to 1) or disables (when set to **0**) code generation of the function OSMutexPendAbort().

OS_CFG_OBJ_TYPE_CHK_EN

OS_CFG_OBJ_TYPE_CHK_EN determines whether most of µC/OS-III functions should check to see if the function is manipulating the proper object. In other words, if attempting to post to a semaphore, is the user in fact passing a semaphore object or another object by mistake? It is recommended to set this #define to **1** until absolutely certain that the code is behaving correctly and the user code is always pointing to the proper objects. You would set this #define to 0 to save code space as well as data space. µC/OS-III object type checking is done nearly 30 times, and it is possible to save a few hundred bytes of code space and processing time by disabling this check.

OS_CFG_PEND_MULTI_EN

This constant determines whether the code to support pending on multiple events (i.e., semaphores or message queues) will be enabled (**1**) or not (0).

OS_CFG_PRIO_MAX

OS_CFG_PRIO_MAX specifies the maximum number of priorities available in the application. Specifying OS_CFG_PRIO_MAX to just the number of priorities the user intends to use, reduces the amount of RAM needed by µC/OS-III.

In µC/OS-III, task priorities can range from 0 (highest priority) to a maximum of 255 (lowest possible priority) when the data type OS_PRIO is defined as a CPU_INT08U. However, in µC/OS-III, there is no practical limit to the number of available priorities. Specifically, if defining OS_PRIO as a CPU_INT16U, there can be up to 65536 priority levels. It is recommended to leave OS_PRIO defined as a CPU_INT08U and use only 256 different priority levels (i.e., 0..255), which is generally sufficient for every application. You should always set the value of OS_CFG_PRIO_MAX to even multiples of 8 (8, 16, **32**, 64, 128, 256, etc.). The higher the number of different priorities, the more RAM µC/OS-III will consume.

An application cannot create tasks with a priority number higher than or equal to OS_CFG_PRIO_MAX. In fact, µC/OS-III reserves priority OS_CFG_PRIO_MAX-2 and OS_CFG_PRIO_MAX-1 for itself; OS_CFG_PRIO_MAX-1 is reserved for the idle task OS_IdleTask(). Additionally, do not use priority 0 for an application since it is reserved by µC/OS-III's ISR handler task. The priorities of the application tasks can therefore take a value between 2 and OS_CFG_PRIO_MAX-3 (inclusive).

To summarize, there are two priority levels to avoid in an application:

Priority	Reserved by µC/OS-III for ...
0	The ISR Handler Task (OS_IntQTask())
1	Reserved
OS_CFG_PRIO_MAX-2	Reserved
OS_CFG_PRIO_MAX-1	The idle task (OS_IdleTask())

OS_CFG_Q_EN

OS_CFG_Q_EN enables (when set to **1**) or disables (when set to 0) code generation of message queue services and data structures. This reduces the amount of code space needed when an application does not require the use of message queues. When OS_CFG_Q_EN is set to 0, you do not need to enable or disable any of the other OS_CFG_Q_XXX #define constants in this section.

OS_CFG_Q_DEL_EN

OS_CFG_Q_DEL_EN enables (when set to 1) or disables (when set to **0**) code generation of the function OSQDel().

OS_CFG_Q_FLUSH_EN

OS_CFG_Q_FLUSH_EN enables (when set to 1) or disables (when set to 0) code generation of the function OSQFlush().

OS_CFG_Q_PEND_ABORT_EN

OS_CFG_Q_PEND_ABORT_EN enables (when set to **1**) or disables (when set to **0**) code generation of the function OSQPendAbort().

OS_CFG_SCHED_LOCK_TIME_MEAS_EN

This constant enables (when set to **1**) or disables (when set to **0**) code generation to measure the amount of time the scheduler is locked. This is useful when determining task latency.

OS_CFG_SCHED_ROUND_ROBIN_EN

This constant enables (when set to **1**) or disables (when set to **0**) code generation for the round-robin feature of µC/OS-III.

OS_CFG_SEM_EN

OS_CFG_SEM_EN enables (when set to **1**) or disables (when set to **0**) code generation of the semaphore manager and associated data structures. This reduces the amount of code and data space needed when an application does not require the use of semaphores. When OS_CFG_SEM_EN is set to 0, it is not necessary to enable or disable any of the other OS_CFG_SEM_XXX #define constants in this section.

OS_CFG_SEM_DEL_EN

OS_CFG_SEM_DEL_EN enables (when set to 1) or disables (when set to **0**) code generation of the function OSSemDel().

OS_CFG_SEM_PEND_ABORT_EN

OS_CFG_SEM_PEND_ABORT_EN enables (when set to **1**) or disables (when set to 0) code generation of the function OSSemPendAbort().

OS_CFG_SEM_SET_EN

OS_CFG_SEM_SET_EN enables (when set to **1**) or disables (when set to 0) code generation of the function OSSemSet().

OS_CFG_STAT_TASK_EN

OS_CFG_STAT_TASK_EN specifies whether or not to enable µC/OS-III's statistic task, as well as its initialization function. When set to **1**, the statistic task OS_StatTask( ) and statistic task initialization function are enabled. OS_StatTask( ) computes the CPU usage of an application, stack usage of each task, the CPU usage of each task at run time and more.

When enabled, OS_StatTask( ) executes at a rate of OS_CFG_STAT_TASK_RATE_HZ (see os_cfg_app.h), and computes the value of OSStatTaskCPUUsage, which is a variable that contains the percentage of CPU used by the application. OS_StatTask( ) calls OSStatTaskHook( ) every time it executes so that the user can add their own statistics as needed. See **os_stat.c** for details on the statistic task. The priority of OS_StatTask( ) is configurable by the application code (see **os_cfg_app.h**).

OS_StatTask( ) also computes stack usage of each task created when the **#define** OS_CFG_STAT_TASK_STK_CHK_EN is set to 1. In this case, OS_StatTask( ) calls OSTaskStkChk( ) for each task and the result is placed in the task's TCB. The .StkFree and .StkUsed field of the task's TCB represents the amount of free space (in bytes) and amount of used space, respectively.

When OS_CFG_STAT_TASK_EN is set to 0, all variables used by the statistic task are not declared (see **os.h**). This, of course, reduces the amount of RAM needed by µC/OS-III when not enabling the statistic task. When setting OS_CFG_STAT_TASK_EN to 1, statistics will be determined at a rate of OS_CFG_STAT_TASK_RATE_HZ (see **os_cfg_app.h**).

OS_CFG_STAT_TASK_STK_CHK_EN

This constant allows the statistic task to call OSTaskStkChk( ) for each task created. For this to happen, OS_CFG_STAT_TASK_EN needs to be set to **1** (i.e., the statistic task needs to be enabled). However, you can call OSStatStkChk( ) from one of the tasks to obtain this information about the task(s).

OS_CFG_STK_SIZE_MIN

This **#define** specifies the minimum stack size (in **CPU_STK** elements) for each task. This is used by µC/OS-III to verify that sufficient stack space is provided for when each task is created. Suppose the full context of a processor consists of 16 registers of 32 bits. Also, suppose CPU_STK is declared as being of type **CPU_INT32U**, at a bare minimum, set OS_CFG_STK_SIZE_MIN to 16. However, it would be quite unwise to not accommodate for storage of local variables, function call returns, and possibly nested ISRs. Refer to the "port" of the processor used to see how to set this minimum. Again, this is a safeguard to make sure task stacks have sufficient stack space.

OS_CFG_TASK_CHANGE_PRIO_EN

OS_CFG_TASK_CHANGE_PRIO_EN enables (when set to **1**) or disables (when set to 0) code generation of the function OSTaskChangePrio().

OS_CFG_TASK_DEL_EN

OS_CFG_TASK_DEL_EN enables (when set to 1) or disables (when set to **0**) code generation of the function OSTaskDel().

OS_CFG_TASK_Q_EN

OS_CFG_TASK_Q_EN enables (when set to **1**) or disables (when set to 0) code generation of the OSTaskQXXX() functions used to send and receive messages directly to/from tasks and ISRs. Sending messages directly to a task is more efficient than sending messages using a message queue because there is no pend list associated with messages sent to a task.

OS_CFG_TASK_Q_PEND_ABORT_EN

OS_CFG_TASK_Q_PEND_ABORT_EN enables (when set to 1) or disables (when set to **0**) code generation of code for the function OSTaskQPendAbort().

OS_CFG_TASK_PROFILE_EN

This constant allows variables to be allocated in each task's OS_TCB to hold performance data about each task. If OS_CFG_TASK_PROFILE_EN is set to **1**, each task will have a variable to keep track of the number of times a task is switched to, the task execution time, the percent CPU usage of the task relative to the other tasks and more. The information made available with this feature is highly useful when debugging, but requires extra RAM.

OS_CFG_TASK_REG_TBL_SIZE

This constant allows each task to have task context variables. Use task variables to store such elements as "**errno**", task identifiers and other task-specific values. The number of variables that a task contains is set by this constant. Each variable is identified by a unique identifier from 0 to OS_CFG_TASK_REG_TBL_SIZE-1. Also, each variable is declared as having an OS_REG data type (see os_type.h). If OS_REG is a CPU_INT32U, all variables in this table are of this type.

OS_CFG_TASK_SEM_PEND_ABORT_EN

OS_CFG_TASK_SEM_PEND_ABORT_EN enables (when set to **1**) or disables (when set to 0) code generation of code for the function OSTaskSemPendAbort().

OS_CFG_TASK_SUSPEND_EN

OS_CFG_TASK_SUSPEND_EN enables (when set to **1**) or disables (when set to 0) code generation of the functions OSTaskSuspend() and OSTaskResume(), which allows the application to explicitly suspend and resume tasks, respectively. Suspending and resuming a task is useful when debugging, especially if calling these functions via a terminal interface at run time.

OS_CFG_TIME_DLY_HMSM_EN

OS_CFG_TIME_DLY_HMSM_EN enables (when set to **1**) or disables (when set to 0) the code generation of the function OSTimeDlyHMSM(), which is used to delay a task for a specified number of hours, minutes, seconds, and milliseconds.

OS_CFG_TIME_DLY_RESUME_EN

OS_CFG_TIME_DLY_RESUME_EN enables (when set to 1) or disables (when set to **0**) the code generation of the function OSTimeDlyResume().

OS_CFG_TLS_TBL_SIZE

OS_CFG_TLS_TBL_SIZE determines the size of the array: .TLS_Tbl[] in each task's OS_TCB. OS_CFG_TLS_TBL_SIZE also serves the purpose of enabling (when > 0) or disabling the TLS (thread-local storage) feature (when == **0**). The TLS feature was added in V3.03.00.

OS_CFG_TMR_EN

Enables (when set to **1**) or disables (when set to 0) the code generation of timer management services.

OS_CFG_TMR_DEL_EN

OS_CFG_TMR_DEL_EN enables (when set to 1) or disables (when set to **0**) the code generation of the function OSTmrDel().

B-2 DATA TYPES (OS_TYPE.H)

os_type.h contains the data types used by µC/OS-III, which should only be altered by the implementer of the µC/OS-III port. You can alter the contents of os_type.h. However, it is important to understand how each of the data types that are being changed will affect the operation of µC/OS-III-based applications.

The reason to change os_type.h is that processors may work better with specific word sizes. For example, a 16-bit processor will likely be more efficient at manipulating 16-bit values and a 32-bit processor more comfortable with 32-bit values, even at the cost of extra RAM. In other words, the user may need to choose between processor performance and RAM footprint.

If changing "any" of the data types, you should copy os_type.h in the project directory and change that file (not the original os_type.h that comes with the µC/OS-III release).

Recommended data type sizes are specified in comments in os_type.h.

B-3 µC/OS-III STACKS, POOLS AND OTHER (OS_CFG_APP.H)

µC/OS-III allows the user to configure the sizes of the idle task stack, statistic task stack, message pool, tick wheel, timer wheel, debug tables, and more. This is done through os_cfg_app.h.

OS_CFG_TASK_STK_LIMIT_PCT_EMPTY

This #define sets the position (as a percentage to empty) of the stack limit for the idle, statistic, tick, interrupt queue handler, and timer tasks stacks. In other words, the amount of space to leave before the stack is empty. For example if the stack contains 1000 CPU_STK entries and the user declares OS_CFG_TASK_STK_LIMIT_PCT_EMPTY to 10, the stack limit will be set when the stack reaches 90% full, or 10% empty.

If the stack of the processor grows from high memory to low memory, the limit would be set towards the "base address" of the stack, i.e., closer to element 0 of the stack.

If the processor used does not offer automatic stack limit checking, you should set this #define to 0.

OS_CFG_IDLE_TASK_STK_SIZE

This #define sets the size of the idle task's stack (in CPU_STK elements) as follows:

    CPU_STK OSCfg_IdleTaskStk[OS_CFG_IDLE_TASK_STK_SIZE];

Note that the stack size needs to be at least greater than OS_CFG_STK_SIZE_MIN.

OS_CFG_INT_Q_SIZE

If OS_CFG_ISR_POST_DEFERRED_EN is set to 1 (see os_cfg.h), this #define specifies the number of entries that can be placed in the interrupt queue. The size of this queue depends on how many interrupts could occur in the time it takes to process interrupts by the ISR Handler Task. The size also depends on whether or not to allow interrupt nesting. A good start point is approximately 10 entries.

OS_CFG_INT_Q_TASK_STK_SIZE

If OS_CFG_ISR_POST_DEFERRED_EN is set to 1 (see os_cfg.h) then this #define sets the size of the ISR handler task's stack (in CPU_STK elements) as follows:

    CPU_STK OSCfg_IntQTaskStk[OS_CFG_INT_Q_TASK_STK_SIZE];

Note that the stack size needs to be at least greater than OS_CFG_STK_SIZE_MIN.

OS_CFG_ISR_STK_SIZE

This specifies the size of µC/OS-III's interrupt stack (in CPU_STK elements). Note that the stack size needs to accommodate for worst case interrupt nesting, assuming the processor supports interrupt nesting. The ISR handler task stack is declared in os_cfg_app.c as follows:

    CPU_STK OSCfg_ISRStk[OS_CFG_ISR_STK_SIZE];

OS_CFG_MSG_POOL_SIZE

This entry specifies the number of OS_MSGs available in the pool of OS_MSGs. The size is specified in number of OS_MSG elements. The message pool is declared in os_cfg_app.c as follows:

    OS_MSG OSCfg_MsgPool[OS_CFG_MSG_POOL_SIZE];

OS_CFG_STAT_TASK_PRIO

This **#define** allows a user to specify the priority assigned to the μC/OS-III statistic task. It is recommended to make this task a very low priority and possibly even one priority level just above the idle task, or, **OS_CFG_PRIO_MAX-2**.

OS_CFG_STAT_TASK_RATE_HZ

This **#define** defines the execution rate (in Hz) of the statistic task. It is recommended to make this rate an even multiple of the tick rate (see **OS_CFG_TICK_RATE_HZ**).

OS_CFG_STAT_TASK_STK_SIZE

This **#define** sets the size of the statistic task's stack (in **CPU_STK** elements) as follows:

```
CPU_STK OSCfg_StatTaskStk[OS_CFG_STAT_TASK_STK_SIZE];
```

Note that the stack size needs to be at least greater than **OS_CFG_STK_SIZE_MIN**.

OS_CFG_TICK_RATE_HZ

This **#define** specifies the rate in Hertz of μC/OS-III's tick interrupt. The tick rate should be set between 10 and 1000 Hz. The higher the rate, the more overhead it will impose on the processor. The desired rate depends on the granularity required for time delays and timeouts.

OS_CFG_TICK_TASK_PRIO

This **#define** specifies the priority to assign to the μC/OS-III tick task. It is recommended to make this task a fairly high priority, but it does not need to be the highest. The priority assigned to this task must be greater than 0 and less than **OS_CFG_PRIO_MAX-1**.

OS_CFG_TICK_TASK_STK_SIZE

This entry specifies the size of μC/OS-III's tick task stack (in **CPU_STK** elements). Note that the stack size must be at least greater than **OS_CFG_STK_SIZE_MIN**. The tick task stack is declared in os_cfg_app.c as follows:

```
CPU_STK  OSCfg_TickTaskStk[OS_CFG_TICK_TASK_STK_SIZE];
```

OS_CFG_TICK_WHEEL_SIZE

This **#define** determines the number of entries in the **OSTickWheel[]** table. This "wheel" reduces the number of tasks to be updated by the tick task. The size of the wheel should be a fraction of the number of tasks expected in the application.

This value should be a number between 4 and 1024. Task management overhead is somewhat determined by the size of the wheel. A large number of entries might reduce the overhead for tick management but would require more RAM. Each entry requires a pointer and a counter of the number of entries in each "spoke" of the wheel. This counter is typically a 16-bit value. It is recommended that **OS_CFG_TICK_WHEEL_SIZE** not be a multiple of the tick rate. If the application has many tasks, a large wheel size is recommended. As a starting value, you should use a prime number (3, 5, 7, 11, 13, 17, 19, 23, etc.).

OS_CFG_TMR_TASK_PRIO

This **#define** allows a user to specify the priority to assign to the µC/OS-III timer task. It is recommended to make this task a medium-to-low priority, depending on how fast the timer task will execute (see **OS_CFG_TMR_TASK_RATE_HZ**), how many timers running in the application, and the size of the timer wheel, etc. The priority assigned to this task must be greater than 0 and less than **OS_CFG_PRIO_MAX-1**.

You should start with these simple rules:

■ The faster the timer rate, the higher the priority to assign to this task.

■ The higher the timer wheel size, the higher the priority to assign this task.

■ The higher the number of timers in the system, the lower the priority.

In other words:

High Timer Rate	Higher Priority
High Timer Wheel Size	Higher Priority
High Number of Timers	Lower Priority

OS_CFG_TMR_TASK_RATE_HZ

This **#define** specifies the rate in Hertz of μC/OS-III's timer task. The timer task rate should typically be set to 10 Hz. However, timers can run at a faster rate at the price of higher processor overhead. Note that **OS_CFG_TMR_TASK_RATE_HZ** MUST be an integer multiple of **OS_CFG_TICK_TASK_RATE_HZ**. In other words, if setting **OS_CFG_TICK_TASK_RATE_HZ** to 1000, do not set **OS_CFG_TMR_TASK_RATE_HZ** to 11 since 90.91 ticks would be required for every timer update, and 90.91 is not an integer multiple. Use approximately 10 Hz in this example.

OS_CFG_TMR_TASK_STK_SIZE

This **#define** sets the size of the timer task's stack (in **CPU_STK** elements) as follows:

```
CPU_STK OSCfg_TmrTaskStk[OS_CFG_TMR_TASK_STK_SIZE];
```

Note that the stack size needs to be at least greater than **OS_CFG_STK_SIZE_MIN**.

OS_CFG_TMR_WHEEL_SIZE

Timers are updated using a rotating wheel mechanism. This "wheel" reduces the number of timers to be updated by the timer manager task. The size of the wheel should be a fraction of the number of timers in the application.

This value should be a number between 4 and 1024. Timer management overhead is somewhat determined by the size of the wheel. A large number of entries might reduce the overhead for timer management but would require more RAM. Each entry requires a pointer and a counter of the number of entries in each "spoke" of the wheel. This counter is typically a 16-bit value. It is recommended that this value *not* be a multiple of the tick rate. If an application has many timers a large wheel size is recommended. As a starting value, you should use a prime number (3, 5, 7, 11, 13, 17, 19, 23, etc.).

Migrating from μC/OS-II to μC/OS-III

μC/OS-III is a completely new real-time kernel with roots in μC/OS-II. Portions of the μC/OS-II Application Programming Interface (API) function names are the same, but the arguments passed to the functions have, in some places, drastically changed.

Appendix C explains several differences between the two real-time kernels. However, access to μC/OS-II and μC/OS-III source files best highlights the differences.

Table C-1 is a feature-comparison chart for μC/OS-II and μC/OS-III.

Feature	μC/OS-II	μC/OS-III
Year of introduction	1998	2009
Book	Yes	Yes
Source code available	Yes	Yes
Preemptive Multitasking	Yes	Yes
Maximum number of tasks	255	Unlimited
Number of tasks at each priority level	1	Unlimited
Round Robin Scheduling	No	Yes
Semaphores	Yes	Yes
Mutual Exclusion Semaphores	Yes	Yes (nestable)
Event Flags	Yes	Yes
Message Mailboxes	Yes	No (not needed)
Message Queues	**Yes**	**Yes**
Fixed Sized Memory Management	Yes	Yes
Signal a task without requiring a semaphore	No	Yes
Send messages to a task without requiring a message queue	No	Yes
Software Timers	Yes	Yes
Task suspend/resume	Yes	Yes (nestable)
Deadlock prevention	Yes	Yes
Scalable	Yes	Yes
Code Footprint	6K to 26K	6K to 24K
Data Footprint	1K+	1K+
ROMable	Yes	Yes
Run-time configurable	No	Yes
Catch a task that returns	No	Yes
Compile-time configurable	Yes	Yes

Feature	µC/OS-II	µC/OS-III
ASCII names for each kernel object	Yes	Yes
Optio to post without scheduling	No	Yes
Pend on multiple objects	Yes	Yes
Task registers	Yes	Yes
Built-in performance measurements	Limited	Extensive
User definable hook functions	Yes	Yes
Time stamps on posts	No	Yes
Built-in Kernel Awareness support	Yes	Yes
Optimizable Scheduler in assembly language	No	Yes
Tick handling at task level	No	Yes
Number of services	~90	~70
MISRA-C:1998	Yes	N/A
MISRA-C:2004	No	Yes
DO178B Level A and EUROCAE ED-12B	Yes	In progress
Medical FDA pre-market notification (510(k)) and pre-market approval (PMA)	Yes	In progress
SIL3/SIL4 IEC for transportation and nuclear systems	Yes	In progress
IEC-61508	Yes	In progress

Table C-1 **µC/OS-II and µC/OS-III features comparison chart**

C-1 DIFFERENCES IN SOURCE FILE NAMES AND CONTENTS

Table C-2 shows the source files used in both kernels. Note that a few of the files have the same or similar name.

µC/OS-II	µC/OS-III	Note
	os_app_hooks.c	(1)
	os_cfg_app.c	(2)
	os_cfg_app.h	(3)
os_cfg_r.h	os_cfg.h	(4)
os_core.c	os_core.c	
os_cpu.h	os_cpu.h	(5)
os_cpu_a.asm	os_cpu_a.asm	(5)
os_cpu_c.c	os_cpu_c.c	(5)
os_dbg_r.c	os_dbg.c	(6)
os_flag.c	os_flag.c	
	os_int.c	(7)
	os_pend_multi.c	(8)
	os_prio.c	(9)
os_mbox.c		(10)
os_mem.c	os_mem.c	
	os_msg.c	(11)
os_mutex.c	os_mutex.c	
os_q.c	os_q.c	
os_sem.c	os_sem.c	
	os_stat.c	(12)
os_task.c	os_task.c	
os_time.c	os_time.c	
os_tmr.c	os_tmr.c	
	os_var.c	(13)
	os_type.h	(14)
ucos_ii.h	os.h	(15)

Table C-2 µC/OS-II and µC/OS-III files

TC-2(1)   µC/OS-II does not have this file, which is now provided for convenience so you can add application hooks. You should copy this file to the application directory and edit the contents of the file to satisfy your application requirements.

TC-2(2)   **os_cfg_app.c** did not exist in µC/OS-II. This file needs to be added to a project build for µC/OS-III.

TC-2(3)   In µC/OS-II, all configuration constants were placed in **os_cfg.h**. In µC/OS-III, some of the configuration constants are placed in this file, while others are in **os_cfg_app.h**. **os_cfg_app.h** contains application-specific configurations such as the size of the idle task stack, tick rate, and others.

TC-2(4)   In µC/OS-III, **os_cfg.h** is reserved for configuring certain features of the kernel. For example, are any of the semaphore services required, and will the application have fixed-sized memory partition management?

TC-2(5)   These are the port files and a few variables and functions will need to be changed when using a µC/OS-II port as a starting point for the µC/OS-III port.

µC/OS-II variable changes from ...	... to these in µC/OS-III
OSIntNesting	OSIntNestingCtr
OSTCBCur	OSTCBCurPtr
OSTCBHighRdy	OSTCBHighRdyPtr
µC/OS-II function changes from ...	**... to these in µC/OS-III**
OSInitHookBegin()	OSInitHook()
OSInitHookEnd()	N/A
OSTaskStatHook()	OSStatTaskHook()
OSTaskIdleHook()	OSIdleTaskHook()
OSTCBInitHook()	N/A
OSTaskStkInit()	OSTaskStkInit()

The name of **OSTaskStkInit()** is the same but it is listed here since the code for it needs to be changed slightly as several arguments passed to this function are different. Specifically, instead of passing the top-of-stack as in µC/OS-II, **OSTaskStkInit()** is passed the base address and the size of the task stack.

TC-2(6)   In µC/OS-III, **os_dbg.c** should always be part of the build. In µC/OS-II, the equivalent file (**os_dbg_r.c**) was optional.

TC-2(7)   **os_int.c** contains the code for the Interrupt Queue handler, which is a new feature in µC/OS-III, allowing post calls from ISRs to be deferred to a task-level handler. This is done to reduce interrupt latency (see Chapter 9, "Interrupt Management" on page 173).

TC-2(8)   Both kernels allow tasks to pend on multiple kernel objects. In µC/OS-II, this code is found in **os_core.c**, while in µC/OS-III, the code is placed in a separate file, **os_pend_multi.c**.

TC-2(9)   The code to determine the highest priority ready-to-run task is isolated in µC/OS-III and placed in **os_prio.c**. This allows the port developer to replace this file by an assembly language equivalent file, especially if the CPU used supports certain bit manipulation instructions and a count leading zeros (CLZ) instruction.

TC-2(10)   µC/OS-II provides message mailbox services. A message mailbox is identical to a message queue of size one. µC/OS-III does not have these services since they can be easily emulated by message queues.

TC-2(11)   Management of messages for message queues is encapsulated in **os_msg.c** in µC/OS-III.

TC-2(12)   The statistics task and its support functions have been extracted out of **os_core.c** and placed in **os_stat.c** for µC/OS-III.

TC-2(13)   All the µC/OS-III variables are instantiated in a file called **os_var.c**.

TC-2(14)   In µC/OS-III, the size of most data types is better adapted to the CPU architecture used. In µC/OS-II, the size of a number of these data types was assumed.

TC-2(15)   In µC/OS-II, the main header file is called **ucos_ii.h**. In µC/OS-III, it is renamed to **os.h**.

C-2 CONVENTION CHANGES

There are a number of convention changes from µC/OS-II to µC/OS-III. The most notable is the use of CPU-specific data types. Table C-3 shows the differences between the data types used in both kernels

µC/OS-II (os_cpu.h)	µC/CPU (cpu.h)	Note
BOOLEAN	CPU_BOOLEAN	
INT8S	CPU_INT08S	
INT8U	CPU_INT08U	
INT16S	CPU_INT16S	
INT16U	CPU_INT16U	
INT32S	CPU_INT32S	
INT32U	CPU_INT32U	
OS_STK	CPU_STK	(1)
OS_CPU_SR	CPU_SR	(2)
µC/OS-II (os_cfg.h)	**µC/CPU (cpu.h)**	
OS_STK_GROWTH	CPU_CFG_STK_GROWTH	(3)

Table C-3 **µC/OS-II vs. µC/OS-III basic data types**

TC-3(1)   A task stack in µC/OS-II is declared as an **OS_STK**, which is now replaced by a CPU specific data type **CPU_STK**. These two data types are equivalent, except that defining the width of the CPU stack in µC/CPU makes more sense.

TC-3(2)   It also makes sense to declare the CPU's status register in µC/CPU.

TC-3(3)   Stack growth (high-to-low or low-to-high memory) is declared in µC/CPU since stack growth is a CPU feature and not an OS one.

Another convention change is the use of the acronym "**CFG**" which stands for configuration. Now, all **#define** configuration constants and variables have the "**CFG**" or "**Cfg**" acronym in them as shown in Table C-4. Table C-4 shows the configuration constants that have been moved from **os_cfg.h** to **os_cfg_app.h**. This is done because μC/OS-III is configurable at the application level instead of just at compile time as with μC/OS-II.

μC/OS-II (os_cfg.h)	μC/OS-III (os_cfg_app.h)	Note
	OS_CFG_MSG_POOL_SIZE	
	OS_CFG_ISR_STK_SIZE	
	OS_CFG_TASK_STK_LIMIT_PCT_EMPTY	
OS_TASK_IDLE_STK_SIZE	OS_CFG_IDLE_TASK_STK_SIZE	
	OS_CFG_INT_Q_SIZE	
	OS_CFG_INT_Q_TASK_STK_SIZE	
	OS_CFG_STAT_TASK_PRIO	
	OS_CFG_STAT_TASK_RATE_HZ	
OS_TASK_STAT_STK_SIZE	OS_CFG_STAT_TASK_STK_SIZE	
OS_TICKS_PER_SEC	OS_CFG_TICK_RATE_HZ	(1)
	OS_CFG_TICK_TASK_PRIO	
	OS_CFG_TICK_TASK_STK_SIZE	
	OS_CFG_TICK_WHEEL_SIZE	
	OS_CFG_TMR_TASK_PRIO	
OS_TMR_CFG_TICKS_PER_SEC	OS_CFG_TMR_TASK_RATE_HZ	
OS_TASK_TMR_STK_SIZE	OS_CFG_TMR_TASK_STK_SIZE	
OS_TMR_CFG_WHEEL_SIZE	OS_CFG_TMR_WHEEL_SIZE	

Table C-4 μC/OS-III uses "CFG" in configuration

TC-4(1) The very useful **OS_TICKS_PER_SEC** in μC/OS-II was renamed to **OS_CFG_TICK_RATE_HZ** in μC/OS-III. The "**HZ**" indicates that this **#define** represents Hertz (i.e., ticks per second).

Table C-5 shows additional configuration constants added to **os_cfg.h**, while several μC/OS-II constants were either removed or renamed.

µC/OS-II (os_cfg.h)	µC/OS-III (os_cfg.h)	Note
OS_APP_HOOKS_EN	OS_CFG_APP_HOOKS_EN	
OS_ARG_CHK_EN	OS_CFG_ARG_CHK_EN	
	OS_CFG_CALLED_FROM_ISR_CHK_EN	
OS_DEBUG_EN	OS_CFG_DBG_EN	(1)
OS_EVENT_MULTI_EN	OS_CFG_PEND_MULTI_EN	
OS_EVENT_NAME_EN		(2)
	OS_CFG_ISR_POST_DEFERRED_EN	
OS_MAX_EVENTS		(3)
OS_MAX_FLAGS		(3)
OS_MAX_MEM_PART		(3)
OS_MAX_QS		(3)
OS_MAX_TASKS		(3)
	OS_CFG_OBJ_TYPE_CHK_EN	
OS_LOWEST_PRIO	OS_CFG_PRIO_MAX	
	OS_CFG_SCHED_LOCK_TIME_MEAS_EN	
	OS_CFG_SCHED_ROUND_ROBIN_EN	
	OS_CFG_STK_SIZE_MIN	
OS_FLAG_EN	OS_CFG_FLAG_EN	
OS_FLAG_ACCEPT_EN		(6)
OS_FLAG_DEL_EN	OS_CFG_FLAG_DEL_EN	
OS_FLAG_WAIT_CLR_EN	OS_CFG_FLAG_MODE_CLR_EN	
OS_FLAG_NAME_EN		(2)
OS_FLAG_NBITS		(4)
OS_FLAG_QUERY_EN		(5)
	OS_CFG_PEND_ABORT_EN	
OS_MBOX_EN		
OS_MBOX_ACCEPT_EN		(6)

µC/OS-II (os_cfg.h)	µC/OS-III (os_cfg.h)	Note
OS_MBOX_DEL_EN		
OS_MBOX_PEND_ABORT_EN		
OS_MBOX_POST_EN		
OS_MBOX_POST_OPT_EN		
OS_MBOX_QUERY_EN		(5)
OS_MEM_EN	OS_CFG_MEM_EN	
OS_MEM_NAME_EN		(2)
OS_MEM_QUERY_EN		(5)
OS_MUTEX_EN	OS_CFG_MUTEX_EN	
OS_MUTEX_ACCEPT_EN		(6)
OS_MUTEX_DEL_EN	OS_CFG_MUTEX_DEL_EN	
	OS_CFG_MUTEX_PEND_ABORT_EN	
OS_MUTEX_QUERY_EN		(5)
OS_Q_EN	OS_CFG_Q_EN	
OS_Q_ACCEPT_EN		(6)
OS_Q_DEL_EN	OS_CFG_Q_DEL_EN	
OS_Q_FLUSH_EN	OS_CFG_Q_FLUSH_EN	
	OS_CFG_Q_PEND_ABORT_EN	
OS_Q_POST_EN		(7)
OS_Q_POST_FRONT_EN		(7)
OS_Q_POST_OPT_EN		(7)
OS_Q_QUERY_EN		(5)
OS_SCHED_LOCK_EN		
OS_SEM_EN	OS_CFG_SEM_EN	
OS_SEM_ACCEPT_EN		(6)
OS_SEM_DEL_EN	OS_CFG_SEM_DEL_EN	
OS_SEM_PEND_ABORT_EN	OS_CFG_SEM_PEND_ABORT_EN	

µC/OS-II (os_cfg.h)	µC/OS-III (os_cfg.h)	Note
OS_SEM_QUERY_EN		(5)
OS_SEM_SET_EN	OS_CFG_SEM_SET_EN	
OS_TASK_STAT_EN	OS_CFG_STAT_TASK_EN	
OS_TASK_STK_CHK_EN	OS_CFG_STAT_TASK_STK_CHK_EN	
OS_TASK_CHANGE_PRIO_EN	OS_CFG_TASK_CHANGE_PRIO_EN	
OS_TASK_CREATE_EN		
OS_TASK_CREATE_EXT_EN		
OS_TASK_DEL_EN	OS_CFG_TASK_DEL_EN	
OS_TASK_NAME_EN		(2)
	OS_CFG_TASK_Q_EN	
	OS_CFG_TASK_Q_PEND_ABORT_EN	
OS_TASK_QUERY_EN		(5)
OS_TASK_PROFILE_EN	OS_CFG_TASK_PROFILE_EN	
	OS_CFG_TASK_REG_TBL_SIZE	
	OS_CFG_TASK_SEM_PEND_ABORT_EN	
OS_TASK_SUSPEND_EN	OS_CFG_TASK_SUSPEND_EN	
OS_TASK_SW_HOOK_EN		
OS_TICK_STEP_EN		(8)
OS_TIME_DLY_HMSM_EN	OS_CFG_TIME_DLY_HMSM_EN	
OS_TIME_DLY_RESUME_EN	OS_CFG_TIME_DLY_RESUME_EN	
OS_TIME_GET_SET_EN		
OS_TIME_TICK_HOOK_EN		
OS_TMR_EN	OS_CFG_TMR_EN	
OS_TMR_CFG_NAME_EN		(2)
OS_TMR_DEL_EN	OS_CFG_TMR_DEL_EN	

Table C-5 **µC/OS-III uses "CFG" in configuration**

721

TC-5(1)   **DEBUG** is replaced with **DBG**.

TC-5(2)   In µC/OS-II, all kernel objects can be assigned ASCII names after creation. In µC/OS-III, ASCII names are assigned when the object is created.

TC-5(3)   In µC/OS-II, it is necessary to declare the maximum number of kernel objects (number of tasks, number of event flag groups, message queues, etc.) at compile time. In µC/OS-III, all kernel objects are allocated at run time so it is no longer necessary to specify the maximum number of these objects. This feature saves valuable RAM as it is no longer necessary to over allocate objects.

TC-5(4)   In µC/OS-II, event-flag width must be declared at compile time through **OS_FLAG_NBITS**. In µC/OS-III, this is accomplished by defining the width (i.e., number of bits) in **os_type.h** through the data type **OS_FLAG**. The default is typically 32 bits.

TC-5(5)   µC/OS-III does not provide query services to the application.

TC-5(6)   µC/OS-III does not directly provide "**accept**" function calls as with µC/OS-II. Instead, **OS???Pend()** functions provide an option that emulates the "**accept**" functionality by specifying **OS_OPT_PEND_NON_BLOCKING**.

TC-5(7)   In µC/OS-II, there are a number of "**post**" functions. The features offered are now combined in the **OS???Post()** functions in µC/OS-III.

TC-5(8)   The µC/OS-View feature **OS_TICK_STEP_EN** is not present in µC/OS-III since µC/OS-View is an obsolete product and in fact, was replaced by µC/Probe.

C-3 VARIABLE NAME CHANGES

Some of the variable names in µC/OS-II are changed for µC/OS-III to be more consistent with coding conventions. Significant variables are shown in Table C-6.

µC/OS-II (ucos_ii.h)	µC/OS-III (os.h)	Note
OSCtxSwCtr	OSTaskCtxSwCtr	
OSCPUUsage	OSStatTaskCPUUsage	(1)
OSIdleCtr	OSIdleTaskCtr	
OSIdleCtrMax	OSIdleTaskCtrMax	
OSIntNesting	OSIntNestingCtr	(2)
OSPrioCur	OSPrioCur	
OSPrioHighRdy	OSPrioHighRdy	
OSRunning	OSRunning	
OSSchedNesting	OSSchedLockNestingCtr	(3)
	OSSchedLockTimeMax	
OSTaskCtr	OSTaskQty	
OSTCBCur	OSTCBCurPtr	(4)
OSTCBHighRdy	OSTCBHighRdyPtr	(4)
OSTime	OSTickCtr	(5)
OSTmrTime	OSTmrTickCtr	

Table C-6 **Changes in variable naming**

TC-6(1)   In µC/OS-II, **OSCPUUsage** contains the total CPU utilization in percentage format. If the CPU is busy 12% of the time, **OSCPUUsage** has the value 12. In µC/OS-III, the same information is provided in **OSStatTaskCPUUsage**. However, as of µC/OS-III V3.03.00, the resolution of **OSStatTaskCPUUsage** is 1/100th of a percent or, 0.00% (value is **0**) to 100.00% (value is **10,000**).

TC-6(2)   In µC/OS-II, **OSIntNesting** keeps track of the number of interrupts nesting. µC/OS-III uses **OSIntNestingCtr**. The "**Ctr**" has been added to indicate that this variable is a counter.

723

TC-6(3)   **OSSchedNesting** represents the number of times **OSSchedLock()** is called. μC/OS-III renames this variable to **OSSchedLockNestingCtr** to better represent the variable's meaning.

TC-6(4)   In μC/OS-II, **OSTCBCur** and **OSTCBHighRdy** are pointers to the **OS_TCB** of the current task, and to the **OS_TCB** of the highest-priority task that is ready-to-run. In μC/OS-III, these are renamed by adding the "**Ptr**" to indicate that they are pointers.

TC-6(5)   The internal counter of the number of ticks since power up, or the last time the variable was changed through **OSTimeSet()**, has been renamed to better reflect its function.

C-4 API CHANGES

The most significant change from μC/OS-II to μC/OS-III occurs in the API. In order to port a μC/OS-II-based application to μC/OS-III, it is necessary to change the way services are invoked.

Table C-7 shows changes in the way critical sections in μC/OS-III are handled. Specifically, μC/OS-II defines macros to disable interrupts, and they are moved to μC/CPU withμC/OS-III since they are CPU specific functions.

μC/OS-II (os_cpu.h)	μC/CPU (cpu.h)	Note
OS_ENTER_CRITICAL()	CPU_CRITICAL_ENTER()	
OS_EXIT_CRITICAL()	CPU_CRITICAL_EXIT()	

Table C-7 **Changes in macro naming**

One of the biggest changes in the μC/OS-III API is its consistency. In fact, based on the function performed, it is possible to guess which arguments are needed, and in what order. For example, "***p_err**" is a pointer to an error-returned variable. When present, "***p_err**" is always the last argument of a function. In μC/OS-II, error-returned values are at times returned as a "***perr**," and at other times as the return value of the function. This inconsistency has been removed in μC/OS-III.

C-4-1 EVENT FLAGS

Table C-8 shows the API for event-flag management.

µC/OS-II (os_flag.c)	µC/OS-III (os_flag.c)	Note

OS_FLAGS
OSFlagAccept(
    OS_FLAG_GRP *pgrp,
    OS_FLAGS   flags,
    INT8U   wait_type,
    INT8U   *perr);
		(1)

OS_FLAG_GRP *
OSFlagCreate(
    OS_FLAGS   flags,
    INT8U   *perr);
	void
	OSFlagCreate(
	    OS_FLAG_GRP *p_grp,
	    CPU_CHAR *p_name,
	    OS_FLAGS flags,
	    OS_ERR *p_err);
		(2)

OS_FLAG_GRP *
OSFlagDel(
    OS_FLAG_GRP *pgrp,
    INT8U   opt,
    INT8U   *perr);
	OS_OBJ_QTY
	OSFlagDel(
	    OS_FLAG_GRP *p_grp,
	    OS_OPT opt,
	    OS_ERR *p_err);	

INT8U
OSFlagNameGet(
    OS_FLAG_GRP *pgrp,
    INT8U   **pname,
    INT8U *perr);		

void
OSFlagNameSet(
    OS_FLAG_GRP *pgrp,
    INT8U   *pname,
    INT8U   *perr);
		(3)

OS_FLAGS
OSFlagPend(
    OS_FLAG_GRP *pgrp,
    OS_FLAGS   flags,
    INT8U   wait_type,
    INT32U   timeout,
    INT8U   *perr);
	OS_FLAGS
	OSFlagPend(
	    OS_FLAG_GRP *p_grp,
	    OS_FLAGS flags,
	    OS_TICK timeout,
	    OS_OPT opt,
	    OS_TS *p_ts,
	    OS_ERR *p_err);	

725

µC/OS-II (os_flag.c)	µC/OS-III (os_flag.c)	Note

`OS_FLAGS`
`OSFlagPendGetFlagsRdy(`
    `void);`
	`OS_FLAGS`
	`OSFlagPendGetFlagsRdy(`
	    `OS_ERR        *p_err);`	

`OS_FLAGS`
`OSFlagPost(`
    `OS_FLAG_GRP   *pgrp,`
    `OS_FLAGS      flags,`
    `INT8U         opt,`
    `INT8U         *perr);`
	`OS_FLAGS`
	`OSFlagPost(`
	    `OS_FLAG_GRP   *p_grp,`
	    `OS_FLAGS      flags,`
	    `OS_OPT        opt,`
	    `OS_ERR        *p_err);`	

`OS_FLAGS`
`OSFlagQuery(`
    `OS_FLAG_GRP   *pgrp,`
    `INT8U         *perr);`
		(4)

Table C-8 **Event Flags API**

TC-8(1)   In µC/OS-III, there is no "accept" API. This feature is actually built-in the **OSFlagPend( )** by specifying the **OS_OPT_PEND_NON_BLOCKING** option.

TC-8(2)   In µC/OS-II, **OSFlagCreate( )** returns the address of an **OS_FLAG_GRP**, which is used as the "handle" to the event-flag group. In µC/OS-III, the application must allocate storage for an **OS_FLAG_GRP**, which serves the same purpose as the **OS_EVENT**. The benefit in µC/OS-III is that it is not necessary to predetermine the number of event flags at compile time.

TC-8(3)   In µC/OS-II, the user may assign a name to an event-flag group after the group is created. This functionality is built-into **OSFlagCreate( )** for µC/OS-III.

TC-8(4)   µC/OS-III does not provide query services, as they were rarely used in µC/OS-II.

C-4-2 MESSAGE MAILBOXES

Table C-9 shows the API for message mailbox management. Note that µC/OS-III does not directly provide services for managing message mailboxes. Given that a message mailbox is a message queue of size one, µC/OS-III can easily emulate message mailboxes.

µC/OS-II (os_mbox.c)	µC/OS-III (os_q.c)	Note
void * OSMboxAccept(OS_EVENT *pevent);		(1)

OS_EVENT *
OSMboxCreate(
    void   *pmsg);
	void
	OSQCreate(
	    OS_Q *p_q,
	    CPU_CHAR *p_name,
	    OS_MSG_QTY max_qty,
	    OS_ERR *p_err);
		(2)

void *
OSMboxDel(
    OS_EVENT   *pevent,
    INT8U   opt,
    INT8U   *perr);
	OS_OBJ_QTY,
	OSQDel(
	    OS_Q *p_q,
	    OS_OPT opt,
	    OS_ERR *p_err);	

void *
OSMboxPend(
    OS_EVENT   *pevent,
    INT32U   timeout,
    INT8U   *perr);
	void *
	OSQPend(
	    OS_Q *p_q,
	    OS_TICK timeout,
	    OS_OPT opt,
	    OS_MSG_SIZE *p_msg_size,
	    CPU_TS *p_ts,
	    OS_ERR *p_err);
		(3)

INT8U
OSMBoxPendAbort(
    OS_EVENT   *pevent,
    INT8U   opt,
    INT8U   *perr);
	OS_OBJ_QTY
	OSQPendAbort(
	    OS_Q *p_q,
	    OS_OPT opt
	    OS_ERR *p_err);	

µC/OS-II (os_mbox.c)	µC/OS-III (os_q.c)	Note

INT8U
OSMboxPost(
    OS_EVENT   *pevent,
    void   *pmsg);
	void
	OSQPost(
	    OS_Q *p_q,
	    Void *p_void,
	    OS_MSG_SIZE msg_size,
	    OS_OPT opt,
	    OS_ERR *p_err);
		(4)

INT8U
OSMboxPostOpt(
    OS_EVENT   *pevent,
    void   *pmsg,
    INT8U   opt);
		(4)

INT8U
OSMboxQuery(
    OS_EVENT   *pevent,
    OS_MBOX_DATA *p_mbox_data);
		(5)

Table C-9 **Message Mailbox API**

TC-9(1)   In µC/OS-III, there is no "accept" API since this feature is built into the OSQPend() by specifying the OS_OPT_PEND_NON_BLOCKING option.

TC-9(2)   In µC/OS-II, OSMboxCreate() returns the address of an OS_EVENT, which is used as the "handle" to the message mailbox. In µC/OS-III, the application must allocate storage for an OS_Q, which serves the same purpose as the OS_EVENT. The benefit in µC/OS-III is that it is not necessary to predetermine the number of message queues at compile time. Also, to create the equivalent of a message mailbox, you would specify 1 for the max_qty argument.

TC-9(3)   µC/OS-III returns additional information about the message received. Specifically, the sender specifies the size of the message as a snapshot of the current timestamp is taken and stored as part of the message. The receiver of the message therefore knows when the message was sent.

TC-9(4)   In µC/OS-III, OSQPost() offers a number of options that replaces the two post functions provided in µC/OS-II.

TC-9(5)   µC/OS-III does not provide query services, as they were rarely used in µC/OS-II.

C-4-3 MEMORY MANAGEMENT

Table C-10 shows the difference in API for memory management.

µC/OS-II (os_mem.c)	µC/OS-III (os_mem.c)	Note
```OS_MEM *``` ```OSMemCreate(``` ``` void *addr,``` ``` INT32U nblks,``` ``` INT32U blksize,``` ``` INT8U *perr);```	```void``` ```OSMemCreate(``` ``` OS_MEM *p_mem,``` ``` CPU_CHAR *p_name,``` ``` void *p_addr,``` ``` OS_MEM_QTY n_blks,``` ``` OS_MEM_SIZE blk_size,``` ``` OS_ERR *p_err);```	(1)
```void *``` ```OSMemGet(``` ``` OS_MEM *pmem,``` ``` INT8U *perr);```	```void *``` ```OSMemGet(``` ``` OS_MEM *p_mem,``` ``` OS_ERR *p_err);```	
```INT8U``` ```OSMemNameGet(``` ``` OS_MEM *pmem,``` ``` INT8U **pname,``` ``` INT8U *perr);```		
```void``` ```OSMemNameSet(``` ``` OS_MEM *pmem,``` ``` INT8U *pname,``` ``` INT8U *perr);```	```void``` ```OSMemPut(``` ``` OS_MEM *p_mem,``` ``` void *p_blk,``` ``` OS_ERR *p_err);```	(2)
```INT8U``` ```OSMemPut(``` ``` OS_MEM *pmem,``` ``` void *pblk);```		
```INT8U``` ```OSMemQuery(``` ``` OS_MEM *pmem,``` ``` OS_MEM_DATA *p_mem_data);```		(3)

Table C-10 **Memory Management API**

TC-10(1)   In µC/OS-II, **OSMemCreate()** returns the address of an **OS_MEM** object, which is used as the "handle" to the newly created memory partition. In µC/OS-III, the application must allocate storage for an **OS_MEM**, which serves the same purpose. The benefit in µC/OS-III is that it is not necessary to predetermine the number of memory partitions at compile time.

TC-10(2)   µC/OS-III does not need an **OSMemNameSet()** since the name of the memory partition is passed as an argument to **OSMemCreate()**.

TC-10(3)   µC/OS-III does not support query calls.

C-4-4 MUTUAL EXCLUSION SEMAPHORES

Table C-11 shows the difference in API for mutual exclusion semaphore management.

µC/OS-II (os_mutex.c)	µC/OS-III (os_mutex.c)	Note

BOOLEAN
OSMutexAccept(
    OS_EVENT   *pevent,
    INT8U   *perr);
		(1)

OS_EVENT *
OSMutexCreate(
    INT8U   prio,
    INT8U   *perr);
	void
	OSMutexCreate(
	    OS_MUTEX *p_mutex,
	    CPU_CHAR *p_name,
	    OS_ERR *p_err);
		(2)

OS_EVENT *
OSMutexDel(
    OS_EVENT   *pevent,
    INT8U   opt,
    INT8U   *perr);
	void
	OSMutexDel(
	    OS_MUTEX *p_mutex,
	    OS_OPT opt,
	    OS_ERR *p_err);	

void
OSMutexPend(
    OS_EVENT   *pevent,
    INT32U   timeout,
    INT8U   *perr);
	void
	OSMutexPend(
	    OS_MUTEX *p_mutex,
	    OS_TICK timeout,
	    OS_OPT opt,
	    CPU_TS *p_ts,
	    OS_ERR *p_err);
		(3)

	OS_OBJ_QTY
	OSMutexPendAbort(
	    OS_MUTEX *p_mutex,
	    OS_OPT opt,
	    OS_ERR *p_err);	

µC/OS-II (os_mutex.c)	µC/OS-III (os_mutex.c)	Note

`INT8U`
`OSMutexPost(`
`    OS_EVENT        *pevent);`
	`void`
	`OSMutexPost(`
	`    OS_MUTEX      *p_mutex,`
	`    OS_OPT        opt,`
	`    OS_ERR        *p_err);`	

`INT8U`
`OSMutexQuery(`
`    OS_EVENT        *pevent,`
`    OS_MUTEX_DATA  *p_mutex_data);`
		(4)

Table C-11 **Mutual Exclusion Semaphore Management API**

TC-11(1)   In µC/OS-III, there is no "accept" API, since this feature is built into the **OSMutexPend()** by specifying the **OS_OPT_PEND_NON_BLOCKING** option.

TC-11(2)   In µC/OS-II, **OSMutexCreate()** returns the address of an **OS_EVENT**, which is used as the "handle" to the message mailbox. In µC/OS-III, the application must allocate storage for an **OS_MUTEX**, which serves the same purpose as the **OS_EVENT**. The benefit in µC/OS-III is that it is not necessary to predetermine the number of mutual-exclusion semaphores at compile time.

TC-11(3)   µC/OS-III returns additional information when a mutex is released. The releaser takes a snapshot of the current time stamp and stores it in the **OS_MUTEX**. The new owner of the mutex therefore knows when the mutex was released.

TC-11(4)   µC/OS-III does not provide query services as they were rarely used.

C-4-5 MESSAGE QUEUES

Table C-12 shows the difference in API for message-queue management.

µC/OS-II (os_q.c)	µC/OS-III (os_q.c)	Note

void *
OSQAccept(
    OS_EVENT *pevent,
    INT8U   *perr);
		(1)

OS_EVENT *
OSQCreate(
    void   **start,
    INT16U   size);
	void
	OSQCreate(
	    OS_Q *p_q,
	    CPU_CHAR *p_name,
	    OS_MSG_QTY max_qty,
	    OS_ERR *p_err);
		(2)

OS_EVENT *
OSQDel(
    OS_EVENT *pevent,
    INT8U   opt,
    INT8U   *perr);
	OS_OBJ_QTY,
	OSQDel(
	    OS_Q *p_q,
	    OS_OPT opt,
	    OS_ERR *p_err);	

INT8U
OSQFlush(
    OS_EVENT *pevent);
	OS_MSG_QTY
	OSQFlush(
	    OS_Q *p_q,
	    OS_ERR *p_err);	

void *
OSQPend(
    OS_EVENT *pevent,
    INT32U   timeout,
    INT8U   *perr);
	void *
	OSQPend(
	    OS_Q *p_q,
	    OS_MSG_SIZE *p_msg_size,
	    OS_TICK timeout,
	    OS_OPT opt,
	    CPU_TS *p_ts,
	    OS_ERR *p_err);
		(3)

INT8U
OSQPendAbort(
    OS_EVENT *pevent,
    INT8U   opt,
    INT8U   *perr);
	OS_OBJ_QTY
	OSQPendAbort(
	    OS_Q *p_q,
	    OS_OPT opt,
	    OS_ERR *p_err);	

INT8U
OSQPost(
    OS_EVENT *pevent,
    void   *pmsg);
	void
	OSQPost(
	    OS_Q *p_q,
	    void *p_void,
	    OS_MSG_SIZE msg_size,
	    OS_OPT opt,
	    OS_ERR *p_err);
		(4)

µC/OS-II (os_q.c)	µC/OS-III (os_q.c)	Note

INT8U
OSQPostFront(
    OS_EVENT *pevent,
    void *pmsg);		

INT8U
OSQPostOpt(
    OS_EVENT *pevent,
    void   *pmsg,
    INT8U   opt);
		(4)

INT8U
OSQQuery(
    OS_EVENT *pevent,
    OS_Q_DATA *p_q_data);
		(5)

Table C-12 **Message Queue Management API**

TC-12(1)   In µC/OS-III, there is no "accept" API as this feature is built into the **OSQPend()** by specifying the **OS_OPT_PEND_NON_BLOCKING** option.

TC-12(2)   In µC/OS-II, **OSQCreate()** returns the address of an **OS_EVENT**, which is used as the "handle" to the message queue. In µC/OS-III, the application must allocate storage for an **OS_Q** object, which serves the same purpose as the **OS_EVENT**. The benefit in µC/OS-III is that it is not necessary to predetermine at compile time, the number of message queues.

TC-12(3)   µC/OS-III returns additional information when a message queue is posted. Specifically, the sender includes the size of the message and takes a snapshot of the current timestamp and stores it in the message. The receiver of the message therefore knows when the message was posted.

TC-12(4)   In µC/OS-III, **OSQPost()** offers a number of options that replaces the three post functions provided in µC/OS-II.

TC-12(5)   µC/OS-III does not provide query services as they were rarely used.

C-4-6 SEMAPHORES

Table C-13 shows the difference in API for semaphore management.

µC/OS-II (os_sem.c)	µC/OS-III (os_sem.c)	Note

`INT16U`
`OSSemAccept(`
    `OS_EVENT    *pevent);`
		(1)

`OS_EVENT *`
`OSSemCreate(`
    `INT16U        cnt);`
	`void`
	`OSSemCreate(`
	    `OS_SEM        *p_sem,`
	    `CPU_CHAR      *p_name,`
	    `OS_SEM_CTR    cnt,`
	    `OS_ERR        *p_err);`
		(2)

`OS_EVENT *`
`OSSemDel(`
    `OS_EVENT    *pevent,`
    `INT8U       opt,`
    `INT8U       *perr);`
	`OS_OBJ_QTY,`
	`OSSemDel(`
	    `OS_SEM      *p_sem,`
	    `OS_OPT      opt,`
	    `OS_ERR      *p_err);`	

`void`
`OSSemPend(`
    `OS_EVENT    *pevent,`
    `INT32U      timeout,`
    `INT8U       *perr);`
	`OS_SEM_CTR`
	`OSSemPend(`
	    `OS_SEM      *p_sem,`
	    `OS_TICK     timeout,`
	    `OS_OPT      opt,`
	    `CPU_TS      *p_ts,`
	    `OS_ERR      *p_err);`
		(3)

`INT8U`
`OSSemPendAbort(`
    `OS_EVENT    *pevent,`
    `INT8U       opt,`
    `INT8U       *perr);`
	`OS_OBJ_QTY`
	`OSSemPendAbort(`
	    `OS_SEM      *p_sem,`
	    `OS_OPT      opt,`
	    `OS_ERR      *p_err);`	

`void`
`OSSemPost(`
    `OS_EVENT    *pevent);`
	`void`
	`OSSemPost(`
	    `OS_SEM      *p_sem,`
	    `OS_OPT      opt,`
	    `OS_ERR      *p_err);`	

`INT8U`
`OSSemQuery(`
    `OS_EVENT    *pevent,`
    `OS_SEM_DATA *p_sem_data);`
		(4)

µC/OS-II (os_sem.c)		µC/OS-III (os_sem.c)		Note
void OSSemSet(		void OSSemSet(		
OS_EVENT	*pevent,	OS_SEM	*p_sem,	
INT16U	cnt,	OS_SEM_CTR	cnt,	
INT8U	*perr);	OS_ERR	*p_err);	

Table C-13 **Semaphore Management API**

TC-13(1)   In µC/OS-III, there is no "accept" API since this feature is built into the OSSemPend( ) by specifying the OS_OPT_PEND_NON_BLOCKING option.

TC-13(2)   In µC/OS-II, OSSemCreate( ) returns the address of an OS_EVENT, which is used as the "handle" to the semaphore. In µC/OS-III, the application must allocate storage for an OS_SEM object, which serves the same purpose as the OS_EVENT. The benefit in µC/OS-III is that it is not necessary to predetermine the number of semaphores at compile time.

TC-13(3)   µC/OS-III returns additional information when a semaphore is signaled. The ISR or task that signals the semaphore takes a snapshot of the current timestamp and stores this in the OS_SEM object signaled. The receiver of the signal therefore knows when the signal was sent.

TC-13(4)   µC/OS-III does not provide query services, as they were rarely used.

C-4-7 TASK MANAGEMENT

Table C-14 shows the difference in API for task-management services.

µC/OS-II (os_task.c)	µC/OS-III (os_task.c)	Note

INT8U
OSTaskChangePrio(
    INT8U   oldprio,
    INT8U   newprio);
	void
	OSTaskChangePrio(
	    OS_TCB *p_tcb,
	    OS_PRIO prio,
	    OS_ERR *p_err);
		(1)

INT8U
OSTaskCreate(
    void   (*task)(void *p_arg),
    void   *p_arg,
    OS_STK   *ptos,
    INT8U   prio);
	void
	OSTaskCreate(
	    OS_TCB *p_tcb,
	    CPU_CHAR *p_name,
	    OS_TASK_PTR *p_task,
	    void *p_arg,
	    OS_PRIO prio,
	    CPU_STK *p_stk_base,
	    CPU_STK_SIZE stk_limit,
	    CPU_STK_SIZE stk_size,
	    OS_MSG_QTY q_size,
	    OS_TICK time_quanta,
	    void *p_ext,
	    OS_OPT opt,
	    OS_ERR *p_err);
		(2)

INT8U
OSTaskCreateExt(
    void   (*task)(void *p_arg),
    void   *p_arg,
    OS_STK   *ptos,
    INT8U   prio,
    INT16U   id,
    OS_STK   *pbos,
    INT32U   stk_size,
    void   *pext,
    INT16U   opt);
	void
	OSTaskCreate(
	    OS_TCB *p_tcb,
	    CPU_CHAR *p_name,
	    OS_TASK_PTR *p_task,
	    void *p_arg,
	    OS_PRIO prio,
	    CPU_STK *p_stk_base,
	    CPU_STK_SIZE stk_limit,
	    CPU_STK_SIZE stk_size,
	    OS_MSG_QTY q_size,
	    OS_TICK time_quanta,
	    void *p_ext,
	    OS_OPT opt,
	    OS_ERR *p_err);
		(2)

INT8U
OSTaskDel(
    INT8U   prio);
	void
	OSTaskDel(
	    OS_TCB *p_tcb,
	    OS_ERR *p_err);	

µC/OS-II (os_task.c)	µC/OS-III (os_task.c)	Note
| ```
INT8U
OSTaskDelReq(
    INT8U      prio);
``` | | |
| ```
INT8U
OSTaskNameGet(
    INT8U      prio,
    INT8U      **pname,
    INT8U      *perr);
``` | | |
| ```
void
OSTaskNameSet(
    INT8U      prio,
    INT8U      *pname,
    INT8U      *perr);
``` | | (3) |
| | ```
OS_MSG_QTY
OSTaskQFlush(
    OS_TCB       *p_tcb,
    OS_ERR       *p_err);
``` | (4) |
| | ```
void *
OSTaskQPend(
    OS_TICK       timeout,
    OS_OPT        opt,
    OS_MSG_SIZE *p_msg_size,
    CPU_TS        *p_ts,
    OS_ERR        *p_err);
``` | (4) |
| | ```
CPU_BOOLEAN
OSTaskQPendAbort(
    OS_TCB       *p_tcb,
    OS_OPT        opt,
    OS_ERR       *p_err);
``` | (4) |
| | ```
void
OSTaskQPost(
    OS_TCB        *p_tcb,
    void          *p_void,
    OS_MSG_SIZE  msg_size,
    OS_OPT        opt,
    OS_ERR        *p_err);
``` | (4) |
| ```
INT32U
OSTaskRegGet(
    INT8U      prio,
    INT8U      id,
    INT8U      *perr);
``` | ```
OS_REG
OSTaskRegGet(
    OS_TCB        *p_tcb,
    OS_REG_ID    id,
    OS_ERR        *p_err);
``` | |
```

µC/OS-II (os_task.c)	µC/OS-III (os_task.c)	Note
``void
OSTaskRegSet(
INT8U   prio,
INT8U   id,
INT32U   value,
INT8U *perr);```	```void
OSTaskRegGet(
OS_TCB   *p_tcb,
OS_REG_ID   id,
OS_REG   value,
OS_ERR *p_err);```	
``INT8U
OSTaskResume(
INT8U prio);```	```void
OSTaskResume(
OS_TCB   *p_tcb,
OS_ERR *p_err);```	
	``OS_SEM_CTR
OSTaskSemPend(
OS_TICK   timeout,
OS_OPT   opt,
CPU_TS   *p_ts,
OS_ERR *p_err);```	(5)
	``CPU_BOOLEAN
OSTaskSemPendAbort(
OS_TCB   *p_tcb,
OS_OPT   opt,
OS_ERR *p_err);```	(5)
	``CPU_BOOLEAN
OSTaskSemPendAbort(
OS_TCB   *p_tcb,
OS_OPT   opt,
OS_ERR *p_err);```	(5)
	``OS_SEM_CTR
OSTaskSemPost(
OS_TCB   *p_tcb,
OS_OPT   opt,
OS_ERR *p_err);```	(5)
	``OS_SEM_CTR
OSTaskSemSet(
OS_TCB   *p_tcb,
OS_SEM_CTR cnt,
OS_ERR *p_err);```	(5)
``INT8U
OSTaskSuspend(
INT8U prio);```	```void
OSTaskSuspend(
OS_TCB   *p_tcb,
OS_ERR *p_err);```	

µC/OS-II (os_task.c)	µC/OS-III (os_task.c)	Note

`INT8U`
`OSTaskStkChk(`
`    INT8U       prio,`
`    OS_STK_DATA *p_stk_data);`
	`void`
	`OSTaskStkChk(`
	`    OS_TCB       *p_tcb,`
	`    CPU_STK_SIZE *p_free,`
	`    CPU_STK_SIZE *p_used,`
	`    OS_ERR       *p_err);`
		(6)

	`void`
	`OSTaskTimeQuantaSet(`
	`    OS_TCB       *p_tcb,`
	`    OS_TICK      time_quanta,`
	`    OS_ERR       *p_err);`
		(7)

`INT8U`
`OSTaskQuery(`
`    INT8U       prio,`
`    OS_TCB      *p_task_data);`
		(8)

Table C-14 **Task Management API**

TC-14(1)   In µC/OS-II, each task must have a unique priority. The priority of a task can be changed at run-time, however it can only be changed to an unused priority. This is generally not a problem since µC/OS-II supports up to 255 different priority levels and is rare for an application to require all levels. Since µC/OS-III supports an unlimited number of tasks at each priority, the user can change the priority of a task to any available level.

TC-14(2)   µC/OS-II provides two functions to create a task: **OSTaskCreate()** and **OSTaskCreateExt()**. **OSTaskCreateExt()** is recommended since it offers more flexibility. In µC/OS-III, only one API is used to create a task, **OSTaskCreate()**, which offers similar features to **OSTaskCreateExt()** and provides additional ones.

TC-14(3)   µC/OS-III does not need an **OSTaskNameSet()** since an ASCII name for the task is passed as an argument to **OSTaskCreate()**.

TC-14(4)   µC/OS-III allows tasks or ISRs to send messages directly to a task instead of having to pass through a mailbox or a message queue as does µC/OS-II.

TC-14(5)   µC/OS-III allows tasks or ISRs to directly signal a task instead of having to pass through a semaphore as does µC/OS-II.

TC-14(6)   In µC/OS-II, the user must allocate storage for a special data structure called **OS_STK_DATA**, which is used to place the result of a stack check of a task. This data structure contains only two fields: **.OSFree** and **.OSUsed**. In µC/OS-III, it is required that the caller pass pointers to destination variables where those values will be placed.

TC-14(7)   µC/OS-III allows users to specify the time quanta of each task on a per-task basis. This is available since µC/OS-III supports multiple tasks at the same priority, and allows for round robin scheduling. The time quanta for a task is specified when the task is created, but it can be changed by the API at run time.

TC-14(8)   µC/OS-III does not provide query services as they were rarely used.

C-4-8 TIME MANAGEMENT

Table C-15 shows the difference in API for time-management services.

µC/OS-II (os_time.c)	µC/OS-III (os_time.c)	Note

void
OSTimeDly(
    INT32U   ticks);
	void
	OSTimeDly(
	    OS_TICK dly,
	    OS_OPT opt,
	    OS_ERR *p_err);
		(1)

INT8U
OSTimeDlyHMSM(
    INT8U   hours,
    INT8U   minutes,
    INT8U   seconds,
    INT16U   ms);
	void
	OSTimeDlyHMSM(
	    CPU_INT16U hours,
	    CPU_INT16U minutes,
	    CPU_INT16U seconds
	    CPU_INT32U milli,
	    OS_OPT opt,
	    OS_ERR *p_err);
		(2)

INT8U
OSTimeDlyResume(
    INT8U   prio);
	void
	OSTimeDlyResume(
	    OS_TCB *p_tcb,
	    OS_ERR *p_err);	

INT32U OSTimeGet(void);	OS_TICK OSTimeGet(OS_ERR *p_err);	

µC/OS-II (os_time.c)	µC/OS-III (os_time.c)	Note

void
OSTimeSet(
    INT32U   ticks);
	void
	OSTimeSet(
	    OS_TICK ticks,
	    OS_ERR *p_err);	

void OSTimeTick(void)	void OSTimeTick(void)	

Table C-15 **Time Management API**

TC-15(1) µC/OS-III includes an option argument, which allows the user to delay a task for a certain number of ticks, periodic mode or wait until the tick counter reaches a certain value. In µC/OS-II, only the former is available.

TC-15(2) **OSTimeDlyHMSM()** in µC/OS-III is more flexible as it allows a user to specify whether to be "strict" about the ranges of hours (0 to 999), minutes (0 to 59), seconds (0 to 59), and milliseconds (0 to 999), or whether to allow any values such as 200 minutes, 75 seconds, or 20,000 milliseconds (non-strict).

C-4-9 TIMER MANAGEMENT

Table C-16 shows the difference in API for timer-management services. The timer management in µC/OS-III is similar to that of µC/OS-II except for minor changes in arguments in **OSTmrCreate()**.

µC/OS-II (os_tmr.c)	µC/OS-III (os_tmr.c)	Note

OS_TMR *
OSTmrCreate(
    INT32U   dly,
    INT32U   period,
    INT8U   opt,
    OS_TMR_CALLBACK callback,
    void   *callback_arg,
    INT8U   *pname,
    INT8U   *perr);
	void
	OSTmrCreate(
	    OS_TMR *p_tmr,
	    CPU_CHAR *p_name,
	    OS_TICK dly,
	    OS_TICK period,
	    OS_OPT opt,
	    OS_TMR_CALLBACK_PTR *p_callback,
	    void *p_callback_arg,
	    OS_ERR *p_err);	

µC/OS-II (os_tmr.c)		µC/OS-III (os_tmr.c)		Note

BOOLEAN
OSTmrDel(
    OS_TMR
    INT8U
	
	*ptmr,
	*perr);
		CPU_BOOLEAN
		OSTmrDel(
		    OS_TMR
		    OS_ERR
			
			*p_tmr,
			*p_err);	

INT8U
OSTmrNameGet(
    OS_TMR
    INT8U
    INT8U
	
	*ptmr,
	**pdest,
	*perr);			

INT32U
OSTmrRemainGet(
    OS_TMR
    INT8U
	
	*ptmr,
	*perr);
		OS_TICK
		OSTmrRemainGet(
		    OS_TMR
		    OS_ERR
			
			*p_tmr,
			*p_err);	

INT8U
OSTmrStateGet(
    OS_TMR
    INT8U
	
	*ptmr,
	*perr);
		OS_STATE
		OSTmrStateGet(
		    OS_TMR
		    OS_ERR
			
			*p_tmr,
			*p_err);	

BOOLEAN
OSTmrStart(
    OS_TMR
    INT8U
	
	*ptmr,
	*perr);
		CPU_BOOLEAN
		OSTmrStart(
		    OS_TMR
		    OS_ERR
			
			*p_tmr,
			*p_err);	

BOOLEAN
OSTmrStop(
    OS_TMR
    INT8U
    void
    INT8U
	
	*ptmr,
	opt,
	*callback_arg,
	*perr);
		CPU_BOOLEAN
		OSTmrStop(
		    OS_TMR
		    OS_OPT
		    void
		    OS_ERR
			
			*p_tmr,
			opt,
			*p_callback_arg,
			*p_err);	

INT8U OSTmrSignal(void);				

Table C-16 **Timer Management API**

C-4-10 MISCELLANEOUS

Table C-17 shows the difference in API for miscellaneous services.

µC/OS-II (os_core.c)	µC/OS-III (os_core.c)	Note

`INT8U`
`OSEventNameGet(`
`    OS_EVENT    *pevent,`
`    INT8U      **pname,`
`    INT8U       *perr);`
		(1)

`void`
`OSEventNameSet(`
`    OS_EVENT    *pevent,`
`    INT8U       *pname,`
`    INT8U       *perr);`
		(1)

`INT16U`
`OSEventPendMulti(`
`    OS_EVENT   **pevent_pend,`
`    OS_EVENT   **pevent_rdy,`
`    void       **pmsgs_rdy,`
`    INT32U       timeout,`
`    INT8U       *perr);`
	`OS_OBJ_QTY`
	`OSPendMulti(`
	`    OS_PEND_DATA  *p_pend_data_tbl,`
	`    OS_OBJ_QTY     tbl_size,`
	`    OS_TICK        timeout,`
	`    OS_OPT         opt,`
	`    OS_ERR        *p_err);`
		(2)

`void`
`OSInit(void)`
	`void`
	`OSInit(`
	`    OS_ERR        *p_err);`
		(3)

`void` `OSIntEnter(void)`	`void` `OSIntEnter(void);`	
`void` `OSIntExit(void)`	`void` `OSIntExit(void)`	
	`void` `OSSched(void);`	

`void`
`OSSchedLock(void)`
	`void`
	`OSSchedLock(`
	`    OS_ERR        *p_err);`
		(4)

	`void`
	`OSSchedRoundRobinCfg(`
	`    CPU_BOOLEAN    en,`
	`    OS_TICK        dflt_time_quanta,`
	`    OS_ERR        *p_err);`
		(5)

	`void`
	`OSSchedRoundRobinYield(`
	`    OS_ERR        *p_err);`
		(6)

`void`
`OSSchedUnlock(void)`
	`void`
	`OSSchedUnlock(`
	`    OS_ERR        *p_err);`
		(7)

µC/OS-II (os_core.c)	µC/OS-III (os_core.c)	Note
void OSStart(void)	void OSStart(void);	
void OSStatInit(void)	void OSStatTaskCPUUsageInit(OS_ERR *p_err);	(8)
INT16U OSVersion(void)	CPU_INT16U OSVersion(OS_ERR *p_err);	(9)

Table C-17 **Miscellaneous API**

TC-17(1)   Objects in µC/OS-III are named when they are created and these functions are not required in µC/OS-III.

TC-17(2)   The implementation of the multi-pend functionality is changed from µC/OS-II. However, the purpose of multi-pend is the same, to allow a task to pend (or wait) on multiple objects. In µC/OS-III, however, it is possible to only multi-pend on semaphores and message queues and not event flags and mutexes.

TC-17(3)   µC/OS-III returns an error code for this function. Initialization is successful if **OS_ERR_NONE** is received from **OSInit( )**. In µC/OS-II, there is no way of detecting an error in the configuration that caused **OSInit( )** to fail.

TC-17(4)   An error code is returned in µC/OS-III for this function.

TC-17(5)   Enable or disable µC/OS-III's round-robin scheduling at run time, as well as change the default time quanta.

TC-17(6)   A task that completes its work before its time quanta expires may yield the CPU to another task at the same priority.

TC-17(7)   An error code is returned in µC/OS-III for this function.

TC-17(8)   Note the change in name for the function that computes the "capacity" of the CPU for the purpose of computing CPU usage at run-time.

TC-17(9)   An error code is returned in µC/OS-III for this function.

C-4-11 HOOKS AND PORT

Table C-18 shows the difference in APIs used to port µC/OS-II to µC/OS-III.

µC/OS-II (os_cpu*.c/h)	µC/OS-III (os_cpu*.c/h)	Note
	`OS_GET_TS();`	(1)
`void` `OSInitHookBegin(void);`	`void` `OSInitHook(void);`	
`void` `OSInitHookEnd(void);`		

`void`
`OSTaskCreateHook(`
`    OS_TCB    *ptcb);`
	`void`
	`OSTaskCreateHook(`
	`    OS_TCB        *p_tcb);`	

`void`
`OSTaskDelHook(`
`    OS_TCB    *ptcb);`
	`void`
	`OSTaskDelHook(`
	`    OS_TCB        *p_tcb);`	

`void` `OSTaskIdleHook(void);`	`void` `OSIdleTaskHook(void);`	

	`void`
	`OSTaskReturnHook(`
	`    OS_TCB        *p_tcb);`
		(2)

`void` `OSTaskStatHook(void)`	`void` `OSStatTaskHook(void);`	

`void`
`OSTaskStkInit(`
`    void      (*task)(void *p_arg),`
`    void      *p_arg,`
`    OS_STK    *ptos,`
`    INT16U    opt);`
	`CPU_STK *`
	`OSTaskStkInit(`
	`    OS_TASK_PTR    p_task,`
	`    void           *p_arg,`
	`    CPU_STK        *p_stk_base,`
	`    CPU_STK        *p_stk_limit,`
	`    CPU_STK_SIZE   size,`
	`    OS_OPT         opt);`
		(3)

`void` `OSTaskSwHook(void)`	`void` `OSTaskSwHook(void);`	

`void`
`OSTCBInitHook(`
`    OS_TCB    *ptcb);`
		(4)

`void` `OSTimeTickHook(void);`	`void` `OSTimeTickHook(void);`	
`void` `OSStartHighRdy(void);`	`void` `OSStartHighRdy(void);`	(5)
`void` `OSIntCtxSw(void);`	`void` `OSIntCtxSw(void);`	(5)

745

µC/OS-II (os_cpu*.c/h)	µC/OS-III (os_cpu*.c/h)	Note
void OSCtxSw(void);	void OSCtxSw(void);	(5)

Table C-18 **Hooks and Port API**

TC-18(1)   µC/OS-III requires that the Board Support Package (BSP) provide a 32-bit free-running counter (from **0x00000000** to **0xFFFFFFFF** and rolls back to **0x00000000**) for the purpose of performing time measurements. When a signal is sent, or a message is posted, this counter is read and sent to the recipient. This allows the recipient to know when the message was sent. If a 32-bit free-running counter is not available, you can simulate one using a 16-bit counter but, this requires more code to keep track of overflows.

TC-18(2)   µC/OS-III is able to terminate a task that returns. Recall that tasks should not return since they should be either implemented as an infinite loop, or deleted if implemented as run once.

TC-18(3)   The code for **OSTaskStkInit()** must be changed slightly in µC/OS-III since several arguments passed to this function are different than in µC/OS-II. Instead of passing the top-of-stack as in µC/OS-II, **OSTaskStkInit()** is passed the base address of the task stack, as well as the size of the stack.

TC-18(4)   This function is not needed in µC/OS-III.

TC-18(5)   These functions are a part of **os_cpu_a.asm**, and should only require name changes for the following variables:

µC/OS-II variable changes from ...	... to this in µC/OS-III
OSIntNesting	OSIntNestingCtr
OSTCBCur	OSTCBCurPtr
OSTCBHighRdy	OSTCBHighRdyPtr

Appendix

D

MISRA-C:2004 and µC/OS-III

MISRA C is a software development standard for the C programming language developed by the Motor Industry Software Reliability Association (MISRA). Its aims are to facilitate code safety, portability, and reliability in the context of embedded systems, specifically those systems programmed in ANSI C. There is also a set of guidelines for MISRA C++.

There are now more MISRA users outside of the automotive industry than within it. MISRA has evolved into a widely accepted model of best practices by leading developers in such sectors as aerospace, telecom, medical devices, defense, railway, and others.

The first edition of the MISRA C standard, "Guidelines for the use of the C language in vehicle based software," was produced in 1998 and is officially known as MISRA-C:1998. MISRA-C:1998 had 127 rules, of which 93 were required and 34 advisory. The rules were numbered in sequence from 1 to 127.

In 2004, a second edition "Guidelines for the use of the C language in critical systems," or MISRA-C:2004 was produced with many substantial changes, including a complete renumbering of the rules.

The MISRA-C:2004 document contains 141 rules, of which 121 are "required" and 20 are "advisory," divided into 21 topical categories, from "Environment" to "Run-time failures."

µC/OS-III follows most of the MISRA-C:2004 except a few of the required rules were suppressed. The reasoning behind this is discussed within this appendix.

IAR Embedded Workbench for ARM (EWARM) V6.2x was used to verify MISRA-C:2004 compliance, which required suppressing the rules to achieve a clean build.

D

D-1 MISRA-C:2004, RULE 8.5 (REQUIRED)

Rule Description

There shall be no definitions of objects or functions in a header file.

Offending code appears as

```
OS_EXT    OS_IDLE_CTR    OSIdleTaskCtr;
```

OS_EXT allows us to declare "extern" and storage using a single declaration in **os.h** but allocation of storage actually occurs in **os_var.c**.

Rule suppressed

The method used in μC/OS-III is an improved scheme as it avoids declaring variables in multiple files.

Occurs in

os.h

D-2 MISRA-C:2004, RULE 8.12 (REQUIRED)

Rule Description:

When an array is declared with external linkage, its size shall be stated explicitly or defined implicitly by initialization.

Offending code appears as

```
extern  CPU_STK       OSCfg_IdleTaskStk[];
```

µC/OS-III can be provided in object form (linkable object), but requires that the value and size of known variables and arrays be declared in application code. It is not possible to know the size of the arrays.

Rule suppressed

There is no choice other than to suppress or add a fictitious size, which would not be proper. For example, we could specify a size of 1 and the MISRA-C:2004 would pass but, we chose not to.

Occurs in:

os.h

D-3 MISRA-C:2004, RULE 14.7 (REQUIRED)

Rule Description

A function shall have a single point of exit at the end of the function.

Offending code appears as

```
if (argument is invalid) {
    Set error code;
    return;
}
```

Rule suppressed

We prefer to exit immediately upon finding an invalid argument rather than create nested "if" statements.

Occurs in

os_core.c
os_flag.c
os_int.c
os_mem.c
os_msg.c
os_mutex.c
os_pend_multi.c
os_prio.c
os_q.c
os_sem.c
os_stat.c
os_task.c
os_tick.c
os_time.c
os_tmr.c

D-4 MISRA-C:2004, RULE 15.2 (REQUIRED)

Rule Description

An unconditional break statement shall terminate every non-empty **switch** clause.

Offending code appears as

```
switch (value) {
    case constant_value:
        /* Code */
        return;
}
```

Rule suppressed

The problem involves using a return statement to exit the function instead of using a **break**. When adding a "**break**" statement after the return, the compiler complains about the unreachable code of the "**break**" statement.

Occurs in

os_flag.c

os_mutex.c

os_q.c

os_tmr.c

D-5 MISRA-C:2004, RULE 17.4 (REQUIRED)

Rule Description

Array indexing shall be the only allowed form of pointer arithmetic.

Offending code appears as

```
   :
 p_tcb++;
   :
```

Rule suppressed

It is common practice in C to increment a pointer instead of using array indexing to accomplish the same thing. This common practice is not in agreement with this rule.

Occurs in

os_core.c

os_cpu_c.c

os_int.c

os_msg.c

os_pend_multi.c

os_prio.c

os_task.c

os_tick.c

os_tmr.c

Appendix

E

Bibliography

Bal Sathe, Dhananjay. 1988. *Fast Algorithm Determines Priority.* EDN (India), September, p. 237.

Comer, Douglas. 1984. *Operating System Design, The XINU Approach.* Englewood Cliffs, New Jersey: Prentice-Hall. ISBN 0-13-637539-1.

Kernighan, Brian W. and Dennis M. Ritchie. 1988. *The C Programming Language, 2nd edition.* Englewood Cliffs, New Jersey: Prentice Hall. ISBN 0-13-110362-8.

Klein, Mark H., Thomas Ralya, Bill Pollak, Ray Harbour Obenza, and Michael Gonzlez. 1993. *A Practioner's Handbook for Real-Time Analysis: Guide to Rate Monotonic Analysis for Real-Time Systems.* Norwell, Massachusetts: Kluwer Academic Publishers Group. ISBN 0-7923-9361-9.

Labrosse, Jean J. 2002, *MicroC/OS-II, The Real-Time Kernel,* CMP Books, 2002, ISBN 1-57820-103-9.

Li, Qing. *Real-Time Concepts for Embedded Systems,* CMP Books, July 2003, ISBN 1-57820-124-1.

The Motor Industry Software Reliability Association, *MISRA-C:2004,* Guidelines for the Use of the C Language in Critical Systems, October 2004. www.misra-c.com.

Appendix E

E

F

Licensing Policy

uC/OS-III is provided in source form for FREE short-term evaluation, for educational use or for peaceful research. If you plan or intend to use uC/OS-III in a commercial application/ product then, you need to contact Micrium to properly license uC/OS-III for its use in your application/product. We provide ALL the source code for your convenience and to help you experience uC/OS-III. The fact that the source is provided does NOT mean that you can use it commercially without paying a licensing fee.

It is necessary to purchase this license when the decision to use µC/OS-III in a design is made, not when the design is ready to go to production.

If you are unsure about whether you need to obtain a license for your application, please contact Micrium and discuss the intended use with a sales representative.

CONTACT MICRIUM

1290 Weston Road, Suite 306
Weston, FL 33326
USA

Phone: +1 954 217 2036
Fax: +1 954 217 2037

E-mail: Licensing@Micrium.com
Web: www.Micrium.com

F

µC/OS-III™
The Real-Time Kernel

and the
Infineon

XMC4500

Jean J. Labrosse

Micriµm
Press
Weston, FL 33326

Micriµm Press
1290 Weston Road, Suite 306
Weston, FL 33326
USA
www.micrium.com

For bulk orders, please contact Micriµm Press at: +1 954 217 2036

ISBN: 978-1-935772-20-0
100-uCOS-III-Infineon-XMC4500-001

Micriµm
Press

1

Introduction

The Infineon *Hexagon Application Kit* is a modular, expandable application board platform for the XMC4000 family of microcontrollers. *Satellite Cards* connected to a central CPU Board enable fast prototyping of specific applications such as motor control, industrial automation, industrial connectivity or any kind of power conversion such as solar inverters.

At the core of this versatile platform is a CPU board powered by the XMC4500 ARM Cortex-M4 microcontroller. A single CPU Board provides up to 3 satellite connectors. A HMI (Human Machine Interface) satellite card provides an OLED display, SDMMC, audio and touch sense functionality. Additional functionality such as Ethernet, CAN and RS-485 can be added via a COM (Communication) satellite card as shown in Figure 1-1:

Figure 1-1 **Infineon Hexagon Application Kit**

In addition to these two satellite cards, developers can also connect not only an Actuator (ACT) satellite card for motor control, but also their own boards.

As you connect more satellite cards or even your own boards to expand the hardware functionality, you also need software to support it.

Micrium's µC/OS-III facilitates the design of embedded systems based on this hexagon platform by allowing you to create multiple tasks.

The second part of this book delivers to the reader the experience of µC/OS-III through the use of the Infineon hexagon application kit, world-class tools and step-by-step instruction.

Here, you will find µC/OS-III examples for the Infineon XMC4500 CPU board that will serve as a solid platform to create more sophisticated embedded applications.

1-1 PART II CHAPTER CONTENTS

Figure 1-2 shows the layout and flow of Part II of the book. This diagram should be useful in understanding the relationship between chapters and appendices.

The first column on the left indicates chapters that should be read in order to understand µC/OS-III's structure as well as examples. The second column shows porting information for the ARM Cortex-M4 CPU. The third column consists of miscellaneous appendices.

Figure 1-2 **Part II Chapter Layout**

Chapter 1, Introduction. This chapter.

Chapter 2, The ARM Cortex-M4. This chapter provides a brief introduction to the ARM Cortex-M4 CPU.

Chapter 3, Setup. This chapter explains how to set up the test environment to run the µC/OS-III examples. The chapter describes how to download the 32K Kickstart edition of the IAR Systems Embedded Workbench for ARM, how to obtain example code that accompanies the book, and how to connect the XMC4500 CPU board to a PC.

Chapter 4, Example #1. This chapter explains how to get µC/OS-III up and running. The project simply blinks an LED on the XMC4500 CPU board. You will also see how easy it is to use µC/Probe to display run-time data in a target.

Chapter 5, Example #2. The chapter shows how to read the on-board potentiometer and display the position in a Windows application.

Chapter 6, Example #3. The chapter shows how to monitor select µC/OS-III performance measurement values.

Chapter 7, Example #4. This chapter shows how to use µC/OS-III to simulate measuring the RPM of a rotating wheel.

Appendix A, µC/OS-III Port for the Cortex-M4. This appendix explains how µC/OS-III was adapted to the Cortex-M4 CPU. The Cortex-M4 contains interesting features specifically designed for real-time kernels, and µC/OS-III makes good use of these.

Appendix B, µC/CPU Port for the Cortex-M4. This appendix describes how the µC/CPU module was adapted to the Cortex-M4.

Appendix C, IAR Systems Embedded Workbench for ARM. This appendix provides a brief description of IAR Systems Embedded Workbench for the ARM architecture (EWARM).

Appendix D, µC/Probe. This appendix provides a brief description of Micriµm's µC/Probe, which is a Windows application that easily allows users to display and change target variables at run time.

Appendix E, XMC4500 CPU Board User's Guide. This appendix provides a description of the XMC4500 CPU board, as well as complete electrical schematics.

Appendix F, Bibliography.

Appendix G, Licensing µC/OS-III.

1-2 ACKNOWLEDGEMENTS

I would like to thank IAR for their support and for providing access to the 32K Kickstart version of the IAR Embedded Workbench for ARM (EWARM). EWARM is an awesome tool and I'm sure readers of this book will appreciate the ability to try out µC/OS-III on the XMC4500 CPU board.

A special thanks to Mr. Rolf Segger for providing the J-Link Pro, which makes debugging and accessing variables with µC/Probe a breeze.

Thank you also to Hitex for providing some of the text for Chapter 2, "The ARM Cortex-M4 and the XMC4500" on page 765.

Finally, thank you to my great team at Micriµm for the help and support they provided for this project, specially Daniel Colls for getting µC/OS-III running on the XMC4500 and Juan Benavides for helping with the second part of this book.

The ARM Cortex-M4 and the XMC4500

The ARM Cortex family is a generation of processors that provides a standard architecture for a wide range of technological demands. Unlike other ARM CPUs, the Cortex family is a complete processor core that provides a standard CPU and system architecture. The Cortex-M4 family is designed for cost-sensitive microcontroller applications.

This chapter provides a brief summary of the Cortex-M4 architecture. Additional reference material is provided in the section "Bibliography" on page 893.

While ARM7 and ARM9 CPUs are successfully integrated into standard microcontrollers, they do show their SoC heritage. Each specific manufacturer has designed an interrupt handling solution. However, the Cortex-M4 provides a standardized microcontroller core, which goes beyond the CPU to provide the complete heart of a microcontroller (including the interrupt system, SysTick timer, debug system and memory map). The 4 Gbyte address space of Cortex-M4 is split into well-defined regions for code, SRAM, peripherals, and system peripherals. Unlike the ARM7, the Cortex-M4 is a Harvard architecture with multiple busses that allow it to perform operations in parallel, boosting overall performance. Unlike earlier ARM architectures, the Cortex family allows unaligned data access. This ensures the most efficient use of the internal SRAM. The Cortex family also supports setting and clearing of bits within two 1Mbyte regions of memory by a method called bit banding. This allows efficient access to peripheral registers and flags located in SRAM memory, without the need for a full Boolean processor.

One of the key components of the Cortex-M4 core is the Nested Vector Interrupt Controller (NVIC). The NVIC provides a standard interrupt structure for all Cortex-based microcontrollers and exceptional interrupt handling. The NVIC provides dedicated interrupt vectors for up to 240 peripheral sources so that each interrupt source can be individually prioritized. In the case of back-to-back interrupts, the NVIC uses a "tail chaining" method that allows successive interrupts to be serviced with minimal overhead. During the interrupt-stacking phase, a high-priority interrupt can preempt a low-priority interrupt without incurring additional CPU cycles. The interrupt structure is also tightly coupled to the low-power modes within the Cortex-M4 core.

Although the Cortex-M4 is designed as a low cost core, it is still a 32-bit CPU with support for two operating modes: Thread mode and Handler mode, which can be configured with their own stacks. This allows more sophisticated software design and support for such real-time kernels as µC/OS-II and µC/OS-III.

The Cortex core also includes a 24-bit auto reload timer that is intended to provide a periodic interrupt for the kernel. While the ARM7 and ARM9 CPUs have two instruction sets (the ARM 32-bit and Thumb 16-bit), the Cortex family is designed to support the ARM Thumb-2 instruction set. This blends both 16-bit and 32-bit instructions to deliver the performance of the ARM 32-bit instruction set with the code density of the Thumb 16-bit instruction set. The Thumb-2 is a rich instruction set designed as a target for C/C++ compilers. This means that a Cortex application can be entirely coded in C.

2-1 THE CORTEX CPU

The Cortex CPU is a 32-bit RISC CPU. This CPU has a simplified version of the ARM7/9 programmer's model, but a richer instruction set with good integer math support, better bit manipulation, and 'harder' real-time performance.

The Cortex CPU includes a Floating Point Unit (FPU) and a Memory Protection Unit (MPU).

- Floating Point Unit (FPU): The FPU provides IEEE754-compliant operations on single precision, 32-bit, floating-point values.

- Memory Protection Unit (MPU): The MPU improves system reliability by defining the memory attributes for different memory regions. It provides fine grain memory control, enabling applications to utilize multiple privilege levels, separating and protecting code, data and stack on a task-by-task basis. Up to eight different regions are supported as well as an optional predefined background region. These features are becoming critical to support safety requirements in many embedded applications.

The Cortex CPU executes most instructions in a single cycle, which is achieved with a three-stage pipeline.

The Cortex CPU is a RISC processor featuring a load and store architecture. In order to perform data processing instructions, the operands must be loaded into CPU registers, the data operation must be performed on these registers, and the results saved back to memory. Consequently, all program activity focuses on the CPU registers.

As shown in Figure 2-1, the CPU registers consist of sixteen 32-bit wide registers. Registers R0-R12 can be used to hold variables or addresses. Registers R13-R15 have special functions within the Cortex CPU. Register R13 is used as a stack pointer. This register is banked, which allows the Cortex CPU to have two operating modes, each with their own separate stack space. In the Cortex CPU the two stacks are called the main stack (ISR stack) and the process stack (Task stack). The next register R14 is called the link register, and it is used to store the return address when a call is made to a function. This allows the Cortex CPU to make a fast entry and exit to a function. If the code calls several levels of subroutines, the compiler automatically stores R14 onto the stack. The final register R15 is the program counter. Since R15 is part of the CPU registers it can be read and manipulated like any other register.

The Cortex-M4 implementation in the XMC4500 includes a Floating Point Unit (FPU) which fully supports single-precision add, subtract, multiply, divide, multiply and accumulate, and square root operations. It also provides conversions between fixed-point and floating-point data formats, and floating-point constant instructions.

The FPU provides floating-point computation functionality that is compliant with the ANSI/IEEE Std 754-2008, IEEE Standard for Binary Floating-Point Arithmetic, referred to as the IEEE 754 standard.

The FPU contains 32 single-precision extension registers, which you can also access as 16 doubleword registers for load, store, and move operations.

The FPU is disabled by default. You must enable it before you can use any floating-point instructions. In order to enable the FPU and µC/OS-III to save and restore the FPU status control registers at each context switch, you need to set **OS_CPU_ARM_FP_EN** to **DEF_ENABLED** as illustrated in Figure 2-1.

Core Registers

◄—— 32 bit ——►

R0
R1
R2
R3
R4
R5
R6
R7
R8
R9
R10
R11
R12

General purpose registers

Stack Pointer	R13 (SP)
Link Register	R14 (LR)
Program Counter	R15 (PC)

R13 (SP)
Banked Version of SP

Program Status Register   PSR

Floating Point Registers

#if (OS_CPU_ARM_FP_EN == DEF_ENABLED)

◄—— 32 bit ——►

FPSCR   Floating-Point Status Control

S0
S1
S2
S3
S4
S5
S6
S7
S8
S9
S10
S11
S12
.
.
.
S31

Floating Point Registers

Figure 2-1 **The Cortex-M4 CPU Registers**

2-1-1 THE PROGRAM STATUS REGISTER

In addition to the CPU registers there is a separate register called the Program Status Register (PSR). The PSR is not part of the main CPU registers and is only accessible through two dedicated instructions. The PSR contains a number of fields that influence the execution of the Cortex CPU. Refer to the Cortex-M4 Technical Reference Manual for details.

31					26	25	24	23		16	15		10	9	8	7		0
N	Z	C	V	Q	ICI/IT		T				ICI/IT					ISR Number		

Figure 2-2 **The Cortex-M4 PSR Register**

While most Thumb-2 instructions execute in a single cycle, some (such as load and store instructions) take multiple cycles. To enable the Cortex CPU to have a deterministic interrupt response time, these instructions are interruptible.

2-1-2 STACKING AND INTERRUPTS

Tasks execute in Thread mode using the process stack; interrupts execute in Handler mode using the main stack. The task context is automatically saved on the process stack when an exception occurs, whereupon the processor moves to Handler mode, making the main stack active. On return from the exception, the task context is restored and Thread mode reinstated.

Figure 2-3 shows the stacking order of the CPU registers during an exception or interrupt. The software only needs to save/restore registers R4-R11 (if required by the Interrupt Service Routine); the other registers are saved automatically by hardware upon accepting the interrupt.

```
#if (OS_CPU_ARM_FP_EN == DEF_DISABLED)
```

Core Registers

R13 (SP_{process})	**Top Of Stack**	

← 32 bit →

Register	
R4	
R5	
R6	Saved by software during context switch
R7	
R8	
R9	
R10	
R11	
R0	
R1	
R2	Automatically saved by hardware during context switch
R3	
R12	
R14 (LR)	
R15 (PC)	
PSR	

Lower Memory Address

Higher Memory Address

Figure 2-3 **Cortex-M4 Register Stacking Order (FPU Disabled)**

If the FPU is enabled by setting OS_CPU_ARM_FP_EN to DEF_ENABLED, then µC/OS-III will also save/restore the Floating-Point Status Control Register (FPSCR) and the 32 Floating-Point Registers (S0-S31) when an exception occurs. In this case, the stacking order starts from the Program Status Register (PSR) in the Core Registers all the way to the General Purpose Register R4 and then continue with the FPU registers from the Floating-Point Status Control Register (FPSCR) all the way to the Floating-Point Register S0, which will be the new top-of-stack as illustrated in Figure 2-4.

```
#if (OS_CPU_ARM_FP_EN == DEF_ENABLED)
```

Floating Point Registers

Top Of Stack

R13 (SP_{process})

◄— **32 bit** —►

| S0 |
| S1 |
| S2 |
| S3 |
| . |
| . |
| . |
| S31 |
| FPSCR |

Saved by software during context switch

Lower Memory Address

| R4 |
| R5 |
| R6 |
| R7 |
| R8 |
| R9 |
| R10 |
| R11 |

Saved by software during context switch

| R0 |
| R1 |
| R2 |
| R3 |
| R12 |
| R14 (LR) |
| R15 (PC) |
| PSR |

Automatically saved by hardware during context switch

◄— **32 bit** —►

Higher Memory Address

Core Registers

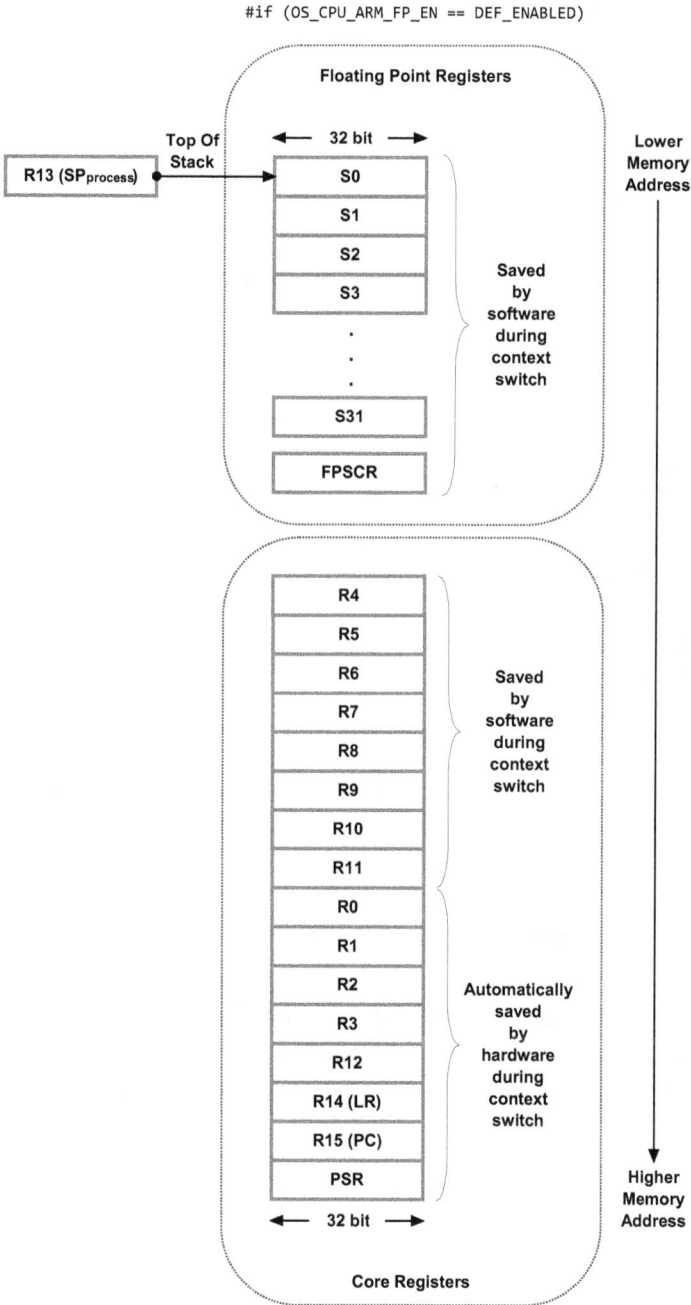

Figure 2-4 **Cortex-M4 Register Stacking Order (FPU Enabled)**

771

2-2 NESTED VECTOR INTERRUPT CONTROLLER (NVIC)

The Cortex-M4 includes not only the core CPU (ALU, control logic, data interface, instruction decoding, etc.), but also several integrated peripherals. Most important is the Nested Vectored Interrupt Controller (NVIC), designed for low latency, efficiency and configurability.

The NVIC saves half of the processor registers automatically upon interrupt, restoring them upon exit, which allows for efficient interrupt handling. Moreover, back-to-back interrupts are handled without saving/restoring registers (since that is unnecessary). This is called Tail Chaining.

The NVIC offers 8 to 256 priority levels, with dynamic priority assignment. The NVIC also is capable of handling between 1 and 240 external interrupt sources.

The NVIC is a standard unit within the Cortex core. This means that all Cortex-based microcontrollers have the same interrupt structure, regardless of the manufacturer. Therefore, application code and operating systems can be easily ported from one microcontroller to another, and the programmer does not need to learn a new set of registers. The NVIC is also designed to have very low interrupt latency. This is both a feature of the NVIC itself and of the Thumb-2 instruction set, which allows such multi-cycle instructions as load and store multiple to be interruptible.

The NVIC peripheral eases the migration between Cortex-M4 processors. This is particularly true for µC/OS-III.

2-3 EXCEPTION VECTOR TABLE

The Cortex vector table starts at the bottom of the address range. However, rather than start at zero, the vector table starts at address 0x00000004 and the first four bytes are used to store the starting address of the stack pointer. The vector table is shown in Table 2-1.

Each of the interrupt vector entries is four bytes wide and holds the start address of each service routine associated with the interrupt. The first 15 entries are for exceptions that occur within the Cortex core. These include the reset vector, non-maskable interrupt, fault and error management, debug exceptions, and the SysTick timer interrupt. The Thumb-2 instruction set also includes system service call instructions which, when executed, generate an exception. The user peripheral interrupts start from entry 16, and will be linked to peripherals as defined by the manufacturer. In software, the vector table is usually maintained in the startup by locating the service routine addresses at the base of memory.

No.	Type	Priority	Type of Priority	Description
1	Reset	-3	Fixed	Reset
2	NMI	-2	Fixed	Non-Maskable Interrupts
3	Hard Fault	-1	Fixed	Default fault if other handler not implemented
4	MemManageFault	0	Settable	MPU violation
5	Bus Fault	1	Settable	Fault if AHB error
6	Usage Fault	2	Settable	Program error exception
7-10	Reserved		N/A	
11	SV Call	3	Settable	System Call Service
12	Debug Monitor	4	Settable	Breakpoints, watchpoints, external debug
13	Reserved	N/A	N/A	
14	PendSV	5	Settable	Pendable request
15	SysTick	6	Settable	System tick timer
16	Interrupt #0	7	Settable	External interrupt #0
:	:	:	Settable	:
:	:	:	Settable	:
256	Interrupt #240	247	Settable	External interrupt #240

Table 2-1 **The Cortex-M4 Exception Table**

The PendSV vector is used by µC/OS-III to perform a context switch, while the SysTick vector is used by µC/OS-III for the clock tick interrupt.

2-4 SYSTICK (SYSTEM TICK)

The Cortex core includes a 24-bit down counter with auto reload and end of count interrupt, called the SysTick. The SysTick was designed to be used as an RTOS clock tick interrupt, and it is present in all Cortex implementations.

The SysTick timer has three registers. The current value and reload value should be initialized with the count period. The control and status register contains an ENABLE bit to start the timer running, and a TICKINT bit to enable its interrupt line.

The SysTick peripheral eases the migration between Cortex-M4 processors, which is particularly true for µC/OS-III.

2-5 MEMORY MAP

Unlike most previous ARM processors, the Cortex-M4 has a fixed-memory map as shown in Figure 2-5.

Figure 2-5 **Cortex-M4 Memory Map**

The first 1.0 Gbyte of memory is split evenly between a code region and a SRAM region. Although code can be loaded and executed from the SRAM, instructions would be fetched using the system bus, which incurs an extra wait state. It is likely that code would run slower from SRAM than from on-chip FLASH memory located in the code region.

The next 0.5 Gbyte of memory is the on-chip peripheral region. All user peripherals provided by the microcontroller vendor will be located in this region.

The first Mbyte of both the SRAM and Peripheral regions is bit-addressable using a technique called bit banding. Since all SRAM and user peripherals on the processor are located in these regions, every memory location of the processor can be manipulated in a word-wide or bitwise fashion.

The next 2.0 Gbytes of address space is allocated to external memory-mapped SRAM and peripherals.

The final 0.5 Gbyte is allocated to the internal Cortex processor peripherals and a region for future vendor-specific enhancements to the Cortex processor. All Cortex processor registers are at fixed locations for all Cortex-based microcontrollers.

2-6 INSTRUCTION SET

The ARM7 and ARM9 CPUs execute two instruction sets: the ARM 32-bit instruction set and the Thumb 16-bit instruction set. This allows developers to optimize a program by selecting the instruction set used for different procedures: for example, 32-bit instructions for speed, and 16-bit instructions for code compression.

The Cortex CPU is designed to execute the Thumb-2 instruction set, which is a blend of 16-bit and 32-bit instructions. The Thumb-2 instruction set yields a 26% code density improvement over the ARM 32-bit instruction set, and a 25% improvement in performance over the Thumb 16-bit instruction set.

The Thumb-2 instruction set has improved multiply instructions, which can execute in a single cycle, and a hardware divide that takes between 2 – 7 cycles.

Of special interest to µC/OS-III is the Count Leading Zeros (CLZ) instruction, which greatly improves the scheduling algorithm, See Chapter 6, "The Ready List" on page 139 in Part I of this book.

2-7 DEBUG AND TRACE FEATURES

The XMC4500 Series Microcontrollers provide a large variety of debug, trace and test features. They are implemented with a standard configuration of the ARM CoreSight^{TM} module together with a daisy chained standard TAP controller.

Debug and trace functions are integrated into the ARM Cortex-M4. The debug system supports serial wire debug (SWD) and trace functions in addition to standard JTAG debug and parallel trace.

The Debug and Trace System implements ARM CoreSight^{TM} debug and trace features with the objective of debugging the entire SoC.

The CoreSight^{TM} infrastructure includes a debug subsystem and a trace subsystem:

■ Debug Subsystem: the debug functionality includes processor halt, single-step, processor core register access, vector catch, unlimited software break points and full system memory access. The debug function includes a breakpoint unit supporting 2 literal comparators and 6 instruction comparators and a watchpoint unit supporting 4 watchpoints. The processing element (CPU) is paired with an instruction/data ETM (ETM-M4).

■ Trace Subsystem: CoreSight^{TM} enables different trace sources to be enabled into one stream. The unique trace stream, marked with suitable identifiers and timestamps. Trace can be done using either a 4-bit parallel or a Serial Wire interface. Less data can be traced with Serial Wire interface, but only one output pin is required for application. Parallel trace has a greater bandwidth, but uses 5 more pins.

The block diagram in Figure 2-6 shows the available features mapped to functions:

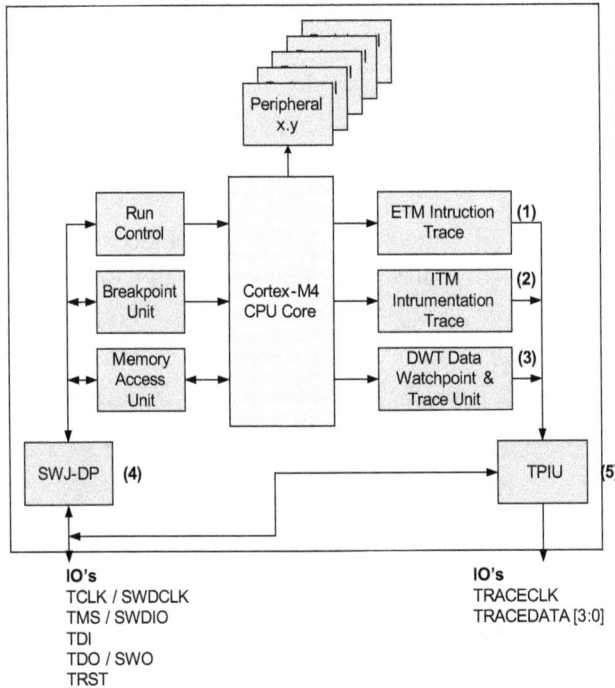

Figure 2-6 **Cortex-M4 Debug and Trace System**

F2-6(1)   The Embedded Trace Macrocell (ETM) provides instruction trace capabilities.

F2-6(2)   Application driven trace source, supports `printf` style debugging. The Instrumentation Trace Macrocell (ITM) generates trace information as packets out of four sources (Software Trace, Hardware Trace, Time Stamping and Global System Time Stamping).

F2-6(3)   Implemented watch points, trigger resources, and system profiling. The DWT contains four comparators that can be configured as a hardware watchpoint, an ETM trigger, a PC sampler event trigger or a data address sampler event trigger, data sampler, interrupt trace and CPU statistics.

F2-6(4)   This debug port provides native JTAG debug capabilities.

F2-6(5)   The TPIU encodes and provides trace information to the debugger. As ports the single wire viewer (TRACESWO) or 4-bit Trace Port (TRACEDATA[3:0], TRACECLK) can be used.

2-8 THE INFINEON XMC4500

The XMC4500 series belongs to the XMC4000 family of industrial microcontrollers based on the ARM Cortex-M4 processor core. The XMC4500 series devices are optimized for electrical motor control, power conversion, industrial connectivity and sense & control applications.

The growing complexity of today's energy efficient embedded control applications are demanding microcontroller solutions with higher performance CPU cores featuring DSP (Digital Signal Processing) and FPU (Floating Point Unit) capabilities as well as integrated peripherals that are optimized for performance. Complemented with a development environment designed to shorten product development time and increase productivity, the XMC4500 series of microcontrollers take advantage of Infineon's decades of experience in microcontroller design, providing an optimized solution to meet the performance challenges of today's embedded control applications.

The XMC4500 series devices combine the extended functionality and performance of the ARM Cortex-M4 core with powerful on-chip peripheral subsystems and on-chip memory units. The following key features are available in the XMC4500 series devices:

2-8-1 CPU SUBSYSTEM

■ CPU Core

  ▨ High Performance 32-bit ARM Cortex-M4 CPU

  ▨ 16-bit and 32-bit Thumb2 instruction set

  ▨ DSP/MAC instructions

  ▨ System timer (SysTick) for Operating System support

■ Floating Point Unit

■ Memory Protection Unit

■ Nested Vectored Interrupt Controller

■ Two General Purpose DMA with up to 12 channels

■ Event Request Unit (ERU) for programmable processing of external and internal service requests

■ Flexible CRC Engine (FCE) for multiple bit error detection

2-8-2 ON-CHIP MEMORIES

■ 16 KB on-chip boot ROM

■ 64 KB on-chip high-speed program memory

■ 64 KB on-chip high speed data memory

■ 32 KB on-chip high-speed communication

■ 1024 KB on-chip Flash Memory with 4 KB instruction cache

2-8-3 COMMUNICATION PERIPHERALS

■ Ethernet MAC module capable of 10/100 Mbit/s transfer rates

■ Universal Serial Bus, USB 2.0 host, Full-Speed OTG, with integrated PHY

■ Controller Area Network interface (MultiCAN), Full-CAN/Basic-CAN with three nodes, 64 message objects, data rate up to 1 Mbit/s

■ Six Universal Serial Interface Channels (USIC), usable as UART, double-SPI, quad-SPI, IIC, IIS and LIN interfaces

■ LED and Touch-Sense Controller (LEDTS) for Human-Machine interface

■ SD and Multi-Media Card interface (SDMMC) for data storage memory cards

■ External Bus Interface Unit (EBU) enabling communication with external memories and off-chip peripherals like SRAM, SDRAM, NOR, NAND and Burst Flash.

2-8-4 ANALOG FRONTEND PERIPHERALS

■ Four Analog-to-Digital Converters (VADC) of 12-bit resolution, 8 channels each with input out-of-range comparators for over-voltage detection

■ Delta Sigma Demodulator with four channels, digital input stage for A/D signal conversion

■ Digital-to-Analog Converter (DAC) with two channels of 12-bit resolution

2-8-5 INDUSTRIAL CONTROL PERIPHERALS

■ Four Capture/Compare Units 4 (CCU4) for use as general purpose timers

■ Two Capture/Compare Units 8 (CCU8) for motor control and power conversion

■ Two Position Interfaces (POSIF) for hall and quadrature encoders and motor positioning

■ Window Watchdog Timer (WDT) for safety sensitive applications

■ Die Temperature Sensor (DTS)

■ Real Time Clock module with alarm support

■ System Control Unit (SCU) for system configuration and control

2-8-6 INPUT/OUTPUT LINES

■ Programmable port driver control module (PORTS)

■ Individually bit addressable

■ Tri-stated in input mode

■ Push/pull or open drain output mode

■ Boundary scan test support over JTAG interface

3

Setup

In this chapter you will learn how to setup an environment to run the μC/OS-III-based projects featured in this book.

It is assumed that the following elements are available:

■ Hardware

  ▦ A Windows™-based PC running Windows-XP or Windows 7

  ▦ The Infineon XMC4500 CPU board

  ▦ Segger's J-Link Pro Debugger

  ▦ J-Link Adapter for Cortex-M

  ▦ A USB cable to power up the CPU board

  ▦ A USB cable to program and debug the μC/OS-III examples

■ Software

  ▦ IAR Systems Embedded Workbench for ARM (EWARM)

  ▦ Micrium's book companion software

The following sections will describe each of the hardware and software requirements.

3-1 HARDWARE

3-1-1 THE INFINEON XMC4500 CPU BOARD

The XMC4500 CPU board shown in Figure 3-1 is available for purchase on the Infineon website at http://www.infineon.com/xmc_kits

Figure 3-1 **Infineon XMC4500 CPU Board**

This CPU board is part of Infineon's Hexagon Application Kits and in their most basic kit, it includes:

■ CPU Board XMC4500 General Purpose (CPU_45A-V2)

■ Pin Extension Board (UNI_EXT01-V2)

■ USB cable

3-1-2 SEGGER'S J-LINK PRO DEBUGGER

The XMC4500 CPU board supports JTAG debugging via 3 different connectors:

▪ Cortex Debug Connector (10-pin)

▪ Cortex Debug+ETM Connector (20-pin)

▪ DriveMonitor2 Connector

J-Link is a JTAG emulator designed for ARM cores and we recommend using the J-Link Pro Debugging Probe from Segger as it not only allows you to download and debug the code but it also makes the interface with µC/Probe ready.

The J-Link Pro shown in Figure 3-2 is available for purchase on Segger's website at:

http://www.segger.com/jlink-pro.html

Figure 3-2 **J-Link Pro Debugger**

Additionally, you will need a J-Link 19-pin Cortex-M Adapter, which allows JTAG, SWD and SWO connections between J-Link and Cortex-M based target hardware systems.

The adapter is also available for purchase on Segger's website at:

`http://www.segger.com/jlink-adapters.html#CM_19pin`

It adapts from the 20-pin 0.1" JTAG connector in the J-Link Pro to the 19-pin 0.05" Samtec FTSH connector onboard the XMC4500 CPU board as defined by ARM.

Figure 3-3 illustrates how to connect the XMC4500 CPU board to a PC.

Figure 3-3 **Connecting a PC to the XMC4500 CPU Board**

3-2 SOFTWARE

To run the examples provided with this book, it will be necessary to download a number of files from the Internet.

3-2-1 IAR EMBEDDED WORKBENCH FOR ARM

The KickStart edition of IAR Embedded Workbench for ARM is a fully functional integrated development environment including project manager, editor, compiler, assembler, linker, librarian and debugger tools.

The examples provided with this book were tested using the IAR Embedded Workbench for ARM V6.40.

The KickStart edition of IAR Embedded Workbench for ARM is completely free of charge and you may use it for as long as you want. The KickStart tools are ideal for creating small applications or for getting started fast on a new project. The only requirement is that you register with IAR to get an evaluation license key.

You can download the IAR Embedded Workbench for ARM from the IAR website at:

`http://www.iar.com/ewarm`

You can use the full version of the IAR Embedded Workbench if you are already a licensee.

3-2-2 MICRIUM BOOK'S COMPANION SOFTWARE

The µC/OS-III book and the XMC4500 CPU board do not include CDs. Instead, project files are actually downloadable from the Micriµm website. This allows samples to be kept up to date.

To obtain the µC/OS-III software and example projects, simply point your favorite browser to:

`http://www.Micrium.com/Books/Micrium-uCOS-III`

You will be required to register. This means that you'll have to provide information about yourself. This information will be used for market research purposes and will allow us to contact you should new updates of µC/OS-III for this book become available. Your information will be held in strict confidence.

Extract to your PC the following zip file:

Micrium-Book-uCOS-III-XMC4500.zip

Figure 3-4 shows the directory structure contained in this zip file.

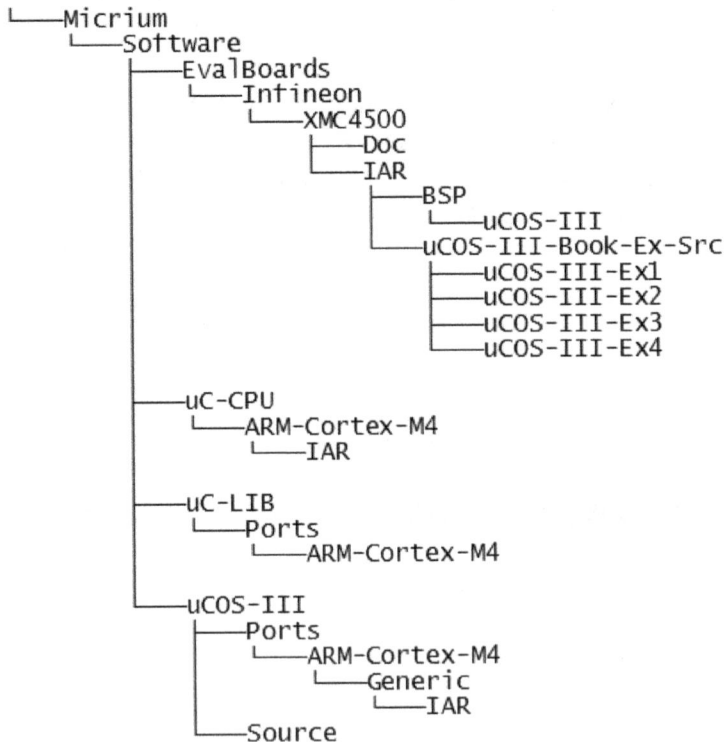

```
└──Micrium
    └──Software
        ├──EvalBoards
        │   └──Infineon
        │       └──XMC4500
        │           ├──Doc
        │           └──IAR
        │               ├──BSP
        │               │   └──uCOS-III
        │               └──uCOS-III-Book-Ex-Src
        │                   ├──uCOS-III-Ex1
        │                   ├──uCOS-III-Ex2
        │                   ├──uCOS-III-Ex3
        │                   └──uCOS-III-Ex4
        ├──uC-CPU
        │   └──ARM-Cortex-M4
        │       └──IAR
        ├──uC-LIB
        │   └──Ports
        │       └──ARM-Cortex-M4
        └──uCOS-III
            ├──Ports
            │   └──ARM-Cortex-M4
            │       └──Generic
            │           └──IAR
            └──Source
```

Figure 3-4 **µC/OS-III Project Directories**

All files are placed under the \Micrium\Software directory. There are four main sub-directories: \EvalBoards, \uC-CPU, \uC-LIB and \uCOS-III as described next.

\EvalBoards

This is the standard Micriµm sub-directory where all evaluation board examples are placed. The sub-directory contains additional sub-directories organizing evaluation boards by manufacturers. In this case, \Infineon is the manufacturer of the XMC4500 CPU board, and projects for this board are placed under: \XMC4500.

The \EvalBoards\Infineon\XMC4500 sub-directory contains further directories.

\Doc contains the XMC4500 datasheet.

\IAR contains the main IAR IDE workspace, which includes the four projects provided with this book. Specifically, the file uCOS-III-Book-Ex-Src.eww is the workspace to open with the IAR Embedded Workbench for ARM.

Projects will be described in the next four chapters. This sub-directory contains five additional sub-directories:

```
\BSP
\uCOS-III-Ex1
\uCOS-III-Ex2
\uCOS-III-Ex3
\uCOS-III-Ex4
```

\IAR\bsp.c contains Board Support Package (BSP) files used to support the peripherals found on the XMC4500 CPU board. The contents of these files will be described as needed within the sample projects. This sub-directory contains the following files:

```
bsp.c
bsp.h
bsp_int.c
cpu_bsp.c
\uCOS-III\bsp_os.c
\uCOS-III\bsp_os.h
```

\IAR\uCOS-III-Book-Ex-Src\uCOS-III-Ex1 presents a simple project that demonstrates how to properly initialize and start a µC/OS-III-based application. This project is described in Chapter 5, "µC/OS-III Example #1" on page 803.

\IAR\uCOS-III-Book-Ex-Src\uCOS-III-Ex2 presents a project that reads the on-board potentiometer and displays the position using µC/Probe. This project will be described in Chapter 6, "µC/OS-III Example #2" on page 817.

\IAR\uCOS-III-Book-Ex-Src\uCOS-III-Ex3 presents a project that measures some performance metrics on µC/OS-III. This project will be described in Chapter 7, "µC/OS-III Example #3" on page 823.

\IAR\uCOS-III-Book-Ex-Src\uCOS-III-Ex4 presents a project that simulates the measurement of a rotating device. This project will be described in Chapter 8, "µC/OS-III Example #4" on page 839.

\uC-CPU

This sub-directory contains the generic and Cortex-M4-specific files for the µC/CPU module. These are described in Appendix B, "µC/CPU Port for the Cortex-M4" on page 877. This sub-directory contains the following files:

> **cpu_core.c**
> **cpu_core.h**
> **cpu_def.h**
> \ARM-Cortex-M4\IAR**cpu.h**
> \ARM-Cortex-M4\IAR**cpu_a.asm**
> \ARM-Cortex-M4\IAR**cpu_c.c**
> \Cfg\Template**cpu_cfg.h**
> \Doc**uC-CPU-Manual.pdf**
> \Doc**uC-CPU-ReleaseNotes.pdf**

*.h

These are the header files that need to be added to the project when using the module along with µC/OS-III.

\uC-LIB

This sub-directory contains compiler-independent library functions to manipulate ASCII strings, perform memory copies, and more. We refer to these files as being part of the µC/LIB module. **lib_def.h** contains a number of useful **#defines**, such as **DEF_FALSE**, **DEF_TRUE**, **DEF_ON**, **DEF_OFF**, **DEF_ENABLED**, **DEF_DISABLED**, and dozens more. µC/LIB also declares such macros as **DEF_MIN( )**, **DEF_MAX( )**, **DEF_ABS( )**, and more.

This sub-directory contains the following files:

```
lib_ascii.c
lib_ascii.h
lib_def.h
lib_math.c
lib_math.h
lib_mem.c
lib_mem.h
lib_str.c
lib_str.h
\Doc\uC-Lib-Manual.pdf
\Doc\uC-Lib-ReleaseNotes.pdf
\Ports\ARM-Cortex-M4\IAR\lib_mem_a.asm
\Doc\uC-Lib_Manual.pdf
\Doc\uC-Lib-ReleaseNotes.pdf
```

*.h
These are header files that need to be added in a project when using this module with µC/OS-III.

\uCOS-III

This sub-directory contains the following files:

```
\Cfg\Template\os_app_hooks.c
\Cfg\Template\os_app_hooks.h
\Cfg\Template\os_cfg.h
\Cfg\Template\os_cfg_app.h
\Ports\ARM-Cortex-M4\Generic\IAR\os_cpu_a.asm
\Ports\ARM-Cortex-M4\Generic\IAR\os_cpu_c.c
```

```
\Ports\ARM-Cortex-M4\Generic\IAR\os_cpu.h
\Source\os_cfg_app.c
\Source\os_core.c
\Source\os_dbg.c
\Source\os_flag.c
\Source\os_int.c
\Source\os_mem.c
\Source\os_msg.c
\Source\os_mutex.c
\Source\os_pend_multi.c
\Source\os_prio.c
\Source\os_q.c
\Source\os_sem.c
\Source\os_stat.c
\Source\os_task.c
\Source\os_tick.c
\Source\os_time.c
\Source\os_tmr.c
\Source\os.h
\Source\os_type.h
\Source\os_var.c
```

*.h

These are the header files that need to be added to a project.

3-2-3 Micriµm's µC/Probe

µC/Probe is a Microsoft Windows-based application that allows users to display or change the value (at run time) of virtually any variable or memory location on a connected embedded target. See Appendix C, "Introduction to µC/Probe" on page 889 for a brief introduction.

µC/Probe is used in the examples described in Chapter 1, "Part II Chapter Contents" on page 760 to gain run-time visibility. There are two versions of µC/Probe:

■ The Full Version allows users to display or change an unlimited number of variables.

■ The Trial Version is not time limited, but only allows users to display or change up to five application variables. However, the trial version also allows users to monitor any µC/OS-III variables because µC/Probe is µC/OS-III aware.

Both versions are available from Micriµm's website. Simply point your browser to:

```
http://www.micrium.com/probe
```

CONFIGURING µC/PROBE TO WORK WITH J-LINK

The J-Link Pro debugger from Segger not only allows you to download and debug the code but also to communicate with µC/Probe. The best thing of all is that you can run IAR's Embedded Workbench for ARM and µC/Probe at the same time as illustrated in Figure 3-5:

Figure 3-5 **µC/Probe and EWARM via J-Link**

If you followed the installation instructions for EWARM, then the J-Link drivers for the J-Link Pro are already installed in your computer.

The only thing necessary is to configure µC/Probe with the path in your file system to the J-Link driver.

Open µC/Probe and click the *Settings* button on the top toolbar and the application will open the configuration screen shown in Figure 3-6:

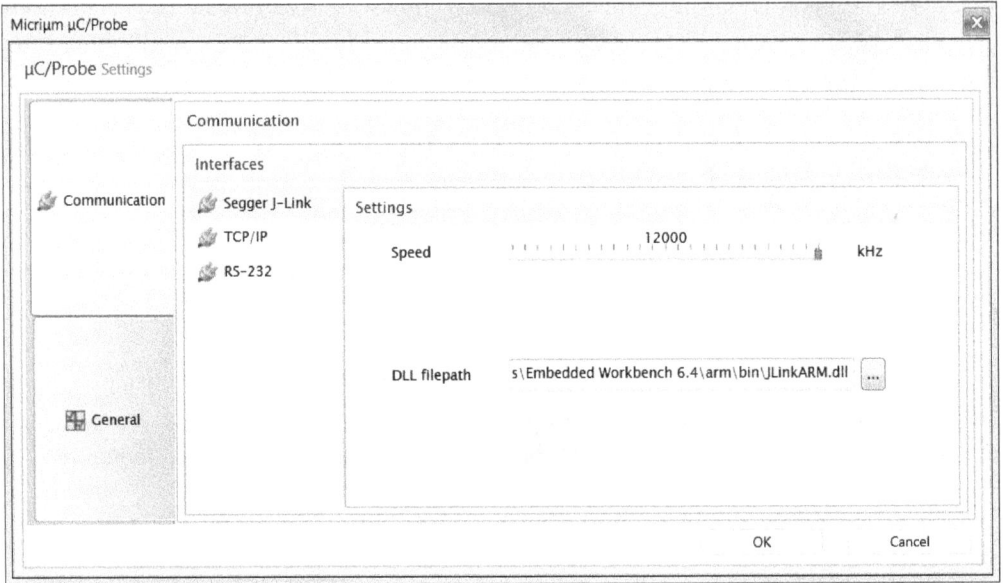

Figure 3-6 **µC/Probe Configuration Screen**

Configure the J-Link driver's DLL path by browsing to the following folder in your file system:

```
$\Program Files (x86)\IAR Systems\Embedded Workbench 6.4\arm
 \bin\JLinkARM.dll
```

Click *OK* and the J-Link driver will be used the next time you want to interface with the XMC4500 CPU board.

This configuration screen also allows you to specify the speed which can be increased for better performance.

IAR Embedded Workbench for ARM (EWARM)

IAR Systems Embedded Workbench for ARM, also known as EWARM, is a complete development and debug environment for applications based on 8, 16 and 32-bit microcontrollers. It incorporates a high performance compiler, an assembler, a linker and a debugger into one integrated development environment (IDE). The entire IDE is developed and supported by IAR Systems which unlike other tools in the market, provides you a single toolbox in which all components integrate seamlessly and are fully tested.

This chapter describes the processes of editing, project managing, building, debugging, and provides related reference information.

If you are new to using this product, we suggest that you first read this chapter before trying the µC/OS-III example projects.

4-1 KEY COMPONENTS

- Integrated development environment with project management tools and editor

- Highly optimizing C and C++ compiler for ARM

- Automatic checking of MISRA C rules (MISRA C:2004)

- ARM EABI and CMSIS compliance

- Extensive HW target system support

- Optional I-jet and JTAGjet hardware debug probes

- Power debugging to visualize power consumption in correlation with source code

4

- Run-time libraries including source code

- Relocating ARM assembler

- Linker and librarian tools

- C-SPY® debugger with ARM simulator, JTAG support and support for RTOS-aware debugging on hardware

- RTOS plugins available from IAR Systems and RTOS vendors such as Micriμm

- Over 3100 sample projects for evaluation boards from many different manufacturers

- User and reference guides in PDF format

- Context-sensitive online help

4-2 OPENING A WORKSPACE

Workspace files have the extension **.eww** and the μC/OS-III project examples featured in this book are contained in a workspace located at:

```
\Micrium\Software\EvalBoards\Infineon\XMC4500\IAR\
 uCOS-III-Book-Ex-Src\uCOS-III-Book-Ex-Src.eww
```

In order to open a workspace select *File -> Open -> Workspace* as shown in Figure 4-1:

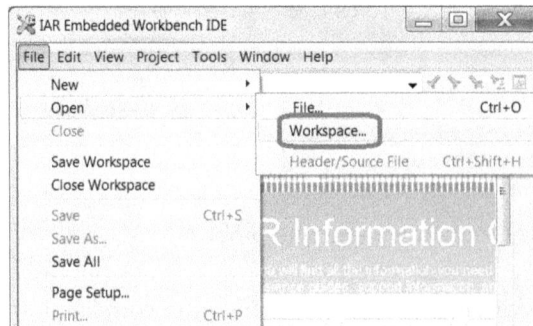

Figure 4-1 **Opening Workspace uCOS-III-Book-Ex-Src.eww**

4-3 SETTING A PROJECT ACTIVE

Once the workspace is open, the workspace explorer window is populated with all the µC/OS-III project examples. Click on one of the tabs at the bottom of the workspace explorer to select a project as indicated in Figure 4-2:

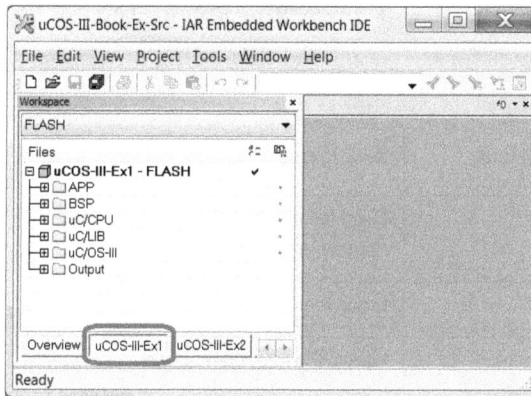

Figure 4-2 **Setting a Project Active**

4-4 COMPILING, PROGRAMMING AND DEBUGGING

Click on the Download and Debug button on the far right in the IAR Embedded Workbench as indicated in Figure 4-3:

Figure 4-3 **Downloading and Debugging**

Embedded Workbench will compile and link the code, program the object file onto Flash, and launch a C-SPY® debugging session, all with the single press of a button.

4-5 DEBUGGING TOOLS

C-SPY® is a high-level-language debugger for embedded applications. It is designed for use with the IAR Systems compilers and assemblers, and is completely integrated in the IDE, providing development and debugging within the same application.

Once a debug session is launched, C-SPY® makes available a debug menu. The debug menu provides commands for executing and debugging the source application as follows:

Command	Shortcut	Description
Go	F5	Executes from the current statement or instruction until a breakpoint or program exit is reached.
Break	N/A	Stops the application execution.
Reset	N/A	Resets the target processor.
Stop Debugging	Ctrl+Shift+D	Stops the debugging session and returns you to the project manager.
Step Over	F10	Executes the next statement, function call, or instruction, without entering C or C++ functions or assembler subroutines.
Step Into	F11	Executes the next statement or instruction, or function call, entering C or C++ functions or assembler subroutines.
Step Out	Shift+F11	Executes from the current statement up to the statement after the call to the current function.
Next Statement	N/A	Executes directly to the next statement without stopping at individual function calls.
Run to Cursor	N/A	Executes from the current statement or instruction up to a selected statement or instruction

Table 4-1 **Debugging Commands**

Most commands are also available as icon buttons on the debug toolbar as shown in Figure 4-4:

Figure 4-4 **Debugging Tools**

4-6 µC/OS-III KERNEL AWARENESS PLUGIN FOR C-SPY®

C-SPY® RTOS Awareness plugin modules give you a high level of control and visibility over an application built on top of a real-time operating system such as Micriµm's µC/OS-III.

The µC/OS-III kernel awareness plugin for C-SPY® is fully integrated with IAR Embedded Workbench and it is part of their official product release.

This plugin installs a number of new windows in C-SPY®, most importantly the task list window where each task's stack usage, CPU usage and other run-time statistics are displayed. Different inspector windows display the contents of µC/OS-III internal data

799

structures such as timers, message queues, semaphores and other kernel objects as shown in Figure 4-5:

Figure 4-5 µC/OS-III Kernel Awareness Plugin for C-SPY®

The new windows can be shown or hidden by selecting them from the new µC/OS-III menu entry in the embedded workbench menu as shown in Figure 4-6.

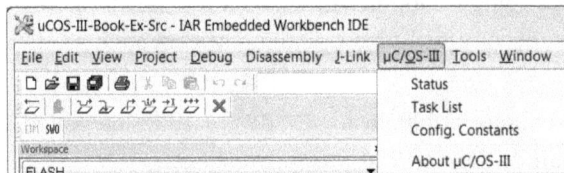

Figure 4-6 µC/OS-III Kernel Awareness Plugin Menu

All the example projects featured in this book are configured to use the μC/OS-III kernel awareness plugin. This is part of the project options under the Debugger category as shown in Figure 4-7:

Figure 4-7 **Configuring an RTOS Plugin into your Project**

Chapter

5

µC/OS-III Example #1

In this chapter you will see how easy it is to put together a µC/OS-III-based application.

This first project will perform the classical 'blink an LED' test. This is not exactly exciting, but it allows us to begin to put all the pieces together.

The GPIO port pin P3.9 on the XMC4500 CPU board is connected to an LED as indicated in Figure 5-1. More user LEDs are available through the I2C GPIO expander on most of the satellite cards.

Figure 5-1 **XMC4500 LED**

5

Set up the required software and hardware as described in Chapter 3, "Setup" on page 783.

Start the IAR Embedded Workbench for ARM and open the following workspace as described in section 4-2 "Opening a Workspace" on page 796:

```
\Micrium\Software\EvalBoards\Infineon\XMC4500\IAR\
  uCOS-III-Book-Ex-Src\uCOS-III-Book-Ex-Src.eww
```

Click on the **uCOS-III-Ex1** tab at the bottom of the workspace explorer to select the first project as described in section 4-3 "Setting a Project Active" on page 797.

Figure 5-2 shows the expanded file tree in the workspace explorer window.

■   The **APP** group is where the actual code for the example is placed, including the files to configure the application. I'll discuss some of the project configurations shortly.

■   The BSP group contains the 'Board Support Package' code to use some of the Input/Output (I/O) devices on the XMC4500 CPU board.

■   The **uC-CPU** group contains source files for the µC/CPU module which defines portable data-types and critical section macros for specific processor architectures and compilers such as the XMC4500 and the IAR compiler. All the examples featured in this book make reference to the portable data types defined by this µC/CPU module.

■   The **uC-LIB** group contains the source files for the µC/LIB module which replaces some of the C standard library functions in order to simplify third-party certification. All the examples make reference to the functions and macros defined by this µC/LIB module.

■   The **uCOS-III** group contains the source files for µC/OS-III. **os_cfg_app.c** needs to be compiled along with your application based on the contents of **os_cfg_app.h**.

```
Files
□ 🗇 uCOS-III-Ex1 - FLASH
  ├─🗀 APP
  │   ├─⊞ 🗎 app.c
  │   ├── 🗎 app_cfg.h
  │   ├── 🗎 cpu_cfg.h
  │   ├── 🗎 includes.h
  │   ├─⊞ 🗎 os_app_hooks.c
  │   ├── 🗎 os_app_hooks.h
  │   ├── 🗎 os_cfg.h
  │   └── 🗎 os_cfg_app.h
  ├─🗀 BSP
  │   ├─⊞ 🗎 bsp.c
  │   ├── 🗎 bsp.h
  │   ├─⊞ 🗎 bsp_int.c
  │   ├─⊞ 🗎 cpu_bsp.c
  │   ├─⊞ 🗎 cstartup.c
  │   └── 🗎 XMC4500_FLASH.icf
  ├─🗀 uC/CPU
  │   ├─🗀 ARM-Cortex-M4
  │   │   └─🗀 IAR
  │   │       ├── 🗎 cpu.h
  │   │       ├─⊞ 🗎 cpu_a.asm
  │   │       └─⊞ 🗎 cpu_c.c
  │   ├─⊞ 🗎 cpu_core.c
  │   ├── 🗎 cpu_core.h
  │   └── 🗎 cpu_def.h
  ├─🗀 uC/LIB
  │   ├─🗀 Ports
  │   │   └─🗀 ARM-Cortex-M4
  │   │       └─🗀 IAR
  │   │           └─⊞ 🗎 lib_mem_a.asm
  │   ├─⊞ 🗎 lib_ascii.c
  │   ├── 🗎 lib_ascii.h
  │   ├── 🗎 lib_def.h
  │   ├─⊞ 🗎 lib_math.c
  │   ├── 🗎 lib_math.h
  │   ├─⊞ 🗎 lib_mem.c
  │   ├── 🗎 lib_mem.h
  │   ├─⊞ 🗎 lib_str.c
  │   └── 🗎 lib_str.h
  ├─🗀 uC/OS-III
  │   ├─🗀 Ports
  │   │   └─🗀 ARM-Cortex-M4
  │   │       └─🗀 Generic
  │   │           └─🗀 IAR
  │   │               ├── 🗎 os_cpu.h
  │   │               ├─⊞ 🗎 os_cpu_a.asm
  │   │               └─⊞ 🗎 os_cpu_c.c
  │   └─🗀 Source
  │       ├── 🗎 os.h
  │       ├─⊞ 🗎 os_cfg_app.c
  │       ├─⊞ 🗎 os_core.c
  │       ├─⊞ 🗎 os_dbg.c
  │       ├─⊞ 🗎 os_flag.c
  │       ├─⊞ 🗎 os_int.c
  │       ├─⊞ 🗎 os_mem.c
  │       ├─⊞ 🗎 os_msg.c
  │       ├─⊞ 🗎 os_mutex.c
  │       ├─⊞ 🗎 os_pend_multi.c
  │       ├─⊞ 🗎 os_prio.c
  │       ├─⊞ 🗎 os_q.c
  │       ├─⊞ 🗎 os_sem.c
  │       ├─⊞ 🗎 os_stat.c
  │       ├─⊞ 🗎 os_task.c
  │       ├─⊞ 🗎 os_tick.c
  │       ├─⊞ 🗎 os_time.c
  │       ├─⊞ 🗎 os_tmr.c
  │       ├── 🗎 os_type.h
  │       └─⊞ 🗎 os_var.c
  └─⊞ 🗀 Output
```

Figure 5-2 **Expanded Project for uCOS-III-Ex1**

805

5-1 RUNNING THE PROJECT

Everything should be in place to run the example project. Connect the USB power cable and the J-Link Pro Debugger as shown in Chapter 3, "Connecting a PC to the XMC4500 CPU Board" on page 786.

Click on the *Download and Debug* button on the far right in the IAR Embedded Workbench as described in section 4-4 "Compiling, Programming and Debugging" on page 797. Embedded Workbench will not only compile and link the example code, but also program the object file onto the Flash of the XMC4500 using the J-Link Pro debugger.

The code will start executing and stop at **main()** in **app.c** as shown in Figure 5-3.

Figure 5-3 **Stops at main() After Code is Downloaded**

Using the debugging tools described in section 4-5 "Debugging Tools" on page 798, click on the debugger's *Go* button to continue execution and verify that the yellow LED right beside the potentiometer on P3.9 is blinking every 1-second.

Stop execution by clicking on the *Break* button and click on the *Reset* button to restart the application.

5-2 HOW THE EXAMPLE PROJECT WORKS

The code for **main()** is duplicated and shown in Listing 5-1 so that it is more readable.

```
int  main (void)
{
    OS_ERR  err;


    BSP_IntDisAll();                                                (1)
    OSInit(&err);                                                   (2)
    OSTaskCreate((OS_TCB     *)&AppTaskStartTCB,                    (3)
                 (CPU_CHAR   *)"App Task Start",
                 (OS_TASK_PTR )AppTaskStart,
                 (void       *)0,
                 (OS_PRIO     )APP_TASK_START_PRIO,
                 (CPU_STK    *)&AppTaskStartStk[0],
                 (CPU_STK_SIZE)APP_TASK_START_STK_SIZE / 10,
                 (CPU_STK_SIZE)APP_TASK_START_STK_SIZE,
                 (OS_MSG_QTY  )5,
                 (OS_TICK     )0,
                 (void       *)0,
                 (OS_OPT      )(OS_OPT_TASK_STK_CHK | OS_OPT_TASK_STK_CLR),
                 (OS_ERR     *)&err);
    OSStart(&err);                                                  (4)
}
```

Listing 5-1 **main() in app.c**

L5-1(1)   **main()** starts by calling **BSP_IntDisAll()**. The code for this function is found in **bsp_int.c**. **BSP_IntDisAll()** simply calls **CPU_IntDis()** to disable all interrupts. The reason a BSP function is used instead of simply calling **CPU_IntDis()** is that on some processors, it is necessary to disable interrupts

5

from the interrupt controller, which would then be appropriately handled by a BSP function. This way, the application code can easily be ported to another processor.

L5-1(2) OSInit() is called to initialize µC/OS-III. Normally, you will want to verify that OSInit() returns without any errors by verifying that **err** contains OS_ERR_NONE (*i.e.* the value 0). You can do this with the debugger by single stepping through the code (step over) and stop after OSInit() returns. Simply 'hover' the mouse over **err** and the current value of **err** will be displayed.

OSInit() creates four internal tasks: the idle task, the tick task, the timer task, and the statistics task. The interrupt handler queue task is not created because in os_cfg.h, OS_CFG_ISR_POST_DEFERRED_EN set to 0.

L5-1(3) OSTaskCreate() is called to create an application task called AppTaskStart(). OSTaskCreate() contains 13 arguments described in Appendix A, *µC/OS-III API Reference Manual* in Part I of this book.

AppTaskStartTCB is the OS_TCB used by the task. This variable is declared in the 'Local Variables' section in **app.c**, just a few lines above **main()**.

AppTaskStartStk[] is an array of **CPU_STKs** used to declare the stack for the task. In µC/OS-III, each task requires its own stack space. The size of the stack greatly depends on the application. In this example, the stack size is declared through APP_TASK_START_STK_SIZE, which is defined in **app_cfg.h**. 128 CPU_STK elements are allocated, which, on the Cortex-M4, corresponds to 512 bytes (each CPU_STK entry is 4 bytes, see cpu.h,) and this should be sufficient stack space for the simple code of AppTaskStart().

APP_TASK_START_PRIO determines the priority of the start task and is defined in app_cfg.h.

L5-1(4) OSStart() is called to start the multitasking process. With the application task, µC/OS-III will be managing five tasks. However, OSStart() will start the highest priority of the tasks created. In our example, the highest priority task is the AppTaskStart() task. OSStart() is not supposed to return. However, it would be wise to still add code to check the returned value.

The code for **AppTaskStart()** is shown in Listing 5-2.

```
static  void  AppTaskStart (void *p_arg)
{
    CPU_INT32U  cpu_clk_freq;
    CPU_INT32U  cnts;
    OS_ERR      err;


    (void)&p_arg;
    BSP_Init();                                                          (1)
    CPU_Init();                                                          (2)
    cpu_clk_freq = BSP_CPU_ClkFreq();                                    (3)
    cnts         = cpu_clk_freq / (CPU_INT32U)OSCfg_TickRate_Hz;
    OS_CPU_SysTickInit(cnts);
#if OS_CFG_STAT_TASK_EN > 0u
    OSStatTaskCPUUsageInit(&err);                                        (4)
#endif
    CPU_IntDisMeasMaxCurReset();                                         (5)
    BSP_LED_Off(0);                                                      (6)
    while (DEF_TRUE) {                                                   (7)
        BSP_LED_Toggle(0);                                              (8)
        OSTimeDlyHMSM(0, 0, 0, 500,                                     (9)
                          OS_OPT_TIME_HMSM_STRICT,
                          &err);
    }
}
```

Listing 5-2 **AppTaskStart() in app.c**

L5-2(1)   **AppTaskStart()** starts by calling **BSP_Init()** (See **bsp.c**) to initialize peripherals used on the XMC4500 CPU board. **BSP_Init()** initializes different clock sources on the XMC4500. The crystal that feeds the XMC4500 runs at 12 MHz and the XMC4500's PLLs (Phase Locked Loops) and dividers are configured such that the CPU operates at 120 MHz.

L5-2(2)   **CPU_Init()** is called to initialize the µC/CPU services. **CPU_Init()** initializes internal variables used to measure interrupt disable time, the time stamping mechanism, and a few other services.

L5-2(3)   The Cortex-M4's system tick timer is initialized. **BSP_CPU_ClkFreq()** returns the frequency (in Hz) of the CPU, which is 120 MHz for the XMC4500. This value is used to compute the reload value for the Cortex-M4's system tick timer.

The computed value is passed to OS_CPU_SysTickInit(), which is part of the μC/OS-III port (os_cpu_c.c). Once the system tick is initialized, the XMC4500 will receive interrupts at the rate specified by OS_CFG_TICK_RATE_HZ (See os_cfg_app.c), which in turn is assigned to OSCfg_TickRate_Hz in os_cfg_app.c. The first interrupt will occur in 1/OS_CFG_TICK_RATE_HZ second, since the interrupt will occur only when the system tick timer reaches zero after being initialized with the computed value, cnts.

L5-2(4)   OSStatTaskCPUUsageInit() is called to determine the 'capacity' of the CPU. μC/OS-III will run 'only' its internal tasks for 1/10 of a second and determine the maximum number of time the idle task loops. The number of loops is counted and placed in the variable OSStatTaskCtr. This value is saved in OSStatTaskCtrMax just before OSStatTaskCPUUsageInit() returns. OSStatTaskCtrMax is used to determine the CPU usage when other tasks are added. Specifically, as you add tasks to the application OSStatTaskCtr (which is reset every 1/10 of a second) is incremented less by the idle task because other tasks consume CPU cycles. CPU usage is determined by the following equation:

$$OSStatTaskCPU\,Usage_{(\%)} = (100 - \frac{100 \times OSStatTaskCtr}{OSStatTaskCtrMax})$$

The value of OSStatTaskCPUUsage can be displayed at run-time by μC/Probe. However, this simple example barely uses any CPU time and most likely CPU usage will be near 0.

Note that as of V3.03.00, OSStatTaskCPUUsage has a range of 0 to 10,000 to represent 0.00 to 100.00%. In other words, OSStatTaskCPUUsage now has a resolution of 0.01% instead of 1%.

L5-2(5)   The μC/CPU module is configured (See cpu_cfg.h) to measure the amount of time interrupts are disabled. In fact, there are two measurements, total interrupt disable time assuming all tasks, and per-task interrupt disable time. Each task's OS_TCB stores the maximum interrupt disable time when the task runs. These values can be monitored by μC/Probe at run time. CPU_IntDisMeasMaxCurReset() initializes this measurement mechanism.

L5-2(6)   BSP_LED_Off() is called to turn off (by passing 0) all user-accessible LEDs on the XMC4500.

L5-2(7)   A typical µC/OS-III task is written as an infinite loop.

L5-2(8)   **BSP_LED_Toggle( )** is called to toggle the LED.

L5-2(9)   Finally, a µC/OS-III task needs to call a µC/OS-III function that will cause the task to wait for an event to occur. In this case, the event to occur is the passage of time. **OSTimeDlyHMSM( )** specifies that the calling task does not need to do anything else until 500 milliseconds expire. Since the LED is toggled, it will blink at a rate of 1 Hz (500 milliseconds on, 500 milliseconds off).

In the absence of any GUI, this blinking rate will allow you to quickly identify that the XMC4500 CPU board is running Example #1 (1 Hz).

5-3 MONITORING VARIABLES USING µC/PROBE

Click the 'Go' button in the IAR C-Spy® debugger in order to resume execution of the code.

Locate the µC/Probe shortcut like the one shown in Figure 5-4 and start µC/Probe.

Figure 5-4 **µC/Probe Icon**

Click File -> Open, in order to open the **uCOS-III-Ex1-Probe.wspx** workspace found in the following directory:

```
$\Micrium\Software\EvalBoards\Infineon\XMC4500\IAR\
  uCOS-III-Book-Ex-Src\uCOS-III-Ex1\
```

The µC/Probe screen should appear as the one shown in Figure 5-5.

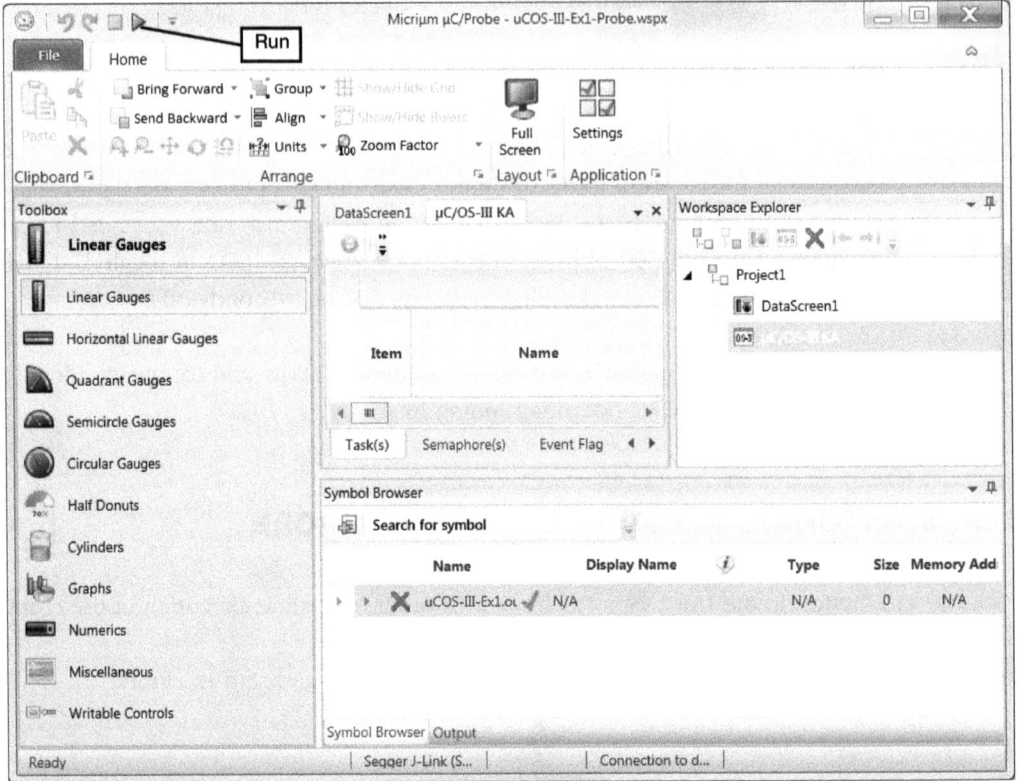

Figure 5-5 **µC/Probe Example #1 Design Mode Screen**

Click on the 'Run' button and see µC/Probe collect run-time data from the XMC4500 CPU board as shown in Figure 5-6. The 'µC/OS-III Tasks' tab shows run-time information about the five µC/OS-III tasks.

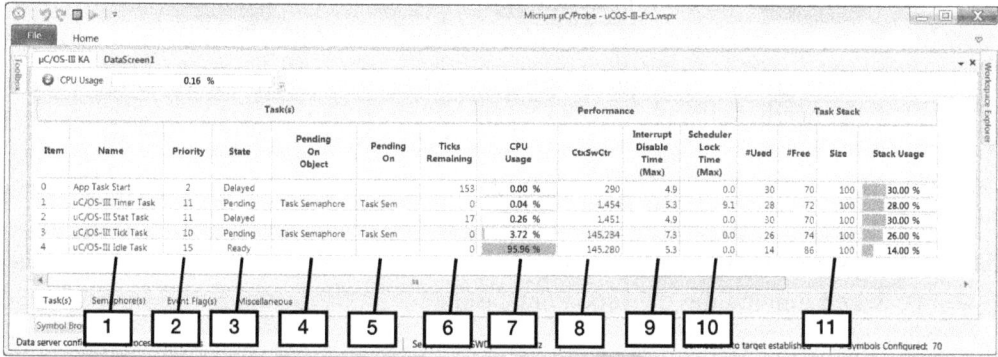

Figure 5-6 **µC/Probe Example #1 Run Mode Screen**

F5-6(1)   The first column displays the name of the task.

F5-6(2)   The priority of each task is displayed in the second column. µC/OS-III was configured to have up to 8 priority levels (0 to 7). The idle task is always assigned the lowest priority (*i.e.* 7). The statistic and timer tasks are executing at the same priority.

F5-6(3)   The next column indicates the state of each task. A task can be in one of eight states as described in Chapter 4, *Task Management* in Part I of this book.

    The idle task will always show that the task is ready. The tick and timer tasks will either be ready or pending because both tasks wait (*i.e.* pend) on their internal task semaphore. The statistics task will show delayed because it calls OSTimeDly() every 1/10th of a second.

F5-6(4)   The '**Pending on Object**' column indicates what a task is pending on if the task is in a pend state.

F5-6(5)   The '**Pending On**' column displays the name of the instance of the kernel object the task is pending on in the task is in the pend state.

F5-6(6)   The '**Ticks Remaining**' column indicates the amount of time left (in clock ticks) until a task time delay expires, or the task times out waiting on a kernel object such as a semaphore, message queue, or other.

5

F5-6(7)   The CPU Usage column indicates the CPU usage of each task relative to other tasks. The example consumes about 0.16% of the CPU. The idle task consumes 95.96% of that 0.16% or, 0.95% of the CPU. The tick task 3.72% and the other tasks nearly nothing.

F5-6(8)   The '**CtxSwCtr**' column indicates the number of times the task executed.

F5-6(9)   This column indicates the maximum amount of time interrupts were disabled when running the corresponding task.

F5-6(10)   This column indicates the maximum amount of time the scheduler was locked when running the corresponding task.

F5-6(11)   The next four columns indicate the stack usage of each task. This information is collected by the statistics task 10 times per second.

5-4 SUMMARY

There are several interesting things to notice.

1   With the on-board J-Link and the Cortex-M4 SWD interface, you can run Embedded Workbench concurrently with µC/Probe, even if you are stepping through the code. In other words, you can stop the debugger at a breakpoint and µC/Probe will continue reading values from the target. This allows you to see changes in variables as they are updated when stepping through code.

2   The display screens in µC/Probe only show µC/OS-III variables. However, µC/Probe allows you to 'see' any variable in the target as long as the variable is declared global or static. In fact, it is fairly easy to add the application task to the task list. This will be

shown in the example in Chapter 6, "µC/OS-III Example #2" on page 817.

3   Variables are updated on the µC/Probe data screen as quickly as the interface permits it. The J-Link interface should update variables at about 300 or so symbols per second. If µC/Probe uses the TCP/IP interface, we've seen updates easily exceeding 1,000 symbols/second. With TCP/IP, however, you will need to add target resident code (provided by Micriµm) and µC/Probe would only be able to update the display when the target is running.

The on-board J-Link and the IAR C-SPY debugger makes it easy to download the application to the target and Flash the XMC4500.

5

µC/OS-III Example #2

The XMC4500 CPU board provides a potentiometer for ease of use and testing of the on-chip analog-to-digital converter. The potentiometer is connected to the analog input G0_CH1 (P14.1) as indicated in Figure 6-1. The analog output of the potentiometer ranges from 0 V to 3.3 V.

The example described in this chapter will read the analog output of the potentiometer and will display the raw count in µC/Probe.

Potentiometer
on AI P14.1

Figure 6-1 **XMC4500 Potentiometer**

Setup the required software and hardware as described in Chapter 3, "Setup" on page 783.

Start the IAR Embedded Workbench for ARM and open the following workspace as described in section 4-2 "Opening a Workspace" on page 796:

```
\Micrium\Software\EvalBoards\Infineon\XMC4500\IAR\
  uCOS-III-Book-Ex-Src\uCOS-III-Book-Ex-Src.eww
```

6

Click on the **uCOS-III-Ex2** tab at the bottom of the workspace explorer to select the second project as described in section 4-3 "Setting a Project Active" on page 797. Notice that the file tree looks identical to the file tree of Example #1. The only file that changed is **app.c**.

6-1 RUNNING THE PROJECT

Connect the USB power cable and the J-Link Pro Debugger as shown in Chapter 3, "Connecting a PC to the XMC4500 CPU Board" on page 786.

Click on the *Download and Debug* button on the far right in the IAR Embedded Workbench as described in section 4-4 "Compiling, Programming and Debugging" on page 797.

Embedded Workbench will not only compile and link the example code, but also program the object file onto the Flash of the XMC4500 using the J-Link Pro debugger.

Notice how the code is almost exactly the same as the one presented in the previous chapter except that we turn on round-robin scheduling (by calling **OSSchedRoundRobinCfg()**) immediately after calling **OSInit()**. You might wonder then how is it possible for the previous example to run multiple tasks at the same priority when round-robin scheduling was turned off? The answer is simple, round robin occurs only when a task requires more processing than its time quanta. If a task takes less processing and calls a blocking function, the task behaves as any other task.

Using the debugging tools described in section 4-5 "Debugging Tools" on page 798, click on the debugger's *Go* button to continue execution and verify that the yellow LED is blinking at a rate of 2 Hz (that will indicate you are running example #2).

Stop execution by clicking on the *Stop* button and then click on the *Reset* button to restart the application.

In the debugger window, scroll down slightly to expose the code for **AppTaskStart()** as shown in Listing 6-1. Two things are different in **AppTaskStart()** from the example in the previous chapter.

6

```
static  void  AppTaskStart (void *p_arg)
{
    CPU_INT32U  cpu_clk_freq;
    CPU_INT32U  cnts;
    OS_ERR      err;


    (void)p_arg;
    BSP_Init();
    CPU_Init();
    cpu_clk_freq = BSP_CPU_ClkFreq();
    cnts         = cpu_clk_freq / (CPU_INT32U)OSCfg_TickRate_Hz;
    OS_CPU_SysTickInit(cnts);
#if OS_CFG_STAT_TASK_EN > 0u
    OSStatTaskCPUUsageInit(&err);
#endif
    CPU_IntDisMeasMaxCurReset();

    AppTaskCreate();                                                (1)
    BSP_LED_Off(0);
    while (DEF_TRUE) {
        BSP_LED_Toggle(1);                                         (2)
        OSTimeDlyHMSM(0, 0, 0, 250,
                      OS_OPT_TIME_HMSM_STRICT,
                      &err);
    }
}
```

Listing 6-1 **AppTaskStart() in app.c**

L6-1(1)   **AppTaskCreate()** is called to create other application tasks. **AppTaskCreate()** is declared after the code for **AppTaskStart()**. **AppTaskCreate()** creates a single task, **AppTaskPot()**. Notice that **AppTaskPot()** could have been created directly in **AppTaskStart()** but it is wise to have a separate function to create other tasks. This makes the code in **AppTaskStart()** neater.

The creation of **AppTaskPot()** looks quite similar to the creation of **AppTaskStart()**. Obviously, different arguments are used to create this task. The priority of the task is defined in **app_cfg.h** and in this example, it is set to the same priority as **AppTaskStart()**.

L6-1(2)   The LED is toggled in this task. The LED will blink at a rate of 2 Hz.

Now, in regards to the code for the potentiometer task **AppTaskPot()**, it is written as an infinite loop as shown in Listing 6-2.

```
static  void  AppTaskPot  (void *p_arg)
{
    OS_ERR      err;


    while (DEF_TRUE) {

        AppPotRawCnt = BSP_PotRd();                              (1)

        OSTimeDlyHMSM(0, 0, 0, 100,
                      OS_OPT_TIME_HMSM_STRICT,
                      &err);
    }
}
```

Listing 6-2 **AppTaskPot() in app.c**

L6-2(1)   The Potentiometer is read every 100 milliseconds and the value, in 12-bit raw counts is placed in **AppPotRawCnt**. You can examine this value by setting a breakpoint using C-SPY or, better yet, monitor the position of the potentiometer live using µC/Probe.

6-2 MONITORING THE POTENTIOMETER USING µC/PROBE

Click on the 'Run' button in Embedded Workbench in order to resume execution of the code.

Start µC/Probe and open the uCOS-III-Ex2-Probe.wspx workspace found in the following directory:

\Micrium\Software\EvalBoards\Infineon\XMC4500\
 IAR\uCOS-III-Book-Ex-Src\uCOS-III-Ex2

The µC/Probe screen should appear as shown in Figure 6-2 once you click on the 'Go' button.

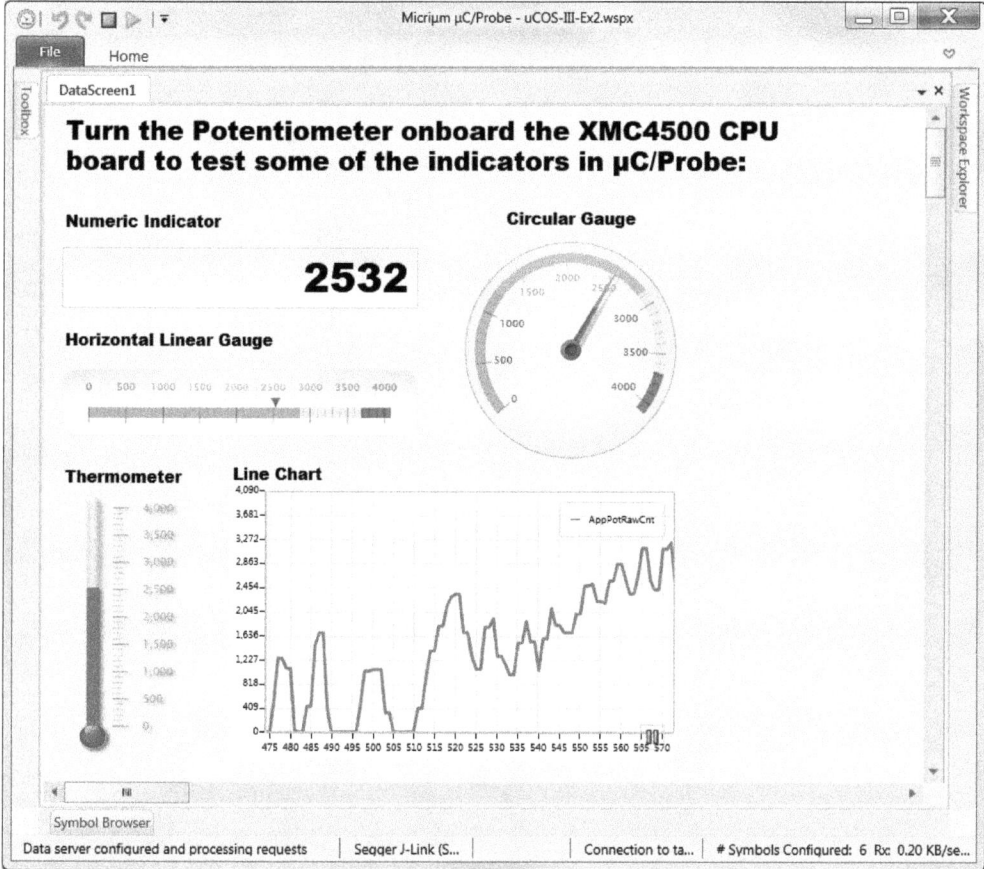

Figure 6-2 **µC/Probe Potentiometer Screen**

Turn the potentiometer onboard the XMC4500 CPU board left and right to test some of the indicators offered by µC/Probe.

μC/OS-III Example #3

The example described in this chapter will display μC/OS-III performance measurements. Specifically, we'll look at the built-in time measurement features of μC/OS-III, as well as compute post-to-pend times for various kernel objects.

We will once again use the XMC4500 CPU board.

It is assumed that you read the previous two chapters and are comfortable with the tools (Embedded Workbench and μC/Probe). It is also assumed that you have the XMC4500 CPU board connected to your PC.

Start the IAR Embedded Workbench for ARM and open the following workspace:

```
\Micrium\Software\EvalBoards\Infineon\XMC4500\IAR\
 uCOS-III-Book-Ex-Src\uCOS-III-Book-Ex-Src.eww
```

Click on the uCOS-III-Ex3 tab at the bottom of the workspace explorer to select the third project. Notice that the file tree looks identical to the file tree of Examples #1 and #2. The only file that changed was **app.c**.

7

7-1 RUNNING THE PROJECT

Connect the USB power cable and the J-Link Pro Debugger as shown in Chapter 3, "Connecting a PC to the XMC4500 CPU Board" on page 786.

Click on the *Download and Debug* button on the far right in the IAR Embedded Workbench as described in section 4-4 "Compiling, Programming and Debugging" on page 797.

Embedded Workbench will not only compile and link the example code, but also program the object file onto the Flash of the XMC4500 using the J-Link Pro debugger.

Using the debugging tools described in section 4-5 "Debugging Tools" on page 798, click on the debugger's *Go* button to continue execution and verify that the yellow LED is blinking at a rate of 3 Hz (that will indicate you are running example #3).

7-2 EXAMINING PERFORMANCE TEST RESULTS WITH μC/PROBE

Start μC/Probe and open the **uCOS-III-Ex3-Probe.wspx** workspace found in the following directory:

```
\Micrium\Software\EvalBoardsInfineon\XMC4500\IAR\
  uCOS-III-Book-Ex-Src\uCOS-III-Ex3\
```

Click on the μC/Probe 'Run' button. The screen should appear as shown in Figure 7-1 (I set the test selector slider control to position 8).

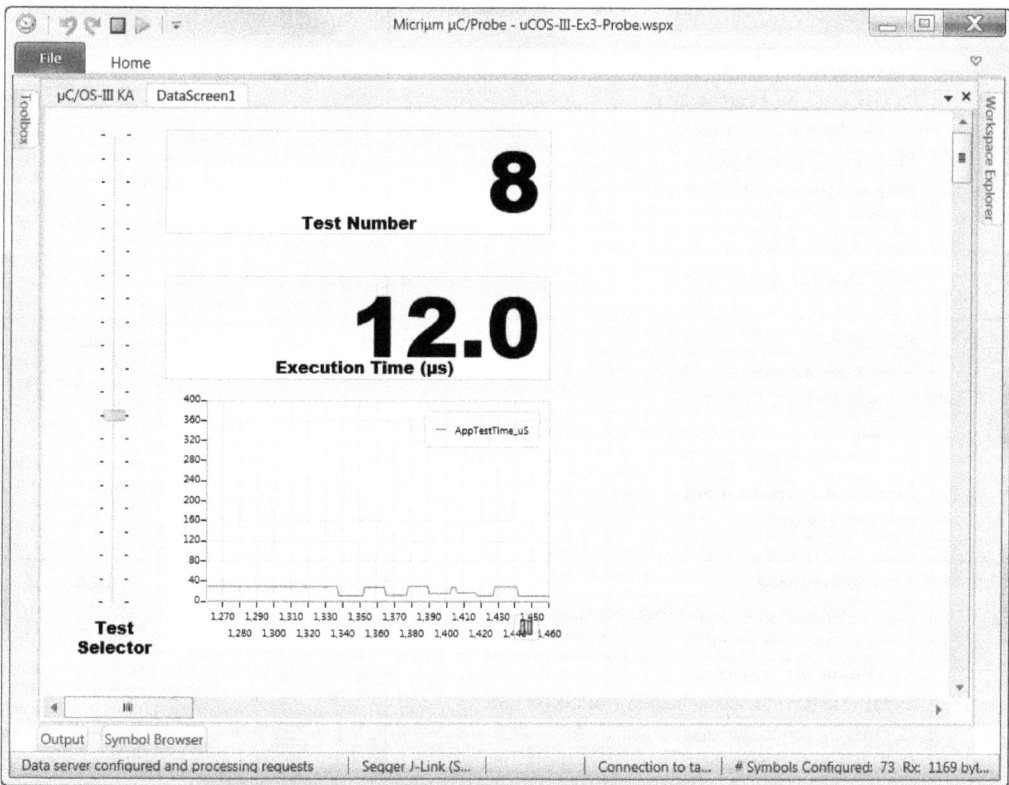

Figure 7-1 **μC/OS-III Performance Tests**

With your mouse, 'grab' the slider control. You should see the number on the 'Test #' indicator reflect the position on the slider. As you slide the control, the 'Execution Time (μS)' indicator will display the execution time for the test being performed.

Example #3 creates two additional tasks used to perform a series of 11 performance measurements. One of the tasks signals or sends messages to the other task, which waits for these signals or messages. The receiving task has a higher priority than the sender.

Table 7-1 summarizes the results.

Test #	Description	Description (Non-optimized) (1)	Execution Time (μS) (Optimized) (2)
0	**Semaphore** Rx task waits on a semaphore Context Switch to Tx task **Start time measurement** Tx task signals the semaphore Context Switch to Rx task Rx task returns from wait **Stop time measurement**	31.0	15.0
1	**Semaphore** **Start time measurement** Rx task signals a semaphore Rx task waits for the semaphore Rx task returns from wait **Stop time measurement** No context switch	13.0	4.0
2	**Task Semaphore** Rx task waits on its internal task semaphore Context Switch to Tx task **Start time measurement** Tx task signals the task semaphore of the Rx task Context Switch to Rx task Rx task returns from wait **Stop time measurement**	29.0	14.0

Test #	Description	Description (Non-optimized) (1)	Execution Time (µS) (Optimized) (2)
3	**Task Semaphore** **Start time measurement** Rx task signals its own task semaphore Rx task waits for its task semaphore Rx task returns from wait **Stop time measurement** No context switch	14.0	5.0
4	**Message Queue** Rx task waits on a message queue Context Switch to Tx task **Start time measurement** Tx task sends a message to the message queue Context Switch to Rx task Rx task returns from wait **Stop time measurement**	32.0	15.0
5	**Message Queue** **Start time measurement** Rx task sends a message to the message queue Rx task waits on the message queue Rx task returns from wait **Stop time measurement** No context switch	19.0	6.0
6	**Task Message Queue** Rx task waits on its internal task message queue Context Switch to Tx task **Start time measurement** Tx task sends a message to the Rx task's internal message queue Context Switch to Rx task Rx task returns from wait **Stop time measurement**	30.0	14.0
7	**Task Message Queue** **Start time measurement** Rx task sends a message to its own task message queue Rx task waits on its task message queue Rx task returns from wait **Stop time measurement** No context switch	19.0	7.0

827

7

Test #	Description	Description (Non-optimized) (1)	Execution Time (μS) (Optimized) (2)
8	**Mutual Exclusion Semaphore** **Start time measurement** Rx task waits on a mutex (mutex is available) Rx task releases the mutex **Stop time measurement** No context switch	14.0	4.0
9	**Event Flags** Rx task waits on an event flag group Context Switch to Tx task **Start time measurement** Tx task sets event flag group bits Context Switch to Rx task Rx task returns from wait **Stop time measurement**	31.0	16.0
10	**Event Flags** **Start time measurement** Rx task sets event flag group bits Rx task waits on the event flag group Rx task returns from wait **Stop time measurement** No context switch	15.0	4.0

Table 7-1 µC/OS-III Performance Test Results

T7-1(1)   In these tests, the compiler was set to 'no-optimization' for best debug capabilities. Also, µC/OS-III was configured to check all arguments, whether some of the functions were called from ISRs, or whether API calls are passed the proper object types, etc. This is the default configuration of the project provided with this book and consists of the following settings (See Appendix B, *µC/OS-III Configuration Manual* in Part I of this book):

```
Compiler Optimization                None
CPU_CFG_INT_DIS_MEAS_EN              Defined
OS_CFG_TS_EN                         DEF_ENABLED
OS_CFG_APP_HOOKS_EN                  1u
OS_CFG_ARG_CHK_EN                    1u
OS_CFG_CALLED_FROM_ISR_CHK_EN        1u
```

OS_CFG_DBG_EN	1u
OS_CFG_OBJ_TYPE_CHK_EN	1u
OS_CFG_SCHED_LOCK_TIME_MEAS_EN	1u
OS_CFG_STAT_TASK_EN	1u
OS_CFG_STAT_TASK_STK_CHK_EN	1u
OS_CFG_TASK_PROFILE_EN	1u

T7-1(2)   For comparison, I ran separate tests using the following configuration settings:

Compiler Optimization	Medium
CPU_CFG_INT_DIS_MEAS_EN	Not Defined
OS_CFG_TS_EN	DEF_ENABLED
OS_CFG_APP_HOOKS_EN	1u
OS_CFG_ARG_CHK_EN	0u
OS_CFG_CALLED_FROM_ISR_CHK_EN	0u
OS_CFG_DBG_EN	0u
OS_CFG_OBJ_TYPE_CHK_EN	0u
OS_CFG_SCHED_LOCK_TIME_MEAS_EN	0u
OS_CFG_STAT_TASK_EN	0u
OS_CFG_STAT_TASK_STK_CHK_EN	0u
OS_CFG_TASK_PROFILE_EN	0u

As you can see, performance is more than doubled with the second configuration. The biggest gain in performance resulted from the disable interrupt disable and scheduler lock time measurement. While developing an application it is useful to keep μC/OS-III's performance measurements enabled. However, when deploying a product, some of the above features could be disabled. I would use the following configuration:

Compiler Optimization	Medium
CPU_CFG_INT_DIS_MEAS_EN	Not Defined
CPU_CFG_TS_EN	DEF_ENABLED
OS_CFG_APP_HOOKS_EN	1u
OS_CFG_ARG_CHK_EN	0u
OS_CFG_CALLED_FROM_ISR_CHK_EN	0u
OS_CFG_DBG_EN	1u
OS_CFG_OBJ_TYPE_CHK_EN	0u
OS_CFG_SCHED_LOCK_TIME_MEAS_EN	0u
OS_CFG_STAT_TASK_EN	1u

```
OS_CFG_STAT_TASK_STK_CHK_EN      1u
OS_CFG_TASK_PROFILE_EN           1u
```

When µC/OS-III is used in safety-critical applications, the following configuration should be considered:

```
Compiler Optimization            Medium
CPU_CFG_INT_DIS_MEAS_EN          Not Defined
CPU_CFG_TS_EN                    DEF_ENABLED
OS_CFG_APP_HOOKS_EN              1u
OS_CFG_ARG_CHK_EN                1u
OS_CFG_CALLED_FROM_ISR_CHK_EN    1u
OS_CFG_DBG_EN                    1u
OS_CFG_OBJ_TYPE_CHK_EN           1u
OS_CFG_SCHED_LOCK_TIME_MEAS_EN   0u
OS_CFG_STAT_TASK_EN              1u
OS_CFG_STAT_TASK_STK_CHK_EN      1u
OS_CFG_TASK_PROFILE_EN           1u
```

Being able to adjust the configuration assumes access to the µC/OS-III source code, which is available to licensees.

Remember that a kernel uses typically 2 to 4% of the CPU time so the fact that the code executes twice as fast with optimization has very little impact on the overall performance of a system. I generally like to leave performance measurement into the code because it gives better visibility into an application and how it's behaving. I also like to keep argument checking as it protects the code in case features are added later. Unless every ounce of performance is required in an application, I would recommend taking the safer approach.

7-3 HOW THE TEST CODE WORKS

main() is identical to **main()** shown in the previous examples.

AppTaskStart() is also nearly identical to the previous examples except that a call was added to a function called **AppObjCreate()**, which is used to initialize kernel objects that are used in this example. **AppObjCreate()** is shown in Listing 7-1.

```
static  void  AppObjCreate (void)
{
    OS_ERR  err;
    OSSemCreate  ((OS_SEM      *)&AppSem,
                  (CPU_CHAR    *)"App Sem",
                  (OS_SEM_CTR  )0,
                  (OS_ERR      *)&err);
    OSFlagCreate ((OS_FLAG_GRP *)&AppFlagGrp,
                  (CPU_CHAR    *)"App Flag Group",
                  (OS_FLAGS    )0,
                  (OS_ERR      *)&err);
    OSQCreate    ((OS_Q        *)&AppQ,
                  (CPU_CHAR    *)"App Queue",
                  (OS_MSG_QTY  )20,
                  (OS_ERR      *)&err);
    OSMutexCreate((OS_MUTEX    *)&AppMutex,
                  (CPU_CHAR    *)"App Mutex",
                  (OS_ERR      *)&err);
}
```

Listing 7-1 **AppObjCreate() in app.c**

AppTaskCreate() creates two tasks called: **AppTaskRx()** and **AppTaskTx()**. These tasks are used in the post-to-pend performance measurements. **AppTaskRx()** has a higher priority than **AppTaskTx**. **AppTaskRx()** will be receiving signals or messages from **AppTaskTx()**.

Figure 7-2 shows how the two tasks interact to perform the tests.

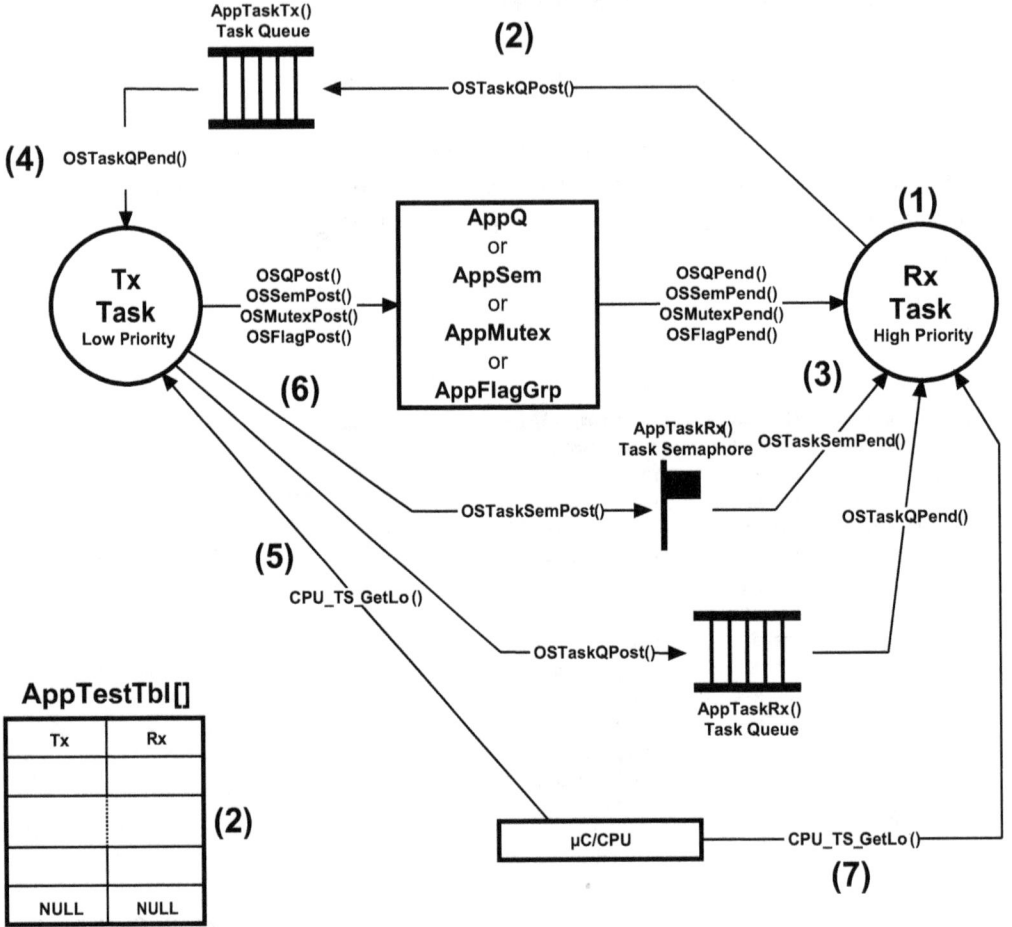

Figure 7-2 **Block Diagram**

F7-2(1)   AppTaskRx() executes first since it has a higher priority than AppTaskTx().

F7-2(2)   AppTaskRx() reads the table AppTestTbl[], which contains pointers to functions that need to be executed by both AppTaskTx() and AppTaskRx(). Each entry contains one test to perform. AppTaskRx() posts the address of the current entry of AppTestTbl[] to AppTaskTx() so that it can perform its test function.

F7-2(3)   **AppTaskRx()** then executes its 'Rx' test as directed by the current table entry. In most cases, this corresponds to pending on one of the 4 kernel objects created or, **AppTaskRx()**'s internal task semaphore or message queue. Since no posts have been performed yet, **AppTaskRx()** blocks waiting for **AppTaskTx()** to send it a signal or a message.

F7-2(4)   **AppTaskTx()** executes and immediately waits on its internal message queue.

F7-2(5)   **AppTaskTx()** reads the current timestamp by invoking the **OS_TS_GET()** macro. The value returned is stored in a RAM array called **AppTS_Start[]** using the index of **AppTestTbl[]** as the index to **AppTS_Start[]**.

F7-2(6)   Since **AppTaskRx()** sent the address of the current **AppTestTbl[]** entry to **AppTaskTx()**, **AppTaskTx()** executes its 'Tx' function from the table. This will most likely correspond to either sending a signal or a message to **AppTaskRx()** based on the test function being executed.

F7-2(7)   Since **AppTaskRx()** has a higher priority, a context switch will occur and **AppTaskRx()** will resume execution. **AppTaskRx()** will then read the current timestamp from the µC/CPU module and store the value in another array, **AppTS_End[]**. **AppTaskRx()** will then compute the difference between the start and end time and save the difference in **AppTS_Delta[]**. Note that all values in the RAM arrays are in **CPU_TS** units.

For the Cortex-M4, a timestamp is obtained by reading the CYCCNT register of the DWT counts as fast as the CPU clock or 120 MHz in the case of the XMC4500 CPU board. Execution time in microseconds simply requires a division by 120 of the **AppTS_Delta[]** entry.

The code for **AppTaskRx()** is shown in Listing 7-2.

```
static  void  AppTaskRx (void *p_arg)
{
    OS_ERR      err;
    CPU_INT08U  i;
    APP_TEST    *p_test;
    CPU_INT32U  clk_freq_mhz;

    (void)p_arg;
    i            = 0;
    p_test       = &AppTestTbl[0];
    AppTestSel   = 0;
    clk_freq_mhz = BSP_CPU_ClkFreq() / (CPU_INT32U)1000000;          (1)
    if (clk_freq_mhz == 0) {
        clk_freq_mhz = 1;
    }

    while (DEF_TRUE) {
        BSP_LED_Toggle(1);
        OSTimeDlyHMSM(0, 0, 0, 50,                                  (2)
                        OS_OPT_TIME_HMSM_STRICT,
                        &err);
        if ((void *)p_test->Tx != (void *)0) {                      (3)
            OSTaskQPost((OS_TCB    *)&AppTaskTxTCB,                  (4)
                        (void      *)p_test,
                        (OS_MSG_SIZE)i,
                        (OS_OPT     )OS_OPT_POST_FIFO,
                        (OS_ERR    *)&err);
            (*(p_test->Rx))(i);                                     (5)
            i++;
            p_test++;
        } else {
            i      = 0;
            p_test = &AppTestTbl[0];
        }
        AppTestTime_uS = AppTS_Delta[AppTestSel] / clk_freq_mhz;    (6)
    }
}
```

Listing 7-2 **AppTaskRx() in app.c**

L7-2(1) The CPU clock frequency in MHz is computed by obtaining the CPU frequency in Hz from the BSP function **BSP_CPU_ClkFreq()**.

L7-2(2) **AppTaskRx()** executes a test every 50 milliseconds, or 20 tests per second.

L7-2(3) **AppTaskRx()** goes through **AppTestTbl[]** until all tests have been performed and continuously restarts the tests from the beginning.

L7-2(4)   **AppTaskRx()** sends the address of the current **AppTestTbl[]** entry to **AppTaskTx()**. Notice that the index into **AppTestTbl[]** is sent as the message size.

L7-2(5)   **AppTaskRx()** then executes the 'Rx' function provided in **AppTestTbl[]** at the current entry.

L7-2(6)   The execution time of the test is computed (in microseconds) so that it can be displayed by µC/Probe. Note that **AppTestSel** corresponds to the value of the virtual slider control on the µC/Probe 'Application' data screen.

The code for **AppTaskTx()** is shown in Listing 7-3.

```
static  void  AppTaskTx (void *p_arg)
{
    OS_ERR       err;
    OS_MSG_SIZE  msg_size;
    CPU_TS       ts;
    APP_TEST     *p_test;


    (void)p_arg;
    while (DEF_TRUE) {
        BSP_LED_Toggle(3);
        p_test = (APP_TEST *)OSTaskQPend((OS_TICK        )0,                          (1)
                                         (OS_OPT         )OS_OPT_PEND_BLOCKING,
                                         (OS_MSG_SIZE *)&msg_size,
                                         (CPU_TS       *)&ts,
                                         (OS_ERR       *)&err);
        (*p_test->Tx)((CPU_INT08U)msg_size);                                          (2)
    }
}
```

Listing 7-3 **AppTaskTx() in app.c**

L7-3(1)   **AppTaskTx()** waits for a message to be sent by **AppTaskRx()**.

L7-3(2)   Once the message is received, **AppTaskTx()** executes the function at the current entry in **AppTestTbl[]**. Note that the 'Tx' function expects the index into **AppTS_Start[]**, **AppTS_End[]**, and **AppTS_Delta[]**, where the measurement results will be saved.

835

7-4 OTHER PERFORMANCE MEASUREMENTS

Run the example code and select the 'µC/OS-III Tasks' screen in µC/Probe. Figure 7-3 shows this screen after running the example code for more than three hours.

Figure 7-3 µC/OS-III Task Screen

F7-3(1)   µC/OS-III's idle task consumes over 95% of the CPU.

F7-3(2)   Worst case interrupt disable time for µC/OS-III's internal task is less than 12.9 µs, and the scheduler is locked for a maximum of 9.5 µs.

F7-3(3)   Based on the stack usage, it would be possible to reduce the RAM requirements of most tasks since none of the tasks never exceed 60% and, in fact, the idle task only uses 14% of its stack space.

F7-3(4)   The tick task and timer tasks are signaled by the tick ISR. The tick task runs within 39.1 µs from the time it is signaled, whereas the timer task runs within 94.8 µs of being signaled. The timer task executes after the tick task because its priority is lower. (task semaphore signal time)

Select the 'µC/OS-III Miscellaneous' screen in µC/Probe. Figure 7-4 shows this screen.

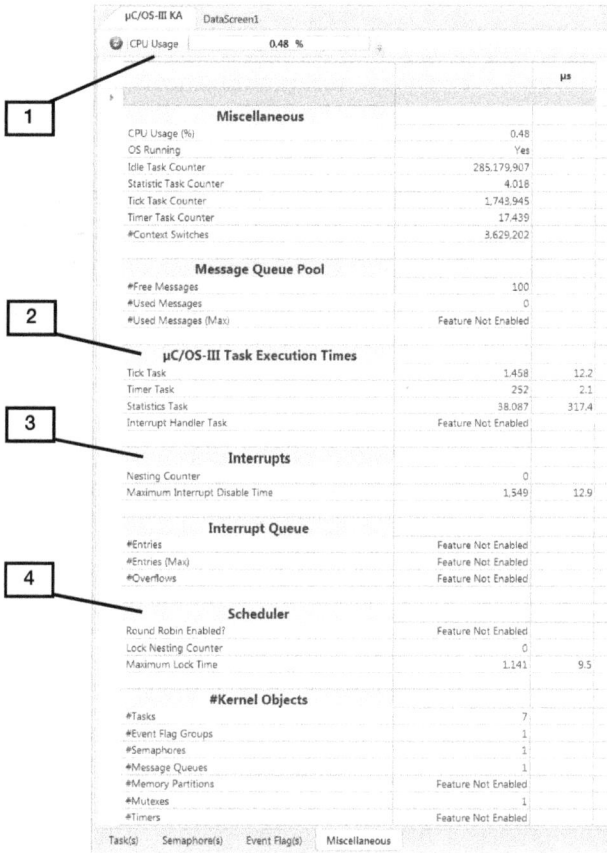

Figure 7-4 **µC/OS-III Miscellaneous Screen**

F7-4(1) The horizontal meter indicates the total CPU usage for the code running this application. As you can see, this represents less than 1%.

F7-4(2) µC/OS-III computes the maximum execution time of the statistic, tick, timer and interrupt handler tasks. These values are shown in both timer counts and microseconds.

F7-4(3) µC/OS-III measures the maximum amount of time interrupts are disabled.

F7-4(4) Finally, µC/OS-III calculates the maximum amount of time the scheduler is locked.

7

7-5 SUMMARY

This example showed only a fraction of the performance measurements performed by µC/OS-III.

In most applications, you should leave performance measurement in the code because it gives better visibility into the application and how it is behaving. Argument checking protects the code in case features are later added. I recommend taking the safer approach unless every ounce of performance is needed in an application. Because µC/OS-III should only use between 2 to 4% of the CPU time, having the best performance out of µC/OS-III should have very little impact on the overall performance of a system.

With µC/Probe, it is possible to show the performance data of the application tasks. However, the Trial Version of µC/Probe limits you to display only 5 of your variables (you can display all of µC/OS-III's variables because µC/Probe is µC/OS-III aware).

8

µC/OS-III Example #4

The Infineon XMC4500 is ideal for supporting sophisticated motor control applications such as servo drives for Computer Numerical Control (CNC) machines. This chapter involves an example using a timer to simulate the rotational speed of a wheel (Revolutions Per Minute (RPM). This is similar to the example provided in Section 14-7 in Part I of this book. Figure 8-1 shows a block diagram of the system.

Figure 8-1 **RPM Measurement**

As you can see, the embedded system will measure and display the RPM of the wheel, as well as indicate the number of revolutions.

The rotating wheel will be simulated using a timer generating a frequency from 17 Hz to 10,000 Hz, which represents 1,000 to 600,000 RPM, respectively. Although it is doubtful that a wheel is able to spin at 600,000 RPM (Turbine engines rotate at about 20,000 RPM), the example causes a lot of interrupts that demonstrates certain aspects of µC/OS-III.

Using µC/Probe, we'll be able to change the frequency of the timer using a 'slider' (*i.e.* virtual potentiometer). µC/Probe will also display the RPM and the number of revolutions along with other interesting values.

It is assumed that you have read the previous three chapters, and are comfortable with the tools (Embedded Workbench and µC/Probe). It is also assumed that you have the XMC4500 CPU board connected to a PC as shown in Chapter 3, "Connecting a PC to the XMC4500 CPU Board" on page 786.

Start the IAR Embedded Workbench for ARM and open the following workspace:

```
\Micrium\Software\EvalBoards\Infineon\XMC4500\IAR\
  uCOS-III-Book-Ex-Src\uCOS-III-Book-Ex-Src.eww
```

Click on the uCOS-III-Ex4 tab at the bottom of the workspace explorer to select the fourth project. Notice that the folder tree looks identical to the one from previous examples. The only file that changed is **app.c**.

8-1 RUNNING THE PROJECT

Click on the Download and Debug button on the far right in the IAR Embedded Workbench as described in section 4-4 "Compiling, Programming and Debugging" on page 797.

Embedded Workbench will not only compile and link the example code, but also program the object file onto the Flash of the XMC4500 using the J-Link Pro debugger.

Using the debugging tools described in section 4-5 "Debugging Tools" on page 798, click on the debugger's Go button to continue execution and verify that the yellow LED is blinking at a rate of 4 Hz (that will indicate you are running example #4).

8-2 DISPLAYING ROTATING WHEEL DATA

Start µC/Probe and open the **uCOS-III-Ex4-Probe.wsp** workspace found in the following directory:

\Micrium\Software\EvalBoards\Infineon\XMC4500\IAR
  uCOS-III-Book-Ex-Src\uCOS-III-Ex4

Click on the µC/Probe 'Run' button. The screen should appear as the one shown in Figure 8-2:

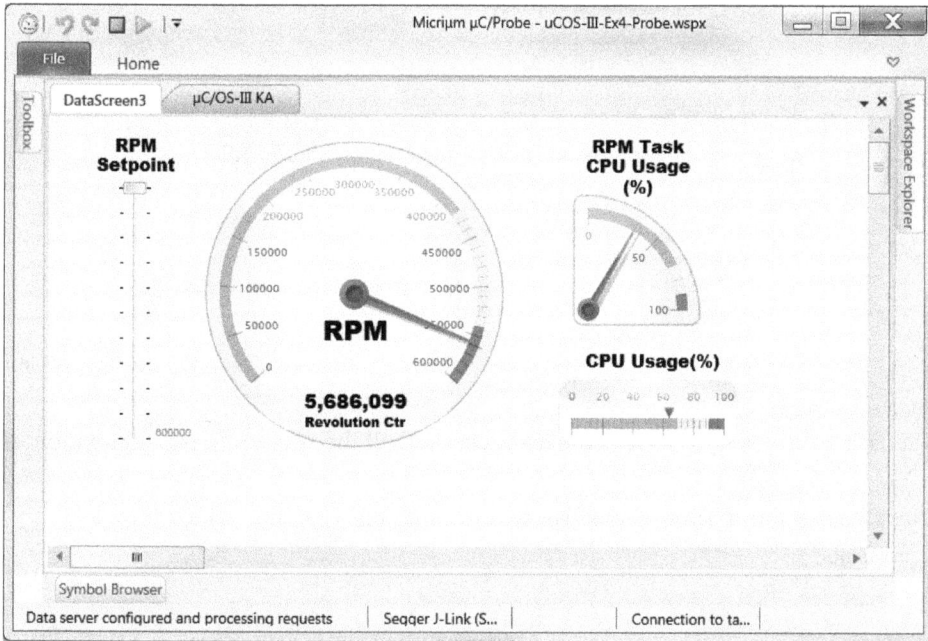

Figure 8-2 **RPM Example User Interface using µC/Probe**

The big meter in the center represents the RPM of the wheel (0 to 600,000).

The numeric display on the bottom of the meter labeled as 'Revolution Ctr' represents the number of revolutions that the wheel performed so far.

The 'RPM Setpoint' slider is used to adjust the RPM of the simulated wheel. This slider changes the frequency of the timer used to simulate the rotation of the wheel. The number on the slider should correspond to the number on the RPM meter.

Two additional meters are shown. The horizontal meter indicates the total CPU usage of the application code. The quadrant meter indicates the percentage of CPU time used by the RPM measurement task (described later) as a percentage of the total CPU time used. As shown on Figure 8-2, the RPM task consumes 34% of the total CPU usage, which is 64%. In other words, the RPM task consumes 21.76% of the total CPU time (34% of 64%).

Figure 8-3 shows the statistics on the µC/OS-III tasks.

									Performance				Task Stack			
Item	Name	Priority	State	Pending On Object	Pending On	Ticks Remaining	CPU Usage	CtxSwCtr	Interrupt Disable Time (Max)	Scheduler Lock Time (Max)	#Used	#Free	Size	Stack Usage
0	UserFlay Task	3	Delayed			1	0.04 %	10.402	5.1	0.0	27	101	128	21.09 %
1	RPM Task	2	Ready		Task Q	0	33.92 %	5.199.342	8.2	0.0	28	100	128	21.88 %
2	App Task Start	1	Delayed			1	0.04 %	9.871	5.2	0.0	31	97	128	24.22 %
3	uC/OS-III Timer Task	6	Pending	Task Semaphore	Task Sem	0	0.10 %	15.167	5.1	29.7	24	104	128	18.75 %
4	uC/OS-III Stat Task	6	Delayed			1	0.61 %	36.315	5.2	0.0	25	103	128	19.53 %
5	uC/OS-III Tick Task	4	Pending	Task Semaphore	Task Sem	0	0.06 %	13.594	15.8	0.0	24	104	128	18.75 %
6	uC/OS-III Idle Task	7	Ready			0	65.20 %	5.159.515	5.2	0.0	17	111	128	13.28 %

µC/OS-III KA   DataScreen3 — CPU Usage 63.94 %

Figure 8-3 **µC/OS-III Tasks**

The idle task indicates 65% since the RPM is cranked all the way up to 600,000 on the slider.

The Tick, Statistics and Timer tasks barely consume any CPU time since they are very low overhead tasks.

8-3 RPM MEASUREMENT SIMULATION IMPLEMENTATION

The Capture/Compare Unit # 4 (CCU4) peripheral on the XMC4500 is a major component for systems that need general purpose timers for signal monitoring/conditioning and Pulse Width Modulation (PWM) signal generation and will be used in this example.

Figure 8-4 shows a block diagram of the ISRs and tasks involved. The example consists of two tasks and an ISR. One task is used to monitor changes of a virtual slider control and switch, both provided by µC/Probe.

Figure 8-4 **Measuring and computing RPM**

F8-4(1) The statistics reset switch is read by the User Interface task every 100 milliseconds. When toggled from off to on, **OSStatReset()** is called. To reset the statistics, return the toggle switch back to the off position and repeat the process.

F8-4(2) The User Interface task also monitors the value of the slider (**AppRPM_Stp**) and converts this value to the reload counts (**AppRPM_TmrReload_Cnts**) used by the timer to simulate the rotation of the wheel (*i.e.* CCU4 Timer of the XMC4500).

F8-4(3) The CCU Timer #4 is a 16-bit down counter that automatically reloads itself when the count reaches zero. As shown, the reference frequency for the timer is set to 1 MHz and thus, the timer can generate frequencies from 15.25 Hz (65535 counts) to 1 MHz (1 count). Upon timing out, the timer will generate an interrupt.

F8-4(4)   The interrupt service routine simulates the reading of an Input Capture (described later) by reading the current timestamp. Recall that on the Cortex-M4, the timestamp comes from the **DWT_CYCCNT** register, which is a 32-bit counter that counts CPU clock cycles. On the XMC4500 CPU board, the counter increments at 120 MHz, providing plenty of resolution. The timestamp is subtracted from the previous timestamp to compute the time between interrupts.

F8-4(5)   The delta time is posted to the RPM task's built-in message queue.

F8-4(6)   When the ISR exits and, if the RPM task is the highest priority task ready to run, then µC/OS-III will context switch to this task. The RPM task extracts the received message from its message queue and computes the RPM, which is given by:

$$\text{AppRPM} = \frac{60}{\text{TimeForOneRevolution}}$$

or,

$$\text{AppRPM} = \frac{60 \times 120{,}000{,}000}{\text{delta\_ts}}$$

The computation is performed using floating-point math because 60 x 120,000,000 exceeds the range of a 32-bit unsigned number.

F8-4(7)   The RPM task also keeps track of the number of revolutions that corresponds to the number of times the task was posted. In fact, this also corresponds to the number of times the task has been context switched to, and this is saved in the task's **OS_TCB**. However, the information in the TCB should not be read by the application code.

The average RPM (**AppRPM_Avg**) is computed by filtering the RPM value by taking 1/16th of the current value and adding 15/16th of the previous value as shown below:

$$\text{AppRPM\_Avg} = \frac{\text{AppRPM}}{16} + \frac{15 \times \text{AppRPM\_Avg}}{16}$$

The RPM task also detects the maximum RPM (**AppRPM_Max**) and the minimum RPM (**AppRPM_Min**).

8-3-1 MEASURING RPM USING AN INPUT CAPTURE

Normally, RPM (or period) measurement is performed using a special timer found on many microcontrollers called an *input capture*. Figure 8-5 shows how this works.

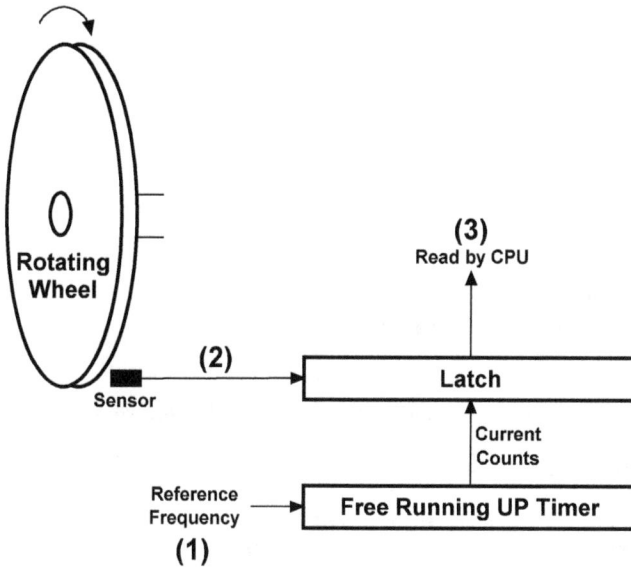

Figure 8-5 **Using an Input Capture to measure RPM**

F8-5(1)   A reference frequency feeds a free running up counter. Many input captures are only 16-bit, which limits the range of values measured. However, modern microcontrollers offer 32-bit input captures, which offer a wide dynamic range.

F8-5(2)   When the sensor detects one revolution of the wheel, it 'latches' (or captures) the current value of the free running timer.

F8-5(3)   The CPU is generally interrupted at the same time and the CPU reads the latched value. The time the wheel took to complete a full revolution is determined by subtracting the current latched value from the previous latched value. The RPM is thus:

$$RPM = \frac{60 \times ReferenceFrequency}{CurrentLatched - PreviousLatched}$$

8-4 HOW THE CODE WORKS

`main()` and `AppTaskStart()` are identical to the previous examples.

The code for the user interface task is shown in Listing 8-1.

```
static  void  AppTaskUserIF (void *p_arg)
{
    OS_ERR        err;


   (void)p_arg;
   while (DEF_TRUE) {
       BSP_LED_Toggle(3);
       OSTimeDlyHMSM(0, 0, 0, 100,
                     OS_OPT_TIME_HMSM_STRICT,
                     &err);
       if (AppRPM_Stp > 1000u) {                                    (1)
           AppRPM_TmrReload_Cnts = (CPU_INT16U)(60000000uL / AppRPM_Stp);
       } else {
           AppRPM_TmrReload_Cnts = (CPU_INT16U)60000u;
       }
       BSP_REG_CCU40_CC40PRS = AppRPM_TmrReload_Cnts;               (2)
       BSP_REG_CCU40_GCSS    = BSP_BIT_CCU4_GCSS_S0SE;              (3)
       if (AppStatResetSw != DEF_FALSE) {                           (4)
           OSStatReset(&err);
           AppStatResetSw = DEF_FALSE;
       }
   }
}
```

Listing 8-1 **AppTaskUserIF()** in app.c

L8-1(1)   The RPM setpoint variable is changed by µC/Probe (the slider). Since a 16-bit timer is used to simulate the RPM, the RPM cannot go lower than 1,000 (16 Hz) based on the 1 MHz reference frequency feeding Timer CCU #4. The reload value is then computed from the setpoint.

L8-1(2)   The reload register of Timer CCU #4 is updated.

L8-1(3)   Enable shadow period transfer for the new reload register's value.

L8-1(4)   The µC/OS-III statistics are reset if the user toggles the switch (See the screenshot of Figure 8-2), which maps to **AppStatResetSw** from µC/Probe.

The code for the RPM task is shown in Listing 8-2.

```
static  void  AppTaskRPM (void *p_arg)
{
    OS_ERR        err;
    CPU_INT32U    cpu_clk_freq_mhz;
    CPU_INT32U    rpm_delta_ic;
    OS_MSG_SIZE   msg_size;
    CPU_TS        ts;
    CPU_TS        ts_start;
    CPU_TS        ts_end;


    (void)p_arg;
    AppRPM_PrevTS    = OS_TS_GET();                                      (1)
    AppTmrInit(200);                                                     (2)
    cpu_clk_freq_mhz = BSP_CPU_ClkFreq() / (CPU_INT32U)1000000;          (3)
    AppRPM_RevCtr    = 0u;
    AppRPM_Max       = (CPU_FP32)0.0;
    AppRPM_Min       = (CPU_FP32)99999999.9;
```

Listing 8-2 **AppTaskRPM() in app.c**

L8-2(1)   The current timestamp is read to initialize the 'previous timestamp value' required when computing the period of a rotation.

L8-2(2)   Timer CCU #4 is initialized.

L8-2(3)   The number of revolutions, as well as the minimum and maximum detectors.

```
    while (DEF_ON) {
        rpm_delta_ic = (CPU_INT32U)OSTaskQPend((OS_TICK      )OSCfg_TickRate_Hz,      (4)
                                              (OS_OPT        )OS_OPT_PEND_BLOCKING,
                                              (OS_MSG_SIZE *)&msg_size,
                                              (CPU_TS      *)&ts,
                                              (OS_ERR      *)&err);
        ts_start = OS_TS_GET();                                                       (5)
        if (err == OS_ERR_TIMEOUT) {                                                  (6)
            AppRPM = (CPU_FP32)0;
        } else {
            AppRPM_RevCtr++;                                                          (7)
            if (rpm_delta_ic > 0u) {
                AppRPM = (CPU_FP32)60 * (CPU_FP32)AppCPU_ClkFreq_Hz                   (8)
                        / (CPU_FP32)rpm_delta_ic;
            } else {
                AppRPM = (CPU_FP32)0;
            }
        }
        if (AppRPM > AppRPM_Max) {                                                    (9)
            AppRPM_Max = AppRPM;
        }
        if (AppRPM < AppRPM_Min) {
            AppRPM_Min = AppRPM;
        }
        AppRPM_Avg             = (CPU_FP32)0.0625 * AppRPM                            (10)
                               + (CPU_FP32)0.9375 * AppRPM_Avg;
        ts_end                 = OS_TS_GET();
        AppRPM_TaskExecTime_uS = (ts_end - ts_start)                                 (11)
                               / cpu_clk_freq_mhz;
        BSP_LED_Toggle(1);
    }
}
```

L8-2(4)   The task then waits until a message is sent to it. The message is actually the 'delta timestamp,' which represents one complete revolution of the simulated wheel.

L8-2(5)   When a message is received, another timestamp is taken, which is used to measure the execution time of this task (See item (11) below).

L8-2(6)   If the pend on the message queue timed out, the RPM is 0 indicating that the wheel is not turning. In our simulation, this should never happen since the minimum frequency is 16 Hz.

L8-2(7)   The revolutions counter is updated.

8

L8-2(8)   The RPM is computed based on the time it took between interrupts. Note that you should always have code that checks for divide by zero.

L8-2(9)   The minimum and maximum RPM detectors are updated.

L8-2(10)   The average RPM is computed using a simple filter.

L8-2(11)   Finally, the execution time of the task is determined (it should be approximately seven microseconds).

The code for the timer ISR (that simulates a input capture) is shown in Listing 8-3.

```
static  void  AppTmrISR_Handler (void)
{
    OS_ERR  err;
    CPU_TS  ts;
    CPU_TS  delta_ts;


    ts         = OS_TS_GET();                              (1)
    delta_ts   = ts - AppRPM_PrevTS;                       (2)
    AppRPM_PrevTS = ts;
    BSP_REG_CCU40_CC40SWR = BSP_BIT_CCU40_SWR_RPM;         (3)
    OSTaskQPost((OS_TCB   *)&AppTaskRPM_TCB,               (4)
                (void      *)delta_ts,
                (OS_MSG_SIZE)sizeof(CPU_TS),
                (OS_OPT    )OS_OPT_POST_FIFO,
                (OS_ERR    *)&err);
}
```

Listing 8-3 **AppTmrISR_Handler() in app.c**

L8-3(1)   The timestamp is read to simulate reading the input capture 'latch' register.

L8-3(2)   The time between interrupts (*i.e.* input captures) is computed.

L8-3(3)   The timer's period match interrupt is cleared to avoid re-entering the same interrupt upon exiting the ISR.

L8-3(4)   The delta counts are posted to the RPM task.

8-5 OBSERVATIONS

μC/OS-III's `OSTaskQPost()` already takes a snapshot of the timestamp when a message is posted. As a result, the ISR and RPM tasks could have been written somewhat differently to make use of this feature. If you are not using an input capture there will be some inaccuracies in the measurement.

Specifically, it is not necessary to read the timestamp in the ISR, compute the delta, and post the delta to the RPM task. Instead, the ISR could have simply done the following:

```
static  void  AppTmrISR_Handler (void)
{
    OSTaskQPost((OS_TCB    *)&AppTaskRPM_TCB,
                (void       *)0,
                (OS_MSG_SIZE)0,
                (OS_OPT     )OS_OPT_POST_FIFO,
                (OS_ERR     *)&err);
    BSP_REG_CCU40_CC40SWR = BSP_BIT_CCU40_SWR_RPM;
}
```

The only difference is that the timestamp is read slightly later (because it is read in `OSTaskQPost()`). However, the timestamp is read fairly early in `OSTaskQPost()`.

There is no need to post anything since the timestamp is what we are looking for when `OSTaskQPend()` returns in the RPM task. Because of this, we could have used `OSTaskSemPost()` and `OSTaskSemPend()` and would have obtained the same result.

The RPM task can also compute deltas to reduce ISR processing time. The RPM task would be as follows (only the changes are shown in bold):

```
while (DEF_TRUE) {
    (void)OSTaskQPend((OS_TICK       )OSCfg_TickRate_Hz,
                      (OS_OPT        )OS_OPT_PEND_BLOCKING,
                      (OS_MSG_SIZE *)&msg_size,
                      (CPU_TS      *)&ts,
                      (OS_ERR      *)&err);
    ts_start = OS_TS_GET();
    if (err == OS_ERR_TIMEOUT) {
        AppRPM = (CPU_FP32)0;
    } else {
        AppRPM_RevCtr++;
        rpm_delta_ic  = ts - AppRPM_PrevTS;
        AppRPM_PrevTS = ts;
        if (rpm_delta_ic > 0u) {
            AppRPM = (CPU_FP32)60 * (CPU_FP32)AppCPU_ClkFreq_Hz
                   / (CPU_FP32)rpm_delta_ic;
        } else {
            AppRPM = (CPU_FP32)0;
        }
    }
    :
    /* Rest of the code here */
    :
}
}
```

8-6 SUMMARY

This example showed how to measure the RPM of a wheel. The wheel was simulated using a timer. The RPM generated was grossly exaggerated to create a high interrupt rate (up to 10,000 Hz).

μC/CPU provides the capability to obtain timestamps, which are used to measure execution times and the time between interrupts.

μC/Probe is a highly useful tool that can display nearly any run-time data from an application. This information is very useful during debugging since it allows you to "see" things that are not visible on most deeply embedded systems.

8

A

µC/OS-III Port for the Cortex-M4

This appendix describes the adaptation of µC/OS-III to the ARM Cortex-M4 which is called a *port*.

The port files are found in the following directories depending on the toolchain of your choice:

■ IAR Systems Embedded Workbench for ARM

\Micrium\Software\uCOS-III\Ports\ARM-Cortex-M4\Generic\IAR\os_cpu.h
\Micrium\Software\uCOS-III\Ports\ARM-Cortex-M4\Generic\IAR\os_cpu_c.c
\Micrium\Software\uCOS-III\Ports\ARM-Cortex-M4\Generic\IAR\os_cpu_a.asm

■ Keil MDK-ARM Microcontroller Development Kit for ARM

\Micrium\Software\uCOS-III\Ports\ARM-Cortex-M4\Generic\RealView\os_cpu.h
\Micrium\Software\uCOS-III\Ports\ARM-Cortex-M4\Generic\RealView\os_cpu_c.c
\Micrium\Software\uCOS-III\Ports\ARM-Cortex-M4\Generic\RealView\os_cpu_a.a
sm

■ Atollic TrueSTUDIO for ARM

\Micrium\Software\uCOS-III\Ports\ARM-Cortex-M4\Generic\GNU\os_cpu.h
\Micrium\Software\uCOS-III\Ports\ARM-Cortex-M4\Generic\GNU\os_cpu_c.c
\Micrium\Software\uCOS-III\Ports\ARM-Cortex-M4\Generic\GNU\os_cpu_a.a

This appendix will describe the µC/OS-III port for the ARM Cortex-M4 based on the compiler for IAR Systems. However, the three ports are very similar except for some differences in regards to peripheral support and assembly syntax as listed in Table A-1:

	IAR Embedded Workbench	Keil MDK-ARM	Atollic TrueSTUDIO
FPU Support	Yes	No	No
Assembly Keywords	EXTERN <Symbol>	IMPORT <Symbol>	.extern <Symbol>
Assembly Keywords	PUBLIC <Symbol>	EXPORT <Symbol>	.global <Symbol>
Assembly Statements	<Symbol> EQU <Expression>	<Symbol> EQU <Expression>	.equ <Symbol>, <Expression>
Assembly Comments	; Comment Here	; Comment Here	@ Comment Here

Table A-1 **µC/OS-III Port Differences Among Toolchains**

A-1 OS_CPU.H

os_cpu.h contains processor- and implementation-specific **#defines** constants, macros, and typedefs. **os_cpu.h** is shown in Listing A-1.

```
#ifndef  OS_CPU_H                                                    (1)
#define  OS_CPU_H
#ifdef   OS_CPU_GLOBALS                                              (2)
#define  OS_CPU_EXT
#else
#define  OS_CPU_EXT  extern
#endif
/*
*********************************************************************************
*                                  MACROS
*********************************************************************************
*/
#ifndef  NVIC_INT_CTRL
#define  NVIC_INT_CTRL          *((CPU_REG32 *)0xE000ED04)
#endif

#ifndef  NVIC_PENDSVSET
#define  NVIC_PENDSVSET         0x10000000
#endif
#define  OS_TASK_SW()           NVIC_INT_CTRL = NVIC_PENDSVSET       (3)
#define  OSIntCtxSw()           NVIC_INT_CTRL = NVIC_PENDSVSET

#if OS_CFG_TS_EN == 1u
#define  OS_TS_GET()            (CPU_TS)CPU_TS_TmrRd()               (4)
#else
#define  OS_TS_GET()            (CPU_TS)0u
/*
*********************************************************************************
*                                PROTOTYPES
*********************************************************************************
*/
void  OSCtxSw              (void);                                   (5)
void  OSIntCtxSw           (void);
void  OSStartHighRdy       (void);
void  OS_CPU_PendSVHandler (void);                                  (6)
void  OS_CPU_SysTickHandler (void);                                 (7)
void  OS_CPU_SysTickInit   (CPU_INT32U  cnts);
#endif
```

Listing A-1 **os_cpu.h**

LA-1(1)   Typical multiple header file inclusion protection.

LA-1(2)   **OS_CPU_GLOBALS** and **OS_CPU_EXT** allow us to declare global variables that are specific to this port. However, the port doesn't contain any global variables and thus these statements are just included for completeness and consistency.

LA-1(3)   The task and ISR level context switch code is performed by triggering the PendSV handler on the Cortex-M4. The PendSV handler is implemented in **os_cpu_a.asm**

LA-1(4)   Timestamps are obtained by calling **CPU_TS_TmrRd()**. On the Cortex-M4, **CPU_TS_TmrRd()** reads the **DWT_CYCCNT** register which is a 32-bit free-running up counter.

LA-1(5)   The prototypes of mandatory µC/OS-III functions.

LA-1(6)   The Cortex-M4 processor provides a special interrupt handler specifically designed for use by context switch code. This is called the PendSV Handler and is implemented by **OS_CPU_PendSVHandler()**. The function is found in **os_cpu_a.asm**

LA-1(7)   The Cortex-M4 has a timer dedicated for RTOS use called the SysTick. The code to initialize and handle the SysTick interrupt is found in **os_cpu_c.c**. Note that this code is part of the µC/OS-III port file and not the Board Support Package (bsp.c), because the SysTick is available to all Cortex-M4 implementations and is always handled the same by µC/OS-III.

A-2 OS_CPU_C.C

A µC/OS-III port requires that the following functions be declared:

```
OSIdleTaskHook()
OSInitHook()
OSStatTaskHook()
OSTaskCreateHook()
OSTaslDelHook()
OSTaskReturnHook()
OSTaskStkInit()
OSTaskSwHook()
OSTimeTickHook()
```

The Cortex-M4 port implements two additional functions as described in the previous sections:

```
OS_CPU_SysTickHandler()
OS_CPU_SysTickInit()
```

A-2-1 os_cpu_c.c – OSIdleTaskHook()

The idle task hook allows the port developer to extend the functionality of the idle task. For example, you can place the processor in low power mode when no other higher-priority tasks are running. This is especially useful in battery-powered applications. Listing A-2 shows the typical code for **OSIdleTaskHook()**.

```
void  OSIdleTaskHook (void)
{
#if OS_CFG_APP_HOOKS_EN > 0u                                    (1)
    if (OS_AppIdleTaskHookPtr != (OS_APP_HOOK_VOID)0) {        (2)
        (*OS_AppIdleTaskHookPtr)();                            (3)
    }
#endif
}
```

Listing A-2 **os_cpu_c.c – OSIdleTaskHook()**

LA-2(1)   Application level hook functions are enabled by **OS_CFG_APP_HOOKS_EN**.

LA-2(2)   If the application developer wants his/her own function to be called on every
iteration of the idle task, the developer needs to initialize the value of
OS_AppIdleTaskHookPtr to point to the desired function to call.

Note that μC/OS-III initializes **OS_AppIdleTaskHookPtr** to **NULL** when
OSInit() is called and therefore, the code must set this pointer only after
calling **OSInit()**.

The application hook function *must not* make any blocking calls because the
idle task must never block. In other words, it cannot call **OSTimeDly()**,
OSTimeDlyHMSM(), or **OSTaskSuspend()** (to suspend 'self'), and any of the
OS???Pend() functions.

Examples of application hooks are found in **os_app_hooks.c**.

LA-2(3)   The application level idle task hook is called without any argument.

A-2-2 os_cpu_c.c – OSInitHook()

Listing A-3 shows the typical code for **OSInitHook()**.

```
void  OSInitHook (void)
{
}
```

Listing A-3 **os_cpu_c.c – OSInitHook()**

OSInitHook() does not call any application level hook functions because it can't and thus,
there are no application hook function pointer. The reason for this is that **OSInit()**
initializes all the application hook pointers to **NULL** and because of that, it would not be
possible to redefine the application init hook pointer before **OSInit()** returns.

A-2-3 os_cpu_c.c – OSStatTaskHook()

OSTaskStatHook() allows you to extend the functionality of the statistic task by allowing him/her to add additional statistics. OSStatTaskHook() is called after computing the total CPU usage (see OS_StatTask() in os_stat.c). Listing A-4 shows the typical code for OSStatTaskHook().

```
void  OSStatTaskHook (void)
{
#if OS_CFG_APP_HOOKS_EN > 0u
    if (OS_AppStatTaskHookPtr != (OS_APP_HOOK_VOID)0) {        (1)
        (*OS_AppStatTaskHookPtr)();                            (2)
    }
#endif
}
```

Listing A-4 **os_cpu_c.c – OSStatTaskHook()**

LA-4(1)   If you wants your own function to be called by µC/OS-III's statistic task (i.e. OS_StatTask()) then the developer needs to initialize the value of OS_AppStatTaskHookPtr to point to the desired function to call.

Note that µC/OS-III initializes **OS_AppStatTaskHookPtr** to **NULL** when OSInit() is called and therefore, the code must set this pointer only after calling OSInit().

The application hook function *must not* make any blocking calls because it would affect the behavior of the statistic task. Examples of application hooks are found in **os_app_hooks.c**.

LA-4(2)   The application-level statistic task hook is called without any argument.

A-2-4 os_cpu_c.c – OSTaskCreateHook()

OSTaskCreateHook() gives the port developer the opportunity to add code specific to the port when a task is created. OSTaskCreateHook() is called once the OS_TCB fields are initialized, but prior to making the task ready to run. Listing A-5 shows the typical code for OSTaskCreateHook().

```
void  OSTaskCreateHook (OS_TCB *p_tcb)
{
#if OS_CFG_APP_HOOKS_EN > 0u
    if (OS_AppTaskCreateHookPtr != (OS_APP_HOOK_TCB)0) {        (1)
        (*OS_AppTaskCreateHookPtr)(p_tcb);                     (2)
    }
#else
    (void)&p_tcb;          /* Prevent compiler warning */
#endif
}
```

Listing A-5 **os_cpu_c.c – OSTaskCreateHook()**

LA-5(1)   If the application developer wants his/her own function to be called when a task is created, the developer needs to initialize the value of **OS_AppTaskCreateHookPtr** to point to the desired function to call.

The application hook function *must not* make any blocking calls and should perform its function as quickly as possible.

Note that µC/OS-III initializes **OS_AppTaskCreateHookPtr** to NULL when OSInit() is called. The code must set this pointer only after calling OSInit().

Examples of application hooks are found in **os_app_hooks.c**.

LA-5(2)   The application level task create hook is passed the address of the OS_TCB of the task being created.

A-2-5 os_cpu_c.c – OSTaskDelHook()

OSTaskDelHook() gives the port developer the opportunity to add code specific to the port when a task is deleted. OSTaskDelHook() is called once the task has been removed from all lists (the ready list, the tick list or a pend list). Listing A-6 shows the typical code for OSTaskDelHook().

```
void  OSTaskDelHook (OS_TCB *p_tcb)
{
#if OS_CFG_APP_HOOKS_EN > 0u
    if (OS_AppTaskDelHookPtr != (OS_APP_HOOK_TCB)0) {       (1)
        (*OS_AppTaskDelHookPtr)(p_tcb);                     (2)
    }
#else
    (void)&p_tcb;         /* Prevent compiler warning */
#endif
}
```

Listing A-6 **os_cpu_c.c – OSTaskDelHook()**

LA-6(1)   If the application developer wants his/her own function to be called when a task is deleted, the developer needs to initialize the value of **OS_AppTaskDelHookPtr** to point to the desired function to call.

The application hook function *must not* make any blocking calls, and should perform its function as quickly as possible.

You should note that µC/OS-III initializes **OS_AppTaskDelHookPtr** to **NULL** when OSInit() is called and the code must set this pointer only after calling OSInit().

Examples of application hooks are found in **os_app_hooks.c**.

LA-6(2)   The application level task delete hook is passed the address of the **OS_TCB** of the task being created.

A-2-6 os_cpu_c.c – OSTaskReturnHook()

With µC/OS-III, a task is never allowed to return. However, if this happens 'accidentally,' µC/OS-III will catch this and delete the offending task. However, **OSTaskDelHook()** will be called before the task is deleted. Listing A-7 shows the typical code for **OSTaskReturnHook()**.

```
void OSTaskReturnHook (OS_TCB *p_tcb)
{
#if OS_CFG_APP_HOOKS_EN > 0u
    if (OS_AppTaskReturnHookPtr != (OS_APP_HOOK_TCB)0) {          (1)
        (*OS_AppTaskReturnHookPtr)(p_tcb);                       (2)
    }
#else
    (void)&p_tcb;          /* Prevent compiler warning */
#endif
}
```

Listing A-7 **os_cpu_c.c – OSTaskReturnHook()**

LA-7(1)   If the application developer wants his/her own function to be called when a task returns, the developer needs to initialize the value of **OS_AppTaskReturnHookPtr** to point to the desired function to call.

The application hook function *must not* make any blocking calls and should perform its function as quickly as possible.

Note that µC/OS-III initializes **OS_AppTaskReturnHookPtr** to **NULL** when **OSInit()** is called and the code must set this pointer only after calling **OSInit()**.

Examples of application hooks are found in **os_app_hooks.c**.

LA-7(2)   The application level task return hook is passed the address of the **OS_TCB** of the task being created.

A-2-7 os_cpu_c.c – OSTaskStkInit()

This function initializes the stack frame of a task being created. When µC/OS-III creates a task it makes its stack look as if an interrupt just occurred and simulates pushing the context of the task onto the task stack. **OSTaskStkInit()** is called by **OSTaskCreate()**.

Listing A-8 shows the Cortex-M4 code for **OSTaskStkInit()**.

```
CPU_STK *OSTaskStkInit (OS_TASK_PTR    p_task,             (1)
                        void          *p_arg,
                        CPU_STK       *p_stk_base,
                        CPU_STK       *p_stk_limit,
                        CPU_STK_SIZE   stk_size,
                        OS_OPT         opt)
{
    CPU_STK  *p_stk;


    (void)&opt;
    (void)&p_stk_limit;
     p_stk   = &p_stk_base[stk_size];             (2)
    *--p_stk = (CPU_INT32U)0x01000000L;           (3)
    *--p_stk = (CPU_INT32U)p_task;                (4)
    *--p_stk = (CPU_INT32U)OS_TaskReturn;         (5)
    *--p_stk = (CPU_INT32U)0x12121212L;           (6)
    *--p_stk = (CPU_INT32U)0x03030303L;
    *--p_stk = (CPU_INT32U)0x02020202L;
    *--p_stk = (CPU_INT32U)p_stk_limit;
    *--p_stk = (CPU_INT32U)p_arg;                 (7)
    *--p_stk = (CPU_INT32U)0x11111111L;           (8)
    *--p_stk = (CPU_INT32U)0x10101010L;
    *--p_stk = (CPU_INT32U)0x09090909L;
    *--p_stk = (CPU_INT32U)0x08080808L;
    *--p_stk = (CPU_INT32U)0x07070707L;
    *--p_stk = (CPU_INT32U)0x06060606L;
    *--p_stk = (CPU_INT32U)0x05050505L;
    *--p_stk = (CPU_INT32U)0x04040404L;
    return (p_stk);                               (9)
}
```

Listing A-8 **os_cpu_c.c – OSTaskStkInit()**

LA-8(1)   **OSTaskStkInit()** is called by **OSTaskCreate()** and is passed six arguments:

1. The task's entry point (i.e. the address of the task).

2. A pointer to an argument that will be passed to the task when the task starts, i.e. **p_arg**.

3. The base address of the storage area in RAM of the stack. Typically a stack is declared as an array of **CPU_STKs** as shown below.

CPU_STK   MyTaskStk[stk_size];

In this case, the base address is simply **&MyTaskStk[0]**.

1. The address of where the stack limit is to point to. This assumes that the CPU supports stack limit checking. If not then this pointer is not used.

2. The size of the stack is also passed to **OSTaskStkInit()**.

3. Finally, the 'opt' argument of **OSTaskCreate()** is passed to **OSTaskStkInit()** in case any of these are needed by **OSTaskStkInit()** for special options.

LA-8(2)   A local pointer is initialized to the top-of-stack to initialize. In the case of the Cortex-M4, the stack grows from high memory to low memory and therefore, the top-of-stack is at the highest address of the stack storage area.

LA-8(3)   The Cortex-M4's PSR register is initialized. The initial value sets the 'T' bit in the PSR, which causes the Cortex-M4 to use Thumb instructions (this should always be the case).

LA-8(4)   This register corresponds to R15 which is the program counter. We initialize this register to point to the task entry point.

LA-8(5)   This register corresponds to R14 (the link register), which contains the return address of the task. As previously mentioned, a task is not supposed to return. This pointer allows us, therefore, to catch this fault and properly terminate the task. µC/OS-III provides a function just for that purpose, **OS_TaskReturn()**.

LA-8(6)   Registers R12, R3, R2 and R1 are initialized to a value that makes it easy for them to be identified when a debugger performs a memory dump.

LA-8(7)   R0 is the register used by the C compiler to pass the first argument to a function. Recall that the prototype for a task looks as shown below.

```
void  MyTask (void *p_arg);
```

In this case, 'p_arg' is simply passed in R0 so that when the task starts, it will think it was called as with any other function.

LA-8(8)   Registers R11, R10, R9 and R8, R7, R6, R5 and R4 are initialized to a value that makes it easy for them to be identified when a debugger performs a memory dump.

LA-8(9)   Notice that the stack pointer is not decremented after the last register is placed onto the stack. This is because the Cortex-M4 assumes that the stack pointer points to the last element pushed onto the stack.

OSTaskStkInit() returns the new top-of-stack pointer to OSTaskCreate(), which will save this value in the task's OS_TCB in the .StkPtr field.

The stack frame of the task being created is shown in Figure A-1.

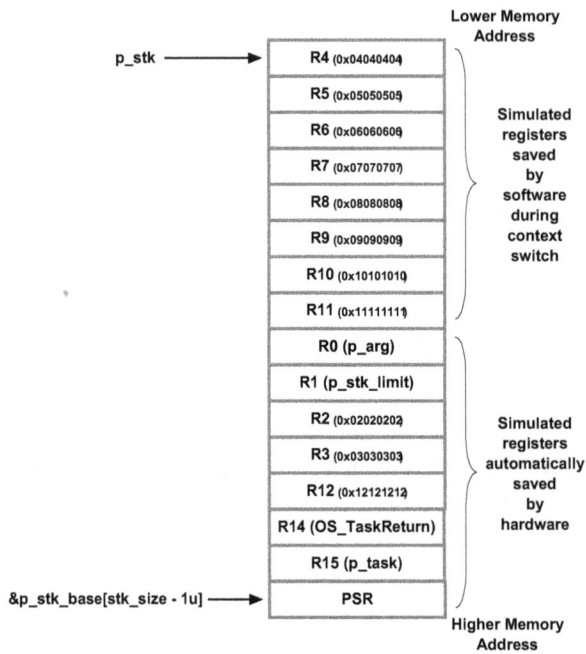

Figure A-1 **Stack frame of task being created.**

A-2-8 os_cpu_c.c – OSTaskSwHook()

OSTaskSwHook() is called when µC/OS-III performs a context switch. If fact, OSTaskSwHook() is called after saving the context of the task being suspended. Also, OSTaskSwHook() is called with interrupts disabled.

Listing A-9 shows the code for OSTaskSwHook(). This function is fairly complex and contains a lot of conditional compilation.

```
void  OSTaskSwHook (void)
{
#if OS_CFG_TASK_PROFILE_EN > 0u
    CPU_TS      ts;
#ifdef  CPU_CFG_INT_DIS_MEAS_EN
    CPU_TS      int_dis_time;
#endif
#endif
#if OS_CFG_APP_HOOKS_EN > 0u
    if (OS_AppTaskSwHookPtr != (OS_APP_HOOK_VOID)0) {        (1)
        (*OS_AppTaskSwHookPtr)();                            (2)
    }
#endif
#if OS_CFG_TASK_PROFILE_EN > 0u
    ts = OS_TS_GET();                                        (3)
    if (OSTCBCurPtr != OSTCBHighRdyPtr) {
        OSTCBCurPtr->CyclesDelta  = ts - OSTCBCurPtr->CyclesStart;
        OSTCBCurPtr->CyclesTotal += (OS_CYCLES)OSTCBCurPtr->CyclesDelta;
    }
    OSTCBHighRdyPtr->CyclesStart  = ts;                      (4)
#ifdef  CPU_CFG_INT_DIS_MEAS_EN
    int_dis_time = CPU_IntDisMeasMaxCurReset();              (5)
    if (int_dis_time > OSTCBCurPtr->IntDisTimeMax) {
        OSTCBCurPtr->IntDisTimeMax = int_dis_time;
    }
#if OS_CFG_SCHED_LOCK_TIME_MEAS_EN > 0u
    if (OSSchedLockTimeMaxCur > OSTCBCurPtr->SchedLockTimeMax) {   (6)
        OSTCBCurPtr->SchedLockTimeMax = OSSchedLockTimeMaxCur;
    }
    OSSchedLockTimeMaxCur = (CPU_TS)0;
#endif
#endif
#endif
}
```

Listing A-9 **os_cpu_c.c – OSTaskSwHook()**

LA-9(1)   If the application developer wants his/her own function to be called when a context switch occurs, the developer needs to initialize the value of **OS_AppTaskSwHookPtr** to point to the desired function to call.

The application hook function *must not* make any blocking calls and should perform its function as quickly as possible.

Note that µC/OS-III initializes **OS_AppTaskSwHookPtr** to **NULL** when **OSInit()** is called and your code must set this pointer only after calling **OSInit()**.

Examples of application hooks are found in **os_app_hooks.c**.

LA-9(2)   The application level task switch hook is not passed any arguments. However, the global µC/OS-III variables **OSTCBCurPtr** and **OSTCBHighRdyPtr** will point to the **OS_TCB** of the task being switched out and the **OS_TCB** of the task being switched in, respectively.

LA-9(3)   This code measures the execution time of each task. This will be used by the statistic task to compute the relative CPU usage (in percentage) that each task uses.

If task profiling is enabled (i.e. **OS_CFG_TASK_PROFILE_EN** is set to 1) then we obtain the current timestamp. If we are switching to a new task, we simply compute how long the task that is being switched out ran for. We then accumulate this in the **.CyclesTotal** field (64 bits) of the **OS_TCB** for that task.

LA-9(4)   **OSTaskSwHook()** stores the timestamp read as the beginning time of the new task being switched in.

Note is that the execution time of each task also includes the execution time of any interrupt that occurred while the task was executing. It would be possible to exclude this, but it would require more overhead on the CPU.

LA-9(5)   If **CPU_CFG_INT_DIS_MEAS_EN** is set to 1, µC/CPU measures the interrupt disable time on a per-task basis. The code simply detects the maximum amount of interrupt disable time for each task and stores it in the **.IntDisTimeMax** field of the **OS_TCB** for the task being switched out.

LA-9(6)   If OS_CFG_SCHED_LOCK_TIME_MEAS_EN is set to 1, μC/OS-III keeps track of the
            maximum amount of time a task will have the scheduler locked for critical
            sections. This value is saved in the .SchedLockTimeMax field of the OS_TCB of
            the task being switched out.

A-2-9 os_cpu_c.c - OSTimeTickHook()

OSTimeTickHook() gives the port developer the opportunity to add code that will be called
by OSTimeTick(). OSTimeTickHook() is called from the tick ISR and must not make any
blocking calls (it would be allowed to anyway) and must execute as quickly as possible.

Listing A-10 shows the typical code for OSTimeTickHook().

```
void  OSTimeTickHook (void)
{
#if OS_CFG_APP_HOOKS_EN > 0u
    if (OS_AppTimeTickHookPtr != (OS_APP_HOOK_VOID)0) {          (1)
        (*OS_AppTimeTickHookPtr)();                              (2)
    }
#else
    (void)&p_tcb;           /* Prevent compiler warning */
#endif
}
```

Listing A-10 **os_cpu_c.c - OSTimeTickHook()**

LA-10(1)   If the application developer wants his/her own function to be called when a
            tick interrupt occurs, the developer needs to initialize the value of
            OS_AppTimeTickHookPtr to point to the desired function to call.

            Note that μC/OS-III initializes OS_AppTimeTickHookPtr to NULL when
            OSInit() is called and the code must set this pointer only after calling
            OSInit().

            Examples of application hooks are found in os_app_hooks.c.

LA-10(2)   The application level time tick hook is not passed any arguments.

A-2-10 os_cpu_c.c – OS_CPU_SysTickHandler()

OS_CPU_SysTickHandler() is automatically invoked by the Cortex-M4 when a SysTick interrupt occurs and interrupts are enabled. For this to happen, however, the address of OS_CPU_SysTickHandler() must be placed in the interrupt vector table at the SysTick entry (the 16th entry in the vector table of the Cortex-M4).

Listing A-11 shows the Cortex-M4 code for OS_CPU_SysTickHandler().

```
void  OS_CPU_SysTickHandler (void)                    (1)
{
    CPU_SR_ALLOC();


    CPU_CRITICAL_ENTER();
    OSIntNestingCtr++;                                (2)
    CPU_CRITICAL_EXIT();
    OSTimeTick();                                     (3)
    OSIntExit();                                      (4)
}
```

Listing A-11 **os_cpu_c.c – OS_CPU_SysTickHandler()**

LA-11(1)   When the Cortex-M4 enters an interrupt, the CPU automatically saves critical registers (R0, R1, R2, R3, R12, PC, LR and XPSR) onto the current task's stack and switches to the Main Stack (MSP) to handle the interrupt.

This means that R4 through R11 are not saved when the interrupt starts and the ARM Architecture Procedure Call Standard (AAPCS) requires that all interrupt handlers preserve the values of the other registers, if they are required during the ISR.

LA-11(2)   The interrupt nesting counter is incremented in a critical section because the **SysTick** interrupt handler could be interrupted by a higher priority interrupt.

LA-11(3)   The µC/OS-III tick interrupt needs to call **OSTimeTick()**.

LA-11(4)   Every interrupt handler must call **OSIntExit()** at the end of the handler.

A-2-11 os_cpu_c.c – OS_CPU_SysTickInit()

`OS_CPU_SysTickInit()` is called by your application code to initialize the `SysTick` interrupt.

Listing A-12 shows the Cortex-M4 code for `OS_CPU_SysTickInit()`.

```
void  OS_CPU_SysTickInit (CPU_INT32U  cnts)                       (1)
{
    CPU_REG_NVIC_ST_RELOAD = cnts - 1u;                           (1)
    CPU_REG_NVIC_SHPRI3    |= 0xFF000000u;                        (2)
    CPU_REG_NVIC_ST_CTRL   |= CPU_REG_NVIC_ST_CTRL_CLKSOURCE
                           | CPU_REG_NVIC_ST_CTRL_ENABLE;
    CPU_REG_NVIC_ST_CTRL   |= CPU_REG_NVIC_ST_CTRL_TICKINT;
}
```

Listing A-12 **os_cpu_c.c – OS_CPU_SysTickInit()**

LA-12(1)   `OS_CPU_SysTickInit()` must be informed about the counts to reload into the `SysTick` timer. The counts to reload depend on the CPU clock frequency and the configured tick rate (i.e. **OS_CFG_TICK_RATE_HZ** in **os_cfg_app.h**).

The reload value is typically computed by the first application task to run as follows:

```
cpu_clk_freq = BSP_CPU_ClkFreq();
cnts         = cpu_clk_freq / (CPU_INT32U)OS_CFG_TICK_RATE_HZ;
```

BSP_CPU_ClkFreq() is a bsp.c function that returns the CPU clock frequency. We then compute reload counts from the tick rate.

LA-12(2)   The **SysTick** interrupt is set to the lowest priority because ticks are mostly used for coarse time delays and timeouts, and we want application interrupts to be handled first.

A-3 OS_CPU_A.ASM

os_cpu_a.asm contains processor-specific code for three functions that must be written in assembly language:

OSStartHighRdy()
OSCtxSw()
OSIntCtxSw()

In addition, the Cortex-M4 requires the definition of a function to handle the PendSV exception.

OS_CPU_PendSVHandler()

A-3-1 os_cpu_a.asm – OSStartHighRdy()

OSStartHighRdy() is called by OSStart() to start the process of multitasking. µC/OS-III will switch to the highest priority task that is ready to run.

Listing A-13 shows the Cortex-M4 code for OSStartHighRdy().

```
OSStartHighRdy
        LDR     R0, =NVIC_SYSPRI14
        LDR     R1, =NVIC_PENDSV_PRI                          (1)
        STRB    R1, [R0]
        MOVS    R0, #0
        MSR     PSP, R0
        LDR     R0, =NVIC_INT_CTRL
        LDR     R1, =NVIC_PENDSVSET                           (2)
        STR     R1, [R0]
        CPSIE   I
                                                             (3)
OSStartHang
        B       OSStartHang
                                                             (4)
```

Listing A-13 **os_cpu_a.asm – OSStartHighRdy()**

LA-13(1)   OSStartHighRdy() starts by setting the priority level of the PendSV handler. The PendSV handler is used to perform all context switches and is always set at the lowest priority so that it executes after the last nested ISR.

LA-13(2)   The PendSV handler is invoked by 'triggering' it. However, the PendSV will not execute immediately because it is assumed that interrupts are disabled.

LA-13(3)   Interrupts are enabled and this should cause the Cortex-M4 processor to vector to the PendSV handler (described later).

LA-13(4)   The PendSV handler should pass control to the highest-priority task that was created and the code should never come back to OSStartHighRdy().

A-3-2 os_cpu_a.asm – OSCtxSw() and OSIntCtxSw()

OSCtxSw() is called by OSSched() and OS_Sched0() to perform a context switch from a task.

OSIntCtxSw() is called by OSIntExit() to perform a context switch after an ISR has completed.

Both of these functions simply 'trigger' the PendSV exception handler, which does the actual context switching.

Listing A-14 shows the Cortex-M4 code for OSCtxSw() and OSIntCtxSw().

```
OSCtxSw
        LDR     R0, =NVIC_INT_CTRL
        LDR     R1, =NVIC_PENDSVSET
        STR     R1, [R0]
        BX      LR
OSIntCtxSw
        LDR     R0, =NVIC_INT_CTRL
        LDR     R1, =NVIC_PENDSVSET
        STR     R1, [R0]
        BX      LR
```

Listing A-14 **os_cpu_a.asm – OSCtxSw() and OSIntCtxSw()**

A-3-3 os_cpu_a.asm – OS_CPU_PendSVHandler()

OS_CPU_PendSVHandler() is the code that performs a context switch initiated by a task, or at the completion of an ISR. OS_CPU_PendSVHandler() is invoked by OSStartHighRdy(), OSCtxSw() and OSIntCtxSw().

Listing A-15 shows the Cortex-M4 code for OS_CPU_PendSVHandler().

```
OS_CPU_PendSVHandler
    CPSID   I                                       (1)
    MRS     R0, PSP                                 (2)
    CBZ     R0, OS_CPU_PendSVHandler_nosave
    SUBS    R0, R0, #0x20                           (3)
    STM     R0, {R4-R11}
    LDR     R1, =OSTCBCurPtr                        (4)
    LDR     R1, [R1]
    STR     R0, [R1]

OS_CPU_PendSVHandler_nosave
    PUSH    {R14}                                   (5)
    LDR     R0, =OSTaskSwHook
    BLX     R0
    POP     {R14}
    LDR     R0, =OSPrioCur                          (6)
    LDR     R1, =OSPrioHighRdy
    LDRB    R2, [R1]
    STRB    R2, [R0]
    LDR     R0, =OSTCBCurPtr                        (7)
    LDR     R1, =OSTCBHighRdyPtr
    LDR     R2, [R1]
    STR     R2, [R0]
    LDR     R0, [R2]                                (8)
    LDM     R0, {R4-R11}                            (9)
    ADDS    R0, R0, #0x20
    MSR     PSP, R0                                 (10)
    ORR     LR, LR, #0x04
    CPSIE   I                                       (11)
    BX      LR                                      (12)
```

Listing A-15 **os_cpu_a.asm – OS_CPU_PendSVHandler()**

LA-15(1) **OS_CPU_PendSVHandler()** starts by disabling all interrupts because interrupt should not occur during a context switch.

LA-15(2) This code skips saving the remaining 8 registers if this is the first time the PendSV is called. In other words, when **OSStartHighRdy()** triggers the PendSV handler, there is nothing to save from the 'previous task' as there is no previous task.

LA-15(3) If **OS_CPU_PendSVHandler()** is invoked from either **OSCtxSw()** or **OSIntCtxSw()**, the PendSV handler saves the remaining eight CPU registers (R4 through R11) onto the stack of the task switched out.

LA-15(4) **OS_CPU_PendSVHandler()** saves the stack pointer of the task switched out into that task's **OS_TCB**. Note that the first field of an **OS_TCB** is **.StkPtr** (the task's stack pointer), which makes it convenient for assembly language code since there are no offsets to determine.

LA-15(5) The task switch hook (**OSTaskSwHook()**) is then called.

LA-15(6) **OS_CPU_PendSVHandler()** copies the priority of the new task into the priority of the current task, i.e.:

```
OSPrioCur = OSPrioHighRdy;
```

LA-15(7) **OS_CPU_PendSVHandler()** copies the pointer to the new task's **OS_TCB** into the pointer to the current task's **OS_TCB**, i.e.:

```
OSTCBCurPtr = OSTCBHighRdyPtr;
```

LA-15(8) **OS_CPU_PendSVHandler()** retrieves the stack pointer from the new task's **OS_TCB**.

LA-15(9) CPU registers R4 through R11 from the new task are loaded into the CPU.

LA-15(10) The task stack pointer is updated with the new top-of-stack pointer.

LA-15(11)   Interrupts are re-enabled since we are finished performing the critical portion of the context switch. If another interrupt occurs before we return from the PendSV handler, the Cortex-M4 knows that there are eight registers still saved on the stack, and there would be no need for it to save them. This is called Tail Chaining and it makes servicing back-to-back interrupts quite efficient on the Cortex-M4.

LA-15(12)   By performing a return from the PendSV handler, the Cortex-M4 processors knows that it is returning from interrupt and will thus restore the remaining registers.

B

µC/CPU Port for the Cortex-M4

µC/CPU consists of files that encapsulate common CPU-specific functionality and CPU compiler-specific data types. Appendix B describes the adaptation of µC/CPU to the Cortex-M4 as it relates to µC/OS-III.

Notice how each variable, function, **#define** constant, or macro is prefixed with **CPU_**. This makes it easier to identify them as belonging to the µC/CPU module when invoked by other modules, or application code.

The µC/CPU files are found in the following directories depending on the toolchain of your choice:

■ All Toolchains

```
\Micrium\Software\uC-CPU\cpu_core.c
\Micrium\Software\uC-CPU\cpu_core.h
\Micrium\Software\uC-CPU\cpu_def.h
\Micrium\Software\uC-CPU\Cfg\Template\cpu_cfg.h
```

■ IAR Systems Embedded Workbench for ARM

```
\Micrium\Software\uC-CPU\ARM-Cortex-M4\IAR\cpu.h
\Micrium\Software\uC-CPU\ARM-Cortex-M4\IAR\cpu_a.asm
\Micrium\Software\uC-CPU\ARM-Cortex-M4\IAR\cpu_c.c
```

■ Keil MDK-ARM Microcontroller Development Kit for ARM

```
\Micrium\Software\uC-CPU\ARM-Cortex-M4\RealView\cpu.h
\Micrium\Software\uC-CPU\ARM-Cortex-M4\RealView\cpu_a.asm
\Micrium\Software\uC-CPU\ARM-Cortex-M4\RealView\cpu_c.c
```

■ Atollic TrueSTUDIO for ARM

```
\Micrium\Software\uC-CPU\ARM-Cortex-M4\GNU\cpu.h
\Micrium\Software\uC-CPU\ARM-Cortex-M4\GNU\cpu_a.asm
\Micrium\Software\uC-CPU\ARM-Cortex-M4\GNU\cpu_c.c
```

This appendix will describe the µC/CPU port for the ARM Cortex-M4 based on the compiler for IAR Systems. However, the three ports are very similar except for some differences in regards to peripheral support and assembly syntax as listed in Table B-1:

	IAR Embedded Workbench	Keil MDK-ARM	Atollic TrueSTUDIO
FPU Support	Yes	No	No
Assembly Keywords	EXTERN <Symbol>	IMPORT <Symbol>	.extern <Symbol>
Assembly Keywords	PUBLIC <Symbol>	EXPORT <Symbol>	.global <Symbol>
Assembly Statements	<Symbol> EQU <Expression>	<Symbol> EQU <Expression>	.equ <Symbol>, <Expression>
Assembly Comments	; Comment Here	; Comment Here	@ Comment Here

Table B-1 µC/CPU Port Differences Among Toolchains

B-1 cpu_core.c

cpu_core.c contains C code that is common to all CPU architectures and this file must not be changed. Specifically, cpu_core.c contains functions to allow µC/OS-III and your application to obtain time stamps, measure the interrupt disable time of the CPU_CRITICAL_ENTER() and CPU_CRITICAL_EXIT() macros, a function that emulates a count leading zeros instruction (if the processor does not have that instruction built-in), and a few other functions.

The application code must call CPU_Init() before it calls any other µC/CPU function. This call can be placed in main() before calling µC/OS-III's OSInit().

B-2 cpu_core.h

cpu_core.h contains function prototypes for the functions provided in **cpu_core.c** and allocation of the variables used by the module to measure interrupt disable time. This file must not be modified.

B-3 cpu_def.h

cpu_def.h contains miscellaneous **#define** constants used by the µC/CPU module. This file must not be modified.

B-4 cpu_cfg.h

cpu_cfg.h contains a template to configure µC/CPU for an actual project. **cpu_cfg.h** determines whether to enable measurement of the interrupt disable time, whether the CPU implements a count leading zeros instruction in assembly language, or whether it will be emulated in C, and more.

You should copy **cpu_cfg.h** to the application directory for a project and modify this file as necessary. This obviously assumes that you have access to the source code. The source code is provided to µC/OS-III licensees.

Listing B-1 shows the recommended values for the Cortex-M4.

```
#define   CPU_CFG_NAME_EN                   DEF_ENABLED        (1)
#define   CPU_CFG_NAME_SIZE                       16u          (2)
#define   CPU_CFG_TS_EN                     DEF_ENABLED        (3)
#define   CPU_CFG_INT_DIS_MEAS_EN           DEF_ENABLED        (4)
#define   CPU_CFG_INT_DIS_MEAS_OVRHD_NBR          1u           (5)
#define   CPU_CFG_LEAD_ZEROS_ASM_PRESENT    DEF_ENABLED        (6)
```

Listing B-1 **cpu_cfg.h recommended values**

LB-1(1)   Assign an ASCII name to the CPU by calling **CPU_NameSet()**. This is useful for debugging purposes.

LB-1(2)   The name of the CPU should be limited to 15 characters plus a NUL, unless this value is changed.

LB-1(3)   This **#define** enables the code to measure timestamps. It is a feature required by µC/OS-III, and should always be set to **DEF_ENABLED**.

LB-1(4)   This **#define** determines whether to measure interrupt disable time. This is a useful feature during development but it may be turned off when deploying a system, as measuring interrupt disable time adds measurement artifacts (i.e. overhead).

LB-1(5)   This **#define** determines how many iterations will be performed when determining the overhead involved in measuring interrupt disable time. For the Cortex-M4, the recommended value is 1.

LB-1(6)   The ARMv7 instruction set of the Cortex-M4 contains a Count Leading Zeros (CLZ) instruction, which significantly improves the performance of the µC/OS-III scheduler and, therefore, this option always needs to be enabled.

B-5 µC/CPU FUNCTIONS IN bsp.c

µC/CPU also requires two Board Support Package (bsp.c) specific functions:

```
CPU_TS_TmrInit()
CPU_TS_TmrRd()
```

These functions are typically implemented in **bsp.c** of the evaluation or target board.

The Cortex-M4's Debug Watch Trace (DWT) contains a 32-bit CPU cycle counter (CYCCNT) that is used by µC/CPU for time stamping. The 32-bit counter is incremented at the CPU clock rate which provides excellent time measurement accuracy. The CYCCNT will overflow and reset from 0 after counting 4,294,967,296 CPU clock cycles. This is not a problem since µC/CPU maintains a 64-bit timestamp using two 32-bit values. The overflows are therefore accounted for. However, for µC/OS-III, we only need the lower 32 bits because that offers sufficient resolution for what µC/OS-III needs to do with it.

A 64-bit timestamp is unlikely to ever overflow for the life of a product. For example, if the Cortex-M4 is clocked at 1 GHz (this is not possible at this time), the 64-bit timestamp would overflow after approximately 585 years!

B-5-1 µC/CPU FUNCTIONS IN bsp.c, CPU_TS_TmrInit()

Listing B-2 shows how to initialize the DWT's cycle counter.

```
#if (CPU_CFG_TS_TMR_EN == DEF_ENABLED)
CPU_INT16U  CPU_TS_TmrInit (void)
{
    DEM_CR      |= (CPU_INT32U)DEM_CR_TRCENA;                        (1)
    DWT_CYCCNT   = (CPU_INT32U)0;
    DWT_CR      |= (CPU_INT32U)0x00000001;                          (2)
    return ((CPU_INT16U)0);                                         (3)
}
#endif
```

Listing B-2 **bsp.c, CPU_TS_TmrInit()**

LB-2(1)   We need to enable the trace module.

LB-2(2)   To initialize the DWT's **CYCCNT** set bit 0 in the DWT's Control Register (**DWT_CR**). A read-modify-write avoids altering the other bits in the **DWT_CR**.

LB-2(3)   **CPU_TS_TmrInit()** requires that the function returns the number of left shifts needed to make **CPU_TS_TmrRd()** (described below) return a 32-bit value. Since **CYCCNT** is already a 32-bit counter, no shifts are needed, and this value is 0.

B-5-2 µC/CPU FUNCTIONS IN bsp.c, CPU_TS_TmrRd()

The DWT's **CYCCNT** register is read by calling **CPU_TS_TmrRd()**. This function is implemented as shown in Listing B-3.

```
#if (CPU_CFG_TS_TMR_EN == DEF_ENABLED)
CPU_TS  CPU_TS_TmrRd (void)
{
    return ((CPU_TS)DWT_CYCCNT);
}
#endif
```

Listing B-3 **bsp.c, CPU_TS_TmrRd()**

B-6 cpu.h

cpu.h contains processor- and implementation-specific **#defines** constants, macros and typedefs.

B-6-1 cpu.h – #DEFINES

cpu.h declares a number of processor specific **#define** constants and macros. The most important ones related to µC/OS-III are shown in Listing B-4.

```
#define  CPU_CFG_STK_GROWTH            CPU_STK_GROWTH_HI_TO_LO           (1)
#define  CPU_CFG_LEAD_ZEROS_ASM_PRESENT                                  (2)
#define  CPU_SR_ALLOC()                CPU_SR  cpu_sr = (CPU_SR)0;       (3)
#define  CPU_CRITICAL_ENTER()          { cpu_sr = CPU_SR_Save(); }       (4)
#define  CPU_CRITICAL_EXIT()           { CPU_SR_Restore(cpu_sr);}        (5)
```

Listing B-4 **cpu.h, #defines**

LB-4(1)   This **#define** specifies that the Cortex-M4 stack grows from high memory to lower-memory addresses.

LB-4(2)   This **#define** indicates that the Cortex-M4 has an assembly language instruction that counts leading zeros in a data word. This feature significantly speeds up µC/OS-III's scheduling algorithm.

LB-4(3)   The macro is used to allocate a local variable in a function that needs to protect a critical section by disabling interrupts. µC/OS-III uses **CPU_SR_ALLOC()** as follows:

```
void  OSFunction (void)
{
    CPU_SR_ALLOC();


    CPU_CRITICAL_ENTER();
    /* Code protected by critical section */
    CPU_CRITICAL_EXIT();
    :

}
```

The macro might not appear necessary if we are only declaring a single variable, but the actual code in **cpu.h** is slightly more complex. Therefore the macro hides this complexity from the user.

LB-4(4)   **CPU_CRITICAL_ENTER( )** is invoked by µC/OS-III to disable interrupts. As shown, the macro calls **CPU_SR_Save( )**, which is declared in **cpu_a.asm** (described later). **CPU_SR_Save( )** saves the current state of the Cortex-M4's PSR and then disables interrupts. The saved value of the PSR is returned to the function that invokes **CPU_CRITICAL_ENTER( )**. The PSR is saved in the local variable allocated by **CPU_SR_ALLOC( )**. **CPU_SR_Save( )** is implemented in assembly language because C cannot access CPU registers.

LB-4(5)   **CPU_CRITICAL_EXIT( )** calls the function **CPU_SR_Restore( )** (See **cpu_a.asm**) to restore the previously saved state of the PSR. The reason the PSR was saved in the first place is because interrupts might already be disabled before invoking **CPU_CRITICAL_ENTER( )** and we want to keep them disabled when we exit the critical section. If interrupts were enabled before calling **CPU_CRITICAL_ENTER( )**, they will be re-enabled by **CPU_CRITICAL_EXIT( )**.

B-6-2 cpu.h – DATA TYPES

Micriµm does not make use of the standard C data types. Instead, data types are declared that are highly portable and intuitive. In addition, all data types are always declared in upper case, which follows Micriµm's coding standard.

Listing B-5 shows the data types used by Micriµm specific to the Cortex-M4 (assuming the IAR C compiler).

B

```
typedef            void       CPU_VOID;
typedef            char       CPU_CHAR;                     /*  8-bit character           */  (1)
typedef   unsigned char       CPU_BOOLEAN;                  /*  8-bit boolean or logical  */  (2)
typedef   unsigned char       CPU_INT08U;                   /*  8-bit unsigned integer    */  (3)
typedef     signed char       CPU_INT08S;                   /*  8-bit   signed integer    */
typedef   unsigned short      CPU_INT16U;                   /* 16-bit unsigned integer    */
typedef     signed short      CPU_INT16S;                   /* 16-bit   signed integer    */
typedef   unsigned int        CPU_INT32U;                   /* 32-bit unsigned integer    */
typedef     signed int        CPU_INT32S;                   /* 32-bit   signed integer    */
typedef   unsigned long long  CPU_INT64U;                   /* 64-bit unsigned integer    */  (4)
typedef     signed long long  CPU_INT64S;                   /* 64-bit   signed integer    */
typedef            float      CPU_FP32;                     /* 32-bit floating point      */  (5)
typedef            double     CPU_FP64;                     /* 64-bit floating point      */
typedef   volatile CPU_INT08U CPU_REG08;                    /*  8-bit register            */
typedef   volatile CPU_INT16U CPU_REG16;                    /* 16-bit register            */
typedef   volatile CPU_INT32U CPU_REG32;                    /* 32-bit register            */
typedef   volatile CPU_INT64U CPU_REG64;                    /* 64-bit register            */
typedef            void       (*CPU_FNCT_VOID)(void);
typedef            void       (*CPU_FNCT_PTR )(void *);
```

Listing B-5 **cpu.h, Data Types**

LB-5(1)   Characters are assumed to be 8-bit quantities on the Cortex-M4.

LB-5(2)   It is often convenient to declare Boolean variables. However, even though a Boolean represents either 1 or 0, a whole byte is used. This is done because ANSI C does not define single bit variables.

LB-5(3)   The signed and unsigned integer data types are declared for 8, 16 and 32-bit quantities.

LB-5(4)   µC/OS-III requires that the compiler defines 64-bit data types. These are used when computing CPU usage on a per-task basis. The 64-bit data types are used when declaring **OS_CYCLES** in **os_type.h**.

LB-5(5)   Most of Micriµm's software components do not use floating-point values. These data types are declared for consistency and to provide portable data types to the application developer.

```
#define   CPU_CFG_ADDR_SIZE        CPU_WORD_SIZE_32                         (6)
#define   CPU_CFG_DATA_SIZE        CPU_WORD_SIZE_32
#if       (CPU_CFG_ADDR_SIZE == CPU_WORD_SIZE_32)
typedef   CPU_INT32U               CPU_ADDR;
#elif     (CPU_CFG_ADDR_SIZE == CPU_WORD_SIZE_16)
typedef   CPU_INT16U               CPU_ADDR;
#else
typedef   CPU_INT08U               CPU_ADDR;
#endif
#if       (CPU_CFG_DATA_SIZE == CPU_WORD_SIZE_32)
typedef   CPU_INT32U               CPU_DATA;
#elif     (CPU_CFG_DATA_SIZE == CPU_WORD_SIZE_16)
typedef   CPU_INT16U               CPU_DATA;
#else
typedef   CPU_INT08U               CPU_DATA;
#endif
typedef   CPU_DATA                 CPU_ALIGN;
typedef   CPU_ADDR                 CPU_SIZE_T;
typedef   CPU_INT16U               CPU_ERR;
typedef   CPU_INT32U               CPU_STK;                                 (7)
typedef   CPU_ADDR                 CPU_STK_SIZE;
typedef   CPU_INT32U               CPU_SR;                                  (8)
```

Listing B-6 **cpu.h, Data Type (Continued)**

LB-6(1)   Miscellaneous types are declared.

LB-6(2)   **CPU_STK** declares the width of a CPU stack entry and they are 32-bits wide on the Cortex-M4. All μC/OS-III stacks must be declared using **CPU_STK**.

LB-6(3)   μC/CPU provides code to protect critical sections by disabling interrupts. This is implemented by **CPU_CRITICAL_ENTER()** and **CPU_CRITICAL_EXIT()**. When **CPU_CRITICAL_ENTER()** is invoked, the current state of the Cortex-M4's Program Status Register (PSR) is saved in a local variable so that it can be restored when **CPU_CRITICAL_EXIT()** is invoked. The local variable that holds the saved PSR is declared as a **CPU_SR**.

B-6-3 cpu.h – FUNCTION PROTOTYPES

cpu.h also contains a number of data types. The most significant prototypes related to µC/OS-III are shown in Listing B-7.

```
CPU_SR     CPU_SR_Save     (void);
void       CPU_SR_Restore  (CPU_SR    cpu_sr);
CPU_DATA   CPU_CntLeadZeros (CPU_DATA  val);
```

Listing B-7 **cpu.h, Data Type**

B-7 cpu_a.asm

cpu_a.asm contains assembly language functions provided by µC/CPU. Three functions of particular importance to µC/OS-III are shown in Listing B-8.

CPU_SR_Save() obtains the current value of the Cortex-M4 PSR and then disables all CPU interrupts. The value of the saved PSR is returned to the caller.

CPU_SR_Restore() reverses the process and restores the PSR to the value passed to

CPU_SR_Restored() as an argument.

CPU_CntLeadZeros() counts the number of zero bits starting from the most significant bit position. This function is implemented in assembly language because the ARMv7 instruction incorporates this functionality.

In all of the functions below, R0 contains the value passed to the function, as well as the returned value.

```
CPU_SR_Save
        MRS     R0, PRIMASK
        CPSID   I
        BX      LR


CPU_SR_Restore
        MSR     PRIMASK, R0
        BX      LR


CPU_CntLeadZeros
        CLZ     R0, R0
        BX      LR
```

Listing B-8 **cpu_a.asm**

C

Introduction to µC/Probe

This appendix aims at briefly introducing µC/Probe. µC/Probe is a Windows application designed to read and write the memory of any embedded target processor during run-time. Memory locations are mapped to a set of virtual controls and indicators placed on a dashboard. Figure C-1 shows an overview of the system and data flow.

Figure C-1 **µC/Probe Data Flow Diagram**

FC-1(1)   You have to provide µC/Probe with an ELF file with DWARF-2 debugging information. The ELF file is generated by IAR EWARM toolchain's linker. µC/Probe parses the ELF file and reads the addresses of each of the embedded target's symbols (i.e. global variables) and creates a catalog known as *symbol browser*, which will be used by you during design-time to select the symbols you want to display on your dashboard. For more information on building ELF files with IAR Embedded Workbench, see section 4-4 "Compiling, Programming and Debugging" on page 797.

FC-1(2)   During design-time, you create a workspace using a Windows PC and µC/Probe. You design your own dashboard by dragging and dropping virtual controls and indicators onto a *data screen*. Each virtual control and indicator needs to be mapped to an embedded target's symbol by selecting it from the symbol browser.

FC-1(3)   Before proceeding to the run-time stage, µC/Probe needs to be configured to use one of the three communication interfaces: J-Link, RS232 or TCP/IP. The examples featured in the book use the J-Link interface, see section "Configuring µC/Probe to work with J-Link" on page 793 for more details. In order to start the run-time stage, you click the *Play* button and µC/Probe starts making requests to read the value of all the memory locations associated with each virtual control and indicator (i.e. buttons and gauges respectively). At the same time, µC/Probe sends commands to write the memory locations associated with each virtual control (i.e. buttons on a click event).

FC-1(4)   In the case of a reading request, the embedded target responds with the latest value. In the case of a write command, the embedded target responds with an acknowledgement. Because the examples in this book use the J-Link interface, no resident firmware is necessary on the XMC4500 CPU board. Any other type of interface such as RS-232 or TCP/IP requires target code which is available from Micrium for most platforms.

FC-1(5)   µC/Probe parses the responses from the embedded target and updates the virtual controls and indicators.

C-1 FURTHER READING

The μC/Probe page on the Micriμm website is filled with instructional videos and the official documentation. Go online to:

`http://www.micrium.com/probe`

- Download the document *μC/Probe Target Manual* for more information about the firmware that resides on the Embedded System.

- Download the document *μC/Probe User's Manual* for more information about the Windows PC side of the system.

Appendix C

Appendix

D

Bibliography

ARM Ltd, *ARM Cortex-M4 Technical Reference Manual*, 110 Fulbourn Road, Cambridge, CB1 9NJ, England, Available at: http://infocenter.arm.com/help/index.jsp

IAR Systems AB, *IAR Embedded Workbench - IDE Project Management and Building Guide*, Second edition, April 2011, Uppsala, Sweden, Available at: http://www.iar.com/en/ Products/IAR-Embedded-Workbench/ARM/User-guides

IAR Systems AB, *IAR Embedded Workbench - C-SPY® Debugging Guide*, Third edition, October 2011, Uppsala, Sweden, Available at: http://www.iar.com/en/Products/ IAR-Embedded-Workbench/ARM/User-guides

Infineon Technologies AG, *Hexagon Application Kit For XMC4000 Family - CPU Board XMC4500 General Purpose - User's Manual*, Rev 1.1, July 2012, Munich, Germany, Available at: http://www.infineon.com/xmc_kits

Segger Microcontroller GmbH & Co. KG, *J-Link / J-Trace User Guide*, September 2012, Available at: http://www.segger.com/jlink-pro.html

D

Licensing Policy

This book contains µC/OS-III in source form for FREE short-term evaluation, for educational use or for peaceful research. If you plan or intend to use µC/OS-III in a commercial application/product then, you need to contact Micriµm to properly license µC/OS-III for its use in your application/product.

We provide ALL the source code for your convenience and to help you experience µC/OS-III. The fact that the source is provided does NOT mean that you can use it commercially without paying a licensing fee. Knowledge of the source code may NOT be used to develop a similar product.

The user may use µC/OS-III with the XMC4500 CPU board and it is not necessary to purchase anything else as long as the initial purchase is used for educational purposes. Once the code is used to create a commercial project/product for profit, however, it is necessary to purchase a license.

It is necessary to purchase this license when the decision to use µC/OS-III in a design is made, not when the design is ready to go to production.

If you are unsure about whether you need to obtain a license for your application, please contact Micriµm and discuss the intended use with a sales representative.

CONTACT MICRIUM

1290 Weston Road, Suite 306
Weston, FL 33326
USA
+1 954 217 2036
+1 954 217 2037 (FAX)
E-mail: sales@micrium.com
Web: www.micrium.com

E

Index

Y

Micrium

Are you Five Years Out?

Most people live in the present. The world of now. But a handful of us work in a unique world that doesn't quite exist yet – the world of Five Years Out.

Five Years Out is the tangible future. And the people who live and work there know that new technologies, new materials, new ideas and new electronics will make life not only different, but better. Not just cheaper, but smarter. Not just easier, but more inspired.

Five Years Out is an exciting place to be. So exciting that, once you've been there, it's hard to get excited about the present. Because we know what's coming is going to be so much better.

Five Years Out is a community of builders, designers, engineers and imaginers who navigate the path between possibility and practicality. Creating the future of everything from cars to coffee makers.

Are you Five Years Out?
Then you're probably working with us.

ΛɾɾⲥW
Five Years Out

⟫ SEGGER Development Tools

J-Link – JTAG-Emulator

- Very easy to use
- #1 emulator for ARM cores
- High-Speed download
- Direct support by major IDEs
- Easy installation on host

- Supports JTAG/SWD/SWO
- Optimized flash algorithms[*]
- Unlimited Flash breakpoints[*]
- Connects via USB or Ethernet[**]
- Integration into Micrium's µC/Probe
- JTAG-isolation-Adapter available

J-Trace

- For use with ETM
- Instruction tracing
- ARM7, ARM9 & Cortex-M3

[*] Add-on: not included in all models
[**] Not available for all models